The Encyclopaedia of

# ATHLETICS

# The Encyclopaedia of
# ATHLETICS

Compiled by

## MELVYN WATMAN

Foreword by

HAROLD ABRAHAMS C.B.E.

## ROBERT HALE · LONDON

© *Melvyn Watman 1964, 1967 and 1973*

*First published in Great Britain 1964*
*Second Edition 1967*
*Third Edition 1973*

Robert Hale & Company
63 Old Brompton Road
London S.W.7

ISBN 0 7091 4010 x

PRINTED IN GREAT BRITAIN BY
BRISTOL TYPESETTING CO. LTD.
BARTON MANOR - ST. PHILIPS
BRISTOL 2

# Foreword

by

# HAROLD ABRAHAMS

This is the third occasion upon which my friend Melvyn Watman has paid me the compliment of asking me to contribute a foreword to his splendid *Encyclopaedia of Athletics*. What can I say that I have not said on the two previous occasions? In my first foreword, in September 1964, I wrote: " It is, alas, only too true that much information herein contained must very quickly become out of date. The solution to that defect is the production of new editions." Since the revised edition was published in 1967, to take but one example, not far short of 250 world records have been passed by the I.A.A.F. The necessity for a third edition is manifest.

Inevitably much included in the two previous editions has had to be omitted. Happy the enthusiast who possesses these two valuable productions to add to this Third Edition. Something like 100 biographies, available in Volumes 1 and 2, have had to disappear from Volume 3, which is surely of an even higher standard than its predecessors.

All of us who enjoy athletics are deeply indebted to Melvyn Watman for his continued incomparable care and never waning enthusiasm.

HAROLD M. ABRAHAMS

London,
June 1973.

# Acknowledgements

I am particularly indebted to Harold Abrahams, Peter Hildreth, Andrew Huxtable, Peter Lovesey, Peter Matthews, Peter Pozzoli and Bob Sparks for their invaluable assistance.

In addition, I have referred frequently to the following magazines: Athletics Weekly, Athletics World, Leichtathletik, Track and Field News and World Athletics—and to the publications of the Amateur Athletic Association, Association of Track and Field Statisticians, British Amateur Athletic Board, English Cross-Country Union, International Amateur Athletic Federation, International Cross-Country Union, National Union of Track Statisticians, Race Walking Association and Women's Amateur Athletic Association.

I would also like to thank all who have notified me of errors or omissions in the previous editions of this book.

M.W.

# Illustrations

## PHOTO CREDITS

Keystone Press Agency Ltd. 1, 2, 9; Ed Lacey, 3, 4, 8, 11, 16; Novosti Press Agency 5; Mark Shearman 6; Tony Duffy 7, 17; Peter Tempest 10; Fionnbar Callanan 12, 13, 14, 15.

To my darling Pat

# Introduction

Much has happened in the development of athletics since the second edition of this encyclopaedia was published in 1967. Two Olympic Games have come and gone; dozens of world records have been created; new techniques, like the "Fosbury Flop" in high jumping, have come into being; more and more countries are engaging in international competition and throwing up athletes of world class; the East German sporting "miracle" has taken place; drugs—mainly in the shape of anabolic steroids—regrettably have become more widely used in the sport; a professional circuit has been established in the United States; all-weather track surfaces have become commonplace; women have been allowed to race at 3,000 metres and 400 metres hurdles.

There are changes, too, in this book. The historical data retained from previous editions have been brought up to date, and there are many fresh entries. The 130 short biographies scattered throughout the book include all the 1972 Olympic champions and most of the current world record holders. The work has been made more international in scope, new sections include American champions and European indoor champions.

I regret that, for production reasons, it was not possible in this edition to print metric as well as Imperial measurements in field event results. However, performances originally measured in metric have been reconverted to feet and inches in accord with the present rules; e.g. no fractions of an inch for distances over 100 feet.

London,                                                    MELVYN WATMAN
June 1973.

## KEY
### to abbreviations of Athletic organisations

AAA— Amateur Athletic Association
AAU— Amateur Athletic Union (of USA)
BAAB— British Amateur Athletic Board
IAAF— International Amateur Athletic
Federation
IOC— International Olympic Committee
RWA— Race Walking Association
WAAA— Women's Amateur Athletic
Association

# A

## ABEBE BIKILA (Ethiopia)

The only man ever to have made a successful defence of an Olympic marathon title, Abebe Bikila is without question the greatest road runner of all time. Previously unheard of outside his own country, he created the biggest upset of the 1960 Olympic Games by winning, barefoot (" just to make history "), in a world's best time of 2 hr. 15 min. 16.2 sec. It transpired that this was his third marathon in three months, having recorded 2 hr. 39 min. 50 sec. in July and 2 hr. 21 min. 23 sec. in August at high altitude.

Four years later, in Tokyo (wearing shoes this time), he produced an even more astonishing performance by defeating the best the world could offer by a margin of over four minutes (three-quarters of a mile) in another world's best of 2 hr. 12 min. 11.2 sec.—an average of about 5 min. 2 sec. per mile for the 26 mi. 385 yd. course. Severe pains in his left leg forced him to drop out of the 1968 Olympic event after about 10 miles, a race won by Ethiopian team-mate Mamo Wolde. Tragically, he received such serious spinal injuries in a car crash in March 1969 that he is unlikely ever to be able to walk again. He was born at Mout on Aug. 7th, 1932.

## ABRAHAMS, H. M. (GB)

In the world of athletics, Harold Abrahams has distinguished himself in at least five spheres: as a performer, administrator, writer, broadcaster and statistician. His greatest success on the track occurred in 1924 when he won the Olympic 100 m. title —the first European and only Briton to achieve that honour. Sprinting in an inspired fashion, he proceeded within the space of 26 hours to equal the Olympic record of 10.6 sec. in the second-round heat, semi-final (despite a dreadful start) and final. His actual time in the final of 10.52 sec. would be recorded as 10.5 sec. under the present rules and was appreciably faster than anything he accomplished before or after the Paris Games.

One month before the Olympics, on the same day that he ran 100 yds. in a wind-assisted 9.6 sec., he long jumped 24 ft. 2½ in.—a mark that stood as an English native record for 32 years. Other personal bests included 9.9 sec. for 100yd., 21.6 sec. for 220 yd. (straight), 22.0 sec. for 200m. (turn) and 50.8 sec. for 440yd. His active career was cut short in 1925 when he broke his leg long jumping.

He has been a leading official since 1926 and was appointed chairman of the British Amateur Athletics Board in 1968 after serving as honorary treasurer for 21 years. He was born at Bedford on Dec. 15th. 1899.

## ADMINISTRATION

See under AMATEUR ATHLETIC ASSOCIATION, AMATEUR ATHLETIC UNION, BRITISH AMATEUR ATHLETIC BOARD, INTERNATIONAL AMATEUR ATHLETIC FEDERATION, INTERNATIONAL OLYMPIC COMMITTEE, NATIONAL COLLEGIATE ATHLETIC ASSOCIATION, and WOMEN'S AMATEUR ATHLETIC ASSOCIATION.

## AFRICAN GAMES

Winners at the first Pan-African Games, held in Brazzaville (Congo) in 1965 and supported by 26 nations: 100 m., G. Kone (Ivory Coast) 10.3 sec.; 200 m., Kone 21.1 sec.; 400 m., W. Kiprugut (Kenya) 46.9 sec.; 800 m., Kiprugut 1 min. 47.4 sec.; 1500 m., K. Keino (Ken) 3 min. 41.1 sec.; 5000 m., Keino 13 min. 44.4 sec.; 3000 m. steeplechase, B. Kogo (Ken) 8 min. 47.4 sec.; 110 m. hurdles, F. Erinle (Nigeria) 14.6 sec.; 400 m. hurdles, K. Songok (Ken) 51.7 sec.; 4 x 100 m. Senegal 40.5 sec.; 4 x 400 m. Senegal 3 min. 11.5 sec.; High jump, S. Igun (Nig) 6ft. 9½in.; Pole vault, B. Elloe

11

(Iv. Coast) 13ft. 7½in.; Long jump, E. Akika (Nig) 24ft. 7in.; Triple jump, Igun (Nig) 53ft 4½in.; Shot, S. Kragbe (Iv. Coast) 53ft. 6½in.; Discus, N. Niare (Mali) 168ft. 0in.; Javelin A. Oyakhire (Nig) 234ft. 8 in.; Women's events—100 m., J. Bodunrin (Nig) 12.4 sec.; 80 m. hurdles, R. Hart (Ghana) 11.7 sec.; 4 x 100 m., Nigeria 48.0 sec.; High jump, A. Okoli (Nig) 5ft. 3¾in.; Long jump, A. Annum (Gha) 18ft. 5¾in.; Javelin, H. Okwara (Nig) 132ft. 2in.

The second African Games, having twice been postponed, were held in Lagos (Nigeria) in January, 1973.

Winners: 100 m. and 200 m., O. Kari Kari (Gha) 10.6 sec. and 21.1 sec.; 400 m., C. Asati (Ken) 46.3 sec.; 800 m., C. Silei (Ken) 1 min. 45.3 sec.; 1500 m., F. Bayi (Tanz) 3 min. 37.2 sec.; 5000 m., B. Jipcho (Ken) 14 min. 07.2 sec.; 10,000 m., M. Yifter (Eth) 29 min. 04.6 sec., Mar., Mamo Wolde (Eth) 2 hr. 27 min. 32 sec.; 3000 m. SC, Jipcho 8 min. 20.8 sec.; 110 m. H, F. Kimaiyo (Ken) 14.1 sec.; 400 m. H, J. Akii-Bua (Uga) 48.5 sec.; 4 x 100 m., Nigeria 39.8 sec.; 4 x 400 m., Kenya 3 min. 06.3 sec.; High Jump, A. Wasughe (Som) 6 ft. 8¼ in.; Pole vault, A. Gheita (Egy) 15 ft. 3 in.; Long jump, J. Owusu (Gha) 26 ft. 3 in.; Triple jump, M. Dia (Sen) 54 ft. 2¾ in.; Shot, N. Asaad (Egy) 63 ft. 11 in.; Discus, N. Niare (Mali) 181 ft. 4 in.; Hammer, Y. Ochola (Uga) 166 ft. 2 in.; Javelin, A. Abehi (Iv C) 253 ft. 4 in. Women: 100 m. and 200 m., A. Annum (Gha) 11.7 sec. and 23.8 sec.; 400 m., T. Chemabwai (Ken) 54.0 sec.; 800 m., C. Anyakun (Uga) 2 min. 09.5 sec.; 1500 m. P. Kesiime (Uga) 4 min. 38.7 sec.; 100 m. High jump and Long jump, M. Oshikoya (Nig) 14.2 sec.; 5 ft. 7¼ in. and 20 ft. 2¼ in.; 4 x 100 m., Ghana 46.2 sec.; 4 x 400 m., Uganda 3 min. 45.4 sec.; Shot, E. Okeke (Nig) 44 ft. 7 in.; Discus, R. Hart (Gha) 134 ft. 8 in.; Javelin, C. Rwabiryage (Uga) 155 ft. 10 in.

# AGE GROUPS

Track and field competition under the jurisdiction of the Amateur Athletic Association is split into four age groups. Seniors are athletes who are at least 19 at midnight on Aug. 31st in the year of competition; juniors are over 17 and under 19, youths over 15 and under 17, boys over 13 and under 15—all as at midnight on Aug. 31st in the year of competition.

Under Women's Amateur Athletic Association rules, an intermediate is an athlete over 15 and under 17, and a junior under 15, at midnight on Aug 31st in the year of competition.

Internationally, juniors are boys under 20 and girls under 19 on December 31st in the year of competition.

See under JUNIORS, OLDEST, VETERANS and YOUNGEST.

# AKII-BUA, J. (Uganda)

In spite of the disadvantage of being drawn in the sharp inside lane, a handicap in particular for a man who hurdles with a right-leg lead, John Akii-Bua not only won the 1972 Olympic 400 metres hurdles title in Munich but smashed David Hemery's prestigious world record into the bargain. The lanky Ugandan was timed in an astonishing 47.8 sec., as against the British athlete's 48.1 sec. recorded under the advantageous altitude conditions of Mexico City.

Akii-Bua's performance—he won the race by the wide margin of 0.7 sec. from Ralph Mann (USA) and Hemery —was hailed as one of the greatest in all athletics history. He ran a technically perfect race, taking 13 strides between the hurdles for five flights before dropping to 14 strides (alternate leg lead) for the remainder.

One of 43 children (his father had eight wives), Akii-Bua took up hurdling in 1967, but it was not until 1970 that he turned seriously to the 400 m. hurdles. He quickly made an impact, finishing fourth in that year's Commonwealth Games, and the following season he won for Africa in a match against the USA in 49.0 sec., the world's second fastest time in 1971.

A fine all-rounder, he has run 400 m. in 46.2 sec., 800 m. in 1 min. 54.1 sec., 110 m. hurdles in 13.8 sec., high jumped 6ft. 4in., thrown the javelin over 200ft. and scored 6,933 pts. in his decathlon debut. Annual progress at 400 m. hurdles: 1968—53.7 (440 yd.); 1970—51.0; 1971—49.0; 1972—47.8. He was born on Dec. 3rd, 1949.

# ALTITUDE

The effect of competing at high altitude was brought home vividly for the first time in 1955 when the Pan-American Games were held in Mexico City, at an elevation of 7,347 ft. The world records for the 400 m. and triple jump were shattered, and sprint and long jump performances were much better than expected. On the other hand, the star American miler, Wes Santee, was sensationally defeated in a slow race by a South American runner who was more familiar with such conditions, and all the long distance events were won in extremely poor times.

The reason for this disparity in performances is that at such an altitude the air is approximately 23 per cent thinner than at sea level. The consequent reduction in air resistance is favourable to sprinters and jumpers, whereas the shortage of oxygen adversely affects athletes in the endurance events (1500 m. upwards).

Long distance runners born and resident at high altitude are able to run more efficiently in those conditions than their lowland rivals—as was proved at the 1968 Olympics in Mexico City. There, such athletes from Kenya, Mexico and Ethiopia placed 1st in the 1,500 m., 2nd, 3rd and 4th in the 5,000 m., 1st, 2nd and 4th in the 10,000 m. 1st in the marathon, and 1st and 2nd in the steeplechase. Mohamed Gammoudi (Tunisia), the 5,000 m. winner, had spent considerable time training at altitude in the French Pyrenees, which helped reduce his physiological disadvantage. An unacclimatised Ron Clarke (Australia), world record holder for both events, could finish only 5th in the 5,000 m. and 6th in the 10,000 m.

The reduced air resistance contributed towards world record performances at the Games in the 100 m. (9.9 sec.), 200 m. (19.8 sec.), 400 m. (43.8 sec.), 400 m. hurdles (48.1 sec.), 4 x 100 m. relay (38.2 sec.), 4 x 400 m. relay (2 min. 56.1 sec.), long jump (29ft. 2½in.), triple jump (57ft. 0¾in.), women's 100 m. (11.0 sec.), women's 200 m. (22.5 sec.), women's 4 x 100 m. relay (42.8 sec.), and women's long jump (22ft. 4½in.).

# AMATEUR ATHLETIC ASSOCIATION

The AAA, which was founded in Oxford on Apr. 24th, 1880, is the governing body for men's athletics in England and Wales.

## Championships

The Annual AAA Championships have long served as the unofficial British Championships, and as from 1972 the first home athlete in each event has been designated " UK champion ".

The inaugural Championships were held at Lillie Bridge Grounds, London, on July 3rd, 1880. Previously, " English Championships " were promoted by the Amateur Athletic Club from 1866 to 1879.

The longest sequence of foreign successes in any one event occurred in the shot-put from 1927 to 1948 inclusive. During this period, the luckless R. L. Howland filled second place on eight occasions!

That graceful and consistent sprinter from Trinidad, E. McDonald Bailey, holds the " record " for the greatest number of AAA titles. Excluding relays, he gained 14 victories between 1946 and 1953.

The most wins in one event is 13 by the Irish shot-putter Dennis Horgan between 1893 and 1912.

Four is the highest total of championships gained in one year—by Walter George in 1882 and 1884 (880 yd., mile, 4 mi. and 10 mi.) and by William Snook in 1885 (mile, 4 mi., 10 mi. and steeplechase).

Five men have won a title seven years running: Dennis Horgan (shot, 1893-99), Don Finlay (120 yd. hurdles, 1932-38), Bert Cooper (2 mi. walk, 1932-38), Harry Whittle (440 yd. hurdles, 1947-53) and Maurice Herriott (3,000 m. steeplechase, 1961-67).

Harry Edward, from British Guiana, took the 100, 220 and 440 yd. on one afternoon in 1922.

The Championships went metric in 1969.

| 100 Yards | | sec. |
|---|---|---|
| 1880 | W. P. Phillips | 10.2 |
| 1881 | W. P. Phillips | 10.2 |
| 1882 | W. P. Phillips | 10.2 |

13

| 1883 | J. M. Cowie | 10.2 | | 1951 | E. McD. Bailey | 9.6 |
|------|------------|------|---|------|----------------|-----|
| 1884 | J. M. Cowie | 10.2 | | 1952 | E. McD. Bailey | 9.6 |
| 1885 | J. M. Cowie | 10.2 | | 1953 | E. McD. Bailey | 9.8 |
| 1886 | A. Wharton | 10.0 | | 1954 | G. S. Ellis | 9.9 |
| 1887 | A. Wharton | 10.1 | | 1955 | E. R. Sandstrom | 10.0 |
| 1888 | F. Westing (USA) | 10.2 | | 1956 | J. R. C. Young | 9.9 |
| 1889 | E. H. Pelling | 10.4 | | 1957 | K. J. Box | 10.0 |
| 1890 | N. D. Morgan (Ireland) | 10.4 | | 1958 | J. S. O. Omagbemi | |
| 1891 | L. H. Cary (USA) | 10.2 | | | (Nigeria) | 9.9 |
| 1892 | C. A. Bradley | 10.2 | | 1959 | P. F. Radford | 9.7 |
| 1893 | C. A. Bradley | 10.0 | | 1960 | P. F. Radford | 9.7 |
| 1894 | C. A. Bradley | 10.2 | | 1961 | H. W. Jerome (Canada) | 9.6 |
| 1895 | C. A. Bradley | 10.0 | | 1962 | S. Antao (Kenya) | 9.8 |
| 1896 | N. D. Morgan (Ireland) | 10.4 | | 1963 | T. B. Jones | 9.7 |
| 1897 | J. H. Palmer | 10.8 | | 1964 | E. Figuerola (Cuba) | 9.4 |
| 1898 | F. W. Cooper | 10.0 | | 1965 | E. Figuerola (Cuba) | 9.6 |
| 1899 | R. W. Wadsley | 10.2 | | 1966 | P. Nash (S. Africa) | 9.6 |
| 1900 | A. F. Duffey (USA) | 10.0 | | 1967 | B. H. Kelly | 9.9 |
| 1901 | A. F. Duffey (USA) | 10.0 | | 1968 | P. Nash (S. Africa) | 9.9 |
| 1902 | A. F. Duffey (USA) | 10.0 | | | | |
| 1903 | A. F. Duffey (USA) | 10.0 | | *100 Metres* | | |
| 1904 | J. W. Morton | 10.0 | | 1969 | R. Jones | 10.7 |
| 1905 | J. W. Morton | 10.2 | | 1970 | R. G. Symonds (Bermuda) | 10.3 |
| 1906 | J. W. Morton | 10.4 | | 1971 | B. W. Green | 10.6 |
| 1907 | J. W. Morton | 10.8 | | 1972 | V. Papageorgopoulos | |
| 1908 | R. Kerr (Canada) | 10.0 | | | (Greece) | 10.2 |
| 1909 | R. E. Walker (S. Africa) | 10.0 | | | (UK champion: B. W. Green 10.4) | |
| 1910 | F. L. Ramsdell (USA) | 10.2 | | | | |
| 1911 | F. L. Ramsdell (USA) | 10.4 | | *220 Yards* | | |
| 1912 | G. H. Patching (S. Africa) | 9.8 | | 1902 | R. W. Wadsley | 22.4 |
| 1913 | W. R. Applegarth | 10.0 | | 1903 | G. F. Brewill | 23.0 |
| 1914 | W. R. Applegarth | 10.0 | | 1904 | C. H. Jupp | 22.8 |
| 1919 | W. A. Hill | 10.0 | | 1905 | H. A. Hyman (USA) | 22.4 |
| 1920 | H. F. V. Edward | 10.0 | | 1906 | C. H. Jupp | 22.6 |
| 1921 | H. F. V. Edward | 10.2 | | 1907 | J. P. George | 22.8 |
| 1922 | H. F. V. Edward | 10.0 | | 1908 | R. Kerr (Canada) | 22.4 |
| 1923 | E. H. Liddell | 9.7 | | 1909 | N. J. Cartmell (USA) | 22.0 |
| 1924 | H. M. Abrahams | 9.9 | | 1910 | F. L. Ramsdell (USA) | 22.4 |
| 1925 | L. C. Murchison (USA) | 9.9 | | 1911 | F. L. Ramsdell (USA) | 22.2 |
| 1926 | R. Corts (Germany) | 10.0 | | 1912 | W. R. Applegarth | 22.0 |
| 1927 | H. Kornig (Germany) | 10.1 | | 1913 | W. R. Applegarth | 21.6 |
| 1928 | W. B. Legg (S. Africa) | 9.9 | | 1914 | W. R. Applegarth | 21.2 |
| 1929 | J. E. London | 10.0 | | 1919 | W. A. Hill | 22.6 |
| 1930 | C. D. Berger (Netherlands) | 9.9 | | 1920 | H. F. V. Edward | 21.6 |
| 1931 | E. L. Page | 10.0 | | 1921 | H. F. V. Edward | 22.2 |
| 1932 | F. P. Reid | 9.9 | | 1922 | H. F. V. Edward | 22.0 |
| 1933 | G. T. Saunders | 9.9 | | 1923 | E. H. Liddell | 21.6 |
| 1934 | J. Sir (Hungary) | 9.9 | | 1924 | H. P. Kinsman (S. Africa) | 21.7 |
| 1935 | A. W. Sweeney | 10.2 | | 1925 | L. C. Murchison (USA) | 21.6 |
| 1936 | M. B. Osendarp (Nether- | | | 1926 | G. M. Butler | 21.9 |
| | lands) | 9.8 | | 1927 | H. Houben (Germany) | 21.8 |
| 1937 | C. B. Holmes | 9.9 | | 1928 | F. W. Wichmann | |
| 1938 | M. B. Osendarp (Nether- | | | | (Germany) | 21.7 |
| | lands) | 9.8 | | 1929 | J. A. T. Hanlon | 21.9 |
| 1939 | A. W. Sweeney | 9.9 | | 1930 | S. E. Englehart | 22.0 |
| 1946 | E. McD. Bailey | 9.8 | | 1931 | R. Murdoch | 22.5 |
| 1947 | E. McD. Bailey | 9.7 | | 1932 | F. P. Reid | 22.0 |
| 1948 | J. F. Treloar (Australia) | 9.8 | | 1933 | C. D. Berger (Netherlands) | 22.0 |
| 1949 | E. McD. Bailey | 9.7 | | 1934 | R. Murdoch | 22.1 |
| 1950 | E. McD. Bailey | 9.9 | | 1935 | M. B. Osendarp (Nether- | |
| | | | | | lands) | 22.2 |

| 1936 | A. W. Sweeney | 21.9 | 1904 | R. L. Watson | 51.8 |
|------|---------------|------|------|--------------|------|
| 1937 | A. W. Sweeney | 21.9 | 1905 | W. Halswelle | 50.8 |
| 1938 | W. van Beveren (Nether- | | 1906 | W. Halswelle | 48.8 |
| | lands) | 22.1 | 1907 | E. H. Montague | 52.6 |
| 1939 | C. B. Holmes | 21.9 | 1908 | W. Halswelle | 49.4 |
| 1946 | E. McD. Bailey | 22.3 | 1909 | A. Patterson | 51.2 |
| 1947 | E. McD. Bailey | 21.7 | 1910 | L. J. de B. Reed | 51.0 |
| 1948 | A. McCorquodale | 22.2 | 1911 | F. J. Halbaus (Canada) | 50.8 |
| 1949 | E. McD. Bailey | 21.7 | 1912 | C. N. Seedhouse | 49.8 |
| 1950 | E. McD. Bailey | 21.8 | 1913 | G. Nicol | 49.4 |
| 1951 | E. McD. Bailey | 21.4 | 1914 | C. N. Seedhouse | 50.0 |
| 1952 | E. McD. Bailey | 21.4 | 1919 | G. M. Butler | 49.2 |
| 1953 | E. McD. Bailey | 21.4 | 1920 | B. G. D'U. Rudd (S. | |
| 1954 | B. Shenton | 21.5 | | Africa) | 49.2 |
| 1955 | G. S. Ellis | 22.0 | 1921 | R. A. Lindsay | 50.4 |
| 1956 | B. Shenton | 21.8 | 1922 | H. F. V. Edward | 50.4 |
| 1957 | D. H. Segal | 21.9 | 1923 | W. E. Stevenson (USA) | 49.6 |
| 1958 | D. H. Segal | 21.4 | 1924 | E. H. Liddell | 49.6 |
| 1959 | D. H. Jones | 21.7 | 1925 | H. B. Stallard | 50.0 |
| 1960 | D. H. Jones | 21.3 | 1926 | J. W. J. Rinkel | 49.8 |
| 1961 | D. H. Jones | 21.4 | 1927 | D. G. A. Lowe | 48.8 |
| 1962 | S. Antao (Kenya) | 21.1 | 1928 | D. G. A. Lowe | 50.0 |
| 1963 | D. H. Jones | 21.3 | 1929 | J. A. T. Hanlon | 49.1 |
| 1964 | W. M. Campbell | 21.1 | 1930 | K. C. Brangwin | 49.8 |
| 1965 | P. J. A. Morrison | 21.8 | 1931 | G. L. Rampling | 48.6 |
| 1966 | P. Nash (S. Africa) | 21.2 | 1932 | C. H. Stoneley | 49.8 |
| 1967 | W. M. Campbell | 21.4 | 1933 | F. F. Wolff | 49.0 |
| 1968 | P. Nash (S. Africa) | 21.2 | 1934 | G. L. Rampling | 49.6 |
| | | | 1935 | W. Roberts | 49.0 |

*200 Metres*

| | | | 1936 | A. G. K. Brown | 48.6 |
|------|---------------|------|------|----------------|------|
| 1969 | D. G. Dear | 21.4 | 1937 | W. Roberts | 48.2 |
| 1970 | M. E. Reynolds | 21.0 | 1938 | A. G. K. Brown | 49.2 |
| 1971 | A. P. Pascoe | 21.1 | 1939 | A. Pennington | 48.8 |
| 1972 | A. P. Pascoe | 20.9 | 1946 | A. S. Wint (Jamaica) | 48.4 |
| | | | 1947 | J. P. Reardon (Ireland) | 48.3 |

*440 Yards*

| | | | 1948 | M. J. Curotta (Australia) | 48.2 |
|------|---------------|------|------|---------------------------|------|
| 1880 | M. Shearman | 52.2 | 1949 | D. C. Pugh | 48.5 |
| 1881 | L. E. Myers (USA) | 48.6 | 1950 | L. C. Lewis | 48.2 |
| 1882 | H. R. Ball | 50.2 | 1951 | D. C. Pugh | 47.9 |
| 1883 | J. M. Cowie | 51.0 | 1952 | A. S. Wint (Jamaica) | 48.1 |
| 1884 | J. M. Cowie | 50.4 | 1953 | P. G. Fryer | 48.9 |
| 1885 | L. E. Myers (USA) | 52.4 | 1954 | P. G. Fryer | 48.4 |
| 1886 | C. G. Wood | 49.8 | 1955 | P. G. Fryer | 47.7 |
| 1887 | C. G. Wood | 51.0 | 1956 | M. K. V. Wheeler | 47.7 |
| 1888 | H. C. L. Tindall | 51.4 | 1957 | F. P. Higgins | 47.6 |
| 1889 | H. C. L. Tindall | 48.5 | 1958 | J. E. Salisbury | 47.2 |
| 1890 | T. L. Nicholas | 51.8 | 1959 | J. D. Wrighton | 47.5 |
| 1891 | M. Remington (USA) | 51.0 | 1960 | Milkha Singh (India) | 46.5 |
| 1892 | C. Dickenson (Ireland) | 50.4 | 1961 | A. P. Metcalfe | 47.6 |
| 1893 | E. C. Bredin | 49.2 | 1962 | R. I. Brightwell | 45.9 |
| 1894 | E. C. Bredin | 50.0 | 1963 | A. P. Metcalfe | 47.3 |
| 1895 | W. Fitzherbert | 49.6 | 1964 | R. I. Brightwell | 47.5 |
| 1896 | J. C. Meredith (Ireland) | 52.0 | 1965 | M. D. Larrabee (USA) | 47.6 |
| 1897 | S. Elliott | 53.2 | 1966 | W. Mottley (Trinidad) | 45.9 |
| 1898 | W. Fitzherbert | 50.0 | 1967 | T. J. M. Graham | 46.6 |
| 1899 | R. W. Wadsley | 54.6 | 1968 | M. J. Winbolt Lewis | 46.9 |
| 1900 | M. W. Long (USA) | 49.8 | | | |
| 1901 | R. W. Wadsley | 49.8 | | *400 Metres* | |
| 1902 | G. W. White | 50.2 | 1969 | D. G. Griffiths | 46.8 |
| 1903 | C. McLachlan | 52.2 | 1970 | M. Bilham | 46.6 |

| 1889 | S. Thomas | 20 31.8 |
| 1890 | J. Kibblewhite | 20 16.4 |
| 1891 | W. H. Morton | 20 53.6 |
| 1892 | J. Kibblewhite | 19 50.6 |
| 1893 | C. Pearce | 20 12.6 |
| 1894 | F. E. Bacon | 19 48.8 |
| 1895 | H. A. Munro | 19 49.4 |
| 1896 | H. Harrison | 20 27.4 |
| 1897 | C. Bennett | 20 52.6 |
| 1898 | C. Bennett | 20 14.4 |
| 1899 | C. Bennett | 20 49.6 |
| 1900 | J. T. Rimmer | 20 11.0 |
| 1901 | A. Shrubb | 20 01.8 |
| 1902 | A. Shrubb | 20 01.4 |
| 1903 | A. Shrubb | 20 06.0 |
| 1904 | A. Shrubb | 19 56.8 |
| 1905 | J. Smith | 21 08.8 |
| 1906 | F. H. Hulford | 20 27.4 |
| 1907 | A. Duncan | 19 51.4 |
| 1908 | E. R. Voigt | 19 47.4 |
| 1909 | E. R. Voigt | 19 57.6 |
| 1910 | A. G. Hill | 20 00.6 |
| 1911 | H. Kolehmainen (Finland) | 20 03.6 |
| 1912 | G. W. Hutson | 20 10.8 |
| 1913 | G. W. Hutson | 19 32.0 |
| 1914 | G. W. Hutson | 19 41.4 |
| 1919 | E. Backman (Sweden) | 19 56.4 |
| 1920 | C. E. Blewitt | 20 10.8 |
| 1921 | W. Monk | 19 59.2 |
| 1922 | P. J. Nurmi (Finland) | 19 52.2 |
| 1923 | C. E. Blewitt | 19 56.6 |
| 1924 | W. M. Cotterell | 19 45.6 |
| 1925 | C. E. Blewitt | 19 54.6 |
| 1926 | J. E. Webster | 19 49.6 |
| 1927 | B. Ohrn (Sweden) | 19 40.8 |
| 1928 | W. Beavers | 19 41.6 |
| 1929 | W. Beavers | 19 49.4 |
| 1930 | L. Virtanen (Finland) | 19 36.2 |
| 1931 | J. A. Burns | 19 49.4 |

*6 Miles*

| 1932 | J. H. Potts | 30 23.2 |
| 1933 | J. T. Holden | 30 32.2 |
| 1934 | J. T. Holden | 30 43.8 |
| 1935 | J. T. Holden | 30 50.6 |
| 1936 | J. Noji (Poland) | 29 43.4 |
| 1937 | J. Kelen (Hungary) | 30 07.8 |
| 1938 | G. Beviacqua (Italy) | 30 06.0 |
| 1939 | S. O. A. Palmer | 30 06.4 |
| 1946 | J. H. Peters | 30 50.4 |
| 1947 | A. H. Chivers | 30 31.4 |
| 1948 | S. E. W. Cox | 30 08.4 |
| 1949 | V. Lillakas | 30 15.0 |
| 1950 | F. E. Aaron | 29 33.6 |
| 1951 | D. A. G. Pirie | 29 32.0 |
| 1952 | D. A. G. Pirie | 28 55.6 |
| 1953 | D. A. G. Pirie | 28 19.4 |
| 1954 | P. B. Driver | 28 34.8 |
| 1955 | K. L. Norris | 29 00.6 |

| 1956 | K. L. Norris | 28 13.6 |
| 1957 | G. Knight | 28 50.4 |
| 1958 | S. E. Eldon | 28 05.0 |
| 1959 | S. E. Eldon | 28 12.4 |
| 1960 | D. A. G. Pirie | 28 09.6 |
| 1961 | W. D. Power (Australia) | 27 57.8 |
| 1962 | H. R. Fowler | 27 49.8 |
| 1963 | R. Hill | 27 49.8 |
| 1964 | M. J. Bullivant | 27 26.6 |
| 1965 | M. Gammoudi (Tunisia) | 27 38.2 |
| 1966 | M. Gammoudi (Tunisia) | 27 23.4 |
| 1967 | J. Haase (E. Germany) | 27 33.2 |
| 1968 | T. F. K. Johnston | 27 22.2 |

*10,000 Metres*

| 1969 | R. G. Taylor | 28 27.6 |
| 1970 | D. C. Bedford | 28 26.4 |
| 1971 | D. C. Bedford | 27 47.0 |
| 1972 | D. C. Bedford | 27 52.8 |

*10 Miles*

| 1880 | C. H. Mason | 56 07.0 |
| 1881 | G. A. Dunning | 54 34.0 |
| 1882 | W. G. George | 54 41.0 |
| 1883 | W. Snook | 57 41.0 |
| 1884 | W. G. George | 54 02.0 |
| 1885 | W. Snook | 53 25.2 |
| 1886 | W. H. Coad | 55 44.2 |
| 1887 | E. C. Carter | 55 09.0 |
| 1888 | E. W. Parry | 53 43.4 |
| 1889 | S. Thomas | 51 31.4 |
| 1890 | J. Kibblewhite | 53 49.0 |
| 1891 | W. H. Morton | 52 33.8 |
| 1892 | S. Thomas | 53 25.2 |
| 1893 | S. Thomas | 52 41.4 |
| 1894 | S. Thomas | 51 37.0 |
| 1895 | F. E. Bacon | 52 43.8 |
| 1896 | G. Crossland | 52 05.0 |
| 1897 | A. E. Tysoe | 55 59.6 |
| 1898 | S. J. Robinson | 53 12.0 |
| 1899 | C. Bennett | 54 18.4 |
| 1900 | S. J. Robinson | 53 14.4 |
| 1901 | A. Shrubb | 53 32.0 |
| 1902 | A. Shrubb | 52 25.4 |
| 1903 | A. Shrubb | 51 55.8 |
| 1904 | A. Shrubb | 54 30.4 |
| 1905 | A. Aldridge | 51 49.0 |
| 1906 | A. Aldridge | 54 07.2 |
| 1907 | A. Underwood | 54 03.0 |
| 1908 | A. Duncan | 53 40.4 |
| 1909 | A. E. Wood | 52 40.0 |
| 1910 | F. O'Neill (Ireland) | 52 41.4 |
| 1911 | W. Scott | 52 26.4 |
| 1912 | W. Scott | 52 35.0 |
| 1913 | E. Glover | 51 56.8 |
| 1914 | T. Fennah | 53 33.4 |
| 1919 | C. E. Blewitt | 53 45.6 |

18

| | | | |
|---|---|---|---|
| 1920 | C. T. Clibbon | 53 | 53.4 |
| 1921 | H. Britton | 54 | 58.2 |
| 1922 | H. Britton | 53 | 24.2 |
| 1923 | E. Harper | 53 | 34.6 |
| 1924 | H. Britton | 52 | 48.8 |
| 1925 | J. E. Webster | 52 | 32.6 |
| 1926 | E. Harper | 52 | 04.0 |
| 1927 | E. Harper | 52 | 21.2 |
| 1928 | J. E. Webster | 52 | 16.2 |
| 1929 | E. Harper | 52 | 15.8 |
| 1930 | J. W. Winfield | 53 | 05.4 |
| 1931 | J. W. Winfield | 54 | 34.4 |
| 1932 | J. F. Wood | 52 | 00.2 |
| 1933 | G. W. Bailey | 50 | 51.0 |
| 1934 | J. T. Holden | 52 | 21.4 |
| 1935 | F. Marsland | 54 | 38.6 |
| 1936 | W. E. Eaton | 50 | 30.8 |
| 1937 | R. Walker | 52 | 33.8 |
| 1938 | R. V. Draper | 52 | 40.6 |
| 1939 | J. Chapelle (Belgium) | 51 | 56.0 |
| 1947 | J. H. Peters | 53 | 21.0 |
| 1958 | F. Norris | 49 | 39.0 |
| 1959 | F. Norris | 48 | 32.4 |
| 1960 | B. B. Heatley | 48 | 18.4 |
| 1961 | B. B. Heatley | 47 | 47.0 |
| 1962 | L. G. Edelen (USA) | 48 | 31.8 |
| 1963 | M. R. Batty | 48 | 13.4 |
| 1964 | M. R. Batty | 47 | 26.8 |
| 1965 | R. Hill | 48 | 56.0 |
| 1966 | R. Hill | 50 | 04.0 |
| 1967 | R. Hill | 47 | 38.6 |
| 1968 | R. Hill | 47 | 02.2 |
| 1969 | R. Hill | 47 | 27.0 |
| 1970 | T. Wright | 47 | 20.2 |
| 1971 | T. Wright | 46 | 51.6 |
| 1972 | B. J. Plain | 48 | 25.8 |

*Marathon*

| | | | | |
|---|---|---|---|---|
| 1925 | S. Ferris | 2 | 35 | 58.2 |
| 1926 | S. Ferris | 2 | 42 | 24.2 |
| 1927 | S. Ferris | 2 | 40 | 32.2 |
| 1928 | H. W. Payne | 2 | 34 | 34.0 |
| 1929 | H. W. Payne | 2 | 30 | 57.6 |
| 1930 | D. McL. Wright | 2 | 38 | 29.4 |
| 1931 | D. McL. Wright | 2 | 49 | 54.2 |
| 1932 | D. McN. Robertson | 2 | 34 | 32.6 |
| 1933 | D. McN. Robertson | 2 | 43 | 13.6 |
| 1934 | D. McN. Robertson | 2 | 41 | 55.0 |
| 1935 | A. J. Norris | 3 | 02 | 57.8 |
| 1936 | D. McN. Robertson | 2 | 35 | 02.4 |
| 1937 | D. McN. Robertson | 2 | 37 | 19.2 |
| 1938 | J. W. Beman | 2 | 36 | 39.6 |
| 1939 | D. McN. Robertson | 2 | 35 | 37.0 |
| 1946 | S. S. Yarrow | 2 | 43 | 14.4 |
| 1947 | J. T. Holden | 2 | 33 | 20.2 |
| 1948 | J. T. Holden | 2 | 36 | 44.6 |
| 1949 | J. T. Holden | 2 | 34 | 10.6 |
| 1950 | J. T. Holden | 2 | 31 | 03.4 |
| 1951 | J. H. Peters | 2 | 31 | 42.6 |
| 1952 | J. H. Peters | 2 | 20 | 42.2 |

| | | | | |
|---|---|---|---|---|
| 1953 | J. H. Peters | 2 | 22 | 29.0 |
| 1954 | J. H. Peters | 2 | 17 | 39.4 |
| 1955 | R. W. McMinnis | 2 | 39 | 35.0 |
| 1956 | H. J. Hicks | 2 | 26 | 15.0 |
| 1957 | E. Kirkup | 2 | 22 | 27.8 |
| 1958 | C. K. Kemball | 2 | 22 | 27.4 |
| 1959 | J. C. Fleming-Smith | 2 | 30 | 11.6 |
| 1960 | B. L. Kilby | 2 | 22 | 48.8 |
| 1961 | B. L. Kilby | 2 | 24 | 37.0 |
| 1962 | B. L. Kilby | 2 | 26 | 15.0 |
| 1963 | B. L. Kilby | 2 | 16 | 45.0 |
| 1964 | B. L. Kilby | 2 | 23 | 01.0 |
| 1965 | W. A. Adcocks | 2 | 16 | 50.0 |
| 1966 | G. A. H. Taylor | 2 | 19 | 04.0 |
| 1967 | J. N. C. Alder | 2 | 16 | 08.0 |
| 1968 | T. F. K. Johnston | 2 | 15 | 26.0 |
| 1969 | R. Hill | 2 | 13 | 42.0 |
| 1970 | D. K. Faircloth | 2 | 18 | 15.0 |
| 1971 | R. Hill | 2 | 12 | 39.0 |
| 1972 | L. Philipp (W. Germany) | | 2 12 | 50.0 |

(UK champion: R. Hill    2 12 51.0)

*Steeplechase (Distance Varied)*

| | |
|---|---|
| 1880 | J. Concannon |
| 1881 | J. Ogden |
| 1882 | T. Crellin |
| 1883 | T. Thornton |
| 1884 | W. Snook |
| 1885 | W. Snook |
| 1886 | M. A. Harrison |
| 1887 | M. A. Harrison |
| 1888 | J. C. Cope |
| 1889 | T. White |
| 1890 | E. W. Parry |
| 1891 | E. W. Parry |
| 1892 | W. H. Smith |
| 1893 | G. Martin |
| 1894 | A. B. George |
| 1895 | E. J. Wilkins |
| 1896 | S. J. Robinson |
| 1897 | G. H. Lee |
| 1898 | G. W. Orton (USA) |
| 1899 | W. Stokes |
| 1900 | S. J. Robinson |
| 1901 | S. J. Robinson |
| 1902 | G. Martin |
| 1903 | S. J. Robinson |
| 1904 | A. Russell |
| 1905 | A. Russell |
| 1906 | A. Russell |
| 1907 | J. C. English |
| 1908 | R. Noakes |
| 1909 | R. Noakes |
| 1910 | J. C. English |
| 1911 | R. Noakes |
| 1912 | S. Frost |

*2 Miles Steeplechase*

| | | |
|---|---|---|
| 1913 | C. H. Ruffell | 11 03.6 |

| 1914 | S. Frost | 11 10.6 |
| 1919 | P. Hodge | 11 53.6 |
| 1920 | P. Hodge | 11 22.8 |
| 1921 | P. Hodge | 10 57.2 |
| 1922 | P. J. Nurmi (Finland) | 11 11.2 |
| 1923 | P. Hodge | 11 13.6 |
| 1924 | C. E. Blewitt | 11 02.0 |
| 1925 | J. E. Webster | 11 01.4 |
| 1926 | J. E. Webster | 10 34.2 |
| 1927 | J. E. Webster | 11 06.0 |
| 1928 | J. E. Webster | 10 44.8 |
| 1929 | E. H. Oliver | 10 53.2 |
| 1930 | G. W. Bailey | 10 55.4 |
| 1931 | T. Evenson | 10 36.4 |
| 1932 | T. Evenson | 10 13.8 |
| 1933 | V. Iso-Hollo (Finland) | 10 06.6 |
| 1934 | S. C. Scarsbrook | 10 48.4 |
| 1935 | G. W. Bailey | 10 20.4 |
| 1936 | T. Evenson | 10 24.8 |
| 1937 | W. C. Wylie | 10 27.0 |
| 1938 | J. H. Potts | 10 39.2 |
| 1939 | J. Chapelle (Belgium) | 10 22.4 |
| 1946 | M. Vandewattyne (Belgium) | 10 27.6 |
| 1947 | H. Hires (Hungary) | 10 39.3 |
| 1948 | T. P. E. Curry | 10 31.8 |
| 1949 | F. T. Holt | 10 29.0 |
| 1950 | P. Segedin (Yugoslavia) | 10 02.4 |
| 1951 | P. Segedin (Yugoslavia) | 9 58.6 |
| 1952 | J. I. Disley | 9 44.0 |
| 1953 | E. G. Ellis | 10 02.8 |

*3000 Metres Steeplechase*

| 1954 | K. E. Johnson | 9 00.8 |
| 1955 | J. I. Disley | 8 56.6 |
| 1956 | E. Shirley | 8 51.6 |
| 1957 | J. I. Disley | 8 56.8 |
| 1958 | E. Shirley | 8 51.0 |
| 1959 | M. Herriott | 8 52.8 |
| 1960 | E. Shirley | 8 51.0 |
| 1961 | M. Herriott | 8 53.6 |
| 1962 | M. Herriott | 8 43.8 |
| 1963 | M. Herriott | 8 47.8 |
| 1964 | M. Herriott | 8 40.0 |
| 1965 | M. Herriott | 8 41.0 |
| 1966 | M. Herriott | 8 37.0 |
| 1967 | M. Herriott | 8 33.8 |
| 1968 | D. G. Bryan-Jones | 8 36.2 |
| 1969 | J. M. Jackson | 8 35.0 |
| 1970 | J. A. Holden | 8 38.0 |
| 1971 | J. A. Holden | 8 38.0 |
| 1972 | S. C. Hollings | 8 31.2 |

*120 Yards Hurdles*    sec.

| 1880 | G. P. C. Lawrence | 16.4 |
| 1881 | G. P. C. Lawrence | 16.2 |
| 1882 | S. Palmer | 16.6 |
| 1883* | S. Palmer | 16.2 |
| 1884 | C. W. Gowthorpe | 16.6 |
| 1885 | C. F. Daft | 16.6 |
| 1886 | C. F. Daft | 16.0 |
| 1887 | J. Le Fleming | 16.2 |
| 1888 | S. Joyce | 16.0 |
| 1889 | C. W. Haward | 16.4 |
| 1890 | C. F. Daft | 16.8 |
| 1891 | D. D. Bulger (Ireland) | 16.6 |
| 1892 | D. D. Bulger (Ireland) | 16.0 |
| 1893 | G. B. Shaw | 16.4 |
| 1894 | G. B. Shaw | 16.6 |
| 1895 | G. B. Shaw | 15.8 |
| 1896 | G. B. Shaw | 15.6 |
| 1897 | A. Trafford | 17.4 |
| 1898 | H. R. Parkes | 16.4 |
| 1899 | W. G. Paget-Tomlinson | 16.4 |
| 1900 | A. C. Kraenzlein (USA) | 15.4 |
| 1901 | A. C. Kraenzlein (USA) | 15.6 |
| 1902 | G. W. Smith (New Zealand) | 16.0 |
| 1903 | G. R. Garnier | 15.8 |
| 1904 | R. S. Stronach | 16.0 |
| 1905 | R. S. Stronach | 16.8 |
| 1906 | R. S. Stronach | 16.6 |
| 1907 | O. Groenings | 16.8 |
| 1908 | V. Duncker (S. Africa) | 16.2 |
| 1909 | A. H. Healey | 15.8 |
| 1910 | G. R. L. Anderson | 16.0 |
| 1911 | P. R. O'R. Philips | 16.2 |
| 1912 | G. R. L. Anderson | 15.6 |
| 1913 | G. H. Gray | 16.0 |
| 1914 | G. H. Gray | 15.8 |
| 1919 | H. E. Wilson (New Zealand) | 15.8 |
| 1920 | G. A. Trowbridge (USA) | 15.4 |
| 1921 | H. Bernard (France) | 15.8 |
| 1922 | F. R. Gaby | 15.6 |
| 1923 | F. R. Gaby | 15.2 |
| 1924 | S. J. M. Atkinson (S. Africa) | 15.1 |
| 1925 | F. R. Gaby | 15.2 |
| 1926 | F. R. Gaby | 15.1 |
| 1927 | F. R. Gaby | 14.9 |
| 1928 | S. J. M. Atkinson (S. Africa) | 14.7 |
| 1929 | Lord Burghley | 15.4 |
| 1930 | Lord Burghley | 15.2 |
| 1931 | Lord Burghley | 14.8 |
| 1932 | D. O. Finlay | 14.9 |
| 1933 | D. O. Finlay | 15.0 |
| 1934 | D. O. Finlay | 14.8 |
| 1935 | D. O. Finlay | 15.0 |
| 1936 | D. O. Finlay | 14.6 |
| 1937 | D. O. Finlay | 14.5 |
| 1938 | D. O. Finlay | 14.4 |
| 1939 | R. J. Brasser (Netherlands) | 14.7 |

| Year | Name | Time |
|---|---|---|
| 1946 | P. Braekman (Belgium) | 14.9 |
| 1947 | P. Braekman (Belgium) | 14.9 |
| 1948 | J. R. Birrell | 15.1 |
| 1949 | D. O. Finlay | 14.6 |
| 1950 | P. B. Hildreth | 15.2 |
| 1951 | F. J. Parker | 14.8 |
| 1952 | R. H. Weinberg (Australia) | 14.4 |
| 1953 | P. B. Hildreth | 14.6 |
| 1954 | F. J. Parker | 14.7 |
| 1955 | F. J. Parker | 14.6 |
| 1956 | P. B. Hildreth | 14.5 |
| 1957 | E. F. Kinsella (Ireland) | 14.7 |
| 1958 | K. A. St. H. Gardner (Jamaica) | 14.1 |
| 1959 | V. C. Matthews | 14.5 |
| 1960 | H. G. Raziq (Pakistan) | 14.6 |
| 1961 | N. Svara (Italy) | 14.4 |
| 1962 | B. Lindgren (USA) | 14.2 |
| 1963 | J. L. Taitt | 14.1 |
| 1964 | J. M. Parker | 14.2 |
| 1965 | J. L. Taitt | 14.3 |
| 1966 | D. P. Hemery | 14.0 |
| 1967 | E. Ottoz (Italy) | 14.0 |
| 1968 | A. P. Pascoe | 14.1 |

* In re-run race after tie.

*110 Metres Hurdles*

| Year | Name | Time |
|---|---|---|
| 1969 | W. Coetzee (S. Africa) | 14.0 |
| 1970 | D. P. Hemery | 13.9 |
| 1971 | A. P. Pascoe | 14.5 |
| 1972 | A. P. Pascoe | 13.9 |

*220 Yards Hurdles*

| Year | Name | Time |
|---|---|---|
| 1952 | P. B. Hildreth | 24.6 |
| 1953 | H. Whittle | 24.2 |
| 1954 | P. B. Hildreth | 24.6 |
| 1955 | P. A. L. Vine | 23.7 |
| 1956 | P. A. L. Vine | 24.5 |
| 1957 | J. R. A. Scott-Oldfield | 24.2 |
| 1958 | K. S. D. Wilmshurst | 24.3 |
| 1959 | J. Metcalf | 23.8 |
| 1960 | C. W. E. Surety | 24.9 |
| 1961 | S. Morale (Italy) | 23.9 |
| 1962 | B. Lindgren (USA) | 23.9 |

(discontinued)

*440 Yards Hurdles*

| Year | Name | Time |
|---|---|---|
| 1914 | J. C. English | 59.8 |
| 1919 | G. H. Gray | 59.8 |
| 1920 | E. W. Wheller | 57.4 |
| 1921 | C. A. Christiernsson (Sweden) | 55.4 |
| 1922 | W. S. Kent-Hughes | 59.0 |
| 1923 | L. H. Phillips | 58.0 |
| 1924 | W. G. Tatham | 57.6 |
| 1925 | I. H. Riley (USA) | 57.8 |
| 1926 | Lord Burghley | 55.0 |
| 1927 | Lord Burghley | 54.2 |
| 1928 | Lord Burghley | 54.0 |
| 1929 | L. Facelli (Italy) | 53.4 |
| 1930 | Lord Burghley | 53.8 |
| 1931 | L. Facelli (Italy) | 54.6 |
| 1932 | Lord Burghley | 54.4 |
| 1933 | L. Facelli (Italy) | 55.6 |
| 1934 | R. K. Brown | 55.4 |
| 1935 | F. A. R. Hunter | 55.3 |
| 1936 | J. Sheffield | 55.6 |
| 1937 | J. Bosmans (Belgium) | 55.0 |
| 1938 | J. Bosmans (Belgium) | 54.1 |
| 1939 | J. Bosmans (Belgium) | 54.9 |
| 1946 | D. R. Ede | 57.0 |
| 1947 | H. Whittle | 55.0 |
| 1948 | H. Whittle | 54.9 |
| 1949 | H. Whittle | 54.9 |
| 1950 | H. Whittle | 55.2 |
| 1951 | H. Whittle | 54.2 |
| 1952 | H. Whittle | 53.3 |
| 1953 | H. Whittle | 52.7 |
| 1954 | H. Kane | 53.4 |
| 1955 | R. D. Shaw | 52.2 |
| 1956 | I. Savel (Rumania) | 52.2 |
| 1957 | T. S. Farrell | 52.1 |
| 1958 | D. F. Lean (Australia) | 51.2 |
| 1959 | C. E. Goudge | 52.7 |
| 1960 | M. G. Boyes | 52.2 |
| 1961 | J. A. Rintamaki (Finland) | 51.5 |
| 1962 | R. Rogers (USA) | 51.0 |
| 1963 | W. Atterberry (USA) | 51.2 |
| 1964 | J. H. Cooper | 51.1 |
| 1965 | W. J. Cawley (USA) | 50.9 |
| 1966 | J. Sherwood | 51.1 |
| 1967 | J. Sherwood | 50.9 |
| 1968 | D. P. Hemery | 50.2 |

*400 Metres Hurdles*

| Year | Name | Time |
|---|---|---|
| 1969 | J. Sherwood | 50.1 |
| 1970 | R. M. Roberts | 52.4 |
| 1971 | J. Sherwood | 51.4 |
| 1972 | D. P. Hemery | 49.7 |

*High Jump*

| Year | Name | ft. | in. |
|---|---|---|---|
| 1880 | J. W. Parsons | 5 | 9¾ |
| 1881 | P. Davin (Ireland) | 6 | 0½ |
| 1882 | R. F. Houghton | 5 | 7¼ |
| 1883 | J. W. Parsons | 6 | 0¼ |
| 1884 | T. Ray | 5 | 7 |
| 1885 | P. J. Kelly (Ireland) | 5 | 11 |
| 1886 | G. W. Rowdon | 5 | 11½ |
| 1887 | G. W. Rowdon and W. B. Page (USA) | 6 | 0 |
| 1888 | G. W. Rowdon | 5 | 8 |
| 1889 | T. Jennings | 5 | 8½ |
| 1890 | C. W. Haward | 5 | 8½ |
| 1891 | T. Jennings | 5 | 9½ |
| 1892 | A. Watkinson | 5 | 8½ |
| 1893 | J. M. Ryan (Ireland) | 6 | 2½ |
| 1894 | R. Williams | 5 | 9¼ |
| 1895 | J. M. Ryan (Ireland) | 5 | 11½ |

| | | | |
|---|---|---|---|
| 1896 | M. O'Brien (Ireland) | 5 | 11 |
| 1897 | C. E. H. Leggatt | 5 | 9 |
| 1898 | P. Leahy (Ireland) | 5 | 11⅝ |
| 1899 | P. Leahy (Ireland) | 5 | 10¼ |
| 1900 | I. K. Baxter (USA) | 6 | 2 |
| 1901 | I. K. Baxter (USA) | 5 | 11 |
| 1902 | S. S. Jones (USA) | 6 | 3 |
| 1903 | P. O'Connor (Ireland) | 5 | 8 |
| 1904 | P. O'Connor (Ireland), R. G. Murray and J. B. Milne | 5 | 9½ |
| 1905 | C. Leahy (Ireland) | 5 | 10¼ |
| 1906 | C. Leahy (Ireland) | 6 | 0 |
| 1907 | C. Leahy (Ireland) | 6 | 0 |
| 1908 | C. Leahy (Ireland) | 5 | 11 |
| 1909 | J. H. Banks | 5 | 9 |
| 1910 | B. H. Baker | 5 | 8½ |
| 1911 | R. Pasemann (Germany) | 6 | 0 |
| 1912 | B. H. Baker | 6 | 0 |
| 1913 | B. H. Baker | 6 | 0 |
| 1914 | W. M. Oler (USA) | 6 | 2½ |
| 1919 | B. H. Baker | 5 | 11 |
| 1920 | B. H. Baker | 6 | 3¾ |
| 1921 | B. H. Baker | 6 | 2¼ |
| 1922 | P. Lewden (France) | 5 | 11 |
| 1923 | P. Lewden (France) | 6 | 4 |
| 1924 | L. Stanley (Ireland) | 6 | 1½ |
| 1925 | H. M. Osborn (USA) | 6 | 4 |
| 1926 | C. T. van Geyzel | 6 | 1 |
| 1927 | H. Adolfsson (Sweden) | 6 | 0 |
| 1928 | C. Menard (France) | 6 | 3 |
| 1929 | C. Kesmarki (Hungary) | 6 | 3 |
| 1930 | C. E. S. Gordon | 6 | 1 |
| 1931 | A. J. Gray | 6 | 0 |
| 1932 | W. A. Land | 6 | 1 |
| 1933 | M. Bodosi (Hungary) | 6 | 3 |
| 1934 | M. Bodosi (Hungary) | 6 | 3 |
| 1935 | S. R. West | 6 | 3 |
| 1936 | J. P. Metcalfe (Australia) | 6 | 1 |
| 1937 | J. L. Newman | 6 | 2 |
| 1938 | R. O'Rafferty (Ireland) | 6 | 1 |
| 1939 | J. L. Newman | 6 | 2 |
| 1946 | A. S. Paterson | 6 | 2 |
| 1947 | Prince Adedoyin (Nigeria) | 6 | 4 |
| 1948 | J. A. Winter (Australia) | 6 | 4 |
| 1949 | A. S. Paterson | 6 | 4 |
| 1950 | A. S. Paterson | 6 | 4 |
| 1951 | R. C. Pavitt | 6 | 5 |
| 1952 | R. C. Pavitt | 6 | 4 |
| 1953 | D. R. J. Cox | 6 | 3 |
| 1954 | B. M. P. O'Reilly (Ireland) | 6 | 5 |
| 1955 | W. Piper | 6 | 3 |
| 1956 | I. Soeter (Rumania) | 6 | 4 |
| 1957 | O. Okuwobi (Nigeria) | 6 | 5 |
| 1958 | P. Etolu (Uganda) | 6 | 8 |
| 1959 | C. W. Fairbrother | 6 | 7 |
| 1960 | R. E. Kotei (Ghana) | 6 | 10 |
| 1961 | C. W. Fairbrother | 6 | 9 |
| 1962 | K. Sugioka (Japan) | 6 | 10½ |
| 1963 | K. Sugioka (Japan) | 6 | 8 |
| 1964 | C. W. Fairbrother | 6 | 8 |
| 1965 | K. A. Nilsson (Sweden) | 6 | 8 |
| 1966 | J. S. O. Kadiri (Nigeria) | 6 | 6 |
| 1967 | E. Lansdell (S. Africa) | 6 | 7 |
| 1968 | D. Mendenhall (USA) | 6 | 10 |
| 1969 | K. Lundmark (Sweden) | 6 | 10¾ |
| 1970 | H. Tomizawa (Japan) | 6 | 9¾ |
| 1971 | M. C. Campbell | 6 | 8¼ |
| 1972 | M. Jarmrich (West Germany) | 6 | 9¾ |

(UK champion: C. Boreham 6 7)

| *Pole Vault* | | ft. | in. |
|---|---|---|---|
| 1880 | E. A. Strachan | 10 | 4 |
| 1881 | T. Ray | 11 | 3 |
| 1882 | T. Ray | 10 | 6 |
| 1883 | H. J. Cobbold | 9 | 6 |
| 1884 | T. Ray | 10 | 4 |
| 1885 | T. Ray | 10 | 0 |
| 1886 | T. Ray | 10 | 11½ |
| 1887 | T. Ray | 11 | 1 |
| 1888 | E. L. Stones and T. Ray | 11 | 0½ |
| 1889 | E. L. Stones | 11 | 1¾ |
| 1890 | R. D. Dickinson | 11 | 0 |
| 1891 | R. Watson | 11 | 3 |
| 1892 | R. Watson and R. D. Dickinson | 11 | 0 |
| 1893 | R. D. Dickinson | 11 | 2 |
| 1894 | R. D. Dickinson | 10 | 11 |
| 1895 | R. D. Dickinson | 10 | 0 |
| 1896 | R. E. Foreshaw | 10 | 0 |
| 1897 | J. Poole | 9 | 10½ |
| 1898 | J. Poole | 10 | 3 |
| 1899 | E. C. Pritchard | 9 | 1 |
| 1900 | B. Johnson (USA) | 11 | 4 |
| 1901 | I. K. Baxter (USA) and W. H. Hodgson | 9 | 10 |
| 1902 | F. J. Kauser (Hungary) | 10 | 8 |
| 1903 | S. Morriss (Germany) | 8 | 6 |
| 1904 | A. Puyseigur (France) | 10 | 6 |
| 1905 | F. Gonder (France) | 10 | 2 |
| 1906 | A. E. A. Harragin (Trinidad) | 10 | 4 |
| 1907 | B. Soderstrom (Sweden) | 10 | 6 |
| 1908 | E. B. Archibald (Canada) | 12 | 0 |
| 1909 | A. E. Flaxman | 9 | 7½ |
| 1910 | K. de Szathmary (Hungary) | 11 | 7½ |
| 1911 | R. Pasemann (Germany) | 12 | 0 |
| 1912 | A. O. Conquest | 9 | 6½ |
| 1913 | C. Gille (Sweden) | 12 | 1 |

| | | | |
|---|---|---|---|
| 1914 | R. Sjoberg (Sweden) | 11 | 2 |
| 1919 | G. Hogstrom (Sweden) | 11 | 0 |
| 1920 | A. Franquenelle (France) | 10 | 6 |
| 1921 | E. Rydberg (Sweden) | 12 | 2¾ |
| 1922 | C. Hoff (Norway) | 12 | 0 |
| 1923 | P. Lewden (France) | jump-over | |
| 1924 | D. J. R. Sumner | 10 | 3 |
| 1925 | P. W. Jones (USA) | 11 | 6 |
| 1926 | F. J. Kelley (USA) | 12 | 0 |
| 1927 | H. Lindblad (Sweden) | 12 | 6 |
| 1928 | F. J. Kelley (USA) | 12 | 7 |
| 1929 | H. Ford | 11 | 9 |
| 1930 | H. Lindblad (Sweden) and A. Van De Zee (Netherlands) | 12 | 0 |
| 1931 | H. Lindblad (Sweden) and A. Van De Zee (Netherlands) | 12 | 6 |
| 1932 | P. B. B. Ogilvie | 12 | 0 |
| 1933 | D. Innocenti (Italy) | 12 | 6 |
| 1934 | F. Phillipson | 12 | 3 |
| 1935 | K. Brown (USA) | 13 | 10 |
| 1936 | F. R. Webster | 12 | 9 |
| 1937 | J. H. Dodd | 12 | 0 |
| 1938 | M. Romeo (Italy) | 13 | 0 |
| 1939 | F. R. Webster | 12 | 3 |
| 1946 | C. Lamoree (Netherlands) | 12 | 10 |
| 1947 | Z. Zitvay (Hungary) | 12 | 6 |
| 1948 | F. R. Webster | 12 | 3 |
| 1949 | P. G. Harwood (USA) | 12 | 6 |
| 1950 | R. Stjernild (Denmark) | 12 | 6 |
| 1951 | T. Bryngeirsson (Iceland) | 13 | 3 |
| 1952 | G. M. Elliott | 13 | 0 |
| 1953 | G. M. Elliott | 13 | 6 |
| 1954 | T. Homonnay (Hungary) | 14 | 0 |
| 1955 | G. M. Elliott | 13 | 6 |
| 1956 | I. Ward | 13 | 0 |
| 1957 | I. Ward | 13 | 5 |
| 1958 | M. D. Richards (New Zealand) | 13 | 6 |
| 1959 | A. Ditta (Pakistan) | 13 | 6 |
| 1960 | S. R. Porter | 13 | 6 |
| 1961 | R. Ankio (Finland) | 14 | 6 |
| 1962 | P. K. Nikula (Finland) | 15 | 3¼ |
| 1963 | J. T. Pennel (USA) | 16 | 8¾ |
| 1964 | F. Hansen (USA) | 15 | 0 |
| 1965 | P. Wilson (USA) | 15 | 6 |
| 1966 | M. A. Bull | 15 | 0 |
| 1967 | M. A. Bull | 15 | 0 |
| 1968 | R. Dionisi (Italy) | 16 | 6 |
| 1969 | M. A. Bull | 15 | 6¼ |
| 1970 | K. Niwa (Japan) | 16 | 4¾ |
| 1971 | M. A. Bull | 16 | 6¾ |
| 1972 | M. A. Bull | 17 | 1 |

*Long Jump*

| | | ft. | in. |
|---|---|---|---|
| 1880 | C. L. Lockton | 22 | 2 |
| 1881 | P. Davin (Ireland) | 22 | 11 |
| 1882 | T. M. Malone (Ireland) | 21 | 9½ |
| 1883 | J. W. Parsons | 23 | 0¼ |
| 1884 | E. Horwood | 21 | 9 |
| 1885 | J. Purcell (Ireland) | 21 | 10½ |
| 1886 | J. Purcell (Ireland) | 22 | 4 |
| 1887 | F. B. Roberts | 22 | 4 |
| 1888 | A. A. Jordan (USA) | 21 | 8¾ |
| 1889 | D. D. Bulger (Ireland) | 21 | 6 |
| 1890 | R. G. Hogarth | 20 | 0 |
| 1891 | D. D. Bulger (Ireland) and M. W. Ford (USA) | 20 | 4 |
| 1892 | D. D. Bulger (Ireland) | 21 | 4½ |
| 1893 | T. M. Donovan (Ireland) | 21 | 11 |
| 1894 | T. M. Donovan (Ireland) | 20 | 8 |
| 1895 | W. J. Oakley | 21 | 6½ |
| 1896 | C. E. H. Leggatt | 23 | 0¾ |
| 1897 | C. E. H. Leggatt | 21 | 4 |
| 1898 | W. J. M. Newburn (Ireland) | 23 | 7 |
| 1899 | W. J. M. Newburn (Ireland) | 22 | 2 |
| 1900 | A. C. Kraenzlein (USA) | 22 | 10¼ |
| 1901 | P. O'Connor (Ireland) | 23 | 8½ |
| 1902 | P. O'Connor (Ireland) | 23 | 7½ |
| 1903 | P. O'Connor (Ireland) | 22 | 9½ |
| 1904 | P. O'Connor (Ireland) | 23 | 2½ |
| 1905 | P. O'Connor (Ireland) | 23 | 9½ |
| 1906 | P. O'Connor (Ireland) | 23 | 5½ |
| 1907 | D. Murray (Ireland) | 22 | 0 |
| 1908 | W. H. Bleaden | 22 | 3½ |
| 1909 | T. J. Ahearne (Ireland) | 22 | 4¼ |
| 1910 | P. Kirwan (Ireland) | 22 | 0¾ |
| 1911 | P. Kirwan (Ireland) | 23 | 5½ |
| 1912 | P. Kirwan (Ireland) | 23 | 2½ |
| 1913 | S. S. Abrahams | 22 | 6 |
| 1914 | P. C. Kingsford | 23 | 3¼ |
| 1919 | W. Bjornemann (Sweden) | 23 | 6¾ |
| 1920 | D. B. Lourie (USA) | 22 | 4 |
| 1921 | H. C. Taylor (USA) | 22 | 1 |
| 1922 | C. Hoff (Norway) | 23 | 3 |
| 1923 | H. M. Abrahams | 23 | 8¾ |
| 1924 | H. M. Abrahams | 22 | 8½ |
| 1925 | R. St. J. Honner (Australia) | 23 | 11½ |
| 1926 | R. St. J. Honner (Australia) | 23 | 8 |
| 1927 | R. Dobermann (Germany) | 23 | 11¾ |
| 1928 | H. De Boer (Netherlands) | 24 | 2¼ |
| 1929 | H. J. Cohen | 22 | 7 |
| 1930 | O. Hallberg (Sweden) | 24 | 2 |

| Year | Name | ft. | in. |
|---|---|---|---|
| 1931 | H. De Boer (Netherlands) | 23 | 8 |
| 1932 | R. M. Evans (S. Africa) | 23 | 2 |
| 1933 | L. Balogh (Hungary) | 23 | $2\frac{1}{4}$ |
| 1934 | R. Paul (France) | 23 | 1 |
| 1935 | R. Paul (France) | 23 | $10\frac{1}{2}$ |
| 1936 | G. T. Traynor | 23 | $2\frac{1}{2}$ |
| 1937 | L. Long (Germany) | 24 | $6\frac{3}{4}$ |
| 1938 | A. Maffei (Italy) | 24 | 8 |
| 1939 | W. E. N. Breach | 23 | 8 |
| 1946 | D. C. V. Watts | 23 | 4 |
| 1947 | H. Whittle | 23 | $9\frac{1}{2}$ |
| 1948 | T. Bruce (Australia) | 23 | $9\frac{1}{2}$ |
| 1949 | H. Whittle | 23 | $5\frac{1}{2}$ |
| 1950 | H. E. Askew | 23 | $2\frac{1}{4}$ |
| 1951 | S. O. Williams (Nigeria) | 23 | $1\frac{1}{2}$ |
| 1952 | S. O. Williams (Nigeria) | 24 | $0\frac{1}{4}$ |
| 1953 | K. A. B. Olowu (Nigeria) | 23 | $5\frac{1}{2}$ |
| 1954 | O. Foldessy (Hungary) | 24 | $6\frac{1}{2}$ |
| 1955 | K. A. B. Olowu (Nigeria) | 24 | 2 |
| 1956 | A. R. Cruttenden | 23 | $9\frac{1}{2}$ |
| 1957 | A. R. Cruttenden | 23 | 10 |
| 1958 | K. A. B. Olowu (Nigeria) | 23 | $10\frac{1}{2}$ |
| 1959 | D. J. Whyte | 23 | 9 |
| 1960 | F. J. Alsop | 23 | 7 |
| 1961 | O. Oladitan (Nigeria) | 24 | $3\frac{1}{4}$ |
| 1962 | J. R. Valkama (Finland) | 25 | $1\frac{1}{4}$ |
| 1963 | F. J. Alsop | 24 | $8\frac{1}{4}$ |
| 1964 | L. Davies | 26 | $1\frac{1}{4}$ |
| 1965 | F. J. Alsop | 24 | $2\frac{3}{4}$ |
| 1966 | L. Davies | 26 | $5\frac{1}{4}$ |
| 1967 | L. Davies | 26 | $0\frac{1}{4}$ |
| 1968 | L. Davies | 26 | $0\frac{1}{2}$ |
| 1969 | L. Davies | 25 | 0 |
| 1970 | A. L. Lerwill | 25 | $0\frac{1}{4}$ |
| 1971 | H. Hines (USA) | 26 | $3\frac{1}{2}$ |
| 1972 | A. L. Lerwill | 26 | 9 |

*Triple Jump*

| Year | Name | ft. | in. |
|---|---|---|---|
| 1914 | I. Sahlin (Sweden) | 46 | $0\frac{1}{4}$ |
| 1920 | C. E. Lively | 43 | $3\frac{1}{2}$ |
| 1921 | F. Jansson (Sweden) | 46 | $6\frac{1}{4}$ |
| 1922 | V. Tuulos (Finland) | 46 | $9\frac{3}{4}$ |
| 1923 | J. Odde | 46 | $4\frac{1}{2}$ |
| 1924 | J. Higginson | 45 | 11 |
| 1925 | E. Somfai (Hungary) | 46 | $10\frac{1}{2}$ |
| 1926 | J. Higginson | 45 | 6 |
| 1927 | W. Peters (Netherlands) | 50 | 9 |
| 1928 | W. Peters (Netherlands) | 48 | 11 |
| 1929 | W. Peters (Netherlands) | 46 | 8 |
| 1930 | W. Peters (Netherlands) | 49 | $6\frac{1}{4}$ |
| 1931 | J. Blankers (Netherlands) | 46 | $7\frac{3}{4}$ |
| 1932 | A. J. Gray | 45 | 4 |
| 1933 | J. Blankers (Netherlands) | 48 | $2\frac{1}{2}$ |
| 1934 | E. Boyce | 47 | $8\frac{1}{4}$ |
| 1935 | W. Peters (Netherlands) | 46 | $10\frac{1}{2}$ |
| 1936 | J. P. Metcalfe (Australia) | 49 | $5\frac{1}{2}$ |
| 1937 | W. Peters (Netherlands) | 47 | 0 |
| 1938 | E. Boyce | 46 | $1\frac{1}{2}$ |
| 1939 | J. Palamiotis (Greece) | 49 | $3\frac{3}{4}$ |
| 1946 | D. C. V. Watts | 46 | $10\frac{1}{2}$ |
| 1947 | D. C. V. Watts | 46 | 9 |
| 1948 | G. G. Avery (Australia) | 46 | 5 |
| 1949 | H. Van Egmond (Netherlands) | 47 | 0 |
| 1950 | S. E. Cross | 46 | $9\frac{1}{2}$ |
| 1951 | S. E. Cross | 47 | 0 |
| 1952 | W. Burgard (Saar) | 47 | $10\frac{1}{2}$ |
| 1953 | K. S. D. Wilmshurst | 47 | $1\frac{1}{2}$ |
| 1954 | K. S. D. Wilmshurst | 48 | $9\frac{1}{2}$ |
| 1955 | K. S. D. Wilmshurst | 49 | $9\frac{1}{2}$ |
| 1956 | K. S. D. Wilmshurst | 49 | 9 |
| 1957 | K. S. D. Wilmshurst | 48 | 9 |
| 1958 | D. S. Norris (New Zealand) | 51 | 4 |
| 1959 | J. E. C. Whall | 49 | $2\frac{1}{4}$ |
| 1960 | F. J. Alsop | 50 | $7\frac{3}{4}$ |
| 1961 | F. J. Alsop | 50 | $5\frac{1}{4}$ |
| 1962 | T. Ota (Japan) | 51 | $4\frac{1}{2}$ |
| 1963 | K. Sakurai (Japan) | 51 | $3\frac{1}{4}$ |
| 1964 | F. J. Alsop | 52 | 3 |
| 1965 | F. J. Alsop | 52 | $1\frac{1}{4}$ |
| 1966 | J. Szmidt (Poland) | 52 | $5\frac{3}{4}$ |
| 1967 | F. J. Alsop | 51 | 5 |
| 1968 | S. Ciochina (Rumania) | 52 | $7\frac{1}{4}$ |
| 1969 | A. E. Wadhams | 51 | $4\frac{1}{2}$ |
| 1970 | M. Muraki (Japan) | 52 | $2\frac{1}{2}$ |
| 1971 | A. E. Wadhams | 49 | 9 |
| 1972 | D. C. Johnson | 51 | 10 |

*Shot*

| Year | Name | ft. | in. |
|---|---|---|---|
| 1880 | W. Y. Winthrop | 37 | 3 |
| 1881 | M. Davin (Ireland) | 39 | $6\frac{1}{2}$ |
| 1882 | G. Ross | 42 | 4 |
| 1883 | O. Harte (Ireland) | 41 | 1 |
| 1884 | O. Harte (Ireland) | 39 | 10 |
| 1885 | D. J. Mackinnon | 43 | $0\frac{1}{2}$ |
| 1886 | J. S. Mitchel (Ireland) | 38 | 1 |
| 1887 | J. S. Mitchel (Ireland) | 39 | $1\frac{1}{2}$ |
| 1888 | G. R. Gray (USA) | 43 | 7 |
| 1889 | W. J. M. Barry (Ireland) and R. A. Green | 39 | 8 |
| 1890 | R. A. Green | 37 | 8 |
| 1891 | W. J. M. Barry (Ireland) | 40 | 8 |
| 1892 | W. J. M. Barry (Ireland) | 42 | $10\frac{1}{2}$ |
| 1893 | D. Horgan (Ireland) | 42 | 9 |
| 1894 | D. Horgan (Ireland) | 42 | 4 |
| 1895 | D. Horgan (Ireland) | 44 | $3\frac{1}{2}$ |
| 1896 | D. Horgan (Ireland) | 43 | $5\frac{1}{2}$ |
| 1897 | D. Horgan (Ireland) | 45 | 4 |
| 1898 | D. Horgan (Ireland) | 45 | 0 |

| | | | |
|---|---|---|---|
| 1899 | D. Horgan (Ireland) | 46 | 0½ |
| 1900 | R. Sheldon (USA) | 45 | 10½ |
| 1901 | W. W. Coe (USA) | 45 | 5½ |
| 1902 | W. W. Coe (USA) | 42 | 10½ |
| 1903 | T. R. Nicolson | 40 | 7½ |
| 1904 | D. Horgan (Ireland) | 45 | 2 |
| 1905 | D. Horgan (Ireland) | 44 | 5½ |
| 1906 | T. Kirkwood | 45 | 4½ |
| 1907 | T. Kirkwood | 44 | 2 |
| 1908 | D. Horgan (Ireland) | 44 | 7 |
| 1909 | D. Horgan (Ireland) | 44 | 1 |
| 1910 | D. Horgan (Ireland) | 42 | 9 |
| 1911 | J. Barrett (Ireland) | 43 | 5 |
| 1912 | D. Horgan (Ireland) | 44 | 10 |
| 1913 | E. Nilsson (Sweden) | 47 | 4½ |
| 1914 | A. R. Taipale (Finland) | 44 | 7½ |
| 1919 | B. Jansson (Sweden) | 42 | 7 |
| 1920 | R. Paoli (France) | 43 | 10 |
| 1921 | B. Jansson (Sweden) | 46 | 2½ |
| 1922 | V. Porhola (Finland) | 47 | 10 |
| 1923 | J. Barrett (Ireland) | 39 | 2½ |
| 1924 | R. S. Woods | 43 | 10 |
| 1925 | H. H. Schwarze (USA) | 47 | 3 |
| 1926 | R. S. Woods | 44 | 11 |
| 1927 | G. Brechenmacher (Germany) | 46 | 6½ |
| 1928 | E. Duhour (France) | 47 | 5 |
| 1929 | J. Daranyi (Hungary) | 46 | 7 |
| 1930 | J. Noel (France) | 45 | 2 |
| 1931 | J. Daranyi (Hungary) | 49 | 11½ |
| 1932 | H. B. Hart (S. Africa) | 48 | 5½ |
| 1933 | Z. Heljasz (Poland) | 51 | 8¼ |
| 1934 | Z. Heljasz (Poland) | 48 | 10¼ |
| 1935 | A. G. J. De Bruyn (Netherlands) | 48 | 9¾ |
| 1936 | A. G. J. De Bruyn (Netherlands) | 46 | 2½ |
| 1937 | H. Woellke (Germany) | 50 | 6 |
| 1938 | C. Profeti (Italy) | 46 | 1¾ |
| 1939 | A. G. J. De Bruyn (Netherlands) | 48 | 6¼ |
| 1946 | A. G. J. De Bruyn (Netherlands) | 43 | 8 |
| 1947 | D. Guiney (Ireland) | 47 | 6¼ |
| 1948 | D. Guiney (Ireland) | 47 | 3½ |
| 1949 | J. A. Giles | 46 | 4½ |
| 1950 | P. Sarcevic (Yugoslavia) | 49 | 11½ |
| 1951 | G. Huseby (Iceland) | 52 | 0¾ |
| 1952 | J. A. Savidge | 54 | 1¾ |
| 1953 | J. A. Savidge | 53 | 0½ |
| 1954 | J. A. Savidge | 51 | 0 |
| 1955 | W. B. L. Palmer | 49 | 7 |
| 1956 | W. B. L. Palmer | 54 | 2 |
| 1957 | A. Rowe | 53 | 9 |
| 1958 | A. Rowe | 56 | 9 |
| 1959 | A. Rowe | 58 | 10¾ |
| 1960 | A. Rowe | 59 | 2½ |
| 1961 | A. Rowe | 60 | 11¾ |
| 1962 | L. J. Silvester (USA) | 59 | 7¾ |
| 1963 | M. R. Lindsay | 57 | 10¾ |
| 1964 | V. Varju (Hungary) | 61 | 10 |
| 1965 | V. Varju (Hungary) | 62 | 5 |
| 1966 | J. Botha (S. Africa) | 56 | 2¾ |
| 1967 | D. Booysen (S. Africa) | 58 | 4½ |
| 1968 | J. Teale | 58 | 2½ |
| 1969 | J. Teale | 60 | 1¼ |
| 1970 | L. R. Mills (NZ) | 61 | 2¾ |
| 1971 | L. R. Mills (NZ) | 63 | 2¾ |
| 1972 | G. L. Capes | 63 | 10½ |

| *Discus* | | ft. | in. |
|---|---|---|---|
| 1914 | A. R. Taipale (Finland) | 144 | 6¼ |
| 1920 | P. Quinn (Ireland) | 123 | 5¼ |
| 1921 | O. Zallhagen (Sweden) | 134 | 6½ |
| 1922 | V. Nittyman (Finland) | 136 | 7 |
| 1923 | G. T. Mitchell | 110 | 3 |
| 1924 | P. J. Bermingham (Ireland) | 135 | 1 |
| 1925 | P. J. Bermingham (Ireland) | 138 | 7½ |
| 1926 | P. J. Bermingham (Ireland) | 142 | 4 |
| 1927 | K. Marvalits (Hungary) | 145 | 8½ |
| 1928 | E. Paulus (Germany) | 147 | 0 |
| 1929 | H. Stenerud (Norway) | 142 | 10 |
| 1930 | J. Noel (France) | 146 | 6 |
| 1931 | E. Madarasz (Hungary) | 141 | 4¾ |
| 1932 | P. J. Bermingham (Ireland) | 139 | 2¾ |
| 1933 | E. Madarasz (Hungary) | 144 | 11¼ |
| 1934 | P. J. Bermingham (Ireland) | 135 | 4¾ |
| 1935 | H. Andersson (Sweden) | 169 | 11¾ |
| 1936 | B. L. Prendergast (Jamaica) | 141 | 5 |
| 1937 | N. Syllas (Greece) | 161 | 4 |
| 1938 | A. Consolini (Italy) | 143 | 0¾ |
| 1939 | N. Syllas (Greece) | 161 | 1¾ |
| 1946 | R. J. Brasser (Netherlands) | 142 | 11¾ |
| 1947 | R. J. Brasser (Netherlands) | 143 | 7 |
| 1948 | C. Clancy (Ireland) | 138 | 6 |
| 1949 | F. Klics (Hungary) | 156 | 4½ |
| 1950 | R. Kintziger (Belgium) | 153 | 4 |
| 1951 | G. Tosi (Italy) | 175 | 9½ |
| 1952 | M. Pharaoh | 146 | 8 |
| 1953 | M. Pharaoh | 156 | 4 |
| 1954 | F. Klics (Hungary) | 168 | 5 |
| 1955 | M. Pharaoh | 156 | 7 |
| 1956 | M. Pharaoh | 164 | 1 |
| 1957 | M. R. Lindsay | 166 | 6 |

| | | | |
|---|---|---|---|
| 1958 | S. J. du Plessis (S. Africa) | 171 | 4 |
| 1959 | M. R. Lindsay | 175 | 8 |
| 1960 | M. R. Lindsay | 172 | 7½ |
| 1961 | E. Malan (S. Africa) | 183 | 10 |
| 1962 | L. J. Silvester (USA) | 199 | 7½ |
| 1963 | D. Weill (USA) | 176 | 10 |
| 1964 | R. A. Hollingsworth (Trinidad) | 179 | 10 |
| 1965 | L. G. Haglund (Sweden) | 176 | 11½ |
| 1966 | W. R. Tancred | 169 | 10 |
| 1967 | W. R. Tancred | 169 | 9 |
| 1968 | W. R. Tancred | 174 | 1 |
| 1969 | W. R. Tancred | 174 | 1 |
| 1970 | W. R. Tancred | 176 | 9 |
| 1971 | L. R. Mills (NZ) | 192 | 4 |
| 1972 | W. R. Tancred | 200 | 4 |

| *Hammer* | | ft. | in. |
|---|---|---|---|
| 1880 | W. Lawrence | 96 | 0 |
| 1881 | M. Davin (Ireland) | 98 | 10 |
| 1882 | E. Baddeley | 96 | 4 |
| 1883 | J. Gruer | 101 | 2½ |
| 1884 | O. Harte (Ireland) | 83 | 5 |
| 1885 | W. J. M. Barry (Ireland) | 108 | 10 |
| 1886 | J. S. Mitchel (Ireland) | 110 | 4 |
| 1887 | J. S. Mitchel (Ireland) | 124 | 0½ |
| 1888 | J. S. Mitchel (Ireland) | 124 | 8 |
| 1889 | W. J. M. Barry (Ireland) | 130 | 0 |
| 1890 | R. Lindsay (New Zealand) | 102 | 2 |
| 1891 | C. A. J. Queckberner (USA) | 129 | 10¼ |
| 1892 | W. J. M. Barry (Ireland) | 133 | 3 |
| 1893 | D. Carey (Ireland) | 123 | 4½ |
| 1894 | W. J. M. Barry (Ireland) | 126 | 8½ |
| 1895 | W. J. M. Barry (Ireland) | 132 | 11½ |
| 1896 | J. J. Flanagan (USA) | 131 | 11 |
| 1897 | T. F. Kiely (Ireland) | 142 | 5 |
| 1898 | T. F. Kiely (Ireland) | 140 | 1 |
| 1899 | T. F. Kiely (Ireland) | 136 | 4½ |
| 1900 | J. J. Flanagan (USA) | 163 | 4 |
| 1901 | T. F. Kiely (Ireland) | 148 | 6½ |
| 1902 | T. F. Kiely (Ireland) | 142 | 9 |
| 1903 | T. R. Nicolson | 142 | 7 |
| 1904 | T. R. Nicolson | 157 | 5½ |
| 1905 | T. R. Nicolson | 155 | 10½ |
| 1906 | H. A. Leeke | 123 | 1 |
| 1907 | T. R. Nicolson | 158 | 9 |
| 1908 | S. P. Gillis (USA) | 164 | 5¼ |
| 1909 | T. R. Nicolson | 164 | 8 |
| 1910 | A. E. Flaxman | 117 | 5½ |
| 1911 | G. E. Putnam (USA) | 147 | 7½ |
| 1912 | T. R. Nicolson | 162 | 2¼ |
| 1913 | C. J. Lindh (Sweden) | 155 | 7½ |
| 1914 | C. J. Lindh (Sweden) | 163 | 3½ |
| 1919 | E. Midtgaard (Denmark) | 144 | 4 |
| 1920 | T. Speers (USA) | 140 | 5½ |
| 1921 | C. J. Lindh (Sweden) | 161 | 11¼ |
| 1922 | C. J. Lindh (Sweden) | 172 | 3½ |
| 1923 | M. C. Nokes | 161 | 4½ |
| 1924 | M. C. Nokes | 167 | 8½ |
| 1925 | M. C. Nokes | 151 | 0½ |
| 1926 | M. C. Nokes | 159 | 6 |
| 1927 | O. Skold (Sweden) | 165 | 0 |
| 1928 | W. Britton | 152 | 11 |
| 1929 | W. Britton | 156 | 2 |
| 1930 | O. Skold (Sweden) | 167 | 9 |
| 1931 | O. Skold (Sweden) | 168 | 6 |
| 1932 | G. Walsh (Ireland) | 141 | 7½ |
| 1933 | W. Britton | 147 | 6½ |
| 1934 | P. O'Callaghan (Ireland) | 168 | 8¾ |
| 1935 | F. Warngard (Sweden) | 146 | 2¾ |
| 1936 | N. H. Drake | 151 | 9 |
| 1937 | K. Hein (Germany) | 183 | 3 |
| 1938 | B. Healion (Ireland) | 172 | 1½ |
| 1939 | B. Healion (Ireland) | 161 | 8½ |
| 1946 | J. H. Houtzager (Netherlands) | 159 | 0½ |
| 1947 | I. Nemeth (Hungary) | 174 | 11¾ |
| 1948 | N. H. Drake | 161 | 6½ |
| 1949 | I. Nemeth (Hungary) | 182 | 5½ |
| 1950 | D. McD. M. Clark | 178 | 4½ |
| 1951 | T. Taddia (Italy) | 177 | 2½ |
| 1952 | D. McD. M. Clark | 173 | 11½ |
| 1953 | D. W. J. Anthony | 174 | 8 |
| 1954 | J. Csermak (Hungary) | 194 | 11 |
| 1955 | E. C. K. Douglas | 185 | 5 |
| 1956 | P. C. Allday | 187 | 11 |
| 1957 | M. J. Ellis | 197 | 9 |
| 1958 | M. J. Ellis | 203 | 2 |
| 1959 | M. J. Ellis | 201 | 0½ |
| 1960 | M. J. Ellis | 210 | 7 |
| 1961 | J. F. Lawlor (Ireland) | 210 | 4½ |
| 1962 | N. Okamoto (Japan) | 204 | 0½ |
| 1963 | T. Sugawara (Japan) | 215 | 1 |
| 1964 | A. H. Payne | 196 | 5½ |
| 1965 | G. Zsivotzky (Hungary) | 223 | 6½ |
| 1966 | G. Zsivotzky (Hungary) | 216 | 8 |
| 1967 | E. Burke (USA) | 221 | 9 |
| 1968 | L. Lovasz (Hungary) | 217 | 2 |
| 1969 | A. H. Payne | 219 | 2 |
| 1970 | A. H. Payne | 222 | 0 |
| 1971 | A. H. Payne | 218 | 0 |
| 1972 | B. Williams | 220 | 7 |

| *Javelin* | | ft. | in. |
|---|---|---|---|
| 1914 | M. Koczan (Hungary) | 195 | 11 |
| 1920 | F. L. Murray (USA) | 149 | 9 |
| 1921 | G. Lindstrom (Sweden) | 205 | 0 |

| | | | |
|---|---|---|---|
| 1922 | P. Johansson (Finland) | 200 | 5 |
| 1923 | J. Dalrymple | 148 | 9½ |
| 1924 | E. G. Sutherland (S. Africa) | 173 | 11 |
| 1925 | B. Szepes (Hungary) | 176 | 11 |
| 1926 | O. Sunde (Norway) | 201 | 3 |
| 1927 | B. Szepes (Hungary) | 212 | 7½ |
| 1928 | S. A. Lay (New Zealand) | 222 | 9 |
| 1929 | B. Szepes (Hungary) | 218 | 10 |
| 1930 | A. Dominutti (Italy) | 202 | 1 |
| 1931 | O. Sunde (Norway) | 199 | 4½ |
| 1932 | O. Jurgis (Latvia) | 211 | 8 |
| 1933 | W. P. Abell | 169 | 1½ |
| 1934 | C. G. Bowen | 169 | 9¼ |
| 1935 | L. Atterwall (Sweden) | 215 | 6¾ |
| 1936 | J. F. Van Der Poll (Netherlands) | 189 | 2 |
| 1937 | S. Wilson | 194 | 2 |
| 1938 | R. E. M. Blakeway (S. Africa) | 197 | 1¼ |
| 1939 | J. A. McD. McKillop | 186 | 7 |
| 1946 | N. B. Lutkeveld (Netherlands) | 185 | 8½ |
| 1947 | J. Stendzenieks | 210 | 7½ |
| 1948 | J. Stendzenieks | 218 | 9 |
| 1949 | A. F. Hignell | 184 | 9½ |
| 1950 | M. J. Denley | 192 | 0¼ |
| 1951 | A. Metteucci (Italy) | 200 | 5 |
| 1952 | M. J. Denley | 216 | 1 |
| 1953 | M. J. Denley | 208 | 7 |
| 1954 | M. Morrell | 198 | 0 |
| 1955 | D. Zamfir (Rumania) | 222 | 9 |
| 1956 | P. S. Cullen | 214 | 2 |
| 1957 | P. S. Cullen | 236 | 7 |
| 1958 | C. G. Smith | 218 | 1 |
| 1959 | C. G. Smith | 229 | 4½ |
| 1960 | M. Nawaz (Pakistan) | 250 | 7½ |
| 1961 | M. Macquet (France) | 253 | 0 |
| 1962 | J. V. McSorley | 260 | 0 |
| 1963 | C. G. Smith | 237 | 9 |
| 1964 | J. FitzSimons | 243 | 1 |
| 1965 | D. H. Travis | 242 | 0 |
| 1966 | J. V. P. Kinnunen (Finland) | 273 | 0 |
| 1967 | J. B. Sanderson | 240 | 11 |
| 1968 | D. H. Travis | 236 | 9 |
| 1969 | W. Nikiciuk (Poland) | 279 | 1 |
| 1970 | D. H. Travis | 252 | 3 |
| 1971 | D. H. Travis | 252 | 7 |
| 1972 | D. H. Travis | 261 | 3 |

*56-lb. Weight* — ft. in.

| | | | |
|---|---|---|---|
| 1920 | W. W. Coe (USA) | 23 | 8 |

*Decathlon* (1950 Tables) — Pts.

| | | |
|---|---|---|
| 1928 | H. B. Hart (S. Africa) | 6016* |
| 1937 | J. Miggins (Ireland) | 4647* |
| 1938 | T. L. Langton-Lockton | 5513* |

| | | |
|---|---|---|
| 1947 | H. J. Moesgaard-Kjeldsen (Denmark) | 5965* |
| 1948 | H. J. Moesgaard-Kjeldsen (Denmark) | 5794* |
| 1949 | H. J. Moesgaard-Kjeldsen (Denmark) | 6138* |
| 1950 | H. Whittle | 6087* |
| 1951 | L. Pinder | 5089 |
| 1952 | L. Pinder | 5504 |
| 1953 | L. Pinder | 5321 |
| 1954 | L. Pinder | 5415 |
| 1955 | M. Dodds | 4690 |
| 1956 | A. G. Brown (Rhodesia) | 4934 |
| 1957 | H. L. Williams | 5370 |
| 1958 | C. J. Andrews | 5113 |
| 1959 | C. J. Andrews | 5517 |
| 1960 | C. J. Andrews | 6176 |
| 1961 | M. D. Burger (Rhodesia) | 6343 |
| 1962 | Z. Sumich (Australia) | 6237 |
| 1963 | Z. Sumich (Australia) | 6538 |
| 1964 | D. S. Clarke | 6084 |
| 1965 | N. Foster | 6840† |
| 1966 | D. S. Clarke | 7001† |
| 1967 | P. J. Gabbett | 6533† |
| 1968 | P. J. Gabbett | 7247† |
| 1969 | P. de Villiers (S. Africa) | 6960† |
| 1970 | P. J. Gabbett | 7331† |
| 1971 | D. F. Kidner | 6691† |
| 1972 | B. J. King | 7346† |

* Scored on 1934 Tables.
† Scored on 1962 Tables.

*2 Miles Walk* — min. sec.

| | | | |
|---|---|---|---|
| 1901 | G. Deyermond (Ireland) | 14 | 17.4 |
| 1902 | W. J. Sturgess | 14 | 46.6 |
| 1903 | E. J. Negus | 14 | 44.4 |
| 1904 | G. E. Larner | 13 | 57.6 |
| 1905 | G. E. Larner | 13 | 50.0 |
| 1906 | A. T. Yeomans | 14 | 20.4 |
| 1907 | R. Harrison | 14 | 01.8 |
| 1908 | G. E. Larner | 13 | 58.4 |
| 1909 | E. J. Webb | 13 | 56.4 |
| 1910 | E. J. Webb | 13 | 54.4 |
| 1911 | H. V. L. Ross | 13 | 55.4 |
| 1912 | R. Bridge | 13 | 55.4 |
| 1913 | R. Bridge | 13 | 51.8 |
| 1914 | R. Bridge | 13 | 57.2 |
| 1919 | R. Bridge | 14 | 18.4 |
| 1920 | C. S. Dowson | 14 | 32.0 |
| 1921 | J. F. Evans | 14 | 40.2 |
| 1922 | U. Frigerio (Italy) | 14 | 30.0 |
| 1923 | G. H. Watts | 14 | 24.0 |
| 1924 | G. R. Goodwin | 14 | 11.2 |
| 1925 | G. R. Goodwin | 14 | 07.4 |
| 1926 | W. N. Cowley | 14 | 32.4 |
| 1927 | A. H. G. Pope | 14 | 21.6 |
| 1928 | A. H. G. Pope | 14 | 04.8 |
| 1929 | A. H. G. Pope | 13 | 57.6 |

| | | | | | | |
|---|---|---|---|---|---|---|
| 1930 | C. W. Hyde | 13 56.4 | | 1889 | W. Wheeler | 56 29.4 |
| 1931 | A. H. G. Pope | 13 52.6 | | 1890 | H. Curtis | 52 28.4 |
| 1932 | A. A. Cooper | 13 44.6 | | 1891 | H. Curtis | 54 00.2 |
| 1933 | A. A. Cooper | 13 39.8 | | 1892 | H. Curtis | 55 56.2 |
| 1934 | A. A. Cooper | 13 41.0 | | 1893 | H. Curtis | 56 37.2 |
| 1935 | A. A. Cooper | 13 46.6 | | 1901 | J. Butler | 54 37.0 |
| 1936 | A. A. Cooper | 13 50.0 | | 1902 | W. J. Sturgess | 52 49.4 |
| 1937 | A. A. Cooper | 13 58.2 | | 1903 | J. Butler | 56 17.2 |
| 1938 | A. A. Cooper | 14 02.2 | | 1904 | G. E. Larner | 52 57.4 |
| 1939 | H. G. Churcher | 13 50.0 | | 1905 | G. E. Larner | 52 34.0 |
| 1946 | L. Hindmar (Sweden) | 13 59.0 | | 1906 | F. T. Carter | 53 20.2 |
| 1947 | L. Hindmar (Sweden) | 13 54.4 | | 1907 | F. B. Thompson | 52 46.6 |
| 1948 | H. G. Churcher | 13 49.8 | | 1908 | E. J. Webb | 53 02.6 |
| 1949 | K. A. Borjesson (Sweden) | 14 06.6 | | 1909 | E. J. Webb | 52 37.0 |
| 1950 | R. Hardy | 13 46.8 | | 1910 | E. J. Webb | 51 37.0 |
| 1951 | R. Hardy | 13 43.2 | | 1911 | G. E. Larner | 52 08.0 |
| 1952 | R. Hardy | 13 27.8 | | 1912 | R. Bridge | 52 45.6 |
| 1953 | G. W. Coleman | 14 02.2 | | 1913 | R. Bridge and H. V. L. Ross | 52 08.4 |
| 1954 | G. W. Coleman | 13 52.0 | | 1914 | R. Bridge | 52 32.0 |
| 1955 | G. W. Coleman | 14 01.0 | | 1919 | W. Hehir | 53 23.6 |
| 1956 | R. F. Goodall | 14 20.8 | | 1920 | C. S. Dowson | 53 50.0 |
| 1957 | S. F. Vickers | 14 05.6 | | 1921 | H. V. L. Ross | 55 48.6 |
| 1958 | S. F. Vickers | 13 33.4 | | 1922 | G. H. Watts | 53 24.2 |
| 1959 | K. J. Matthews | 13 19.4 | | 1923 | G. H. Watts | 54 35.4 |
| 1960 | S. F. Vickers | 13 02.4 | | 1924 | G. R. Goodwin | 52 00.6 |
| 1961 | K. J. Matthews | 13 24.6 | | 1925 | G. H. Watts | 52 53.8 |
| 1962 | K. J. Matthews | 13 59.0 | | 1926 | G. R. Goodwin | 53 56.0 |
| 1963 | K. J. Matthews | 13 18.2 | | 1927 | W. N. Cowley | 55 46.4 |
| 1964 | K. J. Matthews | 13 22.4 | | 1928 | C. W. Hyde | 55 46.2 |
| 1965 | V. P. Nihill | 13 20.0 | | 1929 | C. W. Hyde | 53 38.6 |
| 1966 | R. Wallwork | 13 35.0 | | 1930 | C. W. Hyde | 53 32.4 |
| 1967 | R. E. Wallwork | 13 44.8 | | 1931 | U. Frigerio (Italy) | 54 09.0 |
| 1968 | A. J. Jones | 13 35.6 | | 1932 | A. H. G. Pope | 51 25.4 |
| | | | | 1933 | J. F. Johnson | 52 01.6 |

*3000 Metres Walk*

| | | | | | | |
|---|---|---|---|---|---|---|
| 1969 | R. G. Mills | 12 57.0 | | 1934 | J. F. Johnson | 52 10.4 |
| 1970 | V. P. Nihill | 12 13.8 | | 1935 | H. A. Hake | 53 48.0 |
| 1971 | V. P. Nihill | 12 08.4 | | 1936 | V. W. Stone | 52 21.2 |
| 1972 | R. G. Mills | 12 31.6 | | 1937 | J. F. Mikaelsson (Sweden) | 50 19.2 |
| | | | | 1938 | J. F. Mikaelsson (Sweden) | 51 48.2 |

*4 Miles Walk*

| | | | | | | |
|---|---|---|---|---|---|---|
| 1894 | H. Curtis | 30 05.8 | | 1939 | H. G. Churcher | 52 37.0 |
| 1895 | W. J. Sturgess | 30 17.4 | | 1946 | L. Hindmar (Sweden) | 52 30.0 |
| 1896 | W. J. Sturgess | 28 57.6 | | 1947 | H. G. Churcher | 52 48.4 |
| 1897 | W. J. Sturgess | 28 24.8 | | 1948 | H. G. Churcher | 52 32.8 |
| 1898 | W. J. Sturgess | 29 10.0 | | 1949 | H. G. Churcher | 52 41.8 |
| 1899 | W. J. Sturgess | 29 20.6 | | 1950 | R. Hardy | 50 11.6 |
| 1900 | W. J. Sturgess | 30 20.8 | | 1951 | R. Hardy | 51 14.6 |
| | | | | 1952 | R. Hardy | 50 05.6 |

*7 Miles Walk*

| | | | | | | |
|---|---|---|---|---|---|---|
| 1880 | G. P. Beckley | 56 40.0 | | 1953 | R. Hardy | 51 47.0 |
| 1881 | J. W. Raby | 54 48.2 | | 1954 | G. W. Coleman | 51 22.8 |
| 1882 | H. Whyatt | 55 56.5 | | 1955 | R. Hardy | 53 04.6 |
| 1883 | H. Whyatt | 59 15.0 | | 1956 | G. W. Coleman | 50 19.0 |
| 1884 | W. H. Meek (USA) | 54 27.0 | | 1957 | S. F. Vickers | 51 34.4 |
| 1885 | J. Jervis | 56 10.6 | | 1958 | S. F. Vickers | 51 10.2 |
| 1886 | J. H. Jullie | 56 30.2 | | 1959 | K. J. Matthews | 50 28.8 |
| 1887 | C. W. V. Clarke | 56 59.8 | | 1960 | K. J. Matthews | 49 42.6 |
| 1888 | C. W. V. Clarke | 57 08.6 | | 1961 | K. J. Matthews | 49 43.6 |
| | | | | 1962 | C. Williams | 52 15.0 |

| | | | | | | |
|---|---|---|---|---|---|---|
| 1963 | K. J. Matthews | 49 52.8 | | 1923 | L. C. Murchison | 10.1 |
| 1964 | K. J. Matthews | 48 23.0 | | 1924 | C. W. Paddock | 9.6 |
| 1965 | V. P. Nihill | 51 54.4 | | 1925 | F. Hussey | 9.8 |
| 1966 | V. P. Nihill | 50 52.0 | | 1926 | C. E. Borah | 9.8 |
| 1967 | M. R. Tolley | 52 32.4 | | 1927 | C. Bowman | 9.6 |
| 1968 | V. P. Nihill | 51 10.4 | | 1928 | F. C. Wykoff | 10.6* |
| | | | | 1929 | T. E. Tolan | 10.0 |

*10,000 Metres Walk*

| | | | | | | |
|---|---|---|---|---|---|---|
| 1969 | V. P. Nihill | 44 07.0 | | 1930 | T. E. Tolan | 9.7 |
| 1970 | W. M. S. Sutherland | 45 16.8 | | 1931 | F. C. Wykoff | 9.5 |
| 1971 | P. B. Embleton | 45 26.2 | | 1932 | R. H. Metcalfe | 10.6* |
| 1972 | P. B. Embleton | 44 26.8 | | 1933 | R. H. Metcalfe | 10.5* |
| 1973 | R. G. Mills | 44 38.6 | | 1934 | R. H. Metcalfe | 10.4* |

For indoor champions, see under INDOOR ATHLETICS; for road walking champions, see under WALKING.

## AMATEUR ATHLETIC UNION

Founded in 1888, the AAU is the internationally recognised governing body for track and field athletics (men and women) in the United States.

### Championships

The first American Championships, organised by the New York Athletic Club, were held in 1876. Three years later they were taken over by the National Association of Amateur Athletes of America. The inaugural AAU Championships were staged in 1888 and have continued without break ever since.

The most titles won in any individual men's event is nine—by Joe McCluskey (steeplechase: 1930-33, 35, 38-40, 43), Bob Richards (pole vault: 1948-52, 54-57) and Harold Connolly (hammer: 1955-61, 64, 65). The only men to win eight consecutive titles are James Mitchel in the hammer, 1889-96, and John J. Kelley in the marathon, 1956-63. The most prolific AAU title winner is walker Ronnie Laird, with more than fifty championship wins.

*100 Yards*

| | | |
|---|---|---|
| 1914 | J. Loomis | 10.2 |
| 1915 | J. Loomis | 9.8 |
| 1916 | A. E. Ward | 10.0 |
| 1917 | A. E. Ward | 10.2 |
| 1918 | A. H. Henke | 10.0 |
| 1919 | W. D. Hayes | 10.2 |
| 1920 | L. C. Murchison | 10.0 |
| 1921 | C. W. Paddock | 9.6 |
| 1922 | R. McAllister | 10.0 |

| | | |
|---|---|---|
| 1935 | E. Peacock | 10.2* |
| 1936 | J. C. Owens | 10.4* |
| 1937 | P. Walker | 10.7* |
| 1938 | B. Johnson | 10.7* |
| 1939 | C. Jeffrey | 10.2* |
| 1940 | H. Davis | 10.3* |
| 1941 | H. N. Ewell | 10.3* |
| 1942 | H. Davis | 10.5* |
| 1943 | H. Davis | 10.3* |
| 1944 | C. Young | 10.5* |
| 1945 | H. N. Ewell | 10.3* |
| 1946 | W. Mathis | 10.7* |
| 1947 | W. Mathis | 10.5* |
| 1948 | H. N. Ewell | 10.6* |
| 1949 | A. W. Stanfield | 10.3* |
| 1950 | A. Bragg | 10.4* |
| 1951 | J. Golliday | 10.3* |
| 1952 | F. D. Smith | 10.5* |
| 1953 | A. Bragg | 9.5 |
| 1954 | A. Bragg | 9.5 |
| 1955 | B. J. Morrow | 9.5 |
| 1956 | B. J. Morrow | 10.2* |
| 1957 | L. King | 9.5 |
| 1958 | B. J. Morrow | 9.4 |
| 1959 | O. R. Norton | 10.5* |
| 1960 | O. R. Norton | 10.5* |
| 1961 | F. J. Budd | 9.2 |
| 1962 | R. L. Hayes | 9.3 |
| 1963 | R. L. Hayes | 9.1 |
| 1964 | R. L. Hayes | 10.3* |
| 1965 | G. Anderson | 9.3 |
| 1966 | C. Greene | 9.4 |
| 1967 | J. Hines | 9.3 |
| 1968 | C. Greene | 10.0* |
| 1969 | I. Crockett | 9.3 |
| 1970 | I. Crockett | 9.3 |
| 1971 | D. Meriwether | 9.0 |
| 1972 | R. Taylor | 10.2* |

*220 Yards*

| | | | |
|---|---|---|---|
| | (* 200 Metres) | | sec. |
| 1914 | I. T. Howe | | 22.2 |
| 1915 | R. F. Morse | | 21.2 |
| 1916 | A. E. Ward | | 21.6 |
| 1917 | A. E. Ward | | 22.2 |
| 1918 | L. C. Murchison | | 22.4 |
| 1919 | H. Williams | | 21.8 |

29

| Year | Name | Time | | Year | Name | Time |
|---|---|---|---|---|---|---|
| 1920 | C. W. Paddock | 21.4 | | 1915 | J. E. Meredith | 47.0 |
| 1921 | C. W. Paddock | 21.8 | | 1916 | T. J. Halpin | 49.8 |
| 1922 | J. A. Leconey | 22.1 | | 1917 | F. J. Shea | 49.6 |
| 1923 | L. C. Murchison | 22.3 | | 1918 | C. C. Shaughnessy | 49.4 |
| 1924 | C. W. Paddock | 20.8 | | 1919 | F. J. Shea | 50.2 |
| 1925 | J. V. Scholz | 20.8 | | 1920 | F. J. Shea | 49.0 |
| 1926 | T. Sharkey | 21.4 | | 1921 | W. E. Stevenson | 48.6 |
| 1927 | C. E. Borah | 21.6 | | 1922 | J. W. Driscoll | 49.9 |
| 1928 | C. E. Borah | 21.4* | | 1923 | H. M. Fitch | 50.0 |
| 1929 | T. E. Tolan | 21.9 | | 1924 | J. Burgess | 49.8 |
| 1930 | G. Simpson | 21.3 | | 1925 | C. G. Cooke | 49.2 |
| 1931 | T. E. Tolan | 21.0 | | 1926 | K. Kennedy | 48.6 |
| 1932 | R. H. Metcalfe | 21.5* | | 1927 | H. Phillips | 49.6 |
| 1933 | R. H. Metcalfe | 21.1* | | 1928 | R. J. Barbuti | 51.4* |
| 1934 | R. H. Metcalfe | 21.3* | | 1929 | R. F. Bowen | 48.4 |
| 1935 | R. H. Metcalfe | 21.0* | | 1930 | V. Williams | 48.8 |
| 1936 | R. H. Metcalfe | 21.2* | | 1931 | V. Williams | 48.8 |
| 1937 | J. Weiershauser | 20.9* | | 1932 | W. A. Carr | 46.9* |
| 1938 | M. Robinson | 21.3* | | 1933 | I. Fuqua | 47.7* |
| 1939 | H. N. Ewell | 21.0* | | 1934 | I. Fuqua | 47.4* |
| 1940 | H. Davis | 20.4* | | 1935 | E. O'Brien | 47.6* |
| 1941 | H. Davis | 20.4* | | 1936 | H. Smallwood | 47.3* |
| 1942 | H. Davis | 20.9* | | 1937 | R. Malott | 47.1* |
| 1943 | H. Davis | 20.2* | | 1938 | R. Malott | 47.6* |
| 1944 | C. Parker | 21.3* | | 1939 | E. Miller | 48.3 |
| 1945 | E. Harris | 21.9* | | 1940 | G. Klemmer | 47.0* |
| 1946 | H. N. Ewell | 21.2* | | 1941 | G. Klemmer | 46.0* |
| 1947 | H. N. Ewell | 21.0* | | 1942 | C. F. Bourland | 46.7* |
| 1948 | L. B. La Beach (Panama) | 21.0* | | 1943 | C. F. Bourland | 47.7* |
| 1949 | A. W. Stanfield | 20.4 | | 1944 | E. Harris | 48.0* |
| 1950 | R. Tyler | 21.1* | | 1945 | H. H. McKenley (Jam.) | 48.4* |
| 1951 | J. Ford | 20.8 | | 1946 | E. Harris | 46.3* |
| 1952 | A. W. Stanfield | 21.1* | | 1947 | H. H. McKenley (Jam.) | 47.1* |
| 1953 | A. W. Stanfield | 21.2 | | 1948 | H. H. McKenley (Jam.) | 46.3* |
| 1954 | A. Bragg | 21.1 | | 1949 | V. G. Rhoden (Jam.) | 46.4* |
| 1955 | R. Richard | 21.0 | | 1950 | V. G. Rhoden (Jam.) | 46.5* |
| 1956 | W. T. Baker | 20.6* | | 1951 | V. G. Rhoden (Jam.) | 46.0* |
| 1957 | O. C. Cassell | 21.0 | | 1952 | M. G. Whitfield | 46.4* |
| 1958 | B. J. Morrow | 20.9 | | 1953 | J. W. Mashburn | 47.1 |
| 1959 | O. R. Norton | 20.8* | | 1954 | J. Lea | 46.6 |
| 1960 | O. R. Norton | 20.8* | | 1955 | C. L. Jenkins | 46.7 |
| 1961 | O. P. Drayton | 21.0 | | 1956 | T. W. Courtney | 45.8* |
| 1962 | O. P. Drayton | 20.5 | | 1957 | R. Pearman | 46.4 |
| 1963 | H. Carr and O. P. Drayton | 20.4 | | 1958 | S. E. Southern | 45.8 |
| 1964 | H. Carr | 20.6* | | 1959 | S. E. Southern | 46.1* |
| 1965 | A. C. Plummer | 20.6 | | 1960 | O. C. Davis | 45.8* |
| 1966 | J. Hines | 20.5 | | 1961 | O. C. Davis | 46.1 |
| 1967 | T. C. Smith | 20.4 | | 1962 | U. C. Williams | 45.8 |
| 1968 | T. C. Smith | 20.3* | | 1963 | U. C. Williams | 45.8 |
| 1969 | J. Carlos | 20.2 | | 1964 | M. D. Larrabee | 46.0* |
| 1970 | B. Vaughan | 20.8 | | 1965 | O. C. Cassell | 46.1 |
| 1971 | D. Quarrie (Jamaica) | 20.2 | | 1966 | L. Evans | 45.9 |
| 1972 | C. Smith | 20.7* | | 1967 | L. Evans | 45.3 |
| | | | | 1968 | L. Evans | 45.0* |
| | | | | 1969 | L. Evans | 45.6 |
| | | | | 1970 | J. Smith | 45.7 |
| | | | | 1971 | J. Smith | 44.5 |
| | | | | 1972 | L. Evans | 45.0* |

*440 Yards*
(* 400 Metres)    sec.
1914 J. E. Meredith    50.2

## 880 Yards

| (* 800 Metres) | | min. sec. |
|---|---|---|
| 1914 | H. Baker | 1 57.6 |
| 1915 | L. Campbell | 2 01.0 |
| 1916 | D. M. Scott | 1 54.0 |
| 1917 | M. A. Devaney | 1 57.0 |
| 1918 | T. S. Campbell | 1 56.8 |
| 1919 | J. W. Ray | 1 56.0 |
| 1920 | E. Eby | 1 54.2 |
| 1921 | A. B. Helffrich | 1 54.8 |
| 1922 | A. B. Helffrich | 1 56.3 |
| 1923 | R. B. Watson | 1 57.2 |
| 1924 | E. Kirby | 1 58.9 |
| 1925 | A. B. Helffrich | 1 56.6 |
| 1926 | A. Martin | 1 53.6 |
| 1927 | R. B. Watson | 1 53.6 |
| 1928 | L. Hahn | 1 51.4* |
| 1929 | P. A. Edwards (B. Guiana) | 1 55.7 |
| 1930 | E. Genung | 1 53.4 |
| 1931 | E. Genung | 1 52.6 |
| 1932 | E. Genung | 1 52.6* |
| 1933 | G. Cunningham | 1 51.8* |
| 1934 | B. B. Eastman | 1 50.8* |
| 1935 | E. Robinson | 1 53.1* |
| 1936 | C. Beetham | 1 50.3* |
| 1937 | J. Y. Woodruff | 1 50.0* |
| 1938 | H. Borck | 1 51.5* |
| 1939 | C. Beetham | 1 51.7* |
| 1940 | C. Beetham | 1 51.1* |
| 1941 | C. Beetham | 1 50.2* |
| 1942 | J. Borican | 1 51.2* |
| 1943 | W. Hulse | 1 53.4* |
| 1944 | R. Kelly | 1 51.8* |
| 1945 | R. Kelly | 1 54.1* |
| 1946 | J. Fulton | 1 52.7* |
| 1947 | R. Pearman | 1 50.9* |
| 1948 | H. Barten | 1 51.3* |
| 1949 | M. G. Whitfield | 1 50.5* |
| 1950 | M. G. Whitfield | 1 51.8* |
| 1951 | M. G. Whitfield | 1 52.9* |
| 1952 | R. Pearman | 1 53.5* |
| 1953 | M. G. Whitfield | 1 51.5 |
| 1954 | M. G. Whitfield | 1 50.8 |
| 1955 | A. N. Sowell | 1 47.6 |
| 1956 | A. N. Sowell | 1 47.6* |
| 1957 | T. W. Courtney | 1 50.1 |
| 1958 | T. W. Courtney | 1 49.2 |
| 1959 | T. Murphy | 1 47.9* |
| 1960 | J. Cerveny | 1 48.4* |
| 1961 | J. Dupree | 1 48.5 |
| 1962 | J. Siebert | 1 47.1 |
| 1963 | W. F. Crothers (Can.) | 1 46.8 |
| 1964 | J. Siebert | 1 47.5* |
| 1965 | M. Groth | 1 47.7 |
| 1966 | T. Farrell | 1 47.6 |
| 1967 | W. Bell | 1 46.1 |
| 1968 | W. Bell | 1 45.5* |
| 1969 | B. Dyce (Jamaica) | 1 46.6 |
| 1970 | K. Swenson | 1 47.4 |
| 1971 | J. Luzins | 1 47.1 |
| 1972 | D. Wottle | 1 47.3* |

## Mile

| (* 1500 Metres) | | min. sec. |
|---|---|---|
| 1914 | A. R. Kiviat | 4 25.2 |
| 1915 | J. W. Ray | 4 23.2 |
| 1916 | I. A. Myer | 4 22.0 |
| 1917 | J. W. Ray | 4 18.4 |
| 1918 | J. W. Ray | 4 20.0 |
| 1919 | J. W. Ray | 4 14.4 |
| 1920 | J. W. Ray | 4 16.2 |
| 1921 | J. W. Ray | 4 16.8 |
| 1922 | J. W. Ray | 4 17.0 |
| 1923 | J. W. Ray | 4 18.0 |
| 1924 | R. Buker | 4 24.8 |
| 1925 | R. Buker | 4 19.4 |
| 1926 | L. Hahn | 4 16.0 |
| 1927 | R. Conger | 4 23.6 |
| 1928 | R. Conger | 3 55.0* |
| 1929 | L. Lermond | 4 24.6 |
| 1930 | R. Conger | 4 19.8 |
| 1931 | L. Lermond | 4 15.0 |
| 1932 | N. P. Hallowell | 3 52.7* |
| 1933 | G. Cunningham | 3 52.3* |
| 1934 | W. R. Bonthron | 3 48.8* |
| 1935 | G. Cunningham | 3 52.1* |
| 1936 | G. Cunningham | 3 54.2* |
| 1937 | G. Cunningham | 3 51.8* |
| 1938 | G. Cunningham | 3 52.5* |
| 1939 | B. Rideout | 3 51.5* |
| 1940 | W. Mehl | 3 47.9* |
| 1941 | L. MacMitchell | 3 53.1* |
| 1942 | G. Dodds | 3 50.2* |
| 1943 | G. Dodds | 3 50.0* |
| 1944 | W. Hulse | 3 54.3* |
| 1945 | R. Sink | 3 58.4* |
| 1946 | L. Strand (Swe.) | 3 54.5* |
| 1947 | G. Karver | 3 52.9* |
| 1948 | G. Dodds | 3 52.1* |
| 1949 | J. Twomey | 3 52.6* |
| 1950 | J. Twomey | 3 51.3* |
| 1951 | L. Truex | 3 52.0* |
| 1952 | W. D. Santee | 3 49.3* |
| 1953 | W. D. Santee | 4 07.6 |
| 1954 | F. Dwyer | 4 09.5 |
| 1955 | W. D. Santee | 4 11.5 |
| 1956 | J. Walters | 3 48.4* |
| 1957 | M. Lincoln (Aus.) | 4 06.1 |
| 1958 | H. J. Elliott (Aus.) | 3 57.9 |
| 1959 | D. Burleson | 3 47.5* |
| 1960 | J. Grelle | 3 42.7* |
| 1961 | D. Burleson | 4 04.9 |
| 1962 | J. T. Beatty | 3 57.9 |
| 1963 | D. Burleson | 3 56.7 |
| 1964 | T. O'Hara | 3 38.1* |
| 1965 | J. R. Ryun | 3 55.3 |
| 1966 | J. R. Ryun | 3 58.6 |
| 1967 | J. R. Ryun | 3 51.1 |
| 1968 | J. Mason | 3 43.1* |

31

| | | |
|---|---|---|
| 1969 | M. Liquori | 3 59.5 |
| 1970 | H. Michael | 4 01.8 |
| 1971 | M. Liquori | 3 56.5 |
| 1972 | J. Howe | 3 38.2* |

## 3 Miles

| (* 5000 Metres) | | min. sec. |
|---|---|---|
| 1932 | R. Hill | 14 55.7* |
| 1933 | J. Follows | 15 27.0* |
| 1934 | F. Crowley | 15 18.6* |
| 1935 | J. P. McCluskey | 15 14.1* |
| 1936 | D. Lash | 15 04.8* |
| 1937 | J. P. McCluskey | 15 04.1* |
| 1938 | J. G. Rice | 15 15.0* |
| 1939 | J. G. Rice | 14 50.9* |
| 1940 | J. G. Rice | 14 33.4* |
| 1941 | J. G. Rice | 14 45.2* |
| 1942 | J. G. Rice | 14 39.7* |
| 1943 | G. Hagg (Swe.) | 14 48.5* |
| 1944 | J. Rafferty | 15 22.3* |
| 1945 | J. Kandl | 16 14.4* |
| 1946 | F. Martin | 15 50.7* |
| 1947 | C. Stone | 15 02.7* |
| 1948 | C. Stone | 14 49.1* |
| 1949 | F. Wilt | 14 49.3* |
| 1950 | F. Wilt | 15 19.4* |
| 1951 | F. Wilt | 14 47.5* |
| 1952 | C. Stone | 15 03.3* |
| 1953 | C. Capozzoli | 14 28.2 |
| 1954 | H. Ashenfelter | 14 18.5 |
| 1955 | H. Ashenfelter | 14 45.2 |
| 1956 | R. Hart | 14 47.4* |
| 1957 | J. Macy | 13 55.0 |
| 1958 | A. Henderson | 13 37.0 |
| 1959 | W. Dellinger | 14 47 6 |
| 1960 | W. Dellinger | 14 26.4* |
| 1961 | L. Tabori | 13 50.0 |
| 1962 | M. G. Halberg (NZ) | 13 30.6 |
| 1963 | P. Clohessy (Aus.) | 13 40.4 |
| 1964 | R. K. Schul | 13 56.2* |
| 1965 | R. K. Schul | 13 10.4 |
| 1966 | G. Young | 13 27.4 |
| 1967 | G. Lindgren | 13 10.6 |
| 1968 | R. Day | 13 50.4* |
| 1969 | T. Smith | 13 18.4 |
| 1970 | F. Shorter | 13 24.2 |
| 1971 | S. Prefontaine | 12 58.6 |
| 1972 | M. Keogh (Ire.) | 13 51.8* |

## 6 Miles

| (* 10,000 Metres) | | min. sec. |
|---|---|---|
| 1925 | G. W. Lermond | 31 34.6 |
| 1926 | P. Osif | 31 31.0 |
| 1927 | V. J. Ritola (Fin.) | 30 43.6 |
| 1928 | J. W. Ray | 31 28.4* |
| 1929 | L. Gregory | 33 47.7 |
| 1930 | L. Gregory | 31 31.3 |
| 1931 | L. Gregory | 31 26.4 |
| 1932 | T. Ottey | 32 18.2* |
| 1933 | L. Gregory | 32 39.4* |
| 1934 | E. Pentti | 33 34.2* |
| 1935 | T. Ottey | 32 07.3* |
| 1936 | D. Lash | 31 06.9* |
| 1937 | E. Pentti | 32 02.0* |
| 1938 | E. Pentti | 32 15.6* |
| 1939 | L. Gregory | 33 11.5* |
| 1940 | D. Lash | 32 29.2* |
| 1941 | L. Gregory | 33 11.0* |
| 1942 | J. P. McCluskey | 32 28.3* |
| 1943 | L. Gregory | 33 22.0* |
| 1944 | N. Bright | 33 53.0* |
| 1945 | T. Vogl | 35 30.7* |
| 1946 | E. O'Toole | 32 17.5* |
| 1947 | E. O'Toole | 33 28.3* |
| 1948 | E. O'Toole | 32 29.7* |
| 1949 | F. Wilt | 31 05.7* |
| 1950 | H. Ashenfelter | 32 44.3* |
| 1951 | C. Stone | 32 30.7* |
| 1952 | C. Stone | 30 33.4* |
| 1953 | C. Stone | 31 18.2 |
| 1954 | C. Stone | 31 39.4 |
| 1955 | R. Hart | 31 58.5 |
| 1956 | M. Truex | 30 52.0* |
| 1957 | D. Kyle (Can.) | 29 22.8 |
| 1958 | J. Macy | 29 25.6 |
| 1959 | M. Truex | 31 22.4* |
| 1960 | A. Lawrence (Aus.) | 30 11.4* |
| 1961 | J. Gutknecht | 28 52.6 |
| 1962 | B. Kidd (Can.) | 28 23.2 |
| 1963 | P. McArdle | 28 29.2 |
| 1964 | P. McArdle | 30 11.0* |
| 1965 | W. M. Mills | 27 11.6 |
| 1966 | T. Smith | 28 02.0 |
| 1967 | V. Nelson | 28 18.8 |
| 1968 | T. Smith | 28 47.0* |
| 1969 | J. Bacheler | 28 12.2 |
| 1970 | F. Shorter and J. Bacheler | 27 24.0 |
| 1971 | F. Shorter | 27 27.2 |
| 1972 | G. Fredericks | 28 08.0* |

## Steeplechase

| (* 3000 Metres; Otherwise 2 miles) | | min. sec. |
|---|---|---|
| 1916 | M. A. Devaney | 10 48.0 |
| 1919 | M. A. Devaney | 10 17.4 |
| 1920 | P. Flynn | 9 58.2* |
| 1921 | M. A. Devaney | 11 34.0 |
| 1922 | M. A. Devaney | 11 10.2 |
| 1923 | V. J. Ritola (Fin.) | 10 45.6 |
| 1924 | M. Rick | 10 43.2 |
| 1925 | R. Payne | 10 40.8 |
| 1926 | V. J. Ritola (Fin.) | 10 34.2 |
| 1927 | V. J. Ritola (Fin.) | 10 19.4 |
| 1928 | W. O. Spencer | 9 35.8* |
| 1929 | D. Abbott | 10 59.1 |
| 1930 | J. P. McCluskey | 10 44.2 |
| 1931 | J. P. McCluskey | 10 11.6 |
| 1932 | J. P. McCluskey | 9 14.5* |
| 1933 | J. P. McCluskey | 9 38.5* |

| 1934 | H. Manning | 9 13.1* |
|---|---|---|
| 1935 | J. P. McCluskey | 9 30.3* |
| 1936 | H. Manning | 9 15.1* |
| 1937 | F. Lochner | 9 26.6* |
| 1938 | J. P. McCluskey | 9 23.3* |
| 1939 | J. P. McCluskey | 9 23.1* |
| 1940 | J. P. McCluskey | 9 16.6* |
| 1941 | F. Efaw | 9 13.7* |
| 1942 | G. DeGeorge | 9 16.5* |
| 1943 | J. P. McCluskey | 9 39.7* |
| 1944 | F. Efaw | 9 39.6* |
| 1945 | J. Wisner | 10 00.6* |
| 1946 | J. Rafferty | 10 01.0* |
| 1947 | F. Efaw | 9 32.5* |
| 1948 | F. Efaw | 9 32.9* |
| 1949 | C. Stone | 9 31.0* |
| 1950 | W. Druetzler | 9 33.6* |
| 1951 | H. Ashenfelter | 9 24.5* |
| 1952 | R. McMullen | 9 25.3* |
| 1953 | H. Ashenfelter | 10 02.5 |
| 1954 | W. Ashenfelter | 10 08.2 |
| 1955 | K. Reiser | 10 20.7 |
| 1956 | H. Ashenfelter | 9 04.1* |
| 1957 | C. Jones | 9 49.6 |
| 1958 | C. Jones | 8 57.3* |
| 1959 | P. Coleman | 9 19.3* |
| 1960 | P. Coleman | 8 55.6* |
| 1961 | C. Jones | 8 48.0* |
| 1962 | G. Young | 8 48.2* |
| 1963 | P. Traynor | 8 51.2* |
| 1964 | J. Fishback | 8 43.6* |
| 1965 | G. Young | 8 50.6* |
| 1966 | P. Traynor | 8 40.6* |
| 1967 | P. Traynor | 8 42.0* |
| 1968 | G. Young | 8 30.6* |
| 1969 | M. Manley | 8 36.6* |
| 1970 | W. Reilly | 8 34.8* |
| 1971 | S. Sink | 8 26.4* |
| 1972 | J. Dare | 8 33.8* |

## 120 Yards Hurdles

| | (* 110 Metres Hurdles) | sec. |
|---|---|---|
| 1914 | H. Goelitz | 16.2 |
| 1915 | F. Murray | 15.0 |
| 1916 | R. Simpson | 14.8 |
| 1917 | H. E. Barron | 15.0 |
| 1918 | E. J. Thomson (Can.) | 15.2 |
| 1919 | R. Simpson | 15.2 |
| 1920 | H. E. Barron | 15.2 |
| 1921 | E. J. Thomson (Can.) | 15.0 |
| 1922 | E. J. Thomson (Can.) | 15.3 |
| 1923 | K. W. Anderson | 15.1 |
| 1924 | I. H. Riley | 15.4 |
| 1925 | G. Guthrie | 14.6 |
| 1926 | L. Dye | 14.6 |
| 1927 | C. D. Werner | 14.6 |
| 1928 | S. E. Anderson | 14.8* |
| 1929 | S. E. Anderson | 14.9 |
| 1930 | S. E. Anderson | 14.4 |
| 1931 | P. Beard | 14.2 |

| 1932 | J. Keller | 14.4* |
|---|---|---|
| 1933 | J. Morriss | 14.3* |
| 1934 | P. Beard | 14.6* |
| 1935 | P. Beard | 14.2* |
| 1936 | F. G. Towns | 14.2* |
| 1937 | A. Tolmich | 14.5* |
| 1938 | F. Wolcott | 14.3* |
| 1939 | J. Batiste | 14.1* |
| 1940 | F. Wolcott | 13.9* |
| 1941 | F. Wolcott | 13.7* |
| 1942 | W. Cummins | 14.1* |
| 1943 | W. Cummins | 14.3* |
| 1944 | O. Cassidy | 14.9* |
| 1945 | C. Morgan | 14.9* |
| 1946 | W. H. Dillard | 14.2* |
| 1947 | W. H. Dillard | 14.0* |
| 1948 | W. Porter | 14.1* |
| 1949 | C. Dixon | 13.8* |
| 1950 | R. H. Attlesey | 13.6* |
| 1951 | R. H. Attlesey | 13.8* |
| 1952 | W. H. Dillard | 13.7* |
| 1953 | J. Davis | 13.9 |
| 1954 | J. Davis | 14.0 |
| 1955 | M. Campbell | 13.9 |
| 1956 | L. Q. Calhoun | 13.6* |
| 1957 | L. Q. Calhoun | 14.2 |
| 1958 | H. W. Jones | 13.8 |
| 1959 | L. Q. Calhoun | 14.0* |
| 1960 | H. W. Jones | 13.6* |
| 1961 | H. W. Jones | 13.6 |
| 1962 | J. Tarr | 13.4 |
| 1963 | H. W. Jones | 13.4 |
| 1964 | H. W. Jones | 13.8* |
| 1965 | W. Davenport | 13.6 |
| 1966 | W. Davenport | 13.3 |
| 1967 | W. Davenport | 13.3 |
| 1968 | E. McCullouch | 13.5* |
| 1969 | R. Coleman and W. Davenport | 13.3 |
| 1970 | T. Hill | 13.3 |
| 1971 | R. Milburn | 13.1 |
| 1972 | R. Milburn | 13.4* |

## 440 Yards Hurdles

| | (* 400 Metres Hurdles) | sec. |
|---|---|---|
| 1914 | W. H. Meanix | 57.8 |
| 1915 | W. H. Meanix | 52.6 |
| 1916 | W. A. Hummel | 54.8 |
| 1917 | F. Smart | 54.8 |
| 1918 | D. Hause | 59.0 |
| 1919 | F. Smart | 55.6 |
| 1920 | F. F. Loomis | 55.0 |
| 1921 | A. Desch | 53.4 |
| 1922 | J. Hall | 56.5 |
| 1923 | I. H. Riley | 55.4 |
| 1924 | F. M. Taylor | 54.5 |
| 1925 | F. M. Taylor | 53.8 |
| 1926 | F. M. Taylor | 55.0 |
| 1927 | J. A. Gibson | 52.6 |
| 1928 | F. M. Taylor | 52.0* |

c

| Year | | Time | | Year | | ft. in. |
|---|---|---|---|---|---|---|
| 1929 | G. Allott | 54.3 | | 1927 | R. W. King | 6 2½ |
| 1930 | R. Pomeroy | 53.1 | | 1928 | R. W. King and | |
| 1931 | V. Burke | 54.2 | | | C. E. McGinnis | 6 5 |
| 1932 | J. Healy | 53.5* | | 1929 | H. Lasallette | 6 3½ |
| 1933 | G. F. Hardin | 52.2* | | 1930 | A. B. Burg | 6 4¼ |
| 1934 | G. F. Hardin | 51.8* | | 1931 | A. B. Burg | 6 5¼ |
| 1935 | T. Moore | 53.5* | | 1932 | R. Van Osdel, G. Spitz | |
| 1936 | G. F. Hardin | 51.6* | | | and C. C. Johnson | 6 6½ |
| 1937 | J. Patterson | 52.3* | | 1933 | C. C. Johnson | 6 7 |
| 1938 | J. Patterson | 52.8* | | 1934 | C. C. Johnson and | |
| 1939 | R. V. Cochran | 51.9* | | | W. Marty | 6 8½ |
| 1940 | C. McBain | 51.6* | | 1935 | C. C. Johnson | 6 7 |
| 1941 | A. Erwin | 54.5* | | 1936 | C. C. Johnson | 6 8 |
| 1942 | J. W. Smith | 52.0* | | 1937 | D. Albritton | 6 8½ |
| 1943 | A. Erwin | 53.1* | | 1938 | M. Walker | 6 7 |
| 1944 | A. Erwin | 54.0* | | 1939 | L. Steers | 6 8 |
| 1945 | A. Erwin | 53.7* | | 1940 | L. Steers | 6 8½ |
| 1946 | A. Erwin | 55.5* | | 1941 | W. Stewart | 6 9¼ |
| 1947 | J. W. Smith | 52.3* | | 1942 | A. Berry | 6 7 |
| 1948 | L. V. Cochran | 52.3* | | 1943 | P. Watkins | 6 7¾ |
| 1949 | C. H. Moore | 51.1* | | 1944 | F. Sheffield and | |
| 1950 | C. H. Moore | 53.6* | | | W. Smith | 6 7 |
| 1951 | C. H. Moore | 51.4* | | 1945 | D. Albritton, J. William- | |
| 1952 | C. H. Moore | 51.2* | | | son, R. Schnacke and L. | |
| 1953 | J. Culbreath | 52.5 | | | Howe | 6 5¾ |
| 1954 | J. Culbreath | 52.0 | | 1946 | D. Albritton | 6 6¾ |
| 1955 | J. Culbreath | 52.0 | | 1947 | D. Albritton | 6 6 |
| 1956 | G. A. Davis | 50.9* | | 1948 | T. Scofield and W. A. | |
| 1957 | G. A. Davis | 50.9 | | | Vessie | 6 7½ |
| 1958 | G. A. Davis | 49.9 | | 1949 | R. Phillips | 6 6¾ |
| 1959 | R. Howard | 50.7* | | 1950 | J. Heintzmann, D. Al- | |
| 1960 | G. A. Davis | 50.1* | | | britton, V. Severns and | |
| 1961 | C. Cushman | 50.9 | | | J. Razzeto | 6 5½ |
| 1962 | W. Atterberry | 50.5 | | 1951 | J. L. Hall | 6 8 |
| 1963 | W. J. Cawley | 50.4 | | 1952 | W. F. Davis | 6 10½ |
| 1964 | W. Hardin | 50.1* | | 1953 | W. F. Davis | 6 11½ |
| 1965 | W. J. Cawley | 50.3 | | 1954 | E. Shelton | 6 9¾ |
| 1966 | J. Miller | 50.1 | | 1955 | E. Shelton and C. E. | |
| 1967 | R. Whitney | 50.3 | | | Dumas | 6 10 |
| 1968 | R. Whitney | 49.6* | | 1956 | C. E. Dumas | 6 10 |
| 1969 | R. Mann | 50.1 | | 1957 | C. E. Dumas | 6 10½ |
| 1970 | R. Mann | 49.8 | | 1958 | C. E. Dumas | 6 9¾ |
| 1971 | R. Mann | 49.3 | | 1959 | C. E. Dumas | 6 9 |
| 1972 | R. Bruggeman | 50.0* | | 1960 | J. C. Thomas | 7 2 |
| | | | | 1961 | R. Avant | 7 0 |
| | | | | 1962 | J. C. Thomas | 6 10 |
| | | | | 1963 | G. Johnson | 7 0 |
| *High Jump* | | ft. in. | | 1964 | E. Caruthers | 7 1 |
| 1914 | J. Loomis | 6 1¾ | | 1965 | O. Burrell | 7 0 |
| 1915 | G. Horine | 6 0¾ | | 1966 | O. Burrell | 7 2 |
| 1916 | W. Oler | 6 2 | | 1967 | O. Burrell | 7 0½ |
| 1917 | C. Larsen | 6 2½ | | 1968 | E. Hanks | 6 11 |
| 1918 | C. Rice | 6 1 | | 1969 | O. Burrell | 7 1 |
| 1919 | J. Murphy | 6 3 | | 1970 | R. Brown | 7 1 |
| 1920 | J. Murphy | 6 4¼ | | 1971 | R. Brown | 7 3 |
| 1921 | D. V. Alberts | 6 4 | | 1972 | R. Schur | 7 2 |
| 1922 | D. V. Alberts | 6 5 | | | | |
| 1923 | L. Brown | 6 5½ | | *Pole Vault* | | ft. in. |
| 1924 | R. L. Juday | 6 4 | | 1914 | K. R. Curtis | 12 3 |
| 1925 | H. M. Osborn | 6 7 | | 1915 | S. Bellah | 12 9 |
| 1926 | H. M. Osborn | 6 4½ | | | | |

34

| | | | |
|---|---|---|---|
| 1916 | S. Landers | 12 | 9 |
| 1917 | E. Knourek | 12 | 9 |
| 1918 | C. Buck | 12 | 3 |
| 1919 | F. K. Foss | 12 | 9 |
| 1920 | F. K. Foss | 13 | 1 |
| 1921 | E. Knourek | 12 | 7½ |
| 1922 | E. Knourek | 13 | 0 |
| 1923 | E. E. Meyers | 13 | 1 |
| 1924 | E. E. Meyers | 13 | 0 |
| 1925 | H. Smith | 12 | 11½ |
| 1926 | P. Harrington | 13 | 0 |
| 1927 | L. S. Barnes | 13 | 0 |
| 1928 | L. S. Barnes | 13 | 9 |
| 1929 | F. Sturdy | 13 | 9¼ |
| 1930 | F. Sturdy | 13 | 6 |
| 1931 | J. Wool | 13 | 4½ |
| 1932 | W. Graber | 14 | 4¼ |
| 1933 | M. Gordy and K. Brown | 14 | 0 |
| 1934 | K. Brown, W. Graber and W. Thompson | 13 | 11¼ |
| 1935 | E. E. Meadows and W. H. Sefton | 13 | 10¼ |
| 1936 | G. Varoff | 14 | 6½ |
| 1937 | W. H. Sefton | 14 | 7½ |
| 1938 | C. A. Warmerdam | 14 | 5½ |
| 1939 | G. Varoff | 14 | 4 |
| 1940 | C. A. Warmerdam | 15 | 1 |
| 1941 | C. A. Warmerdam | 15 | 0 |
| 1942 | C. A. Warmerdam | 15 | 2½ |
| 1943 | C. A. Warmerdam | 15 | 0 |
| 1944 | C. A. Warmerdam | 15 | 0 |
| 1945 | A. R. Morcom and R. Phelps | 13 | 6 |
| 1946 | I. Moore | 14 | 4¾ |
| 1947 | A. R. Morcom | 14 | 0 |
| 1948 | R. E. Richards and A. R. Morcom | 14 | 6 |
| 1949 | R. E. Richards | 14 | 4 |
| 1950 | R. E. Richards | 14 | 8 |
| 1951 | R. E. Richards | 14 | 4 |
| 1952 | R. E. Richards and D. Laz | 14 | 8 |
| 1953 | D. Laz and G. Mattos | 14 | 1 |
| 1954 | R. E. Richards | 15 | 3½ |
| 1955 | R. E. Richards | 15 | 0 |
| 1956 | R. E. Richards | 15 | 0 |
| 1957 | R. E. Richards | 15 | 1½ |
| 1958 | R. Morris | 14 | 9 |
| 1959 | D. G. Bragg | 15 | 3¼ |
| 1960 | A. Dooley | 15 | 0¾ |
| 1961 | R. Morris | 15 | 8 |
| 1962 | R. Morris | 16 | 0¼ |
| 1963 | B. H. Sternberg | 16 | 4 |
| 1964 | F. M. Hansen | 17 | 0 |
| 1965 | J. T. Pennel | 17 | 0 |
| 1966 | R. Seagren | 17 | 0 |
| 1967 | P. Wilson | 17 | 8 |
| 1968 | R. Railsback | 17 | 0¼ |
| 1969 | R. Seagren | 17 | 6 |
| 1970 | R. Seagren | 17 | 2 |
| 1971 | J. Johnson | 17 | 0 |
| 1972 | D. Roberts | 18 | 0¼ |

*Long Jump*

| | | ft. | in. |
|---|---|---|---|
| 1914 | P. Adams | 23 | 2 |
| 1915 | H. T. Worthington | 23 | 10 |
| 1916 | H. T. Worthington | 23 | 2½ |
| 1917 | J. Irish | 22 | 4¾ |
| 1918 | D. Politzer | 22 | 4 |
| 1919 | F. Smart | 22 | 7¼ |
| 1920 | S. Butler | 24 | 8 |
| 1921 | E. O. Gourdin | 23 | 7¾ |
| 1922 | D. Hubbard | 24 | 5 |
| 1923 | D. Hubbard | 24 | 7¾ |
| 1924 | D. Hubbard | 24 | 0 |
| 1925 | D. Hubbard | 25 | 4¼ |
| 1926 | D. Hubbard | 25 | 2½ |
| 1927 | D. Hubbard | 25 | 8¾ |
| 1928 | E. B. Hamm | 25 | 11 |
| 1929 | E. I. Gordon | 24 | 4¼ |
| 1930 | A. H. Bates | 24 | 3¾ |
| 1931 | A. H. Bates | 24 | 7 |
| 1932 | E. Gordon | 25 | 3¼ |
| 1933 | J. C. Owens | 24 | 6¼ |
| 1934 | J. C. Owens | 25 | 0¾ |
| 1935 | E. Peacock | 26 | 3 |
| 1936 | J. C. Owens | 26 | 3 |
| 1937 | K. King | 25 | 1½ |
| 1938 | W. Lacefield | 25 | 0¼ |
| 1939 | W. Lacefield | 25 | 5½ |
| 1940 | W. Brown | 25 | 1 |
| 1941 | W. Brown | 25 | 4½ |
| 1942 | W. Brown | 24 | 3½ |
| 1943 | W. Christopher | 24 | 4½ |
| 1944 | W. Lund | 23 | 3½ |
| 1945 | H. Douglas | 24 | 0 |
| 1946 | W. Steele | 24 | 0 |
| 1947 | W. Steele | 24 | 9¼ |
| 1948 | F. Johnson | 25 | 4½ |
| 1949 | G. Bryan | 25 | 1½ |
| 1950 | J. Holland | 25 | 9 |
| 1951 | G. Brown | 25 | 8½ |
| 1952 | G. Brown | 25 | 9 |
| 1953 | G. Brown | 25 | 10¾ |
| 1954 | J. Bennett | 24 | 10¼ |
| 1955 | G. C. Bell | 26 | 0½ |
| 1956 | E. Shelby | 26 | 1¼ |
| 1957 | E. Shelby | 25 | 2½ |
| 1958 | E. Shelby | 25 | 10¼ |
| 1959 | G. C. Bell | 26 | 1¼ |
| 1960 | H. Visser (*Neth.*) | 25 | 2 |
| 1961 | R. H. Boston | 26 | 11¼ |
| 1962 | R. H. Boston | 26 | 6 |
| 1963 | R. H. Boston | 26 | 10 |
| 1964 | R. H. Boston | 26 | 7½ |
| 1965 | R. H. Boston | 26 | 3½ |
| 1966 | R. H. Boston | 26 | 3¼ |
| 1967 | J. Proctor | 26 | 0¾ |
| 1968 | R. Beamon | 27 | 4 |

| 1969 | R. Beamon | 26 | 11 | | 1968 | A. Walker | 53 | 9¼ |
| 1970 | B. Moore | 26 | 2¼ | | 1969 | J. Craft | 52 | 9¼ |
| 1971 | A. Robinson | 26 | 10¼ | | 1970 | M. Tiff | 53 | 0 |
| 1972 | A. Robinson | 26 | 5¼ | | 1971 | J. Craft | 54 | 7 |
| | | | | | 1972 | J. Craft | 54 | 10 |

**Triple Jump** — ft. in.    **Shot** — ft. in.

| Year | Triple Jump | ft. | in. | | Year | Shot | ft. | in. |
|---|---|---|---|---|---|---|---|---|
| 1914 | D. F. Ahearn | 48 | 6 | | | *Shot* | | |
| 1915 | D. F. Ahearn | 50 | 11 | | 1914 | P. J. McDonald | 46 | 3½ |
| 1916 | D. F. Ahearn | 46 | 0½ | | 1915 | A. W. Mucks | 48 | 11½ |
| 1917 | D. F. Ahearn | 47 | 8 | | 1916 | A. W. Mucks | 47 | 2 |
| 1918 | D. F. Ahearn | 46 | 3¾ | | 1917 | A. W. Mucks | 45 | 10¼ |
| 1919 | S. G. Landers | 47 | 8½ | | 1918 | A. Richards | 42 | 3¼ |
| 1920 | S. G. Landers | 48 | 7¾ | | 1919 | P. J. McDonald | 45 | 8 |
| 1921 | K. Geist | 46 | 3 | | 1920 | P. J. McDonald | 47 | 0½ |
| 1922 | D. Hubbard | 48 | 1½ | | 1921 | C. L. Houser | 46 | 11½ |
| 1923 | D. Hubbard | 47 | 0½ | | 1922 | P. J. McDonald | 46 | 11½ |
| 1924 | H. Martin | 45 | 8½ | | 1923 | O. Wanzer | 47 | 0½ |
| 1925 | H. Martin | 47 | 11¼ | | 1924 | R. G. Hills | 46 | 5¾ |
| 1926 | L. Casey | 49 | 4¼ | | 1925 | C. L. Houser | 50 | 1 |
| 1927 | L. Casey | 48 | 4¾ | | 1926 | H. Schwarze | 49 | 10¼ |
| 1928 | L. Casey | 48 | 10 | | 1927 | J. Kuck | 48 | 5 |
| 1929 | R. Kelley | 48 | 6¾ | | 1928 | H. Brix | 50 | 11¼ |
| 1930 | L. Casey | 47 | 11½ | | 1929 | H. Brix | 50 | 2½ |
| 1931 | R. Kelley | 47 | 7½ | | 1930 | H. Brix | 52 | 5½ |
| 1932 | S. Bowman | 48 | 11¼ | | 1931 | H. Brix | 50 | 8¼ |
| 1933 | N. Blair | 47 | 3 | | 1932 | L. J. Sexton | 52 | 8 |
| 1934 | D. Wilkins | 48 | 0 | | 1933 | J. Torrance | 51 | 4¼ |
| 1935 | R. Romero | 50 | 4¾ | | 1934 | J. Torrance | 55 | 5 |
| 1936 | W. Brown | 49 | 2 | | 1935 | J. Torrance | 51 | 6¼ |
| 1937 | W. Brown | 49 | 7¼ | | 1936 | D. Zaitz | 50 | 7½ |
| 1938 | H. Neil | 48 | 0 | | 1937 | J. Reynolds | 51 | 7 |
| 1939 | H. Neil | 47 | 9¾ | | 1938 | F. Ryan | 52 | 1½ |
| 1940 | W. Brown | 50 | 2½ | | 1939 | L. Williams | 53 | 7 |
| 1941 | W. Brown | 50 | 11½ | | 1940 | A. Blozis | 55 | 0¼ |
| 1942 | W. Brown | 48 | 11½ | | 1941 | A. Blozis | 54 | 0½ |
| 1943 | W. Brown | 45 | 8 | | 1942 | A. Blozis | 53 | 8¼ |
| 1944 | D. Barksdale | 47 | 2¾ | | 1943 | E. Audet | 52 | 11¼ |
| 1945 | B. Cox | 45 | 10¼ | | 1944 | E. Audet | 52 | 8 |
| 1946 | R. Tate | 47 | 11¼ | | 1945 | W. Bangert | 52 | 10 |
| 1947 | R. Beckus | 45 | 11¼ | | 1946 | W. Bangert | 52 | 2½ |
| 1948 | G. Bryan | 47 | 11¼ | | 1947 | F. Delaney | 52 | 9½ |
| 1949 | G. Bryan | 49 | 1 | | 1948 | F. Delaney | 53 | 8¼ |
| 1950 | G. Bryan | 47 | 11 | | 1949 | J. Fuchs | 57 | 2 |
| 1951 | G. Bryan | 46 | 11½ | | 1950 | J. Fuchs | 57 | 2 |
| 1952 | W. Ashbaugh | 50 | 8¾ | | 1951 | W. P. O'Brien | 55 | 9¼ |
| 1953 | G. Shaw | 47 | 8 | | 1952 | W. P. O'Brien | 57 | 4¼ |
| 1954 | C. Cabrejas (*Cuba*) | 47 | 3 | | 1953 | W. P. O'Brien | 55 | 10¼ |
| 1955 | V. Hernandez (*Cuba*) | 50 | 4 | | 1954 | W. P. O'Brien | 58 | 11¼ |
| 1956 | W. Hollie | 49 | 6 | | 1955 | W. P. O'Brien | 58 | 5¼ |
| 1957 | W. Sharpe | 50 | 4¼ | | 1956 | K. Bantum | 59 | 1½ |
| 1958 | I. Davis | 50 | 8¼ | | 1957 | W. H. Nieder | 61 | 6½ |
| 1959 | I. Davis | 50 | 6½ | | 1958 | W. P. O'Brien | 61 | 11¼ |
| 1960 | I. Davis | 53 | 4½ | | 1959 | W. P. O'Brien | 62 | 2¼ |
| 1961 | W. Sharpe | 52 | 4¾ | | 1960 | W. P. O'Brien | 62 | 6¼ |
| 1962 | W. Sharpe | 52 | 1¼ | | 1961 | D. C. Long | 62 | 2 |
| 1963 | K. Floerke | 51 | 7¾ | | 1962 | G. Gubner | 63 | 6½ |
| 1964 | C. Mousiadis (*Greece*) | 53 | 1 | | 1963 | D. Davis | 62 | 5½ |
| 1965 | A. Walker | 53 | 1 | | 1964 | J. R. Matson | 64 | 11 |
| 1966 | A. Walker | 53 | 8 | | 1965 | J. McGrath | 63 | 0 |
| 1967 | C. Craig | 53 | 1½ | | 1966 | J. R. Matson | 64 | 2¼ |

| | | | |
|---|---|---|---|
| 1967 | J. R. Matson | 66 | 11 |
| 1968 | J. R. Matson | 67 | 5 |
| 1969 | N. Steinhauer | 67 | 4 |
| 1970 | J. R. Matson | 67 | 10¼ |
| 1971 | K. Salb | 67 | 2¾ |
| 1972 | J. R. Matson | 69 | 6½ |

*Discus*

| | | ft. | in. |
|---|---|---|---|
| 1914 | E. Muller | 137 | 0½ |
| 1915 | A. W. Mucks | 146 | 9¼ |
| 1916 | A. W. Mucks | 145 | 4½ |
| 1917 | A. W. Mucks | 140 | 1½ |
| 1918 | E. Muller | 136 | 0 |
| 1919 | A. W. Mucks | 143 | 9¾ |
| 1920 | A. R. Pope | 146 | 5 |
| 1921 | A. R. Pope | 144 | 0 |
| 1922 | A. R. Pope | 145 | 11 |
| 1923 | T. J. Lieb | 151 | 3¾ |
| 1924 | T. J. Lieb | 144 | 7¼ |
| 1925 | C. L. Houser | 156 | 6 |
| 1926 | C. L. Houser | 153 | 6½ |
| 1927 | E. C. W. Krenz | 146 | 0 |
| 1928 | C. L. Houser | 153 | 6¼ |
| 1929 | E. C. W. Krenz | 157 | 0 |
| 1930 | P. B. Jessup | 169 | 8¾ |
| 1931 | P. B. Jessup | 152 | 5¼ |
| 1932 | J. Anderson | 165 | 0 |
| 1933 | J. Anderson | 165 | 1½ |
| 1934 | R. Jones | 155 | 11 |
| 1935 | K. K. Carpenter | 158 | 11½ |
| 1936 | K. K. Carpenter | 166 | 2 |
| 1937 | P. Levy | 163 | 7¾ |
| 1938 | P. Zagar | 167 | 3¼ |
| 1939 | P. Fox | 172 | 4½ |
| 1940 | P. Fox | 170 | 4½ |
| 1941 | A. Harris | 167 | 9½ |
| 1942 | R. Fitch | 166 | 10 |
| 1943 | H. S. Cannon | 161 | 2 |
| 1944 | H. S. Cannon | 162 | 1 |
| 1945 | J. Donaldson | 151 | 2 |
| 1946 | R. Fitch | 179 | 0 |
| 1947 | F. E. Gordien | 174 | 1½ |
| 1948 | F. E. Gordien | 168 | 5 |
| 1949 | F. E. Gordien | 174 | 5¼ |
| 1950 | F. E. Gordien | 173 | 2½ |
| 1951 | R. Doyle | 175 | 6½ |
| 1952 | J. Dillion | 175 | 3½ |
| 1953 | F. E. Gordien | 183 | 9½ |
| 1954 | F. E. Gordien | 182 | 2 |
| 1955 | W. P. O'Brien | 175 | 7 |
| 1956 | R. Drummond | 180 | 3 |
| 1957 | A. A. Oerter | 181 | 6 |
| 1958 | R. Babka | 187 | 10 |
| 1959 | A. A. Oerter | 186 | 5 |
| 1960 | A. A. Oerter | 193 | 9½ |
| 1961 | L. J. Silvester | 195 | 8 |
| 1962 | A. A. Oerter | 202 | 2 |
| 1963 | L. J. Silvester | 198 | 11½ |
| 1964 | A. A. Oerter | 201 | 1½ |

| | | | |
|---|---|---|---|
| 1965 | L. Danek (*Czech.*) | 205 | 7 |
| 1966 | A. A. Oerter | 193 | 9 |
| 1967 | G. Carlsen | 205 | 10 |
| 1968 | L. J. Silvester | 203 | 9 |
| 1969 | J. Cole | 208 | 10 |
| 1970 | L. J. Silvester | 205 | 4 |
| 1971 | T. Vollmer | 208 | 4 |
| 1972 | L. J. Silvester | 213 | 0 |

*Hammer*

| | | ft. | in. |
|---|---|---|---|
| 1914 | P. J. Ryan | 183 | 3¾ |
| 1915 | P. J. Ryan | 176 | 2¾ |
| 1916 | P. J. Ryan | 174 | 8 |
| 1917 | P. J. Ryan | 168 | 7½ |
| 1918 | M. J. McGrath | 173 | 11¼ |
| 1919 | P. J. Ryan | 175 | 5¾ |
| 1920 | P. J. Ryan | 169 | 4 |
| 1921 | P. J. Ryan | 170 | 7½ |
| 1922 | M. J. McGrath | 155 | 9 |
| 1923 | F. D. Tootell | 173 | 6½ |
| 1924 | F. D. Tootell | 173 | 11¼ |
| 1925 | M. J. McGrath | 172 | 0½ |
| 1926 | M. J. McGrath | 162 | 10¼ |
| 1927 | J. Merchant | 170 | 7½ |
| 1928 | E. Black | 166 | 4¼ |
| 1929 | J. Merchant | 170 | 6 |
| 1930 | N. G. Wright | 163 | 9¼ |
| 1931 | E. F. Flanagan | 158 | 8 |
| 1932 | F. Conner | 170 | 10¾ |
| 1933 | P. O'Callaghan (*Ire.*) | 161 | 3¼ |
| 1934 | D. Favor | 163 | 5¾ |
| 1935 | H. Dreyer | 168 | 8½ |
| 1936 | W. Rowe | 175 | 7 |
| 1937 | I. Folwartshny | 173 | 7½ |
| 1938 | I. Folwartshny | 179 | 3 |
| 1939 | C. Cruikshank | 174 | 1½ |
| 1940 | S. Johnson | 182 | 6¼ |
| 1941 | I. Folwartshny | 175 | 6 |
| 1942 | C. Cruikshank | 173 | 8½ |
| 1943 | H. Dreyer | 164 | 6¼ |
| 1944 | H. Dreyer | 166 | 6½ |
| 1945 | H. Dreyer | 166 | 11½ |
| 1946 | I. Folsworth | 169 | 8 |
| 1947 | R. Bennett | 180 | 11 |
| 1948 | R. Bennett | 175 | 7 |
| 1949 | S. Felton | 176 | 10 |
| 1950 | S. Felton | 187 | 3¾ |
| 1951 | S. Felton | 184 | 2¾ |
| 1952 | T. Bane | 179 | 11½ |
| 1953 | M. Engel | 186 | 9 |
| 1954 | R. Backus | 189 | 3 |
| 1955 | H. V. Connolly | 199 | 8 |
| 1956 | H. V. Connolly | 205 | 10½ |
| 1957 | H. V. Connolly | 216 | 3 |
| 1958 | H. V. Connolly | 225 | 4 |
| 1959 | H. V. Connolly | 216 | 10 |
| 1960 | H. V. Connolly | 224 | 4½ |
| 1961 | H. V. Connolly | 213 | 6½ |

| | | | |
|---|---|---|---|
| 1962 | A. Hall | 219 | 3 |
| 1963 | A. Hall | 214 | 11 |
| 1964 | H. V. Connolly | 226 | 5½ |
| 1965 | H. V. Connolly | 232 | 1 |
| 1966 | E. Burke | 220 | 0 |
| 1967 | E. Burke | 235 | 11 |
| 1968 | E. Burke | 217 | 0 |
| 1969 | T. Gage | 228 | 5 |
| 1970 | G. Frenn | 230 | 0 |
| 1971 | G. Frenn | 230 | 1 |
| 1972 | A. Schoterman | 228 | 1 |

*Javelin*

| | | ft. | in. |
|---|---|---|---|
| 1914 | G. A. Bronder | 166 | 8½ |
| 1915 | G. A. Bronder | 177 | 7¾ |
| 1916 | G. A. Bronder | 190 | 6 |
| 1917 | G. A. Bronder | 184 | 0½ |
| 1918 | G. A. Bronder | 169 | 10½ |
| 1919 | G. A. Bronder | 176 | 6 |
| 1920 | M. S. Angier | 192 | 10¾ |
| 1921 | M. S. Angier | 189 | 3¼ |
| 1922 | F. Hanner | 193 | 2¼ |
| 1923 | H. Hoffman | 194 | 7½ |
| 1924 | J. Leyden | 181 | 0 |
| 1925 | H. Bonura | 213 | 10½ |
| 1926 | J. Kuck | 199 | 7 |
| 1927 | C. Harlow | 193 | 3½ |
| 1928 | C. B. Hines | 202 | 1¾ |
| 1929 | J. P. Mortensen | 204 | 11½ |
| 1930 | J. DeMers | 222 | 6¾ |
| 1931 | J. DeMers | 211 | 5¼ |
| 1932 | M. Metcalf | 219 | 8 |
| 1933 | L. Bartlett | 209 | 6¾ |
| 1934 | R. Legore | 216 | 0 |
| 1935 | H. O'Dell | 217 | 1½ |
| 1936 | J. Mottram | 214 | 7¼ |
| 1937 | W. Reitz | 224 | 9¼ |
| 1938 | N. Vukmanic | 218 | 7¾ |
| 1939 | B. Brown | 215 | 10¾ |
| 1940 | B. Brown | 223 | 1¼ |
| 1941 | B. Brown | 218 | 3 |
| 1942 | B. Brown | 216 | 7½ |
| 1943 | M. Biles | 202 | 5 |
| 1944 | M. Biles | 211 | 0 |
| 1945 | E. Marshall | 215 | 4 |
| 1946 | G. Adair | 213 | 7 |
| 1947 | S. Seymour | 248 | 10 |
| 1948 | S. Seymour | 230 | 5 |
| 1949 | F. D. Held | 232 | 2½ |
| 1950 | S. Seymour | 228 | 10¾ |
| 1951 | F. D. Held | 241 | 0¾ |
| 1952 | W. Miller | 236 | 1 |
| 1953 | F. D. Held | 242 | 7 |
| 1954 | F. D. Held | 249 | 8½ |
| 1955 | F. D. Held | 260 | 3 |
| 1956 | C. Young | 247 | 11½ |
| 1957 | R. Voiles | 251 | 5½ |
| 1958 | F. D. Held | 252 | 0½ |
| 1959 | A. Cantello | 246 | 9 |
| 1960 | A. Cantello | 271 | 9 |

| | | | |
|---|---|---|---|
| 1961 | J. Fromm | 249 | 11½ |
| 1962 | D. Studney | 246 | 6 |
| 1963 | L. Stuart | 255 | 3 |
| 1964 | F. Covelli | 253 | 7 |
| 1965 | W. Floerke | 258 | 7 |
| 1966 | J. Tushaus | 260 | 8 |
| 1967 | D. McNab | 268 | 3 |
| 1968 | F. Covelli | 269 | 6 |
| 1969 | M. Murro | 284 | 3 |
| 1970 | W. Skinner | 276 | 7 |
| 1971 | W. Skinner | 267 | 2 |
| 1972 | F. Luke | 277 | 5 |

*Decathlon*

(Scored per tables of the day)

| | | Pts. |
|---|---|---|
| 1915 | A. Richards | 6858 |
| 1920 | B. Hamilton | 7022 |
| 1921 | D. Shea | 5849 |
| 1922 | S. H. Thomson | 6890 |
| 1923 | H. M. Osborn | 7351 |
| 1924 | A. J. Plansky | 5901 |
| 1925 | H. M. Osborn | 7706 |
| 1926 | H. M. Osborn | 7187 |
| 1927 | F. Elkins | 7574 |
| 1928 | J. K. Doherty | 7600 |
| 1929 | J. K. Doherty | 7784 |
| 1930 | W. Charles | 7313 |
| 1931 | J. P. Mortensen | 8166 |
| 1932 | J. A. Bausch | 8103 |
| 1933 | B. F. Berlinger | 7597 |
| 1934 | R. Clark | 7966 |
| 1935 | R. Clark | 7929 |
| 1936 | G. E. Morris | 7880 |
| 1938 | J. Scott | 6486 |
| 1939 | J. Scott | 6671 |
| 1940 | W. Watson | 7523 |
| 1941 | J. Borican | 5666 |
| 1942 | W. Terwilliger | 6802 |
| 1943 | W. Watson | 5994 |
| 1944 | I. Mondschein | 5748 |
| 1945 | C. Beaudry | 5886 |
| 1946 | I. Mondschein | 6466 |
| 1947 | I. Mondschein | 6715 |
| 1948 | R. B. Mathias | 7224 |
| 1949 | R. B. Mathias | 7556 |
| 1950 | R. B. Mathias | 8042 |
| 1951 | R. E. Richards | 7834 |
| 1952 | R. B. Mathias | 7825 |
| 1953 | M. Campbell | 7235 |
| 1954 | R. E. Richards | 6501 |
| 1955 | R. E. Richards | 6873 |
| 1956 | R. L. Johnson | 6873 |
| 1957 | C. Pratt | 7164 |
| 1958 | R. L. Johnson | 7754 |
| 1959 | C. K. Yang (*Taiwan*) | 7549 |
| 1960 | R. L. Johnson | 8683 |
| 1961 | P. Herman | 7142 |
| 1962 | C. K. Yang (*Taiwan*) | 8249 |
| 1963 | S. Pauly | 7852 |

| Year | Name | Score |
|---|---|---|
| 1964 | C. K. Yang (*Taiwan*) | 8641 |
| 1965 | W. Toomey | 7764 |
| 1966 | W. Toomey | 8234 |
| 1967 | W. Toomey | 7880 |
| 1968 | W. Toomey | 8037 |
| 1969 | W. Toomey | 7818 |
| 1970 | J. Warkentin | 8026 |
| 1971 | R. Wanamaker | 7989 |
| 1972 | J. Bennett | 7910 |

*Marathon*

| Year | Name | hr. | min. | sec. |
|---|---|---|---|---|
| 1925 | C. L. Mellor | 2 | 33 | 00.6 |
| 1926 | C. DeMar | 2 | 45 | 05.2 |
| 1927 | C. DeMar | 2 | 40 | 22.2 |
| 1928 | C. DeMar | 2 | 37 | 07.8 |
| 1929 | J. C. Miles | 2 | 33 | 08.8 |
| 1930 | K. Koski | 2 | 25 | 21.2 |
| 1931 | W. A. Agee | 2 | 32 | 38.0 |
| 1932 | C. D. Martak | 2 | 58 | 18.0 |
| 1933 | D. Komonen | 2 | 53 | 43.0 |
| 1934 | D. Komonen | 2 | 43 | 26.6 |
| 1935 | F. Dengis | 2 | 53 | 53.0 |
| 1936 | W. T. McMahon | 2 | 38 | 14.2 |
| 1937 | M. Porter | 2 | 44 | 22.0 |
| 1938 | F. Dengis | 2 | 39 | 38.2 |
| 1939 | F. Dengis | 2 | 33 | 45.2 |
| 1940 | G. Cote | 2 | 34 | 06.0 |
| 1941 | J. Smith | 2 | 36 | 06.8 |
| 1942 | F. A. McGlone | 2 | 37 | 54.0 |
| 1943 | G. Cote | 2 | 38 | 35.3 |
| 1944 | C. Robbins | 2 | 40 | 48.6 |
| 1945 | C. Robbins | 2 | 37 | 14.0 |
| 1946 | G. Cote | 2 | 47 | 53.6 |
| 1947 | T. Vogel | 2 | 40 | 11.0 |
| 1948 | J. A. Kelley | 2 | 48 | 32.3 |
| 1949 | V. Dyrgall | 2 | 38 | 48.9 |
| 1950 | J. A. Kelley | 2 | 45 | 55.3 |
| 1951 | J. Van Zant | 2 | 37 | 12.5 |
| 1952 | V. Dyrgall | 2 | 38 | 24.4 |
| 1953 | K. G. Leandersson | 2 | 48 | 12.5 |
| 1954 | T. Corbitt | 2 | 46 | 13.9 |
| 1955 | N. Costes | 2 | 31 | 12.4 |
| 1956 | J. J. Kelley | 2 | 24 | 52.2 |
| 1957 | J. J. Kelley | 2 | 24 | 55.2 |
| 1958 | J. J. Kelley | 2 | 21 | 00.4 |
| 1959 | J. J. Kelley | 2 | 21 | 54.4 |
| 1960 | J. J. Kelley | 2 | 24 | 18.5 |
| 1961 | J. J. Kelley | 2 | 26 | 53.4 |
| 1962 | J. J. Kelley | 2 | 27 | 39.0 |
| 1963 | J. J. Kelley | 2 | 25 | 17.6 |
| 1964 | L. Edelen | 2 | 24 | 25.6 |
| 1965 | G. Williams | 2 | 33 | 50.6 |
| 1966 | N. Higgins | 2 | 22 | 50.0 |
| 1967 | R. Daws | 2 | 40 | 07.0 |
| 1968 | G. Young | 2 | 30 | 48.0 |
| 1969 | —— | | | |
| 1970 | R. Fitts | 2 | 24 | 10.6 |
| 1971 | K. Moore | 2 | 16 | 48.6 |
| 1972 | E. Norris | 2 | 24 | 42.8 |

*20 Kilometres Walk*

| Year | Name | hr. | min. | sec. |
|---|---|---|---|---|
| 1938 | J. Rahkonen | 1 | 51 | 57.0 |
| 1939 | J. Deni | 1 | 49 | 55.4 |
| 1940 | L. Schnepel | 1 | 56 | 03.0 |
| 1941 | W. Wilson | 2 | 18 | 04.0 |
| 1942 | W. Mihalo | 1 | 39 | 07.0 |
| 1943 | S. Carlsson | 2 | 02 | 04.0 |
| 1944 | J. Megyesy | 1 | 44 | 48.0 |
| 1945 | J. Megyesy | 1 | 58 | 15.0 |
| 1946 | J. Deni | 1 | 53 | 10.0 |
| 1947 | E. Weber | 1 | 47 | 55.0 |
| 1948 | M. Fleischer | 2 | 10 | 07.0 |
| 1949 | W. Mihalo | 2 | 03 | 06.0 |
| 1950 | A. Weinacker | 1 | 40 | 10.8 |
| 1951 | H. H. Laskau | 1 | 38 | 14.3 |
| 1952 | H. H. Laskau | 1 | 37 | 04.0 |
| 1953 | H. H. Laskau | 1 | 43 | 09.3 |
| 1954 | H. H. Laskau | 1 | 44 | 53.3 |
| 1955 | H. H. Laskau | 1 | 44 | 08.0 |
| 1956 | A. Oakley (*Can.*) | 1 | 39 | 06.0 |
| 1957 | R. Haluza | 1 | 49 | 16.0 |
| 1958 | R. Laird | 1 | 40 | 09.0 |
| 1959 | R. Haluza | 1 | 32 | 36.0 |
| 1960 | R. Haluza | 1 | 34 | 12.0 |
| 1961 | R. Zinn | 1 | 41 | 51.0 |
| 1962 | R. Zinn | 1 | 43 | 59.0 |
| 1963 | R. Laird | 1 | 34 | 52.0 |
| 1964 | R. Laird | 1 | 34 | 44.6 |
| 1965 | R. Laird | 1 | 38 | 38.0 |
| 1966 | R. Haluza | 1 | 36 | 16.0 |
| 1967 | R. Laird | 1 | 38 | 40.0 |
| 1968 | R. Laird | 1 | 33 | 00.0 |
| 1969 | R. Laird | 1 | 33 | 10.4 |
| 1970 | D. Romansky | 1 | 35 | 05.0 |
| 1971 | T. Dooley | 1 | 32 | 18.0 |
| 1972 | L. Young | 1 | 35 | 56.4 |
| 1973 | W. Ranney | 1 | 34 | 15.0 |

*50 Kilometres Walk*

| Year | Name | hr. | min. | sec. |
|---|---|---|---|---|
| 1929 | M. Weiss | 4 | 52 | 45.0 |
| 1930 | H. Cieman | 4 | 47 | 48.0 |
| 1931 | H. L. Clark | 5 | 26 | 41.8 |
| 1932 | P. Jachelski | 5 | 27 | 05.0 |
| 1933 | P. Jachelski | 5 | 11 | 30.0 |
| 1934 | H. Cieman | 4 | 58 | 55.2 |
| 1935 | H. Cieman | 4 | 57 | 29.0 |
| 1936 | E. Crosbie | 5 | 16 | 16.0 |
| 1937 | A. Mangan | 5 | 00 | 03.0 |
| 1938 | L. Schnepel | 5 | 18 | 50.2 |
| 1939 | E. Crosbie | 5 | 19 | 33.3 |
| 1940 | W. Mihalo | 5 | 07 | 25.0 |
| 1941 | J. Deni | 5 | 19 | 43.0 |
| 1942 | W. Mihalo | 5 | 06 | 45.0 |
| 1943 | W. Mihalo | 5 | 15 | 45.0 |
| 1944 | W. Fleming | 5 | 22 | 49.5 |
| 1945 | J. J. Abbate | 5 | 35 | 20.0 |
| 1946 | G. Wieland | 5 | 17 | 25.0 |
| 1947 | J. J. Abbate | 5 | 12 | 52.0 |
| 1948 | E. Crosbie | 5 | 04 | 30.0 |

| | | | | |
|---|---|---|---|---|
| 1949 | A. Weinacker | 5 | 13 | 30.0 |
| 1950 | J. Deni | 5 | 41 | 32.0 |
| 1951 | W. Mihalo | 5 | 25 | 39.0 |
| 1952 | L. Sjogren | 4 | 46 | 51.5 |
| 1953 | L. Sjogren | 4 | 56 | 59.9 |
| 1954 | L. Sjogren | 4 | 43 | 44.4 |
| 1955 | L. Sjogren | 4 | 30 | 57.0 |
| 1956 | A. Weinacker | 4 | 38 | 57.5 |
| 1957 | J. Hewson | 5 | 06 | 39.0 |
| 1958 | J. Hewson | 4 | 43 | 40.0 |
| 1959 | E. H. Denman | 5 | 07 | 47.0 |
| 1960 | R. Laird | 4 | 40 | 09.0 |
| 1961 | J. W. Allen | 4 | 38 | 19.6 |
| 1962 | R. Laird | 5 | 25 | 30.0 |
| 1963 | C. McCarthy | 4 | 44 | 55.0 |
| 1964 | C. McCarthy | 4 | 45 | 31.0 |
| 1965 | D. Rasmussen | 5 | 03 | 33.0 |
| 1966 | L. Young | 4 | 38 | 24.6 |
| 1967 | L. Young | 4 | 33 | 03.0 |
| 1968 | L. Young | 4 | 12 | 12.0 |
| 1969 | B. Overton | 4 | 56 | 00.0 |
| 1970 | J. Knifton | 4 | 35 | 02.0 |
| 1971 | L. Young | 4 | 18 | 29.2 |
| 1972 | L. Young | 4 | 13 | 04.4 |
| 1973 | W. Weigle | 4 | 22 | 27.0 |

# Women's Championships

With the exception of 1934, AAU Women's Championships have been held each year since 1923.

The most titles won in a single event is 12 by Willye White in the long jump: 1959-66, 68-70, 72. Dorothy Dodson won the javelin title 11 years running, from 1939 to 1949. Stella Walsh (Polish-born Stanislawa Walasiewicz), between 1930 and 1951, won 11 titles in the 200 m. and 220 yds., 11 in the long jump, 4 in the 100 yd. and 100 m., and 2 in the discus.

## 100 Metres

(* 100 Yards)

| | | |
|---|---|---|
| 1923 | F. Ruppert | 12.0* |
| 1924 | F. Ruppert | 12.0* |
| 1925 | H. Filkey | 11.4* |
| 1926 | R. M. Grosse (Can) | 11.8* |
| 1927 | E. Cartwright | 11.4* |
| 1928 | E. Cartwright | 12.4 |
| 1929 | B. Robinson | 11.2* |
| 1930 | S. Walsh | 11.2* |
| 1931 | E. Egg | 11.4* |
| 1932 | W. von Bremen | 12.3 |
| 1933 | A. Rogers | 12.2 |
| 1935 | H. H. Stephens | 11.6 |
| 1936 | H. H. Stephens | 11.7 |
| 1937 | C. Isicson | 12.8 |
| 1938 | L. Hymes | 12.4 |
| 1939 | O. Hasenfus | 12.6 |
| 1940 | J. Lane | 12.0 |
| 1941 | J. Lane | 12.4 |
| 1942 | A. Coachman | 12.1 |
| 1943 | S. Walsh | 11.6 |
| 1944 | S. Walsh | 12.0 |
| 1945 | A. Coachman | 12.0 |
| 1946 | A. Coachman | 12.3 |
| 1947 | J. Watson | 13.1 |
| 1948 | S. Walsh | 12.9 |
| 1949 | J. Patton | 12.1 |
| 1950 | J. Patton | 13.3 |
| 1951 | M. McNabb | 12.2 |
| 1952 | C. Hardy | 12.3 |
| 1953 | B Jones | 11.9 |
| 1954 | B. Jones | 12.0 |
| 1955 | M. Faggs | 10.8* |
| 1956 | M. Faggs | 11.7 |
| 1957 | B. Jones | 10.9* |
| 1958 | M. Matthews | 11.1* |
| 1959 | W. Rudolph | 12.1 |
| 1960 | W. Rudolph | 11.5 |
| 1961 | W. Rudolph | 10.8* |
| 1962 | W. Rudolph | 10.8* |
| 1963 | E. McGuire | 11.0* |
| 1964 | W. Tyus | 11.5 |
| 1965 | W. Tyus | 10.5* |
| 1966 | W. Tyus | 10.5* |
| 1967 | B. Ferrell | 11.1 |
| 1968 | M. Bailes | 11.1 |
| 1969 | B. Ferrell | 10.7* |
| 1970 | Chi Cheng (Taiwan) | 10.2* |
| 1971 | I. Davis | 11.2 |
| 1972 | A. Annum (Ghana) | 11.5 |

## 200 Metres

(* 220 Yards)

| | | sec. |
|---|---|---|
| 1926 | F. Keddie | 28.6* |
| 1927 | E. Brough | 26.8* |
| 1928 | F. Wright | 27.4* |
| 1929 | M. Gilliland | 27.4* |
| 1930 | S. Walsh | 25.4* |
| 1931 | S. Walsh | 26.4* |
| 1932 | O. Hasenfus | 26.5* |
| 1933 | O. Hasenfus | 26.2 |
| 1935 | H. H. Stephens | 24.6 |
| 1936 | B. Hobbs | 26.6 |
| 1937 | G. Johnson | 26.0 |
| 1938 | F. Vitale | 26.7 |
| 1939 | S. Walsh | 25.5 |
| 1940 | S. Walsh | 26.1 |
| 1941 | J. Lane | 25.2 |
| 1942 | S. Walsh | 25.4 |
| 1943 | S. Walsh | 26.3 |
| 1944 | S. Walsh | 24.6 |
| 1945 | S. Walsh | 26.6 |
| 1946 | S. Walsh | 26.3 |
| 1947 | S. Walsh | 26.2 |
| 1948 | S. Walsh | 25.5 |

| | | | | | | |
|---|---|---|---|---|---|---|
| 1949 | N. Jackson | 24.2 | 1970 | C. Toussaint | 2 05.1* |
| 1950 | N. Jackson | 25.0 | 1971 | C. Toussaint | 2 04.3 |
| 1951 | J. Patton | 25.4 | 1972 | C. Hudson | 2 06.7 |
| 1952 | C. Hardy | 25.5 | | | |
| 1953 | D. Dwyer | 24.4 | *1500 Metres* | | min. sec. |
| 1954 | M. Faggs | 24.5 | 1965 | M. Mulder | 4 36.5 |
| 1955 | M. Faggs | 25.1* | 1966 | D. Brown | 4 20.2 |
| 1956 | M. Faggs | 24.6* | 1967 | N. Rocha | 4 29.0 |
| 1957 | I. Daniels | 24.7* | 1968 | J. Hill | 4 46.5 |
| 1958 | L. Williams | 24.3* | 1969 | D. Brown | 4 27.3 |
| 1959 | I. Daniels | 24.1 | 1970 | F. Larrieu | 4 20.8 |
| 1960 | W. Rudolph | 22.9 | 1971 | K. Gibbons | 4 19.2 |
| 1961 | L. O'Neal | 25.0* | 1972 | F. Larrieu | 4 18.4 |
| 1962 | V. Brown | 24.1* | | | |
| 1963 | V. Brown | 24.4* | *3000 Metres* | | min. sec. |
| 1964 | E. McGuire | 23.6 | 1972 | T. Anex | 9 42.6 |
| 1965 | E. McGuire | 23.6* | | | |
| 1966 | W. Tyus | 23.8* | *2 Miles* | | min. sec. |
| 1967 | D. Wilson | 23.6 | 1971 | D. Brown | 10 07.0 |
| 1968 | W. Tyus | 23.5 | | | |
| 1969 | B. Ferrell | 23.8* | *80 Metres Hurdles* | | sec. |
| 1970 | Chi Cheng (*Taiwan*) | 22.4* | 1929 | H. Filkey | 12.6 |
| 1971 | K. Boyle (*Aus*) | 23.1 | 1930 | E. Hall | 13.0 |
| 1972 | A. Annum (*Ghana*) | 23.4 | 1931 | M. Didrikson | 12.0 |

*400 Metres*
(* 440 Yards)

| | | | | | |
|---|---|---|---|---|---|
| | | sec. | 1932 | M. Didrikson | 12.1 |
| 1958 | C. McKenzie (*GB*) | 61.5* | 1933 | S. Schaller | 12.1 |
| 1959 | K. Polson | 59.0 | 1935 | J. Hiller | 13.0 |
| 1960 | I. Robertson (*GB*) | 57.6 | 1936 | A. O'Brien | 12.0 |
| 1961 | J. Peterson | 59.5* | 1937 | C. Gaines | 12.8 |
| 1962 | S. Knott | 58.1* | 1938 | M. Cotrell | 13.0 |
| 1963 | S. Knott | 57.0* | 1939 | M. Cotrell | 12.5 |
| 1964 | J. Smith | 54.7 | 1940 | S. Cooper | 13.1 |
| 1965 | J. Smith | 55.1* | 1941 | L. Perry | 13.2 |
| 1966 | C. Cooke | 53.4* | 1942 | L. Purifoy | 12.6 |
| 1967 | C. Cooke | 52.5 | 1943 | N. Phillips | 12.3 |
| 1968 | J. Scott | 52.9 | 1944 | L. Purifoy | 12.8 |
| 1969 | K. Hammond | 54.4* | 1945 | L. Purifoy | 12.5 |
| 1970 | M. Laing | 52.9* | 1946 | N. Phillips | 12.2 |
| 1971 | M. Fergerson | 53.3 | 1947 | N. Phillips | 12.6 |
| 1972 | K. Hammond | 52.3 | 1948 | B. Robinson | 12.1 |
| | | | 1949 | B. Robinson | 11.9 |
| | | | 1950 | E. Lawler | 11.9 |
| | | | 1951 | N. Phillips | 12.2 |

*800 Metres*
(* 880 Yards)

| | | | | | |
|---|---|---|---|---|---|
| | | min. sec. | 1952 | C. Darnowski | 12.1 |
| 1927 | M. Barkley | 2 36.6 | 1953 | N. Phillips | 12.2 |
| 1928 | R. B. Wilson | 2 32.6 | 1954 | C. Darnowski | 12.2 |
| 1958 | F. McArdle | 2 26.7* | 1955 | B. Diaz (*Cuba*) | 11.5 |
| 1959 | G. Butcher | 2 21.2 | 1956 | B. Diaz (*Cuba*) | 11.1 |
| 1960 | P. Bank | 2 17.5 | 1957 | S. Crowder | 12.4 |
| 1961 | P. Bank | 2 19.2* | 1958 | B. Diaz (*Cuba*) | 11.4 |
| 1962 | L. Bennett | 2 12.3* | 1959 | S. Crowder | 11.7 |
| 1963 | S. Knott | 2 12.5* | 1960 | J. A. Terry | 11.4 |
| 1964 | S. Knott | 2 10.4 | 1961 | C. Sherrard | 11.5 |
| 1965 | M. Mulder | 2 11.1* | 1962 | C. Sherrard | 11.3 |
| 1966 | C. Cooke | 2 05.0* | 1963 | R. Bonds | 11.3 |
| 1967 | M. Jackson | 2 03.6 | 1964 | R. Bonds | 10.8 |
| 1968 | D. Brown | 2 05.1 | 1966 | C. Sherrard | 10.7 |
| 1969 | M. Jackson | 2 11.1* | 1967 | M. Rallins | 10.9 |
| | | | 1968 | M. Rallins | 10.6 |

41

*100 Metres Hurdles*

| | | sec. |
|---|---|---|
| 1965 | C. Sherrard | 13.6 |
| 1969 | Chi Cheng (*Taiwan*) | 13.7 |
| 1970 | M. Rallins | 13.4 |
| 1971 | P. Johnson | 13.5 |
| 1972 | M. Rallins | 13.5 |

*200 Metres Hurdles*

| | | sec. |
|---|---|---|
| 1965 | J. Meldrum (*Can*) | 27.5 |
| 1966 | P. Johnson | 27.6 |
| 1967 | P. Johnson | 27.8 |
| 1968 | P. Johnson | 27.3 |
| 1969 | P. Hawkins | 27.4 |
| 1970 | P. Hawkins | 26.1 |
| 1971 | P. Hawkins | 26.1 |
| 1972 | P. Hawkins | 26.3 |

*High Jump*

| | | ft. | in. |
|---|---|---|---|
| 1923 | C. M. Wright | 4 | 7½ |
| 1925 | E. Stine | 4 | 10 |
| 1926 | C. Maguire | 4 | 11¼ |
| 1927 | C. Maguire | 5 | 0½ |
| 1928 | M. Wiley | 4 | 11¾ |
| 1929 | J. Shiley | 4 | 9¾ |
| 1930 | J. Shiley | 5 | 1 |
| 1931 | J. Shiley | 5 | 2 |
| 1932 | M. Didrikson and J. Shiley | 5 | 3 |
| 1933 | A. Arden | 5 | 3¼ |
| 1935 | B. Howe | 4 | 11 |
| 1936 | A. Rogers | 5 | 2½ |
| 1937 | M. Bergmann | 4 | 11½ |
| 1938 | M. Bergmann | 5 | 2 |
| 1939 | A. Coachman | 5 | 2 |
| 1940 | A. Coachman | 4 | 11 |
| 1941 | A. Coachman | 5 | 2¾ |
| 1942 | A. Coachman | 4 | 8 |
| 1943 | A. Coachman | 5 | 0 |
| 1944 | A. Coachman | 5 | 1½ |
| 1945 | A. Coachman | 5 | 0 |
| 1946 | A. Coachman | 5 | 0 |
| 1947 | A. Coachman | 5 | 1 |
| 1948 | A. Coachman | 5 | 0 |
| 1949 | G. Orr | 5 | 0 |
| 1950 | D. Chisholm | 4 | 8¼ |
| 1951 | M. Boos | 4 | 9¾ |
| 1952 | M. Boos | 4 | 11½ |
| 1953 | M. McDaniel | 5 | 1½ |
| 1954 | J. Cantrell | 5 | 0¼ |
| 1955 | M. McDaniel | 5 | 6½ |
| 1956 | M. McDaniel | 5 | 4 |
| 1957 | V. Thomas and H. Ulmer | 4 | 10 |
| 1958 | B. Brown and R. Robinson | 5 | 2½ |
| 1959 | L. Josefson | 5 | 4 |
| 1960 | L. Josefson | 5 | 4¼ |
| 1961 | L. Josefson | 5 | 1 |
| 1962 | K. Tsutsumi (*Japan*) | 5 | 3 |
| 1963 | E. Montgomery | 5 | 8 |
| 1964 | E. Montgomery | 5 | 8 |
| 1965 | E. Montgomery | 5 | 7 |
| 1966 | E. Montgomery | 5 | 7 |
| 1967 | E. Montgomery | 5 | 6¼ |
| 1968 | T. Thrasher | 5 | 6 |
| 1969 | E. Montgomery | 5 | 11 |
| 1970 | S. Plihal | 5 | 8 |
| 1971 | L. Iddings | 5 | 8 |
| 1972 | A. Reid (*Jamaica*) | 6 | 0½ |

*Long Jump*

| | | ft. | in. |
|---|---|---|---|
| 1923 | H. Dinnehey | 15 | 4 |
| 1924 | D. Walsh | 15 | 3 |
| 1925 | H. Filkey | 17 | 0 |
| 1926 | N. Todd | 16 | 7¼ |
| 1927 | E. Egg | 17 | 1¾ |
| 1928 | E. Cartwright | 16 | 10¾ |
| 1929 | N. Todd | 17 | 3¼ |
| 1930 | S. Walsh | 18 | 9¼ |
| 1931 | M. Didrikson | 17 | 11½ |
| 1932 | N. Todd | 17 | 6 |
| 1933 | G. Valvoda | 17 | 2¾ |
| 1935 | E. Tate | 16 | 6 |
| 1936 | M. Smith | 18 | 0 |
| 1937 | L. Hymes | 17 | 8½ |
| 1938 | L. Hymes | 17 | 2 |
| 1939 | S. Walsh | 19 | 4¾ |
| 1940 | S. Walsh | 17 | 7½ |
| 1941 | S. Walsh | 18 | 6¾ |
| 1942 | S. Walsh | 17 | 11 |
| 1943 | S. Walsh | 19 | 1 |
| 1944 | S. Walsh | 17 | 11 |
| 1945 | S. Walsh | 18 | 3 |
| 1946 | S. Walsh | 17 | 0¾ |
| 1947 | L. Purifoy | 17 | 6 |
| 1948 | S. Walsh | 17 | 8½ |
| 1949 | M. Landry | 17 | 5 |
| 1950 | M. Landry | 17 | 5¾ |
| 1951 | S. Walsh | 17 | 3 |
| 1952 | M. Landry | 18 | 1½ |
| 1953 | M. Landry | 18 | 7½ |
| 1954 | M. Landry | 17 | 11 |
| 1955 | N. Phillips | 17 | 5¾ |
| 1956 | M. Matthews | 19 | 4 |
| 1957 | M. Matthews | 19 | 5½ |
| 1958 | M. Matthews | 20 | 1 |
| 1959 | W. White | 19 | 4½ |
| 1960 | W. White | 19 | 1½ |
| 1961 | W. White | 19 | 11½ |
| 1962 | W. White | 20 | 3 |
| 1963 | W. White | 19 | 4¾ |
| 1964 | W. White | 21 | 1 |
| 1965 | W. White | 20 | 5½ |
| 1966 | W. White | 20 | 7½ |
| 1967 | P. Bank | 20 | 8¼ |
| 1968 | W. White | 20 | 11¼ |
| 1969 | W. White | 19 | 8¾ |
| 1970 | W. White | 21 | 1 |

| | | ft. | in. |
|---|---|---|---|
| 1971 | K. Attlesey | 20 | 8¾ |
| 1972 | W. White | 20 | 6¼ |

*Shot*

| | | ft. | in. |
|---|---|---|---|
| 1923 | B. Christophel | 30 | 10½ |
| 1924 | E. Behring | 30 | 1½ |
| 1925 | L. Copeland | 32 | 10½ |
| 1926 | L. Copeland | 38 | 3¾ |
| 1927 | L. Copeland | 39 | 6 |
| 1928 | L. Copeland | 40 | 4¼ |
| 1929 | R. McDonald | 42 | 3 |
| 1930 | R. McDonald | 38 | 11½ |
| 1931 | L. Copeland | 40 | 2¼ |
| 1932 | M. Didrikson | 39 | 6¼ |
| 1933 | C. Rutherford | 38 | 11 |
| 1935 | R. McDonald | 38 | 3¾ |
| 1936 | H. H. Stephens | 41 | 8½ |
| 1937 | M. Bergmann | 37 | 6¾ |
| 1938 | C. Fellmeth | 38 | 5¾ |
| 1939 | C. Fellmeth | 41 | 1¾ |
| 1940 | C. Fellmeth | 38 | 3½ |
| 1941 | C. Fellmeth | 37 | 0¼ |
| 1942 | R. Harris | 37 | 10½ |
| 1943 | F. Kuszubski | 37 | 11 |
| 1944 | D. Dodson | 36 | 0¼ |
| 1945 | F. Kuszubski | 37 | 9¾ |
| 1946 | D. Dodson | 38 | 10¾ |
| 1947 | D. Dodson | 37 | 11 |
| 1948 | F. Kuszubski | 40 | 5¾ |
| 1949 | A. Bert | 39 | 8¼ |
| 1950 | F. Kuszubski | 39 | 3¾ |
| 1951 | A. Bert | 41 | 3 |
| 1952 | A. Bert and J. Dicks | 37 | 9 |
| 1953 | A. Bert | 40 | 2½ |
| 1954 | L. Testa | 40 | 2½ |
| 1955 | W. Wejzgrow | 37 | 4½ |
| 1956 | E. Brown | 45 | 0 |
| 1957 | E. Brown | 43 | 0¼ |
| 1958 | E. Brown | 47 | 5½ |
| 1959 | E. Brown | 46 | 4¾ |
| 1960 | E. Brown | 49 | 8½ |
| 1961 | E. Brown | 47 | 8½ |
| 1962 | E. Brown | 48 | 10¾ |
| 1963 | S. Sheppard | 48 | 3½ |
| 1964 | E. Brown | 46 | 11 |
| 1965 | L. Graham | 47 | 7 |
| 1966 | L. Graham | 47 | 11¾ |
| 1967 | M. Seidler | 46 | 10 |
| 1968 | M. Seidler | 50 | 3¾ |
| 1969 | L. Graham | 48 | 11¾ |
| 1970 | L. Graham | 49 | 10 |
| 1971 | L. Graham | 52 | 0 |
| 1972 | M. Seidler | 52 | 9 |

*Discus*

| | | ft. | in. |
|---|---|---|---|
| 1923 | B. M. Wolbert | 71 | 9½ |
| 1924 | R. Ranck | 70 | 0 |
| 1925 | M. Reichardt | 87 | 2¾ |
| 1926 | L. Copeland | 101 | 1 |
| 1927 | L. Copeland | 103 | 8¼ |
| 1928 | M. Reichardt | 116 | 9¼ |
| 1929 | R. McDonald | 113 | 4 |
| 1930 | E. Ferrara | 111 | 6 |
| 1931 | E. Ferrara | 108 | 10½ |
| 1932 | R. Osborn | 133 | 0¾ |
| 1933 | R. Osborn | 123 | 0¼ |
| 1935 | M. Wright | 113 | 9½ |
| 1936 | H. H. Stephens | 121 | 6½ |
| 1937 | E. Lindsey | 107 | 11 |
| 1938 | C. Fellmeth | 126 | 0¼ |
| 1939 | C. Fellmeth | 113 | 7½ |
| 1940 | C. Fellmeth | 114 | 11 |
| 1941 | S. Walsh | 113 | 10¼ |
| 1942 | S. Walsh | 110 | 11¾ |
| 1943 | F. Kuszubski | 109 | 6¼ |
| 1944 | H. Turner | 101 | 7¾ |
| 1945 | F. Kuszubski | 103 | 0¼ |
| 1946 | D. Dodson | 102 | 6 |
| 1947 | F. Kuszubski | 110 | 4¾ |
| 1948 | F. Kuszubski | 124 | 3¼ |
| 1949 | F. Kuszubski | 123 | 9 |
| 1950 | F. Kuszubski | 113 | 4¾ |
| 1951 | F. Kuszubski | 121 | 0 |
| 1952 | J. Dicks | 137 | 9 |
| 1953 | J. Dicks | 123 | 2 |
| 1954 | M. Larney | 120 | 11½ |
| 1955 | A. Ibarra (*Cuba*) | 117 | 8 |
| 1956 | P. Kurrell | 140 | 11 |
| 1957 | O. Connolly | 147 | 8 |
| 1958 | E. Brown | 152 | 5½ |
| 1959 | E. Brown | 153 | 8 |
| 1960 | O. Connolly | 159 | 6½ |
| 1961 | E. Brown | 149 | 4½ |
| 1962 | O. Connolly | 172 | 2 |
| 1963 | S. Sheppard | 150 | 6 |
| 1964 | O. Connolly | 158 | 4 |
| 1965 | L. Graham | 157 | 9 |
| 1966 | C. Frost | 159 | 8 |
| 1967 | C. Frost | 152 | 5 |
| 1968 | O. Connolly | 170 | 10 |
| 1969 | C. Frost | 167 | 3 |
| 1970 | C. Frost | 172 | 3 |
| 1971 | J. De La Vina (*Phil*) | 179 | 6 |
| 1972 | J. De La Vina (*Phil*) | 172 | 0 |

*Javelin*

| | | ft. | in. |
|---|---|---|---|
| 1923 | R. G. Ranck | 59 | 7¾ |
| 1924 | E. Spargo | 72 | 5¾ |
| 1925 | A. Silva | 105 | 8 |
| 1926 | L. Copeland | 112 | 5½ |
| 1927 | M. Jenkins | 127 | 3½ |
| 1928 | M. Jenkins | 112 | 5½ |
| 1929 | E. Hill | 100 | 5 |
| 1930 | M. Didrikson | 133 | 3 |
| 1931 | L. Copeland | 116 | 1½ |
| 1932 | M. Didrikson | 139 | 3 |
| 1933 | N. Gindele | 130 | 2¼ |
| 1935 | S. Broman | 102 | 7½ |
| 1936 | M. Worst | 125 | 0¼ |
| 1937 | R. Auerbach | 123 | 5½ |

| | | | |
|---|---|---|---|
| 1938 | R. Auerbach | 121 | 6¾ |
| 1939 | D. Dodson | 130 | 9½ |
| 1940 | D. Dodson | 126 | 1 |
| 1941 | D. Dodson | 128 | 7 |
| 1942 | D. Dodson | 122 | 10½ |
| 1943 | D. Dodson | 111 | 3 |
| 1944 | D. Dodson | 123 | 1½ |
| 1945 | D. Dodson | 124 | 10 |
| 1946 | D. Dodson | 120 | 2 |
| 1947 | D. Dodson | 122 | 5 |
| 1948 | D. Dodson | 125 | 10¼ |
| 1949 | D. Dodson | 123 | 1 |
| 1950 | A. Bert | 115 | 1¾ |
| 1951 | F. Licata | 120 | 0½ |
| 1952 | M. Larney | 126 | 3¾ |
| 1953 | A. Wershoven | 124 | 7 |
| 1954 | K. Andersen | 127 | 1 |
| 1955 | K. Andersen | 150 | 1¼ |
| 1956 | K. Andersen | 159 | 1 |
| 1957 | M. Larney | 187 | 8* |
| 1958 | M. Larney | 153 | 7½ |
| 1959 | M. Larney | 152 | 9½ |
| 1960 | M. Larney | 151 | 10½ |
| 1961 | F. Davenport | 137 | 8 |
| 1962 | K. Mendyka | 158 | 5 |
| 1963 | F. Davenport | 166 | 2½ |
| 1964 | R. Bair | 173 | 4½ |
| 1965 | R. Bair | 175 | 0½ |
| 1966 | R. Bair | 174 | 10 |
| 1967 | R. Bair | 196 | 3 |
| 1968 | B. Friedrich | 178 | 10 |
| 1969 | K. Schmidt | 177 | 4 |
| 1970 | S. Calvert | 184 | 9 |
| 1971 | S. Calvert | 179 | 7 |
| 1972 | S. Calvert | 184 | 0 |

* " Spanish " style, later illegal

| Pentathlon | | Pts. |
|---|---|---|
| 1959 | A. Roniger | —— |
| 1960 | J. A. Terry | —— |
| 1961 | P. Bank | —— |
| 1962 | P. Bank | —— |
| 1963 | P. Bank | —— |
| 1964 | P. Bank | —— |
| 1965 | P. Bank | —— |
| 1966 | P. Bank | —— |
| 1967 | P. Bank | 4824 |
| 1968 | Chi Cheng (*Taiwan*) | 4823 |
| 1969 | J. Glotzer | 4544 |
| 1970 | P. Bank | 4735 |
| 1971 | M. King | 4731 |
| 1972 | J. Meldrum (*Can*) | 4251* |

(* New scoring table)

## AMATEUR DEFINITION

The International Amateur Athletic Federation defines an amateur as " one who competes for the love of sport and as a means of recreation, without any motive of securing any material gain from such competition."

## ASIAN GAMES

The Asian Games were inaugurated in New Delhi in 1951 and have been held subsequently in Manila (1954), Tokyo (1958), Djakarta (1962) and Bangkok (1966 and 1970). The 1974 Games will be staged in Iran. With China a continual absentee, Japanese athletes have dominated—winning 104 of 195 gold medals up to and including 1970.

| 100 Metres | | sec. |
|---|---|---|
| 1951 | L. Pinto (India) | 10.8 |
| 1954 | A. Khaliq (Pakistan) | 10.6 |
| 1958 | A. Khaliq (Pak) | 10.9 |
| 1962 | M. Sarengat (Indonesia) | 10.4 |
| 1966 | M. Jegathesan (Malaysia) | 10.5 |
| 1970 | M. Jinno (Japan) | 10.5 |

| 200 Metres | | sec. |
|---|---|---|
| 1951 | L. Pinto (India) | 22.0 |
| 1954 | M. S. Butt (Pak) | 21.9 |
| 1958 | Milkha Singh (India) | 21.6 |
| 1962 | M. Jegathesan (Malaya) | 21.3 |
| 1966 | M. Jegathesan (Malaysia) | 21.5 |
| 1970 | A. Ratanapol (Thai) | 21.1 |

| 400 Metres | | sec. |
|---|---|---|
| 1951 | E. Okano (Japan) | 50.7 |
| 1954 | K. Akagi (Jap) | 48.5 |
| 1958 | Milkha Singh (India) | 47.0 |
| 1962 | Milkha Singh (India) | 46.9 |
| 1966 | Ajmer Singh (India) | 47.1 |
| 1970 | Y. Tomonaga (Japan) | 46.6 |

| 800 Metres | | min. sec. |
|---|---|---|
| 1951 | Ranjit Singh (India) | 1 59.3 |
| 1954 | Y. Muroya (Jap) | 1 54.5 |
| 1958 | Y. Muroya (Jap) | 1 52.1 |
| 1962 | M. Morimoto (Jap) | 1 52.6 |
| 1966 | B. S. Barua (India) | 1 49.4 |
| 1970 | J. Crampton (Burma) | 1 47.9 |

| 1500 Metres | | min. sec. |
|---|---|---|
| 1951 | Nikka Singh (India) | 4 04.1 |
| 1954 | C. Y. Chil (Korea) | 3 56.2 |
| 1958 | M. Khaligh (Iran) | 3 57.6 |
| 1962 | Mohinder Singh (India) | 3 48.6 |
| 1966 | K. Sawaki (Japan) | 3 47.3 |
| 1970 | S. Noro (Japan) | 3 53.0 |

| 5000 Metres | | min. | sec. |
|---|---|---|---|
| 1951 | Baghbanbashi (Iran) | 15 | 54.2 |
| 1954 | O. Inoue (Jap) | 15 | 00.2 |
| 1958 | O. Inoue (Jap) | 14 | 39.4 |
| 1962 | Mubarak Shah (Pak) | 14 | 27.2 |
| 1966 | K. Sawaki (Japan) | 14 | 22.0 |
| 1970 | L. Rosa (Ceylon) | 14 | 32.2 |

| 10,000 Metres | | min. | sec. |
|---|---|---|---|
| 1951 | S. Tamoi (Jap) | 33 | 49.6 |
| 1954 | C. S. Sik (Korea) | 33 | 06.0 |
| 1958 | T. Baba (Jap) | 30 | 48.4 |
| 1962 | Tarlok Singh (India) | 30 | 21.4 |
| 1966 | K. Tsuchiya (Japan) | 30 | 27.8 |
| 1970 | L. Rosa (Ceylon) | 29 | 55.6 |

| Marathon | | hr. | min. | sec. |
|---|---|---|---|---|
| 1951 | Chhota Singh (India) | 2 | 42 | 58.6 |
| 1954 | Not held | | | |
| 1958 | C. H. Lee (Kor) | 2 | 32 | 55.0 |
| 1962 | M. Nagata (Jap) | 2 | 34 | 54.2 |
| 1966 | K. Kimihara (Jap.) | 2 | 33 | 22.8 |
| 1970 | K. Kimihara (Japan) | 2 | 21 | 03.0 |

| 3000 m. Steeplechase | | min. | sec. |
|---|---|---|---|
| 1951 | S. Takahashi (Jap) | 9 | 30.4 |
| 1954 | S. Takahashi (Jap) | 9 | 15.0 |
| 1958 | Mubarak Shah (Pak) | 9 | 03.0 |
| 1962 | Mubarak Shah (Pak) | 8 | 57.8 |
| 1966 | T. Saruwatari (Jap.) | 8 | 53.6 |
| 1970 | Y. Miura (Japan) | 8 | 48.8 |

| 110 Metres Hurdles | | sec. |
|---|---|---|
| 1951 | L. Chiang (Singapore) | 15.2 |
| 1954 | Sarwan Singh (India) | 14.7 |
| 1958 | G. Raziq (Pak) | 14.4 |
| 1962 | M. Sarengat (Indonesia) | 14.3 |
| 1966 | G. Raziq (Pak.) | 14.4 |
| 1970 | C. Watanabe (Japan) | 14.7 |

| 400 Metres Hurdles | | sec. |
|---|---|---|
| 1951 | E. Okano (Japan) | 54.2 |
| 1954 | Mirza Khan (Pak) | 54.1 |
| 1958 | Tsai Cheng Fu (Taiwan) | 52.4 |
| 1962 | K. Ogushi (Jap) | 52.2 |
| 1966 | K. Yui (Japan) | 51.7 |
| 1970 | Y. Shigeta (Japan) | 52.6 |

| 4 x 100 Metres | | sec. |
|---|---|---|
| 1951 | Japan | 42.7 |
| 1954 | Japan | 41.2 |
| 1958 | Philippines | 41.4 |
| 1962 | Philippines | 41.3 |
| 1966 | Malaysia | 40.6 |
| 1970 | Thailand | 40.4 |

| 4 x 400 Metres | | min. | sec. |
|---|---|---|---|
| 1951 | India | 3 | 24.2 |
| 1954 | Japan | 3 | 17.2 |
| 1958 | Japan | 3 | 13.9 |
| 1962 | India | 3 | 10.2 |
| 1966 | Japan | 3 | 09.1 |
| 1970 | Japan | 3 | 10.0 |

| High Jump | | ft. | in. |
|---|---|---|---|
| 1951 | A. Franco (Phil) | 6 | 4 |
| 1954 | Ajit Singh (India) | 6 | 4¾ |
| 1958 | N. Ethirveerasingam (Ceylon) | 6 | 8 |
| 1962 | K. Sugioka (Japan) | 6 | 9½ |
| 1966 | Bhim Singh (India) | 6 | 8¾ |
| 1970 | T. Ghiassi (Iran) | 6 | 9 |

| Pole Vault | | ft. | in. |
|---|---|---|---|
| 1951 | B. Sawada (Jap) | 13 | 5¾ |
| 1954 | B. Sawada (Jap) | 13 | 3¾ |
| 1958 | N. Yasuda (Jap) | 13 | 9½ |
| 1962 | H. Morita (Jap) | 14 | 5¼ |
| 1966 | T. Hirota (Japan) | 15 | 5 |
| 1970 | K. Inoue (Japan) | 15 | 9 |

| Long Jump | | ft. | in. |
|---|---|---|---|
| 1951 | M. Tajima (Jap) | 23 | 5¼ |
| 1954 | N. Sagawa (Jap) | 23 | 0½ |
| 1958 | Y. J. Suh (Kor) | 24 | 9 |
| 1962 | T. Okazaki (Jap) | 24 | 3¾ |
| 1966 | H. Yamada (Japan) | 24 | 6½ |
| 1970 | S. Ogura (Japan) | 25 | 0 |

| Triple Jump | | ft. | in. |
|---|---|---|---|
| 1951 | Y. Imuro (Jap) | 49 | 9¾ |
| 1954 | N. Sagawa (Jap) | 49 | 8 |
| 1958 | Mohinder Singh (India) | 51 | 3 |
| 1962 | T. Sakurai (Jap) | 51 | 1 |
| 1966 | K. Gushiken (Jap.) | 51 | 2½ |
| 1970 | Mohinder Singh Gill (India) | 52 | 10¼ |

| Shot | | ft. | in. |
|---|---|---|---|
| 1951 | M. Lal (India) | 45 | 2½ |
| 1954 | Parduman Singh (India) | 46 | 4¾ |
| 1958 | Parduman Singh (India) | 49 | 4¼ |
| 1962 | T. Itokawa (Jap) | 51 | 1 |
| 1966 | Joginder Singh (India) | 53 | 2½ |
| 1970 | Joginder Singh (India) | 56 | 1 |

| Discus | | ft. | in. |
|---|---|---|---|
| 1951 | Makhan Singh (India) | 130 | 11 |
| 1954 | Parduman Singh (India) | 142 | 4 |
| 1958 | Balkar Singh (India) | 156 | 4 |
| 1962 | S. Yanagawa (Japan) | 156 | 6 |
| 1966 | P. Kumar (India) | 162 | 9 |
| 1970 | P. Kumar (India) | 171 | 8 |

| Hammer | | ft. | in. |
|---|---|---|---|
| 1951 | F. Kamamoto (Japan) | 153 | 0 |
| 1954 | Y. Kojima (Japan) | 177 | 1 |
| 1958 | M. Iqbal (Pak) | 200 | 0 |
| 1962 | N. Okamoto (Jap) | 209 | 7 |
| 1966 | T. Sugawara (Jap.) | 206 | 4 |
| 1970 | S. Murofushi (Jap) | 220 | 1 |

| Javelin | | ft. | in. |
|---|---|---|---|
| 1951 | H. Nagayasu (Jap) | 209 | 10 |
| 1954 | M. Nawaz (Pak) | 210 | 11 |
| 1958 | M. Nawaz (Pak) | 227 | 8 |
| 1962 | T. Miki (Japan) | 244 | 7 |
| 1966 | Nashatar Singh Sidhu (Malaysia) | 239 | 3 |
| 1970 | H. Yamamoto (Jap) | 233 | 9 |

| Decathlon (1950 Tables) | | Pts. |
|---|---|---|
| 1951 | F. Nishiuchi (Jap) | 6,324 |
| 1954 | C. K. Yang (Taiwan) | 5,454 |
| 1958 | C. K. Yang (Taiwan) | 7,101 |
| 1962 | Gurbachan Singh (India) | 6,739 |
| 1966 | Wu Ah-Min (Taiwan) | †7,003 |
| 1970 | J. Onizuka (Japan) | †7,073 |
| † 1962 Tables | | |

| 10,000m Walk | | min. | sec. |
|---|---|---|---|
| 1951 | M. Prasad (India) | 52 | 31.4 |

| 50,000m Walk | | hr. | min. | sec. |
|---|---|---|---|---|
| 1951 | Bakhtawar Singh (India) | 5 | 44 | 07.4 |

WOMEN'S EVENTS

| 100 Metres | | sec. |
|---|---|---|
| 1951 | K. Sugimura (Jap) | 12.6 |
| 1954 | A. Nambu (Jap) | 12.5 |
| 1958 | I. Solis (Phil) | 12.5 |
| 1962 | M. Sulaiman (Phil) | 11.8 |
| 1966 | M. Sato (Japan) | 12.3 |
| 1970 | Chi Cheng (Taiwan) | 11.6 |

| 200 Metres | | sec. |
|---|---|---|
| 1951 | K. Okamoto (Jap) | 26.0 |
| 1954 | M. Tanaka (Jap) | 26.0 |
| 1958 | Y. Kobayashi (Jap) | 25.9 |
| 1962 | M. Sulaiman (Phil) | 24.5 |
| 1966 | D. Markus (Israel) | 25.3 |
| 1970 | K. Yamada (Jap) | 25.0 |

| 400 Metres | | sec. |
|---|---|---|
| 1966 | M. Rajamani (Malaysia) | 56.3 |
| 1970 | K. Sandhu (India) | 57.3 |

| 800 Metres | | min. | sec. |
|---|---|---|---|
| 1962 | C. Tanaka (Jap) | 2 | 18.2 |
| 1966 | H. Shezifi (Israel) | 2 | 10.5 |
| 1970 | H. Shezifi (Israel) | 2 | 06.5 |

| 1500 Metres | | | |
|---|---|---|---|
| 1970 | H. Shezifi (Israel) | 4 | 25.1 |

| 80 Metres Hurdles | | sec. |
|---|---|---|
| 1951 | K. Yoneda (Jap) | 12.8 |
| 1954 | M. Iwamoto (Jap) | 11.7 |
| 1958 | M. Iwamoto (Jap) | 11.6 |
| 1962 | I. Yoda (Jap) | 11.5 |
| 1966 | R. Sukegawa (Jap) | 11.2 |

| 100 Metres Hurdles | | |
|---|---|---|
| 1970 | E. Shachamarov (Israel) | 14.0 |

| 4 x 100 Metres | | sec. |
|---|---|---|
| 1951 | Japan | 51.4 |
| 1954 | India | 49.5 |
| 1958 | Japan | 48.6 |
| 1962 | Philippines | 48.6 |
| 1966 | Japan | 47.1 |
| 1970 | Japan | 47.2 |

| High Jump | | ft. | in. |
|---|---|---|---|
| 1951 | K. Yoneda (Jap) | 4 | 10¾ |
| 1954 | A. Kraus (Israel) | 5 | 1 |
| 1958 | E. Kamiya (Jap) | 5 | 2¼ |
| 1962 | K. Tsutsumi (Jap) | 5 | 3 |
| 1966 | M. Takeda (Jap) | 5 | 3 |
| 1970 | M. Inaoka (Jap) | 5 | 7 |

| Long Jump | | ft. | in. |
|---|---|---|---|
| 1951 | K. Sugimura (Jap) | 19 | 4¾ |
| 1954 | Y. Takahashi (Jap) | 18 | 7¾ |
| 1958 | V. Badana (Phil) | 18 | 6 |
| 1962 | S. Kishimoto (Jap) | 18 | 10½ |
| 1966 | Chi Cheng (Taiwan) | 19 | 6¼ |
| 1970 | H. Yamashita (Jap) | 19 | 9 |

| Shot | | ft. | in. |
|---|---|---|---|
| 1951 | T. Yoshino (Jap) | 39 | 0½ |
| 1954 | T. Yoshino (Jap) | 40 | 4¾ |
| 1958 | S. Obonai (Jap) | 43 | 6 |
| 1962 | S. Obonai (Jap) | 46 | 0¾ |
| 1966 | R. Sugiyama (Jap) | 47 | 6 |
| 1970 | Baik Ok-ja (S. Kor) | 47 | 9¼ |

| Discus | | ft. | in. |
|---|---|---|---|
| 1951 | T. Yoshino (Jap) | 138 | 1 |
| 1954 | T. Yoshino (Jap) | 140 | 8 |
| 1958 | H. Uchida (Jap) | 137 | 5 |
| 1962 | K. Murase (Jap) | 150 | 7 |
| 1966 | J. De la Vina (Phil) | 156 | 1 |
| 1970 | T. Yagishita (Jap) | 156 | 6 |

| *Javelin* | | ft. | in. |
|---|---|---|---|
| 1951 | T. Yoshino (Jap) | 118 | 10 |
| 1954 | A. Kurihara (Jap) | 144 | 7 |
| 1958 | Y. Shida (Jap) | 154 | 8 |
| 1962 | H. Sato (Jap) | 157 | 11 |
| 1966 | M. Katayama (Jap) | 162 | 2 |
| 1970 | N. Morita (Jap) | 163 | 6 |

| *Pentathlon* | | Pts. |
|---|---|---|
| 1966 | M. Okamoto (Jap) | 4,426 |
| 1970 | E. Shachamarov (Israel) | 4,530 |

## AVILOV, N. (USSR)

Nikolay Avilov laid a strong claim to being considered the greatest all-round athlete in history by his victory in the 1972 Olympic decathlon. His winning margin of 419 points was the widest at an Olympics for twenty years and his score of 8,454 points surpassed the world record of 8,417 set by Bill Toomey (U.S.A.) in 1969.

Avilov, whose highest score prior to Munich was 8,115 made a few weeks earlier, beat or equalled personal bests in no fewer than six of the ten events, as noted below:

| Event | Munich | Prev. best |
|---|---|---|
| 100m. | 11.0 sec. | 10.8 sec. |
| Long Jump | 25 ft. 2½ in. | 25 ft. 3½ in. |
| Shot | 47 ft. 1½ in. | 46 ft. 3½ in. |
| High Jump | 6 ft. 11¼ in. | 6 ft. 11¼ in. |
| 400m. | 48.5 sec. | 48.9 sec. |
| Hurdles | 14.3 sec. | 14.0 sec. |
| Discus | 154 ft. 1 in. | 153 ft. 0 in. |
| Pole Vault | 14 ft. 11 in. | 14 ft. 5¼ in. |
| Javelin | 202 ft. 3 in. | 203 ft. 10 in. |
| 1,500m. | 4 min. 22.8 sec. | 4 min. 23.0 sec. |

European junior long jump champion in 1966, Avilov began his decathlon career in 1967. The following year, in only his fourth decathlon, he was placed fourth at the Olympics. His annual progress: 1967—7.505; 1968—7,909; 1969—7,945; 1970—7,874; 1971—8,096; 1972—8,454. He was born in Odessa (Ukraine) on August 6th, 1948—the day on which Bob Mathias (U.S.A.) won the first of his two Olympic decathlon titles.

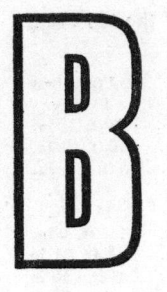

## BALAS, I. (Rumania)

Iolanda Balas, who stands 6ft. 0¾in. tall, utterly dominated the realm of women's high jumping from 1958 to 1966. Probably no other athlete in history has enjoyed such a wide measure of supremacy over such a long period.

Miss Balas set the first of her 14 world records in July 1956. In December of that year she placed fifth at the Olympic Games, her only defeat until injury brought her career to an end in 1966.

Her championship honours include the Olympic gold in 1960 and 1964, the European title in 1958 and 1962 (having finished second in 1954), and her final world record of 6ft. 3¼in was 3in. higher than the best then achieved by any other woman—a remarkable margin. She cleared 6ft. or higher in more than 50 competitions between 1958 and 1966. She married her coach, Ion Soeter, in 1967.

Her exceptional height and phenomenally long legs would appear to have been of advantage, but on account of her physique she was unable to master either the straddle or western roll style and had to settle for a modified version of the outmoded scissors. She was born at Timosoaru on Dec. 12th, 1936.

## BALZER, K. (East Germany)

No other hurdler, male or female, has accumulated as many major championship medals as Karin Balzer (née Richert). Between 1960 and 1972 she competed in every Olympic Games and European Championships, hurdling over 80m. until 1968 and 100m. since 1969, and her tally stands at an Olympic gold (1964) and bronze (1972), plus three European golds (1966, 1969 and 1971), and a silver (1962). In addition she was European 1967 to 1971, and is a former world indoor champion every year from record holder at both 80 m. and 100 m. hurdles.

Her best performances include 11.3 sec. for 100m., 23.4 sec. for 200 m., 55.1 sec. for 400 m., 10.5 sec. for 80 m. hurdles, 12.6 sec. for 100 m. hurdles, 20 ft. 4½ in. long jump and 4,790 pts. pentathlon (old tables).

Annual hurdling progress: 1954— 12.6 (80 m.); 1955—11.9; 1956—11.7; 1957—11.3; 1958—11.0; 1959—11.0; 1960—10.7; 1961—10.9; 1962—10.6; 1963—10.7; 1964—10.5; 1965—gave birth to son; 1966—10.6; 1967—10.7; 1968—10.5; 1969—12.9 (100 m.); 1970 —12.7; 1971—12.6; 1972—12.7. She was born in Magdeburg on June 5th, 1938.

## BANNISTER, R. G. (GB)

No single athletic performance either before or since has attracted quite as much publicity and acclaim as Roger Bannister's 3 min. 59.4 sec. mile at the Iffley Road track, Oxford, on May 6th, 1954. His feat of becoming the first man to break four minutes —a barrier referred to as the " Everest " of athletics—captured the headlines all over the world.

Bannister was the first to acknowledge his debt to his friends Chris Chataway and Chris Brasher, who shared pacemaking duties. The final time clipped almost two seconds from the world record set by Gunder Hagg (Sweden) in 1945, yet within seven weeks the Australian John Landy had run even faster. Such is the ephemeral nature of even the most celebrated of athletic achievements.

That first four-minute mile was the prelude to two magnificent competitive performances in 1954. At the Commonwealth Games in Vancouver in August he defeated Landy in his fastest time of 3 min. 58.8 sec. following the most dramatic miling duel in history; and later in the month he captured the European 1500 metres crown with another display of masterly tactics. This, his final season, more than made up for his Olympic disappointment of two years earlier.

Jesse Owens (USA), *left*, pictured with his great sprint rival, Ralph Metcalfe (USA).

Paavo Nurmi (Finland), the most successful Olympic competitor in history.

*Left:* Herb Elliott (Australia) during one of his 17 sub-four minute miles; on this occasion a 3 min. 58.6 sec. performance in London in 1960.

*Right:* Peter Snell (NZ) completes a half-mile relay stage in an unprecedented 1 min. 44·9 sec. in London shortly after the 1960 Olympics.

Ever since 1949, when he clocked 4 min. 11.1 sec. at the age of 20, Bannister had been considered a candidate for the very highest honours. He finished a close third in the 1950 European 800 metres final and improved his mile time to 4 min. 09.9 sec. In 1951 he brought his time down to 4 min. 07.8 sec. and thrilled the crowds with his spectacular finishing powers.

Shortly before the 1952 Olympics he ran a three-quarter mile time trial in a staggering 2 min. 52.9 sec., 3.7 sec. faster than the unofficial world record held by Arne Andersson (Sweden). He seemed destined to follow in the footsteps of the 1936 Olympic 1500 metres champion, New Zealander Jack Lovelock, who like Bannister had studied medicine at Exeter College, Oxford.

The stage was set . . . but at short notice a round of semi-finals was inserted because of the large entry. It was a death blow to Bannister, a relatively delicate athlete who had not prepared for three hard, nerve-racking races on three consecutive days. In fact, he finished fourth in the UK record time of 3 min. 46.0 sec.

His personal best marks included 1 min. 50.7 sec. for 880 yd., 3 min. 42.2 sec. for 1500 m., 3 min. 58.8 sec. for the mile, and 9 min. 09.2 sec. for 2 mi. Dr. Bannister was appointed chairman of the Sports Council in 1971. He was born at Harrow on Mar. 23rd, 1929.

# BEAMON, R. (USA)

World records are made to be broken; progress is such that few survive more than a year or two. Among the hundreds of world records established in the Olympic range of events since the end of the Second World War only three have lasted a decade: Peter Snell's 1 min. 44.3 sec. 800 m. Martin Lauer's 13.2 sec. 110 m. hurdles and Iolanda Balas's 6 ft. 3¼ in. high jump. Yet it is quite feasible that Bob Beamon's figures of 29 ft. 2½ in. during the 1968 Olympic Games in Mexico City will stand as the ultimate in long jumping until the next century.

This incredible leap, widely accepted as the most astonishing single exploit in track and field history, is generations ahead of its time. It took 30 years for the record to creep up from 26 ft. 8¼ in. (by Jesse Owens in 1935), to the mark which Beamon beat: 27 ft. 5 in. by Ralph Boston. Suddenly not only the 28 ft. barrier, but the undreamt of 29 ft. was broken. No one, in the four subsequent seasons, has reached 27½ ft.

Beamon himself was often an unreliable performer, prone to frequent no-jumping, although his prodigious talent was never in question. His best prior to Mexico was 27 ft. 4 in. but in later seasons, struggling unsuccessfully to live up to his own impossible standard, he never did better than 26 ft. 11 in. He turned professional in 1973. A 9.5 sec. sprinter (100 yd.), he was born in New York on Aug. 29th, 1946.

# BEDFORD, D. C. (GB)

A combination of flamboyant front-running and a cheeky attitude off the track has made Dave Bedford the most publicised of currently active British athletes. His presence has been largely responsible for several capacity crowds at London's Crystal Palace Stadium.

His only major international championship success has been winning the International Cross-Country title in 1971, his reputation having been based upon prolific record breaking. As at the end of 1972 he held all the U.K. records from 2,000 m. to 10,000 m. with the exception of the 2 miles. At one time he was second only to Ron Clarke on the world all-time list at 3 miles, 5000 m., 6 miles and 10,000 m., and in a rare attempt at the steeplechase he became, in 1971, the first Briton to better 8½ min. He was only 19 when he set his first British record, 28 min. 24.4 sec. for 10,000 m., in 1969. He finished 6th in the 10,000 m. at both the 1971 European Championships and 1972 Olympics, a disappointment to him and his supporters.

His best marks include 3 min. 47.0 sec. for 1500 m., 4 min. 02.9 sec. for the mile, 5 min. 03.2 sec. for 2000 m. 7 min. 46.2 sec. for 3000 m., 12 min. 52.0 sec. for 3 mi., 13 min. 17.2 sec. for 5000 m., 26 min. 51.6 sec. for 6 mi., 27 min. 47.0 sec. for 10,000 m. and 8 min. 28.6 sec. for 3000 m.

steeplechase. Annual progress at 5000 and 10,000 m.; 1966—14:43.0 (3 mi.), 31:24.2 (6 mi.); 1967—14:13.2 (3 mi.), 29:15.8 (6 mi.); 1968—13:54.6 (3 mi.), 32:16.0; 1969—13:42.8, 28:24.4; 1970—13:54.8, 28:06.2; 1971—13:22.2, 27:47.0; 1972—13:17.2, 27:52.4. He was born in London on Dec. 30th, 1949.

## BIKILA ABEBE (Ethiopia)
See ABEBE BIKILA.

## BLAGOYEVA, Y. (Bulgaria)

On two counts Yordanka Blagoyeva (actually Mrs. Dimitrova) is the highest jumper among women: she is the world record holder with 6 ft. 4¼ in. and, in clearing that height in September 1972, she leapt 7¾ in. above her own head—also a record.

She achieved an early international success when winning the World Student Games title in 1965 but she had to wait until 1969, when she first jumped 6 ft., before joining the world's elite.

Only 19 days after placing 2nd with 6 ft. 2 in. at the Munich Olympics she straddled over 6 ft. 4¼ in. at the second attempt to add ¾ in. to the world record shared by Ilona Gusenbauer and Olympic champion Ulrike Meyfarth. She even attempted 6 ft. 5 in.—a height exceeded by only ten British men in 1972!

Annual progress: 1961—4 ft. 3¼ in.; 1962—4 ft. 11 in.; 1963—5 ft. 1 in.; 1964—5 ft. 4½ in.; 1965—5 ft. 6½ in.; 1966—5 ft. 3 in.; 1967—5 ft. 7 in.; 1968—5 ft. 10½ in.; 1969—6 ft. 0 in.; 1970—6 ft. 0½ in. (indoors); 1971—6 ft. 2¾ in.; 1972—6 ft. 4¼ in. She was born at Mikhailovgrad on Jan. 19th, 1947.

## BLANKERS-KOEN, F. E. (Netherlands)

Mrs. Fanny Blankers-Koen became the most famous woman athlete in history when, at the age of 30 (13 years after she made her debut as an 800 m. runner with a time of 2 min. 29.0 sec.), she collected four gold medals at the 1948 Olympic Games in London. She triumphed in the 100 m., 200 m. and 80 m. hurdles, and anchored the Dutch 4 x 100 m. relay team to victory.

Always a superb competitor, she won eight medals in three European Championship meetings: gold in the 1946 hurdles and relay and the 1950 100 m., 200 m. and hurdles; silver in the 1950 relay; and bronze in the 1938 100 m. and 200 m.

Between 1938 and 1951 she set official world records in no fewer than seven individual events: 100 yd., 100 m., 220 yd., 80 m. hurdles, high jump, long jump and pentathlon. She unofficially equalled the 100 m. record of 11.5 sec. in 1952, the following year her hurdles time of 11.1 sec. was the fastest in the world that season, and even as late as 1956 (aged 38) she was timed at 11.3 sec. in a wind assisted hurdles race.

Her best marks included 10.8 sec. for 100 yd., 11.5 sec. for 100 m., 23.9 sec. for 200 m., 24.2 sec. for 220 yd., 11.0 sec. for 80 m. hurdles, 5ft. 7¼in. high jump, 20ft. 6in. long jump, 39 ft. 6¾ in. shot, 120 ft. 6 in. discus, and 4,692 point pentathlon. She was born in Amsterdam on Apr. 26th, 1918.

## BOARD, L. B. (GB)

The world of athletics was robbed of one of its most talented, delightful and sporting personalities with the tragic death, of cancer, of Lillian Board at the age of 22.

During her lamentably brief career she achieved much of distinction—she was Olympic 400 m. silver medallist in 1968 (overhauled in the last few strides by Colette Besson), European gold medallist in the 800 m. and 4 x 400 m. relay in 1969—but almost certainly her greatest triumphs lay ahead of her. When she spreadeagled the European 800 m. field in 2 min. 01.4 sec. she was nowhere near her fittest due to back trouble and it is not unreasonable to assume that she might have gone on to become the first woman to break 2 min. for the distance officially. The run for which she will be best remembered was her anchor leg in the relay at Athens when she pipped Besson on the tape after a most thrilling chase.

Lillian, who first made her mark as a long jumper (English Schools junior champion at the age of 14), built up the finest collection of times by any British girl runner: 100 yd. in wind-assisted 10.6 sec., 100 m. in 11.9 sec.,

50

200 m. in 23.4 sec., 400 m. in 52.1 sec., 800 m. in 2 min. 01.4 sec., mile in 4 min. 44.6 sec., plus a long jump of 19 ft. 0¼ in. She was born in Durban (South Africa) of British parents, on Dec. 13th, 1948, and died in a Munich hospital on Dec. 26th, 1970.

## BONDARCHUK, A. (USSR)

Like many another hammer thrower, Anatoliy Bondarchuk was a late developer. Although he began in 1958 it was not until nine years later, when he was 27, that he broke into top class with a distance of 228 ft. 1 in. He made his international debut in 1968 and, although he did not qualify for the USSR Olympic team, the very next season he was crowned European champion. That was a momentous competition for the Ukrainian, as he broke the world record into the bargain with a toss of 245 ft. 0 in., defeating his mentor, 1964 Olympic champion Romuald Klim.

He slipped to 3rd in the 1971 European Championships but reached new heights in 1972, improving to 248 ft. 7 in. and winning the Olympic title with his opening throw of 247 ft. 8 in. The average for his six throws in the Munich final was an all-time best of 240 ft. 7 in. Bondarchuk claims he has thrown the hammer more than 100,000 times in training during the past 13 years!

His annual progress: 1965—208ft. 6in.; 1966—214ft. 5in.; 1967—228ft. 1in.; 1968—232ft. 0in.; 1969—247ft. 8in.; 1970—246ft. 2in.; 1971—244ft. 9in.; 1972—248ft. 7in. He was born at Rovno on May 31st, 1940.

## BORZOV, V. (USSR)

The only European ever to win the Olympic sprint double for men, Valeriy Borzov can claim a perfect record in major championship events. He contested, and won, the 1968 European junior 100 and 200 m., 1969 European 100 m., 1970 and 1971 European indoor 60 m., 1971 European 100 and 200 m., 1972 European indoor 50 m., and 1972 Olympic 100 and 200 m. One of the smoothest, most relaxed speedsters ever seen, he is strong in every department of sprinting—start, pick-up, mid-race and finish, not to mention temperament. His only fault is a habit of looking round at the opposition.

Soviet sports authorities say that Borzov the sprinter was made rather than born. A team of scientists in Kiev studied all the facets of sprinting and, based on their findings, Prof. Valentin Petrovsky guided Borzov on his technique and training. Progress was swift and in Dec. 1968 (aged 19) he equalled the world indoor 60 m. best of 6.4 sec. In 1969 he ran his first 10.0 sec. 100 m. to tie the European record.

His Olympic victories in Munich were clear cut. The USA's two 9.9 sec. performers, Eddie Hart and Rey Robinson, failed to show up in time for their 100 m. quarter-final races, but Borzov appeared to have plenty in hand as he took the final, easing up, by a metre in 10.1 sec. In the 200 m., an event he runs infrequently, he won by 2 m. in 20.0 sec., a European record.

His annual progress at 100 and 200 m.: 1966—10.5, 22.0; 1967—10.5, 21.4; 1968—10.2, 21.0; 1969—10.0, 20.8 (and 47.6 sec. for 400 m.); 1970—10.3, 20.5; 1971—10.0, 20.2; 1972—10.0, 20.0. He was born near Lvov (Ukraine) on Oct. 20th, 1949.

## BOSTON, R. H. (USA)

Ralph Boston will be remembered by posterity not only as Olympic champion in 1960 but as the man who broke Jesse Owens' long jump world record after 25 years and became the first to leap over 27 ft.

He reached world class in 1959 and during the next two seasons carried the world record out to 27 ft. 2 in. In 1962 he lost it to Igor Ter-Ovanesyan, his Soviet rival, but regained it in 1964 and the following season improved the mark to 27ft. 5in. In 1966 he actually covered 28ft. 1in. but fell back for a measurement of 27ft. 0in. He was placed second behind Britain's Lynn Davies in the 1964 Olympics, and third in the 1968 Games, where Bob Beamon shattered his world record.

A talented all-rounder, Boston's best marks in other events include a 9.6 sec. 100 yd., 21.0 sec. straight 220 yd., 48.5 sec. 440 yd., 13.7 sec. 120 yd. hurdles, 22.4 sec. straight 220 yd. hurdles, 6 ft. 9in. high jump, 13ft. 9in. pole vault, 52ft. 1½in. triple jump and 210ft. javelin.

His annual long jumping progress: 1954—20ft. 10in., 1955—21ft. 5½in., 1956—22ft. 7in., 1957—24ft. 0in., 1958 —24ft. 0in., 1959—25ft. 3in., 1960— 26ft. 11¼in., 1961—27ft. 2in., 1962— 26ft. 6in., 1963—26ft. 11in., 1964— 27ft. 4½in. (and 27ft. 10¾in. wind assisted), 1965—27ft. 5in., 1966—27ft. 0in., 1967—27ft. 2½in., 1968—27ft. 1½ in., 1969—25ft. 1in., 1970—25ft. 2¼in., 1971—25ft. 9½in., 1972—26ft. 5¾in. (wind assisted). He was born at Laurel, Mississippi, on May 9th, 1939.

## BRAGINA, L. (USSR)

Incredulity was the general reaction to the news of Lyudmila Bragina's first world record. Running in the USSR Championships on July 18th, 1972, she cut 2.7 sec. off the previous mark with a time of 4 min. 06.9 sec. for 1500 m., and that was in her heat! It was no fluke. In Munich, where the event was being staged for the first time in Olympic history, she won her heat on Sept. 4th in 4 min. 06.5 sec., her semi-final on Sept. 7th in 4 min. 05.1 sec., and the final on Sept. 9th in 4 min. 01.4 sec.—all world record runs. Usually an uncompromising front-runner, she held back in the final prior to launching a devastating last two laps, covered in an astonishing 2 min. 07.4 sec. Her winning time was faster than Albert Hill's Olympic gold medal performance in 1920!

An apparent lack of basic speed (her fastest 800 m. is a modest 2 min. 05.7 sec.) is more than compensated by tremendous stamina, as witness her world's best 3000 m. time of 8 min. 53.0 sec. in 1972. In previous major international championship events she had placed 4th in the 1969 European 1500 m. and 2nd three years running in the European Indoor Championships.

Her annual progression at 1500 m.: 1967—4:22.2, 1968—4:17.0, 1969— 4:13.2, 1970—4:13.4, 1971—4:13.9, 1972—4:01.4. She was born at Sverdlovsk on July 24th, 1943.

## BRASHER, C. W. (GB)

The career of Chris Brasher is an inspiration to all. For years he was simply a capable middle distance runner (3 min. 54.0 sec. 1500 m. and 14 min. 22.4 sec. 3 mi. in 1951) who appeared to lack that extra something which is required of the absolute top liner.

Realising his limitations on the flat, he switched his attention to the steeplechase—an undulating event appropriate to his mountaineering skill (he was on the short list for an Everest expedition). He clocked a modest but promising 9 min. 21.8 sec. in 1951 and next year won his way into the Olympic team. At Helsinki he improved over 10 seconds on his best by returning 9 min. 03.2 sec. in his heat, and in the final he pluckily finished 11th out of 12 after injuring himself on the second lap.

Throughout the next two seasons Brasher became better known as Roger Bannister's pacemaker and training companion than as an athlete in his own right, though he did cut his mile time to 4 min. 09.0 sec. in 1954.

He returned to serious steeplechasing in 1955, and progressed to 8 min. 49.2 sec. that year. He improved to 8 min. 47.2 sec. in Aug. 1956 but he travelled to Melbourne for the Olympic Games very much as John Disley's second string. Shortly before the Games, Brasher knocked almost 13 sec. off his best 2 mi. flat time with 8 min. 45.6 sec. and in the Olympic final he ran the race of his life to win in the Olympic and U.K. record time of 8 min. 41.2 sec.

At first he was disqualified for an alleged obstruction during the race but was rightfully reinstated by the jury of appeal. Thus the man who had never even won an AAA title succeeded where his two more celebrated partners, Roger Bannister and Chris Chataway, failed.

Other best marks included 3 min. 53.6 sec. for 1500 m., 4 min. 06.8 sec. for the mile and 8 min. 15.4 sec. for 3000 m. He was born in Georgetown (Guyana) on Aug. 21st, 1928.

## BRIGHTWELL, A. E. (GB)

See PACKER, A. E.

## BRITISH AMATEUR ATHLETIC BOARD

The BAAB, founded in 1932, is affiliated to the International Amateur Athletic Federation as the governing athletic association for the United Kingdom of Great Britain and Northern Ireland. The Board is responsible for the control of international athletics in Britain and selects and manages teams to represent Britain.

## BRITISH ATHLETICS LEAGUE

See NATIONAL ATHLETICS LEAGUE

## BRITISH EMPIRE AND COMMONWEALTH GAMES

See COMMONWEALTH GAMES.

## BRITISH EMPIRE AND COMMONWEALTH RECORDS

See COMMONWEALTH RECORDS.

## BRITISH RECORDS

See UNITED KINGDOM RECORDS.

## BROAD JUMP

See LONG JUMP.

## BRUMEL, V. (USSR)

Siberian-born Valeriy Brumel held the high jump world record for 10 years, his best leap—using the straddle style—being 7 ft. 5¾ in. in 1963. That was a record 17 in. above his own head.

He began jumping at the age of 11 but progress was slow until, between 1956 and 1957, he shot up over a foot. While still only 18 he set a European record of 7 ft. 2¾ in. in 1960, and that year—in his first big international test—won the silver medal at the Olympic Games. He shared the Olympic record of 7 ft. 1 in. with his colleague Robert Shav-

lakadze, with the odds-on favourite John Thomas (USA) only third.

Brumel raised the outdoor world record six times between 1961 and 1963.

He won the 1964 Olympic title as expected, although John Thomas shared the winning height of 7 ft. 1¾ in., but disaster struck when he sustained serious leg and foot injuries in a motor-cycle accident in the autumn of 1965. Following a series of major operations he made a miraculous comeback in 1969, jumping 6 ft. 9 in., and in 1970 he cleared 6 ft. 11¾ in.

Other best marks include 10.5 sec. for 100 m., 13ft. 9¼in., pole vault, 25ft. 1¼in., long jump, 51ft. 11¾in., shot and 195ft. 2in. javelin. He was born at Tolbuzino on Apr. 14th, 1942.

## BURGHLEY, LORD (GB)

Lord Burghley, now the 6th Marquess of Exeter, enjoyed one of the most successful careers of any British athlete. Though he made no mark on the playing fields of Eton and failed to gain his " blue " in his first year at Cambridge he did qualify at the age of 19 for the 1924 Olympic team as a 110 m. hurdler.

Equally adept at all three types of hurdle racing, he held the British records for 120 yd. from 1927 to 1936, for 220 yd. from 1925 to 1950, for 400 m. from 1928 to 1954 and for 440 yd. from 1926 to 1949.

His championship record was first class: Olympic 400 m. hurdles winner in 1928 and fourth (in his fastest time) in 1932; silver medallist in the 1932 Olympic 4 x 400 m. relay (running his stage in 46.7 sec.); triple gold medallist at the 1930 Commonwealth Games—120 yd. hurdles, 440 yd. hurdles and 4 x 440 yd. relay.

Best marks included 14.5 sec., 24.3 sec., 52.2 sec. and 53.8 sec. for the four hurdle events mentioned in the second paragraph. The Marquess has been president of the AAA since 1936 and of the International Amateur Athletic Federation since 1946. He was born at Stamford on Feb. 9th, 1905.

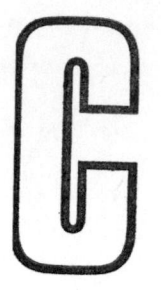

## CALHOUN L. Q. (USA)

The only man to win the Olympic 110 m. hurdles crown twice is Lee Calhoun, who performed the trick in 1956 and 1960. As a co-holder of world records for 110 m. and 120 yd. hurdles at 13.2 sec. (in 1960), he has strong claims to being considered the finest high hurdling exponent of all-time.

He began his athletic career at the age of 17 as a high jumper and was helped by his predecessor as Olympic champion, Harrison Dillard, when he decided to switch to hurdling in 1951. After five seasons his best stood at only 14.4 sec., but in 1956 he improved sensationally to 13.5 sec.

Between his two Olympic triumphs he was suspended by the Amateur Athletic Union of the USA, after appearing with his bride on a television " give-away " show and receiving nearly £1,000 worth of gifts. Penalised for capitalising on his athletic fame, he missed the 1958 season but came back better than ever.

His best marks in other events included 9.7 sec. for 100 yd., 22.9 sec. for 220 yd. hurdles (turn) and 6 ft. 3 in. high jump. He was born at Laurel, Mississippi (Ralph Boston's home town) on Feb. 23rd, 1933.

## CARLOS, J. W. (USA)

Controversy surrounded John Carlos during his brief but tempestuous sprinting career. In 1967, the year he reached world class with 220 yd. in 20.3 sec., he withdrew from East Texas State University claiming colour prejudice, and he also supported the Olympic boycott threatened by militant black athletes. There was no boycott, in fact, and Carlos ran at the Mexico City Games of 1968 where he was placed 3rd in the 200 m. after leading for two-thirds of the race. During the medal presentation ceremony he and winner Tommie Smith staged a demonstration to draw attention to racial inequality which led to their expulsion from the Olympic Village.

Even Carlos's greatest run, 19.7 sec. for 200 m. in the 1968 US Olympic Trials—three tenths of a second inside the world record—provoked controversy, for he was wearing " brush " shoes containing 68 tiny spikes which were against the rules. The IAAF has never ratified the performance, which four years later remained unmatched.

He enjoyed a sparkling season in 1969, which included his equalling the world indoor 60 yd. record of 5.9 sec. and the outdoor 100 yd. figures of 9.1 sec., as well as becoming the first man to clock 9 sec. dead (wind assisted). He forfeited his amateur status following the 1970 season. His best times were 9.1 sec. for 100 yd., 10.0 sec. for 100 m. and 19.7 sec. for 200 m. He was born in New York on June 5th, 1945.

## CHATAWAY, C. J. (GB)

Few athletes have enjoyed such widespread popularity as Chris Chataway, whose personal appeal and exceptional ability contributed greatly to the British athletics boom of the 1950s. His bobbing red hair and fiery finish were characteristics that attracted thousands to the big White City meetings, and he rarely let his public down.

It is fitting, perhaps, that he was the winner of what is generally considered to be the finest race ever to grace a British track: his duel over 5000 m. with Vladimir Kuts in the London v. Moscow match of 1954. In a memorable finish he thrust his chest ahead in the last stride for victory in the world record time of 13 min. 51.6 sec. He thus gained swift revenge over his conqueror of the European Championships a few weeks earlier.

His silver medal in that race was the nearest he got to a world title (though he won the 1954 Commonwealth Games 3 mi.), for as an inexperienced 21-year-old at the 1952 Olympics he was placed fifth after tripping over while rounding the final bend and in 1956 he fell away to 11th place suffering from severe stomach cramp.

Considering it was Chataway who pulled Roger Bannister to the first four-minute mile and pushed John Landy to the second, it was only poetic justice that he himself broke the barrier in 1955.

Best marks: 3 min. 43.6 sec. for 1500 m., 3 min. 59.8 sec. for the mile, 5 min. 09.4 sec. for 2000 m., 8 min. 06.2 sec. for 3000 m., 8 min. 41.0 sec. for 2 mi., 13 min. 23.2 sec. for 3 mi. and 13 min. 51.6 sec. for 5000 m. Chataway, a Minister in Edward Heath's Government, was born at Chelsea on Jan. 31st, 1931.

## CHI CHENG (Taiwan)

One Olympic medal—the bronze for the 80 m. hurdles in 1968—is no indication at all of the impact that Chi Cheng has made on women's athletics.

During 1969 and 1970 she won 153 out of her 154 competitions, the only loss being a disputed 100 yd. verdict against American sprint star Barbara Ferrell. World records fell to her in the 100 yd. (a staggering 10.0 sec. flat, three-tenths inside the previous mark), 100 m., 200 m., 220 yd., 100 m. hurdles and 200 m. hurdles—and she missed the 440 yd. record by just a tenth!

Unfortunately injuries have played havoc with this Chinese girl's career and she was present at the 1972 Olympics, where she would have been co-favourite with Renate Stecher for the sprint titles, only in the roles of flag-bearer and coach to the Taiwan team. She has been resident in California for many years and is married to her coach, Vince Reel.

Her best marks are 10.0 sec. for 100 yd., 11.0 sec. for 100 m., 22.4 sec. for 200 m., 22.6 sec. (and wind assisted 22.4 sec.) for 220 yd., 52.5 sec. for 440 yd., 10.3 sec. for 80 m. hurdles, 12.8 sec. for 100 m. hurdles, 26.2 sec. for 200 m. hurdles, 5 ft. 1¼ in. high jump, 20 ft. 10 in. long jump, 36 ft. 8 in. shot and 4,844 pts. pentathlon (old tables).

Annual progression at 100 yd. or 100 m., 200 m. and hurdles: 1962—

12.7 (100 m.), 26.9, 11.9; 1963—11.7 (100 yd.), 26.2, 11.4; 1964—11.1 (100 yd.), 25.0, 11.1; 1965—11.7 (100 m.), 25.4, 10.8; 1966—10.5 (100 yd.), 24.5, 10.7; 1967—10.9 (100 yd.), 10.8; 1968—11.2 (100 m.) 23.6, 10.4; 1969—10.3 (100 yd.), 11.3 (100 m.), 23.1, 13.3 (100 m.); 1970—10.0 (100 yd., 11.0 (100 m.), 22.4, 12.8; 1971—10.3 (100 yd.), 24.1 (220 yd.). She was born at Hsin-chu on March 15th, 1944.

## CHIZHOVA, N. (USSR)

There is only one blot on the remarkable shot-putting career record of Nadyezhda Chizhova: her defeat at the 1968 Olympics where, a solid favourite, she placed no higher than third behind the East Germans, Margitta Gummel and Marita Lange.

Apart from that it has been titles and records all the way, ever since winning the European junior championship in 1964. She was crowned European champion outdoors in 1966, 1969 and 1971, indoors in 1967, 1968, 1970, 1971 and 1972, and Olympic champion in 1972, with Gummel second. She made no mistake in her second crack at the Olympic title, for with her opening put she added over a foot to her previous world record with a phenomenal 69 ft. 0 in. Only four years earlier a put of 61 ft. 3 in. had sufficed to gain her first IAAF world record plaque.

Annual progress: 1963—49ft. 5¾in., 1964—54ft. 5½in., 1965—57ft. 7½in., 1966—56ft. 10¼in., 1967—60ft. 2in., 1968—61ft. 3in., 1969—67ft. 0½in., 1970—64ft. 7¼in., 1971—67ft. 0½in., 1972—69ft. 0in. She was born at Usolye-Sibirskoye (Siberia) on Sept. 29th, 1945.

## CLARKE, R. W. (Australia)

Few athletes have made such an impact on the world record books as Ron Clarke, setter of global marks for 3 mi., 5000 m., 6 mi., 10,000 m., 10 mi., 20,000 m. and one hour. Only one runner before him has managed to set records in all seven of those events: the immortal Paavo Nurmi, and even he did not hold the complete set simultaneously, as did Clarke for a few months. Clarke later set world records for 2 mi. also.

It was Clarke who was mainly responsible for the astonishing upsurge in distance running standards during the last decade. As at November, 1963 the best times recorded for 3 mi., 5000 m., 6 mi., and 10,000 m. were respectively 13 min. 10.0 sec., 13 min. 35.0 sec., 27 min. 43.8 sec. and 28 min. 18.2 sec. Clarke produced times of 12 min. 50.4 sec., 13 min. 16.6 sec., 26 min. 47.0 sec. and 27 min. 39.4 sec.! So much for the theory that world records will be broken by ever narrower margins.

In spite of innumerable successes against the stopwatch and several brilliant victories against top opposition, Clarke never quite made his mark as a major championship competitor. He was favoured to win the Olympic 10,000 m. in 1964 but was beaten into third place; while at the 1966 Commonwealth Games he collected another two silver medals to add to the one he gained in the 3 mi. four years earlier. The problems of altitude gave him no chance at the 1968 Olympics, and he bowed out at the 1970 Commonwealth Games with yet another silver medal in the 10,000 m.

Clarke was labelled a boy wonder when he set junior world " records " of 3 min. 49.8 sec. for 1500 m., 4 min. 06.8 sec. for the mile and 9 min. 01.8 sec. for 2 mi. early in 1956 at the age of 18. He did not make the Australian Olympic team that year but was awarded the honour of carrying the Olympic torch at the opening of the Melbourne Games. He slipped into obscurity soon afterwards and it was not until 1961 that he launched his comeback.

Personal best performances include: 3 min. 44.1 sec. for 1500 m., 4 min. 00.2 sec. for the mile, 7 min. 47.2 sec. for 3000 m., 8 min. 19.6 sec. for 2 mi., 12 min. 50.4 sec. for 3 mi., 13 min. 16.6 sec. for 5000 m., 26 min. 47.0 sec. for 6 mi., 27 min. 39.4 sec. for 10,000 m., 47 min. 12.8 sec. for 10 mi., 59 min. 22.8 sec. for 20,000 m., 12 mi. 1,006 yd. for one hour, 2 hr. 20 min. 26.8 sec. for the marathon. He was born in Melbourne on Feb. 21st, 1937.

## CLAYTON, D. (Australia)

Repeated leg injuries have prevented Derek Clayton from showing his true form in major championship races but he has since 1967 held the world's best time for the marathon.

This native of Lancashire, who emigrated to Australia in 1963, graduated to marathon running in 1965 but his career nearly came to a premature end when, early in 1967, he was operated on for a broken Achilles tendon. Amazingly, he recovered to such effect that in December of that year he became the first man to average under 5 min. per mile for the journey in winning a Japanese race in 2 hr. 9 min. 36.4 sec—nearly 2½ min. inside the previous world's best held by Morio Shigematsu of Japan.

Cartilage trouble destroyed his Olympic prospects in 1968 and he did well to finish 7th. Following another operation he returned in 1969 to set another world's best time of 2 hr. 8 min. 33.6 sec. in Antwerp. Further injuries prevented his finishing in the 1970 Commonwealth Games and held him down to 13th place in the 1972 Olympics.

His best track times include 13 min. 45.4 sec. for 5000 m. and 28 min. 45.2 sec. for 10,000 m. His annual marathon progress: 1965—2:22:12, 1967—2:09:36.4, 1968—2:14:47.8, 1969—2:08:33.6, 1970—2:13:39, 1971—2:11:08.8, 1972—2:16:19. He was born at Barrow-in-Furness (England) on Nov. 17th, 1942.

## CLUBS

Athletic clubs form the backbone of the sport in Britain and most other countries, although the club system is not yet well developed in the USA.

### Oldest Clubs

Probably the first athletic club was the Necton Guild in Norfolk, founded in 1817, but no trace can be found of it after 1826. The oldest existing club is Exeter College (Oxford) AC, founded in Dec. 1850. Its members have included the world beating milers, Jack Lovelock and Roger Bannister.

The open clubs with the longest histories are Olympic Club of San Francisco (founded May 1860), London AC (April 1864) and New York AC (June 1866).

# COMMONWEALTH GAMES

The first British Empire Games were staged at Hamilton, Canada, in 1930, although the idea of such an event was mooted as early as 1891 by a Mr. Astley Cooper and an "Inter-Empire Championships" was held at London's Crystal Palace in 1911. The driving force behind the Hamilton Games was Mr. M. M. Robinson, manager of the Canadian athletics team at the 1928 Olympic Games.

Women's events were introduced at the second Empire Games in London in 1934. Subsequent meetings were held in Sydney (1938), Auckland (1950), Vancouver (1954), Cardiff (1958), Perth, Western Australia (1962), Kingston, Jamaica (1966) and Edinburgh (1970). The 1974 Games have been awarded to Christchurch (NZ) and the 1978 Games to Edmonton (Canada). This sporting festival is officially entitled the British Commonwealth Games. The Games went metric in 1970.

## Champions

| 100 Yards | | sec. |
|---|---|---|
| 1930 | P. Williams (Canada) | 9.9 |
| 1934 | A. W. Sweeney (England) | 10.0 |
| 1938 | C. B. Holmes (England) | 9.7 |
| 1950 | J. F. Treloar (Australia) | 9.7 |
| 1954 | M. G. R. Agostini (Trinidad) | 9.6 |
| 1958 | K. A. St. H. Gardner (Jamaica) | 9.4 |
| 1962 | S. Antao (Kenya) | 9.5 |
| 1966 | H. W. Jerome (Canada) | 9.4 |

| 100 Metres | | |
|---|---|---|
| 1970 | D. Quarrie (Jamaica) | 10.2 |

| 220 Yards | | sec. |
|---|---|---|
| 1930 | S. E. Englehart (England) | 21.8 |
| 1934 | A. W. Sweeney (England) | 21.9 |
| 1938 | C. B. Holmes (England) | 21.2 |
| 1950 | J. F. Treloar (Australia) | 21.5 |
| 1954 | D. W. Jowett (New Zealand) | 21.5 |
| 1958 | T. A. Robinson (Bahamas) | 21.0 |
| 1962 | S. Antao (Kenya) | 21.1 |
| 1966 | S. F. Allotey (Ghana) | 20.7 |

| 200 Metres | | |
|---|---|---|
| 1970 | D. Quarrie (Jamaica) | 20.5 |

| 440 Yards | | sec. |
|---|---|---|
| 1930 | A. Wilson (Canada) | 48.8 |
| 1934 | G. L. Rampling (England) | 48.0 |
| 1938 | W. Roberts (England) | 47.9 |
| 1950 | E. W. Carr (Australia) | 47.9 |
| 1954 | R. K. Gosper (Australia) | 47.2 |
| 1958 | Milkha Singh (India) | 46.6 |
| 1962 | G. E. Kerr (Jamaica) | 46.7 |
| 1966 | W. Mottley (Trinidad) | 45.0 |

| 400 Metres | | |
|---|---|---|
| 1970 | C. Asati (Kenya) | 45.0 |

| 880 Yards | | min. sec. |
|---|---|---|
| 1930 | T. Hampson (England) | 1 52.4 |
| 1934 | P. A. Edwards (Brit. Guiana) | 1 54.2 |
| 1938 | V. P. Boot (New Zealand) | 1 51.2 |
| 1950 | H. J. Parlett (England) | 1 53.1 |
| 1954 | D. J. N. Johnson (England) | 1 50.7 |
| 1958 | H. J. Elliott (Australia) | 1 49.3 |
| 1962 | P. G. Snell (New Zealand) | 1 47.6 |
| 1966 | N. S. Clough (Australia) | 1 46.9 |

| 800 Metres | | |
|---|---|---|
| 1970 | R. Ouko (Kenya) | 1 46.8 |

| Mile | | min. sec. |
|---|---|---|
| 1930 | R. H. Thomas (England) | 4 14.0 |
| 1934 | J. E. Lovelock (New Zealand) | 4 12.8 |
| 1938 | J. W. Ll. Alford (Wales) | 4 11.6 |
| 1950 | C. W. Parnell (Canada) | 4 11.0 |
| 1954 | R. G. Bannister (England) | 3 58.8 |
| 1958 | H. J. Elliott (Australia) | 3 59.0 |
| 1962 | P. G. Snell (New Zealand) | 4 04.6 |
| 1966 | K. Keino (Kenya) | 3 55.3 |

| 1500 Metres | | |
|---|---|---|
| 1970 | K. Keino (Kenya) | 3 36.6 |

| 3 Miles | | min. sec. |
|---|---|---|
| 1930 | S. A. Tomlin (England) | 14 27.4 |
| 1934 | W. J. Beavers (England) | 14 32.6 |
| 1938 | C. H. Matthews (New Zealand) | 13 59.6 |
| 1950 | L. Eyre (England) | 14 23.6 |
| 1954 | C. J. Chataway (England) | 13 35.2 |
| 1958 | M. G. Halberg (New Zealand) | 13 15.0 |
| 1962 | M. G. Halberg (New Zealand) | 13 34.2 |

| 1966 | K. Keino (Kenya) | 12 57.4 |

*5000 Metres*

| 1970 | I. Stewart (Scotland) | 13 22.8 |

*6 Miles* min. sec.

| 1930 | W. J. Savidan (New Zealand) | 30 49.6 |
| 1934 | A. W. Penny (England) | 31 00.6 |
| 1938 | C. H. Matthews (New Zealand) | 30 14.5 |
| 1950 | W. H. Nelson (New Zealand) | 30 29.6 |
| 1954 | P. B. Driver (England) | 29 09.4 |
| 1958 | W. D. Power (Australia) | 28 47.8 |
| 1962 | B. Kidd (Canada) | 28 26.6 |
| 1966 | N. Temu (Kenya) | 27 14.6 |

*10,000 Metres*

| 1970 | J. L. Stewart (Scotland) | 28 11.8 |

*Marathon* hr. min. sec.

| 1930 | D. McL. Wright (Scotland) | 2 43 43.0 |
| 1934 | H. Webster (Canada) | 2 40 36.0 |
| 1938 | J. L. Coleman (S. Africa) | 2 30 49.8 |
| 1950 | J. T. Holden (England) | 2 32 57.0 |
| 1954 | J. McGhee (Scotland) | 2 39 36.0 |
| 1958 | W. D. Power (Australia) | 2 22 45.6 |
| 1962 | B. L. Kilby (England) | 2 21 17.0 |
| 1966 | J. N. C. Alder (Scotland) | 2 22 07.8 |
| 1970 | R. Hill (England) | 2 09 28.0 |

*Steeplechase* min. sec.

| 1930 | G. W. Bailey (England) | 9 52.0 |
| 1934 | S. C. Scarsbrook (England) | 10 23.4 |

*3000 Metres Steeplechase* min. sec.

| 1962 | T. A. Vincent (Australia) | 8 43.4 |
| 1966 | R. P. Welsh (New Zealand) | 8 29.6 |
| 1970 | A. P. Manning (Australia) | 8 26.2 |

*120 Yards Hurdles* sec.

| 1930 | Lord Burghley (England) | 14.6 |
| 1934 | D. O. Finlay (England) | 15.2 |
| 1938 | T. P. Lavery (S. Africa) | 14.0 |
| 1950 | P. J. Gardner (Australia) | 14.3 |
| 1954 | K. A. St. H. Gardner (Jamaica) | 14.2 |

| 1958 | K. A. St. H. Gardner (Jamaica) | 14.0 |
| 1962 | H. G. Raziq (Pakistan) | 14.3 |
| 1966 | D. P. Hemery (England) | 14.1 |

*110 Metres Hurdles*

| 1970 | D. P. Hemery (England) | 13.6 |

*440 Yards Hurdles* sec.

| 1930 | Lord Burghley (England) | 54.4 |
| 1934 | F. A. R. Hunter (Scotland) | 55.2 |
| 1938 | J. W. Loaring (Canada) | 52.9 |
| 1950 | D. White (Ceylon) | 52.5 |
| 1954 | D. F. Lean (Australia) | 52.4 |
| 1958 | G. C. Potgieter (S. Africa) | 49.7 |
| 1962 | K. J. Roche (Australia) | 51.5 |
| 1966 | K. J. Roche (Australia) | 51.0 |

*400 Metres Hurdles*

| 1970 | J. Sherwood (England) | 50.0 |

*4 x 110 Yards Relay* sec.

| 1930 | Canada (J. R. Brown, L. Miller, R. A. Adams J. R. Fitzpatrick) | 42.2 |
| 1934 | England (E. I. Davis, W. Rangeley, G. T. Saunders, A. W. Sweeney) | 42.2 |
| 1938 | Canada (J. Brown, P. Haley, J. W. Loaring, L. G. O'Connor) | 41.6 |
| 1950 | Australia (A. W. de Gruchy, D. Johnson, A. K. Gordon, J. F. Treloar) | 42.2 |
| 1954 | Canada (J. D. Macfarlane, D. R. Stonehouse, H. Nelson, B. Springbett) | 41.3 |
| 1958 | England (P. F. Radford, D. H. Segal, E. R. Sandstrom, A. Breacker) | 40.7 |
| 1962 | England (P. F. Radford, L. W. Carter, A. Meakin, D. H. Jones) | 40.6 |
| 1966 | Ghana (E. C. Addy, B. K. Mends, J. A. Addy, S. F. Allotey) | 39.8 |

*4 x 100 Metres Relay*

| 1970 | Jamaica (E. Stewart, L. Miller, C. Lawson, D. Quarrie) | 39.4 |

*4 x 440 Yards Relay* min. sec.

| 1930 | England (Lord Burghley, K. C. Brangwin, R. Leigh-Wood, H. S. Townend) | 3 19.4 |

| 1934 | England (D. L. Rathbone, C. H. Stoneley, G. N. Blake, G. L. Rampling) | 3 16.8 |
| 1938 | Canada (W. Dale, J. Frazer, J. W. Loaring, J. Orr) | 3 16.9 |
| 1950 | Australia (R. E. Price, G. V. Gedge, J. W. Humphreys, E. W. Carr) | 3 17.8 |
| 1954 | England (F. P. Higgins, A. Dick, P. G. Fryer, D. J. N. Johnson) | 3 11.2 |
| 1958 | South Africa (G. R. Day, G. G. Evans, G. C. Potgieter, M. C. Spence) | 3 08.1 |
| 1962 | Jamaica (L. Khan, Mal Spence, Mel Spence, G. E. Kerr) | 3 10.2 |
| 1966 | Trinidad & Tobago (L. Yearwood, K. Bernard, E. Roberts, W. Mottley) | 3 02.8 |

*4 x 400 Metres Relay*

| 1970 | Kenya (H. Nyamau, J. Sang, R. Ouko, C. Asati) | 3 03.6 |

*High Jump* ft. in.

| 1930 | J. H. Viljoen (S. Africa) | 6 | 3 |
| 1934 | E. T. Thacker (S. Africa) | 6 | 3 |
| 1938 | E. T. Thacker (S. Africa) | 6 | 5 |
| 1950 | J. A. Winter (Australia) | 6 | 6 |
| 1954 | E. A. Ifeajuna (Nigeria) | 6 | 8 |
| 1958 | E. Haisley (Jamaica) | 6 | 9 |
| 1962 | P. F. Hobson (Australia) | 6 | 11 |
| 1966 | L. Peckham (Australia) | 6 | 10 |
| 1970 | L. Peckham (Australia) | 7 | 0¼ |

*Pole Vault* ft. in.

| 1930 | V. W. Pickard (Canada) | 12 | 3 |
| 1934 | C. J. S. Apps (Canada) | 12 | 6 |
| 1938 | A. S. du Plessis (S. Africa) | 13 | 5¾ |
| 1950 | T. D. Anderson (England) | 13 | 0 |
| 1954 | G. M. Elliott (England) | 14 | 0 |
| 1958 | G. M. Elliott (England) | 13 | 8 |
| 1962 | T. S. Bickle (Australia) | 14 | 9 |
| 1966 | T. S. Bickle (Australia) | 15 | 9 |
| 1970 | M. A. Bull (N. Ireland) | 16 | 8¾ |

*Long Jump* ft. in.

| 1930 | L. Hutton (Canada) | 23 | 7½ |
| 1934 | S. Richardson (Canada) | 23 | 6¼ |
| 1938 | H. Brown (Canada) | 24 | 4¾ |
| 1950 | N. G. Price (S. Africa) | 24 | 0 |
| 1954 | K. S. D. Wilmshurst (England) | 24 | 8¾ |
| 1958 | P. Foreman (Jamaica) | 24 | 6¼ |
| 1962 | M. Ahey (Ghana) | 26 | 5 |
| 1966 | L. Davies (Wales) | 26 | 2¾ |
| 1970 | L. Davies (Wales) | 26 | 5½ |

*Triple Jump* ft. in.

| 1930 | G. C. Smallacombe (Canada) | 48 | 5 |
| 1934 | J. P. Metcalfe (Australia) | 51 | 3½ |
| 1938 | J. P. Metcalfe (Australia) | 50 | 10 |
| 1950 | B. T. Oliver (Australia) | 51 | 2½ |
| 1954 | K. S. D. Wilmshurst (England) | 50 | 1½ |
| 1958 | I. R. Tomlinson (Australia) | 51 | 7¼ |
| 1962 | I. R. Tomlinson (Australia) | 53 | 2 |
| 1966 | S. Igun (Nigeria) | 53 | 9¾ |
| 1970 | P. J. May (Australia) | 54 | 10¼ |

*Shot* ft. in.

| 1930 | H. B. Hart (S. Africa) | 47 | 10 |
| 1934 | H. B. Hart (S. Africa) | 48 | 1¾ |
| 1938 | L. A. Fouche (S. Africa) | 47 | 6 |
| 1950 | M. Tuicakau (Fiji) | 48 | 0¼ |
| 1954 | J. A. Savidge (England) | 55 | 0¼ |
| 1958 | A. Rowe (England) | 57 | 8 |
| 1962 | M. T. Lucking (England) | 59 | 4 |
| 1966 | D. Steen (Canada) | 61 | 8 |
| 1970 | D. Steen (Canada) | 63 | 0¼ |

*Discus* ft. in.

| 1930 | H. B. Hart (S. Africa) | 135 | 11 |
| 1934 | H. B. Hart (S. Africa) | 136 | 3 |
| 1938 | E. E. Coy (Canada) | 146 | 10 |
| 1950 | I. M. Reed (Australia) | 156 | 7 |
| 1954 | S. J. du Plessis (S. Africa) | 169 | 7½ |
| 1958 | S. J. du Plessis (S. Africa) | 183 | 6½ |
| 1962 | W. P. Selvey (Australia) | 185 | 3½ |
| 1966 | L. R. Mills (New Zealand) | 184 | 4 |
| 1970 | G. Puce (Canada) | 193 | 8 |

*Hammer* ft. in.

| 1930 | M. C. Nokes (England) | 154 | 7½ |
| 1934 | M. C. Nokes (England) | 158 | 3½ |
| 1938 | G. W. Sutherland (Canada) | 159 | 10 |

| 1950 | D. McD. M. Clark (Scotland) | 163 | 10¼ |
|------|-----------------------------|-----|-----|
| 1954 | M. Iqbal (Pakistan) | 181 | 8 |
| 1958 | M. J. Ellis (England) | 206 | 4½ |
| 1962 | A. H. Payne (England) | 202 | 3 |
| 1966 | A. H. Payne (England) | 203 | 4 |
| 1970 | A. H. Payne (England) | 222 | 5 |

**Javelin** ft. in.

| 1930 | S. A. Lay (New Zealand) | 207 | 1½ |
|------|-------------------------|-----|-----|
| 1934 | R. Dixon (Canada) | 196 | 11 |
| 1938 | J. A. Courtwright (Canada) | 206 | 0¾ |
| 1950 | L. J. Roininen (Canada) | 187 | 4½ |
| 1954 | J. D. Achurch (Australia) | 224 | 9½ |
| 1958 | C. G. Smith (England) | 233 | 10½ |
| 1962 | A. E. Mitchell (Australia) | 256 | 3 |
| 1966 | J. H. P. FitzSimons (England) | 261 | 9 |
| 1970 | D. H. Travis (England) | 260 | 10 |

**Decathlon** pts.

| 1966 | R. A. Williams (New Zealand) | 7270 |
|------|------------------------------|------|
| 1970 | G. J. Smith (Australia) | 7492 |

**20 Miles Walk** hr. min. sec.

| 1966 | R. Wallwork (England) | 2 44 42.8 |
|------|-----------------------|-----------|
| 1970 | N. F. Freeman (Australia) | 2 33 33.0 |

## Women Champions

**100 Yards** sec.

| 1934 | E. M. Hiscock (England) | 11.3 |
|------|-------------------------|------|
| 1938 | D. Norman (Australia) | 11.1 |
| 1950 | M. Jackson (Australia) | 10.8 |
| 1954 | M. Nelson (Australia)* | 10.7 |
| 1958 | M. J. Willard (Australia) | 10.6 |
| 1962 | D. Hyman (England) | 11.2 |
| 1966 | D. Burge (Australia) | 10.6 |

* née Jackson

**100 Metres**

| 1970 | R. A. Boyle (Australia) | 11.2 |
|------|-------------------------|------|

**220 Yards** sec.

| 1934 | E. M. Hiscock (England) | 25.0 |
|------|-------------------------|------|
| 1938 | D. Norman (Australia) | 24.7 |
| 1950 | M. Jackson (Australia) | 24.3 |
| 1954 | M. Nelson (Australia)* | 24.0 |
| 1958 | M. J. Willard (Australia) | 23.6 |
| 1962 | D. Hyman (England) | 23.8 |
| 1966 | D. Burge (Australia) | 23.8 |

* née Jackson

**200 Metres**

| 1970 | R. A. Boyle (Australia) | 22.7 |
|------|-------------------------|------|

**440 Yards** sec.

| 1966 | J. Pollock (Australia) | 53.0 |
|------|------------------------|------|

**400 Metres**

| 1970 | M. Neufville (Jamaica) | 51.0 |
|------|------------------------|------|

**880 Yards** min. sec.

| 1934 | G. A. Lunn (England) | 2 19.4 |
|------|----------------------|--------|
| 1962 | D. Willis (Australia) | 2 03.7 |
| 1966 | A. Hoffman (Canada) | 2 04.3 |

**800 Metres**

| 1970 | R. O. Stirling (Scotland) | 2 06.2 |
|------|---------------------------|--------|

**1500 Metres** min. sec.

| 1970 | R. Ridley (England) | 4 18.8 |
|------|---------------------|--------|

**80 Metres Hurdles** sec.

| 1934 | M. R. Clark (S. Africa) | 11.8 |
|------|-------------------------|------|
| 1938 | B. Burke (S. Africa) | 11.7 |
| 1950 | S. B. Strickland (Australia) | 11.6 |
| 1954 | E. M. Maskell (N. Rhodesia) | 10.9 |
| 1958 | N. C. Thrower (Australia) | 10.7 |
| 1962 | P. Kilborn (Australia) | 10.9 |
| 1966 | P. Kilborn (Australia) | 10.9 |

**100 Metres Hurdles**

| 1970 | P. Kilborn (Australia) | 13.2 |
|------|------------------------|------|

**110 x 220 x 110 Yards Relay** sec.

| 1934 | England (N. Halstead E. Maguire, E. M. Hiscock) | 49.4 |
|------|-------------------------------------------------|------|
| 1938 | Australia (J. Coleman, A. E. Wearne, D. Norman) | 49.1 |
| 1950 | Australia (M. Jackson, S. B. Strickland, V. Johnston) | 47.9 |

**4 x 110 Yards Relay**

| 1954 | Australia (G. Wallace, N. A. Fogarty, W. Cripps, M. Nelson) | 46.8 |
|------|------------------------------------------------------------|------|
| 1958 | England (V. M. Weston, J. F. Paul, D. Hyman, H. J. Young) | 45.3 |
| 1962 | Australia (J. Bennett, G. Beasley, B. Cox, B. Cuthbert) | 46.6 |
| 1966 | Australia (J. Lamy, P. Kilborn, J. Bennett, D. Burge) | 45.3 |

*4 x 100 Metres Relay*
1970 Australia (J. Lamy, P.
  Kilborn, M. Hoffman,
  R. A. Boyle)          44.1

*660 Yards Relay*        min. sec.
1934 Canada (L. Palmer, B.
  White, A. A. Meagher,
  A. Dearnley)          1 14.4
1938 Australia (J. Coleman,
  D. Norman, T. Peake,
  J. Woodland)          1 15.2
1950 Australia (S. B. Strick-
  land, V. Johnston, M.
  Jackson, A. Shanley)  1 13.4

*High Jump*              ft. in.
1934 M. R. Clark (S. Africa) 5  3
1938 D. J. B. Odam (England) 5  3
1950 D. J. B. Tyler (England)* 5 3
1954 T. E. Hopkins (N. Ireland)                 5  6
1958 M. M. Mason (Australia) 5 7
1962 R. Woodhouse
  (Australia)           5 10
1966 M. M. Brown
  (Australia)†          5  8
1970 D. Brill (Canada)   5 10
        * *née* Odam
        † *née* Mason

*Long Jump*              ft. in.
1934 P. Bartholomew (Eng-
  land)                 17 11¼
1938 D. Norman (Australia) 19 0¼
1950 Y. W. Williams (New
  Zealand)              19 4½
1954 Y. W. Williams (New
  Zealand)              19 11½
1958 S. H. Hoskin (England) 19 9
1962 P. Kilborn (Australia) 20 6¾
1966 M. D. Rand (England) 20 10½
1970 S. Sherwood (England) 22 1

*Shot*                   ft. in.
1954 Y. W. Williams (New
  Zealand)              45 9½
1958 V. I. Sloper (New Zealand)                 51 0
1962 V. I. Young (New Zealand)*                49 11½
1966 V. I. Young (New Zealand)                 54 1¾
1970 M. E. Peters (N. Ireland)                 52 3¼
        * *née* Sloper

*Discus*                 ft. in.
1954 Y. W. Williams (New
  Zealand)              147 8

1958 S. Allday (England)  150  7½
1962 V. I. Young (New
  Zealand)              164  8½
1966 V. I. Young (New
  Zealand)              163  4
1970 C. R. Payne (Scotland) 178 8

*Javelin*                ft. in.
1934 G. A. Lunn (England) 105  7¼
1938 R. Higgins (Canada)  125  7¼
1950 C. C. McGibbon
  (Australia)           127  5¼
1954 M. C. Swanepoel (S.
  Africa)               143  9½
1958 A. Pazera (Australia) 188 4
1962 S. Platt (England)   164 10¼
1966 M. Parker (Australia) 168 7
1970 P. Rivers (Australia) 170 7

*Pentathlon*                 Pts.
1970 M. E. Peters (N. Ireland) 5148


## Distribution of Gold Medals

Gold medals in the men's events
have been won as follows:—

*1930:* England 9, Canada 6, South
  Africa, 3, New Zealand 2,
  Scotland 1.
*1934:* England 10, Canada 4, South
  Africa 3, Australia, British
  Guiana, New Zealand, Scot-
  land 1 each.
*1938:* Canada 7, South Africa 5, England, New Zealand 3 each,
  Australia, Wales 1 each.
*1950:* Australia 9, England 4, Canada
  2, Ceylon, Fiji, New Zealand,
  Scotland, South Africa 1 each.
*1954:* England 9, Australia 3, Canada,
  Jamaica, New Zealand, Nigeria,
  Pakistan, Scotland, South
  Africa, Trinidad 1 each.
*1958:* Australia, England 5 each,
  Jamaica 4, South Africa 3,
  Bahamas, India, New Zealand 1
  each.
*1962:* Australia 7, England 4, New
  Zealand 3, Jamaica, Kenya 2
  each, Canada, Ghana, Pakistan 1 each.
*1966:* Australia, England 4 each,
  Kenya, New Zealand 3 each,
  Canada, Ghana, Trinidad 2
  each, Nigeria, Scotland, Wales
  1 each.

*1970:* Australia, England 5 each, Kenya 4, Jamaica 3, Canada, Scotland 2 each, N. Ireland, Wales 1 each.

*Aggregate:* England 53, Australia 35, Canada 25.

Figures for the women's events:—

*1934:* England 6, South Africa 2 Canada 1.
*1938:* Australia 5, Canada, England South Africa 1 each.
*1950:* Australia 6, England, New Zealand 1 each.
*1954:* Australia, New Zealand 3 each, Northern Ireland, Northern Rhodesia, South Africa 1 each.
*1958:* Australia 5, England 3, New Zealand 1.
*1962:* Australia 5, England 3, New Zealand 2.
*1966:* Australia 7, New Zealand 2, Canada, England 1 each.
*1970:* Australia 5, England, N. Ireland, Scotland 2 each, Canada, Jamaica 1 each.

*Aggregate:* Australia 36, England 17, New Zealand 9.

## English Medallists

The following athletes, listed in alphabetical order, have won Commonwealth Games medals while representing England. G signifies gold (1st), S silver (2nd) and B bronze (3rd).

Adcocks, W. A., 1966, marathon (S).
Adey, J. A., 1966, 4 x 440 yd. (B).
Allday, P. C., 1958, hammer (B).
Allen, C. K., 1934, 3 mi. (S).
Alsop, F. J., 1962, triple jump (B); 1966, triple jump (B).
Anderson, T. D., 1950, pole vault (G).
Archer, J., 1950, 4 x 110 yd. (S).
Bailey, G. W., 1930, Steep. (G); 1934, Steep. (B).
Bannister, R. G., 1954, mile (G).
Beavers, W. J., 1934, 3 mi. (G).
Bell, D. R., 1934, discus (S).
Bilham, M., 1970, 4 x 400 m. (B).
Blake, G. N., 1934, 4 x 440 yd. (G).
Boyd, I. H., 1954, 880 yd. (B).
Brangwin, K. C., 1930, 4 x 440 yd. (G).
Breacker, A., 1958, 4 x 110 yd. (G).
Brightwell, R. I., 1962, 440 yd. (S); 4 x 440 yd. (S).
Brown, R. K., 1934, 440 hurdles (B).

Burghley, Lord, 1930, 120 yd. hurdles (G), 440 yd. hurdles (G) and 4 x 440 yd. (G).
Burns, J. A., 1934, 3 mi. (B).
Carr, G. A., 1958, discus (B).
Carter, L. W., 1962, 4 x 110 yd. (G).
Chataway, C. J., 1954, 3 mi. (G).
Chivers, A. H., 1950, 3 mi. (B).
Cohen, H. J., 1930, 4 x 110 yd. (S).
Cornes, J. F., 1930, mile (B); 1934, mile (B).
Davis, E. I., 1934, 4 x 110 yd. (G).
Dear, D. G., 1970, 4 x 100 m. (B).
Dick, A., 1954, 4 x 440 yd. (G).
Driver, P. B., 1954, 6 mi. (G).
Duncan, K. S., 1938, 4 x 110 yd. (S).
Elliott, G. M., 1954, pole vault (G); 1958, pole vault (G).
Ellis, M. J., 1958, hammer (G).
Englehart, S. E., 1930, 220 yd. (G) and 4 x 110 yd. (S).
Evenson, T., 1930, 6 mi. (B); 1934, Steep. (S).
Eyre, L., 1950, 3 mi. (G) and mile (S).
Faircloth, D. K., 1970, marathon (B).
Ferris, S., 1930, marathon (S).
Finlay, D. O., 1934, 120 yd. hurdles (G).
FitzSimons, J. H. P., 1966, javelin (G), 1970, javelin (B).
Ford, H., 1930, pole vault (S).
Foster, B., 1970, 1500 m. (B).
Fraser, B., 1970, hammer (S).
Fryer, P. G., 1954, 4 x 440 yd. (G).
Furze, A. F., 1934, 6 mi. (B).
Gabbett, P. J., 1970, decathlon (S).
Gaby, F. R., 1930, 120 yd. hurdles (B).
Graham, T. J. M., 1966, 4 x 440 yd. (B).
Green, B. W., 1970, 4 x 100 m. (B).
Green, F., 1954, 3 mi. (S).
Green, I. D., 1970, 4 x 100 m. (B).
Hampson, T., 1930, 880 yd. (G).
Handley, F. R., 1938, 880 yd. (S) and 4 x 440 yd. (S).
Hanlon, J. A. T., 1930, 4 x 110 yd. (S).
Harper, E., 1930, 6 mi. (S).
Hauck, M. A., 1970, 4 x 400 m. (B).
Heap, J. C., 1930, 4 x 110 yd. (S).
Hemery, D. P., 1966, 120 yd. hurdles (G), 1970, 120 yd. hurdles (G).
Herriott, M., 1962, 3000 m. steeplechase (S).
Hewson, B. S., 1954, 880 yd. (S); 1958, 880 yd. (S).
Higgins, F. P., 1954, 4 x 440 yd. (G).
Higgins, T. L., 1950, 4 x 440 yd. (S).
Higham, C. E. E., 1954, 120 yd. hurdles (S).

Hill, R., 1970, marathon (G).
Holden, J. T., 1950, marathon (G).
Holmes, C. B., 1938, 100 yd. (G), 220 yd. (G) and 4 x 110 yd. (S).
Howland, R. L., 1930, shot (S); 1934, shot (S).
Jackson, B. D., 1962, 4 x 440 yd. (S).
Johnson, D. J. N., 1954, 880 yd. (G) and 4 x 440 yd. (G); 1958, 4 x 440 yd. (S).
Jones, D. H., 1962, 4 x 110 yd. (G) and 220 yd. (S).
Kane, H., 1954, 440 yd. hurdles (S).
Kilby, B. L., 1962, marathon (G).
King, B. J., 1970, decathlon (B).
Leigh-Wood, R., 1930, 4 x 440 yd. (G) and 440 yd. hurdles (S).
Lerwill, A. L., 1970, long jump (B).
Lewis, L. C., 1950, 440 yd. (S), 4 x 110 yd. (S) and 4 x 440 yd. (S).
Lucking, M. T., 1958, shot (S); 1962, shot (G).
McCabe, B. F., 1938, 4 x 440 yd. (S).
McSorley, J. V., 1970, javelin (S).
Meakin, A., 1962, 4 x 110 yd. (G).
Metcalfe, A. P., 1962, 4 x 440 yd. (S).
Middleton, R. C., 1966, 20 miles walk (S).
Moody, H. E. A., 1950, shot (S).
Morgan, V. E., 1930, steeplechase (B).
Neame, D. M. L., 1930, 440 yd. hurdles (B).
Nokes, M. C., 1930, hammer (G); 1934, hammer (G).
Norris, A. J., 1938, marathon (S).
Pack, H. E., 1938, 4 x 440 yd. (S).
Page, E. L., 1930, 100 yd. (S).
Parker, J. M., 1966, 120 yd. hurdles (S).
Parlett, H. J., 1950, 880 yd. (G) and 4 x 440 yd. (S).
Payne, A. H., 1962, hammer (G); 1966, hammer (G); 1970, hammer (G).
Penny, A. W., 1934, 6 mi. (G).
Peters, J. H., 1954, 6 mi. (B).
Pharaoh, M., 1954, discus (B).
Pilbrow, A. G., 1934, 120 yd. hurdles (B).
Pridie, K. H., 1934, shot (B).
Pugh, D. C., 1950, 4 x 440 yd. (S).
Radford, P. F., 1958, 4 x 110 yd. (G); 1962, 4 x 110 yd. (G).
Rampling, G. L., 1934, 440 yd. (G) and 4 x 440 yd. (G).
Rangeley, W., 1934, 4 x 110 yd. (G) and 220 yd. (B).
Rathbone, D. L., 1934, 4 x 440 yd. (G).
Rawson, M. A., 1958, 880 yd. (B).

Revans, R. W., 1930, long jump (S) and triple jump (S).
Reynolds, M. E., 1970, 4 x 100 m. (B).
Richardson, K. J., 1938, 4 x 110 yd. (S).
Roberts, W., 1934, 440 yd. (S); 1938, 440 yd. (G) and 4 x 440 yd. (S).
Rowe, A., 1958, shot (G).
Rushmer, A. T., 1966, 3 mi. (B).
Salisbury, J. E., 1958, 4 x 440 yd. (S).
Sampson, E. J., 1958, 4 x 440 yd. (S).
Sando, F. D., 1954, 6 mi. (S) and 3 mi. (B).
Sandstrom, E. R., 1958, 4 x 110 yd. (G).
Saunders, G. T., 1934, 4 x 110 yd. (G).
Savidge, J. A., 1954, shot (G).
Scarsbrook, S. C., 1934, steeplechase (G).
Segal, D. H., 1958, 4 x 110 yd. (G).
Setti, R. E. F., 1962, 4 x 440 yd. (S).
Sheldrick, J. W., 1962, discus (B).
Shenton, B., 1950, 4 x 110 yd. (S); 1954, 220 yd. (S).
Sherwood, J., 1970, 400 m. hurdles (G), and 4 x 400 m. (B).
Simpson, A., 1966, mile (S).
Smith, C. G., 1958, javelin (G); 1962 javelin (S).
Stacey, N. D., 1950, 4 x 110 yd. (S).
Stoneley, C. H., 1934, 4 x 440 yd. (G) and 440 yd. (B).
Sweeney, A. W., 1934, 100 yd. (G), 220 yd. (G) and 4 x 110 yd. (G).
Taitt, J. L., 1962, 120 yd. hurdles (B).
Trancred, W. R., 1970, discus (B).
Taylor, R. G., 1970, 10,000 m. (B).
Teale, J., 1970, shot (S).
Thomas, R. H., 1930, mile (G) and 880 yd. (S).
Tomlin, S. A., 1930, 3 mi. (G).
Townend, H. S., 1930, 4 x 440 yd. (G.)
Travis, D. H., 1970, javelin (G).
Wallace, L. M., 1938, 4 x 110 yd. (S).
Wallwork, R., 1966, 20 miles walk (G).
Walters, L. B., 1970, 4 x 400 m. (B).
Ward, P. D. H., 1938, 3 mi. (S).
Warden, P., 1966, 440 yd. hurdles (B) and 4 x 440 yd. (B).
Wilkinson, P. A., 1958, marathon (B).
Williams, B., 1970, hammer (B).
Wilmshurst, K. S. D., 1954, long jump (G) and triple jump (G).
Winbolt Lewis, M. J., 1966, 4 x 440 yd. (B).
Winfield, J. W., 1930, 3 mi. (B).
Wooderson, S. C., 1934, mile (S).

63

Wrighton, J. D., 1958, 4 x 440 yd. (S).

## Women

Allday, S., 1954, discus (S); 1958, discus (G) and shot (S); 1962, shot (B).
Bartholomew, P., 1934, long jump (G).
Batter, D., 1950, 660 yd. relay (S).
Bell, C., 1970, 100 m. hurdles (B).
Burgess, S., 1954, 4 x 110 yd. (S).
Butterfield, D., 1934, 880 yd. (B).
Chalmers, L., 1934, 100 yd. (B).
Cheeseman, S., 1950, 660 yd. relay (S) and 440 yd. relay (B).
Cobb, V. M., 1958, 4 x 110 yd. (G) and 100 yd. (B); 1970, 4 x 100 m. (S).
Cox, M., 1934, javelin (B).
Critchley, M. A., 1970, 200 m. (B) and 4 x 100 m. (S).
Crowther, B., 1950, high jump (S).
Farquhar, A., 1970, javelin (S).
Gardner, D. K., 1938, high jump (S).
Green, E., 1934, 80 m. hurdles (B).
Hall, D. G., 1950, 660 yd. relay (S) and 440 yd. relay (B).
Hall, J. A., 1966, 100 yd. (B) and 4 x 110 yd. (S).
Halstead, E., 1934, javelin (S).
Halstead, N., 1934, 440 yd. relay (G), 660 yd. relay (S) and 220 yd. (B).
Hiscock, E., 1934, 100 yd. (G), 220 yd. (G), 440 yd. relay (G) and 660 yd. relay (S).
Hoskin, S. H., 1958, long jump (G).
Hyman, D., 1958, 4 x 110 yd. (G); 1962, 100 yd. (G), 220 yd. (G) and 4 x 110 yd. (S).
Johnson, E., 1934, 660 yd. relay (S).
Jones, I., 1934, 880 yd. (S).
Jordan, J. W., 1962, 880 yd. (B).
Jordan, W., 1938, 660 yd. relay (S) and 440 yd. relay (B).
Lowe, P. B., 1970, 800 m. (S).
Lunn, G. A., 1934, 880 yd. (G) and javelin (G); 1938, javelin (B).
Maguire, E., 1934, 440 yd. relay (G).
Moore, B. R. H., 1962, 80 m. hurdles (S) and 4 x 110 yd. (S).
Morgan, R., 1962, javelin (S).
Neil, D. A., 1970, 4 x 100 m. (S).
Packer, A. E., 1962, 4 x 110 yd. (S).
Page, J. F., 1970, 1500 m. (S).
Pashley, A., 1954, 4 x 110 yd. (S).
Paul, J. F., 1958, 4 x 110 yd. (G).
Peat, V., 1970, 4 x 100 m. (S).
Pickering, J. C., 1954, 80 m. hurdles (B) and long jump (B).

Pirie, S., 1954, 4 x110 yd. (S) and 220 yd. (B).
Platt, S. M., 1962, javelin (G).
Quinton, C. L., 1958, 80 m. hurdles (S).
Raby, E., 1938, long jump (S) and 660 yd. relay (S).
Rand, M. D., 1958, long jump (S); 1966, long jump (G).
Ridley, R., 1970, 1500 m. (G).
Saunders, D., 1938, 660 yd. relay (S) and 440 yd. relay (B).
Sherwood, S. H., 1966, long jump (S); 1970, long jump (G).
Shirley, D. A., 1966, high jump (S).
Simpson, J. M., 1966, 4 x 110 yd. (S).
Slater, D., 1962, 4 x 110 yd. (S); 1966, 4 x 110 yd. (S).
Smith, A. R., 1966, 880 yd. (B).
Stokes, K., 1938, 660 yd. relay (S) and 440 yd. relay (B).
Tranter, M. D., 1966, 4 x 110 yd. (S).
Tyler, D. J. B., 1938, high jump (G); 1950, high jump (G); 1954, high jump (S).
Walker, I., 1934, 660 yd. relay (S).
Walker, M., 1950, 660 yd. relay (S) and 440 yd. relay (B).
Watkinson, D. A., 1966, 440 yd. (S).
Webb, V., 1934, long jump (B).
Williams, A. M., 1958, javelin (B).
Wilson, A. S., 1970, high jump (S); long jump (S) and pentathlon (S).
Young, H. J., 1954, 4 x 110 yd. (S); 1958, 4 x 110 yd. (G), 100 yd. (S) and 220 yd. (B).

## Scottish Medallists

Alder, J. N. C., 1966, marathon (G) and 6 mi. (B); 1970, marathon (S).
Brownlee, D. A., 1934, 4 x 110 yd. (B).
Clark, D. McD. M., 1950, hammer (G).
Douglas, E. C. K., 1954, hammer (B).
Forbes, A., 1950, 6 mi. (S).
Hunter, F. A. R., 1934, 440 yd. hurdles (G) and 4 x 440 yd. (B).
Lindsay, M. R., 1962, shot (S) and discus (S).
McCafferty, I., 1970, 5000 m. (S).
McGhee, J., 1954, marathon (G).
Mackenzie, W., 1934, hammer (B).
Michie, J. F., 1934, high jump (B).
Murdoch, R. L., 1934, 4 x 110 yd. (B).
Paterson, A. S., 1950, high jump (S).
Robertson, D. McN., 1934, marathon (S).
Stewart, I., 1970, 5000 m. (G).

Valeriy Brumel (USSR), 1964 Olympic champion—straddle jumper.

Dick Fosbury (USA), 1968 Olympic champion—flopper.

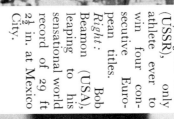

*Left:* Janis Lusis (USSR), only athlete ever to win four consecutive European titles.

*Right:* Bob Beamon (USA), leaping to his sensational world record of 29 ft 2½ in. at Mexico City.

Stewart, J. L., 1970, 10,000 m. (G).
Stothard, J. C., 1934, 880 yd. (B) and
4 x 440 yd. (B).
Sutherland, W. M. S., 1970, 20 mi.
walk (B).
Turner, A. D., 1934, 4 x 110 yd. (B).
Wallace, R. H. H., 1934, 4 x 440 yd.
(B).
Wright, D. McL., 1930, marathon (G);
1934, marathon (B).
Wylde, R. B., 1934, 4 x 440 yd. (B).
Young, D., 1938, discus (S).
Young, I. C., 1934, 100 yd. (B) and
4 x 110 yd. (B).

*Women*
Cunningham, J., 1934, 660 yd. relay
(B).
Dobbie, S., 1934, 660 yd. relay (B).
Jackson, C., 1934, 660 yd. relay (B).
Mackenzie, M., 1934, 660 yd. relay
(B).
Payne, C. R., 1970, discus (G).
Stirling, R. O., 1970, 800 m. (G).
Walls, M. L., 1970, high jump (B).

## Welsh Medallists

Alford, J. W. Ll., 1938, mile (G).
Davies, L., 1966, long jump (G); 1970,
long jump (G).
England, D. M., 1962, 4 x 110 yd. (B).
Jones, K. J., 1954, 220 yd. (B).
Jones, R., 1962, 4 x 110 yd. (B).
Jones, T. B., 1962, 4 x 110 yd. (B).
Longe, C. C. O., 1966, decathlon (S).
Merriman, J. L., 1958, 6 mi. (S); 1962,
6 mi. (B).

# COMMONWEALTH RECORDS

Shaw, R. D., 1954, 440 yds. hurdles
(B).
Whitehead, J. N., 1962, 4 x 110 yd.
(B).

## Northern Irish Medallists

Bull, M. A., 1966, pole vault (S); 1970,
pole vault (G).
Hopkins, T. E., 1954, Women's high
jump (G) and long jump (S).
Peters, M. E., 1966, Women's shot (S);
1970, shot (G) and pentathlon
(G).

## Record Achievements

The most victories recorded is seven
by sprinter Marjorie Nelson, *née*
Jackson (Australia) in 1950 and 1954.
Another Australian, Decima Norman,
obtained five gold medals in 1938:
100 yards, 220 yards, long jump and
two relays. Dorothy Tyler (England),
who as Dorothy Odam won the 1938
high jump title, retained her laurels in
1950 and placed second in 1954—
clearing 5ft. 3in. each time.

The most prolific male gold
medallist was Harry Hart (South
Africa), who won both shot and discus in 1930 and 1934.

Two athletes have won three successive titles: Howard Payne (England),
hammer in 1962, 1966 and 1970; and
Pam Kilborn (Australia), 80 m.
hurdles in 1962 and 1966, 100 m.
hurdles in 1970.

The best performances on record in the
standard international events by citizens of
the British Commonwealth, as at June 1,
1973:

| | | | | |
|---|---|---|---|---|
| *100 m.* | | 10.0 | Harry Jerome (Canada) | July 15 1960 |
| | | 10.0 | Lennox Miller (Jamaica) | June 20 1968 |
| | | 10.0 | Lennox Miller (Jamaica) | Oct. 14 1968 |
| | | 10.0 | Lennox Miller (Jamaica) | Nov. 2 1968 |
| *200 m.* | | 19.8 | Don Quarrie (Jamaica) | Aug. 3 1971 |
| *400 m.* | | 44.9 | Julius Sang (Kenya) | Sept. 7 1972 |
| *800 m.* | 1 | 44.3 | Peter Snell (New Zealand) | Feb. 3 1962 |
| | 1 | 44.3 | Ralph Doubell (Australia) | Oct. 15 1968 |
| *1500 m.* | 3 | 34.9 | Kip Keino (Kenya) | Oct. 20 1968 |
| *5000 m.* | 13 | 16.6 | Ron Clarke (Australia) | July 5 1966 |
| *10,000 m.* | 27 | 39.4 | Ron Clarke (Australia) | July 14 1965 |
| *Marathon* | 2 08 | 33.6 | Derek Clayton (Australia) | May 30 1969 |
| *3000 m. steeplechase* | 8 | 20.8 | Ben Jipcho (Kenya) | Jan. 15 1973 |
| *110 m. hurdles* | | 13.6 | David Hemery (England) | July 5 1969 |
| | | 13.6 | David Hemery (England) | Sept. 13 1970 |
| | | 13.6 | Godfrey Murray (Jamaica) | June 1 1972 |
| *120 y. hurdles* | | 13.5 | Danny Smith (Bahamas) | May 5 1972 |

| | | | | |
|---|---|---|---|---|
| *400 m. hurdles* | | 47.8 | John Akii-Bua (Uganda) | Sept. 2 1972 |
| *High Jump* | 7ft. | 3 in. | Peter Boyce (Australia) | Mar. 30 1968 |
| *Pole Vault* | 17ft. | 6¼in. | Kirk Bryde (Canada) | July 20 1972 |
| *Long Jump* | 27ft. | 0 in. | Lynn Davies (Wales) | June 30 1968 |
| *Triple Jump* | 55ft. | 10¼in. | Phil May (Australia) | Oct. 17 1968 |
| *Shot* | 66ft. | 2½in. | Geoff Capes (England) | July 26 1972 |
| *Discus* | 211ft. | 3 in. | George Puce (Canada) | Mar. 16 1968 |
| *Hammer* | 228ft. | 8 in. | Peter Farmer (Australia) | May 11 1973 |
| *Javelin* | 273ft. | 9 in. | David Travis (England) | Aug. 2 1970 |
| *Decathlon* | | 8,040 | Peter Gabbett (England) | May 21/2 1972 |
| *4 x 100 m.* | | 38.3 | Jamaica (Errol Stewart, Mike Fray, Clifton Forbes, Lennox Miller) | Oct. 19 1968 |
| *4 x 400 m.* | | 2 59.6 | Kenya (Charles Asati, Hezekiah Nyamau, Naftali Bon, Daniel Rudisha) | Oct. 20 1968 |

## Women

| | | | | |
|---|---|---|---|---|
| *100 m.* | | 11.1 | Raelene Boyle (Australia) | Oct. 15 1968 |
| | | 11.1 | Raelene Boyle (Australia) | Oct. 15 1968 |
| | | 11.1 | Alice Annum (Ghana) | Sept. 11 1971 |
| *200 m.* | | 22.5 | Raelene Boyle (Australia) | Sept. 7 1972 |
| *400 m.* | | 51.0 | Marilyn Neufville (Jamaica) | July 23 1970 |
| *800 m.* | | 2 00.2 | Rosemary Stirling (Scotland) | Sept. 3 1972 |
| | | 2 00.2 | Abigail Hoffman (Canada) | Sept. 3 1972 |
| *1500 m.* | | 4 04.8 | Sheila Carey (England) | Sept. 9 1972 |
| *3000 m.* | | 9 05.8 | Joyce Smith (England) | Sept. 19 1972 |
| *100 m. hurdles* | | 12.5 | Pam Ryan (Australia) | June 28 1972 |
| *200 m. hurdles* | | 25.7 | Pam Ryan (Australia) | Nov. 25 1971 |
| *High Jump* | 6ft. | 1½in. | Debbie Brill (Canada) | Aug. 5 1972 |
| | 6ft. | 1¼in. | Barbara Inkpen (England) | Sept. 15 1972 |
| *Long Jump* | 22ft. | 2¼in. | Mary Rand-Toomey (England) | Oct. 14 1964 |
| *Shot* | 56ft. | 7½in. | Valerie Young (New Zealand) | Oct. 20 1964 |
| *Discus* | 190ft. | 4 in. | Rosemary Payne (Scotland) | June 3 1972 |
| *Javelin* | 204ft. | 2 in. | Petra Rivers (Australia) | Dec. 2 1972 |
| *Pentathlon* | | 4,801 | Mary Peters (N. Ireland) | Sept. 2/3 1972 |
| *4 x 100 m.* | | 43.4 | Australia (Jenny Lamy, Joyce Bennett, Raelene Boyle, Dianne Burge) | Oct. 20 1968 |
| *4 x 400 m.* | | 3 28.7 | Great Britain (Verona Bernard, Janet Simpson, Jannette Roscoe, Rosemary Stirling) | Sept. 10 1972 |

# CROSS-COUNTRY
## English:

The first English Cross-Country Championship was held in Epping Forest in 1876, but all 32 runners went off course and the race was declared void. The inaugural champion, in 1877, was P. H. Stenning, who retained his title for the next three years. Only one man has equalled Stenning's feat of four consecutive victories: Alf Shrubb. The Championship is organised annually by the English Cross-Country Union (founded 1883).

Individual and team champions:

| *Individual* | | *Team* | *No. of Starters* |
|---|---|---|---|
| 1877 | P. H. Stenning | Thames Hare and Hounds | 33 |
| 1878 | P. H. Stenning | Spartan Harriers | 33 |
| 1879 | P. H. Stenning | Thames Hare and Hounds | 41 |
| 1880 | P. H. Stenning | Birchfield Harriers | 88 |

| | | | |
|---|---|---|---|
| 1881 | G. A. Dunning | Moseley Harriers | 105 |
| 1882 | W. G. George | Moseley Harriers | 107 |
| 1883 | G. A. Dunning | Moseley Harriers | 91 |
| 1884 | W. G. George | Moseley Harriers | 56 |
| 1885 | W. Snook | Liverpool Harriers | 66 |
| 1886 | J. E. Hickman | Birchfield Harriers | 58 |
| 1887 | J. E. Hickman | Birchfield Harriers | 54 |
| 1888 | E. W. Parry | Birchfield Harriers | 88 |
| 1889 | E. W. Parry | Salford Harriers | 82 |
| 1890 | E. W. Parry | Salford Harriers | 80 |
| 1891 | J. Kibblewhite | Birchfield Harriers | 88 |
| 1892 | H A. Heath | Birchfield Harriers | 91 |
| 1893 | H. A. Heath | Essex Beagles | 81 |
| 1894 | G. Crossland | Salford Harriers | 83 |
| 1895 | S. Cottrill | Birchfield Harriers | 149 |
| 1896 | G. Crossland | Salford Harriers | 104 |
| 1897 | S. J. Robinson | Salford Harriers, Manchester Harriers | 98 |
| 1898 | S. J. Robinson | Salford Harriers | 80 |
| 1899 | C. Bennett | Highgate Harriers | 116 |
| 1900 | C. Bennett | Finchley Harriers | 93 |
| 1901 | A. Shrubb | Essex Beagles | 113 |
| 1902 | A. Shrubb | Highgate Harriers | 159 |
| 1903 | A. Shrubb | Birchfield Harriers | 146 |
| 1904 | A. Shrubb | Highgate Harriers | 114 |
| 1905 | A. Aldridge | Highgate Harriers | 125 |
| 1906 | C. J. Straw | Sutton Harriers | 162 |
| 1907 | G. Pearce | Birchfield Harriers | 186 |
| 1908 | A. J. Robertson | Hallamshire Harriers | 252 |
| 1909 | J. Murphy | Birchfield Harriers | 163 |
| 1910 | F. C. Neaves | Hallamshire Harriers | 247 |
| 1911 | F. N. Hibbins | Hallamshire Harriers | 240 |
| 1912 | F. N. Hibbins | Hallamshire Harriers | 173 |
| 1913 | E. Glover | Birchfield Harriers | 211 |
| 1914 | C. H. Ruffell | Surrey Athletic Club | 273 |
| 1920* | C. T. Clibbon | Birchfield Harriers | 271 |
| 1921 | W. Freeman | Birchfield Harriers | 205 |
| 1922* | H. Eckersley | Birchfield Harriers | 236 |
| 1923 | C. E. Blewitt | Birchfield Harriers | 327 |
| 1924 | W. M. Cotterell | Birchfield Harriers | 219 |
| 1925 | W. M. Cotterell | Birchfield Harriers | 245 |
| 1926 | J. E. Webster | Birchfield Harriers | 321 |
| 1927 | E. Harper | Hallamshire Harriers | 429 |
| 1928 | J. E. Webster | Birchfield Harriers | 375 |
| 1929 | E. Harper | Birchfield Harriers | 247 |
| 1930 | W. B. Howard | Birchfield Harriers | 334 |
| 1931 | J. H. Potts | Birchfield Harriers | 348 |
| 1932 | J. A. Burns | Birchfield Harriers | 289 |
| 1933 | T. Evenson | Birchfield Harriers | 344 |
| 1934 | S. Dodd | Birchfield Harriers | 297 |
| 1935 | F. Close | Belgrave Harriers | 295 |
| 1936 | J. H. Potts | Birchfield Harriers | 285 |
| 1937 | H. D. Clark | Birchfield Harriers | 315 |
| 1938 | J. T. Holden | Mitcham Athletic Club | 288 |
| 1939 | J. T. Holden | Belgrave Harriers | 392 |
| 1946 | J. T. Holden | Belgrave Harriers | 239 |
| 1947 | A. A. Robertson | Sutton Harriers | 274 |
| 1948 | S. C. Wooderson | Belgrave Harriers | 402 |
| 1949 | F. E. Aaron | Sutton Harriers | 449 |
| 1950 | F. E. Aaron | Sutton Harriers | 493 |

| 1951 | F. E. Aaron | Sutton Harriers | 350 |
|------|-------------|-----------------|-----|
| 1952 | W. Hesketh | Victoria Park AAC | 418 |
| 1953 | D. A. G. Pirie | Birchfield Harriers | 473 |
| 1954 | D. A. G. Pirie | Bolton United Harriers | 419 |
| 1955 | D. A. G. Pirie | South London Harriers | 544 |
| 1956 | K. L. Norris | Sheffield United Harriers | 509 |
| 1957 | F. D. Sando | South London Harriers | 717 |
| 1958 | A. F. Perkins | South London Harriers | 574 |
| 1959 | F. Norris | Sheffield United Harriers | 617 |
| 1960 | B. B. Heatley | Derby and County AC | 662 |
| 1961 | B. B. Heatley | Derby and County AC | 796 |
| 1962 | Gerry A. North | Derby and County AC | 696 |
| 1963 | B. B. Heatley | Coventry Godiva Harriers | 857 |
| 1964 | M. R. Batty | Portsmouth AC | 840 |
| 1965 | M. R. Batty | Portsmouth AC | 908 |
| 1966 | R. Hill | North Staffs & Stone H | 919 |
| 1967 | R. G. Taylor | Portsmouth AC | 831 |
| 1968 | R. Hill | Coventry Godiva Harriers | 944 |
| 1969 | M. J. Tagg | Tipton Harriers | 1046 |
| 1970 | T. Wright | City of Stoke AC | 1023 |
| 1971 | D. C. Bedford | Shettleston Harriers | 914 |
| 1972 | M. Thomas | Tipton Harriers | 1021 |
| 1973† | D. C. Bedford | Gateshead Harriers | 1195 |

\* Actual winner was J. Guillemot (France).  † Actual winner was R. Dixon (N.Z.)

(Women champions: See under WOMEN'S AAA CHAMPIONSHIPS)

## International

The first international cross-country race on record was held between England and France at Ville d'Avray on Mar. 20th, 1898. The English scored an absolute clean sweep, all eight of their runners finishing before the first Frenchman. The individual winner was S. J. Robinson.

The International Cross-Country Championship was instituted at Hamilton Park Racecourse in Scotland on Mar. 28th, 1903. Alf Shrubb was the individual winner and he led England to victory in the team race over Ireland, Scotland and Wales. France began competing in 1907 and in 1922 became the first team to defeat England.

Jack Holden (England), Alain Mimoun (France) and Gaston Roelants (Belgium) have won the race four times, one more than the next best—Jean Bouin (France). Holden and Bouin were victorious three years running. Marcel Vandewattyne (Belgium), runner-up in the 1946 race, placed 2nd again in 1962 and was a member of Belgium's winning team in 1963. The following year he made his 19th Championship appearance.

Individual and Team Champions:
(note B—Belgium, E—England, F—France, I—Ireland, M—Morocco, S—Scotland, Sp—Spain, T—Tunisia, Y—Yugoslavia, Fi—Finland).

| | Individual | Team |
|------|-----------|------|
| 1903 | A. Shrubb (E) | England |
| 1904 | A. Shrubb (E) | England |
| 1905 | A. Aldridge (E) | England |
| 1906 | C. J. Straw (E) | England |
| 1907 | A. Underwood (E) | England |
| 1908 | A. J. Robertson (E) | England |
| 1909 | A. E. Wood (E) | England |
| 1910 | A. E. Wood (E) | England |
| 1911 | J. Bouin (F) | England |
| 1912 | J. Bouin (F) | England |
| 1913 | J. Bouin (F) | England |
| 1914 | A. H. Nicholls (E) | England |
| 1920 | J. Wilson (S) | England |
| 1921 | W. Freeman (E) | England |
| 1922 | J. Guillemot (F) | France |
| 1923 | C. E. Blewitt (E) | France |
| 1924 | W. M. Cotterell (E) | England |
| 1925 | J. E. Webster (E) | England |
| 1926 | E. Harper (E) | France |
| 1927 | L. Payne (E) | France |
| 1928 | H. Eckersley (E) | France |
| 1929 | W. M. Cotterell (E) | France |
| 1930 | T. Evenson (E) | England |
| 1931 | T. F. Smythe (I) | England |
| 1932 | T. Evenson (E) | England |

| | | |
|---|---|---|
| 1933 | J. T. Holden (E) | England |
| 1934 | J. T. Holden (E) | England |
| 1935 | J. T. Holden (E) | England |
| 1936 | W. E. Eaton (E) | England |
| 1937 | J. C. Flockhart (S) | England |
| 1938 | C. A. J. Emery (E) | England |
| 1939 | J. T. Holden (E) | France |
| 1946 | R. Pujazon (F) | France |
| 1947 | R. Pujazon (F) | France |
| 1948 | J. Doms (B) | Belgium |
| 1949 | A. Mimoun (F) | France |
| 1950 | L. Theys (B) | France |
| 1951 | G. B. Saunders (E) | England |
| 1952 | A. Mimoun (F) | France |
| 1953 | F. Mihalic (Y) | England |
| 1954 | A. Mimoun (F) | England |
| 1955 | F. D. Sando (E) | England |
| 1956 | A. Mimoun (F) | France |
| 1957 | F. D. Sando (E) | Belgium |
| 1958 | S. E. Eldon (E) | England |
| 1959 | F. Norris (E) | England |
| 1960 | A. Rhadi (M) | England |
| 1961 | B. B. Heatley (E) | Belgium |
| 1962 | G. Roelants (B) | England |
| 1963 | H. R. Fowler (E) | Belgium |
| 1964 | F. Arizmendi (Sp) | England |
| 1965 | J. C. Fayolle (F) | England |
| 1966 | A. El Ghazi (M) | England |
| 1967 | G. Roelants (B) | England |
| 1968 | M. Gammoudi (T) | England |
| 1969 | G. Roelants (B) | England |
| 1970 | M. J. Tagg (E) | England |
| 1971 | D. C. Bedford (E) | England |
| 1972 | G. Roelants (B) | England |
| 1973 | P. Paivarinta (Fi) | Belgium |

**Women**

The first women's international cross-country race on record, including English, French and Belgian runners, was held at Douai (France) in 1931. Gladys Lunn led England to victory.

Regular International Championships have been held since 1967. Individual and team champions:

| | Individual | Team |
|---|---|---|
| 1967 | D. Brown (USA) | England |
| 1968 | D. Brown (USA) | USA |
| 1969 | D. Brown (USA) | USA |
| 1970 | D. Brown (USA) | England |
| 1971 | D. Brown (USA) | England |
| 1972 | J. Smith (Eng) | England |
| 1973 | P. Cacchi (Italy) | England |

## CUTHBERT, B. (Australia)

As a triple gold medallist, the then 18-year-old Betty Cuthbert was naturally the heroine of the Melbourne Olympics in 1956. Her successes came in the 100 m., 200 m. and 4 x 100 m. relay.

Later championships were less rewarding. She was overshadowed by team-mate Marlene Willard at the 1958 Commonwealth Games, injured at the 1960 Olympics and showed indifferent form at the 1962 Commonwealth Games prior to anchoring the Australian relay team to victory. But at the 1964 Olympics, her final competition, she re-established herself as one of the all-time greats of women's athletics by winning the 400 m. in 52.0 sec.

She set a dozen individual world records between 1956 and 1963 at events ranging from 60 m. to 440 yd.

Her best marks were 7.2 sec. for 60 m.,; 10.4 sec. for 100 yd.; 11.4 sec. for 100 m.; 23.2 sec. for 200 m. and 220 yd., 52.0 sec. for 400 m., 53.3 sec. for 440 yd. and 2 min. 17.0 sec. for 880 yd. She was born at Merrylands, near Sydney, on Apr. 20th, 1938.

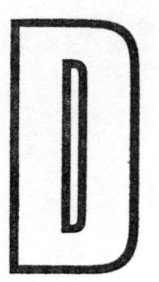

## DANEK, L. (Czechoslovakia)

For many years Ludvik Danek was burdened with the reputation of being a great discus thrower who had the unhappy knack of being unable to produce anywhere near his best form in major championships. He set world records of 211 ft. 9 in. in 1964, 213 ft. 11 in. in 1965 and 216 ft. 9 in. (unratified) in 1966, a European record of 218 ft. 2 in. in 1969 and a personal best of 219 ft. 7 in. in 1971, but his competitive record was less impressive. At the 1964 Olympics he led for four rounds before being overtaken by Al Oerter. eventually finishing 2nd with a throw of 13 ft. below his best; he was 5th in the 1966 European Championships, 3rd in the 1968 Olympics and 4th in the 1969 European.

It was not until 1971, aged 34, that he came into his own as he won the European title at his fourth attempt (he was placed 9th in 1962). The following year he triumphed at the Olympics; only 5th when he stepped into the circle for his final throw, he flung the discus 211 ft. 3 in. to deprive Jay Silvester of the first Olympic gold medal to be won in this event, other than by Oerter, for 20 years.

His annual progress: 1955—134ft. 3in., 1956—140ft. 0in., 1957—150ft. 0in., 1959—141ft. 9in., 1960—165ft. 3in., 1961—168ft. 10in., 1962—185ft. 7in., 1963—200ft. 0in., 1964—211ft. 9in., 1965—214ft. 0in., 1966—216ft. 9in., 1967—212ft. 5in., 1968—206ft. 5in., 1969—218ft. 1in., 1970—210ft. 4in., 1971—219ft. 7in., 1972—217ft. 5in. He was born at Horice on Jan. 6th, 1937.

## DA SILVA, A. F. (Brazil)

Between 1951 and 1959 Adhemar Ferreira da Silva—South America's most distinguished athlete—won every major triple jump title open to him: Olympic champion in 1952 and 1956, Pan-American titlist in 1951, 1955 and 1959. He was placed 14th in his farewell Olympic appearance in 1960, aged 32.

The lithe Brazilian jumped over 52 feet for 11 seasons running (1950-1960) and he held the world record from 1950 to 1953 and from 1955 to 1958. In his ultimate world record of 54 ft. 4 in. in 1955 he hopped 20 ft. $7\frac{1}{4}$ in., stepped 16 ft. 3 in. and jumped 17 ft. $5\frac{3}{4}$ in.

Other best marks included 11.1 sec. for 100 m., 21.0 sec. (wind assisted) for straight 220 yd., 6 ft. $0\frac{1}{4}$ in. high jump and 24 ft. $0\frac{1}{2}$ in. long jump. He was born at Sao Paulo on Sept. 29th, 1927.

## DAVIES, L. (GB)

Lynn Davies made important British athletics history in Tokyo on Oct. 18th, 1964 for in defeating Ralph Boston (USA) and Igor Ter-Ovanesyan (USSR)—the world's only 27ft. long jumpers—he became Wales' first Olympic champion and the first man from Great Britain to win an Olympic field event. Tim Ahearne, the 1908 triple jump victor, was an Irishman.

Davies' triumph was utterly unexpected; even he would have been happy with third place. The damp and desolate conditions were probably less alien to Davies than to most of his rivals but the measure of his achievement was that he was the only competitor to set a personal best, his 26ft. $5\frac{3}{4}$in. in the 5th round being accomplished off a soggy runway and into an 0.7 m. per sec. breeze. Truly magnificent jumping.

He went on to complete a unique set of gold medals by capturing the Commonwealth (26 ft. $2\frac{3}{4}$ in.) and European (26 ft $2\frac{1}{4}$ in.) titles in 1966, and the following year he won the European indoor championships. Hopes of retaining his Olympic laurels in 1968, the year in which he jumped exactly 27 feet, were dashed by Bob Beamon's awe-inspiring opening leap and a deflated Davies merely went through the motions in placing 9th.

Three more medals were added to his collection when he took 2nd place in the 1969 European Championships, indoors and out, and retained his Commonwealth title (26 ft. 5¼ in. wind assisted) in 1970. He finished a close 4th in the 1971 European Championships, a mere 2¾ in. behind the winner, in spite of suffering from tonsillitis but injury proved too much for him in 1972 and in his Olympic farewell he failed to qualify for the final.

During his career he raised the UK record by almost two feet and jumped 26 feet or better 67 times in competition. He was also one of Britain's finest sprinters and, as a junior, a most promising triple jumper.

His best marks: 9.5 sec. for 100 yd., 10.4 sec. for 100 m., 21.2 sec. for 220 yd., 6ft. 2in. high jump (in training), 27ft 0in. long jump and 50ft. 7½in. triple jump. His annual long jump progress: 1960—22ft. 11in., 1961—23ft. 5½in., 1962—25ft. 4in., 1963—25ft. 0in., 1964—26ft. 5⅜in., 1965—25ft. 10¾in., 1966—26ft. 10in., 1967—26ft. 8¼in., 1968—27ft. 0in., 1969—26ft. 8½in., 1970—25ft. 10½in. (and wind assisted 26ft. 5½in.), 1971—26ft. 0in., 1972—25ft. 6in. He was born at Nantymoel, Glamorgan, on May 20th, 1942.

## DAVIS, G. A. (USA)

Glenn Davis is the only man to have won the Olympic 400 m. hurdles twice, in 1956 and 1960. He captured another gold medal in Rome, running a 45.4 sec. leg for the US team that won the 4 x 400 m. relay in the world record time of 3 min. 02.2 sec.

Previously a "one-man team" in high school, Davis made his 400 m. hurdling debut in Apr. 1956, and returned an unexceptional 54.4 sec. So swiftly did he improve, though, that only two months later he sliced no less than nine-tenths of a second off the world record with a time of 49.5 sec.!

He set further world records at 440 yd. flat (45.7 sec.), 400 m. hurdles (49.2 sec.) and 440 yd. hurdles (49.9 sec.) in 1958 and two seasons later, just prior to successfully defending his Olympic laurels, he equalled the world record of 22.5 sec. for 200 m. hurdles (turn).

Other best marks: 100 yd. in 9.7 sec., 100 m. in 10.3 sec., 200 m. (turn) in 21.0 sec., 400 m. in 45.5 sec., 120 yd. hurdles in 14.3 sec., high jump of 6ft. 3½in. (indoors) and long jump of 24ft. 0¼in. He was born at Wellsburg, West Virginia, on Sept. 12th, 1934.

## DECATHLON

A decathlon consists of ten events, four track and six field, which are held on two consecutive days in the following order. First day: 100 m., long jump, shot, high jump and 400 m. Second day: 110 m. hurdles, discus, pole vault, javelin and 1500 m.

An athlete is allowed three trials in the long jump and throwing events. A special rule applicable to the decathlon is that two (as distinct from one) false starts can be committed in the track events without incurring disqualification. The decathlon competitor must start in each of the ten events, or else he will be considered to have abandoned the competition and will not figure in the final classification.

Placings in a decathlon competition are determined by the total number of points scored by each competitor per the International Amateur Athletic Federation scoring tables. In theory it is possible for an athlete to win a decathlon without actually placing first in any of the ten events.

The current scoring tables were adopted by the IAAF in 1962 and used for the first time in 1964. Each performance recorded by a competitor is worth a certain number of points ranging from 1 to 1,200. The first class decathlon exponent averages about 800 points per event.

The decathlon entered the Olympic programme in 1912 and right away became the centre of fierce controversy. The event was won by a handsome margin by Jim Thorpe (USA), who was later branded as a professional and whose name was deleted from the official results. His score (converted to the 1950 tables) of 6,267 points was not bettered until 1930, although it must be pointed out that

71

the 1912 Olympic event was spread over three days.

Harold Osborn (USA) was the first to score over 6,000 points in normal conditions when he added the 1924 Olympic title to his gold medal in the high jump. Ten years later the European champion Hans-Heinrich Sievert (Germany) led the way past 7,000 points.

The next great name was Glenn Morris (USA), later to portray Tarzan on the screen, who won the 1936 Olympic honours with the record score of 7,310. That mark withstood all assaults until 1950 when Bob Mathias (USA), who had two years earlier become the youngest ever Olympic athletics champion, set the first of three records which culminated in his scoring 7,887 in defence of his title in 1952.

The distinction of cracking 8,000 points for the first time was won by Vasiliy Kuznyetsov (USSR), three times European champion, in 1958. Rafer Johnson (USA) seized the record after barely two months but the Russian recaptured the mark the following season. Johnson replied with 8,683 in 1960, won the Olympic title after a thrilling battle with his friend Yang Chuan-kwang (Taiwan) and retired.

The next world record holder, who was Yang Chuan-kwang, caused no little embarrassment during the course of his 1963 record (9,121) by vaulting 15ft. 10½in. The scoring tables were made redundant by this performance as points were listed only up to 15ft. 9¾in.

Under the new tables, Yang's record score became 8,089 points, a mark that was bettered in 1966 by Bill Toomey (USA). Toomey was succeeded in 1972 as Olympic titlist and world record holder (8,417) by Nikolay Avilov (USSR) with a score of 8,454.

Britain's greatest all-rounder is Peter Gabbett, Commonwealth silver medallist in 1970 and 6th in the 1971 European Championships. He scored over 8000 pts. in 1972 but failed to finish at the Olympics, the highest British placing remaining 9th by Geoff Elliott in 1952.

See also under AVILOV, N., JOHN-SON, R. L.; MATHIAS, R. B.; THORPE, J. H.; TOOMEY, W.

## DE LA HUNTY, S. B. (Australia)

No other woman athlete has garnered such a dazzling array of Olympic medals as Mrs. Shirley De La Hunty (née Strickland). The 80 m. hurdles champion in 1952 and 1956 (a unique double), having finished third in 1948, she was also 100 m. bronze medallist in 1948 and 1952 and as a member of the Australian relay team picked up a silver in 1948 and her third gold in 1956. Her Commonwealth Games tally of two gold and two silver medals adds still further lustre to her collection.

Although best known as a hurdler (the first woman to break 11 sec.), Shirley's fastest time of 10.7 sec. was perhaps surpassed by her former world record of 11.3 sec. for 100 m.

In 1960, when well into her thirties, she ran 100 yd. in 10.9 sec. Her father was a professional athlete and her brother placed fourth in the 1953 Australian 220 yd. hurdles championship. Born at Guildford, Western Australia, on July 18th, 1925, her best marks in addition to the above are 10.6 sec. for 100 yd., 24.1 sec. for 200 m. and 56.9 sec. for 440 yd.

## DILLARD, W. H. (USA)

It was the sight of Jesse Owens being cheered through the streets of Cleveland following his 1936 Olympic triumphs that inspired 13-year-old Harrison Dillard to try his luck at athletics. Helped in his formative years by Owens himself, Dillard developed after the war into a superb hurdler and sprinter.

He posted his first world record in 1946 at 220 yd. hurdles, an event in which Owens was a previous record-holder. Between May 1947 and June 1948 he won 82 successive sprint and hurdle races—an incredible run of success. His winning streak included a world record 120 yd. hurdles time of 13.6 sec. in Apr. 1948 but tragedy befell him in the US Olympic trials when he took a spill and failed to make the team as a hurdler.

Fortunately he qualified as third string in the 100 m., and at Wembley he scored a dramatic victory in 10.3 sec. to equal Jesse's Olympic record. Four years later he made up for his previous lapse by taking the high hurdles and for the second time was a member of the winning 4 x 100 m. relay team. He made a comeback at 33 in an attempt to defend his Olympic title but he finished sixth in the US trials.

His explosive start was particularly well suited to indoor racing and he won the AAU 60 yd. hurdles title seven years running. Only 5 ft. 10 in. tall, Dillard proved that a great hurdler need not of necessity be long and lanky.

Best marks: 9.4 sec. for 100 yd., 10.3 sec. for 100 m., 20.8 sec. for 200 m. (turn), 13.6 sec. for 120 yd. hurdles, 22.3 sec. for 220 yd. hurdles (straight), 23.0 sec. for 220 yd. hurdles (turn), 53.7 sec. for 400 m. hurdles. He was born in Cleveland on July 8th, 1923.

# DISCUS

Discus throwing was popular among the ancient Greeks, but the event as it is known today dates from the closing years of the 19th century. The minimum weight of the implement was fixed at 2 Kg. (4 lb. 6½ oz.) but for some years there were three sizes of throwing area in use: a 7 ft. circle in the USA, 7 ft. square in Central Europe, 8 ft. 10¼ in. circle in Scandinavia. The inside diameter of the throwing circle was standardised at 2.50 m. (8 ft. 2½ in.) by 1912.

The International Amateur Athletic Federation rules that " the body of the discus shall be made of wood or other suitable material with metal plates set flush into the sides and shall have, in the exact centre of the circle framed by the metal rim, a means of securing the correct weight."

A throw, to be recorded as valid, must fall within a 45 deg. sector. A foul is recorded when a competitor, after he has stepped into the circle and started to make his throw, touches the ground outside the circle or the top of the circle with any part of his body.

The first great figure in discus throwing was Irish-born Martin Sheri-

dan (USA), who between 1902 and 1909 increased the world record eight times, starting with 129 ft. 4 in. and ending with 144 ft. 0 in. He was Olympic champion in 1904 (after a throw-off with team-mate Ralph Rose) and 1908. Two other men have retained an Olympic title: Clarence Houser (USA), champion in 1924 and 1928; and Al Oerter (USA), gold medallist in 1956, 1960, 1964, and 1968 and the first man to exceed 200ft. (in 1962).

Previously the 150 ft. landmark had been reached first by James Duncan (USA) in 1912, 160 ft. by Hans Hoffmeister (Germany) in 1928, 170 ft. by the American-born Swede, Harold Andersson, in 1934, 180 ft. by Bob Fitch (USA) in 1946, 190 ft. by Sim Iness (USA) in 1953 and 60 m. (196 ft. 10 in.) by yet another American, Jay Silvester, in 1961. Silvester is the current world record holder.

Discus throwers tend to enjoy longer careers in top-flight competition than most of their athletic brethren. For example, Adolfo Consolini (Italy), the 1948 Olympic winner and three times European champion, was throwing over 180 ft. at the age of 43, and Ludvik Danek (Czechoslovakia) won the 1972 Olympic title aged 35.

Britain has little in the way of tradition in this event. The highest Olympic placing is fourth in 1956 by Mark Pharaoh, who succeeded in raising the national record over 22 ft. in three years, whilst no UK athlete has ever won the Commonwealth title or even placed in the first six at the European Championships, Bill Tancred became the first Briton over 200 ft. in 1972.

See also under DANEK, L., OERTER, A. A. and SILVESTER, L. J.

# Women

Female competitors of all age groups use a 1 kg. discus. Nina Dumbadze (USSR) was responsible for transforming the event. When she began her career in 1936 the world record stood at 158 ft. 6 in. by Gisela Mauermeyer (Germany), but by 1952 she had raised the mark to 187 ft. 2 in. Liesel Westermann (W. Germany), was the first to reach the twin landmarks of 60 m. and 200 ft. (in 1967) and six years later the world record was standing at 221 ft. 3 in. by Faina Melnik of the USSR. Also in 1972 Rosemary Payne raised the UK record, at the age of 39, to 190 ft. 4 in.

See also under MELNIK, F. and MENIS, A.

# DOUBELL, R. D. (Australia)

It was an Australian—Edwin Flack —who won the first Olympic 800 m. title back in 1896 (time: 2 min. 11 sec.!), but no other Australian subsequently placed even in the first six until Ralph Doubell's upset victory in the 1968 Olympics. Doubell's performance was all the more startling since he equalled Peter Snell's world record of 1 min. 44.3 sec. in unfamiliar high altitude conditions. To win an Olympic gold medal with a world record is the ultimate in athletic achievement, so Doubell must be rated one of the all-time greats of 800 m. running even though he never approached that run either before or since.

He disappointed at the 1966 Commonwealth Games where he was placed only sixth in the 880 yd. but he gave a better indication of his Olympic prospects when winning the 800 m. from European record holder Franz-Josef Kemper in the 1967 World Student Games.

In Mexico City he ran a faultless race. A comfortable fourth at halfway he moved into second along the back straight and burst past the pace-setter Wilson Kiprugut 50 m. from home.

His pre-Mexico best time had stood at 1 min. 46.2 secs.

Doubell went on to score some notable indoor successes in the USA, including a world best of 2 min. 05.5 sec. for 1000 yd. early in 1970, but was completely off form at the Commonwealth Games later that year— again placing sixth. A severe Achilles tendon injury forced him into premature retirement early in 1972. His best performances included 1 min. 44.3 sec. for 800 m., 2 min. 20.8 sec. for 1000 m. and 4 min. 00.5 sec. for the mile. He was born on Feb. 11th, 1945.

# DUMAS, C. E. (USA)

The first man to high jump 7 ft. in authentic competition was 6 ft. 1 in. tall Charles Dumas (USA). He performed this historic feat in June 1956 aged 19, by straddling 7 ft. 0½ in. Later that year he captured the Olympic title.

Dumas was an outstanding competitor—winner of the US championship five successive years (1955-59) and Pan-American champion in 1959. He did not compete in 1961, 1962 or 1963 but made a brilliant comeback in Apr. 1964 with a leap of 7ft. 0¼in.

Far from extraordinary as a 14-year-old (best of only 4 ft. 11 in.) or 15-year-old (5 ft. 6 in.) he improved rapidly to 6 ft. 2 in. at 16, 6 ft. 5½ in. at 17 and 6 ft. 10¼ in. at 18. In Nov. 1956 he attained 7 ft. 0¼ in. in an exhibition. He was also a useful high hurdler, with a best time of 14.1 sec. for 120 yd. He was born at Tulsa, Oklahoma, on Feb. 12th, 1937.

## EHRHARDT, A.
### (East Germany)

European junior 80 m. hurdles (2 ft. 6 in.) champion in 1968, under her maiden name of Jahns, Annelie Ehrhardt made an unspectacular start to her career at 100 m. hurdles (2 ft. 9 in.) when this event replaced the shorter distance in 1969. She ran only a mediocre 14.1 sec. that season. Just a year later, though, she was universally acknowledged as one of the great hurdlers, with a best time of 12.9 sec. and a share in the world record of 25.8 sec. for 200 m. hurdles.

But she was still overshadowed by her illustrious East German colleague Karin Balzer, 12 years her senior, during 1971 (Annelie finished second to her in the European Championships) but in 1972 she emerged as the world's undisputed number one. Significantly faster on the flat (11.3 sec. for 100 m.), and even more efficient in her hurdling form, she cut the world record to 12.5 sec. and swept to Olympic victory by the remarkably wide margin of a quarter of a second. In Munich she was timed at 12.59 sec. (electrical) into a breeze of 0.6 metres per second, the finest performance yet by a woman hurdler.

Her best marks include 11.3 sec. for 100 m., 12.5 sec. for 100 m. hurdles, 25.8 sec. for 200 m. hurdles and 20 ft. 2¼ in. long jump. Annual hurdling progress: 1964—11.5 (80 m.); 1965—11.3; 1966—11.1; 1967—11.0; 1968—11.0, 15.2 (100 m.); 1969—14.1, 27.6 (200 m.); 1970—12.9, 25.8; 1971—12.7, 26.8; 1972—12.5. She was born at Ohrsleben on June 18th, 1950.

## ELLIOTT, H. J. (Australia)

From 1954, when at the age of 16 he commenced serious training, until his retirement in 1962 Herb Elliott never lost a mile or 1500 m. race. The greatest mile competitor of them all won each of the three major championships he contested: the 880 yd. and mile at the 1958 Commonwealth Games and the 1960 Olympic 1500 m. He broke 4 min. for the mile on 17 occasions.

Here are some of the highlights of his glittering career:—1954: 1 min. 58.2 sec. 880 yd. and 4 min. 25.6 sec. mile (56.8 sec. first lap!) at the age of 16.

1955: Improved to 1 min. 55.8 sec. and 4 min. 20.8 sec. while still 16; later in the year ran 4 min. 20.4 sec. Percy Cerutty saw him win a 4 min. 22 sec. mile, said " this boy can be coached to break Landy's world mile record of 3 min. 57.9 sec. by the end of 1958 " and proceeded to do just that.

1957: Still 18, set world junior bests of 3 min. 47.8 sec. for 1500 m., 4 min. 04.3 sec. for the mile, 9 min. 01.0 sec. for 2 mi. and 14 min. 02.4 sec. for 3 mi., plus a personal best half-mile of 1 min. 50.8 sec. Shortly after his 19th birthday he won the Australian mile (4 min. 00.4 sec.) and 880 yd. (1 min. 49.3 sec.) titles.

1958: Ran his first four-minute mile before his 20th birthday; posted world records for the mile (3 min. 54.5 sec.) and 1500 m. (3 min. 36.0 sec.); won two titles at the Commonwealth Games in Cardiff; set Commonwealth 880 yd. record of 1 min. 47.3 sec.; in the space of eight days successively ran 3 min. 36.0 sec. for 1500 m., 3 min. 58.0 sec. mile, 3 min. 55.4 sec. mile and 3 min. 37.4 sec. 1500 m. Rejected an £89,000 offer to turn professional.

1959: No overseas competition but ran 3 min. 58.9 sec. mile and contributed to a world record in the 4 x mile relay.

1960: Won the Olympic 1500 m. by the extraordinary margin of 20 yards in a world record of 3 min. 35.6 sec.

Elliott's personal best marks were 50.7 sec. for 440 yd., 1 min. 47.3 sec. for 880 yd., 2 min. 19.1 sec. for 1000 m., 3 min. 35.6 sec. for 1500 m., 3 min. 54.5 sec. for the mile, 8 min. 09.5 sec. for 3000 m., 8 min. 37.6 sec.

for 2 mi. and 14 min. 09.9 sec. for 5000 m. He was born at Subiaco, near Perth, on Feb. 25th, 1938.

# EUROPEAN CHAMPION-SHIPS

The European Championships were started in Turin in 1934. The driving force behind their establishment was a Hungarian, Szilard Stankovits. Subsequently, Championships were held in Paris (1938), Oslo (1946), Brussels (1950), Berne (1954), Stockholm (1958). Belgrade (1962), Budapest (1966), Athens (1969) and Helsinki (1971). The next Championships will be staged in Rome in 1974. Britain did not send a team to the 1934 Championships; the Soviet Union competed for the first time in 1946. A separate Women's Championships took place in Vienna in 1938, but since 1946 the Championships have featured men's and women's events.

The West German team withdrew from all the individual events at the 1969 Championships in protest against the IAAF's ruling that a member of that team, Jurgen May (who defected from East Germany in 1967) was ineligible to compete.

## British Medallists

The following athletes, listed in alphabetical order, have won European Championship medals while representing Britain. G signifies gold (1st), S silver (2nd) and B bronze (3rd).

Alder, J. N. C., 1969, marathon (B).
Archer, J., 1946, 100 m. (G).
Baldwin, A. G., 1938, 4 x 400 m. (S).
Bannister, R. G., 1950, 800 m. (B); 1954, 1500 m. (G).
Barnes, J. G., 1938, 4 x 400 m. (S).
Blinston, J. A., 1969, 5000 m. (B).
Box, K. J., 1954, 4 x 100 m. (S).
Breacker, A., 1958, 4 x 100 m. (S).
Brightwell, R. I., 1962, 400 m. (G) and 4 x 400 m. (S).
Brown, A. G. K., 1938, 400 m. (G), 4 x 400 m. (S) and 4 x 100 m. (B).
Carter, A. W., 1971, 800 m. (B).
Chataway, C. J., 1954, 5000 m. (S).
Clark, D. McD. M., 1946, hammer (B).

Davies, L., 1966, long jump (G); 1969, long jump (S).
Ede, D. R., 1946, 4 x 400 m. (S).
Elliott, B. W., 1946, 4 x 400 m. (S).
Elliott, G. M., 1954, pole vault (B).
Ellis, G. S., 1954, 4 x 100 m. (S), 100 m. (B) and 200 m. (B).
Finlay, D. O., 1938, 110 m. hurdles (G).
Forbes, H., 1946, 50 km. walk (S).
Foster, B., 1971, 1500 m. (B).
Fowler, H. R., 1962, 10,000 m. (B).
Hemery, D. P., 1969, 110 m. hurdles (S).
Hewson, B. S., 1958, 1500 m. (G).
Hildreth, P. B., 1950 110 m. hurdles (B).
Hill, R., 1969, marathon (G); 1971, marathon (B).
Hogan, J. J., 1966, marathon (G).
Holden, J. T., 1950, marathon (G).
Jackson, B. D., 1962, 4 x 400 m. (S).
Jenkins, D. A., 1971, 400 m. (G).
Jones, D. H., 1962, 4 x 100 m. (B).
Jones, K. J., 1954, 4 x 100 m. (S).
Jones, R., 1962, 4 x 100 m. (B).
Jones, T. B., 1962, 4 x 100 m. (B).
Kilby, B. L., 1962, marathon (G).
Lewis, L. C., 1950, 4 x 400 m. (B).
MacIsaac, J., 1958, 4 x 400 m. (G).
Matthews, K. J., 1962, 20 km. walk (G).
Meakin, A., 1962, 4 x 100 m. (B).
Megnin, C., 1946, 50 km. walk (B).
Metcalfe, A. P., 1962, 4 x 400 m. (S).
Nankeville, G. W., 1950, 1500 m. (B).
Nihill, V. P., 1969, 20 km. walk (G); 1971, 20 km. walk (B).
Norris, F., 1958, marathon (B).
Page, E. L., 1938, 4 x 100 m. (B).
Parker, F. J., 1954, 110 m. hurdles (S).
Parlett, H. J., 1950, 800 m. (G).
Pascoe, A. P., 1969, 110 m. hurdles (B); 1971, 110 m. hurdles (S).
Paterson, A. S., 1946, high jump (S); 1950, high jump (G).
Pennington, A., 1938, 4 x 400 m. (S) and 200 m. (B).
Pike, M. W., 1950, 4 x 400 m. (G).
Pirie, D. A. G., 1958, 5000 m. (B).
Pugh, D. C., 1946, 4 x 400 m. (S) and 400 m. (B); 1950, 400 m. (G) and 4 x 400 m. (G).
Radford, P. F., 1958, 4 x 100 m. (S) and 100 m. (B).
Rawson, M. A., 1958, 800 m. (G).
Roberts, W., 1946, 4 x 400 m. (S).
Rowe, A., 1958, shot (G).
Salisbury, J. E., 1958, 4 x 400 m. (G) and 400 m. (S).

76

Sampson, E. J., 1958, 4 x 400 m. (G).
Sando, F. D., 1954, 10,000 m. (B).
Sandstrom, E. R., 1958, 4 x 100 m. (S).
Scarr, M. M., 1938, 4 x 100 m. (B).
Scott, A. W., 1950, 4 x 400 m. (G).
Segal, D. H., 1958, 200 m. (S) and 4 x 100 m. (S).
Shenton, B., 1950, 200 m. (G); 1954, 4 x 100 m. (S).
Sherwood, J., 1969, 400 m. hurdles (S).
Stewart, I., 1969, 5000 m. (G).
Sweeney, A. W., 1938, 4 x 100 m. (B).
Tagg, M. J., 1969, 10,000 m. (S).
Thompson, D. J., 1962, 50 km. walk (B).
Todd, A. C., 1969, 400 m. hurdles (B).
Tulloh, M. B. S., 1962, 5000 m. (G).
Vickers, S. F., 1958, 20 km. walk (G).
Whetton, J. H., 1969, 1500 m. (G).
Whitlock, H. H., 1938, 50 km. walk (G).
Whittle, H., 1950, 400 m. hurdles (B).
Wilcock, K. J., 1962, 4 x 400 m. (S).
Wooderson, S. C., 1938, 1500 m. (G); 1946, 5000 m. (G).
Wright, T., 1971, marathon (S).
Wrighton, J. D., 1958, 400 m. (G) and 4 x 400 m. (G).
Yarrow, S. S., 1938, marathon (S).

*Women*
Arden, D., 1962, 4 x 100 m. (B).
Board, L. B., 1969, 800 m. (G). and 4 x 400 m. (G).
Cobb, V. M., 1958, 4 x 100 m. (S).
Cooper, S. A., 1969, 4 x 100 m. (B).
Crowther, B., 1950, pentathlon (S).
Desforges, J. C., 1950, 4 x 100 m. (G); 1954, long jump (G).
Dew, M. C., 1958, 4 x 100 m. (S).
Elliott, P. G., 1954, 80 m. hurdles (B).
Gardner, M. A. J., 1950, 80 m. hurdles (S).
Grieveson, E. J., 1962, 400 m. (S).
Hall, D. G., 1950, 4 x 100 m. (G) and 200 m. (B).
Hay, E., 1950, 4 x 100 m. (G).
Hiscox, M. E., 1958, 400 m. (B).
Hopkins, T. E., 1954, high jump (G).
Hyman, D., 1958, 4 x 100 m. (S); 1962, 100 m. (G), 200 m. (S) and 4 x 100 m. (B).
Inkpen, B. J., 1971, high jump (S).
Jordan, W., 1946, 100 m. (S) and 200 m. (S).
Knowles, L. Y., 1962, high jump (B).
Leather, D. S., 1954, 800 m. (S); 1958, 800 m. (S).

Lerwill, S. W., 1950, high jump (G).
Lowe, P. B., 1969, 4 x 400 m. (G); 1971, 800 m. (S).
Neil, D. A., 1969, 100 m. (B), and 4 x 100 m. (B).
Packer, A. E., 1962, 4 x 100 m. (B).
Pashley, A., 1954, 100 m. (B).
Paul, J. F., 1950, 4 x 100 m. (G) and 100 m. (B).
Peat, V., 1969, 200 m. (B), and 4 x 100 m. (B).
Pirie, S., 1954, 200 m. (B).
Quinton, C. L., 1958, 4 x 100 m. (S).
Ramsden, D. I., 1969, 4 x 100 m. (B).
Rand, M. D., 1962, long jump (B) and 4 x 100 m. (B).
Shirley, D. A., 1958, high jump (B).
Simpson, J. M., 1969, 4 x 400 m. (G).
Stirling, R. O., 1969, 4 x 400 m. (G); 1971, 800 m. (B).
Tyler, D. J. B., 1950, high jump (S).
Young, H. J., 1958, 100 m. (G).

## Champions

| *100 Metres* | | sec. |
|---|---|---|
| 1934 | C. D. Berger (Netherlands) | 10.6 |
| 1938 | M. B. Osendarp (Netherlands) | 10.5 |
| 1946 | J. Archer (GB) | 10.6 |
| 1950 | E. Bally (France) | 10.7 |
| 1954 | H. Futterer (Germany) | 10.5 |
| 1958 | A. Hary (Germany) | 10.3 |
| 1962 | C. Piquemal (France) | 10.4 |
| 1966 | W. J. Maniak (Poland) | 10.5 |
| 1969 | V. Borzov (USSR) | 10.4 |
| 1971 | V. Borzov (USSR) | 10.3 |

| *200 Metres* | | sec. |
|---|---|---|
| 1934 | C. D. Berger (Netherlands) | 21.5 |
| 1938 | M. B. Osendarp (Netherlands) | 21.2 |
| 1946 | N. Karakulov (USSR) | 21.6 |
| 1950 | B. Shenton (GB) | 21.5 |
| 1954 | H. Futterer (Germany) | 20.9 |
| 1958 | M. Germar (Germany) | 21.0 |
| 1962 | O. Jonsson (Sweden) | 20.7 |
| 1966 | R. Bambuck (France) | 20.9 |
| 1969 | P. Clerc (Switzerland) | 20.6 |
| 1971 | V. Borzov (USSR) | 20.3 |

| *400 Metres* | | sec. |
|---|---|---|
| 1934 | A. Metzner (Germany) | 47.9 |
| 1938 | A. G. K. Brown (GB) | 47.4 |
| 1946 | N. Holst Sorensen (Denmark) | 47.9 |
| 1950 | D. C. Pugh (GB) | 47.3 |
| 1954 | A. Ignatyev (USSR) | 46.6 |
| 1958 | J. D. Wrighton (GB) | 46.3 |
| 1962 | R. I. Brightwell (GB) | 45.9 |

77

| 1966 | S. Gredzinski (Poland) | 46.0 |
|------|------------------------|------|
| 1969 | J. Werner (Poland) | 45.7 |
| 1971 | D. A. Jenkins (GB) | 45.5 |

**800 Metres** — min. sec.

| 1934 | M. Szabo (Hungary) | 1 | 52.0 |
|------|--------------------|---|------|
| 1938 | R. Harbig (Germany) | 1 | 50.6 |
| 1946 | R. Gustafsson (Sweden) | 1 | 51.0 |
| 1950 | H. J. Parlett (GB) | 1 | 50.5 |
| 1954 | L. Szentgali (Hungary) | 1 | 47.1 |
| 1958 | M. A. Rawson (GB) | 1 | 47.8 |
| 1962 | M. Matuschewski (Germany) | 1 | 50.5 |
| 1966 | M. Matuschewski (E. Germany) | 1 | 45.9 |
| 1969 | D. Fromm (E. Germany) | 1 | 45.9 |
| 1971 | Y. Arzhanov (USSR) | 1 | 45.6 |

**1500 Metres** — min. sec.

| 1934 | L. Beccali (Italy) | 3 | 54.6 |
|------|--------------------|---|------|
| 1938 | S. C. Wooderson (GB) | 3 | 53.6 |
| 1946 | L. Strand (Sweden) | 3 | 48.0 |
| 1950 | W. F. Slijkhuis (Netherlands) | 3 | 47.2 |
| 1954 | R. G. Bannister (GB) | 3 | 43.8 |
| 1958 | B. S. Hewson (GB) | 3 | 41.9 |
| 1962 | M. Jazy (France) | 3 | 40.9 |
| 1966 | B. Tummler (W. Germany) | 3 | 41.9 |
| 1969 | J. H. Whetton (GB) | 3 | 39.4 |
| 1971 | F. Arese (Italy) | 3 | 38.4 |

**5000 Metres** — min. sec.

| 1934 | R. Rochard (France) | 14 | 36.8 |
|------|---------------------|----|------|
| 1938 | T. A. Maki (Finland) | 14 | 26.8 |
| 1946 | S. C. Wooderson (GB) | 14 | 08.6 |
| 1950 | E. Zatopek (Czecho-slovakia) | 14 | 03.0 |
| 1954 | V. Kuts (USSR) | 13 | 56.6 |
| 1958 | Z. Krzyszkowiak (Poland) | 13 | 53.4 |
| 1962 | M. B. S. Tulloh (GB) | 14 | 00.6 |
| 1966 | M. Jazy (France) | 13 | 42.8 |
| 1969 | I. Stewart (GB) | 13 | 44.8 |
| 1971 | J. Vaatainen (Finland) | 13 | 32.6 |

**10,000 Metres** — min. sec.

| 1934 | I. Salminen (Finland) | 31 | 02.6 |
|------|-----------------------|----|------|
| 1938 | I. Salminen (Finland) | 30 | 52.4 |
| 1946 | V. J. Heino (Finland) | 29 | 52.0 |
| 1950 | E. Zatopek (Czecho-slovakia) | 29 | 12.0 |
| 1954 | E. Zatopek (Czecho-slovakia) | 28 | 58.0 |
| 1958 | Z. Krzyszkowiak (Poland) | 28 | 56.0 |
| 1962 | P. Bolotnikov (USSR) | 28 | 54.0 |
| 1966 | J. Haase (E. Germany) | 28 | 26.0 |
| 1969 | J. Haase (E. Germany) | 28 | 41.6 |
| 1971 | J. Vaatainen (Finland) | 27 | 52.8 |

**Marathon** — hr. min. sec.

| 1934 | A. A. Toivonen (Finland) | 2 | 52 | 29.0 |
|------|--------------------------|---|----|------|
| 1938 | V. Muinonen (Finland) | 2 | 37 | 28.8 |
| 1946* | M. Hietanen (Finland) | 2 | 24 | 55.0 |
| 1950 | J. T. Holden (GB) | 2 | 32 | 13.2 |
| 1954 | V. L. Karvonen (Finland) | 2 | 24 | 51.6 |
| 1958 | S. Popov (USSR) | 2 | 15 | 17.0 |
| 1962 | B. L. Kilby (GB) | 2 | 23 | 18.8 |
| 1966 | J. J. Hogan (GB) | 2 | 20 | 04.6 |
| 1969 | R. Hill (GB) | 2 | 16 | 47.8 |
| 1971 | K. Lismont (Belgium) | 2 | 13 | 09.0 |

\* Under standard distance of 26 mi. 385 yd.

**3000 Metres Steeplechase** — min. sec.

| 1938 | L. A. Larsson (Sweden) | 9 | 16.2 |
|------|------------------------|---|------|
| 1946 | R. Pujazon (France) | 9 | 01.4 |
| 1950 | J. Roudny (Czecho-slovakia) | 9 | 05.4 |
| 1954 | S. Rozsnyoi (Hungary) | 8 | 49.6 |
| 1958 | J. Chromik (Poland) | 8 | 38.2 |
| 1962 | G. Roelants (Belgium) | 8 | 32.6 |
| 1966 | V. Kudinskiy (USSR) | 8 | 26.6 |
| 1969 | M. Zhelev (Bulgaria) | 8 | 25.0 |
| 1971 | J-P. Villain (France) | 8 | 25.2 |

**110 Metres Hurdles** — sec.

| 1934 | J. Kovacs (Hungary) | 14.8 |
|------|---------------------|------|
| 1938 | D. O. Finlay (GB) | 14.3 |
| 1946 | E. H. Lidman (Sweden) | 14.6 |
| 1950 | A. J. Marie (France) | 14.6 |
| 1954 | Y. Bulanchik (USSR) | 14.4 |
| 1958 | K. M. Lauer (Germany) | 13.7 |
| 1962 | A. Mikhailov (USSR) | 13.8 |
| 1966 | E. Ottoz (Italy) | 13.7 |
| 1969 | E. Ottoz (Italy) | 13.5 |
| 1971 | F. Siebeck (E. Germany) | 14.0 |

**400 Metres Hurdles** — sec.

| 1934 | H. Scheele (Germany) | 53.2 |
|------|----------------------|------|
| 1938 | P. Joye (France) | 53.1 |
| 1946 | B. Storskrubb (Finland) | 52.2 |
| 1950 | A. Filiput (Italy) | 51.9 |
| 1954 | A. Yulin (USSR) | 50.5 |
| 1958 | Y. Lituyev (USSR) | 51.1 |
| 1962 | S. Morale (Italy) | 49.2 |
| 1966 | R. Frinolli (Italy) | 49.8 |
| 1969 | V. Skomorokhov (USSR) | 49.7 |
| 1971 | J-C Nallet (France) | 49.2 |

**4 x 100 Metres Relay** — sec.

| 1934 | Germany (E. Schein, E. Gillmeister, G. Hornberger, E. Borchmeyer) | 41.0 |
|------|---|---|

| | | |
|---|---|---|
| 1938 | Germany (M. Kersch, G. Hornberger, K. Neckermann, J. Scheuring) | 40.9 |
| 1946 | Sweden (S. Danielsson, I. Nilsson, O. Laessker, S. Hakansson) | 41.5 |
| 1950 | USSR (V. Sukharyev, L. Kalyayev, L. Sanadze, N. Karakulov) | 41.5 |
| 1954 | Hungary (L. Zarandi, G. Varasdi, G. Csanyi, B. Goldovanyi) | 40.6 |
| 1958 | Germany (W. Mahlendorf, A. Hary, H. Futterer, M. Germar) | 40.2 |
| 1962 | Germany (K. Ulonska, P. Gamper, H. J. Bender, M. Germar) | 39.5 |
| 1966 | France (M. Berger, J. Delecour, C. Piquemal, R. Bambuck) | 39.4 |
| 1969 | France (A. Sarteur, P. Bourbeillon, G. Fenouil, F. Saint-Gilles) | 38.8 |
| 1971 | Czechoslovakia (L. Kriz, J. Demec, J. Kynos, L. Bohman) | 39.3 |

| *4 x 400 Metres Relay* | | min. sec. |
|---|---|---|
| 1934 | Germany (H. Hamann, H. Scheele, H. Voigt, A. Metzner) | 3 14.1 |
| 1938 | Germany (H. Blazejezak, M. Bues, E. Linnhoff, R. Harbig) | 3 13.7 |
| 1946 | France (B. Santona, Y. Cros, R. Chefd'hotel, J. Lunis) | 3 14.4 |
| 1950 | GB (M. W. Pike, L. C. Lewis, A. W. Scott, D. C. Pugh) | 3 10.2 |
| 1954* | France (P. Haarhoff, J. Degats, J. P. Martin du Gard, J. P. Goudeau) | 3 08.7 |
| 1958 | GB (E. J. Sampson, J. MacIsaac, J. D. Wrighton, J. E. Salisbury) | 3 07.9 |
| 1962 | Germany (M. Kinder, W. Kindermann, H. J. Reske, J. Schmitt) | 3 05.8 |
| 1966 | Poland (J. Werner, E. Borowski, S. Gredzinski, A. Badenski) | 3 04.5 |
| 1969 | France (G. Bertould, C. Nicolau, J. Carette, J-C. Nallet) | 3 02.3 |
| 1971 | W. Germany (H-R. Schloske, T. Jordan, M. Jellinghaus, H. Kohler) | 3 02.9 |

* GB (F. P. Higgins, A. Dick, P. G. Fryer, D. J. N. Johnson), 1st in 3 08.2, disqualified.

| *High Jump* | | ft. in. |
|---|---|---|
| 1934 | K. Kotkas (Finland) | 6 6¾ |
| 1938 | K. Lundqvist (Sweden) | 6 5½ |
| 1946 | A. Bolinder (Sweden) | 6 6¼ |
| 1950 | A. S. Paterson (GB) | 6 5 |
| 1954 | B. Nilsson (Sweden) | 6 7½ |
| 1958 | R. Dahl (Sweden) | 6 11½ |
| 1962 | V. Brumel (USSR) | 7 3 |
| 1966 | J. Madubost (France) | 6 11½ |
| 1969 | V. Gavrilov (USSR) | 7 1½ |
| 1971 | K. Sapka (USSR) | 7 2½ |

| *Pole Vault* | | ft. in. |
|---|---|---|
| 1934 | G. Wegner (Germany) | 13 1½ |
| 1938 | K. Sutter (Germany) | 13 3½ |
| 1946 | A. Lindberg (Sweden) | 13 8¼ |
| 1950 | R. L. Lundberg (Sweden) | 14 1¼ |
| 1954 | E. Landstrom (Finland) | 14 5¼ |
| 1958 | E. Landstrom (Finland) | 14 9 |
| 1962 | P. Nikula (Finland) | 15 9 |
| 1966 | W. Nordwig (E. Germany) | 16 8¾ |
| 1969 | W. Nordwig (E. Germany) | 17 4½ |
| 1971 | W. Nordwig (E. Germany) | 17 6½ |

| *Long Jump* | | ft. in. |
|---|---|---|
| 1934 | W. Leichum (Germany) | 24 5½ |
| 1938 | W. Leichum (Germany) | 25 0¾ |
| 1946 | O. Laessker (Sweden) | 24 4¼ |
| 1950 | T. Bryngeirsson (Iceland) | 24 0¼ |
| 1954 | O. Foldessy (Hungary) | 24 7¾ |
| 1958 | I. Ter-Ovanesyan (USSR) | 25 7½ |
| 1962 | I. Ter-Ovanesyan (USSR) | 26 10½ |
| 1966 | L. Davies (GB) | 26 2¼ |
| 1969 | I. Ter-Ovanesyan (USSR) | 26 9¾ |
| 1971 | M. Klauss (E. Germany) | 26 0 |

| *Triple Jump* | | ft. in. |
|---|---|---|
| 1934 | W. Peters (Netherlands) | 48 10¼ |
| 1938 | O. Rajasaari (Finland) | 50 3¼ |
| 1946 | K. J. V. Rautio (Finland) | 49 9¼ |
| 1950 | L. Shcherbakov (USSR) | 50 6 |
| 1954 | L. Shcherbakov (USSR | 52 2 |
| 1958 | J. Szmidt (Poland) | 53 11 |
| 1962 | J. Szmidt (Poland) | 54 3¾ |
| 1966 | G. Stoikovski (Bulgaria) | 54 8¼ |

| | | | |
|---|---|---|---|
| 1969 | V. Saneyev (USSR) | 56 | 10¾ |
| 1971 | J. Drehmel | | |
| | (E. Germany) | 56 | 3¾ |

**Shot** ft. in.

| | | | |
|---|---|---|---|
| 1934 | A. Viiding (Estonia) | 49 | 10 |
| 1938 | A. Kreek (Estonia) | 51 | 11¼ |
| 1946 | G. Huseby (Iceland) | 51 | 0¾ |
| 1950 | G. Huseby (Iceland) | 54 | 11¼ |
| 1954 | J. Skobla (Czecho- | | |
| | slovakia) | 56 | 5¼ |
| 1958 | A. Rowe (GB) | 58 | 4 |
| 1962 | V. Varju (Hungary) | 62 | 5 |
| 1966 | V. Varju (Hungary) | 63 | 9 |
| 1969 | D. Hoffmann | | |
| | (E. Germany) | 66 | 0¼ |
| 1971 | H. Briesenick | | |
| | (E. Germany) | 69 | 2 |

**Discus** ft. in.

| | | | |
|---|---|---|---|
| 1934 | H. Andersson | | |
| | (Sweden) | 165 | 3 |
| 1938 | W. Schroeder (Ger- | | |
| | many) | 163 | 1 |
| 1946 | A. Consolini (Italy) | 174 | 7 |
| 1950 | A. Consolini (Italy) | 176 | 4 |
| 1954 | A. Consolini (Italy) | 175 | 4 |
| 1958 | E. Piatkowski (Poland) | 176 | 11 |
| 1962 | V. Trusenyov (USSR) | 187 | 4 |
| 1966 | D. Thorith | | |
| | (E. Germany) | 188 | 5 |
| 1969 | H. Losch (E. Germany) | 202 | 10 |
| 1971 | L. Danek (Czecho- | | |
| | slovakia) | 209 | 8 |

**Hammer** ft. in.

| | | | |
|---|---|---|---|
| 1934 | V. Porhola (Finland) | 165 | 2 |
| 1938 | K. Hein (Germany) | 192 | 9 |
| 1946 | B. Ericson (Sweden) | 185 | 2 |
| 1950 | S. Strandli (Norway) | 182 | 9 |
| 1954 | M. Krivonosov (USSR) | 207 | 10 |
| 1958 | T. Rut (Poland) | 212 | 6 |
| 1962 | G. Zsivotzky | | |
| | (Hungary) | 228 | 6 |
| 1966 | R. Klim (USSR) | 229 | 9 |
| 1969 | A. Bondarchuk (USSR) | 245 | 0 |
| 1971 | U. Beyer | | |
| | (W. Germany) | 237 | 5 |

**Javelin** ft. in.

| | | | |
|---|---|---|---|
| 1934 | M. H. Jarvinen (Fin- | | |
| | land) | 251 | 6 |
| 1938 | M. H. Jarvinen (Fin- | | |
| | land) | 252 | 2 |
| 1946 | A. L. F. Atterwall | | |
| | (Sweden) | 225 | 6 |
| 1950 | T. Hyytiainen (Fin- | | |
| | land) | 233 | 9 |
| 1954 | J. Sidlo (Poland) | 250 | 5 |
| 1958 | J. Sidlo (Poland) | 263 | 1 |

| | | | |
|---|---|---|---|
| 1962 | J. Lusis (USSR) | 269 | 2 |
| 1966 | J. Lusis (USSR) | 277 | 2 |
| 1969 | J. Lusis (USSR) | 300 | 3 |
| 1971 | J. Lusis (USSR) | 297 | 6 |

**Decathlon (1962 Tables)** Pts.

| | | |
|---|---|---|
| 1934 | H. H. Sievert (Germany) | 6858 |
| 1938 | O. Bexell (Sweden) | 7120 |
| 1946 | G. Holmvang (Norway) | 6760 |
| 1950 | I. Heinrich (France) | 7009 |
| 1954 | V. Kuznyetsov (USSR) | 7043 |
| 1958 | V. Kuznyetsov (USSR) | 7697 |
| 1962 | V. Kuznyetsov (USSR) | 7770 |
| 1966 | W. von Moltke | |
| | (W. Germany) | 7740 |
| 1969 | J. Kirst (E. Germany) | 8041 |
| 1971 | J. Kirst (E. Germany) | 8196 |

**10,000 Metres Walk** min. sec.

| | | | |
|---|---|---|---|
| 1946 | J. F. Mikaelsson | | |
| | (Sweden) | | 46 05.2 |
| 1950 | F. Schwab (Switzer- | | |
| | land) | | 46 01.8 |
| 1954 | J. Dolezal (Czecho- | | |
| | slovakia) | | 45 01.8 |

**20,000 Metres Walk** hr. min. sec.

| | | | | |
|---|---|---|---|---|
| 1958 | S. F. Vickers (GB) | 1 | 33 | 09.0 |
| 1962 | K. J. Matthews (GB) | 1 | 35 | 54.8 |
| 1966 | D. Lindner | | | |
| | (E. Germany) | 1 | 29 | 25.0 |
| 1969 | V. P. Nihill (GB) | 1 | 30 | 41.0 |
| 1971 | N. Smaga (USSR) | 1 | 27 | 20.2 |

**50,000 Metres Walk** hr. min. sec.

| | | | | |
|---|---|---|---|---|
| 1934 | J. Dalins (Latvia) | 4 | 49 | 52.6 |
| 1938 | H. H. Whitlock (GB) | 4 | 41 | 51.0 |
| 1946 | J. Ljunggren | | | |
| | (Sweden) | 4 | 38 | 20.0 |
| 1950 | G. Dordoni (Italy) | 4 | 40 | 42.6 |
| 1954 | V. Ukhov (USSR) | 4 | 22 | 11.2 |
| 1958 | Y. Maskinskov | | | |
| | (USSR) | 4 | 17 | 15.4 |
| 1962 | A. Pamich (Italy) | 4 | 18 | 46.6 |
| 1966 | A. Pamich (Italy) | 4 | 18 | 42.2 |
| 1969 | C. Hohne | | | |
| | (E. Germany) | 4 | 13 | 32.0 |
| 1971 | V. Soldatenko | | | |
| | (USSR) | 4 | 02 | 22.0 |

## Women Champions

**100 Metres** sec.

| | | |
|---|---|---|
| 1938 | S. Walasiewicz (Poland) | 11.9 |
| 1946 | Y. Sechenova (USSR) | 11.9 |
| 1950 | F. E. Blankers-Koen | |
| | (Netherlands) | 11.7 |
| 1954 | I. Turova (USSR) | 11.8 |
| 1958 | H. J. Young (GB) | 11.7 |
| 1962 | D. Hyman (GB) | 11.3 |

| | | |
|---|---|---|
| 1966 | E. Klobukowska (Poland) | 11.5 |
| 1969 | P. Vogt (E. Germany) | 11.6 |
| 1971 | R. Stecher (E. Germany) | 11.4 |

*200 Metres*

| | | sec. |
|---|---|---|
| 1938 | S. Walasiewicz (Poland) | 23.8 |
| 1946 | Y. Sechenova (USSR) | 25.4 |
| 1950 | F. E. Blankers-Koen (Netherlands) | 24.0 |
| 1954 | M. Itkina (USSR) | 24.3 |
| 1958 | B. Janiszewska (Poland) | 24.1 |
| 1962 | J. Heine (Germany) | 23.5 |
| 1966 | I. Kirszenstein (Poland) | 23.1 |
| 1969 | P. Vogt (E. Germany) | 23.2 |
| 1971 | R. Stecher (E. Germany) | 22.7 |

*400 Metres*

| | | sec. |
|---|---|---|
| 1958 | M. Itkina (USSR) | 53.7 |
| 1962 | M. Itkina (USSR) | 53.4 |
| 1966 | A. Chmelkova (Czechoslovakia) | 52.9 |
| 1969 | S. Duclos (France) | 51.7 |
| 1971 | H. Seidler (E. Germany) | 52.1 |

*800 Metres*

| | | min. | sec. |
|---|---|---|---|
| 1954 | N. Otkalenko (USSR) | 2 | 08.8 |
| 1958 | Y. Yermolayeva (USSR) | 2 | 06.3 |
| 1962 | G. Kraan (Netherlands) | 2 | 02.8 |
| 1966 | V. Nikolic (Yugoslavia) | 2 | 02.8 |
| 1969 | L. B. Board (GB) | 2 | 01.4 |
| 1971 | V. Nikolic (Yugoslavia) | 2 | 00.0 |

*1500 Metres*

| | | min. | sec. |
|---|---|---|---|
| 1969 | J. Jehlickova (Czechoslovakia) | 4 | 10.7 |
| 1971 | K. Burneleit (E. Germany) | 4 | 09.6 |

*80 Metres Hurdles*

| | | sec. |
|---|---|---|
| 1938 | C. Testoni (Italy) | 11.6 |
| 1946 | F. E. Blankers-Koen (Netherlands) | 11.8 |
| 1950 | F. E. Blankers-Koen (Netherlands) | 11.1 |
| 1954 | M. Golubnichaya (USSR) | 11.0 |
| 1958 | G. Bystrova (USSR) | 10.9 |
| 1962 | T. Ciepla (Poland) | 10.6 |
| 1966 | K. Balzer (E. Germany) | 10.7 |

*100 Metres Hurdles*

| | | sec. |
|---|---|---|
| 1969 | K. Balzer (E. Germany) | 13.3 |
| 1971 | K. Balzer (E. Germany) | 12.9 |

*4 x 100 Metres Relay*

| | | sec. |
|---|---|---|
| 1938 | Germany (F. Kohl, K. Krauss, E. Albus, I. Kuhnel) | 46.8 |
| 1946 | Netherlands (G. J. M. Koudijs, N. Timmer, J. Adema, F. E. Blankers-Koen) | 47.8 |
| 1950 | GB (E. Hay, J. C. Desforges, D. G. Hall, J. F. Foulds) | 47.4 |
| 1954 | USSR (V. Krepkina, R. Ulitkina, M. Itkina, I. Turova) | 45.8 |
| 1958 | USSR (V. Krepkina, L. Kepp, N. Polyakova, V. Maslovskaya) | 45.3 |
| 1962 | Poland (M. Piatkowska, B. Sobotta,* E. Szyroka, T. Ciepla) | 44.5 |
| 1966 | Poland (E. Bednarek, D. Straszynska, I. Kirszenstein, E. Klobukowska) | 44.4 |
| 1969 | E. Germany (R. Hofer, R. Stecher, B. Podeswa, P. Vogt) | 43.6 |
| 1971 | W. Germany (E. Schittenhelm, I. Helten, A. Irrgang, I. Mickler) | 43.3 |

* formerly Janiszewska.

*4 x 400 Metres Relay*

| | | min. | sec. |
|---|---|---|---|
| 1969 | GB (R. O. Stirling, P. B. Lowe, J. M. Simpson, L. B. Board) | 3 | 30.8 |
| 1971 | E. Germany (R. Kuhne, I. Lohse, H. Seidler, M. Zehrt) | 3 | 29.3 |

*High Jump*

| | | ft. | in. |
|---|---|---|---|
| 1938 | I. Csak (Hungary) | 5 | 4½ |
| 1946 | A. Colchen (France) | 5 | 3 |
| 1950 | S. Alexander (GB) | 5 | 4¼ |
| 1954 | T. E. Hopkins (GB) | 5 | 5¾ |
| 1958 | I. Balas (Rumania) | 5 | 9¾ |
| 1962 | I. Balas (Rumania) | 6 | 0 |
| 1966 | T. Chenchik (USSR) | 5 | 8¾ |
| 1969 | M. Rezkova (Czechoslovakia) | 6 | 0 |
| 1971 | I. Gusenbauer (Austria) | 6 | 1½ |

*Long Jump*

| | | ft. | in. |
|---|---|---|---|
| 1938 | I. Praetz(Germany) | 19 | 3½ |
| 1946 | G. J. M. Koudijs (Netherlands) | 18 | 7¼ |
| 1950 | V. Bogdanova (USSR) | 19 | 1¼ |
| 1954 | J. C. Desforges (GB) | 19 | 9¾ |
| 1958 | L. Jacobi (Germany) | 20 | 1¾ |
| 1962 | T. Shchelkanova (USSR) | 20 | 10½ |
| 1966 | I. Kirszenstein (Poland) | 21 | 6 |
| 1969 | M. Sarna (Poland) | 21 | 3½ |
| 1971 | I. Mickler (W. Germany) | 22 | 2¼ |

*Shot*

| | | ft. | in. |
|---|---|---|---|
| 1938 | H. Schroder (Germany) | 43 | 7¼ |

| | | | |
|---|---|---|---|
| 1946 | T. Sevryukova (USSR) | 46 | 5½ |
| 1950 | A. Andreyeva (USSR) | 46 | 11¾ |
| 1954 | G. Zybina (USSR) | 51 | 4¼ |
| 1958 | M. Werner (Germany) | 51 | 7¾ |
| 1962 | T. Press (USSR) | 60 | 10½ |
| 1966 | N. Chizhova (USSR) | 56 | 6 |
| 1969 | N. Chizhova (USSR) | 67 | 0½ |
| 1971 | N. Chizhova (USSR) | 66 | 1¾ |

*Discus* — ft. in.

| | | | |
|---|---|---|---|
| 1938 | G. Mauermeyer (Germany) | 147 | 0 |
| 1946 | N. Dumbadze (USSR) | 146 | 1 |
| 1950 | N. Dumbadze (USSR) | 157 | 6 |
| 1954 | N. Ponomaryeva (USSR) | 157 | 6 |
| 1958 | T. Press (USSR) | 171 | 8 |
| 1962 | T. Press (USSR) | 186 | 8 |
| 1966 | C. Spielberg (E. Germany) | 189 | 6 |
| 1969 | T. Danilova (USSR) | 194 | 6 |
| 1971 | F. Melnik (USSR) | 210 | 8 |

*Javelin* — ft. in.

| | | | |
|---|---|---|---|
| 1938 | L. Gelius (Germany) | 149 | 6 |
| 1946 | K. Mayuchaya (USSR) | 151 | 8 |
| 1950 | N. Smirnitskaya (USSR) | 156 | 0 |
| 1954 | D. Zatopkova (Czechoslovakia) | 173 | 7 |
| 1958 | D. Zatopkova (Czechoslovakia) | 183 | 9 |
| 1962 | E. Ozolina (USSR) | 180 | 2 |
| 1966 | M. Luttge (E. Germany) | 192 | 8 |
| 1969 | A. Ranky (Hungary) | 196 | 1 |
| 1971 | D. Jaworska (Poland) | 200 | 1 |

*Pentathlon* — Pts.

| | | |
|---|---|---|
| 1950 | A. Ben Hamo (France) | 4023 |
| 1954 | A. Chudina (USSR) | 4526 |
| 1958 | G. Bystrova (USSR) | 4733 |
| 1962 | G. Bystrova (USSR) | 4833 |
| 1966 | V. Tikhomirova (USSR) | 4787 |
| 1969 | L. Prokop (Austria) | 5030 |
| 1971 | H. Rosendahl (W. Germany) | 5299 |

## National Scores

National team point scores are not maintained officially but they do provide a guide to the relative strength of individual countries. Scoring: 7 points for a winner, 5 for 2nd, 4 for 3rd, 3 for 4th, 2 for 5th and 1 for 6th.

### 1934

| | | |
|---|---|---|
| 1. | Germany | 82 |
| 2. | Finland | 80 |
| 3. | Hungary | 56 |
| 4. | Italy and Sweden | 52 |
| 6. | France | 35 |

### 1938

| | | |
|---|---|---|
| 1. | Germany | 110 |
| 2. | Finland | 83 |
| 3. | Sweden | 77½ |
| 4. | Great Britain | 57½ |
| 5. | Italy | 41 |
| 6. | Netherlands | 29 |

### 1946

| | | |
|---|---|---|
| 1. | Sweden | 153 |
| 2. | Finland | 70 |
| 3. | Great Britain | 51 |
| 4. | France | 46 |
| 5. | Norway | 34 |
| 6. | Soviet Union | 28 |

### 1950

| | | |
|---|---|---|
| 1. | France | 75 |
| 2. | Great Britain | 72 |
| 3. | Sweden | 69 |
| 4. | Italy | 58 |
| 5. | Finland | 49 |
| 6. | Soviet Union | 41 |

### 1954

| | | |
|---|---|---|
| 1. | Soviet Union | 106 |
| 2. | Hungary | 64 |
| 3. | Finland | 53½ |
| 4. | Great Britain | 50½ |
| 5. | Czechoslovakia | 49 |
| 6. | Sweden | 44 |

### 1958

| | | |
|---|---|---|
| 1. | Soviet Union | 118 |
| 2. | Great Britain | 93 |
| 3. | Poland | 79 |
| 4. | Germany | 75 |
| 5. | Sweden | 39 |
| 6. | Italy | 18 |

### 1962

| | | |
|---|---|---|
| 1. | Soviet Union | 133 |
| 2. | Germany | 88½ |
| 3. | Poland | 60½ |
| 4. | Great Britain | 59 |
| 5. | France | 35 |
| 6. | Italy | 30 |

### 1966

| | | |
|---|---|---|
| 1. | Soviet Union | 88 |
| 2. | West Germany | 85 |
| 3. | East Germany | 78 |
| 4. | France | 74 |

| | |
|---|---|
| 5. Poland | 58 |
| 6. Hungary | 35 |

### 1969
| | |
|---|---|
| 1. East Germany | 119 |
| 2. Soviet Union | 117 |
| 3. Great Britain | 69 |
| 4. France | 44 |
| 5. Poland | 34 |
| 6. Italy | 19 |

### 1971
| | |
|---|---|
| 1. East Germany | 114½ |
| 2. Soviet Union | 107 |
| 3. Great Britain | 52 |
| 4. West Germany | 51 |
| 5. Poland | 33 |
| 6. Finland | 31½ |

## Women
### 1946
| | |
|---|---|
| 1. Soviet Union | 68 |
| 2. Netherlands | 38 |
| 3. France | 27 |
| 4. Great Britain | 17 |
| 5. Sweden | 14 |
| 6. Poland | 11 |

### 1950
| | |
|---|---|
| 1. Soviet Union | 77 |
| 2. Great Britain | 44 |
| 3. Netherlands | 33 |
| 4. France | 29 |
| 5. Italy | 8 |
| 6. Czechoslovakia | 6 |

### 1954
| | |
|---|---|
| 1. Soviet Union | 106 |
| 2. Great Britain | 39 |
| 3. Germany | 31 |
| 4. Czechoslovakia | 20 |
| 5. Poland | 13 |
| 6. Italy | 7 |

### 1958
| | |
|---|---|
| 1. Soviet Union | 114 |
| 2. Germany | 60 |
| 3. Great Britain | 36 |
| 4. Poland | 18 |
| 5. Czechoslovakia | 14 |
| 6. Rumania | 8 |

### 1962
| | |
|---|---|
| 1. Germany | 65½ |
| 2. Soviet Union | 63 |
| 3. Great Britain | 44 |
| 4. Poland | 33½ |
| 5. Netherlands | 14 |
| 6. Rumania | 13 |

### 1966
| | |
|---|---|
| 1. Soviet Union | 56 |
| 2. Poland | 46 |
| 3. East Germany | 44 |
| 4. West Germany | 43 |
| 5. Hungary | 20 |
| 6. Czechoslovakia | 14 |

### 1969
| | |
|---|---|
| 1. East Germany | 71 |
| 2. Soviet Union | 51 |
| 3. Great Britain | 31 |
| 4. France | 22 |
| 5. Netherlands and Czechoslovakia | 18 |

### 1971
| | |
|---|---|
| 1. East Germany | 90 |
| 2. West Germany | 72 |
| 3. Soviet Union | 39 |
| 4. Poland | 31 |
| 5. Great Britain | 23½ |
| 6. Hungary | 12 |

## Record Achievements

One man has won a title four times running: Janis Lusis (USSR), javelin champion in 1962, 1966, 1969 and 1971.

The most successful female competitor is Fanny Blankers-Koen (Netherlands) with five titles: 80 m. hurdles and 4 x 100 m. relay in 1946; 100 m., 200 m. and hurdles in 1950.

Britain's most prolific medallists, with four apiece, are Derek Pugh (400 m. and 4 x 400 m. relay in 1946 and 1950) and Dorothy Hyman (relay in 1958, both sprints and relay in 1962).

## EUROPEAN CUP

Conceived by the late Bruno Zauli, former president of the IAAF's European Committee, and named after him, a European Cup tournament was instituted in 1965. Nations are represented by one athlete per event. Results of finals:

### 1965 (Men; at Stuttgart)
| | |
|---|---|
| 1. Soviet Union | 86 |
| 2. West Germany | 85 |
| 3. Poland | 69 |
| 4. East Germany | 69 |
| 5. France | 60 |
| 6. Great Britain | 48 |

### 1965 (Women; at Kassel)
| | |
|---|---|
| 1. Soviet Union | 56 |

| | |
|---|---|
| 2. East Germany | 42 |
| 3. Poland | 38 |
| 4. West Germany | 37 |
| 5. Hungary | 32 |
| 6. Netherlands | 25 |

(GB eliminated by Hungary and Netherlands in semi-final)

### 1967 (Men; at Kiev)

| | |
|---|---|
| 1. Soviet Union | 81 |
| 2. West Germany | 80 |
| 3. East Germany | 80 |
| 4. Poland | 68 |
| 5. France | 57 |
| 6. Hungary | 53 |

(GB eliminated by West Germany and Hungary in semi-final)

### 1967 (Women; at Kiev)

| | |
|---|---|
| 1. Soviet Union | 51 |
| 2. East Germany | 43 |
| 3. West Germany | 36 |
| 4. Poland | 35 |
| 5. Great Britain | 34 |
| 6. Hungary | 32 |

### 1970 (Men; at Stockholm)

| | |
|---|---|
| 1. East Germany | 102 |
| 2. Soviet Union | 92½ |
| 3. West Germany | 91 |
| 4. Poland | 82 |
| 5. France | 77½ |
| 6. Sweden | 68 |
| 7. Italy | 47 |

(GB eliminated by France and Soviet Union in semi-final)

### 1970 (Women; at Budapest)

| | |
|---|---|
| 1. East Germany | 70 |
| 2. West Germany | 63 |
| 3. Soviet Union | 43 |
| 4. Poland | 33 |
| 5. Great Britain | 32 |
| 6. Hungary | 32 |

The finals of the 1973 European Cup tournament are scheduled for Edinburgh.

Leading individual performances in the Cup finals of 1965-70: 100m., 10.3 sec. M. Dudziak (Pol) 1965 and V. Sapeya (USSR) 1967; 200m., 20.7 sec. S. Schenke (EG) 1970; 400m., 45.9 sec. A. Badenski (Pol) 1965 and J. Werner (Pol) 1970; 800m., 1 min. 46.9 sec. M. Matuschewski (EG) and F-J. Kemper (WG) 1967; 1500m., 3 min. 40.2 sec. M. Matuschewski (EG) 1967; 5000m., 14 min. 18.0 sec. H. Norpoth (WG) 1965; 10,000m., 28 min. 26.8 sec. J. Haase (EG) 1970; 3000m. Steeplechase, 8 min. 31.6 sec. V. Dudin (USSR) 1970; 110m. Hurdles, 13.7 sec. G. Drut (Fra) 1970; 400m. Hurdles, 50.1 sec. J-C. Nallet (Fra) 1970; 4 x 100m. Relay, 39.2 sec. France 1967; 4 x 400m. Relay, 3 min. 04.4 sec. Poland 1967; High jump, 7 ft. 0½ in. V. Brumel (USSR) 1965 and K. Lundmark (Swe) 1970; Pole vault, 17 ft. 6½ in. W. Nordwig (EG) 1970; Long jump, 26 ft. 8¼ in. I. Ter-Ovanesyan (USSR) 1970; Triple jump, 56 ft. 2½ in. J. Drehmel (EG) 1970; Shot. 67 ft. 5¼ in. H. Briesenick (EG) 1970; Discus, 212 ft. 10 in. R. Bruch (Swe) 1970; Hammer, 231 ft. 7 in. R. Klim (USSR) 1967; Javelin, 280 ft. 1 in. J. Lusis (USSR) 1967.

Women—100m., 11.2 sec. I. Szewinska (Pol) 1967; 200m., 23.0 sec. E. Klobukowska (Pol) 1965 and I. Szewinska (Pol) 1967; 400m., 53.2 sec. H. Seidler (EG) 1970; 800m., 2 min. 04.3 sec. H. Suppe (EG) 1965; 1500m., 4 min. 16.3 sec. E. Tittel (WG) 1970; 100m. Hurdles, 13.1 sec. K. Balzer (EG) 1970; 4 x 100m. Relay, 43.9 sec. W. Germany 1970; 4 x 400m. Relay, 3 min. 37.0 sec. E. Germany 1970; High jump, 6 ft. 0½ in. R. Schmidt (EG) and A. Lazareva (USSR) 1970; Long jump, 22 ft. 3¾ in. H. Rosendahl (WG) 1970; Shot, 63 ft. 8¼ in. N. Chizhova (USSR) 1970; Discus, 202 ft. 1 in. K. Illgen (EG) 1970; Javelin, 198 ft. 10 in. R. Fuchs (EG) 1970.

The only British athlete to have won an event in a European Cup final was Lillian Board, 400m. (53.7 sec.) in 1967.

## EUROPEAN INDOOR CHAMPIONSHIPS

See under INDOOR ATHLETICS.

## EUROPEAN JUNIOR CHAMPIONSHIPS

See under JUNIORS.

84

**EUROPEAN RECORDS** — international events, as ratified by the IAAF or awaiting ratification, as at European records in the standard June 1, 1973:

| | | | | |
|---|---|---|---|---|
| *100 m.* | 10.0 | Armin Hary (W. Germany) | June 21 | 1960 |
| | 10.0 | Roger Bambuck (France) | June 20 | 1968 |
| | 10.0 | Vladislav Sapeya (USSR) | Aug. 16 | 1968 |
| | 10.0 | Valeriy Borzov (USSR) | Aug. 18 | 1969 |
| | 10.0 | Gerd Metz (W. Germany) | Sept. 6 | 1970 |
| | 10.0 | Manfred Kokot (E. Germany) | May 15 | 1971 |
| | 10.0 | Valeriy Borzov (USSR) | June 21 | 1971 |
| | 10.0 | Vasilios Papageorgopoulos (Greece) | June 3 | 1972 |
| | 10.0 | Valeriy Borzov (USSR) | June 16 | 1972 |
| | 10.0 | Pietro Mennea (Italy) | June 16 | 1972 |
| | 10.0 | Valeriy Borzov (USSR) | July 18 | 1972 |
| | 10.0 | Raimo Vilen (Finland) | July 27 | 1972 |
| *200 m.* | 20.0 | Valeriy Borzov (USSR) | Sept. 4 | 1972 |
| *400 m.* | 44.7 | Karl Honz (W. Germany) | July 21 | 1972 |
| *800 m.* | 1 44.5 | Pekka Vasala (Finland) | Aug. 20 | 1972 |
| *1500 m.* | 3 34.0 | Jean Wadoux (France) | July 23 | 1970 |
| *5000 m.* | 13 13.0 | Emiel Puttemans (Belgium) | Sept. 20 | 1972 |
| *10,000 m.* | 27 38.4 | Lasse Viren (Finland) | Sept. 3 | 1972 |
| *Marathon* (unofficial) | 2 09 28.0 | Ron Hill (GB) | July 23 | 1970 |
| *3000 m. Steeplechase* | 8 20.8 | Anders Garderud (Sweden) | Sept. 14 | 1972 |
| *110 m. hurdles* | 13.2 | Martin Lauer (W. Germany) | July 7 | 1959 |
| *400 m. hurdles* | 48.1 | David Hemery (GB) | Oct. 15 | 1968 |
| *High Jump* | 7ft. 5¾in. | Valeriy Brumel (USSR) | July 21 | 1963 |
| *Pole Vault* | 18ft. 4¼in. | Kjell Isaksson (Sweden) | May 23 | 1972 |
| *Long Jump* | 27ft. 4¾in. | Igor Ter-Ovanesyan (USSR) | Oct. 19 | 1967 |
| | 27ft. 4¾in. | Josef Schwarz (W. Germany) | July 15 | 1970 |
| *Triple Jump* | 57ft. 2½in. | Viktor Saneyev (USSR) | Oct. 18 | 1972 |
| *Shot* | 70ft. 8in. | Hartmut Briesenick (E. Germany) | Aug. 25 | 1972 |
| *Discus* | 224ft. 5in. | Ricky Bruch (Sweden) | July 5 | 1972 |
| *Hammer* | 250ft. 8in. | Walter Schmidt (W. Germany) | Sept. 4 | 1971 |
| *Javelin* | 308ft. 8in. | Klaus Wolfermann (W. Germany) | May 5 | 1973 |
| *Decathlon* | 8,454 | Nikolay Avilov (USSR) | Sept. 7/8 | 1972 |
| *4 x 100 m.* | 38.4 | France (Gerard Fenouil, Jocelyn Delecour, Claude Piquemal, Roger Bambuck) | Oct. 20 | 1968 |
| *4 x 400 m.* | 3 00.5 | W. Germany (Helmar Muller, Gerhard Hennige, Manfred Kinder, Martin Jellinghaus) | Oct. 20 | 1968 |
| | 3 00.5 | Poland (Stanislaw Gredzinski, Jan Balachowski, Jan Werner, Andrzej Badenski) | Oct. 20 | 1968 |
| | 3 00.5 | GB (Martin Reynolds, Alan Pascoe, David Hemery, David Jenkins) | Sept. 10 | 1972 |

## Women

| | | | | |
|---|---|---|---|---|
| *100 m.* | 11.0 | Renate Stecher (E. Germany) | Aug. 2 | 1970 |
| | 11.0 | Renate Stecher (E. Germany) | July 31 | 1971 |
| | 11.0 | Renate Stecher (E. Germany) | June 3 | 1972 |
| | 11.0 | Ellen Stropahl (E. Germany) | June 15 | 1972 |

| | | | |
|---|---|---|---|
| | 11.0 | Eva Gleskova (Czechoslovakia) | July 1 1972 |
| | 11.0 | Renate Stecher (E. Germany) | Aug. 20 1972 |
| *200 m.* | 22.4 | Renate Stecher (E. Germany) | Sept. 7 1972 |
| *400 m.* | 51.0 | Monika Zehrt (E. Germany) | July 4 1972 |
| *800 m.* | 1 58.5 | Hildegard Falck (W. Germany) | July 11 1971 |
| *1500 m.* | 4 01.4 | Lyudmila Bragina (USSR) | Sept. 9 1972 |
| *3000 m.* | 8 53.0 | Lyudmila Bragina (USSR) | Aug. 12 1972 |
| *100 m. hurdles* | 12.5 | Annelie Ehrhardt (E. Germany) | June 15 1972 |
| | 12.5 | Annelie Ehrhardt (E. Germany) (twice) | Aug. 13 1972 |
| *200 m. hurdles* | 25.8 | Annelie Ehrhardt (E. Germany) | July 5 1970 |
| | 25.8 | Teresa Sukniewicz (Poland) | Aug. 9 1970 |
| *High Jump* | 6ft. 4¼in. | Yordanka Blagoyeva (Bulgaria) | Sept. 24 1972 |
| *Long Jump* | 22ft. 5¼in. | Heide Rosendahl (W. Germany) | Sept. 3 1970 |
| *Shot* | 69ft. 0in. | Nadyezhda Chizhova (USSR) | Sept. 7 1972 |
| *Discus* | 221ft. 3in. | Faina Melnik (USSR) | May 25 1973 |
| *Javelin* | 213ft. 5in. | Ruth Fuchs (E. Germany) | June 11 1972 |
| *Pentathlon* | 4,801 | Mary Peters (GB and NI) | Sept. 2/3 1972 |
| *4 x 100 m.* | 42.8 | West Germany (Christiane Krause, Ingrid Mickler, Annegret Richter, Heide Rosendahl) | Sept. 10 1972 |
| *4 x 400 m.* | 3 23.0 | East Germany (Dagmar Kasling, Rita Kuhne, Helga Seidler, Monika Zehrt) | Sept. 10 1972 |

## EVANS, L. E. (USA)

For a period of several seasons from 1966, when he was only 19, Lee Evans was firmly entrenched as the world's leading 400 m. runner. His thrusting stride and head-rolling action would not have won him any prizes for style but they carried him to victory after victory, usually in very fast times. His powerful finish and astounding consistency in an event all too easy to misjudge became legendary.

He won many honours: Olympic champion in 1968 (with a world record of 43.8 sec. which still stood four years later), Pan-American champion in 1967, American champion from 1966 to 1969 and again in 1972. He gained further gold medals in the 4 x 400 m. relay at the Olympics and Pan-American Games and, but for the inability of the USA to field a relay team at the Munich Olympics following the ban imposed on Vince Matthews and Wayne Collett, another gold would probably have come his way there. In addition he set world records in the 4 x 200 m., 4 x 220 yd. and 4 x 400 m. relays, and created a world's best 600 m. time of 74.3 sec.

Even on the rare occasions he lost, he would usually turn in a sizzling performance; e.g. 45.3 for 440 yd. behind Tommie Smith and 45.1 for 400 m. behind Vince Matthews in 1967, and 45.1 for 440 yd. behind Curtis Mills in 1969. In spite of winning the American 400 m. title in 1972, defeating his eventual Olympic successor Vince Matthews, Evans was deprived of a chance of defending his crown by finishing only fourth in the US Olympic Trials. He turned professional later in the year.

His best performances include 20.4 sec. for 200 m. and 43.8 sec. for 400 m., and his annual progress at 440 yd. has been: 1961—62.0, 1962—55.0, 1963—52.3, 1964—48.2, 1965—46.9, 1966—45.2 (400 m.), 1967—44.9 (400), 1968—43.8 (400), 1969—44.5 (400), 1970—45.5 (400), 1971—45.9, 1972—44.9. He was born at Madera, California, on Feb. 25th, 1947.

## EXETER, MARQUESS OF

See under BURGHLEY, LORD.

86

## FALCK, H. (West Germany)

Tall, blonde and elegant, Hildegard Falck (née Janze) came to athletics from swimming in 1967 and won the West German 800 m. title in her first season. Three years later she broke into world class with victory in the European Cup final and times of 2 min. 02.8 sec. and 2 min. 00.6 sec. (relay leg).

She won the race to be the first woman to break 2 minutes officially (the IAAF never ratified the 1 min. 58.0 sec. and 1 min. 59.1 sec. attributed to the mysterious Sin Kim Dan of North Korea) when taking the 1971 West German title in 1 min. 58.5 sec. —a full 2 seconds inside Vera Nikolic's listed record. Unhappily she fell during the European 800 m. final a month later, the gold medal going to Nikolic in 2 minutes flat.

Her competitive qualities were put to the test, however, at the Munich Olympics and she quashed any doubts on that score (she had lost in her national championships a few weeks earlier after running the first lap too fast) by triumphing in 1 min. 58.6 sec. She picked up a bronze medal in the 4 x 400 m. relay, her contribution being an excellent 51.2 sec. stage.

Her best performances include 53.7 sec. for 400 m. (51.2 sec. relay), 1 min. 58.5 sec. for 800 m. and 4 min. 14.6 sec for 1500 m. Annual progress at 800 m. 1967—2:11.3, 1968—2:08.9, 1969—2:11.9, 1970—2:02.8, 1971—1:58.5, 1972—1:58.6. She was born at Nettelrede on June 8th, 1949.

## FINLAY, D. O. (GB)

Don Finlay, one of the most remarkable figures in athletics history, made his international debut in 1929 —placed 6th and last in the long jump against France—and closed his British international career in another match against France exactly 20 years later by winning the 120 yd. hurdles in the national record time of 14.4 sec.

His first great success occurred at the 1932 Olympics when he split the redoubtable American trio to take third place in the 110 m. hurdles. Four years later, having in the meantime won the Commonwealth title, he uncorked a spectacular finish to seize second spot in the Olympic final behind world record holder Forrest Towns (USA).

He was already 29 when he triumphed at the 1938 European Championships in his best time of 14.3 sec., but his career was by no means over. He came back in 1947 with two clockings of 14.6 sec. and the following year he competed once again in the Olympics but suffered the misfortune of falling while leading in his heat.

He enjoyed a marvellous season in 1949 (aged 40!), winning his eighth AAA high hurdles title, setting the British record referred to earlier and defeating Dick Attlesey (USA), who the following year was destined to reduce the world record to 13.5 sec. His final fling at international competition was at the 1950 Commonwealth Games where he placed fourth in 14.7 sec.

Finlay was a miraculously consistent competitor, and from 1933 to 1939 inclusive he lost only nine races, three of them to John Thornton—the only British athlete to defeat him during this period.

His best marks included 14.3 sec. for 110 m. hurdles (and 14.1 sec. wind-assisted), 24.2 sec. for 200 m. hurdles (turn), 6ft. 0in. high jump and 22ft. 10½in. long jump. He was born at Christchurch, Hampshire, on May 27th, 1909 and died on April 18th, 1970.

## FOSBURY, R. (USA)

Even if he never recaptures the form that won him the Olympic high jump title in 1968, the name of Fos-

87

bury will always be remembered and honoured. It was Dick Fosbury, a lanky 6 ft. 4 in. tall American, who hit upon the idea of propelling himself across the bar head-first on his back.

That style, known as the "Fosbury Flop", caught the imagination of the world as demonstrated so superbly by its inventor at the Mexico City Olympics, and in subsequent seasons his disciples achieved great success: the 1971 European champion Kestutis Sapka and 1972 Olympic women's champion Ulrike Meyfarth are both floppers, as is Mary Peters, whose amazing high jump progress since taking up this style was the single most important factor in her pentathlon victory.

Fosbury's experiments with a back lay-out technique date back to when he was 16. An exponent of the unsophisticated scissors style and dissatisfied with his results, he felt he could improve by lowering his centre of gravity in going over on his back. His best jump immediately shot up from 5 ft. 4 in. to 5 ft. 10 in. By the time he left high school two years later he was up to 6 ft. 7 in. and indoors in January 1968 he jumped 7 feet for the first time. He won the US Olympic Trial with a personal best of 7 ft. 3 in. and in Mexico City became the most popular champion of the Games as he cleared 7 ft. 4¼ in. at his final attempt. Lacking in motivation since then, his appearances have been spasmodic and largely unsuccessful. He turned professional in 1973.

His annual progress: 1958—3ft. 10in., 1959—4ft. 6in., 1960—4ft. 8in., 1961—4ft. 10in., 1962—5ft. 4in., 1963—5ft. 10in., 1964—6ft. 3½in., 1965—6ft. 7in., 1966—6ft. 7¼in., 1967—6ft. 10¾in., 1968—7ft. 4¼in., 1969—7ft. 2¼in., 1971—7ft. 0in. He was born in Portland, Oregon, on March 6th, 1947.

# FRENKEL, P. (East Germany)

Peter Frenkel wanted to be a successful middle distance runner but, hampered by Achilles tendon trouble, his best 1500 m. time after several years of training was a mediocre 4 min. 9 sec. So he took up walking instead.

His first major international appearance, at the 1968 Olympics, was a disappointment. In contention for a medal at the halfway mark in the 20 km. walk, he fell back to finish tenth in 1 hr. 37 min. 20.8 sec—over 11 minutes outside his best time. In 1970 he collected his first world record plaque, clocking 1 hr. 25 min. 50 sec. on the track, and another came his way in 1971 when he covered 16 miles 993 yards in two hours. He placed 4th in that season's European 20 km. championship but in 1972 he finally came into his own as a competitor, at the age of 33. Accelerating throughout the race (his 5 km. splits were 22:16, 21:41, 21:25 and 21:20.4) he won the Olympic title in 1 hr. 26 min. 42.4 sec. Earlier in the year he had reduced his world record to 1 hr. 25 min. 19.4 sec., and set new 10 km. figures of 41 min. 35 sec. He is acknowledged as one of the fairest stylists in international walking.

His annual progress at 20 km. walk: 1960—1:43:07, 1961—1:42:03, 1962—1:34:03, 1963—1:33:04, 1964—1:32:10.6, 1965—1:29:46.6, 1966—1:30:12.6, 1967—1:29:38, 1968—1:26:09, 1969—1:27:53.6, 1970—1:25:50, 1971—1:27:52.8, 1972—1:25:19.4. He was born at Eckartsberge on May 13th, 1939.

# FUCHS, R. (East Germany)

While the women's world record for the shot had been improved by nearly 7 feet and for the discus by some 20 feet since 1964, the javelin record—set by Yelena Gorchakova (USSR) in the Olympic qualifying round at Toyko—had stood obstinately at 204 ft. 8 in. . . . that is, until June 11th, 1972. On that day it was broken at two separate meetings: Eva Gryziecka of Poland threw 205 ft. 8 in. at Bucharest, followed less than an hour later by a phenomenal 213 ft. 5 in. from Ruth Fuchs (née Gamm) at Potsdam. Ruth had a supporting throw of 207 ft. 0 in., and her new record represented the biggest improvement in the event since official world records have been kept.

Although she began javelin throwing at the age of 14 it was not until a decade later, when placing 3rd in the 1971 European Championships that she first appeared in a major "Games". She maintained a brilliant standard of performance throughout 1972 and at the Munich Olympics she had one brilliant throw, in the 5th round, of 209 ft. 7 in. which ensured her expected victory.

A fine all-rounder, she has high jumped 5 ft. 2¼ in., long jumped 19 ft. 3¼ in. and thrown the discus 152 ft. 7 in. Her annual progress with the javelin: 1961—117ft 0in., 1962—120ft. 2in., 1963—141ft. 10in., 1964—152ft. 7in., 1965—169ft. 10in., 1966—168ft. 4in., 1967—184ft. 0in., 1968—189ft. 4in., 1969—182ft 7in., 1970—198ft. 10in., 1971—198ft. 8 in., 1972—213ft. 5in. She was born at Egeln on Dec. 14th, 1946.

Certainly, he was a man who was years ahead of his time, and in fact it was his form of training that inspired the celebrated Swedish coach Gosta Holmer to devise the popular fartlek system. Born at Calne, Wiltshire, on Sept. 9th, 1858, he lived to a great age (he died on June 4th, 1943) and is buried at his birthplace.

## GEORGE, W. G. (GB)

Walter George achieved enough during his amateur career to warrant lasting fame: world records in 1884 for the mile (4 min. 18.4 sec.), 2 mi. (9 min. 17.4 sec.), 3 mi. (14 min. 39.0 sec.), 6 mi. (30 min. 21.5 sec.), 10 mi. (51 min. 20.0 sec.), and one hour (11 mi. 932 yd.), together with numerous English titles at every event from 880 yd. to 10 mi. plus cross-country.

What ensured his immortality, though, was a professional mile race he won in 1886. He was pitted against the Scotsman William Cummings, holder of the professional record of 4 min. 16.2 sec., whom he had defeated in a 4 min. 20.2 race the previous year.

The return match attracted enormous interest (not to mention stakes) and the large crowd was not disappointed. George ran the legs off his opponent by reeling off laps in 58.5, 63.3, 66.0 and 65.0 sec. for a total time of 4 min. 12.8 sec. (actually 4 min. 12¾ sec.). This was a phenomenal time, for it was not until 1915 that any athlete—amateur or professional—bettered it. George is said to have clocked 4 min. 10.2 sec. (mile), 49 min. 29 sec. (10 mi.) and 59 min. 29 sec. (12 mi.) in training!

## GOLUBNICHIY, V. (USSR)

No walker in history can rival the medal-winning achievements of Vladimir Golubnichiy. Over a 12-year span he has never been worse than third in his six Olympic and European 20 kilometre races.

He was only 19 when he set his first world record, 90 min. 02.8 sec. in 1955, but another five years went by before he made his international championship debut. And what a start: he won the 1960 Olympic title, in hot and humid conditions. He lost his crown in 1964, placing third in a race won by Britain's Ken Matthews, but he regained it in the rarefied atmosphere of Mexico City in 1968 as he prevailed in the face of a blatant late run by Mexico's Jose Pedraza. He was back again in 1972, clocking a brilliant 86 min. 55.2 sec., and failing by a mere 12.8 sec. to hold East Germany's Peter Frenkel in Munich. In his two bids for the European title, he was third in 1962 and second in 1966.

His annual progress at the 20 km. walk: 1955—90:02.8, 1957—92:01, 1958—87:05, 1959—87:03.6, 1960—89:37, 1961—91:55, 1962—89:11, 1963—92:02, 1964—90:17.2, 1965—89:36, 1966—89:10, 1967—88:54, 1968—85:26, 1969—92:11, 1970—87:21.4, 1972—86:55.2. He was born at Sumy (Ukraine) on June 2nd, 1936.

# HAGG, G. (Sweden)

The name of Sweden's Gunder Hagg is inextricably bound up with that of his countryman and arch-rival Arne Andersson. These two tall, powerful runners together revolutionised accepted miling standards and Hagg also accomplished phenomenal records at longer distances.

Hagg was certainly the more successful from a record point of view (he set 15 world marks against Andersson's three) but there was little between them over a mile. Andersson ran a 4 min. 01.6 sec. in 1944, Hagg 4 min. 01.3 sec. in 1945—no other runner had ever beaten 4 min. 04.6 sec. at this time.

Hagg began as a 5000 m. runner in 1936, set his first national 1500 m. record in 1940 and the following year broke Jack Lovelock's celebrated world record of 3 min. 47.8 sec. Between July and Sept. 1942 he set no fewer than ten world records at seven different distances!

One of the marks was 13 min. 58.2 sec. for 5000 m., over ten seconds faster than the previous best and destined to withstand all assaults for nearly 12 years. It was his only serious attempt at the event, his next best time being only 14 min. 24.8 sec. in 1944. Both Hagg and Andersson were disqualified for professionalism in Nov. 1945 at the height of their powers and while in training for their first European Championships.

Hagg's best performances were 1 min. 52.8 sec. for 800 m., 3 min. 43.0 sec. for 1500 m., 4 min. 01.3 sec. for the mile, 5 min. 11.8 sec. for 2000 m., 8 min. 01.2 sec. for 3000 m., 8 min. 42.8 sec. for 2 mi., 13 min. 32.4 sec. for 3 mi., 13 min. 58.2 sec. for 5000 m. and 9 min. 28.4 sec. for 3000 m. steeplechase. He was born at Sorbygden on Dec. 31st, 1918.

# HALBERG, M. G.
## (New Zealand)

Not just a promising track career, but life itself, was threatened when young Murray Halberg was grievously injured playing rugby in 1950. Doctors doubted at first whether he would survive; they predicted at best he would be permanently crippled. They reckoned without Halberg's fantastic will power. Although his left arm is withered as a result of the accident he fought his way to the top of the tree as an athlete.

He first shook the track world in Feb. 1954 when, aged 20, he improved his mile time almost eight seconds to 4 min. 04.4 sec. He placed fifth in that year's epic Commonwealth Games mile in Vancouver but two years later was only 11th in the Olympic 1500 m. final.

His momentous string of championship honours commenced in 1958 when he ran clean away from the field over the final three laps of the Commonwealth Games 3 mi. He repeated these tactics with equal success in the 1960 Olympic 5000 m., and in 1962 he retained his Commonwealth title.

Halberg, who trained under Arthur Lydiard from 1952 and is now a coach in his own right, is a former world record holder at 2 mi. and 3 mi.

His best marks show the breadth of his range: 52.0 sec. for 440 yd., 1 min. 51.7 sec. for 800 m., 3 min. 38.8 sec. for 1500 m., 3 min. 57.5 sec. for the mile, 7 min. 57.6 sec. for 3000 m., 8 min. 30.0 sec. for 2 mi., 13 min. 10.0 sec. for 3 mi., 13 min. 35.2 sec. for 5000 m., 27 min. 32.8 sec. for 6 mi., 28 min. 33.0 sec. for 10,000 m. and 2 hr. 28 min. 36 sec. for the marathon. He was born at Eketahuna on July 7th, 1933.

# HAMMER

The hammer, as thrown today, is a metal ball and handle weighing together not less than 16 pounds. The spherical head is of solid iron or other metal not softer than brass, filled with lead or other material. The handle, connected to the head by means of a swivel, is made of a single unbroken and straight length of steel wire. The total length of the complete hammer is just under four feet. The implement is thrown from a circle 7 ft. in diameter and it must land within a 45 deg. sector. Competitors are allowed to wear gloves.

Prior to standardisation in 1908, the hammer was thrown under several sets of rules. When the event was included at the first Oxford University Sports in 1860 the handle was wooden and an unlimited forward run was permitted, the throw being measured from the front foot at time of delivery. Six years later a scratch line was innovated. This " freestyle " method continued at English universities until 1881. Elsewhere in England, from 1876 to 1886, the hammer (complete with 3 ft. 6 in. long wooden handle) was thrown from a 7 ft. circle. In 1887 the circle was enlarged to 9 ft. and in 1896 the AAA allowed a metal handle.

A dynasty of Irish-born athletes held possession of the world record from 1885 to 1949, a remarkably lengthy period of domination. The first great name was John Flanagan, who raised the record from a puny 145 ft. 10½ in. in 1895 to 184 ft. 4 in. in 1909. He won the Olympic title three times to complete a perfect career.

He was succeeded as record holder and champion by Matt McGrath, whose best was 187 ft. 4 in. in 1911. McGrath hurt his knee at the 1920 Olympics and placed only fifth but in 1924, at the age of 46, he took the silver medal. The 1920 champion was Pat Ryan, who had seven years earlier relieved McGrath of the record with 189 ft. 6½ in., a performance that went unbeaten until 1937 when the last of the Irish masters, Pat O'Callaghan, reached 195 ft. 4½in. The latter won the Olympic gold medal in 1928 and 1932.

The honour of hitting 200 feet first in official competition fell to Sverre Strandli (Norway) in 1952, though it is claimed that Fred Tootell (USA), the 1924 Olympic champion with a best amateur mark of 185 ft. 0 in., threw 210 ft. 7 in. as a professional.

It took 43 years for the record to progress from 180 to 200 feet, yet in the brief space of four years Mikhail Krivonosov (USSR) carried the world record over 220 feet. Even he was quickly superseded and in Nov. 1956 Hal Connolly (USA) seized control of the record with 224 ft. 10½ in. and narrowly defeated the Russian at the Olympics. Connolly blazed the trail over 230 ft. and Gyula Zsivotzky (Hungary) led the way past 240 ft. Walter Schmidt (W. Germany) set the current world record of 250 ft. 8 in. in 1971 but the following year he did not even make the Olympic team, and the gold medal in Munich went to Anatoliy Bondarchuk (USSR), the outstanding competitor in recent years.

Despite the successes achieved by her Irish neighbours, Britain has a fairly unimpressive record in this event. The only Olympic medallist was Malcolm Nokes, who was third in 1924, whilst Scotsman Duncan Clark placed third in the 1946 European Championships. Mike Ellis became the first Briton to surpass 200 ft. in 1957, and Howard Payne, who succeeded him as the record-holder, won the Commonwealth title in 1962, 1966 and 1970.

See also under BONDARCHUK, A., SCHMIDT, W.

## HAMPSON, T. (GB)

Tom Hampson was one of those fortunate athletes who managed to run the race of his life on the day it mattered most. Well known as an even pace runner, he kept cool in the headlong rush of the 1932 Olympic 800 m. final. The early pace was tremendously fast (24.4 sec. for the first 200 m.) and at the half-way stage Phil Edwards (Canada) led in 52.3 sec. Hampson was some 20 yd. down in 54.8 sec. but by maintaining his speed while the leader was forced to decelerate he drew level with Edwards halfway around the second lap and fought it out with another Canadian, Alex Wilson, for the remainder of the race. The Englishman, who only three years earlier had trailed in a poor last in something over two minutes in the Oxford v. Cambridge half-mile, proved just the stronger and won by a foot or two in 1 min. 49.7 sec. to become the first man to crack 1 min. 50 sec.

Five days later he collected a silver medal in the 4 x 400 m. relay, covering his leg in 47.6 sec. Two years prior, he had won the Commonwealth 880 yd. title in his best time of 1 min. 52.4 sec. His fastest mile time was 4 min. 17.0 sec. He was born in London on Oct. 28th, 1907 and died on Sept. 4th, 1965.

## HARBIG, R. (Germany)

Rudolf Harbig's 1 min. 46.6 sec. for 800 m. in 1939 is widely regarded as one of the most amazing individual achievements in track and field history. No one had previously run faster than 1 min. 48.4 sec. (Britain's Sydney Wooderson) and 16 years were to pass before Roger Moens, of Belgium, finally removed the world record.

In this famous race, on the fast 500 m. track in Milan, Harbig led only for the final 100 m. (reputedly covered in just 12 sec.!)—arch rival Mario Lanzi (Italy) having set a swift pace for 700 m. Harbig broke another world record in 1939, clocking 46.0 sec. for 400 m. Two years later he set a kilometre record of 2 min. 21.5 sec.

He was only a 48.8 sec./1 min. 52.2 sec. performer in 1936 when he won a bronze medal in the Berlin Olympic 4 x 400 m., but by 1938 he had attained sufficient stature to capture the European 800 m. title, as well as assisting Germany to victory in the relay.

He won 55 consecutive races at all distances from 50 to 1000 m. between Aug. 1938 and Sept. 1940. His last race was a 1 min. 54.2 sec. 800 m. in Oct. 1942. Best marks: 10.6 sec. for 100 m., 21.5 sec. for 200 m., 46.0 sec. for 400 m., 1 min. 46.6 sec. for 800 m., 2 min. 21.5 sec. for 1000 m., 4 min. 01.0 sec. for 1500 m., 5ft. 8in. high jump and 22ft. 6½in. long jump.

Harbig, who was born in Dresden on Nov. 8th, 1913, and was killed at the Eastern front on Mar. 5th, 1944, was trained by Waldemar Gerschler —later the coach to Josy Barthel (Luxemburg), the 1952 Olympic 1500 m. champion, and Britain's Gordon Pirie.

## HARDIN, G. F. (USA)

Another athlete years ahead of his time was Glenn Hardin, whose mark of 50.6 sec. for 400 m. hurdles in a race he won by 40 yd. survived as the world record from 1934 to 1953. In the same year he posted the second fastest 440 yd. on record (46.8 sec.) and unofficially tied the 220 yd. hurdles (straight) record of 22.7 sec.

Two years earlier he had experienced a somewhat bizarre season. At the American championships he broke the tape in the 400 m. hurdles only to find himself disqualified for running out of his lane. Later, in the Olympic final, because of the rules relating to the knocking down of hurdles then in force, he was credited with equalling the world record of 52.0 sec. though the race and Olympic record went to Irishman Bob Tisdall in 51.7 sec!

He won the Olympic title at the second attempt in 1936 and promptly retired. However, the name of Hardin again became prominent in athletic circles when his son Billy made the USA Olympic team in 1964 as a 400 m. hurdler.

Glenn Hardin's best marks included 21.4 sec. for 220 yd., 46.8 sec. for 440 yd., 1 min. 53.0 sec. for an 880 yd. relay leg, 15.4 sec. for 110 m. hurdles, 22.7 sec. for 220 yd. hurdles and 50.6 sec. for 400 m. hurdles. He was born at Derma, Mississippi, on July 1st, 1910.

## HAYES, R. L. (USA)

Bob Hayes, perhaps the fastest runner ever, began sprinting in 1959 when he was 16, and a mere two years later became the 13th man to tie Mel Patton's 100 yd. world record of 9.3 sec. That same season he was only a tenth of a second outside the straight 220 yd. record of 20.0 sec.

The following year he matched Frank Budd's new record of 9.2 sec. and in 1963 he finally made the world mark his own by streaking over 100 yd. of the rapid asphalt-rubber track in St. Louis in 9.1 sec. with the wind-gauge registering a breeze of only 0.8 m. per second behind him. Earlier in the season he had tied the then world records for 200 m. and 220 yd. (turn) of 20.5 sec.

One of his greatest displays occurred in Hanover in 1963 when, unleashing the most devastating burst of speed, he made up over four yards in a relay leg against Alfred Hebauf (W. Germany), who had run 100 m. in 10.3 sec. previously that day. The 6ft. 0in., 190 lb. American must have exceeded 26 m.p.h.

Early in 1964 he made further history by recording 5.9 sec. for 60 yd. to become the first man to break six seconds for this classic indoor event, but the climax to a brilliant career came, appropriately, at the Olympic Games. After scorching to victory in his 100 m. semi-final in a wind assisted 9.9 sec. he recorded a legal, world record equalling 10.0 sec. (on the unflattering electrical timing) in the final to win by a good two yards—the widest margin in Olympic 100 m. history. Six days later he produced an astonishing anchor leg to capture the 4 x 100 m. relay for the USA in world record time.

That proved to be Hayes' final race, for on returning to the United States he signed a professional football contract with the Dallas Cowboys and became one of the game's outstanding players.

Best marks: 9.1 sec. for 100 yd., 10.0 sec. for 100 m., 20.1 sec. for 220 yd. (straight), 20.5 sec. for 220 yd. (turn). He was born in Jacksonville, Florida, on Dec. 20th, 1942.

# HEMERY, D. P. (GB)

David Hemery, who announced his retirement following the 1972 season, was to a unique degree a product of both British and American athletics. Olympic champions are by implication outstanding athletes, but the skilled coaching of Fred Housden in London and Billy Smith in Boston, allied to his own natural talent and capacity for hard work, all combined to make of Hemery an outstanding champion even among champions.

Born in Gloucestershire, he moved with his family to the United States when he was 12. After graduating from high school in Massachusetts he returned to Britain in 1962. The following year he won the AAA junior 120 yd. hurdles title and, more significantly, made his 440 yd. hurdles debut—clocking 58.6 sec. for third in the Midland Championships.

He entered Boston University in the autumn of 1964 and steady progress was made at both hurdling events and on the flat. Particularly exciting were his European indoor records, early in 1966, of 1 min. 09.8 sec. for 600 yd. and 7.1 sec. for 60 yd. hurdles. Outdoors he ran only a handful of quarter hurdles (52.8 sec. in 1965 and 51.8 sec. in 1966) and concentrated on the "highs" to good effect. He won the 1966 Commonwealth title and, back in Europe, equalled the UK record of 13.9 sec. Hamstring trouble caused him to miss the 1967 outdoor season but, discouraging as it was to him at the time, that enforced rest enabled him to undertake a gruelling non-stop 60-week build up for the Mexico City Olympics.

He began his 1968 outdoor season by equalling his best 440 yd. hurdles time of 51.8 sec. and improved practically week by week so that in his final American race he won the National Collegiate 400 m. hurdles title in 49.8 sec. He trimmed that to 49.6 sec. in Britain and was ready for the Olympic challenge. Content to ease through his heat and semi-final (the latter in 49.3 sec.), he unleashed a staggering performance in the final. Running at a speed and with an attack never before witnessed in this event Hemery won by the huge margin of seven metres and, in clocking 48.1 sec., sliced no less than seven-tenths off the previous world record!

Having achieved the ultimate in 400 m. hurdling, Hemery turned to other challenges in his next two years. Although weak in several of the events he tackled the decathlon with gusto and only one British-born all-rounder bettered his score of 6,893 pts. in 1969. That season he cut the UK 110 m. hurdles record to 13.6 sec. and won the silver medal in the European Championships. In 1970 he retained his Commonwealth title and not only ran another 13.6 but also was timed at a remarkable 13.4 sec. in a European Cup semi-final in Zurich— a mark that was not ratified. He took 1971 off in a repetition of his preparations of four years earlier and returned to his best event in 1972. This time he did not win the Olympic title but he ran with characteristic panache in Munich to take the bronze medal in 48.6 sec., a performance comparable to his high-altitude 48.1 sec. in Mexico City. He completed a set of Olympic medals by winning a silver in the 4 x 400 m. relay

His best marks included 10.9 sec. for 100 m., 21.8 sec. for 200 m., 47.1 sec. for 400 m. (44.8 sec. in relay), 1 min. 52 sec. for 800 m. (in training), 13.6 sec. for 110 m. hurdles, 34.6 sec. for 300 m. hurdles (best on record), 48.1 sec. for 400 m. hurdles, 6 ft. 1¼ in. high jump, 23 ft. 6½ in. long jump and 6,893 pts. decathlon. He was born at Cirencester on July 18th, 1944.

# HIGH JUMP

A high jumper may set about his task of clearing the maximum possible height in any manner he likes—except that he is obliged to take off from one foot, he may not employ weights or grips of any kind, and the sole of his shoe must not be more than half an inch thick nor must the thickness of the heel exceed that of the sole by more than a quarter of an inch. This last measure came into effect in 1958 to combat the growing practice of jumpers using "built-up shoes" for extra leverage.

Three consecutive failures result in the elimination of a competitor. Since 1927 the rules have stipulated that the crossbar must rest in such a manner that it can fall either forwards or backwards.

There are three styles of high jumping commonly in use: the straddle, where the athlete drapes himself face down across the bar (as used by the world record holders Pat Matzdorf and Yordanka Blagoyeva); the Fosbury-flop, where the athlete employs a back lay-out and goes over head first (as originated by 1968 Olympic champion Dick Fosbury and used by 1972 champion Ulrike Meyfarth); and the Western roll, where an athlete crosses the bar on his side.

The first jumper to lift himself over six feet was the English rugby international, the Hon. Marshall Brooks, who in 1876 "cat jumped" 6 ft. 0¼ in. and subsequently 6 ft. 2½ in. It is said that at the English Championships of 1876 the unchallenged Brooks took one disdainful jump at 6 ft. 0 in., landing with both the crossbar and his top hat intact!

Pioneer of the eastern cut-off was Mike Sweeney, an Irish-American, who set world marks of 6 ft. 5 in. and 6 ft. 5½ in. in 1895. His record stood until 1912, in which year George Horine (USA)—inventor of the western roll—went 6 ft. 6 in. and 6ft. 7 in.

Dave Albritton, who tied with fellow-American Cornelius Johnson at the world record height of 6 ft. 9¾ in. in 1936, was the first great straddle exponent. Another straddle jumper, Les Steers (USA) raised the record three times in 1941 ending with 6 ft. 11 in.

The magical seven-foot jump could not be far away, it seemed, but in fact another 15 years were to flit past before its realisation in *bona fide* competition. The hero was Charles Dumas (USA), whose silken straddle carried him over 7 ft. 0½ in. in 1956.

Perhaps the first to jump seven feet under any circumstances was Bill Stewart (USA), who held the world record of 6 ft. 10¼ in. for literally an hour or two in 1941. That same year he is said to have cleared 7 ft. 0¼ in. in training shortly before losing his life.

John Thomas (USA) swept the world record upwards in four stages to 7 ft. 3¾ in. in 1960 and he was succeeded by another straddle jumper Valeriy Brumel (USSR) who was credited with six records culminating with 7 ft. 5¾ in. in 1963. Brumel's record stood until Pat Matzdorf (USA) cleared 7 ft. 6¼ in. in 1971, a height reported to have been jumped by China's Ni Chih-chin (who is only 6 ft. 0½ in. tall) in Nov. 1970. Ni's best official jump is 7 ft. 5¼ in. in 1966.

Excluding a number of talented Irishmen (including the Leahy brothers, Pat and Con, who placed second in the 1900 and 1908 Olympics respectively) British high jumpers have had a lean time since the turn of the century.

The one bright exception was the

Scotsman Alan Paterson, who won the European title in 1950. His best was 6 ft. 7¼ in. in 1947.

See also under BRUMEL, V., DUMAS, C. E., FOSBURY, R., MATZDORF P., and TARMAK, J.

## Women

It took 80 years for the men's record to climb from 6 to 7 ft., but in the women's event, where standards are roughly a foot lower, only 33 years elapsed between the first five-foot clearance by Phyllis Green (GB) in 1925 and the initial six-footer by Iolanda Balas (Rumania) in 1958. Balas dominated the event for practically a decade and her final world record of 6 ft. 3¼ in. survived from 1961 to 1971, when Ilona Gusenbauer (Austria) added a quarter-inch. Yordanka Blagoyeva (Bulgaria) jumped 6 ft. 4¼ in., a height no man bettered until 1895, in 1972.

The three outstanding British jumpers, all world record holders in their time, have been Dorothy Tyler (*née* Odam), Sheila Lerwill (*née* Alexander), the first female straddle stylist, and Thelma Hopkins. Each of these athletes also won an Olympic silver medal (two in Mrs. Tyler's case); in fact it was Britain's misfortune to have been placed second in every Olympic competition from 1936 to 1960 inclusive! Two British-born girls have jumped 6 feet: Barbara Inkpen and Linda Hedmark (*née* Knowles).

See also under BALAS, I., BLAGOYEVA, Y., BLANKERS-KOEN, F. E., MEYFARTH, U., and TYLER, D. J. B.

## HILL, A. G. (GB)

Albert Hill is surprisingly little remembered these days when one considers the magnitude of his achievement in winning both the 800 and 1500 m. at the 1920 Olympic Games. That double triumph came at the age of 31, fully ten years after he won his first AAA title . . . at 4 miles.

In the space of four days he ran a total of five races, winning the 800 m. by a yard in the British record time of 1 min. 53.4 sec. and the 1500 m. by four yards from his colleague Philip Baker (who as Philip Noel-Baker won the Nobel Peace Prize in 1959) in 4 min. 01.8 sec.

The following year he won the AAA mile in 4 min. 13.8 sec. to slash a full three seconds from the British record he shared with Joe Binks. Hill was coached by Sam Mussabini, the trainer of Harold Abrahams and Willie Applegarth among other notables, and he in turn later coached the great Sydney Wooderson. He was born on Mar. 24th, 1889 and died in Canada on Jan. 8th, 1969.

## HILL, R. (GB)

Throughout the 1960s Ron Hill was one of Britain's most prominent track, road and cross-country runners, but it was not until 1969—eight years after his debut at the event—that he emerged as a great marathon competitor.

Due to indiscriminate racing he never did himself justice in several international championship appearances prior to 1968: he failed to finish in the 1962 European marathon, placed 19th in the 1964 Olympic marathon (he was the world's second fastest of all time prior to the race) and 18th in the 10,000 m., 5th in the 1966 Commonwealth Games 6 mi. and —victim of a stomach disorder—12th in the European marathon a few weeks later.

In 1968, however, he adopted a more thoughtful approach to racing and was rewarded by placing 7th in the Olympic 10,000 m., the first finisher among those who had not trained for long periods, or lived, at altitude. He enjoyed a great run of success between Nov. 1968 and July 1970, during which he produced a world record of 46 min. 44.0 sec for 10 mi. (to add to the world records for 15 mi. and 25 km. he set in 1965), won the European and Commonwealth marathon titles (the latter in 2 hr. 9 min. 28 sec., second fastest ever), beat world record holder Derek Clayton in the Maxol Marathon and scored a resounding victory in the famous Boston Marathon (2 hr. 10 min. 30 sec.). The magic had gone for two races Hill had expected to win, the 1971 European (3rd) and 1972 Olympic (6th) marathons, but he remains a potential world beater on his day.

His best marks include 4 min. 10.1 sec. for the mile, 8 min. 41 sec for 2 mi., 13 min. 27.2 sec, for 3 mi., 27 min. 26 sec. for 6 mi., 46 min. 44 sec. for 10 mi., 58 min. 39 sec. for 20 km., 12 mi. 1268 yd. in the hour, 1 hr. 12 min. 48.2 sec. for 15 mi., 1 hr. 15 min. 22.6 sec. for 25 km., 1 hr. 36 min. 28 sec. for 20 mi. (road) and 2 hr. 9 min. 28 sec. for the marathon.

Annual marathon progress: 1961—2:24:22, 1962—2:21:59, 1963—2:18:06, 1964—2:14:12, 1965—2:26:33, 1966—2:20:55, 1967—2:23:43, 1968—2:17:11, 1969—2:11:54, 1970—2:09:28, 1971—2:12:39, 1972—2:12:51. He was born at Accrington (Lancashire) on Sept. 25th, 1938.

## HINES, J. R. (USA)

As the first man to better 10 sec. for 100 metres, the place of Jim Hines in the history of sprinting is assured. The occasion was the American AAU Championships at Sacramento in June 1968 and after a wind-assisted 9.8 sec. heat he established a new world record of 9.9 sec. in his semi.

The final was an anti-climax in that he suffered a bad start and lost narrowly to Charlie Greene, both clocking a windy 10.0 sec. At Mexico City later in the season he made no mistake and won the Olympic crown by a full metre in an electrically timed 9.90 sec.—a world record equalling mark that on hand timing would probably have been registered as 9.8 sec., the fastest sprint to date. He also ran a dynamic anchor leg in the 4 x 100 m. relay, taking his team both to victory and a world record 38.2 sec.

Hines, who was coached by 1956 Olympic sprint hero Bobby Morrow, also equalled the world records of 5.9 for indoor 60 yd. and 9.1 sec. for 100 yd. and was timed at 45.5 sec. for a 440 yd. relay leg. As a profesional in 1969 he ran 220 yd in 20.2 sec. . . . against a racehorse! He was born at Dumas, Arkansas, on Sep. 10th, 1946.

## HISTORY OF ATHLETICS

Men have run, jumped and thrown things in competition with one another for thousands of years. The

Lugnasad, or Tailteann Games, in Ireland are thought to have been founded as far back as 1829 B.C., some four and a half centuries before the Olympic Games are believed to have been started in Greece.

The first Olympic champion whose name we know is Coroebus, winner of the stade (202 yd.) foot race in the Games of 776 B.C. Thirty Olympiads later, in 656 B.C., a Spartan athlete called Chionis long jumped 23 ft. 1½ in.—the earliest measured performance known to posterity.

Following the abolition of the Olympic Games in A.D. 393 athletics plunged into the Dark Ages. There are vague reports of spasmodic athletic activity in medieval England but it was not until the 19th century that the sport became popular.

Mention should be made, though, of the sport of pedestrianism, which began in 17th century England, in which men of means waged on the road running ability of their footmen.

The world's first athletic club, the Necton Guild, was established in Norfolk in 1817. By then regular competitions were already being held at the Royal Military Academy at Sandhurst.

The 11¼ mile Crick Run at Rugby School (as described in *Tom Brown's Schooldays*) was instituted in 1837 and soon afterwards other public schools started to introduce athletics into the sporting curriculum. In 1839 a meeting was held near Toronto, the first on record in North America.

An important landmark was reached in 1850—the formation of the oldest surviving club, Exeter College (Oxford) AC. The same year the first organised meeting was held at Oxford University, six years before athletics got under way at Cambridge.

Below are some of the key dates in athletics history since then:—

1860 Foundation of the Olympic Club of San Francisco.
1862 First open amateur meeting held in England, organised by West London Rowing Club.
1863 Mincing Lane AC (renamed London AC in 1866) founded.
1864 Annual Oxford v. Cambridge match inaugurated.

| 1866 | Amateur Athletic Club promoted the first English Championships. |
|---|---|
| 1868 | First indoor meeting was promoted by New York AC. |
| 1874 | English students staged the Continent's first meeting in Dresden. |
| 1876 | American Championships held for the first time. A team from London AC won a match in Ireland, the first instance of international competition. |
| 1877 | First English cross-country championship. |
| 1880 | Formation of the Amateur Athletic Association and inauguration of AAA Championships. |
| 1888 | Foundation of the Amateur Athletic Union of the USA. |
| 1896 | Olympic Games revived in Athens. |
| 1903 | First international cross-country championship. |
| 1913 | Establishment of the International Amateur Athletic Federation. |
| 1917 | First women's governing body founded in France. |
| 1921 | First full international match between France and England held in Paris. |
| 1922 | Foundation of the Women's Amateur Athletic Association. |
| 1928 | Women's events added to the Olympic Games athletics programme. |
| 1930 | Establishment of the British Commonwealth Games. |
| 1934 | Establishment of the European Championships. |
| 1958 | First match between USA and USSR. |
| 1965 | Establishment of European Cup Tournament. |
| 1966 | Establishment of European Indoor Games (Championships from 1970). |

# HURDLES

There are three forms of hurdle racing: high (3ft. 6in.) hurdling over 120 yd. and 110 m.; intermediate (3ft. 0in.) hurdling over 440 yd. and 400 m.; and low (2ft. 6in.) hurdling over 220 yd. and 200 m. Ten flights of hurdles are negotiated in each of these races.

# High Hurdles

The first reference to a 120 yards event dates back to the Oxford University Sports of 1864. The barriers were crude sheep hurdles, about 3ft. 6in. high, staked in the ground. They were standardised at 3ft. 6in. in 1866.

The high hurdling pioneers used an ungainly bent-leg clearance style. Arthur Croome, an Oxford student, is credited with being the first man to lead over the hurdles with a straight leg in 1886. Alvin Kraenzlein (USA), winner of four gold medals at the 1900 Olympics, brought the record down to 15.2 sec. in 1898 but progress was slow until 1916, when Robert Simpson (USA) twice clocked 14.6 sec. The next record holder (14.4 sec. in 1920), Earl Thomson (Canada), was the first hurdler to use a double-shift arm action.

Shortly after the 1936 Olympics the biggest sensation in hurdling history occurred when Forrest Towns (USA), the newly crowned champion, cut all of four-tenths of a second from the world record with a dazzling time of 13.7 sec. for 110 m.

It was only in 1948 that this record was trimmed to 13.6 sec. by Harrison Dillard (USA), the one man to win both the Oympic 100 m. and 110 m. hurdles. Inches behind Dillard at the 1952 Games was Jack Davis (USA), who shared the winner's Olympic record. Davis ran the first 13.4 sec. in 1956 but in that year's Olympics he underwent the traumatic experience of again sharing the winner's time in second place. The championship went to Lee Calhoun (USA), who successfully defended his laurels in 1960. Martin Lauer (W. Germany), the first man to run the event in 13.2 sec., finished fourth.

That metric 13.2 sec. has survived through 1972 but Rod Milburn (USA), the 1972 Olympic champion, clocked 13.0 for 120 yd. (only 10 inches less than 110 m.) in 1971.

Britain possessed two world class high hurdlers in the 1930s in Lord Burghley, whose 14.5 sec. clocking in 1930 was only a tenth outside the existing world record, and Don Finlay, twice an Olympic medallist. Finlay was Britain's number one from 1932 to 1949 and for most of the following decade or so Peter Hildreth (once Britain's most "capped" international) was his country's first string —thus two athletes dominated the event for close on 30 years between them. Mike Parker became the first Briton to duck under 14 seconds by returning 13.9 sec. late in 1963.

David Hemery won the Commonwealth title in 1966 and gained a European silver medal in 1969, a distinction achieved by Alan Pascoe in 1971.

## Intermediate Hurdles

A 440 yard race over 12 flights was held at the 1860 Oxford University Sports. Although the event received Olympic recognition in 1900 it did not feature in the AAA and AAU Championships until 1914.

The four big names in pre-war intermediate hurdling tangled at the 1932 Olympics. Winner was Bob Tisdall (Ireland), whose time of 51.7 sec. for 400 m. was not officially accepted as a world record because he knocked down the final hurdle, which was against the rules for records then in force. His was one of the most startling breakthroughs in Olympic history, for he was only a novice at the event and his best time prior to the Games was but 54.2 sec.

Runner-up, but absurdly credited with the world record, was Glenn Hardin (USA), who in 1934 was to smash Tisdall's mark by over a second with a resounding 50.6 sec. and two years later was to succeed the Irishman as Olympic champion. In third place was Morgan Taylor (USA), who had won the 1924 title but like Tisdall had lost a record through clipping a hurdle. Placing fourth in 52.2 sec., a British record for 22 years, was the defending champion Lord Burghley.

Yuriy Lituyev (USSR) broke Hardin's record by a fifth of a second in 1953 but the next advance was a dramatic one. Glenn Davis (USA)—in his FIRST year of quarter mile hurdling—ran 49.5 sec. for the metric event and went on to take the Olympic title, which four years later in 1960 he retained. Davis set a new mark of 49.2 sec. in 1958, a time matched by Salvatore Morale (Italy) in winning the 1962 European crown,

and bettered by the 1964 Olympic champion, American Rex Cawley (49.1 sec.).

The event's standards were transformed in 1968 when Geoff Vanderstock (USA) ran 48.8 sec. and David Hemery (GB) dominated the Olympic final in 48.1 sec.—both times being run at high altitude. Hemery's record stood unchallenged until the Munich Olympics, where John Akii-Bua (Uganda) clocked a phenomenal 47.8 sec. at close to sea level. Hemery finished third to add to his previous gold medal and the silver gained by John Cooper in 1964.

## Low Hurdles

Apart from a half-share in the current 200 m. world record (turn) by Martin Lauer, of West Germany, the low hurdles event has always been practically an American preserve. Now that the event has been dropped from championship competition in the USA, it has become almost extinct. It was included in the AAA Championships schedule only from 1952 to 1962.

Don Styron (USA), the present world record holder on a straight track, is the only man to have completed the race inside "even time," his record being 21.9 sec. for 220 yards.

See also AKII-BUA, J., BURGHLEY, LORD, CALHOUN, L. Q., DAVIS, G. A., DILLARD, W. H.; FINLAY, D. O.; HARDIN, G. F.; HEMERY, D. P.; MILBURN, R.; OWENS, J. C.; and TOWNS, F. G.

## Women

The standard hurdling event for women, since 1969, has been 100 m. over ten flights of 2ft. 9in hurdles. Previously the race run at Olympic, European and Commonwealth Games was 80 m. in length, over 8 flights of 2 ft. 6 in. hurdles. The 100 m. record of 12.5 sec. is shared by Annelie Ehrhardt (E. Germany) and Pam Ryan (Australia).

Another event on the world record schedule, although rarely run internationally, is the 200m. hurdles, comprising 10 flights of 2 ft. 6 in. hurdles. Best on record is 25.7 sec. by Pam

Ryan. It is possible that, in years to come, this will be replaced by 400 m. hurdles. A few experimental races have already been held, the fastest time yet being 58.6 sec. by the Austrian, Maria Sykora.

See also BALZER, K.; BLANKERS-KOEN, F. E.; CHI CHENG; DELAHUNTY, S. B.; EHRHARDT, A.; and RYAN, P.

# HYMAN, D. (GB)

The most prolific medal winner in the annals of British athletics, Dorothy Hyman retired after collecting four gold, four silver and three bronze awards in Olympic, European and Commonwealth Games competition. All this was achieved before her 24th birthday.

She made her international bow in 1957 and gained major honours in every subsequent season, with the exception of 1961 which she missed through injury.

1958: Gold medallist in Commonwealth 4 x 110 yd. relay won in world record time of 45.3 sec., and silver medallist in European 4 x 100 m.

1959: WAAA 100 and 220 yd. champion.

1960: WAAA 100 m. and 220 yd. champion; Olympic silver medallist in 100 m. and bronze medallist in 200 m.

1962: WAAA 100 and 220 yd. champion; European 100 m. champion, runner-up in 200 m. and bronze medallist in relay; Commonwealth 100 and 220 yd. champion and relay silver medal winner.

1963: WAAA 100 and 220 yd. champion and unbeaten all season.

1964: despite early season injury, reached Olympic 100 m. final and gained bronze medal in 4 x 100 m. relay.

Her tally in international matches, 1957 to 1964, was equally extraordinary. Excluding relays she won 21 of her 30 races, including 18 victories out of 21 since 1960. She held or shared European records at 100 yd., 100 m. and 200 m., holds the UK records for those three events, and was a member of the world record (45.2 sec.) 4 x 110 yd. relay team in 1963. Her best times were 10.6 sec. for 100 yd., 11.3 sec. for 100 m., 23.2 sec. for 200 m. and 23.7 sec. for 220 yd.

Although barred from international competition because of money received from a book, Dorothy made a great comeback in 1969, winning the WAAA 200 m., placing 2nd to Chi Cheng in the 100 m. and clocking times of 11.3 sec. (wind assisted) and 23.5 sec. She returned 11.5 sec in her final race in 1970. She was born at Cudworth, Yorkshire, on May 9th. 1941.

for 3000 m., 8 min. 41.2 sec. for 2 mi., 13 min. 20.8 sec. for 3 mi., 13 min. 54.4 sec. for 5000 m. and 28 min. 52.0 sec. for 6 mi. He was born in Huddersfield on June 17th, 1932.

## INDOOR ATHLETICS

The world's first indoor meeting was promoted by the New York Athletic Club on Nov. 11th, 1868, but it was not until 1906 that the Amateur Athletic Union of the United States instituted national indoor championships.

English Championships were organised by the AAA at Wembley from 1935 to 1939, and were revived in 1962. The Championships have been staged at Cosford since 1965. An inaugural European Indoor Games, paving the way to a full-scale Championships, was held in Dortmund in 1966. Subsequent venues: 1967—Prague, 1968—Madrid, 1969—Belgrade, 1970—Vienna (first official Championships), 1971—Sofia, 1972—Grenoble, 1973—Rotterdam.

## IBBOTSON, G. D. (GB)

No post-war British athlete has endeared himself to the general public to quite the same degree as Derek Ibbotson. His cheerful personality, allied to exceptional running ability, made him the leading box office attraction in British athletics for several seasons.

He shot into world class as a three-miler in 1955, the following year winning the bronze medal in the Olympic 5000 m. behind Vladimir Kuts and Gordon Pirie. His most startling achievement in 1956 came over a mile, though. Despite a previous best of only 4 min. 07.0 sec. he sensationally equalled Roger Bannister's British record of 3 min. 59.4 sec.

In July 1957 he made not only the national record, but the world record also, his own property with a scintillating run of 3 min. 57.2 sec. The race was a complete triumph for Ibbotson, for he convincingly defeated the most formidable opposition the world could offer. Ron Delany (Ireland), the Olympic champion, finished second ten yards behind, with Stanislav Jungwirth, the Czech who had broken the world 1500 m. record the previous week, and Ken Wood (Britain) also inside four minutes.

Ibbotson ran several fine races in the seasons that followed without ever quite recapturing his 1957 sparkle. Perhaps the outstanding achievement of his later years was his 1962 indoor campaign when he posted European bests at 2 and 3 mi.

Best marks: 1 min. 52.2 sec. for 880 yd., 3 min. 41.9 sec. for 1500 m., 3 min. 57.2 sec. for the mile, 5 min. 12.8 sec. for 2000 m., 8 min. 00.0 sec.

## A.A.A. Champions

| 60 Yards | | sec. |
|---|---|---|
| 1962 | D. H. Jones | 6.5 |
| 1963 | H. J. Bender (W. Germany) | 6.4 |
| 1964 | A. Meakin | 6.4 |
| 1965 | R. M. Frith | 6.3 |
| 1966 | B. H. Kelly | 6.3 |
| 1967 | R. M. Frith | 6.3 |

| 60 Metres | | sec. |
|---|---|---|
| 1968 | R. M. Frith | 6.8 |
| 1969 | R. M. Frith | 6.9 |
| 1970 | P. Pinnington | 6.8 |
| 1971 | D. G. Halliday | 6.8 |
| 1972 | B. H. Kelly | 6.8 |
| 1973 | B. W. Green | 6.8 |

| 70 Yards | | sec. |
|---|---|---|
| 1935 | K. S. Duncan | 7.5 |
| 1936 | C. B. Holmes | 7.4 |
| 1937 | C. B. Holmes | 7.3 |
| 1938 | E. L. Page | 7.4 |
| 1939 | B. Giles | 7.5 |

| 220 Yards | | sec. |
|---|---|---|
| 1965 | D. G Dear | 22.8 |
| 1966 | D. G. Dear | 23.1 |
| 1967 | T. J. Smith | 22.7 |

| 200 Metres | | sec. |
|---|---|---|
| 1968 | R. Banthorpe | 22.8 |
| 1969 | P. Wiltshire | 22.6 |
| 1970 | K. Meredith | 23.0 |

| 440 Yards | | sec. |
|---|---|---|
| 1965 | M. A. Rawson | 49.6 |
| 1966 | W. Mottley (Trinidad) | 47.3 |
| 1967 | C. W. A. Campbell | 49.8 |

| 400 Metres | | sec. |
|---|---|---|
| 1968 | C. W. A. Campbell | 47.9 |
| 1969 | D. G. Griffiths | 48.9 |
| 1970 | D. G. Griffiths | 49.0 |
| 1971 | J. W. Aukett | 48.2 |
| 1972 | J. W. Aukett | 48.9 |
| 1973 | J. W. Aukett | 47.9 |

| 600 Yards | | min. sec. |
|---|---|---|
| 1936 | J. V. Powell | 1 19.5 |
| 1962 | B. H. A. Morris | 1 16.3 |
| 1963 | W. F. Crothers (Canada) | 1 12.1 |
| 1964 | W. F. Crothers (Canada) | 1 10.0 |

| 880 Yards | | min. sec. |
|---|---|---|
| 1937 | J. V. Powell | 2 03.3 |
| 1938 | A. C. Pettit | 2 04.4 |
| 1939 | G. F. Morris | 2 00.4 |
| 1965 | P. J. Beacham | 1 52.5 |
| 1966 | J. Gingell | 1 52.3 |
| 1967 | A. D. Middleton | 1 51.5 |

| 800 Metres | | min. sec. |
|---|---|---|
| 1968 | J. Gingell | 1 52.0 |
| 1969 | R. S. Adams | 1 51.1 |
| 1970 | C. W. A. Campbell | 1 49.6 |
| 1971 | P. J. Lewis | 1 50.2 |
| 1972 | C. F. Cusick | 1 51.2 |
| 1973 | A. K. Gibson | 1 52.0 |

| 1000 Yards | | min. sec. |
|---|---|---|
| 1962 | T. J. B. Bryan | 2 17.9 |
| 1963 | W. F. Crothers (Canada) | 2 14.0 |
| 1964 | J. Whetton | 2 12.2 |

| Mile | | min. sec. |
|---|---|---|
| 1962 | W. Olivier (S. Africa) | 4 12.1 |
| 1963 | J. Whetton | 4 13.3 |
| 1964 | J. Whetton | 4 07.9 |
| 1965 | J. Whetton | 4 06.3 |
| 1966 | J. Whetton | 4 04.7 |
| 1967 | J. Whetton | 4 09.9 |

| 1500 Metres | | min. sec. |
|---|---|---|
| 1968 | J. Whetton | 3 51.0 |
| 1969 | W. Wilkinson | 3 49.3 |
| 1970 | W. Wilkinson | 3 48.0 |
| 1971 | J. Davies | 3 46.9 |
| 1972 | F. J. Clement | 3 46.4 |
| 1973 | J. McGuinness | 3 50.6 |

| 2 Miles | | min. sec. |
|---|---|---|
| 1937 | R. Thorogood | 9 38.0 |
| 1938 | R. Thorogood | 9 33.6 |
| 1939 | T. N. Rowe | 9 27.2 |
| 1962 | G. D. Ibbotson | 8 52.2 |
| 1963 | J. Cooke | 8 57.4 |
| 1964 | B. Kidd (Canada) | 8 39.0 |
| 1965 | G. D. Ibbotson | 8 42.6 |
| 1966 | A. Simpson | 8 45.6 |
| 1967 | I. McCafferty | 8 36.4 |

| 3000 Metres | | min. sec. |
|---|---|---|
| 1968 | I. McCafferty | 8 00.4 |
| 1969 | I. McCafferty | 8 08.4 |
| 1970 | R. S. Wilde | 7 59.2 |
| 1971 | P. J. Stewart | 8 00.4 |
| 1972 | I. Stewart | 7 50.0 |
| 1973 | I. Stewart | 7 58.0 |

| 2000 m. Steeplechase | | min. sec. |
|---|---|---|
| 1967 | R. McAndrew | 5 42.4 |
| 1968 | P. A. Morris | 5 35.0 |
| 1969 | B. D. Blakeley | 5 36.6 |
| 1970 | R. McAndrew | 5 36.8 |
| 1971 | B. Hayward | 5 34.8 |
| 1972 | R. McAndrew | 5 32.4 |
| 1973 | R. McAndrew | 5 36.8 |

| 60 Yards Hurdles | | sec. |
|---|---|---|
| 1962 | J. M. W. Hogan | 7.7 |
| 1963 | J. L. Taitt | 7.6 |
| 1964 | J. M. Parker | 7.4 |
| 1965 | J. M. Parker | 7.4 |
| 1966 | J. M. Parker | 7.4 |
| 1967 | A. P. Pascoe | 7.5 |

| 60 Metres Hurdles | | sec. |
|---|---|---|
| 1968 | A. P. Pascoe | 8.1 |
| 1969 | A. P. Pascoe | 7.8 |
| 1970 | A. P. Pascoe | 7.8 |
| 1971 | B. Price | 7.9 |
| 1972 | G. J. Gower | 7.9 |
| 1973 | A. P. Pascoe | 8.0 |

| 70 Yards Hurdles | | sec. |
|---|---|---|
| 1935 | A. G. Pilbrow | 9.0 |
| 1936 | E. D. Mitchell | 9.3 |
| 1937 | D. O. Finlay | 9.0 |
| 1938 | D. O. Finlay | 8.9 |
| 1939 | T. L. Lockton | 8.9 |

| High Jump | | ft. in. |
|---|---|---|
| 1935 | S. R. West | 6 0 |
| 1936 | J. L. Newman | 5 10 |
| 1937 | J. L. Newman | 6 2 |
| 1938 | R. K. Kennedy | 6 1 |
| 1939 | J. L. Newman | 5 10 |
| 1962 | G. A. Miller | 6 8 |
| 1963 | C. W. Fairbrother | 6 7 |
| 1964 | H. Wadsworth (USA) | 6 7 |

102

| | | ft. | in. |
|---|---|---|---|
| 1965 | G. A. Miller | 6 | 8 |
| 1966 | C. W. Fairbrother | 6 | 7 |
| 1967 | M. C. Campbell | 6 | 5 |
| 1968 | M. C. Campbell | 6 | 5 |
| 1969 | M. C. Campbell | 6 | 4 |
| 1970 | D. N. Wilson | 6 | 4¾ |
| 1971 | D. J. Livesey | 6 | 10¼ |
| 1972 | M. C. Campbell | 6 | 6¾ |
| 1973 | A. Sneazwell (Aus) | 6 | 10¾ |

*Pole Vault*

| | | ft. | in. |
|---|---|---|---|
| 1935 | F. R. Webster | 12 | 3 |
| 1936 | F. R. Webster | 12 | 3 |
| 1937 | F. R. Webster | 12 | 9½ |
| 1938 | F. R. Webster | 12 | 3 |
| 1939 | H. W. Yielder | 12 | 0 |
| 1962 | T. P. Burton | 13 | 9 |
| 1963 | M. R. Higdon | 13 | 0 |
| 1964 | R. Schmelz (W. Germany) | 15 | 5 |
| 1965 | D. D. Stevenson | 14 | 9 |
| 1966 | M. R. Higdon | 14 | 0 |
| 1967 | M. A. Bull | 15 | 1 |
| 1968 | M. A. Bull | 15 | 7¼ |
| 1969 | M. A. Bull | 16 | 3 |
| 1970 | M. A. Bull | 16 | 0¾ |
| 1971 | M. A. Bull | 15 | 6¼ |
| 1972 | M. A. Bull | 16 | 0¾ |
| 1973 | B. R. L. Hooper | 15 | 9 |

*Long Jump*

| | | ft. | in. |
|---|---|---|---|
| 1935 | K. S. Duncan | 22 | 9 |
| 1936 | R. C. Crombie | 21 | 3 |
| 1937 | J. P. Daniel | 22 | 4½ |
| 1938 | R. A. Powell | 21 | 9 |
| 1939 | R. A. Powell | 21 | 8 |
| 1962 | F. J. Alsop | 23 | 7 |
| 1963 | L. Davies | 24 | 6¾ |
| 1964 | O. Oladitan (Nigeria) | 24 | 0½ |
| 1965 | F. J. Alsop | 23 | 8¼ |
| 1966 | L. Davies | 25 | 9 |
| 1967 | P. S. Templeton | 23 | 9½ |
| 1968 | D. Walker | 24 | 2¼ |
| 1969 | P. N. Scott | 23 | 9¾ |
| 1970 | A. L. Lerwill | 24 | 9¼ |
| 1971 | A. L. Lerwill | 25 | 0½ |
| 1972 | L. Davies | 24 | 7¾ |
| 1973 | A. L. Lerwill | 25 | 0½ |

*Triple Jump*

| | | ft. | in. |
|---|---|---|---|
| 1965 | F. J. Alsop | 50 | 10¾ |
| 1966 | M. Ralph | 48 | 3¾ |
| 1967 | F. J. Alsop | 49 | 6 |
| 1968 | F. J. Alsop | 50 | 9¾ |
| 1969 | D. C. J. Boosey | 50 | 9¼ |
| 1970 | D. C. J. Boosey | 51 | 5½ |
| 1971 | A. E. Wadhams | 50 | 7½ |
| 1972 | D. C. J. Boosey | 49 | 9¼ |
| 1973 | C. P. Colman | 50 | 6¼ |

*Shot*

| | | ft. | in. |
|---|---|---|---|
| 1935 | R. L. Howland | 42 | 1¾ |
| 1936 | L. R. Carter | 43 | 1½ |
| 1937 | P. Hincks | 45 | 1¾ |
| 1938 | R. L. Howland | 44 | 1½ |
| 1939 | H. Merz | 42 | 0¼ |
| 1962 | M. T. Lucking | 58 | 8 |
| 1963 | A. Carter | 51 | 7½ |
| 1964 | M. R. Lindsay | 57 | 6¾ |
| 1965 | A. Carter | 57 | 2½ |
| 1966 | M. R. Lindsay | 55 | 2½ |
| 1967 | A. E. Elvin | 54 | 4¼ |
| 1968 | J. Teale | 58 | 2 |
| 1969 | W. R. Tancred | 56 | 9½ |
| 1970 | J. Teale | 56 | 4¾ |
| 1971 | G. L. Capes | 59 | 3½ |
| 1972 | G. L. Capes | 61 | 2¼ |
| 1973 | M. A. Winch | 61 | 3 |

*Mile Walk*

| | | min. | sec. |
|---|---|---|---|
| 1936 | A. A. Cooper | 6 | 59.4 |

## WAAA Champions

(No championships in 1968)

*60 Yards*

| | | sec. |
|---|---|---|
| 1962 | D. Arden | 7.1 |
| 1963 | D. Arden | 7.1 |
| 1964 | D. Arden | 7.1 |
| 1965 | E. A. Gill | 6.9 |
| 1966 | D. Slater (Arden) | 7.1 |

*60 Metres*

| | | sec. |
|---|---|---|
| 1935 | K. Stokes | 8.2 |
| 1936 | E. Hiscock | 8.1 |
| 1937 | B. Burke (S. Africa) | 8.1 |
| 1938 | B. Lock | 8.0 |
| 1939 | B. Lock | 7.9 |
| 1967 | D. P. James | 7.5 |
| 1969 | V. M. Cobb | 7.5 |
| 1970 | J. Stroud | 7.4 |
| 1971 | S. M. Lannaman | 7.5 |
| 1972 | V. M. Cobb | 7.4 |
| 1973 | J. A. C. Lynch | 7.4 |

*220 Yards*

| | | sec. |
|---|---|---|
| 1966 | M. D. Tranter | 24.8 |
| 1967 | J. B. Pawsey | 25.2 |

*200 Metres*

| | | sec. |
|---|---|---|
| 1969 | D. P. James | 25.5 |

*440 Yards*

| | | sec. |
|---|---|---|
| 1966 | G. Dourass | 58.0 |
| 1967 | R. O. Stirling | 56.3 |

*400 Metres*

| | | sec. |
|---|---|---|
| 1969 | R. O. Stirling | 56.0 |
| 1970 | M. F. Neufville | 54.9 |

| | | |
|---|---|---|
| 1971 | J. V. Roscoe | 56.1 |
| 1972 | V. M. Bernard | 55.9 |
| 1973 | V. M. Bernard | 54.6 |

| *600 Yards* | | min. sec. |
|---|---|---|
| 1962 | P. E. M. Perkins | 1 28.6 |
| 1963 | B. J. Cook | 1 28.4 |
| 1964 | P. J. Piercy | 1 27.3 |

| *712 Yards* | | min. sec. |
|---|---|---|
| 1938 | E. Forster | 1 56.4 |
| 1939 | E. Forster | 1 55.0 |

| *880 Yards* | | min. sec. |
|---|---|---|
| 1965 | M. T. Campbell | 2 22.1 |
| 1966 | M. T. Campbell | 2 16.6 |
| 1967 | S. J. Taylor | 2 14.8 |

| *800 Metres* | | min. sec. |
|---|---|---|
| 1969 | S. J. Carey (Taylor) | 2 10.8 |
| 1970 | R. O. Stirling | 2 06.5 |
| 1971 | R. O. Stirling | 2 08.0 |
| 1972 | M. A. Beacham | 2 09.4 |
| 1973 | N. D. Braithwaite | 2 10.4 |

| *Mile* | | min. sec. |
|---|---|---|
| 1966 | J. Smith | 5 03.6 |
| 1967 | D. I. Elliott | 5 02.1 |

| *1500 Metres* | | min. sec. |
|---|---|---|
| 1969 | C. T. Gould | 4 42.4 |
| 1970 | G. A. Tivey | 4 32.8 |
| 1971 | M. A. Beacham | 4 20.5 |
| 1972 | J. M. Lochhead | 4 26.9 |
| 1973 | J. M. Lochhead | 4 30.6 |

| *3000 Metres* | | min. sec. |
|---|---|---|
| 1973 | E. Connors | 9 36.0 |

| *60 Yards Hurdles* | | sec. |
|---|---|---|
| 1962 | D. J. Window | 8.2 |
| 1963 | P. A. Nutting | 8.1 |
| 1964 | M. Y. Botley | 7.9 |
| 1965 | M. Y. Botley | 7.9 |
| 1966 | M. D. Rand | 7.8 |

| *60 Metres Hurdles* | | sec. |
|---|---|---|
| 1935 | V. Webb | 9.5 |
| 1936 | E. Ball | 8.9 |
| 1937 | B. Burke (S. Africa) | 8.6 |
| 1967 | P. Whitehead | 8.9 |
| 1969 | C. Perera | 8.8 |
| 1970 | M. E. Peters | 8.5 |
| 1971 | A. S. Wilson | 8.9 |
| 1972 | A. S. Wilson | 8.6 |
| 1973 | J. A. Vernon | 8.6 |

| *High Jump* | | ft. in. |
|---|---|---|
| 1935 | M. Milne | 4 11 |
| 1936 | M. Dumbrill and D. J. B. Odam | 5 2 |
| 1937 | D. J. B. Odam | 5 2½ |
| 1938 | D. J. B. Odam | 5 1 |
| 1939 | D. J. B. Odam | 5 1 |
| 1962 | F. M. Slaap | 5 7 |
| 1963 | L. Y. Knowles | 5 4 |
| 1964 | F. M. Slaap | 5 6 |
| 1965 | D. A. Shirley | 5 4 |
| 1966 | M. D. Rand | 5 5 |
| 1967 | L. Y. Knowles | 5 6½ |
| 1969 | B. J. Inkpen | 5 8 |
| 1970 | B. J. Inkpen | 5 6½ |
| 1971 | A. S. Wilson | 5 7 |
| 1972 | R. Few | 5 7¼ |
| 1973 | B. J. Inkpen | 6 1¼ |

| *Long Jump* | | ft. in. |
|---|---|---|
| 1935 | E. Raby | 16 6¼ |
| 1936 | E. Raby | 16 11 |
| 1937 | E. Raby | 16 10½ |
| 1938 | E. Raby | 17 6¾ |
| 1939 | E. Raby | 18 0 |
| 1962 | S. Parkin | 19 1 |
| 1963 | S. Parkin | 18 11¼ |
| 1964 | L. A. Jamieson | 19 11¼ |
| 1965 | S. Parkin | 19 2¾ |
| 1966 | M. D. Rand | 20 1¾ |
| 1967 | B. Inkpen | 18 10¼ |
| 1969 | S. D. Scott | 19 3 |
| 1970 | A. S. Wilson | 19 8 |
| 1971 | R. Martin-Jones | 19 9 |
| 1972 | M. A. Chitty | 20 10¼ |
| 1973 | B-A. Barrett | 19 9 |

| *Shot* | | ft. in. |
|---|---|---|
| 1935 | K. Tilley | 30 8 |
| 1936 | K. Tilley | 30 10¼ |
| 1937 | K. Tilley | 34 4½ |
| 1938 | B. Reid | 36 4¾ |
| 1939 | B. Reid | 36 10½ |
| 1962 | S. Allday | 45 2 |
| 1963 | S. Allday | 46 4¼ |
| 1964 | M. E. Peters | 49 1¼ |
| 1965 | M. E. Peters | 46 3¼ |
| 1966 | M. E. Peters | 50 2¼ |
| 1967 | B. R. Bedford | 45 7½ |
| 1969 | B. R. Bedford | 47 6½ |
| 1970 | M. E. Peters | 52 0½ |
| 1971 | B. R. Bedford | 46 4¾ |
| 1972 | M. E. Peters | 53 4¼ |
| 1973 | B. R. Bedford | 47 10½ |

| *1½ Miles Walk* | | min. sec. |
|---|---|---|
| 1966 | J. U. Farr | 12 29.2 |
| 1967 | D. Cotterill | 12 33.8 |

# EUROPEAN INDOOR CHAMPIONSHIPS

*British Medallists*

The following athletes, listed in alphabetical order, have won medals while representing Britain in the European Indoor Games or Championships. G signifies gold (1st), S silver (2nd) and B bronze (3rd).

Davies, L., 1967, long jump (G); 1969, long jump (S).
Frith, R. M., 1968, 50m. (S); 1969 50 m. (B).
Kelly, B. H., 1966 60m. (G).
Lewis, P. J., 1971, 800 m. (S).
Parker, J. M., 1966, 60 m. hurdles (S).
Pascoe, A. P., 1969, 50 m. hurdles (G).
Stewart, I., 1969, 3000 m. (G).
Stewart, P. J., 1971, 3000 m. (G).
Whetton, J., 1966, 1500 m. (G); 1967, 1500 m. (G); 1968, 1500 m. (G).
Wilde, R. S., 1970, 3000 m. (G).
Wilkinson, W., 1969, 1500 (B).

*Women*
Beacham, M. A., 1971, 1500 m. (G).
Bernard, V. M., 1973, 400 m. (G).
Cobb, V. M., 1969, 50 m. (B).
Knowles, L. Y., 1967, high jump (S).
Neufville, M. F., 1970, 400 m. (G).
Perera, C., 1969, 50 m. hurdles (B).
Rand, M. D., 1966, 60 m. (B), high jump (B), long jump (S).
Scott, S. D., 1969, long jump (S).
Stirling, R. O., 1969, 400 m. (B); 1971, 800 m. (B).

*European Champions*

| 50/60 Metres | | sec. |
|---|---|---|
| 1966 | B. H. Kelly (GB) | 6.6 |
| 1967 | P. Giannattasio (Italy) | 5.7 |
| 1968 | J. Hirscht (W. Germany) | 5.7 |
| 1969 | Z. Nowosz (Poland) | 5.8 |
| 1970 | V. Borzov (USSR) | 6.6 |
| 1971 | V. Borzov (USSR) | 6.6 |
| 1972 | V. Borzov (USSR) | 5.8 |
| 1973 | Z. Nowosz (Poland) | 6.6 |

| 400 Metres | | sec. |
|---|---|---|
| 1966 | H. Koch (E. Germany) | 47.9 |
| 1967 | M. Kinder (W. Germany) | 48.4 |
| 1968 | A. Badenski (Poland) | 47.0 |
| 1969 | J. Balachowski (Poland) | 47.3 |
| 1970 | A. Bratchikov (USSR) | 46.8 |
| 1971 | A. Badenski (Poland) | 46.8 |
| 1972 | G. Nuckles (W. Germany) | 47.2 |
| 1973 | L. Susanj (Yugoslavia) | 46.4 |

| 800 Metres | | min. sec. |
|---|---|---|
| 1966 | N. Carroll (Ireland) | 1 49.7 |
| 1967 | N. Carroll (Ireland) | 1 49.6 |
| 1968 | N. Carroll (Ireland) | 1 56.6 |
| 1969 | D. Fromm (E. Germany) | 1 46.6 |
| 1970 | Y. Arzhanov (USSR) | 1 51.0 |
| 1971 | Y. Arzhanov (USSR) | 1 48.7 |
| 1972 | J. Plachy (Czech) | 1 48.8 |
| 1973 | F. Gonzalez (France) | 1 49.2 |

| 1500 Metres | | min. sec. |
|---|---|---|
| 1966 | J. Whetton (GB) | 3 43.8 |
| 1967 | J. Whetton (GB) | 3 48.7 |
| 1968 | J. Whetton (GB) | 3 50.9 |
| 1969 | E. Salve (Belgium) | 3 45.9 |
| 1970 | H. Szordykowski (Poland) | 3 48.8 |
| 1971 | H. Szordykowski (Poland) | 3 41.4 |
| 1972 | J. Boxberger (France) | 3 45.7 |
| 1973 | H. Szordykowski (Pol) | 3 43.0 |

| 3000 Metres | | min. sec. |
|---|---|---|
| 1966 | H. Norpoth (W. Germany) | 7 56.0 |
| 1967 | W. Girke (W. Germany) | 7 58.6 |
| 1968 | V. Kudinskiy (USSR) | 8 10.2 |
| 1969 | I. Stewart (GB) | 7 55.4 |
| 1970 | R. S. Wilde (GB) | 7 47.0 |
| 1971 | P. J. Stewart (GB) | 7 53.6 |
| 1972 | Y. Grustinsh (USSR) | 8 03.0 |
| 1973 | E. Puttemans (Bel) | 7 44.6 |

| 50/60 Metres Hurdles | | sec. |
|---|---|---|
| 1966 | E. Ottoz (Italy) | 7.7 |
| 1967 | E. Ottoz (Italy) | 6.4 |
| 1968 | E. Ottoz (Italy) | 6.5 |
| 1969 | A. P. Pascoe (GB) | 6.6 |
| 1970 | G. Nickel (W. Germany) | 7.8 |
| 1971 | E. Berkes (W. Germany) | 7.8 |
| 1972 | G. Drut (France) | 6.5 |
| 1973 | F. Siebeck (E. Germany) | 7.7 |

| High Jump | | ft. | in |
|---|---|---|---|
| 1966 | V. Skvortsov (USSR) | 7 | 1½ |
| 1967 | A. Moroz (USSR) | 7 | 0¼ |
| 1968 | V. Skvortsov (USSR) | 7 | 1¼ |
| 1969 | V. Gavrilov (USSR) | 7 | 0¼ |
| 1970 | V. Gavrilov (USSR) | 7 | 2½ |
| 1971 | I. Major (Hungary) | 7 | 1½ |
| 1972 | I. Major (Hungary) | 7 | 4¼ |
| 1973 | I. Major (Hungary) | 7 | 2½ |

| Pole Vault | | ft. | in. |
|---|---|---|---|
| 1966 | G. Bliznyetsov (USSR) | 16 | 0¾ |
| 1967 | I. Feld (USSR) | 16 | 4¾ |
| 1968 | W. Nordwig | | |
| | (E. Germany) | 17 | 0¾ |
| 1969 | W. Nordwig | | |
| | (E. Germany) | 17 | 0¾ |
| 1970 | F. Tracanelli (France) | 17 | 4½ |
| 1971 | W. Nordwig | | |
| | (E. Germany) | 17 | 8½ |
| 1972 | W. Nordwig | | |
| | (E. Germany) | 17 | 8½ |
| 1973 | R. Dionisi (Italy) | 17 | 8½ |

| Long Jump | | ft. | in. |
|---|---|---|---|
| 1966 | I. Ter-Ovanesyan | | |
| | (USSR) | 27 | 0 |
| 1967 | L. Davies (GB) | 25 | 9¼ |
| 1968 | I. Ter-Ovanesyan | | |
| | (USSR) | 26 | 9¼ |
| 1969 | K. Beer (E. Germany) | 25 | 6 |
| 1970 | T. Lepik (USSR) | 26 | 5 |
| 1971 | H. Baumgartner | | |
| | (W. Germany) | 26 | 7¾ |
| 1972 | M. Klauss | | |
| | (E. Germany) | 26 | 3¾ |
| 1973 | H. Baumgartner | | |
| | (W. Germany) | 25 | 9¼ |

| Triple Jump | | ft. | in. |
|---|---|---|---|
| 1966 | S. Ciochina (Rumania) | 53 | 11 |
| 1967 | P. Nemsovsky (Czech) | 54 | 4½ |
| 1968 | N. Dudkin (USSR) | 54 | 10 |
| 1969 | N. Dudkin (USSR) | 54 | 10¾ |
| 1970 | V. Saneyev (USSR) | 55 | 7½ |
| 1971 | V. Saneyev (USSR) | 55 | 2¾ |
| 1972 | V. Saneyev (USSR) | 55 | 8¼ |
| 1973 | C. Corbu (Rumania) | 55 | 1½ |

| Shot | | ft. | in. |
|---|---|---|---|
| 1966 | V. Varju (Hungary) | 62 | 6 |
| 1967 | N. Karasyov (USSR) | 63 | 2¼ |
| 1968 | H. Birlenbach | | |
| | (W. Germany) | 61 | 2¼ |
| 1969 | H. Birlenbach | | |
| | (W. Germany) | 64 | 0¼ |
| 1970 | H. Briesenick | | |
| | (E. Germany) | 66 | 4¼ |
| 1971 | H. Briesenick | | |
| | (E. Germany) | 66 | 3 |
| 1972 | H. Briesenick | | |
| | (E. Germany) | 67 | 9¾ |
| 1973 | J. Brabec (Czech) | 66 | 7 |

**Women Champions**

| 50/60 Metres | | sec. |
|---|---|---|
| 1966 | M. Nemeshazi (Hungary) | 7.3 |
| 1967 | M. Nemeshazi (Hungary) | 6.3 |
| 1968 | S. Telliez (France) | 6.2 |
| 1969 | I. Szewinska (Poland) | 6.4 |
| 1970 | R. Stecher (E. Germany) | 7.4 |
| 1971 | R. Stecher (E. Germany) | 7.3 |
| 1972 | R. Stecher (E. Germany) | 6.3 |
| 1973 | A. Richter (W. Germany) | 7.3 |

| 400 Metres | | sec. |
|---|---|---|
| 1966 | H. Henning (W. Germany) | 56.9 |
| 1967 | K. Wallgren (Sweden) | 55.7 |
| 1968 | N. Pechenkina (USSR) | 55.2 |
| 1969 | C. Besson (France) | 54.0 |
| 1970 | M. F. Neufville (GB) | 53.0 |
| 1971 | V. Popkova (USSR) | 53.7 |
| 1972 | C. Frese (W. Germany) | 53.4 |
| 1973 | V. M. Bernard (GB) | 53.0 |

| 800 Metres | | min. | sec. |
|---|---|---|---|
| 1966 | Z. Szabo (Hungary) | 2 | 07.9 |
| 1967 | K. Kessler | | |
| | (W. Germany) | 2 | 08.2 |
| 1968 | K. Burneleit | | |
| | (E. Germany) | 2 | 07.6 |
| 1969 | B. Wieck (E. Germany) | 2 | 05.3 |
| 1970 | M. Sykora (Austria) | 2 | 07.0 |
| 1971 | H. Falck (W. Germany) | 2 | 06.1 |
| 1972 | G. Hoffmeister | | |
| | (E. Germany) | 2 | 04.8 |
| 1973 | S. Yordanova (Bul) | 2 | 02.7 |

| 1500 Metres | | min. | sec. |
|---|---|---|---|
| 1971 | M. A. Beacham (GB) | 4 | 17.2 |
| 1972 | T. Pangelova (USSR) | 4 | 14.6 |
| 1973 | E. Tittel (W. Germany) | 4 | 16.2 |

| 50/60 Metres Hurdles | | sec. |
|---|---|---|
| 1966 | I. Press (USSR) | 8.1 |
| 1967 | K. Balzer (E. Germany) | 6.9 |
| 1968 | K. Balzer (E. Germany) | 7.0 |
| 1969 | K. Balzer (E. Germany) | 7.2 |
| 1970 | K. Balzer (E. Germany) | 8.2 |
| 1971 | K. Balzer (E. Germany) | 8.1 |
| 1972 | A. Ehrhardt (E. Germany) | 6.9 |
| 1973 | A. Ehrhardt (E. Germany) | 8.0 |

| High Jump | | ft. | in. |
|---|---|---|---|
| 1966 | I. Balas (Rumania) | 5 | 9¼ |
| 1967 | T. Chenchik (USSR) | 5 | 9¼ |
| 1968 | R. Schmidt (E. Germany) | 6 | 0½ |
| 1969 | R. Schmidt (E. Germany) | 5 | 11½ |
| 1970 | I. Gusenbauer (Austria) | 6 | 2 |
| 1971 | M. Karbanova (Czech) | 5 | 10¾ |

| | | | | | | | |
|---|---|---|---|---|---|---|---|
| 1972 | R. Schmidt (E. Germany) 6 | 2¾ | | 1972 | B. Roesen | | |
| 1973 | Y. Blagoyeva (Bul) | 6 3½ | | | (W Germany) | 21 | 7¼ |
| | | | | 1973 | D. Yorgova (Bul) | 21 | 2 |

| *Long Jump* | | ft. in. | | *Shot* | | ft. | in. |
|---|---|---|---|---|---|---|---|
| 1966 | T. Shchelkanova | | | 1966 | M. Gummel | | |
| | (USSR) | 22 1 | | | (E. Germany) | 56 | 9¼ |
| 1967 | B. Berthelsen (Norway) | 21 4¼ | | 1967 | N. Chizhova (USSR) | 57 | 2¾ |
| 1968 | B. Berthelsen (Norway) | 21 1¼ | | 1968 | N. Chizhova (USSR) | 59 | 7¾ |
| 1969 | I. Szewinska (Poland) | 20 11¼ | | 1969 | M. Lange (E. Germany) | 57 | 3¾ |
| 1970 | V. Viscopoleanu | | | 1970 | N. Chizhova (USSR) | 61 | 0¼ |
| | (Rumania) | 21 6¼ | | 1971 | N. Chizhova (USSR) | 64 | 7¾ |
| 1971 | H. Rosendahl | | | 1972 | N. Chizhova (USSR) | 63 | 8¼ |
| | (W. Germany) | 21 9½ | | 1973 | H. Fibingerova (Cz) | 62 | 7¼ |

## INDOOR BEST PERFORMANCES

Owing to the wide variations in the size of tracks, and the varying surfaces, indoor records are not officially ratified. Below are the best performances on record (on any indoor surface) on tracks up to 220 yards in circumference.

### United Kingdom

| | min. sec. | | |
|---|---|---|---|
| *50 m.* | 5.5 | Peter Radford | 1958 |
| | 5.5 | Bob Frith | 1963 |
| *60 m.* | 6.6 | Barrie Kelly | 1966 |
| | 6.6 | Brian Green | 1973 |
| *400 m.* | 47.4 | Colin Campbell | 1969 |
| *800 m.* | 1 48.1 | John Davies | 1971 |
| *1500 m.* | 3 42.8 | Ray Smedley | 1973 |
| *Mile* | 3 59.5 | Bob Maplestone | 1972 |
| *3000 m.* | 7 47.0 | Ricky Wilde | 1970 |
| *2 Mi.* | 8 28.4 | Ian Stewart | 1973 |
| *50 m. Hurdles* | 6.6 | Alan Pascoe | 1969 |
| | 6.6 | Graham Gower | 1971 |
| | 6.6 | Berwyn Price | 1971 |
| *60 m. Hurdles* | 7.7 | Alan Pascoe | 1972 & 1973 |
| | ft. in. | | |
| *High Jump* | 6 10¼ | Dave Livesey | 1971 |
| *Pole Vault* | 16 6¾ | Mike Bull | 1972 |
| *Long Jump* | 26 2 | Lynn Davies | 1966 |
| *Triple Jump* | 52 5½ | Derek Boosey | 1969 |
| *Shot* | 65 9 | Geoff Capes | 1973 |

### Women

| | min. sec. | | |
|---|---|---|---|
| *50 m.* | 6.2 | Sonia Lannaman | 1971 |
| *60 m.* | 7.3 | Sonia Lannaman | 1972 and 1973 |
| *400 m.* | 53.0 | Marilyn Neufville | 1970 |
| | 53.0 | Verona Bernard | 1973 |
| *800 m.* | 2 06.5 | Rosemary Stirling | 1970 |
| *1500 m.* | 4 17.2 | Margaret Beacham | 1971 |
| *50 m. Hurdles* | 7.0 | Mary Peters | 1970 |
| *60 m. Hurdles* (6 flights) | 8.5 | Mary Peters | 1970 |
| | ft. in. | | |
| *High Jump* | 6 1¼ | Barbara Inkpen | 1973 |

|  | ft. | in. |  |  |
|---|---|---|---|---|
| *Long Jump* | 21 | 5¼ | Mary Rand | 1966 |
| *Shot* | 53 | 9¾ | Mary Peters | 1970 |

# World

|  | sec. |  |  |
|---|---|---|---|
| *50 yd.* | 5.0 | Kirk Clayton (USA) | 1970 |
|  | 5.0 | Herb Washington (USA) | 1972 & 1973 |
|  | 5.0 | Mel Pender (USA) | 1972 |
| *50 m.* | 5.4 | Bill Gaines (USA) | 1968 |
|  | 5.4 | Manfred Kokot (E. Germany) | 1971 |
| *60 yd.* | 5.8 | Herb Washington (USA) | 1972 |
| *60 m.* | 6.4 | Fyodor Pankratov (USSR) | 1967 |
|  | 6.4 | Valeriy Borzov (USSR) | 1968 |
|  | 6.4 | Aleksandr Kornelyuk (USSR) | 1972 and 1973 |
|  | 6.4 | Erik Gustafsson (Finland) | 1972 |
|  | 6.4 | Zenon Nowosz (Poland) | 1972 |
| *400 m.* | 46.1 | Marcello Fiasconaro (Italy) | 1972 |
| *440 yd.* | 46.2 | Tommie Smith (USA) | 1967 |
| *500 yd.* | 54.4 | Lee Evans (USA) | 1971 |

|  | min. sec. |  |  |
|---|---|---|---|
| *600 yd.* | 1 07.6 | Martin McGrady (USA) | 1970 |
| *800 m.* | 1 46.6 | Dieter Fromm (E. Germany) | 1969 |
| *880 yd.* | 1 47.9 | Ralph Doubell (Australia) | 1969 |
| *1000 yd.* | 2 05.1 | Mark Winzenried (USA) | 1972 |
| *1000 m.* | 2 20.4 | Ruden (USA) | 1971 |
| *1500 m.* | 3 37.8 | Harald Norpoth (W. Germany) | 1971 |
| *Mile* | 3 56.4 | Tom O'Hara (USA) | 1964 |
|  | 3 56.4 | Jim Ryun (USA) | 1971 |
| *3000 m.* | 7 39.2 | Emiel Puttemans (Belgium) | 1973 |
| *2 Mi.* | 8 13.2 | Emiel Puttemans (Belgium) | 1973 |
| *3 Mi.* | 13 07.2 | Tracy Smith (USA) | 1973 |
| *50 m. Hurdles* | 6.2 | Gunter Nickel (W. Germany) | 1970 |
| *60 yd. Hurdles* | 6.8 | Hayes Jones (USA) | 1964 |
|  |  | Earl McCullouch (USA) | 1968 |
|  |  | Willie Davenport (USA) | 1969 and 1970 |

|  | ft. | in. |  |  |
|---|---|---|---|---|
| *High Jump* | 7 | 4½ | Valeriy Brumel (USSR) | 1961 |
| *Pole Vault* | 18 | 0¼ | Steve Smith (USA) | 1973 |
| *Long Jump* | 27 | 2¾ | Bob Beamon (USA) | 1968 |
| *Triple Jump* | 55 | 8¼ | Viktor Saneyev (USSR) | 1972 |
| *Shot* | 69 | 9½ | George Woods (USA) | 1973 |

# Women

|  | min. sec. |  |  |
|---|---|---|---|
| *50 yd.* | 5.5 | Iris Davis (USA) | 1973 |
| *50 m.* | 6.0 | Barbara Ferrell (USA) | 1968 and 1969 |
|  | 6.0 | Renate Stecher (E. Germany) | 1971 |
| *60 yd.* | 6.5 | Wyomia Tyus (USA) | 1966 |
|  | 6.5 | Mattline Render (USA) | 1972 |
|  | 6.5 | Alfreda Daniels (USA) | 1972 |
| *60 m.* | 7.1 | Tatyana Shchelkanova (USSR | 1962 |
|  |  | Renate Stecher (E. Germany) | 1971 |
|  |  | Sylvie Telliez (France) | 1973 |
| *400 m.* | 53.0 | Marilyn Neufville (GB) | 1970 |
|  |  | Verona Bernard (GB) | 1973 |
| *800 m.* | 2 02.7 | Stefka Yordanova (Bulgaria) | 1973 |
| *1000 m.* | 2 44.8 | Tamara Kazachkova (USSR) | 1973 |

| | min. | sec. | | |
|---|---|---|---|---|
| *1500 m.* | 4 | 14.6 | Tamara Pangelova (USSR) | 1972 |
| *Mile* | 4 | 35.6 | Francie Larrieu (US) | 1973 |
| *50 m. Hurdles* | | 6.6 | Annelie Ehrhardt (E. Germany) | 1972 |
| *60 yd. Hurdles* | | 7.4 | Karin Balzer (E. Germany) | 1970 |
| | | | Patty Johnson (USA) | 1972 |
| | | 7.9 | Valeria Bufanu (Rumania) | 1973 |
| | ft. | in. | | |
| *High Jump* | 6 | 3½ | Yordanka Blagoyeva (Bulgaria) | 1973 |
| *Long Jump* | 22 | 1 | Tatyana Shchelkanova (USSR | 1966 |
| *Shot* | 64 | 7¾ | Nadyezhda Chizhova (USSR) | 1971 |

# INTERNATIONAL AMATEUR ATHLETIC FEDERATION

The IAAF is the supreme governing body controlling international athletics throughout the world. It was founded in Stockholm on July 17th, 1912 to draw up and enforce rules and regulations and a common amateur definition, and to recognise world records.

Following exploratory discussions by a provisional committee formed under the patronage of the Crown Prince of Sweden, the inaugural meeting of the IAAF was held in Berlin on August 20th-23rd, 1913. Countries represented were: Australia, Austria, Belgium, Canada, Denmark, Egypt, Finland, France, Germany, Hungary, Norway, South Africa, Sweden, Switzerland, United Kingdom of Great Britain and Ireland, and the United States of America.

Member countries now number over 140, the only notable absentee being the Chinese People's Republic which withdrew on political grounds.

# INTERNATIONAL MATCHES

The earliest instance of international competition dates back to 1866 when a team of English Athletes competed in Brittany. An England v. Ireland match was held in 1876.

International university encounters started in 1894 with Oxford defeating Yale in London. The following year New York Athletic Club, at home, resoundingly defeated London AC.

It was not until 1921 that full-scale matches between the best athletes of two countries were instituted. The pioneers were France and Britain (styled "England" prior to 1933) who met in Paris. The following month, again in Paris, the same countries fought out the first (unofficial) women's international match.

## British Men's Matches

Britain—the United Kingdom of Great Britain and Northern Ireland to be precise—has won 53 of her 111 men's matches from 1921 to 1972 inclusive. The easiest victory was gained against France in 1953 (127 points to 79), the heaviest defeat was suffered at the hands of the USA in 1967 (84 against 139). One match has been drawn: against Poland in 1964. The longest unbroken run of victories was eight between 1949 and 1953.

The most "capped" British international is the high jumper Crawford Fairbrother, with 53 full international selections, 1957-69. Athlete with the longest span as an international is high hurdler, Don Finlay (1929-49).

Results of Britain's matches:—

| | | | |
|---|---|---|---|
| 1921 *v.* France | won | 123 | —118 |
| 1922 *v.* France | won | 57 | — 42 |
| 1923 *v.* France | won | 69 | — 42 |
| 1925 *v.* France | lost | 53 | — 58 |
| 1926 *v.* France | won | 63 | — 48 |
| 1927 *v.* France | won | 66 | — 45 |
| 1929 *v.* France | lost | 58 | — 62 |
| 1929 *v.* Germany | lost | 4 | — 8 |
| | | (events) | |
| 1930 *v.* France | lost | 55 | — 65 |
| 1931 *v.* France | won | 67 | — 53 |
| 1931 *v.* Italy | won | 83½ | — 62½ |
| 1931 *v.* Germany | lost | 4½ | — 7½ |
| | | (events) | |
| 1933 *v.* France | won | 65¼ | — 54¼ |
| 1933 *v.* Germany | lost | 59 | — 75 |

1933 v. Italy lost 62 — 85
1934 v. France won 66½— 53½
1935 v. Finland lost 70 — 78
1935 v. France won 64 — 56
1935 v. Germany lost 61 — 75
1937 v. France won 66 — 54
1937 v. Germany won 69 — 67
1937 v. Finland lost 67 — 82
1937 v. Norway lost 65 — 74
1938 v. Norway won 72 — 67
1938 v. France won 70 — 50
1939 v. Germany lost 42½— 93½
1945 v. France lost 29 — 73
1946 v. France won 72 — 57
1947 v. France lost 56 — 73
1949 v. France won 82 — 65
1950 v. France won 106 — 99
1951 v. France won 115 — 89
1951 v. Yugoslavia won 102½— 89½
1951 v. Greece won 96 — 84
1951 v. Turkey won 103 — 75
1952 v. France won 120 — 85
1953 v. France won 127 — 79
1953 v. W. Germany lost 94 —112
1953 v. Sweden lost 103 —109
1955 v. W. Germany won 111 — 95
1955 v. Hungary lost 93½—116½
1955 v. France won 128 — 85
1955 v. USSR lost 93 —137
1955 v. Czechoslovakia
won 117 —95
1956 v. Czechoslovakia
won 119 — 93
1956 v. Hungary lost 104 —108
1957 v. France won 118 — 94
1957 v. USSR lost 93 —119
1957 v. Poland lost 101 —111
1957 v. W. Germany lost 92½—119½
1958 v. Commonwealth
lost 162 —199
1958 v. France won 124 — 88
1959 v. W. Germany lost 95 —117
1959 v. Poland lost 99 —106
1959 v. USSR lost 95 —129
1959 v. Finland won 126 —104
1960 v. France won 116½— 95½
1961 v. USA lost 88 —122
1961 v. Hungary won 110 —102
1961 v. W. Germany lost 98 —113
1961 v. Poland lost 105 —106
1961 v. France lost 99 —113
1962 v. W. Germany*
won 69 — 56½
1962 v. Poland lost 104 —108
1963 v. W. Germany*
lost 58 — 92
1963 v. USA lost 91 —120
1963 v. W. Germany lost 101 —109
1963 v. Sweden won 126 — 86

1963 v. Russian SFSR
won 112 — 99
1963 v. Hungary won 106½—105½
1964 v. Finland* won 59 — 47
1964 v. Finland won 129 — 83
1964 v. Poland tied 106 —106
1964 v. France won 110 —102
1965 v. USA* lost 47 — 70
1965 v. Finland* won 64 — 42
1965 v. Poland lost 93 —118
1965 v. Hungary won 114 — 96
1965 v. W. Germany lost 91 —121
1966 v. USSR lost 87 —134
1966 v. Sweden lost 100 —112
1966 v. France lost 98 —113
1966 v. Finland won 122 — 90
1967 v. France* lost 57 — 71
1967 v. Hungary won 113 — 99
1967 v. Poland lost 99 —113
1967 v. USA lost 84 —139
1967 v. W. Germany lost 90 —121
1968 v. W. Germany*
lost 67 — 78
1968 v. Switzerland won 128 — 84
1968 v. Poland lost 91 —109
1969 v. Czechoslovakia
won 119 —103
1969 v. USA lost 90 —131
1969 v. Italy won 114 —109
1969 v. Czechoslovakia
won 121 —101
1969 v. France (3) lost 199½—209½
1969 v. W. Germany
lost 97 —115
1969 v. Finland won 118 — 93
1970 v. E. Germany*
lost 54½ — 73½
1970 v. E. Germany lost 97 —114
1970 v. Poland lost 85 —126
1971 v. E. Germany* lost 52 — 76
1971 v. France* won 71½— 55½
1971 v. France (3) lost 201½—206½
1971 v. W. Germany lost 94 —118
1972 v. Spain* won 76 — 52
1972 v. Poland lost 92½—117½
1972 v. Greece (123) and
Netherlands (83) won with 132 pts
1972 v. Finland lost 89 —123
1972 v. Spain won 128 — 81
1972 v. France won 123 — 89
1973 v. E. Germany* lost 56 — 79
* Indoor match (3) 3-a-side

## British Women's Matches

Britain has notched 49 wins in 76 women's matches from 1923 to 1972. The widest margin of victory was achieved against France in 1961 (73-

33), the heaviest defeats inflicted by the Soviet Union in 1955 (48-83) and 1959 (41-76). The longest unbroken run of victories was seven between 1953 and 1955.

The most " capped " international is Mary Rand, who has 40 full internationals to her credit from 1957-67. High jumper Dorothy Tyler's international span extended over 20 years: 1936 to 1956.

Results of Britain's matches:—

| | | | | |
|---|---|---|---|---|
| 1923 | v. France | won | 60 — | 37 |
| 1929 | v. Germany | lost | 45½— | 53½ |
| 1930 | v. Germany | won | 51 — | 47 |
| 1931 | v. Germany | won | 53 — | 48 |
| 1947 | v. France | won | 26 — | 24 |
| 1950 | v. France | won | 58 — | 45 |
| 1951 | v. France | won | 61 — | 43 |
| 1952 | v. France | won | 60 — | 43 |
| 1952 | v. Italy | lost | 46 — | 47 |
| 1953 | v. France | won | 69 — | 33 |
| 1953 | v. W. Germany | won | 49 — | 47 |
| 1954 | v. Hungary | won | 59 — | 54 |
| 1954 | v. Czechoslovakia | | | |
| | | won | 58 — | 48 |
| 1955 | v. W. Germany | won | 53 — | 50 |
| 1955 | v. Hungary | won | 60 — | 53 |
| 1955 | v. France | won | 60 — | 46 |
| 1955 | v. USSR | lost | 48 — | 83 |
| 1955 | v. Czechoslovakia | | | |
| | | won | 58 — | 48 |
| 1956 | v. Czechoslovakia | | | |
| | | won | 58 — | 46 |
| 1956 | v. Hungary | won | 70 — | 43 |
| 1957 | v. France | won | 68 — | 38 |
| 1957 | v. USSR | lost | 40 — | 73 |
| 1957 | v. Poland | won | 57 — | 49 |
| 1957 | v. W. Germany | lost | 48½— | 58½ |
| 1958 | v. Commonwealth | | | |
| | | lost | 84 — | 91 |
| 1958 | v. France | won | 68 — | 38 |
| 1959 | v. W. Germany | won | 64 — | 51 |
| 1959 | v. Poland | lost | 50 — | 54 |
| 1959 | v. USSR | lost | 41 — | 76 |
| 1960 | v. Italy | won | 58 — | 45 |
| 1960 | v. France | won | 71 — | 35 |
| 1961 | v. USA | won | 56 — | 50 |
| 1961 | v. Hungary | won | 61 — | 45 |
| 1961 | v. W. Germany | lost | 45 — | 61 |
| 1961 | v. Poland | lost | 46 — | 60 |
| 1961 | v. France | won | 73 — | 33 |
| 1962 | v. W. Germany* | | | |
| | | lost | 43 — | 52 |
| 1962 | v. Poland | won | 54 — | 52 |
| 1963 | v. W. Germany* | | | |
| | | lost | 42 — | 64 |
| 1963 | v. USA | won | 65½— | 51½ |

| | | | | |
|---|---|---|---|---|
| 1963 | v. W. Germany | won | 75½— | 63½ |
| 1963 | v. Netherlands | won | 74 — | 43 |
| 1963 | v. Russian SFSR | | | |
| | | lost | 56 — | 62 |
| 1963 | v. Hungary | lost | 48 — | 55 |
| 1964 | v. Poland | lost | 57 — | 60 |
| 1964 | v. Netherlands | won | 70 — | 47 |
| 1965 | v. USA* | lost | 33½— | 38½ |
| 1965 | v. Poland | lost | 58 — | 59 |
| 1965 | v. Hungary | won | 63 — | 52 |
| 1965 | v. W. Germany | lost | 57 — | 67 |
| 1966 | v. USSR | lost | 53 — | 71 |
| 1966 | v. France | won | 59 — | 57 |
| 1967 | v. Hungary | won | 78 — | 51 |
| 1967 | v. Poland | lost | 55 — | 62 |
| 1967 | v. W. Germany | won | 66 — | 65 |
| 1968 | v. W. Germany | lost | 62 — | 66 |
| 1968 | v. Poland | won | 64 — | 46 |
| 1969 | v. Czechoslovakia | | | |
| | | won | 68 — | 67 |
| 1969 | v. France | won | 84 — | 48 |
| 1969 | v. USA | won | 67 — | 66 |
| 1969 | v. W. Germany | won | 73 — | 62 |
| 1969 | v. Rumania | won | 71 — | 62 |
| 1970 | v. E. Germany* | lost | 39 — | 56 |
| 1970 | v. Netherlands | won | 77 — | 58 |
| 1970 | v. E. Germany | lost | 55 — | 80 |
| 1970 | v. Poland | won | 70 — | 65 |
| 1970 | v. Rumania | won | 70 — | 65 |
| 1970 | v. Hungary | won | 69 — | 66 |
| 1971 | v. E. Germany* | lost | 41 — | 54 |
| 1971 | v. France* | won | 56 — | 36 |
| 1971 | v. W. Germany | lost | 54 — | 81 |
| 1972 | v. E. Germany | lost | 51 — | 83 |
| 1972 | v. Netherlands | won | 75 — | 60 |
| 1972 | v. Poland | lost | 66 — | 67 |
| 1972 | v. Greece | won | 56 — | 27 |
| 1972 | v. Finland | won | 82 — | 53 |

* Indoor match

## USA v. USSR Matches

The most publicised series of track and field international matches, between the United States and the Soviet Union, began in 1958. Between then and 1971, the USA men's team won eight of the ten encounters, the USSR women's team won nine times.

The matches have yielded a large number of world records, no fewer than seven in the 1961 clash alone.

1958 (Moscow) USA won 126 —109
(women) USSR won 63 — 44
1959 (Philadelphia)
USA won 127 —108
(women) USSR won 67 — 40

111

```
1961 (Moscow) USA won 124 —111
     women) USSR won  68 — 39
1962 (Los Altos)
            USA  won 128 —107
    (women) USSR won  66 — 41
1963 (Moscow) USA won 119 —114
    (women) USSR won  75 — 28
1964 (Los Angeles)
            USA  won 139 — 97
    (women) USSR won  59 — 48
1965 Kiev   USSR won 118 —112
    (women) USSR won  63½— 43½
1969 (Los Angeles)
            USA  won 125 —110
    (women) USA  won  70 — 67
1970 (Leningrad)
            USSR won 122 —114
    (women) USSR won  78 — 59
1971 (Berkeley)
            USA  won 126 —110
    (women) USSR won  76 — 60
Indoors:
1972 (Richmond)
            USA  won  79 — 69
    (women) USA  won  52 — 43
```

```
1973 (Richmond)
            USSR won  84 — 76
    (women) USA  won  65 — 62
Juniors:
1972 (Sacramento)
            USSR won 123 —109
```

# INTERNATIONAL
# OLYMPIC COMMITTEE

The IOC, to which the Congress of Paris on June 23rd, 1894 entrusted the control and development of the modern Olympic Games, is responsible for the regular celebration of the Games and ensuring they live up to the ideals of Baron Pierre de Coubertin (the man behind their revival) by promoting friendship between the amateur sportsmen of all countries.

# J

## JARVINEN, M. H. (Finland)

During the 1930s the javelin record book was completely rewritten by Matti Jarvinen, the outstanding member of a fabulously successful family of athletes. He raised the world record in ten instalments, starting with 234 ft. 9 in. in 1930 and culminating with 253 ft. 4 in. six years later.

A marvellous competitor in a notoriously erratic event, he won the Olympic crown in 1932 and the European title in 1934 and 1938. Only a back injury held him down to fifth place at the 1936 Olympics. He continued to compete after the war, throwing 235 ft. 6 in. in 1945 and even in 1952 (aged 43) he achieved 209 ft. 5 in. Between 1932 and 1940 he exceeded 240 ft. in over 50 different meetings.

As befits the brother of a great decathlon exponent, Matti was himself a superb all-rounder. His best marks included 11.1 sec. for 100 m., 23ft. 10in. long jump, 46ft. 10¼in. triple jump, 47ft. 1in. shot and 154ft. 0in. discus (this last a training mark). He was born at Tampere on Feb. 18th, 1909.

## JAVELIN

A javelin weighs a minimum of 800 grammes (1 lb. 12¼ oz.) and consists of three parts: a pointed metal head, a shaft and a cord grip. The shaft may be constructed of either wood or metal. The complete javelin measures between 8 ft. 6¼ in. and 8 ft. 10¼ in. in length.

It is thrown following a running approach. It must be thrown over the shoulder or upper part of the throwing arm and must not be slung nor hurled. At no time after preparing to throw until the javelin has been discharged into the air may the competitor turn completely around, so that his back is towards the throwing arc. (This rule was introduced when, in 1956, a Spanish athlete achieved phenomenal distances by spinning round with the javelin in the manner of a discus thrower). A throw is not valid unless the tip of the metal head strikes the ground before any part of the javelin.

The event has largely been dominated by throwers from the Nordic lands. Erik Lemming (Sweden) led the way to the 200 ft. marker in the early years of the century. He threw 198 ft. 11 in. in 1912 to win his second Olympic title but the first 200-footer materialised only two days later when Juho Saaristo (Finland) threw 200 ft. 1 in. Lemming came back later in the season with 204 ft. 5 in. Jonni Myyra (Finland) was the next outstanding figure, raising the record to 216 ft. 10 in. in 1919 and taking Olympic honours in 1920 and 1924.

Matti Jarvinen, another Finn, transformed the event in the 30s. He pushed the record up from 234 ft. 9 in. in 1930 to 253 ft. 4 in. in 1936 and collected the 1932 Olympic gold medal on the way. Two years later Jarvinen's protégé, Yrjo Nikkanen (Finland), carried the mark out to 258 ft. 2 in. and there the record stood for almost 15 years until an American, Franklin " Bud " Held, took over the world leadership.

It was his brother, Dick Held, who was chiefly responsible for the spectacular advance in javelin distances during the 1950's. Following research into the characteristics of flight and landing attitudes of javelins, he designed the first aerodynamic model.

Terje Pedersen (Norway) improved the record over 16 ft. during 1964, reaching 300 ft. 11 in., and he was succeeded in 1968 by Janis Lusis (USSR), the greatest javelin thrower of all time. Olympic champion in 1968, four times European gold medallist, he held the world record with 307 ft. 9 in. That mark was beaten by Klaus Wolfermann (W. Germany) with 308 ft. 8 in. in 1973.

See also JARVINEN, M. H.; LUSIS, J.; and WOLFERMANN, K.

## Women

The women's javelin weighs a minimum of 600 grammes (1 lb. 5¼ oz.) and is between 7 ft. 2¼ in. and 7 ft. 6½ in. in length.

The first woman to reach 200 ft. was Yelena Gorchakova (USSR), with 204 ft. 8 in. in the 1964 Olympic qualifying round. This stood as the world record until, on one day in 1972, it was broken almost simultaneously by Ewa Gryziecka (Poland). 205 ft. 8 in.. and Ruth Fuchs (E. Germany), 213 ft. 5 in. Easily Britain's finest thrower is Susan Platt, who would have gained the Olympic silver medal in 1960 had she not stepped across the line.

See also FUCHS, R.

## JENKINS, D. A. (GB)

Britain's only winner in the 1971 European Championships was David Jenkins, who took the 400 m. title at the age of 19 in the UK record time of 45.5 sec. Born at Pointe à Pierre (Trinidad) of British parents on May 25th, 1952, he ran his first quarter in 1967 and only the following year he made his debut for Britain's international junior team.

Apart from a narrow defeat in the Schools' International 440 yd. in 1968 he went unbeaten in one-lap finals until the 1972 Olympics where he disappointed by failing to reach the final. However, he made amends in the 4 x 400 m. relay where he anchored the British team from 4th into 2nd place with a leg timed in 44.1 sec. During 1972 he set UK records of 10.1 sec. (unofficially) for 100 m., 20.3 sec. for 200 m. and 45.3 sec. for 400 m.

His annual progress: 1966—27.5 (220 yd.); 1967——10.8 (100 yd.), 23.9, 53.7 (440 yd.); 1968—10.3, 22.5, 49.0; 1969—10.8 (100 m.), 22.1 (200 m.), 46.5 (400 m.); 1970—10.6, 21.1, 46.9; 1971—10.6, 20.6, 45.5; 1972—10.1, 20.3, 45.3.

## JIPCHO, B. (Kenya)

Ben Jipcho's targets for 1972 were to win the Olympic Steeplechase title and to capture the world record. He did not succeed on either count, but 1973 was barely a fortnight old before he entered the world record lists. Running in the 2nd African Games at Lagos, he won the steeplechase in 8 min. 20.8 sec. to equal the mark set a few months earlier by Sweden's Anders Garderud. His actual time on the electrical apparatus was 8:20.69, which under IAAF regulations is rounded off to 8:20.8.

Jipcho is a good competitor. He was a finalist in the 1968 Olympic 1500 m. and silver medallist in the 1970 Commonwealth Games steeplechase with an African record of 8 min. 29.6 sec. He really came alight in Sept. 1971 when, in the space of six days, he scored four great victories in Europe: an 8 min. 29.6 sec. steeplechase in spite of two falls; a 13 min. 40.8 sec. 5000 m. ahead of Ian Stewart and Lasse Viren; a 3 min. 56.4 sec. mile to defeat Kip Keino among others; and a 3 min. 57.4 sec. mile to beat European champion Francesco Arese. He was not quite at his best at the 1972 Olympics but still took the silver medal in the steeplechase behind Keino in personal best time.

His annual steeplechasing progress: 1968—9:16.2, 1969—8:48.8, 1970—8:29.6, 1971—8:29.6, 1972—8:24.6, 1973—8:20.8. Other best marks include 1 min. 50.7 sec. for 880 yd. and 7 min. 58.2 sec. for 3000 m. He was born on March 1st, 1943.

## JOHNSON, R. L. (USA)

Despite being handicapped by the after effects of an injury sustained in 1948 when he caught his left foot in a conveyor belt (necessitating 23 stitches and several weeks on crutches) and a knee injury in 1956 which caused him to divert his attention from hurdling and long jumping to the throwing events, Rafer Johnson was the most gifted all-round athlete of his, and perhaps any other, time.

He made his decathlon debut in 1954 (5,874 points), yet only the following year he set world record figures of 7,985! Standing 6 ft. 3in. and weighing 200 lb., he placed second in the 1956 Olympic decathlon and triumphed in 1960. His best score was 8,683 points (8,063 when converted to 1962 Tables) in his final season, 1960. He competed in eleven decathlons during his career, winning nine.

His best marks, the finest series collected by any athlete, were 10.3 sec. for 100 m., 21.0 sec. for 220 yds. (straight), 47.9 sec. for 400 m., 4 min. 49.7 sec. for 1500 m., 13.8 sec. for 110 m. hurdles, 22.7 sec. for 220 yd. hurdles (straight), 6ft. 3in. high jump, 13ft. 5½in., pole vault, 25ft. 5¾in. long jump, 54ft. 11½in. shot, 172ft. 3in. discus and 251 ft. 9 in. javelin. He was born at Hillsboro, Texas, on Aug. 18th, 1934.

# JUNIORS

*Best Performances*

The best marks on record by junior athletes (i.e. boys under 20 and girls under 19 on Dec. 31st in the year of competition) are:
*100 m.*: *9.9* R. R. Smith (USA/49) 1968. *200 m.*: 20.1 Willie Turner (USA/48) 1967, Marshall Dill (USA/52) 1971. *400 m.*: 44.9 sec. Wayne Collett (USA/49) 1968. *800 m/1500m/ 1 mile*: 1 min. 44.9 sec./3 min. 36.1 sec./3 min. 51.3 sec. Jim Ryun (USA/47) 1966. *3000 m.*: 7 min. 58.0 sec. Gerry Lindgren (USA/46) 1965, 2 mi.: 8 min. 25.2 sec. Ryun 1966. *3 mi.*: 13 min. 04.2 sec. Lindgren 1965. *5000 m.*: 13 min. 37.4 sec. Dave Black (GB/52) 1971, *6 mi.*: 27 min. 11.6 sec. Lindgren 1965. *10,000 m.*: 28 min. 50.4 sec. Garry Bjorklund (USA/51) 1970. *3000 m. steeplechase*: 8 min. 40.4 sec. Todd Lathers (USA/52) 1971. *110 m. hurdles*: 13.3 sec. Alejandro Casanas (Cuba/54) 1972. *400 m. hurdles*: 49.7 sec. Eddie Southern (USA/38) 1956. *High jump*: 7ft. 4½in. Valeriy Brumel (USSR/42) 1961. *Pole vault*: 17ft. 8½in. Francois Trancanelli (France/51) 1970. *Long jump*: 27ft. 4½in. Randy Williams (USA/53) 1972. *Triple jump*: 57ft. 1in. Pedro Perez (Cuba/52) 1971. *Shot*: 66ft. 3¼in. Randy Matson (USA/45) 1964. *Discus*: 191ft. 2in. Boris Karayev (USSR/50) 1969. *Hammer*: 223ft. 11in. Jacques Accambray (France/50) 1969. *Javelin*: 273ft. 0in. Mark Murro (USA/49) 1968. *Decathlon*: 7,842 pts. Josef Zeilbauer (Austria/52) 1971.
(Girls) *100 m.*: 11.1 sec. Raelene Boyle (Australia/51) 1968, Silvia Chivas (Cuba/54) 1972. *200 m.*: 22.7

sec. Boyle 1968. *400 m.*: 51.0 sec. Marilyn Neufville (Jamaica/52) 1970. *800 m.*: 2 min. 02.7 sec. Barbara Wieck (E. Germany/51) 1969. *1500 m.*: 4 min. 06.7 sec. Glenda Reiser (Canada/55) 1972. *3000 m.*: 9 min. 16.6 sec. Inge Knutsson (Sweden/55) 1972. *100 m. hurdles*: 13.4 sec. Gabrielle Schnicke (E. Germany/53) 1971, Monika Hys (E. Germany/53) 1971, Iwona Dega (Poland/55) 1972. *200 m. hurdles*: 26.7 sec. Maureen Caird (Australia/51) 1969, Sharon Colyear (GB/55) 1971. *High jump*: 6 ft. 3½ in. Ulrike Meyfarth (W. Germany/56) 1972. *Long jump*: 21 ft. 8 in. Irena Kirszenstein, later Szewinska (Poland/46) 1964. *Shot*: 55 ft. 5¾ in. Gabrielle Moritz (E. Germany/ 52) 1970. *Discus*: 184 ft. 3 in. Irina Sapronova (USSR/53) 1971. *Javelin*: 205 ft. 2 in. Jacqueline Todten (E. Germany/54) 1972. *Pentathlon*: (new tables) 4,442 pts. Debbie Van Kiekebelt (Canada/53) 1971.

*European Junior Championships*
The first official European Junior Championships were staged in Paris in 1970. Winners—100/200: F-P. Hofmeister (W. Germany) 10.4/21.4; 400: P. Beaven (GB) 47.0; 800: H-H. Ohlert (E. Germany) 1:50.9; 1500: K-P. Justus (E. Germany) 3:51.3; 3000: H. Mignon (Belgium) 8:08.6; 2000 m. steeplechase: B. Malinowski (Poland) 5:44.0; 110 m. hurdles: B. Price (GB) 14.1; 400 m. hurdles: D. Stukalov (USSR) 50.2; High jump: J. Palkovsky (Czech) 7ft. 1¾in.; Pole vault: F. Tracanelli (France) 17ft. 0¾in.; Long jump/Triple jump: V. Podluzhniy (USSR) 25ft. 10in. and 53ft. 3¼in.; Shot: W. Barthel (W. Germany) 59ft. 4¾in.; Discus: A. Nazhimov (USSR 177ft. 9in.; Hammer: T. Manolov (Bulgaria) 213ft. 9in.; Javelin: A. Pusko (Finland) 252ft. 7in.; Decathlon: A. Blinyayev (USSR) 7,632 pts.; 10,000 m. walk: L. Lipowski (E. Germany) 43:35.6; Relays: USSR 40.1/3:11.2.
(Girls) 100: H. Kerner (Poland) 12.0; 200: H. Golden (GB) 24.3; 400: M. Zehrt (E. Germany) 54.0; 800: W. Pohland (E. Germany) 2:05.2; 1500: K. Clausnitzer (E. Germany) 4:24.0; 100 m. hurdles: G. Rabsztyn (Poland) 13.9; High-jump: M. van Doorn (Netherlands) 5ft. 8½in.; Long jump:

J. Nygrynova (Czech) 20ft. 7in.; Shot: G. Moritz (E. Germany) 55ft. 5¾in.; Discus: K. Pogyor (Hungary) 158ft. 4in.; Javelin: J. Todten (E. Germany) 181ft. 1 in.; Pentathlon: (old tables) M. Peikert (E. Germany) 4,578 pts.; 4 x 100 m.: Poland 45.2; 4 x 400 m.: E. Germany 3:40.2.

Apart from the three gold medals, other medals gained by British athletes were: (silver) John Boggis, 3000 m.; Andrea Lynch, 100 m.; Christine Haskett, 1500 m.; Moira Walls, long jump; (bronze) Helen Golden, 100 m. Two years later, Monika Zehrt won the Olympic 400 m. title and Jacqueline Todten the silver medal in the javelin.

## KANNENBERG, B.
### (West Germany)

After a mere three years as a race walker, Bernd Kannenberg enjoyed a momentous season in 1972—setting a world's best 50 km. time. on the road, of 3 hr. 52 min. 44.6 sec. (7 min. 29 sec. mile speed) and winning the Olympic title in 3 hr. 56 min. 11.6 sec. after a classic duel with the European champion Veniamin Soldatenko (USSR). The pair matched strides until 38 km., at which point Kannenberg began to draw away to win by over two minutes.

Three days earlier, in the Olympic 20 km. walk, he had been a close third at the halfway point, but he withdrew 2 km. later after having been accidentally tripped. A former weight lifter, he is extremely fast with times of 41 min. 36.2 sec. (10 km.) and 88 min. 22 sec. (20 km.) to his credit but his style is considered very fair. He was 9th in the 1971 European 20 km.

His annual progress at 50 km. : 1970 —4:21:43, 1971—4:17:26, 1972— 3.52:44.6. He was born at Königsberg on Aug. 20th, 1942.

## KEINO, K. (Kenya)

Although inspired as a schoolboy by the deeds of his country's first great runner, Nyandika Maiyoro (7th in the 1956 Olympic 5000 m.), it was not until 1962 that Kipchoge Keino began to take athletics seriously. He started with 3 mi. in 14 min. 17.0 sec. and within a few months was Kenyan and East African champion. International competition brought the best out of him even in those early days for at the 1962 Commonwealth Games in Australia he finished 11th in the 3 mi. (in 13 min. 50.0 sec.) and set a national record of 4 min. 07.0 sec. in the mile heats.

At the 1964 Olympics he finished 5th in the 5000 m., less than a dozen yards behind the winner.

Keino set Europe's tracks alight in 1965. He beat Ron Clarke in two races out of three over 5000 m. set a 3000 m. world record of 7 min. 39.6 sec. and came close to the mile record with 3 min. 54.2 sec. Also during the year he won the 1500 m. and 5000 m. at the first African Games and, in New Zealand, temporarily relieved Clarke of the 5000 m. world record with 13 min. 24.2 sec. He carried all before him in 1966, his most notable success including a magnificent double in the Commonwealth Games (12 min. 57.4 sec. 3 mi., 3 min. 55.3 sec. mile) and the then second fastest mile in history (3 min. 53.4 sec.).

During the next six years Kip raced incessantly throughout the world, exciting crowds everywhere with his fabulous loping stride and displaying his talent to good effect at all distances from 800 m. to 10,000 m. plus —in 1972—the steeplechase. Gold medals came his way in the 1968 Olympic 1500 m. (a sensational 3 min. 34.9 sec. at high altitude), 1970 Commonwealth 1500 m. (3 min. 36.6 sec.) and 1972 Olympic steeplechase (8 min. 23.6 sec.), an event he had not previously taken seriously. He did lose some important events—1968 Olympic 5000 m., 1970 Commonwealth 5000 m. and 1972 Olympic 1500 m., but still finished among the medals each time.

His best times include 1 min. 46.4 sec. for 800 m., 3 min. 34.9 sec. for 1500 m., 3 min. 53.1 sec. for the mile, 7 min. 39.6 sec. for 3000 m., 12 min. 57.4 sec. for 3 mi., 13 min. 24.2 sec. for 5000 m., 28 min. 06.4 sec. for 10,000 m. and 8 min. 23.6 sec. for 3000 m. steeplechase.

Annual progress at mile and 3 mi. : 1962—4:07.0, 13:45.0; 1963—4:11.0, 13:47.4; 1964—4:01.5 (and 3:41.9 1500 m.), 13:49.6 (5000 m.); 1965— 3:54.2, 12:58.6 (and 13:24.2 5000 m.); 1966—3:53.4, 12:57.4 (and 13:26.6 5000 m.); 1967—3:53.1, 13:36.8 (5000); 1968—3:55.5 (and 3:34.9 1500), 13:35.8 (5000). 1969—3.37.3 (1500); 1970—3.59.2 (and 3:36.6 1500), 13:27.6 (5000); 1971—3:54.4

(and 3:36.8 1500), 13:25.8 (5000); 1972 —3:59.4 (and 3:36.8 1500). He was born at Kipsamo on Jan. 17th, 1940. He now runs professionally.

## KIRSZENSTEIN, I. (Poland)

See under SZEWINSKA, I.

## KOLEHMAINEN, H. (Finland)

Hannes Kolehmainen was the first of the long line of Finnish distance running masters. He won three Olympic gold medals in 1912: at 5000 m., 10,000 m. and cross-country. His most celebrated race was the 5000 m. in which he defeated Jean Bouin (France) in a desperate finish in 14 min. 36.6 sec. No man had previously beaten 15 min.!

The time lasted ten years until broken by Paavo Nurmi, who as a boy had been inspired to take up running because of that very performance. Kolehmainen won the 1920 Olympic marathon on a course which was 605 yd. over the standard distance of 26 mi. 385 yd. in 2 hr. 32 min. 35.8 sec.—equivalent of close to 2½ hr. for the normal distance—and held world records at numerous events from 3000 to 30,000 m.

His best marks: 8 min. 36.9 sec. for 3000 m., 14 min. 36.6 sec. for 5000 m., 30 min. 20.4 sec. for 6 mi., 31 min. 20.4 sec. for 10,000 m., 51 min. 03.4 sec. for 10 mi. He was born on Dec. 9th, 1889 and died in Jan. 1966. Tatu Kolehmainen, his brother, was also a distinguished marathon runner.

## KOMAR, W. (Poland)

The 1972 Olympic shot competition was confidently expected to involve a private battle for the medals between the Americans and East Germans. However, Wladyslaw Komar, ranked only sixth among the Munich contenders, confounded everyone by putting a personal best of 69 ft. 6 in. with his first effort in the final—and although three men approached to within 1½ in. of that distance none was able to overhaul him.

It was Komar's third Olympic appearance, having placed 9th in 1964 and 6th in 1968. His highest position in the European Championships was 3rd in 1966 and 1971.

Before he filled out his 6 ft. 5¼ in. frame to almost 280 lb. he was a talented all rounder, able to high jump 6 ft. 2¾ in. and long jump over 23 ft. His annual shot progress: 1959— 45ft. 2¼in.; 1960—50ft. 9½in.; 1961— 56ft. 1¼in.; 1962—60ft. 2in.; 1963— 61ft. 8½in.; 1964—63ft. 11¾in.; 1965— 61ft. 4in.; 1966—64ft. 4in.; 1967— 62ft. 7¾in.; 1968—64ft. 0½in.; 1969— 62ft. 9½in.; 1970—66ft. 4¼in.; 1971— 67ft. 5in.; 1972—69ft. 6in. He was born at Kaunas (Lithuania) on Apr. 11th, 1940.

## KUTS, V. (USSR)

It was Vladimir Kuts who succeeded Emil Zatopek as the world's fastest and most effective distance runner. He began running in 1949, when he was 22, and broke into world class in 1953 when he won his first national titles and was unofficially timed at 13 min. 31.4 sec. for 3 mi.— a second faster than Gunder Hagg's world record—during a 5000 m. race.

He quickly made a reputation for himself by the way he would try to run his rivals into the ground in the early stages of a race, often " blowing up" himself instead. However, in 1954 he scored a dramatic *coup* in the European 5000 m. championship when he did not come back to the field and proceeded to win by a wide margin from Chris Chataway and Zatopek in the world record time of 13 min. 56.6 sec.

Later in the season he lost a 5000 m. race (and the record) to Chataway in a classic duel in London, but recaptured it only ten days afterwards with 13 min. 51.2 sec.

His next major defeat occurred in June 1956 when Gordon Pirie beat him in world record time over 5000 m. in Norway. He obtained adequate revenge a few months later at the Melbourne Olympics when he killed off the Englishman in the 10,000 m. and came back to complete a double by winning the 5000, with Pirie a distant second.

Just prior to the Olympics he had set a world record for 10,000 m. of 28 min. 30.4 sec. and to this he added a 5000 m. mark of 13 min. 35.0 sec. in 1957, which survived for as long as seven years. His final track race took place in 1959 when he was just a pale shadow of his former self and he is now a prominent coach.

His best marks: 400 m. in 52.8 sec., 1500 m. in 3 min. 50.8 sec., 3000 m. in 8 min. 01.4 sec., 3 mi. in 13 min. 13.0 sec. (unofficial timing), 5000 m. in 13 min. 35.0 sec., 6 mi. in 27 min. 54.5 sec. (unofficial timing), 10,000 m. in 28 min. 30.4 sec. and 3000 m. steeplechase in 9 min. 13.0 sec. He was born at Aleksino on Feb. 7th, 1927.

## LIDDELL, E. H. (GB)

The 1924 Olympic Games was a wonderful occasion for British sprinting. Harold Abrahams upset the form book by taking the 100 m. and the Scot, Eric Liddell, did likewise by scoring a memorable victory in the 400 m.

Liddell, who withdrew from the 100 m. because the heats were run on a Sunday, directed all his religious fervour to winning that 400 m. Though he had not previously bettered 49 sec. for the quarter-mile he won his semi-final in 48.2 sec. In the final he amazed everyone by shooting off in the outside lane at unprecedented speed. He flashed by 200 m. in an unofficial 22.2 sec. and hit the straight four yards ahead. Though fading somewhat in the closing stages he held on to win by three yards in the glorious time of 47.6 sec. Two days earlier he had gained a bronze medal in the 200 m.

Liddell never raced seriously again after 1925, though in 1929 he is reputed to have recorded 49.0 sec. for 400 m. in China, where he was a missionary.

This Scottish rugby international was an exceptional performer at the short sprint, too. His 100 yd. time of 9.7 sec. in 1923 stood unbeaten as the UK record for 35 years. Other best times were 21.6 sec. for 220 yd. and 49.2 sec. for 440 yd. He was born at Tientsin, China, on Jan. 16, 1902, and died in Japanese captivity in 1945.

## LONG DISTANCE RUNNING

Opinions vary as to where middle-distance running leaves off and long-distance takes over. For the purpose of this section, long-distance comprises events from 3 mi. upwards.

The following track events in this category are included in the IAAF's schedule of world records: 3 mi., 5000 m. (3 mi. 188 yd.), 6 mi., 10,000 m. (6 mi. 376 yd.), 10 mi., 20,000 m. (12 mi. 753 yd.), 1 hour run, 15 mi., 25,000 m. (15 mi. 941 yd.) and 30,000 m. (18 mi. 1,129 yd). Two of these events, the 5000 and 10,000 m. feature in the Olympic programme.

Walter George, Sid Thomas and Alf Shrubb were the pre-eminent long distance runners of the late 19th and early 20th centuries, but British supremacy was terminated by the Finns. Hannes Kolehmainen led the way with his double at the 1912 Olympics and from then until 1948 only twice did the Olympic title at 5000 and 10,000 m. slip from Finland's possession.

Kolehmainen's successor as the individual champion of champions was Paavo Nurmi, the most prolific of all Olympic gold medallists and holder of countless world records.

Emil Zatopek (Czechoslovakia), winner of an unprecedented Olympic treble (5000, 10,000 and marathon) in 1952, was an even more comprehensive record breaker. Of the events listed in the second paragraph, only the 3 mi. record eluded him—and that because he was not timed *en route* to his fastest 5000 m. races rather than any shortcomings on his part.

The outstanding competitors of the post-Zatopek era have ben Vladimir Kuts (USSR) and Lasse Viren, one of a great new wave of Finnish runners —both gained an Olympic 5000 and 10,000 double, in 1956 and 1972 respectively.

The dominant figure in the 1960s, even though he won no major title, was Ron Clarke (Australia). Among his 21 world records, indoors and out, from 2 miles to the hour were such landmarks as the first 3 mi. inside 13 min., the first 6 mi. inside 27 min. and the first 10,000 m. inside 28 min.

Although no Briton has ever won the Olympic 5000 or 10,000, several UK distance runners have performed with great credit since the war—including Sydney Wooderson, famous as a half-miler and miler but who spreadeagled a fine field in the 1946 European 5000 m. championship; Gordon Pirie, the man who by his own example lifted British distance running to its present position; Chris Chataway, conqueror of Kuts in a never to be forgotten 5000 m. race; Bruce Tulloh, who ran a flawless tactical race to win the European 5000 m. in 1962; Ian Stewart, European 5000 m. champion at the age of 20 (1969) and Commonwealth winner the next year; and multi-record breaker Dave Bedford, who for a while ranked second only to Clarke on the world all-time lists.

See also under BEDFORD, D. C.; CHATAWAY, C. J.; CLARKE, R. W.; GEORGE, W. G.; HAGG, G.; HALBERG, M. G.; HILL, R.; IBBOTSON, G. D.; KEINO, K.; KOLEHMAINEN, H.; KUTS, V.; NURMI, P. J.; PIRIE, D. A. G.; PUTTEMANS, E.; ROELANTS, G.; SHRUBB, A.; VIREN, L.; WOODERSON, S. C. and ZATOPEK, E.

# LONG JUMP

The long jump take-off is marked by a board sunk level with the runway and the surface of the landing area (sand pit), the edge of which nearer to the landing area is called the take-off line. A competitor can take off wherever he pleases before the line but if he oversteps the line the jump is counted as a failure. Jumps are measured from the nearest break in the sand made by any part of the athlete's body or limbs to the take-off line and at right angles to such line.

As was the case in so many events, British, Irish and American athletes tended to dominate the proceedings in the formative years of modern athletics—say from 1870 to the outbreak of the First World War.

It is recorded that one Chionis, of Sparta, jumped 23 ft. 1½ in. in 656 B.C., a mark equalled just 2,530 years later by John Lane, of Ireland. Charles Fry (C. B. Fry of cricketing fame) entered his name in the record books with a leap of 23 ft. 6½ in. in 1893 and five years later William Newburn (Ireland) led the way over 24 ft.

The inaugural Olympic title in 1896 went for a paltry 20 ft. 10 in. but the standard was much more respectable in 1900, with Alvin Kraenzlein (USA) winning by a single centimetre from his Polish-born team-mate, Myer Prinstein, the world record holder with 24 ft. 7½ in.—both men leaping over 23 ft. 6 in. Later that season Peter O'Connor (Ireland) took possession of the world record which he lengthened to the somewhat frustrating distance of 24 ft. 11¾ in. in 1901.

That was that so far as records were concerned for 20 years, until Ed Gourdin (USA) achieved 25 ft. 3 in. The first to surpass 26 ft. was Silvio Cator, Haiti's sole but distinguished contribution to international athletics, in 1928, though William DeHart Hubbard (USA)—history's first consistent 25 ft. performer—was unlucky when in 1927 he jumped 26 ft. 2½ in. only to find the take-off board was one inch higher than the pit's surface, and thus a record was ruled out.

The next landmark in view was 8 metres (26 ft. 3 in.) and this duly fell in 1935 to the incomparable Jesse Owens with 26 ft. 8¼ in. The record stood inviolate for 25 long years until Ralph Boston (USA) assumed world leadership. It was Boston who became the first 27-footer. Both the 28 and 29-foot barriers were broken simultaneously when Bob Beamon (USA) touched down at 29 ft. 2½ in. at the 1968 Olympics—perhaps the most sensational exploit in the entire history of athletics.

Rather depressingly, Harold Abrahams' English record of 24 ft. 2½ in. (a fine performance in 1924) stood up for 32 years, but in 1964 Lynn Davies added a new dimension to British long jumping history by defeating Ralph Boston for the Olympic title. Davies, a 9.5 sec. sprinter, proved himself one of the greatest competitors of all time by winning the Commonwealth (for Wales) and European Championships in 1966—a unique treble. He retained his Commonwealth title in 1970 and became, in 1968, Britain's first 27-footer.

See also: BEAMON, R.; BOSTON, R. H.; DAVIES, L.; OWENS, J. C.; and WILLIAMS, R.

## Women

The long jump made its Olympic debut as late as 1948. The two big names in the event's history before then were Kinue Hitomi (Japan), an astonishing all-rounder who raised the world record by 15 in. to 19 ft. 7½ in. in 1928, and an even more distinguished example of athletic versatility in Fanny Blankers-Koen, who leapt 20 ft. 6 in. in 1943.

German athletes were the first to attain the 20 and 21 feet landmarks, respectively Christel Schulz (1939) and Hildrun Claus (1960). Mary Rand's victory in Tokyo, with a world record distance of 22 ft. 2¼ in., was the first ever Olympic gold medal success by a British woman athlete. In spite of the advantage of all-weather runways in later years, the current world record is only a few inches longer: 22 ft. 5¼ in. by Heide Rosendahl (W. Germany).

See also BLANKERS-KOEN, F. E., RAND, M. D., ROSENDAHL, H.. SZEWINSKA, I., and WALASIEWICZ, S.

## LOVELOCK, J. E.
### (New Zealand)

Jack Lovelock was a competitor *par excellence* whose victory in the 1936 Olympic 1500 m. in the world record time of 3 min. 47.8 sec. is widely considered to be one of the supreme races ever run. His final 400 m. was covered in a revolutionary 55.7 sec., the last 800 m. in 1 min. 57.7 sec.

A New Zealander by birth, he came up on a Rhodes Scholarship to Exeter College, Oxford, in the autumn of 1931. The following season he set a British mile record of 4 min. 12.0 sec. before placing seventh in the Olympic 1500 m. final. He posted a world record of 4 min. 07.6 sec. the next year, and in 1934 won the Commonwealth mile.

Lovelock frequently lost relatively unimportant races; his whole training and racing programme was directed towards one major event per year. During his final triumphant season (1936) he also recorded personal bests of 1 min. 55.0 sec. for 880 yd., 9 min. 03.8 sec. for 2 mi. and 14 min. 14.8

sec. for 3 mi. He was born at Cushington on Jan. 5th, 1910, and died in a New York subway accident on Dec. 28th, 1949.

## LOWE, D. G. A. (GB)

A remarkable anomaly in Douglas Lowe's glorious career is that he became Olympic 800 m. champion in 1924 before he ever managed to win an AAA title. Four years later he made history by retaining his gold medal, on that occasion lowering the Olympic record to 1 min. 51.8 sec.

Midway between his Olympic triumphs Lowe was defeated in one of the most celebrated track duels of all time. The event was the 1926 AAA 880 yd., and after a tremendous scrap (in which Lowe led at the bell in 54.6 sec.) Germany's Dr. Otto Peltzer won by three yards in 1 min. 51.6 sec. with Lowe (untimed, but estimated at 1 min. 52.0 sec.) also inside the world record figures of 1 min. 52.2 sec. Only the previous week Lowe had set up a world record of 1 min. 10.4 sec. for 600 yd., a distance then recognised by the IAAF.

His final race was run in Berlin shortly after the 1928 Olympics and he closed his career with a brilliant four yard victory over Peltzer in his fastest 800 m. time of 1 min. 51.2 sec. He was also a capable performer at 440 yd. (best of 48.8 sec.) and 1500 m. (fourth at 1924 Olympics in 3 min. 57.0 sec.). Later he became a leading administrator of the sport, serving as honorary secretary of the AAA from 1931 to 1938. He was born in Manchester on Aug. 7th, 1902.

## LUGANO CUP

This coveted trophy (for the IAAF Walking Team Competition) is contested usually every other year by the world's top walkers. Points are awarded for placings in the two road races, 20 km. and 50 km. and added together to determine the team positions.

Britain won the inaugural Cup Final in Lugano in 1961, scoring 54 pts. as did Sweden. The Cup was awarded to Britain as, under the competition rules, the formula to decide a tie was the position of the first competitor in the 50 km. Don Thompson finished 2nd in that race, one place ahead of the first Swede. Ken Matthews won the 20 km. on that occasion and in 1963 when Britain scored an easy team victory. The East Germans have subsequently dominated the tournament.

*1961:* 1, GB 54 pts; 2, Sweden 54; 3, Italy 28. Individual winners: 20 km: K. Matthews (GB) 1 hr. 30 min. 54.2 sec.; 50 km: A. Pamich (Italy) 4 hr. 25 mins. 38 sec.

*1963:* 1, GB 93; 2, Hungary 64; 3, Sweden 63. 20 km: K. Matthews (GB) 1 hr. 30 min. 10 sec.; 50 km: I. Havasi (Hungary) 4 hr. 14 min. 24 sec.

*1965:* 1, East Germany 117; 2, GB 89; 3, Hungary 64. 20 km: D. Lindner (E. Ger) 1 hr. 28 min. 09 sec.; 50 km: C. Hohne (E. Ger) 4 hr. 03 min. 14 sec.

*1967:* 1, East Germany 128; 2, USSR 107; 3, GB 104. 20 km: N. Smaga (USSR) 1 hr. 28 min. 38 sec.; 50 km: C. Hohne (E. Ger) 4 hr. 09 min. 09 sec.

*1970:* 1, East Germany 134; 2, USSR 125; 3, West Germany 88; 4, GB 65. 20 km: H-G. Reimann (E. Ger) 1 hr. 26 min. 54 sec.; 50 km: C. Hohne (E. Ger) 4 hr. 04 min. 35 sec.

## LUSIS, J. (USSR)

In an event—the javelin—in which an athlete's performance often fluctuates wildly, Janis Lusis has been the personification of consistency. A combination of outstanding competitive ability over a period of many years plus a smattering of world record throws makes him the greatest javelin artist of all time—surpassing even the achievements of Finland's Matti Jarvinen.

Lusis is the only athlete, in any event, to have won four consecutive European titles (1962, 1966, 1969, 1971); on top of that he can point to Olympic gold (1968), silver (1972) and bronze (1964) medals . . . and that silver in Munich would have been a gold had his final throw of 296 ft. 9 in. travelled just one inch farther. He was the second man to reach the 300 ft. line, seizing the world record in 1968 from Terje Pedersen (Norway) with 301 ft. 9 in. He lost it to Finland's Jorma Kinnunen the following year but regained the record in 1972 with 307 ft. 9 in.

In his younger and lighter days he was an excellent all-rounder, having scored 7,483 pts. in the decathlon, high jumped 6 ft. 3½ in., long jumped 23 ft. 8¼ in. and triple jumped 47 ft. 3½ in. His annual javelin progress: 1957—175 ft. 1 in; 1958—207 ft. 8 in.; 1959—238 ft. 3 in.; 1960—245 ft. 8 in.; 1961—265 ft. 9 in.; 1962—282 ft. 3 in.; 1963—274 ft. 5 in.; 1964—270 ft. 11 in.; 1965—284 ft. 0 in.; 1966—281 ft. 2 in.; 1967 298 ft. 6 in.; 1968—301 ft. 9 in.; 1969—300 ft. 3 in.; 1970—288 ft. 9 in.; 1971—297 ft. 6 in.; 1972—307 ft. 9 in. He was born at Jelgava (Latvia) on May 19th, 1939. His wife, Elvira (née Ozolina) was Olympic javelin champion in 1960 and the first woman to reach 200 ft.

# MARATHON

The marathon is the longest of all running events in such international celebrations as the Olympic Games, European Championships and Commonwealth Games. The race, all but a few hundred yards of which is contested on the road, was run over 26 mi. 385 yd. at the 1908 Olympics, and that is recognised as the standard distance for a marathon course.

No other athletics event has given rise to so much drama. The history of the sport is littered with marathon race incidents, some inspiring, many heartbreaking.

Under the latter category the two most notable victims were an Italian, Dorando Pietri, and an Englishman, Jim Peters. Pietri was the first to reach the White City Stadium at the 1908 Olympics but was in a dire state. After collapsing several times during the final lap of the track he was finally helped over the finish—and thus disqualified as a competitor may not be physically assisted during a race.

Nearly half a century later—the occasion being the 1954 Commonwealth Games in Vancouver—Britain's champion, Jim Peters, was brought down by a combination of the heat and his own uncompromising speed. He entered the stadium literally miles in front but, staggering and falling like a drunken man, he took eleven minutes to cover half a lap and was carried off the track when he collapsed just 200 yards from the end. These two men will never be forgotten, yet the victors of those two races, John Hayes (USA) and Joe McGhee (Scotland), are virtually unknown.

As for the inspiring occasions, none

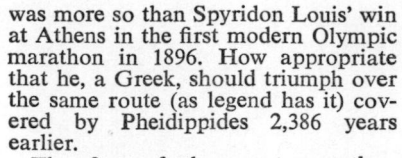

was more so than Spyridon Louis' win at Athens in the first modern Olympic marathon in 1896. How appropriate that he, a Greek, should triumph over the same route (as legend has it) covered by Pheidippides 2,386 years earlier.

The first of the great marathon runners was Hannes Kolehmainen whose time of 2 hr. 32 min. 35.8 sec. in winning the 1920 Olympic title on an over-distance course was worth very close to 2½ hours for the correct distance. Nevertheless, he won by less than 13 sec. from the Estonian, Juri Lossman—the closest result in Olympic marathoning history.

Kitei Son, a Korean running for Japan, brought the Olympic record under 2½ hr. in 1936. That record was beaten by Emil Zatopek, who in 1952 followed up his track double with a marathon in 2 hr. 23 min. 03.2 sec. He was succeeded in 1956 by his former track shadow, Alain Mimoun (France), who like Zatopek four years earlier was making his competitive debut in the event. The 1960 gold medal went to a previously unknown, barefooted Ethiopian, Abebe Bikila, in the then world's fastest time of 2 hr. 15 min. 16.2 sec. and it was he who triumphed again (wearing shoes this time) in Tokyo—winning by the remarkable margin of 4 minutes in 2 hr. 12 min. 11.2 sec.

Owing to the disparity in the nature, if not distance, of various courses, marathon times should not be taken too seriously. The "world record" has progressed as follows since the war:

| Time | Runner | Year |
|---|---|---|
| 2:26 07.0 | Choi Yoon Chil (Korea) | 1951 |
| 2:20 42.2 | Jim Peters (GB) | 1952 |
| 2:18 40.2 | Jim Peters (GB) | 1953 |
| 2:18 34.8 | Jim Peters (GB) | 1953 |
| 2:17 39.4 | Jim Peters (GB) | 1954 |
| 2:15 17.0 | Sergey Popov (USSR) | 1958 |
| 2:15 16.2 | Abebe Bikila (Ethiopia) | 1960 |
| 2:15 15.8 | Toru Terasawa (Japan) | 1963 |
| 2:14 28.0* | Buddy Edelen (USA) | 1963 |
| 2:14 43.0 | Brian Kilby (GB) | 1963 |

* 36 yd. (about 6 sec.) under standard distance.

| | | |
|---|---|---|
| 2:13 55.0 | Basil Heatley (GB) | 1964 |
| 2:12 11.2 | Abebe Bikila (Ethiopia) | 1964 |
| 2:12 00.0 | Morio Shigematsu (Japan) | 1965 |
| 2:09 36.4 | Derek Clayton (Australia) | 1967 |
| 2:08 33.6 | Derek Clayton (Australia) | 1969 |

Though yet to provide an Olympic winner, Britain has a fine record in marathon running. Silver medals have been gained by Sam Ferris (1932), who won the famous Polytechnic marathon from Windsor to Chiswick eight times in eight attempts, Ernie Harper (1936), Tom Richards (1948) and Basil Heatley (1964). Jack Holden, at the age of 43, won both Commonwealth and European titles in 1950, a feat achieved also by Brian Kilby in 1962 and Ron Hill in 1969/ 1970. Jim Peters transformed the event in terms of time and though he failed to win a major title his overall record in international races was a good one.

The fastest marathon time on record by a woman is 2 hr. 49 min. 40 sec. by the American cross-country international Cheryl Bridges in 1971.

See also under ABEBE BIKILA; CLAYTON, D.; HILL, R.; KOLEHMAINEN, H.; PETERS, J. H.; SHORTER, F.; and ZATOPEK, E.

## MATHIAS, R. B. (USA)

Bob Mathias was only 17½ when he won a gold medal at Wembley in 1948 to become the youngest male Olympic champion (in the sphere of athletics). What made the feat doubly astonishing was that Mathias' success came in the most searching test of the track and field programme, the decathlon. He went on to break the world record three times and successfully defend his laurels in 1952.

Mathias was one of that extraordinary number of outstanding athletes who overcame the most gigantic odds to become world champion. He suffered from anaemia as a boy, but so successful was his fight to become strong that by the time he was 16 he held the California schoolboy discus record.

He made his decathlon debut in June 1948 and won all ten of the competitions he contested from then until 1956. Actually he forfeited his amateur status in 1953 but continued to compete in the Services for the following three years. As late as 1959 he threw the discus 176 ft. in training.

His best marks included 10.8 sec. for 100 m., 50.2 sec. for 400 m., 4 min. 50.8 sec. for 1500 m., 13.8 sec. for 110 m. hurdles, 23.2 sec. for 220 yd. hurdles (straight), 6 ft. 2¾ in. high jump, 13 ft. 1½ in. pole vault, 22 ft. 10¾ in. long jump, 52 ft. 8 in. shot, 173 ft. 4 in. discus, 204 ft. 1 in. javelin and 7,887 point decathlon. Mathias, who starred in the Hollywood version of his own life story, was born at Tulare, California, on Nov. 17th, 1930, and in 1972 was re-elected to Congress.

## MATSON, J. R. (USA)

It took 38 years for the world record in the shot-put to advance from 40ft. to 50ft., and a further 45 years before Parry O'Brien opened the 60ft. era in 1954. At that rate of progress 70ft. looked a long way off but a young Texan by the name of Randy Matson had other ideas. He was barely 18 and still at school when he crashed the 60ft. barrier in 1963— and this before he concentrated on weight training and with little coaching.

Matson's improvement in 1964 was sensational: he bettered his season's target of 62ft. during the indoor season, then topped 63 . . . 64 . . . 65ft. He defeated Dallas Long for the American title and came close to repeating the dose in the Olympics with a silver medal winning 66ft. 3½in. Matson, by now standing 6ft. 6½in. and weighing 258lb., succeeded Long as world record holder in April 1965 with 67ft. 11¼in. Within a month the record stood at the fabulous distance of 70ft. 7¼in.—nearly a yard further than any other man had yet achieved.

He improved to 71 ft. 5½ in. during 1967, the year he threw the discus 213 ft. 9 in. for an American record. He won the 1968 Olympic title as expected but, sensationally failed to qualify for the 1972 Olympic team and announced his retirement from amateur competition.

His annual progress in the shot has been: 1962—64 ft. 7 in. (12 lb.); 1963 —60 ft. 6 in.; 1964— 66 ft. 3¼ in,; 1965—70 ft. 7¼ in.; 1966—69 ft. 2½ in.; 1967—71 ft. 5½ in.; 1968—69 ft. 10¼ in.; 1969—66 ft. 7½ in.; 1970—71 ft. 4¼ in.; 1971—68 ft. 8 in.; 1972— 69 ft. 6¼ in. He was born at Kilgore (Texas) on March 5th, 1945.

## MATTHEWS K. J. (GB)

Superbly consistent, Ken Matthews won four of his five major international 20 kilometres (12mi. 753yd.) walk tests: the European title in 1962, the Lugano Trophy finals of 1961 and 1963 . . . and the ultimate, an Olympic gold medal to seal his career in 1964.

His one slip in an otherwise brilliant record occurred at the 1960 Olympics where he led for eight kilometres before the heat and his own imprudent speed took their toll. A scrupulously fair walker and winner of countless style prizes. Matthews held the unofficial world's best for 5 and 10 mi. and the UK records at all events from 5 mi. to 2 hrs.

Best marks included 2 mi. in 13 min. 09.6 sec., 5 mi. in 34 min. 21.2 sec., 10,000 m. in 42 min. 35.6 sec., 7 mi. in 48 min. 22.2 sec., 8 mi. 1,151 yd. in the hour, 10 mi. in 69 min. 40.6 sec., 20 kilometres (road) in 88 min. 15 sec., and 20 mi. (road) in 2 hr. 38 min. 39 sec. He was born in Birmingham on June 21st, 1934.

## MATTHEWS, V. (USA)

Vince Matthews, who was only 19 when he first broke into world class 400 m. running in 1967—the year he won the America v. Europe match event in 45.0 sec. and came second in the Pan-American Games—just failed to make the squad for the 1968 Olympic 400 m. As fourth placer in the US Trials he gained his position in the 4 x 400 m. relay team, and contributed to the USA's victory in a world record of 2 min. 56.1 sec.—but missing his chance of individual glory was a great disappointment to a man who had fleetingly held the world record (unratified as he was wearing

shoes ruled illegal) at 44.4 sec.

He retired, but the lure of the Games in 1972 brought him back into competition (he was still only 24). This time he finished third in the Trials and, in Munich, he brought off an unexpected victory over team-mate Wayne Collett in 44.7 sec. He lost his opportunity of another gold medal in the relay when he and Collett were disqualified from further Olympic competition after what was considered by the Executive Board of the IOC to be disrespectful behaviour during the victory ceremony. He has since turned professional.

His best marks include 20.7 sec. for 200 m., and 44.4 sec. for 400 m. Annual progress at 440 yd.: 1965— 48.0; 1966—46.2; 1967—45.0 (400 m.); 1968—44.4 (400 m.); 1972—44.7 (400 m.). He was born in Queens, New York, on Dec. 16th, 1947.

## MATZDORF, P. (USA)

On July 3rd, 1971, during a match between the USA, USSR and a 'World All Stars' team, Pat Matzdorf—who had never previously jumped higher than 7 ft. 2 in. outdoors—broke one of the oldest and most revered of all world records: Valeriy Brumel's 7 ft. 5¾ in. established in 1963. In a staggering break-through, the 6 ft. 3 in. tall Matzdorf cleared 7 ft. 6¼ in.

A straddle jumper with an unusual bent lead-leg style, he first topped 7 feet in 1970. in which year he won the National Collegiate title but placed only 4th in the World Student Games. Early in 1971 he equalled the American indoor record of 7 ft. 3 in. His best leap since the world record has been 7 ft. 4 in. a fortnight later. Only fifth in the US Trials, he failed to make the Olympic team in 1972.

A 9.8 sec. sprinter for 100 yd., he has shown the following high jumping progress: 1966—6 ft. 0 in.; 1967—6 ft. 6 in.; 1968—6 ft. 11 in.; 1969—6 ft. 10¼ in.; 1970—7 ft. 1¾ in.; 1971— 7ft. 6¼ in.; 1972—7 ft. 1 in. (and 7 ft. 2½ in. indoors). He was born at Sheboygan, Wisconsin, on Dec. 26th, 1949.

## MELNIK, F. (USSR)

In just two seasons Faina Melnik achieved enough to justify being considered the greatest female discus thrower of all time.

She made her international championship debut at the 1971 European Championships a memorable one, for she crushed the opposition with her final throw of 210 ft. 8 in., a world record. A few weeks later, in Munich, she improved to 212 ft. 10 in. Three times in 1972 she extended the world record and on the basis of her 219 ft. 0 in. performance she was rated a strong favourite for the Olympic title. She won it all right, but not without some anxious moments on the way. After three rounds she was only fifth but a magnificent fourth-round throw of 218 ft. 7 in. drew her clear of Argentina Menis.

In May 1973 she regained the world record she had lost to Menis with 221 ft. 3 in.

She is also a first-class shot-putter, with a best of 60 ft. 7¼ in. Annual discus progress: 1965—144 ft. 4 in.; 1966—161 ft. 9 in.; 1967—158 ft. 7 in.; 1968—166 ft. 5 in.; 1969—179 ft. 8 in.; 1970—202 ft. 9 in.; 1971—212 ft. 10 in.; 1972—219 ft. 0 in. She was born at Bakota (Ukraine) on June 9th, 1945.

## MENIS, A. (Rumania)

Thanks largely to a prodigious weight training schedule, Argentina Menis so increased her strength and general proficiency as a discus thrower that, after taking three years to improve merely from 170 ft. to 180 ft., she shot up beyond 200 ft. in 1971 (and placed 4th in the European Championships) and ended 1972 by snatching the world record from Faina Melnik (USSR) with the extraordinary distance of 220 ft. 10 in. During those two eventful years her weight increased from 165 lb. to 190 lb.

One of the very few rivals ever to have defeated Melnik more than once, she gave the Soviet star a tough fight at the Munich Olympics. Menis opened with 210 ft. 11 in. and held the lead until the 4th round in which she improved to 213 ft. 5 in. but where Melnik reached 218 ft. 7 in.

Her annual progress: 1964—118 ft. 4 in.; 1965—147 ft 4 in.; 1966—154 ft. 3 in.; 1967—163 ft. 2 in.; 1968—170 ft. 7 in.; 1969—174 ft. 8 in.; 1970

—180 ft. 11 in.; 1971—200 ft. 5 in.; 1972—220 ft. 10 in. She was born at Craiova on July 19th, 1948.

## MEYFARTH, U. (West Germany)

When the 6 ft. 0½ in. tall Ulrike Meyfarth sent the Munich crowd roaring as she arched successfully over a world record equalling height of 6 ft. 3½ in., she became the youngest Olympic champion and individual world record holder in athletics history. On that heady evening of Sept. 4th, 1972, this Fosbury-flopping schoolgirl was just 16 years and 4 months old.

No one gave her a chance, herself included. Her only previous big-time experience was at the previous year's European Championships where, as a non-qualifier for the final, she had placed equal 30th of 35 competitors with a modest enough leap of 5 ft. 6 in.

She only scraped into the Olympic team and although she progressed to 6 ft. 0¾ in. shortly before the Games there was no indication of the sensational break-through that was to occur. In the final she won the title by clearing 6 ft. 2¾ in. on her second attempt and then, quite inspired, mastered 6 ft. 3½ in. Her annual progress: 1968—4 ft. 10½ in.; 1969—5 ft. 1¾ in.; 1970—5 ft. 6 in.; 1971—5 ft. 10¾ in.; 1972—6 ft. 3½ in. She was born at Frankfurt/Main on May 4th, 1956.

## MIDDLE DISTANCE RUNNING

The province of middle distance running may, for the purposes of this section, be said to stretch from 800 m. (875 yd.) to 2 mi. Olympic and European championships are staged at 800 m. and 1500 m. (120 yd. less than a mile); world records are officially recognised at 800 m., 880 m., 1000 m. (1,093 yd.), 1500 m., mile, 2000 m. (1 mi. 427 yd.), 3000 m. (1 mi. 1,521 yd.) and 2 mi.

## 800 Metres & 880 Yards

The first of the "modern" half-milers is generally acknowledged to be Mel Sheppard (USA), winner of the

127

1908 Olympic 800 m. in a world record of 1 min. 52.8 sec. after covering the first 400 m. in a sparkling 53.0 sec. He was succeeded by James "Ted" Meredith, another American, who not only won the 1912 gold medal in the world record time of 1 min. 51.9 sec. but carried on for another five yards to complete 880 yd. in 1 min. 52.5 sec.—another record.

Albert Hill, the 800 and 1500 m. champion in 1920, began a wonderful string of Olympic successes for Britain. Douglas Lowe triumphed in 1924 and 1928, and Tom Hampson carried on the tradition in 1932, in the process clocking 1 min. 49.7 sec. to become the first man to run two laps inside 1 min. 50 sec. Two years later Ben Eastman (USA) lowered the 880 yd. record to 1 min. 49.8 sec.

John Woodruff (USA) took the 1936 title but though he never officially broke any world records his amazing 880 yd. time of 1 min. 47.7 sec. on a 264 yd. indoor track in 1940 testifies to his tremendous ability. Sydney Wooderson (GB) captured both the 800 m. and 880 yd. records in 1938 but was relieved of the metric standard within a year by Rudolf Harbig (Germany), whose time of 1 min. 46.6 sec. would today still be reckoned as world class.

Mal Whitfield (USA), who broke Wooderson's half-mile record in 1953, equalled Lowe's feat by winning the Olympic crown in 1948 and 1952, on both occasions clocking 1 min. 49.2 sec. and defeating Jamaica's Arthur Wint by a yard. Harbig's record finally tumbled in 1955 when Roger Moens (Belgium) was timed in 1 min. 45.7 sec. ahead of the Norwegian, Audun Boysen (1 min. 45.9 sec.).

Tom Courtney (USA), who narrowly defeated British record holder Derek Johnson in the 1956 Olympics, recorded a 1 min. 46.8 sec. 880 yd. in 1957, yet even this seemed pedestrian when in 1962 Peter Snell (New Zealand) stopped the watches at 1 min. 45.1 sec. after passing 800 m. in 1 min. 44.3 sec. Snell was Olympic champion in 1960 and 1964.

The next gold medallist, Ralph Doubell (Australia), ran a record equalling 1 min. 44.3 sec. in winning his title and in turn his successor, Dave Wottle (USA) also clocked that time in 1972.

Rick Wohlhuter's 880 yd. world record of 1 min. 44.6 sec. is intrinsically better.

Britain has produced several half-milers of the highest class since the War: John Parlett, Commonwealth and European champion in 1950; Derek Johnson, Brian Hewson, John Boulter, Chris Carter and Andy Carter among them.

See also DOUBELL, R.; ELLIOTT, H. J.; HAMPSON, T.; HARBIG, R.; HILL, A. G.; LOWE, D. G. A.; MYERS, L. E.; RYUN, J. R.; SNELL, P. G.; VASALA, P.; WHITFIELD, M. G.; WOODERSON, S. C.; and WOTTLE, D.

## Women

Four names overshadow all others in the realm of women's half-miling: Nina Otkalenko (USSR), who in five seasons (1951-55) hacked down the world record for 800 m. from 2 min. 12.0 sec. to 2 min. 05.0 sec.; the almost legendary Sin Kim Dan (North Korea), who became the first woman to break two minutes with a breathtaking 1 min. 59.1 sec. for the distance in 1963 (and improved to 1 min. 58.0 sec, in 1964); Britain's Ann Packer, who in her first and only season at the event won the 1964 Olympic 800m. crown in 2 min. 01.1 sec.; and Hildegard Falck (W. Germany), official world record holder with 1 min. 58.5 sec. and 1972 Olympic champion in a tenth slower. Commonwealth champion Rosemary Stirling holds the UK record of 2 min. 00.2 sec.

See also BOARD, L. B.; FALCK, H.; and PACKER, A. E.

## MILBURN, R. (USA)

For a whole decade the world high hurdles record of 13.2 sec. by Martin Lauer (W. Germany) in 1959 stood unbroken. Then along came Rod Milburn to astonish the track world with a 1971 season that ranks among the most momentous of any athlete. He went through 28 races unbeaten; and two of them were sensational. On June 4th he was timed at 13.0 sec. with wind assistance over the limit, and three weeks later—at the AAU Championships—he clocked 13 sec-

Fanny Blankers-Koen (Netherlands), nearest camera, on the way to winning the 1948 Olympic 80 metres hurdles from Maureen Gardner (GB) and Shirley Strickland (Australia), number 668.

Lillian Board (UK), European 800 metres champion in 1969, who died of cancer at the age of 22.

Britain's golden girl of the 1972 Olympics, pentathlon champion Mary Peters.

Valeriy Borzov (USSR), Olympic and European sprint champion.

David Hemery (UK), 1968 Olympic champion, defeats his successor John Akii-Bua (Uganda) in 1972 AAA 400 metres hurdles.

onds flat again for the 120 yd. hurdles, and this time legally. Indeed, the electric photo-timer registered 12.94 sec., so he was unlucky not to be credited officially with 12.9 sec. No less an authority than Lee Calhoun expressed the opinion that Milburn was capable of 12.7 sec. but it is possible that the lure of professional football will cause a premature end to a sparkling career.

He encountered some problems in 1972, barely qualifying for the Olympic team, but he struck top form on the big day in Munich and won the gold medal in 13.2 sec., equalling the world record for the 110 m. event which is some ten inches longer than 120 yd. He never races on the flat but he believes he is worth 9.2/9.3 sec. for 100 yd., an estimate borne out by his tremendous leg speed.

His annual progression: 1967—14.2 (3 ft. 3 in. hurdles); 1968—14.2; 1969 —13.7; 1970—13.5; 1971—13.0; 1972 —13.2 and 13.0 wind assisted. He was born at Opelousas, Louisiana, on May 18th, 1950.

## MILE

No other athletic event has captured the public's imagination to quite the same degree as the mile. Even men and women who could not tell a discus from a javelin are aware of the worth of a mile covered in four minutes. That figure four—4 minutes to run 4 laps—developed a mystical quality over the years and even now, when the four-minute " barrier " has been broken hundreds of times, the magic persists.

The first great miler was Englishman Walter George, who set an amateur best of 4 min. 18.4 sec. in 1884 and a professional record of 4 min. 12.75 sec. two years later. He is said to have run 4 min. 10.2 sec. in a time trial. So far ahead of his time was George that it was not until 1931 that 4 min. 10 sec. was officially beaten in competition . . . by the Frenchman, Jules Ladoumegue (4 min. 09.2 sec.).

The Swedish pair, Gunder Hagg and Arne Andersson, beat 4 min. 03 sec. five times between 1943 and 1945 but they were disqualified in the latter year for professionalism. It was left to Britain's Roger Bannister to earn immortality in three minutes and fifty nine point four seconds at Oxford on May 6th, 1954. The lap times on that historic occasion were 57.5, 60.7, 62.3 and 58.9 sec.

John Landy (Australia) and Derek Ibbotson (GB) succeeded Bannister as world record holder but it was left to Herb Elliott (Australia), the greatest mile competitor in history, to drag the record under 3 min. 55 sec. Peter Snell (New Zealand) and Michel Jazy (France) knocked off a few tenths each before Jim Ryun (USA), aged only 19, brought 3 min. 50 sec. within range with times of 3 min. 51.3 sec. in 1966 and 3 min. 51.1 sec. in 1967. Meanwhile, the British record was lowered to 3 min. 55.7 sec. in 1965 by Alan Simpson, a mark that stood until Peter Stewart ran 3 min. 55.3 sec. in 1972.

The metric, and therefore Olympic, equivalent of the mile is 1500 m.—a little under 120 yd. short of the English distance. Approximately 18 sec. is the usual conversion factor for top-class performances.

Winning an Olympic crown in world record time is just about the supreme achievement possible for a runner, and Elliott's 1960 win emulated that of New Zealand's Jack Lovelock, who in 1936 stormed home in 3 min. 47.8 sec.

The first man to break 3 min. 40 sec. was Stanislav Jungwirth (Czechoslovakia), who once handed Roger Bannister a defeat in the latter's great 1954 season, with an almost unbelievable 3 min. 38.1 sec. in 1957, roughly two seconds faster than John Landy's then record mile of 3 min. 57.9 sec. Even the Czech's time lasted barely a year, for Elliott clocked 3 min. 36.0 sec. in 1958 and 3 min. 35.6 sec. in 1960. Ryun smashed that record with his 3 min. 33.1 sec. timing in 1967, although some believe that Kip Keino's 1968 Olympic victory in 3 min. 34.9 sec. at high altitude is an even greater run.

See also BANNISTER, R. G.; ELLIOTT, H. J.; GEORGE, W. G.; HAGG, G.; HILL, A. G.; IBBOTSON, G. D.; KEINO, K.; LOVELOCK, J. E.; NURMI, P. J.; RYUN, J. R.; SNELL, P. G.; VASALA, P.; and WOODERSON, S. C.

I

## Women

Diane Leather (GB) was the first to break 5 min., in 1954. The present best mile time is 4 min. 35.3 sec. by Ellen Tittel (W. Germany) in 1971, but that bears no comparison to the world 1500 m. record of 4 min. 01.4 sec. by Lyudmila Bragina (USSR) in the inaugural Olympic race of 1972. See also BRAGINA, L.

## MORROW, B. J. (USA)

Regarded by some as among the greatest—though not necessarily fastest—sprint competitors to date is Bobby Morrow. Between 1955 and 1958, against the strongest opposition in the world, he lost only one championship race; and at the 1956 Olympics he scored a grand slam by winning the 100 and 200 m. and contributing to the United States' relay victory.

He was far from outstanding as a youngster, his best times at the age of 16 being only 10.5 sec. for 100 yd. and 22.8 sec. for 220 yd., but he developed quickly in his later teens.

He held individual world records at 100 yd. and 200 m. (turn), was credited with running 300 yd. in 29.2 sec. during training (0.2 sec. faster than the unofficial world's best) and was timed in 46.6 sec. for a 440 yd. relay leg. His best official times were 9.3 sec. for 100 yd., 10.2 sec. for 100 m., 20.6 sec. for 200 m. (turn) and 20.4 sec. for 220 yd. (straight).

Morrow, who narrowly failed to make the USA Olympic team in 1960, had two unusual honours accorded him by fellow Texans after returning from Melbourne: Feb. 23rd, 1957, was designated "Bobby Morrow Day" throughout the state and a plaque worded "Bobby Morrow Slept Here" was installed in an Abilene hotel room! He was born at Harlingen on Oct. 15th, 1935.

## MYERS, L. E. (USA)

Just as Walter George was clearly the outstanding middle and long distance runner of the 19th century, so Laurence "Lon" Myers was undisputed master of the short distances. Standing 5 ft. 8 in. and weighing a mere 110 lb., but possessed of disproportionately long legs, Myers began racing in Nov. 1878. The following year he set the first of his numerous world records.

From 1880 to 1888 he held the world records for 100 yd. (equal), 440 yd. and 880 yd.—a feat that, needless to add, has never been duplicated. The quarter-mile was his best event and he was responsible for reducing the best on record from 50.4 sec. to 48.8 sec. In 1880 he succeeded in winning eight national titles in a week: first the American and then the Canadian championships at 100, 220, 440 and 880 yd.

As an amateur his best times included 5.5 sec. for 50 yds., 10.0 sec. for 100 yd., 22.5 sec. for 220 yd., 48.8 sec. for 440 yd., 1 min. 55.4 sec. for 880 yd., 3 min. 13.0 sec. for ¾ mi. He turned professional in 1885 and the following year defeated even George over 880 yd., ¾ mi. and mile. He was born at Richmond, Virginia, on Feb. 16th, 1858, and died of pneumonia on Feb. 15th, 1899.

# NATIONAL ATHLETICS LEAGUE

The National Athletics League was formed in 1969 with the purpose of providing more meaningful competition for clubs—the foundations of British athletics—and to help improve standards, particularly in the comparatively neglected field events. It proved to be an immediate success, with club spirit very much in evidence at fixtures.

The League is split into four divisions of six clubs each, with four matches per season. For example in 1973 the Division 1 meetings are being held at West London Stadium, Wolverhampton, Cwmbran and Edinburgh —thus justifying the League's new name, the British Athletics League. Each club fields two athletes per event.

Final placings in Division 1: 1969—1, Birchfield 15 pts; 2, Cardiff 14; 3, Thames Valley 12; 4, Brighton & Hove 10; 5, Polytechnic 9; 6, Blackheath, 3.

1970—1, Thames Valley 22; 2, Birchfield 19; 3, Cardiff 16; 4, Hillingdon 12; 5, Brighton & Hove 11; 6, Surrey 4.

1971—1, Thames Valley 23; 2, Birchfield 21; 3, Cardiff 15; 4, Edinburgh Southern 11; 5, Hillingdon 10; 6, Sale 4.

1972—1, Cardiff 22; 2, Thames Valley 21; 3, Wolverhampton & Bilston 14; 4, Edinburgh Southern 13; 5, Birchfield 8; 6, Brighton & Hove 6.

In addition to the League, a British Athletics Club Cup knock-out tournament was being arranged for 1973, with one competitor per club per event.

# NATIONAL COLLEGIATE ATHLETIC ASSOCIATION

Founded in 1906 as the Inter-collegiate Athletic Association, the NCAA (as it became known in 1910) is an important administrative body in the United States and since 1921 has promoted annual campionships which invariably produce brilliant results as the leading American collegiate athletes battle for the NCAA's prestigious titles. Indoor championships have been staged since 1965.

# NEUFVILLE, M. F. (Jamaica)

During one action-packed but controversial season (1970) Marilyn Neufville was transformed from a promising British international into the world's fastest female 400 m. runner, wearing the colours of Jamaica—and she was only 17.

Marilyn, born in Jamaica, came with her family to Britain when she was eight. From the age of 11 she was a member of the South London club, Cambridge Harriers. A precocious 220 yd. runner she was, at 15, invited to represent Jamaica in the 1968 Olympics, an offer she declined as she felt then that her international future lay with the British team. The following year she did begin to race for Britain.

Although a novice at that type of running, she created a stir at the 1970 European Indoor Championships as she defeated Olympic champion Colette Besson (France) in a world indoor best time of 53.0 sec. Suddenly she was an internationally acclaimed star and with the Commonwealth Games imminent she decided to compete in Edinburgh for her native land. This action caused resentment in some quarters but the furore did not affect Marilyn's running, for she smashed the world record as she won in 51.0 sec.

Although it appears she was not officially eligible to represent Jamaica in the 1971 Pan-American Games, she won the 400 m. title there in 52.3 sec. and contributed a spectacular 50.8 sec.

relay leg. But her Olympic ambitions were shattered when she tore an Achilles tendon early in 1972. Her best marks include 11.9 sec. for 100 m. (and wind assisted 11.7 sec.), 23.6 sec. for 200 m. and 51.0 sec. for 400 m. Annual 400 m. progress: 1968—57.1 (440 yd.); 1969—54.2; 1970—51.0; 1971—52.3. She was born at Hectors River (Jamaica) on Nov. 16th, 1952.

## NIHILL, V. P. (GB)

Paul Nihill, born in Essex but of Irish descent, has enjoyed a varied career in athletics. He started out as a sprinter and hurdler as a young boy, from 1954 to 1959 he was chiefly a cross-country runner (of county standard), and in 1960 he started training seriously for walking. He won his first national title (the Irish mile) in 1962 and only two years later he finished less than 20 sec. behind the great Italian, Abdon Pamich, for second place in the Olympic 50km. in 4 hr. 11 min. 31.2 sec.—the fastest time by a British walker.

Nihill is also Britain's fastest 'sprint' walker and his best event has proved to be 20 km. He was European champion in 1969, and a close third in 1971; while a month before the 1972 Olympics he clocked the world's fastest ever time for 20 km. (road) of 84 min. 50 sec. in the Isle of Man. At the Games, though, leg trouble held him down to sixth place.

His best walking performances include 11 min. 51.2 sec. for 3000 m., 84 min. 50 sec. for 20,000 m., and 4 hr. 11 min. 31.2 sec. for 50,000m.

Annual progress at 20,000 m. and 50,000 m.; 1961—1:42:07; 1962—1:36:58, 4:51:32; 1963—1:32:09, 4:26:06; 1964—1:31:39, 4:11:31.2; 1965—1:33:33, 4:26:32; 1966—1:33:03; 1968—1:31:19, 4:18:59; 1969—1:28:29; 1970—1:30:55; 1971—1:27:34, 4:14:05; 1972—1:24:50, 4:14.09.4. He was born in Colchester on Sept. 5th, 1939, and announced his retirement in 1973.

## NORDWIG, W. (East Germany)

A rock-steady competitor throughout his international career, it was appropriate that the man who should become the first non-American ever to win the Olympic pole vault was Wolfgang Nordwig, universally acknowledged as this intricate event's finest technician.

Nordwig, born of a German father and French mother, took up pole vaulting when he was 14, using a clothes line as a bar in those early days. He shot up over two feet the year he switched to a fibre-glass pole (1963) and three seasons later he won the European title—which he successfully defended in 1969 and 1971. At the 1968 Olympics he suffered the galling experience of clearing the same height as winner Bob Seagren (USA)—a personal best of 17 ft. 8½ in.—but having to be content with the bronze medal.

The first European to vault 17 ft. (in 1966), Nordwig held the world record briefly in 1970 with 17 ft. 10½ in. and then 17 ft. 11 in., and those remained his best heights until, in the final international competition of his career, he flew over 18 ft. 0½ in. at the 1972 Olympics to defeat Seagren. In all, he vaulted 17 ft. 4½ in. (5.30 metres) or higher in 37 separate competitions . . . a brilliant record of consistency.

His best marks include 100 m. in 10.7 sec., 400 m. in 49.8 sec., 110 m. hurdles in 15.5 sec., 6 ft 0¾ in. high jump, 18 ft. 0½ in. pole vault, 24 ft. 2¼ in. long jump and 7,331 pts. decathlon. Annual pole vault progress: 1958—8 ft. 10¼ in., 1959—11 ft. 2¼ in., 1960—12 ft. 1½ in., 1961—13 ft. 2½ in., 1962—13 ft. 5¾ in., 1963—15 ft. 6½ in., 1964—16 ft. 5¼ in., 1965—16 ft. 6¾ in., 1966—17 ft. 1¾ in., 1967—16 ft. 10¾ in., 1968—17 ft. 8½ in., 1969—17 ft. 6½ in., 1970—17 ft. 11 in., 1971—17 ft. 8½ in., 1972—18 ft. 0½ in. He was born at Siegmar on Aug. 27th, 1943.

## NURMI, P. J. (Finland)

Fifty years after his greatest exploits, Paavo Nurmi remains a household name. No other athlete has won such wide and lasting fame. During his long career he amassed practically every honour open to him, notably nine Olympic gold medals (six individual and three team) collected over three Olympiads and a score of world

132

records over distances ranging from 1500 to 20,000 m.

He opened his Olympic account in 1920 by succeeding his idol, Hannes Kolehmainen, as 10,000 m. and cross-country champion, and he also won a silver medal in the 5000 m. In 1924 he won all four of his races—1500 m., 5000 m. (these two within 1½ hours!), cross-country and 3000 m. team race. Four years later he recaptured his 10,000 m. crown and placed second in the 5000 m. and 3000 m. steeplechase.

But for an untimely disqualification for professionalism he might well have climaxed his career with victory in the 1932 Olympic marathon, for earlier that year he ran 40,200 m. (24 mi. 1,506 yd.) in 2 hr. 22 min. 03.8 sec., the equivalent of under 2½ hr. for the full marathon distance. The Olympic race was won in 2 hr. 31 min. 36 sec.

As for world records, his first came at 6 mi. in 1921 and his last at 2 mi. in 1931. His most spectacular achievement in this department was his pair of world records within one hour a few weeks before the 1924 Olympics —3 min. 52.6 sec. for 1500 m. and 14 min. 28.2 sec. for 5000 m. Another indication of his greatness was the longevity of his world records. His 6 mi. mark stood 15 years, that for

10 mi. almost 17 years.

Even American indoor racing, the downfall of many a European champion, came naturally to him. During his epic campaign of 1925 he won all but one of his numerous races and among his crop of indoor records was a mark of 8 min. 58.2 sec. for 2 mi.— which was over 11 sec. faster than the official outdoor record of the time.

He ran his last important race in 1933, aged 36, winning the Finnish 1500 m. title as a " national amateur " in 3 min. 55.8 sec. A statue of him stands outside Helsinki's Olympic Stadium and it was he who was given the honour of carrying the Olympic torch at the opening ceremony of the 1952 Games. He was born at Turku on June 13th, 1897.

His best marks were 1 min. 56.3 sec. for 800 m., 3 min. 52.6 sec. for 1500 m., 4 min. 10.4 sec. for the mile, 5 min. 24.6 sec. for 2000 m., 8 min. 20.4 sec. for 3000 m., 8 min. 59.5 sec. for 2 mi., 14 min. 02.0 sec. for 3 mi., 14 min. 28.2 sec. for 5000 m., 19 min. 18.7 sec. for 4 mi., 29 min. 07.1 sec. for 6 mi., 30 min. 06.1 sec. for 10,000 m., 50 min. 15.0 sec. for 10 mi., 11 mi. 1,648 yd. in the hour, 64 min. 38.4 sec. for 20,000 m. and 9 min. 30.8 sec. for 3000 m. steeplechase.

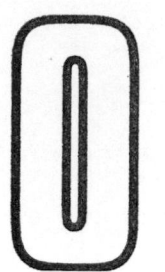

## O'BRIEN, W. P. (USA)

Without question the most significant individual in the history of shot-putting is Parry O'Brien, who revolutionised the event by the introduction of the technique that bears his name. He developed this new method following the 1951 season, during which he had terminated Jim Fuchs' long supremacy by beating him for the USA title. Ridiculed at first, O'Brien quickly silenced all criticism by winning the 1952 Olympic title.

For many years he utterly dominated the speciality. Between July 7th, 1952 and June 15th, 1956 he won 116 consecutive competitions; in 1953 he broke Fuchs' world record of 58 ft. 10¾ in. and in 14 instalments carried the record out to 63 ft. 2 in. in 1956, thus being the first man to achieve 59, 60, 61, 62 and 63 ft.; he successfully defended his Olympic crown in 1956 and also won the Pan-American title in 1955 and 1959.

Dallas Long relieved him of the world mark for two months in 1959 before O'Brien came back with records of 63 ft. 2½ in. and 63 ft. 4 in. Experience finally gave way to youth when Long recaptured the standard in 1960, in which year O'Brien took the Olympic silver medal behind Bill Nieder after leading until the penultimate round.

He made the Olympic team yet again in 1964 and placed 4th, but this was not the signal to retire. Although unable to reach the distances of Long and Randy Matson, O'Brien continued to be a formidable competitor and in 1966, his 19th season, he improved to 64 ft. 7¼ in. Fast (10.8 sec. 100 m. in 1953) as well as strong (6 ft. 3 in., 250 lb.), he was also a top-flight discus thrower—American champion in 1955. He was born at Santa Monica, California, on Jan. 28th, 1932.

## OERTER, A. A. (USA)

Four times acclaimed Olympic champion, the first man to exceed 200 ft. in competition: Al Oerter is the nonpareil of discus throwing.

He seemed destined for greatness when he set an American schoolboy discus (3 lb. 9 oz.) record of 184 ft. 2 in. in 1954 but few could have anticipated he would develop so speedily that only two years later he won an Olympic gold medal. His repeat victory in 1960 was less surprising. Oerter's third triumph in 1964 ranks among the greatest competitive efforts in athletics history for he was in acute pain throughout.

His achievement in winning an unprecedented fourth Olympic title in 1968 made him the most outstanding competitor in the annals of athletics. On paper, his fellow-American Jay Silvester—who had recently set a world record of 224 ft. 5 in.—should have won but once again Oerter rose splendidly to the occasion, unleashing a personal best of 212 ft. 6 in. As Silvester once remarked: "When you throw against Oerter, you don't expect to win. You just hope."

It was not until 1962 that he laid claim to the world record. He made history by throwing 200 ft. 5 in., lost the record just 17 days later to Vladimir Trusenyov (USSR) and recaptured it with 204 ft. 10 in. after a further lapse of 27 days. He improved to 205 ft. 5 in. in 1963 and 206 ft. 6 in. in 1964 for further world records, but distances were always secondary to him. He was the competitor supreme, and it was a relief to those with 1972 Olympic aspirations that Oerter decided not to try for a fifth victory. He was born at Astoria, New York, on Sept. 19th, 1936.

## OLDEST
### Men

Oldest Olympic champion was Pat McDonald (USA), winner of the 56 lb. weight in 1920 at the age of 41. In a standard event—Tommy Green (GB), 50 km. walk in 1932 aged 39.

Oldest European champion: Jack Holden (GB), Marathon in 1950, aged 43.

Oldest Commonwealth champion: Jack Holden (England), Marathon in 1950, aged 42.

Oldest British champion: T. Lloyd Johnson, RWA 50 km. walk in 1949, aged 49.

Oldest British internationals: T. Lloyd Johnson (1948 Olympic 50 km. walk) and Harold Whitlock (1952 Olympic 50 km. walk), aged 48.

Oldest world record breaker: Gerhard Weidner (W. Germany) 30 mi. and 50 km. walk in 1973, aged 40.

Oldest UK record breaker in a track and field event: Don Finlay, 120 yd. hurdles in 1949, aged 40.

## Women

Oldest Olympic champion: Lia Manoliu (Rumania), discus in 1968, aged 36.

Oldest European champion and world record breaker: Dana Zatopkova (Czechoslovakia), javelin in 1958, aged 35.

Oldest Commonwealth champion: Rosemary Payne (Scotland), discus in 1970, aged 37.

Oldest British champion, British international and UK record breaker: Rosemary Payne, discus in 1972, aged 39.

## OLYMPIC GAMES

The precise origins of the Olympic Games are shrouded by the mists of Greek antiquity. As the most famous of a cycle which included the Pythian, Nemean and Isthmian Games, the ancient Olympic Games have been traced back as far as the 13th century B.C. The first Olympic champion known to posterity was one Coroebus, winner of the stade foot-race in the Games of 776 B.C.

From that date, for the next 1,170 years, the Games were staged every four years (an Olympiad). In deference to the Olympic Games and its ideals all battles were halted for the five-days duration of each celebration. The Games, which featured track and field events, wrestling, boxing and chariot racing, were held at Olympia, situated on a plain in the

Elis province of Southern Greece. The horseshoe-shaped stadium, some 230 yards long and 34 yards wide, held 40,000 spectators. As the Greek civilisation declined so, too, did the Olympic Games and in A.D. 393 they were abolished altogether by the decree of the Roman emperor Theodosius.

A little over 15 centuries were to pass before the Olympic Games were brought back to life. The revival was the brainchild of a French baron, Pierre de Coubertin. Three years after making public his intention, the first modern Olympic Games were held, appropriately, in Athens in the spring of 1896.

Subsequent venues: 1900—Paris; 1904—St. Louis; 1908—London; 1912—Stockholm; 1920—Antwerp; 1924—Paris; 1928—Amsterdam; 1932—Los Angeles; 1936—Berlin; 1948—London; 1952—Helsinki; 1956—Melbourne; 1960—Rome; 1964—Tokyo; 1968—Mexico City; 1972—Munich. War has caused the cancellation of the Games on three occasions: in 1916 (scheduled for Berlin), 1940 (awarded first to Toyko, then to Helsinki) and 1944 (London). The 1976 Games will be held in Montreal.

The Games have grown steadily since their modest beginnings in Athens, where 59 athletes from 10 countries contested the track and field events. No fewer than 104 countries sent athletic teams to the 1972 Games.

The athletics events of the Olympics are officially designated "World Championships" by the IAAF, the body which is delegated by the IOC to supervise and control all the technical arrangements. Events for women were introduced in 1928, but Britain did not send a ladies' team on that occasion.

## British Medallists

The following athletes, listed in alphabetical order, have won Olympic medals while representing Great Britain & Northern Ireland or, prior to 1924, Great Britain & Ireland. G signifies gold (1st), S silver (2nd) and B bronze (3rd).

Abrahams, H. M., 1924, 100 m. (G) and 4 x 100 m. (S).

Ahearne, T. J., 1908, triple jump (G).

Ainsworth-Davis, J. C., 1920, 4 x 400 m. (G).
Applegarth, W. R., 1912, 4 x 100 m. (G) and 200 m. (B).
Archer, J., 1948, 4 x 100 m. (S).
Bailey, E. McD., 1952, 100 m. (B).
Baker, P. J. (Noel-), 1920, 1500 m. (S).
Bennett, C., 1900, 1500 m. (G), 5000 m. team (G) and 4000 m. steeplechase (S).
Blewitt, C. E., 1920, 3000 m. team (S).
Brasher, C. W., 1956, 3000 m. steeplechase (G).
Brightwell, R. I., 1964, 4 x 400 m. (S).
Brown, A. G. K., 1936, 4 x 400 m. (G) and 400 m. (S).
Burghley, Lord, 1928, 400 m. hurdles (G); 1932, 4 x 400 m. (S).
Butler, G. M., 1920, 4 x 400 m. (G) and 400 m. (S); 1924, 400 m. (B) and 4 x 400 m. (B).
Coales, W., 1908, 3 mi. team (G).
Cooper, J. H., 1964, 400 m. hurdles (S); 4 x 400 m. (S).
Cornes, J. F., 1932, 1500 m. (S).
Cottrill, W., 1912, 3000 m. team (B).
d'Arcy, V. H. A., 1912, 4 x 100 m. (G).
Davies, L., 1964, long jump (G).
Deakin, J. E., 1908, 3 mi. team (G).
Disley, J. I., 1952, 3000 m. steeplechase (B).
Edward, H. F. V., 1920, 100 m. (B) and 200 m. (B).
Evenson, T., 1932, 3000 m. steeplechase (S).
Ferris, S., 1932, Marathon (S).
Finlay, D. O., 1932, 110 hurdles (B); 1936, 110 hurdles (S).
Gill, C. W., 1928, 4 x 100 m. (B).
Glover, E., 1912, Cross-country team (B).
Goodwin, G. R., 1924, 10,000 m. walk (S).
Goulding, G. T. S., 1896, 110 m. hurdles (S).
Graham, T. J. M., 1964, 4 x 400 m. (S).
Green, T. W., 1932, 50 km. walk (G).
Gregory, J. A., 1948, 4 x 100 m. (S).
Griffiths, C. R., 1920, 4 x 400 m. (G).
Gunn, C. E. J., 1920, 10,000 m. walk (B).
Hallows, N. F., 1908, 1500 m. (B).
Halswelle, W., 1908, 400 m. (G).
Hampson, T., 1932, 800 m. (G) and 4 x 400 m. (S).

Harper, E., 1936, Marathon (S).
Heatley, B. B., 1964, Marathon (S).
Hegarty, A., 1920, Cross-country team (S).
Hemery, D. P., 1968, 400 m. hurdles (G); 1972, 400 m. hurdles (B) and 4 x 400 m. (S).
Henley, E. J., 1912, 4 x 400 m. (B).
Herriott, M., 1964, 3000 m. steeplechase (S).
Hibbins, F. N., 1912, Cross-country team (B).
Higgins, F. P., 1956, 4 x 400 m. (B).
Hill, A. G., 1920, 800 m. (G), 1500 m. (G) and 3000 m. team (S).
Hodge, P., 1920, 3000 m. steeplechase (G).
Horgan, D., 1908, Shot (S).
Humphreys, T., 1912, Cross-country team (B).
Hutson, G. W., 1912, 5000 m. (B) and 3000 m. team (B).
Ibbotson, G. D., 1956, 5000 m. (B).
Jackson, A. N. Strode-, 1912, 1500 m. (G).
Jacobs, D. H., 1912, 4 x 100 m. (G).
Jenkins, D. A., 1972, 4 x 400 m. (S).
Johnson, D. J. N., 1956, 800 m. (S) and 4 x 400 m. (B).
Johnson, T. Lloyd, 1948, 50 km. walk (B).
Johnston, H. A., 1924, 3000 m. team (S).
Jones, D. H., 1960, 4 x 100 m. (B).
Jones, K. J., 1948, 4 x 100 m. (S).
Larner, G. E., 1908, 3500 m. walk (G) and 10 mi. walk (G).
Leahy, C., 1900, long jump (B); 1908, high jump (S).
Leahy, P. J., 1900, high jump (S).
Liddell, E. H., 1924, 400 m. (G) and 200 m. (B).
Lindsay, R. A., 1920, 4 x 400 m. (G).
London, J. E., 1928, 100 m. (S) and 4 x 100 m. (B).
Lowe, D. G. A., 1924, 800 m. (G); 1928, 800 m. (G).
McCorquodale, A., 1948, 4 x 100 m. (S).
MacDonald, B., 1924, 3000 m. team (S).
Macintosh, H. M., 1912, 4 x 100 m. (G).
Matthews, K. J., 1964, 20 km. walk (G).
Metcalfe, A. P., 1964, 4 x 400 m. (S).
Nichol, W. P., 1924, 4 x 100 m. (S).
Nichols, A. H., 1920, Cross-country team (S).

136

Nicol, G., 1912, 4 x 400 m. (B).
Nihill, V. P., 1964, 50 km. walk (S).
Nokes, M. C., 1924, hammer (B).
Owen, E., 1908, 5 mi. (S).
Pascoe, A. P., 1972, 4 x 400 m. (S).
Pirie, D. A. G., 1956, 5000 m. (S).
Porter, C. H. A., 1912, 3000 m. team (B).
Radford, P. F., 1960, 100 m. (B) and 4 x 100 m. (B).
Rampling, G. L., 1932, 4 x 400 m. (S); 1936, 4 x 400 m. (G).
Rangeley, W., 1924, 4 x 100 m. (S); 1928, 200 m. (S) and 4 x 100 m. (B).
Renwick, G. R., 1924, 4 x 400 m. (B).
Reynolds, M. E., 1972, 4 x 400 m. (S).
Richards, T., 1948, Marathon (S).
Rimmer, J. T., 1900, 4000 m. steeplechase (G) and 5000 m. team (G).
Ripley, R. N., 1924, 4 x 400 m. (B).
Roberts, W., 1936, 4 x 400 m. (G).
Robertson, A. J., 1908, 3 mi. team (G) and 3200 m. steeplechase (S).
Robinson, S. J., 1900, 5000 m. team (G), 2500 m. steeplechase (S) and 4000 m. steeplechase (B).
Royle, L. C., 1924, 4 x 100 m. (S).
Russell, A., 1908, 3200 m. steeplechase (G).
Salisbury, J. E., 1956, 4 x 400 m. (B).
Seagrove, W. R., 1920, 3000 m. team (S).
Seedhouse, C. N., 1912, 4 x 400 m. (B).
Segal, D. H., 1960, 4 x 100 m. (B).
Sherwood, J., 1968, 400 m. hurdles (B).
Smouha, E. R., 1928, 4 x 100 m. (B).
Soutter, J. T., 1912, 4 x 400 m. (B).
Spencer, E. A., 1908, 10 mi. walk (B).
Stallard, H. B., 1924, 1500 m. (B).
Stewart, I., 1972, 5000 m. (B).
Stoneley, C. H., 1932, 4 x 400 m. (S).
Thompson, D. J., 1960, 50 km. walk (G).
Toms, E. J., 1924, 4 x 400 m. (B).
Tremeer, L. F., 1908, 400 m. hurdles (B).
Tysoe, A. E., 1900, 800 m. (G) and 5000 m. team (G).
Vickers, S. F., 1960, 20 km. walk (B).
Voigt, E. R., 1908, 5 mi. (G).
Webb, E. J., 1908, 3500 m. walk (S) and 10 mi. walk (S); 1912, 10,000 m. walk (S).
Webber, G. J., 1924, 3000 m. team (S).

Wheeler, M. K. V., 1956, 4 x 400 m. (B).
Whitehead, J. N., 1960, 4 x 100 m. (B).
Whitlock, H. H., 1936, 50 km. walk (G).
Wilson, H. A., 1908, 1500 m. (S).
Wilson, J., 1920, Cross-country team (S) and 10,000m. (B).
Wolff, F., 1936, 4 x 400 m. (G).

*Women*

Arden, D., 1964, 4 x 100 m. (B).
Armitage, H. J., 1952, 4 x 100 m. (B); 1956, 4 x 100 m. (S).
Board, L. B., 1968, 400 m. (S).
Brown, A., 1936, 4 x 100 m. (S).
Burke, B., 1936, 4 x 100 m. (S).
Cawley, S., 1952, long jump (B).
Cheeseman, S., 1952, 4 x 100 m. (B).
Desforges, J. C., 1952, 4 x 100 m. (B).
Gardner, M. A. J., 1948, 80 m. hurdles (S).
Halstead, N., 1932, 4 x 100 m. (B).
Hiscock, E. M., 1932, 4 x 100 m. (B); 1936, 4 x 100 m. (S).
Hopkins, T. E., 1956, high jump (S).
Hyman, D., 1960, 100 m. (S) and 200 m. (B), 1964, 4 x 100 m. (B).
Lerwill, S., 1952, high jump (S).
Manley, D. G., 1948, 100 m. (S).
Olney, V., 1936, 4 x 100 m. (S).
Packer, A. E., 1964, 800 m. (G); 400 m. (S).
Pashley, A., 1956, 4 x 100 m. (S).
Paul, J. F., 1952, 4 x 100 m. (B); 1956, 4 x 100 m. (S).
Peters, M. E., 1972, Pentathlon (G).
Porter, G. A., 1932, 4 x 100 m. (B).
Quinton, C. L., 1960, 80 m. hurdles (S).
Rand, M. D., 1964, long jump (G); Pentathlon (S); 4 x 100 m. (B).
Scrivens, J. E., 1956, 4 x 100 m. (S).
Sherwood, S. H., 1968, long jump (S).
Shirley, D. A., 1960, high jump (S).
Simpson, J. M., 1964, 4 x 100 m. (B).
Tyler, D. J. B., 1936, high jump (S); 1948, high jump (S).
Webb, V., 1932, 4 x 100 m. (B).
Williamson, A. D., 1948, 200 m. (S).

## Champions

| 60 Metres | sec. |
| --- | --- |
| 1900 A. C. Kraenzlein (USA) | 7.0 |
| 1904 A. Hahn (USA) | 7.0 |

137

| 100 Metres | | sec. |
|---|---|---|
| 1896 | T. E. Burke (USA) | 12.0 |
| 1900 | F. W. Jarvis (USA) | 11.0 |
| 1904 | A. Hahn (USA) | 11.0 |
| 1908 | R. E. Walker (S. Africa) | 10.8 |
| 1912 | R. C. Craig (USA) | 10.8 |
| 1920 | C. W. Paddock (USA) | 10.8 |
| 1924 | H. M. Abrahams (GB) | 10.6 |
| 1928 | P. Williams (Canada) | 10.8 |
| 1932 | T. E. Tolan (USA) | 10.3 |
| 1936 | J. C. Owens (USA) | 10.3 |
| 1948 | W. H. Dillard (USA) | 10.3 |
| 1952 | L. J. Remigino (USA) | 10.4 |
| 1956 | B. J. Morrow (USA) | 10.5 |
| 1960 | A. Hary (Germany) | 10.2 |
| 1964 | R. L. Hayes (USA) | 10.0 |
| 1968 | J. R. Hines (USA) | 9.9 |
| 1972 | V. Borzov (USSR) | 10.1 |

| 200 Metres | | sec. |
|---|---|---|
| 1900 | J. W. B. Tewksbury (USA) | 22.2 |
| 1904* | A. Hahn (USA) | 21.6 |
| 1908 | R. Kerr (Canada) | 22.6 |
| 1912 | R. C. Craig (USA) | 21.7 |
| 1920 | A. Woodring (USA) | 22.0 |
| 1924 | J. V. Scholz (USA) | 21.6 |
| 1928 | P. Williams (Canada) | 21.8 |
| 1932 | T. E. Tolan (USA) | 21.2 |
| 1936 | J. C. Owens (USA) | 20.7 |
| 1948 | M. E. Patton (USA) | 21.1 |
| 1952 | A. W. Stanfield (USA) | 20.7 |
| 1956 | B. J. Morrow (USA) | 20.6 |
| 1960 | L. Berruti (Italy) | 20.5 |
| 1964 | H. Carr (USA) | 20.3 |
| 1968 | T. C. Smith (USA) | 19.8 |
| 1972 | V. Borzov (USSR) | 20.0 |

* straight course

| 400 Metres | | sec. |
|---|---|---|
| 1896 | T. E. Burke (USA) | 54.2 |
| 1900 | M. W. Long (USA) | 49.4 |
| 1904 | H. L. Hillman (USA) | 49.2 |
| 1908* | W. Halswelle (GB) | 50.0 |
| 1912 | C. D. Reidpath (USA) | 48.2 |
| 1920 | B. G. D. Rudd (S. Africa) | 49.6 |
| 1924 | E. H. Liddell (GB) | 47.6 |
| 1928 | R. J. Barbuti (USA) | 47.8 |
| 1932 | W. A. Carr (USA) | 46.2 |
| 1936 | A. F. Williams (USA) | 46.5 |
| 1948 | A. S. Wint (Jamaica) | 46.2 |
| 1952 | V. G. Rhoden (Jamaica) | 45.9 |
| 1956 | C. L. Jenkins (USA) | 46.7 |
| 1960 | O. C. Davis (USA) | 44.9 |
| 1964 | M. D. Larrabee (USA) | 45.1 |
| 1968 | L. Evans (USA) | 43.8 |
| 1972 | V. Matthews (USA) | 44.7 |

* walk-over

| 800 Metres | | min. | sec. |
|---|---|---|---|
| 1896 | E. H. Flack (Australia) | 2 | 11.0 |
| 1900 | A. E. Tysoe (GB) | 2 | 01.2 |
| 1904 | J. D. Lightbody (USA) | 1 | 56.0 |
| 1908 | M. W. Sheppard (USA) | 1 | 52.8 |
| 1912 | J. E. Meredith (USA) | 1 | 51.9 |
| 1920 | A. G. Hill (GB) | 1 | 53.4 |
| 1924 | D. G. A. Lowe (GB) | 1 | 52.4 |
| 1928 | D. G. A. Lowe (GB) | 1 | 51.8 |
| 1932 | T. Hampson (GB) | 1 | 49.7 |
| 1936 | J. Y. Woodruff (USA) | 1 | 52.9 |
| 1948 | M. G. Whitfield (USA) | 1 | 49.2 |
| 1952 | M. G. Whitfield (USA) | 1 | 49.2 |
| 1956 | T. W. Courtney (USA) | 1 | 47.7 |
| 1960 | P. G. Snell (New Zealand) | 1 | 46.3 |
| 1964 | P. G. Snell (New Zealand) | 1 | 45.1 |
| 1968 | R. Doubell (Australia) | 1 | 44.3 |
| 1972 | D. Wottle (USA) | 1 | 45.9 |

| 1500 Metres | | min. | sec. |
|---|---|---|---|
| 1896 | E. H. Flack (Australia) | 4 | 33.2 |
| 1900 | C. Bennett (GB) | 4 | 06.2 |
| 1904 | J. D. Lightbody (USA) | 4 | 05.4 |
| 1908 | M. W. Sheppard (USA) | 4 | 03.4 |
| 1912 | A. N. S. Jackson (GB) | 3 | 56.8 |
| 1920 | A. G. Hill (GB) | 4 | 01.8 |
| 1924 | P. J. Nurmi (Finland) | 3 | 53.6 |
| 1928 | H. E. Larva (Finland) | 3 | 53.2 |
| 1932 | L. Beccali (Italy) | 3 | 51.2 |
| 1936 | J. E. Lovelock (New Zealand) | 3 | 47.8 |
| 1948 | H. Eriksson (Sweden) | 3 | 49.8 |
| 1952 | J. Barthel (Luxembourg) | 3 | 45.1 |
| 1956 | R. M. Delany (Ireland) | 3 | 41.2 |
| 1960 | H. J. Elliott (Australia) | 3 | 35.6 |
| 1964 | P. G. Snell (New Zealand) | 3 | 38.1 |
| 1968 | K. Keino (Kenya) | 3 | 34.9 |
| 1972 | P. Vasala (Finland) | 3 | 36.3 |

*3000 Metres Team*
1912 USA (T. S. Berna, N. S. Taber, G. V. Bonhag) 8:44.6
1920 USA (H. H. Brown, A. A. Schardt, I. C. Dresser) 8:45.4
1924 Finland (P. J. Nurmi, V. J. Ritola, E. Katz) 8:32.0

*3 Miles Team*
1908 GB (J. E. Deakin, A. J. Robertson, W. Coales) 14:39.6

*5000 Metres Team*
1900 GB (C. Bennett, J. T. Rimmer, A. E. Tysoe,

138

S. J. Robinson, S.
Rowley)                          15.20.0

*5000 Metres*                    min. sec.
1912  H. Kolehmainen (Fin-
      land)                       14 36.6
1920  J. Guillemot (France)       14 55.6
1924  P. J. Nurmi (Finland)       14 31.2
1928  V. J. Ritola (Finland)      14 38.0
1932  L. A. Lehtinen (Fin-
      land)                       14 30.0
1936  G. Hockert (Finland)        14 22.2
1948  G. E. G. Reiff
      (Belgium)                   14 17.6
1952  E. Zatopek (Czecho-
      slovakia)                   14 06.6
1956  V. Kuts (USSR)              13 39.6
1960  M. G. Halberg (New
      Zealand)                    13 43.4
1964  R. K. Schul (USA)           13 48.8

1968  M. Gammoudi
      (Tunisia)                   14 05.0
1972  L. Viren (Finland)          13 26.4

*4 Miles Team*
1904  New York A.C., USA (A. L.
      Newton, G. Under-
      wood, P. H. Pilgrim,
      H. Valentine, D. C.
      Munson)                     21:17.8

*5 Miles*                         min. sec.
1908  E. R. Voigt (GB)            25 11.2

*10,000 Metres*                   min. sec.
1912  H. Kolehmainen (Fin-
      land)                       31 20.8
1920  P. J. Nurmi (Finland)       31 45.8
1924  V. J. Ritola (Finland)      30 23.2
1928  P. J. Nurmi (Finland)       30 18.8
1932  J. Kusocinski (Poland)      30 11.4
1936  I. Salminen (Finland)       30 15.4
1948  E. Zatopek (Czecho-
      slovakia)                   29 59.6
1952  E. Zatopek (Czecho-
      slovakia)                   29 17.0
1956  V. Kuts (USSR)              28 45.6
1960  P. Bolotnikov (USSR)        28 32.2
1964  W. M. Mills (USA)           28 24.4
1968  N. Temu (Kenya)             29 27.4
1972  L. Viren (Finland)          27 38.4

*Marathon*                        hr. min. sec.
1896* S. Louis (Greece)         2 58 50.0
1900* M. Theato (France)        2 59 45.0
1904* T. J. Hicks (USA)         3 28 53.0
1908(1)J. J. Hayes (USA)        2 55 18.4
1912* K. K. McArthur (S.
      Africa)                   2 36 54.8

1920  H. Kolehmainen (Fin-
      land)                     2 32 35.8
1924  A. O. Stenroos (Fin-
      land)                     2 41 22.6
1928  El Ouafi (France)         2 32 57.0
1932  J. C. Zabala (Argen-
      tine)                     2 31 36.0
1936  K. Son (Japan)            2 29 19.2
1948  D. Cabrera (Argen-
      tine)                     2 34 51.6
1952  E. Zatopek (Czecho-
      slovakia)                 2 23 03.2
1956  A. Mimoun (France)        2 25 00.0
1960  Abebe Bikila
      (Ethiopia)                2 15 16.2
1964  Abebe Bikila
      (Ethiopia)                2 12 11.2
1968  M. Wolde (Ethiopia)       2 20 26.4
1972  F. Shorter (USA)          2 12 19.8
* under standard distance of 26 mi.
  385 yd.

(1) D. Pietri (Italy), 1st in 2:54:46.4,
    disqualified.

*2500 Metres Steeplechase*       min .sec.
1900  G. W. Orton (USA)           7 34.4
1904  J. D. Lightbody (USA)       7 39.6

*3000 Metres Steeplechase*       min. sec.
1920  P. Hodge (GB)              10 00.4
1924  V. J. Ritola (Finland)      9 33.6
1928  T. A. Loukola (Finland)     9 21.8
1932* V. Iso-Hollo (Finland)     10 33.4
1936  V. Iso-Hollo (Finland)      9 03.8
1948  T. Sjostrand (Sweden)       9 04.6
1952  H. Ashenfelter (USA)        8 45.4
1956  C. W. Brasher (GB)          8 41.2
1960  Z. Krzyszkowiak
      (Poland)                    8 34.2
1964  G. Roelants (Belgium)       8 30.8
1968  A. Biwott (Kenya)           8 51.0
1972  K. Keino (Kenya)            8 23.6

* 460 metres over distance

*3200 Metres Steeplechase*       min. sec.
1908  A. Russell (GB)            10 47.8

*4000 Metres Steeplechase*       min. sec.
1900  J. T. Rimmer (GB)          12 58.4

*8000 Metres Cross-Country*
1912  Sweden (H. Andersson, J. Eke,
      J. Ternstrom). Winner: H.
      Kolehmainen (Finland).
1920  Finland (P. J. Nurmi, winner;
      H. Liimatainen, T. Kosken-
      niemi)

*10,000 Metres Cross-Country*
1924  Finland (P. J. Nurmi, winner;
      V. J. Ritola, H. Liimatainen).

| *100 Metres Hurdles* (3ft. 3in.) | sec. |
|---|---|
| 1896  T. P. Curtis (USA) | 17.6 |

| *110 Metres Hurdles* (3ft. 6in.) | sec. |
|---|---|
| 1900  A. C. Kraenzlein (USA) | 15.4 |
| 1904  F. W. Schule (USA) | 16.0 |
| 1908  F. C. Smithson (USA) | 15.0 |
| 1912  F. W. Kelly (USA) | 15.1 |
| 1920  E. J. Thomson (Canada) | 14.8 |
| 1924  D. C. Kinsey (USA) | 15.0 |
| 1928  S. J. M. Atkinson (S. Africa) | 14.8 |
| 1932  G. J. Saling (USA) | 14.6 |
| 1936  F. G. Towns (USA) | 14.2 |
| 1948  W. F. Porter (USA) | 13.9 |
| 1952  W. H. Dillard (USA) | 13.7 |
| 1956  L. Q. Calhoun (USA) | 13.5 |
| 1960  L. Q. Calhoun (USA) | 13.8 |
| 1964  H. W. Jones (USA) | 13.6 |
| 1968  W. Davenport (USA) | 13.3 |
| 1972  R. Milburn (USA) | 13.2 |

| *200 Metres Hurdles* (2ft. 6in.) | sec. |
|---|---|
| 1900  A. C. Kraenzlein (USA) | 25.4 |
| 1904  H. L. Hillman (USA) | 25.4 |

| *400 Metres Hurdles* (2ft. 6in.) | sec. |
|---|---|
| 1904  H. L. Hillman (USA) | 53.0 |

| *400 Metres Hurdles* (3ft. 0in.) | sec. |
|---|---|
| 1900  J. W. B. Tewksbury (USA) | 57.6 |
| 1908  C. J. Bacon (USA) | 55.0 |
| 1920  F. F. Loomis (USA) | 54.0 |
| 1924  F. M. Taylor (USA) | 52.6 |
| 1928  Lord Burghley (GB) | 53.4 |
| 1932  R. M. N. Tisdall (Ireland) | 51.7 |
| 1936  G. F. Hardin (USA) | 52.4 |
| 1948  L. V. Cochran (USA) | 51.1 |
| 1952  C. H. Moore (USA) | 50.8 |
| 1956  G. A. Davis (USA) | 50.1 |
| 1960  G. A. Davis (USA) | 49.3 |
| 1964  W. J. Cawley (USA) | 49.6 |
| 1968  D. P. Hemery (GB) | 48.1 |
| 1972  J. Akii-Bua (Uganda) | 47.8 |

| *4 x 100 Metres Relay* | sec. |
|---|---|
| 1912  GB (D. H. Jacobs, H. M. Macintosh, V. H. A. d'Arcy, W. R. Applegarth) | 42.4 |
| 1920  USA (C. W. Paddock, J. V. Scholz, L. C. Murchison, M. M. Kirksey) | 42.2 |

| 1924  USA (F. Hussey, L. A. Clarke, L. C. Murchison, J. A. Leconey) | 41.0 |
|---|---|
| 1928  USA (F. C. Wykoff, J. F. Quinn, C. E. Borah, H. A. Russell) | 41.0 |
| 1932  USA (R. A. Kiesel, E. Toppino, H. M. Dyer, F. C. Wykoff) | 40.0 |
| 1936  USA (J. C. Owens, R. H. Metcalfe, F. Draper, F. C. Wykoff) | 39.8 |
| 1948  USA (H. N. Ewell, L. C. Wright, W. H. Dillard, M. E. Patton) | 40.6 |
| 1952  USA (F. D. Smith, W. H. Dillard, L. J. Remigino, A. W. Stanfield) | 40.1 |
| 1956  USA (I. J. Murchison, L. King, W. T. Baker, B. J. Morrow) | 39.5 |
| 1960*  Germany (B. Cullmann, A. Hary, W. Mahlendorf, K. M. Lauer) | 39.5 |
| 1964  USA (O. P. Drayton, G. H. Ashworth, R. V. Stebbins, R. L. Hayes) | 39.0 |
| 1968  USA (C. Greene, M. Pender, R. R. Smith, J. R. Hines) | 38.2 |
| 1972  USA (L. Black, R. Taylor, G. Tinker, E. Hart) | 38.2 |

* USA (F. J. Budd, O. R. Norton, S. E. Johnson, D. W. Sime) 1st in 39.4, disqualified.

| *1600 Metres Medley Relay* | min. sec. |
|---|---|
| 1908  USA (W. F. Hamilton, N. J. Cartmell, J. B. Taylor, M. W. Sheppard) | 3 29.4 |

*4 x 400 Metres Relay*

| | min. sec. |
|---|---|
| 1912  USA (M. W. Sheppard, E. F. J. Lindberg, J. E. Meredith, C. D. Reidpath) | 3 16.6 |
| 1920  GB (C. R. Griffiths, R. A. Lindsay, J. C. Ainsworth-Davis, G. M. Butler) | 3 22.2 |
| 1924  USA (C. S. Cochrane, W. E. Stevenson, J. O. McDonald, A. B. Helffrich) | 3 16.0 |

| | | | |
|---|---|---|---|
| 1928 | USA (G. Baird, E. M. Spencer, E. P. Alderman, R. J. Barbuti) | 3 | 14.2 |
| 1932 | USA (I. Fuqua, E. A. Ablowich, K. D. Warner, W. A. Carr) | 3 | 08.2 |
| 1936 | GB (F. F. Wolff, G. L. Rampling, W. Roberts, A. G. K. Brown) | 3 | 09.0 |
| 1948 | USA (A. H. Harnden, C. F. Bourland, L. V. Cochran, M. G. Whitfield) | 3 | 10.4 |
| 1952 | Jamaica (A. S. Wint, L. A. Laing, H. H. McKenley, V. G. Rhoden) | 3 | 03.9 |
| 1956 | USA (C. L. Jenkins, L. W. Jones, J. W. Mashburn, T. W. Courtney) | 3 | 04.8 |
| 1960 | USA (J. L. Yerman, E. V. Young, G. A. Davis, O. C. Davis) | 3 | 02.2 |
| 1964 | USA (O. C. Cassell, M. D. Larrabee, U. C. Williams, H. Carr) | 3 | 00.7 |
| 1968 | USA (V. Matthews, R. Freeman, L. James, L. Evans) | 2 | 56.1 |
| 1972 | Kenya (C. Asati, H. Nyamau, R. Ouko, J. Sang) | 2 | 59.8 |

| *High Jump* | | ft. | in. |
|---|---|---|---|
| 1896 | E. H. Clark (USA) | 5 | 11¼ |
| 1900 | I. K. Baxter (USA) | 6 | 2¾ |
| 1904 | S. S. Jones (USA) | 5 | 11 |
| 1908 | H. F. Porter (USA) | 6 | 3 |
| 1912 | A. W. Richards (USA) | 6 | 4 |
| 1920 | R. W. Landon (USA) | 6 | 4¼ |
| 1924 | H. M. Osborn (USA) | 6 | 6 |
| 1928 | R. W. King (USA) | 6 | 4¼ |
| 1932 | D. McNaughton (Canada) | 6 | 5½ |
| 1936 | C. C. Johnson (USA) | 6 | 8 |
| 1948 | J. A. Winter (Australia) | 6 | 6 |
| 1952 | W. F. Davis (USA) | 6 | 8¼ |
| 1956 | C. E. Dumas (USA) | 6 | 11½ |
| 1960 | R. Shavlakadze (USSR) | 7 | 1 |
| 1964 | V. Brumel (USSR) | 7 | 1¾ |
| 1968 | R. Fosbury (USA) | 7 | 4¼ |
| 1972 | J. Tarmak (USSR) | 7 | 3¾ |

| *Standing High Jump* | | ft. | in. |
|---|---|---|---|
| 1900 | R. C. Ewry (USA) | 5 | 5 |
| 1904 | R. C. Ewry (USA) | 4 | 11 |
| 1908 | R. C. Ewry (USA) | 5 | 2 |
| 1912 | P. Adams (USA) | 5 | 4¼ |

| *Pole Vault* | | ft. | in. |
|---|---|---|---|
| 1896 | W. W. Hoyt (USA) | 10 | 10 |
| 1900 | I. K. Baxter (USA) | 10 | 10 |
| 1904 | C. E. Dvorak (USA) | 11 | 6 |
| 1908 | E. T. Cooke (USA) and A. C. Gilbert (USA) | 12 | 2 |
| 1912 | H. S. Babcock (USA) | 12 | 11½ |
| 1920 | F. K. Foss (USA) | 13 | 5 |
| 1924 | L. S. Barnes (USA) | 12 | 11½ |
| 1928 | S. W. Carr (USA) | 13 | 9¼ |
| 1932 | W. W. Miller (USA) | 14 | 1¾ |
| 1936 | E. E. Meadows (USA) | 14 | 3¼ |
| 1948 | O. G. Smith (USA) | 14 | 1¼ |
| 1952 | R. E. Richards (USA) | 14 | 11 |
| 1956 | R. E. Richards (USA) | 14 | 11½ |
| 1960 | D. G. Bragg (USA) | 15 | 5 |
| 1964 | F. M. Hansen (USA) | 16 | 8¾ |
| 1968 | R. Seagren (USA) | 17 | 8½ |
| 1972 | W. Nordwig (E. Germany) | 18 | 0½ |

| *Long Jump* | | ft. | in. |
|---|---|---|---|
| 1896 | E. H. Clark (USA) | 20 | 10 |
| 1900 | A. C. Kraenzlein (USA) | 23 | 7 |
| 1904 | M. Prinstein (USA) | 24 | 1 |
| 1908 | F. C. Irons (USA) | 24 | 6½ |
| 1912 | A. L. Gutterson (USA) | 24 | 11¼ |
| 1920 | W. Pettersson (Sweden)* | 23 | 5½ |
| 1924 | W. De H. Hubbard (USA) | 24 | 5¼ |
| 1928 | E. B. Hamm (USA) | 25 | 4½ |
| 1932 | E. L. Gordon (USA) | 25 | 0¾ |
| 1936 | J. C. Owens (USA) | 26 | 5½ |
| 1948 | W. S. Steele (USA) | 25 | 8 |
| 1952 | J. C. Biffle (USA) | 24 | 10 |
| 1956 | G. C. Bell (USA) | 25 | 8¼ |
| 1960 | R. H. Boston (USA) | 26 | 7¾ |
| 1964 | L. Davies (GB) | 26 | 5¾ |
| 1968 | R. Beamon (USA) | 29 | 2½ |
| 1972 | R. Williams (USA) | 27 | 0½ |

* later known as Bjorneman

| *Standing Long Jump* | | ft. | in. |
|---|---|---|---|
| 1900 | R. C. Ewry (USA) | 10 | 6¼ |
| 1904 | R. C. Ewry (USA) | 11 | 4½ |
| 1908 | R. C. Ewry (USA) | 10 | 11¼ |
| 1912 | C. Tsiclitiras (Greece) | 11 | 0¾ |

| *Triple Jump* | | ft. | in. |
|---|---|---|---|
| 1896* | J. V. Connolly (USA) | 44 | 11¾ |
| 1900 | M. Prinstein (USA) | 47 | 5¾ |
| 1904 | M. Prinstein (USA) | 47 | 1 |
| 1908 | T. J. Ahearne (GB) | 48 | 11¼ |
| 1912 | G. Lindblom (Sweden) | 48 | 5¼ |
| 1920 | V. Tuulos (Finland) | 47 | 7 |
| 1924 | A. W. Winter (Australia) | 50 | 11¼ |
| 1928 | M. Oda (Japan) | 49 | 11 |
| 1932 | C. Nambu (Japan) | 51 | 7 |
| 1936 | N. Tajima (Japan) | 52 | 6 |
| 1948 | A. P. Ahman (Sweden) | 50 | 6¼ |

| | | | |
|---|---|---|---|
| 1952 | A. F. da Silva (Brazil) | 53 | 2¾ |
| 1956 | A. F. da Silva (Brazil) | 53 | 7¾ |
| 1960 | J. Szmidt (Poland) | 55 | 2 |
| 1964 | J. Szmidt (Poland) | 55 | 3½ |
| 1968 | V. Saneyev (USSR) | 57 | 0¾ |
| 1972 | V. Saneyev (USSR) | 56 | 11¼ |

* two hops and one jump

| *Standing Triple Jump* | | ft. | in. |
|---|---|---|---|
| 1900 | R. C. Ewry (USA) | 34 | 8¼ |
| 1904 | R. C. Ewry (USA) | 34 | 7¼ |

| *Shot* | | ft. | in. |
|---|---|---|---|
| 1896* | R. S. Garrett (USA) | 36 | 9¾ |
| 1900* | R. Sheldon (USA) | 46 | 3¼ |
| 1904 | R. W. Rose (USA) | 48 | 7 |
| 1908 | R. W. Rose (USA) | 46 | 7½ |
| 1912 | P. J. McDonald (USA) | 50 | 4 |
| 1920 | V. Porhola (Finland) | 48 | 7¼ |
| 1924 | C. L. Houser (USA) | 49 | 2¼ |
| 1928 | J. Kuck (USA) | 52 | 0¾ |
| 1932 | L. J. Sexton (USA) | 52 | 6¼ |
| 1936 | H. Woellke (Germany) | 53 | 1¾ |
| 1948 | W. M. Thompson (USA) | 56 | 2 |
| 1952 | W. P. O'Brien (USA) | 57 | 1½ |
| 1956 | W. P. O'Brien (USA) | 60 | 11¼ |
| 1960 | W. H. Nieder (USA) | 64 | 6¾ |
| 1964 | D. C. Long (USA) | 66 | 8½ |
| 1968 | J. R. Matson (USA) | 67 | 4¾ |
| 1972 | W. Komar (Poland) | 69 | 6 |

* from 7 ft. square

| *Shot* (Both Hands) | | ft. | in. |
|---|---|---|---|
| 1912 | R. W. Rose (USA) | 90 | 10¼ |

| *Discus* | | ft. | in. |
|---|---|---|---|
| 1896 | R. S. Garrett (USA) | 95 | 7¾ |
| 1900 | R. Bauer (Hungary) | 118 | 3 |
| 1904 | M. J. Sheridan (USA) | 128 | 10 |
| 1908 | M. J. Sheridan (USA) | 134 | 2 |
| 1912 | A. R. Taipale (Finland) | 148 | 3 |
| 1920 | E. Niklander (Finland) | 146 | 7 |
| 1924 | C. L. Houser (USA) | 151 | 5 |
| 1928 | C. L. Houser (USA) | 155 | 3 |
| 1932 | J. F. Anderson (USA) | 162 | 4 |
| 1936 | K. K. Carpenter (USA) | 165 | 7 |
| 1948 | A. Consolini (Italy) | 173 | 2 |
| 1952 | S. G. Iness (USA) | 180 | 6 |
| 1956 | A. A. Oerter (USA) | 184 | 11 |
| 1960 | A. A. Oerter (USA) | 194 | 2 |
| 1964 | A. A. Oerter (USA) | 200 | 1 |
| 1968 | A. A. Oerter (USA) | 212 | 6 |
| 1972 | L. Danek (Czech) | 211 | 3 |

| *Discus* (Greek Style) | | ft. | in. |
|---|---|---|---|
| 1908 | M. J. Sheridan (USA) | 124 | 8 |

| *Discus* (Both Hands) | | ft | in. |
|---|---|---|---|
| 1912 | A. R. Taipale (Finland) | 271 | 10¼ |

| *Hammer* | | ft. | in. |
|---|---|---|---|
| 1900* | J. J. Flanagan (USA) | 163 | 1 |
| 1904 | J. J. Flanagan (USA) | 168 | 0 |
| 1908 | J. J. Flanagan (USA) | 170 | 4 |
| 1912 | M. J. McGrath (USA) | 179 | 7 |
| 1920 | P. J. Ryan (USA) | 173 | 6 |
| 1924 | F. D. Tootell (USA) | 174 | 10 |
| 1928 | P. O'Callaghan (Ireland) | 168 | 7 |
| 1932 | P. O'Callaghan (Ireland) | 176 | 11 |
| 1936 | K. Hein (Germany) | 185 | 4 |
| 1948 | I. Nemeth (Hungary) | 183 | 11 |
| 1952 | J. Csermak (Hungary) | 197 | 11 |
| 1956 | H. V. Connolly (USA) | 207 | 3 |
| 1960 | V. Rudenkov (USSR) | 220 | 2 |
| 1964 | R. Klim (USSR) | 228 | 10 |
| 1968 | G. Zsivotzky (Hungary) | 240 | 8 |
| 1972 | A. Bondarchuk (USSR) | 247 | 8 |

* from 9 ft. circle

| *Javelin* | | ft. | in. |
|---|---|---|---|
| 1908 | E. V. Lemming (Sweden) | 179 | 10 |
| 1912 | E. V. Lemming (Sweden) | 198 | 11 |
| 1920 | J. J. Myyra (Finland) | 215 | 10 |
| 1924 | J. J. Myyra (Finland) | 206 | 7 |
| 1928 | E. H. Lundkvist (Sweden) | 218 | 6 |
| 1932 | M. H. Jarvinen (Finland) | 238 | 6 |
| 1936 | G. Stock (Germany) | 235 | 8 |
| 1948 | K. T. Rautavaara (Finland) | 228 | 10 |
| 1952 | C. C. Young (USA) | 242 | 1 |
| 1956 | E. Danielsen (Norway) | 281 | 2 |
| 1960 | V. Tsibulenko (USSR) | 277 | 8 |
| 1964 | P. L. Nevala (Finland) | 271 | 2 |
| 1968 | J. Lusis (USSR) | 295 | 7 |
| 1972 | K. Wolfermann (W. Germany) | 296 | 10 |

| *Javelin* (Free Style) | | ft. | in. |
|---|---|---|---|
| 1908 | E. V. Lemming (Sweden) | 178 | 7½ |

| *Javelin* (Both Hands) | | ft. | in. |
|---|---|---|---|
| 1912 | J. Saaristo (Finland) | 358 | 11 |

| *56 lb. Weight* | | ft. | in. |
|---|---|---|---|
| 1904 | E. Desmartreau (Canada) | 34 | 4 |
| 1920 | P. McDonald (USA) | 37 | 0¼ |

*Pentathlon*
1912* F. Bie (Norway)
1920 E. Lehtonen (Finland)
1924 E. Lehtonen (Finland)
* J. H. Thorpe (USA), 1st, subsequently debarred.

| *Decathlon* (1962 Tables) | Pts. |
|---|---|
| 1912* H. Wieslander (Sweden) | 6161 |
| 1920 H. Lovland (Norway) | 5970 |
| 1924 H. M. Osborn (USA) | 6668 |
| 1928 P. I. Yrjola (Finland) | 6774 |
| 1932 J. A. B. Bausch (USA) | 6896 |
| 1936 G. E. Morris (USA) | 7421 |
| 1948 R. B. Mathias (USA) | 6825 |
| 1952 R. B. Mathias (USA) | 7731 |
| 1956 M. G. Campbell (USA) | 7708 |
| 1960 R. L. Johnson (USA) | 8001 |
| 1964 W. Holdorf (Germany) | 7887 |
| 1968 W. Toomey (USA) | 8193 |
| 1972 N. Avilov (USSR) | 8454 |

* J. II. Thorpe (USA), 1st with 6845, subsequently debarred.

| *3000 Metres Walk* | min. sec. |
|---|---|
| 1920 U. Frigerio (Italy) | 13 14.2 |

| *3500 Metres Walk* | min. sec. |
|---|---|
| 1908 G. E. Larner (GB) | 14 55.0 |

| *10,000 Metres Walk* | min. sec |
|---|---|
| 1912 G. H. Goulding (Canada) | 46 28.4 |
| 1920 U. Frigerio (Italy) | 48 06.2 |
| 1924 U. Frigerio (Italy) | 47 49.0 |
| 1948 J. F. Mikaelsson (Sweden) | 45 13.2 |
| 1952 J. F. Mikaelsson (Sweden) | 45 02.8 |

| *10 Mile Walk* | hr. min. sec. |
|---|---|
| 1908 G. E. Larner (GB) | 1 15 57.4 |

| *20,000 Metres Walk* | hr. min. sec. |
|---|---|
| 1956 L. Spirin (USSR) | 1 31 27.4 |
| 1960 V. Golubnichiy (USSR) | 1 34 07.2 |
| 1964 K. J. Matthews (GB) | 1 29 34.0 |
| 1968 V. Golubnichiy (USSR) | 1 33 58.4 |
| 1972 P. Frenkel (E. Germany) | 1 26 42.4 |

| *50,000 Metres Walk* | hr. min. sec. |
|---|---|
| 1932 T. W. Green (GB) | 4 50 10.0 |
| 1936 H. H. Whitlock (GB) | 4 30 41.4 |
| 1948 J. A. Ljunggren (Sweden) | 4 41 52.0 |
| 1952 G. Dordoni (Italy) | 4 28 07.8 |

| | | |
|---|---|---|
| 1956 N. R. Read (New Zealand) | 4 30 | 42.8 |
| 1960 D. J. Thompson (GB) | 4 25 | 30.0 |
| 1964 A. Pamich (Italy) | 4 11 | 12.4 |
| 1968 C. Hohne (E. Germany) | 4 20 | 13.6 |
| 1972 B. Kannenberg (W. Germany) | 3 56 | 11.6 |

# WOMEN CHAMPIONS

| *100 Metres* | sec. |
|---|---|
| 1928 E. Robinson (USA) | 12.2 |
| 1932 S. Walasiewicz (Poland) | 11.9 |
| 1936 H. H. Stephens (USA) | 11.5 |
| 1948 F. E. Blankers-Koen (Netherlands) | 11.9 |
| 1952 M. Jackson (Australia) | 11.5 |
| 1956 B. Cuthbert (Australia) | 11.5 |
| 1960 W. G. Rudolph (USA) | 11.0 |
| 1964 W. Tyus (USA) | 11.4 |
| 1968 W. Tyus (USA) | 11.0 |
| 1972 R. Stecher (E. Germany) | 11.1 |

| *200 Metres* | sec. |
|---|---|
| 1948 F. E. Blankers-Koen (Netherlands) | 24.4 |
| 1952 M. Jackson (Australia) | 23.7 |
| 1956 B. Cuthbert (Australia) | 23.4 |
| 1960 W. G. Rudolph (USA) | 24.0 |
| 1964 E. M. McGuire (USA) | 23.0 |
| 1968 I. Szewinska (Poland) | 22.5 |
| 1972 R. Stecher (E. Germany) | 22.4 |

| *400 Metres* | sec. |
|---|---|
| 1964 B. Cuthbert (Australia) | 52.0 |
| 1968 C. Besson (France) | 52.0 |
| 1972 M. Zehrt (E. Germany) | 51.1 |

| *800 Metres* | min. sec. |
|---|---|
| 1928 L. Radke (Germany) | 2 16.8 |
| 1960 L. Lysenko (USSR) | 2 04.3 |
| 1964 A. E. Packer (GB) | 2 01.1 |
| 1968 M. Manning (USA) | 2 00.9 |
| 1972 H. Falck (W. Germany) | 1 58.6 |

| *1500 Metres* | min. sec. |
|---|---|
| 1972 L. Bragina (USSR) | 4 01.4 |

| *80 Metres Hurdles* | sec. |
|---|---|
| 1932 M. Didrikson (USA) | 11.7 |
| 1936 T. Valla (Italy) | 11.7 |
| 1948 F. E. Blankers-Koen (Netherlands) | 11.2 |
| 1952 S. B. De La Hunty (Australia) | 10.9 |
| 1956 S. B. De La Hunty (Australia) | 10.7 |
| 1960 I. Press (USSR) | 10.8 |

| 1964 | K. Balzer (Germany) | 10.5 |
| 1968 | M. Caird (Australia) | 10.3 |

| 1972 | U. Meyfarth |   |   |
|   | (W. Germany) | 6 | 3½ |

### 100 Metres Hurdles
sec.
1972 A. Ehrhardt
(E. Germany)  12.6

### 4 x 100 Metres Relay
sec.
1928 Canada (F. Rosenfeld,
F. Bell, E. Smith, M.
Cook)  48.4
1932 USA (M. L. Carew, E.
Furtsch, A. J. Rogers,
W. von Bremen)  47.0
1936 USA (H. C. Bland, A. J.
Rogers, E. Robinson,
H. H. Stephens)  46.9
1948 Netherlands (X. Stad-de-
Jongh, J. M. Witziers,
G. J. M. Koudijs,
F. E. Blankers-Koen)  47.5
1952 USA (M. E. Faggs, B. P.
Jones, J. T. Moreau,
C. Hardy)  45.9
1956 Australia (S. B. De La
Hunty, N. W. Croker,
F. N. Mellor, B. Cuth-
bert)  44.5
1960 USA (M. Hudson, L.
Williams, B. P. Jones,
W. G. Rudolph)  44.5
1964 Poland (T. B. Ciepla, I. Kirs-
zenstein, H. Gorecka, E.
Klobukowska)  43.6
1968 USA (B. Ferrell. M.
Bailes, M. Netter, W.
Tyus)  42.8
1972 W. Germany (C. Krause,
I. Mickler, A. Richter,
H. Rosendahl)  42.8

### 4 x 400 Metres Relay
min. sec.
1972 E. Germany (D. Kas-
ling, R. Kuhne, H.
Seidler, M. Zehrt)  3 23.0

### High Jump
ft. in.
1928 E. Catherwood (Canada) 5 2½
1932 J. H. Shiley (USA)  5 5¼
1936 I. Csak (Hungary)  5 3
1948 A. Coachman (USA)  5 6
1952 E. C. Brand (S. Africa)  5 5¾
1956 M. I. McDaniel (USA)  5 9¼
1960 I. Balas (Rumania)  6 0¾
1964 I. Balas (Rumania)  6 2¾
1968 M. Rezkova
(Czechoslovakia)  5 11¾

### Long Jump
ft. in.
1948 V. O. Gyarmati
(Hungary)  18 8¼
1952 Y. W. Williams (New
Zealand)  20 5¾
1956 E. Krzesinska (Poland) 20 10
1960 V. Krepkina (USSR)  20 10¾
1964 M. D. Rand (GB)  22 2¼
1968 V. Viscopoleanu
(Rumania)  22 4½
1972 H. Rosendahl
(W. Germany)  22 3

### Shot
ft. in.
1948 M. O. M. Ostermeyer
(France)  45 1½
1952 G. I. Zybina (USSR)  50 1¾
1956 T. A. Tyshkevich
(USSR)  54 5¼
1960 T. Press (USSR)  56 10
1964 T. Press (USSR)  59 6¼
1968 M. Gummel
(E. Germany)  64 4
1972 N. Chizhova (USSR)  69 0

### Discus
ft. in.
1928 H. Konopacka
(Poland)  130 0
1932 L. Copeland (USA)  133 2
1936 G. Mauermeyer (Ger-
many)  156 3
1948 M. O. M. Ostermeyer
(France)  137 6
1952 N. Romashkova
(USSR)*  168 8
1956 O. Fikotova (Czecho-
slovakia)  176 1
1960 N. Ponomaryeva
(USSR)  180 9
1964 T. Press (USSR)  187 10
1968 L. Manoliu (Rumania) 191 2
1972 F. Melnik (USSR)  218 7
* later Ponomaryeva

### Javelin
ft. in.
1932 M. Didrikson (USA)  143 4
1936 T. Fleischer (Germany) 148 3
1948 H. Bauma (Austria)  149 6
1952 D. Zatopkova (Czechoslovakia)  165 7
1956 I. Jaunzeme (USSR)  176 8
1960 E. Ozolina (USSR)  183 8
1964 M. Penes (Rumania)  198 7
1968 A. Nemeth (Hungary)  198 0
1972 R. Ruchs
(E. Germany)  209 7

*Left:* Bob Seagren (USA), world pole vault record holder.

*Right:* Mary Rand, the first Briton to win an Olympic women's athletics title.

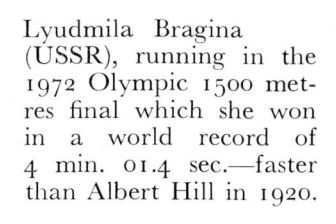

Lyudmila Bragina (USSR), running in the 1972 Olympic 1500 metres final which she won in a world record of 4 min. 01.4 sec.—faster than Albert Hill in 1920.

Lasse Viren (Finland), wins the Munich Olympic 5000 metres ahead of 904, Mohamed Gammoudi (Tunisia), and 309, Ian Stewart (UK). No. 61 is Emiel Puttemans (Belgium).

| | | pts. |
|---|---|---|
| 1964 | I. Press (USSR) | 5246 |
| 1972 | I. Becker (W. Germany) | 5098 |
| 1972† | M. E. Peters (GB & NI) | 4801 |

† Scored on 1970 Tables.

## National Scores

Although, to quote Fundamental Principle No. 7, " the Games are contests between individuals and not between countries," the Olympic Games are in fact riddled with nationalism. Athletes wear their nation's colours and emblem, flags are raised to medal winners and the appropriate national anthem is played in honour of each champion.

The Games provide an opportunity to compare the all-round worth of different countries although points tables are officially frowned upon by the Olympic authorities. The table below lists the six leading nations at each Games since 1908—the first reasonably representative contest. Only those events currently in the Olympic programme have been considered and scoring was 7 points for a winner, 5 for 2nd, 4 for 3rd, 3 for 4th, 2 for 5th and 1 for 6th.

### 1908
| | | |
|---|---|---|
| 1. | United States | 170½ |
| 2. | Great Britain | 52 |
| 3. | Canada | 36 |
| 4. | Sweden | 14 |
| 5. | South Africa | 12 |
| 6. | Finland and Norway | 9 |

### 1912
| | | |
|---|---|---|
| 1. | United States | 217 |
| 2. | Sweden | 60 |
| 3. | Finland | 42 |
| 4. | Great Britain | 30 |
| 5. | Canada | 18 |
| 6. | Germany | 16 |

### 1920
| | | |
|---|---|---|
| 1. | United States | 165 |
| 2. | Sweden | 76 |
| 3. | Finland | 75 |
| 4. | Great Britain | 63 |
| 5. | France | 28 |
| 6. | South Africa | 18 |

### 1924
| | | |
|---|---|---|
| 1. | United States | 198 |
| 2. | Finland | 99 |

| | | |
|---|---|---|
| 3. | Great Britain | 61 |
| 4. | Sweden | 32 |
| 5. | France | 17 |
| 6. | Switzerland | 13 |

### 1928
| | | |
|---|---|---|
| 1. | United States | 149 |
| 2. | Finland | 87 |
| 3. | Germany | 44 |
| 4. | Sweden | 41 |
| 5. | Great Britain | 40 |
| 6. | Canada | 31 |

### 1932
| | | |
|---|---|---|
| 1. | United States | 185 |
| 2. | Finland | 63 |
| 3. | Great Britain | 49 |
| 4. | Germany | 35 |
| 5. | Japan | 32 |
| 6. | Canada | 31 |

### 1936
| | | |
|---|---|---|
| 1. | United States | 167 |
| 2. | Finland | 71½ |
| 3. | Germany | 60¼ |
| 4. | Japan | 45½ |
| 5. | Great Britain | 37 |
| 6. | Canada | 22 |

### 1948
| | | |
|---|---|---|
| 1. | United States | 165 |
| 2. | Sweden | 74 |
| 3. | France | 28 |
| 4. | Finland | 25 |
| 5. | Great Britain | 23 |
| 6. | Australia | 22 |

### 1952
| | | |
|---|---|---|
| 1. | United States | 182 |
| 2. | Soviet Union | 52 |
| 3. | Great Britain | 36 |
| 4. | Jamaica | 33 |
| 5. | Czechoslovakia and Germany | 30 |

### 1956
| | | |
|---|---|---|
| 1. | United States | 187 |
| 2. | Soviet Union | 90 |
| 3. | Great Britain | 39 |
| 4. | Germany | 31 |
| 5. | Australia | 28 |
| 6. | Hungary | 21 |

### 1960
| | | |
|---|---|---|
| 1. | United States | 136 |
| 2. | Soviet Union | 93½ |
| 3. | Germany | 63 |
| 4. | Poland | 31 |
| 5. | Great Britain | 25 |
| 6. | New Zealand | 22 |

#### 1964
1. United States — 144
2. Soviet Union — 64
3. Great Britain — 52
4. Germany — 47½
5. Poland — 26
6. Hungary — 20

#### 1968
1. United States — 162
2. Soviet Union — 60
3. Kenya — 45
4. East Germany — 39
5. West Germany — 38
6. Hungary — 22
(Great Britain 8th—17)

#### 1972
1. United States — 133
2. Soviet Union — 84½
3. East Germany — 54
4. West Germany — 46
5. Kenya — 41
6. Finland — 31
7. Great Britain — 19

*Women*

#### 1928
1. Canada — 28
2. United States — 25
3. Germany — 21
4. Sweden — 8
5. Netherlands and Poland — 7

#### 1932
1. United States — 62
2. Germany — 18
3. Canada — 15
4. Poland — 12
5. Great Britain — 8
6. Netherlands and South Africa — 6

#### 1936
1. Germany — 45
2. United States — 16½
3. Poland — 14
4. Italy — 13
5. Great Britain — 10
6. Canada — 8

#### 1948
1. Netherlands — 37
2. France — 28
3. Great Britain — 26
4. Austria — 17
5. Australia — 16
6. United States — 14

#### 1952
1. Soviet Union — 64
2. Australia — 33
3. Germany — 27
4. Great Britain — 18
5. South Africa — 13
6. Czechoslovakia — 9

#### 1956
1. Soviet Union — 54½
2. Australia — 45
3. Germany — 24
4. United States — 23
5. Great Britain — 12½
6. Czechoslovakia — 10

#### 1960
1. Soviet Union — 74
2. Germany — 40
3. United States — 26
4. Great Britain — 23¾
5. Poland — 17½
6. Rumania — 11

#### 1964
1. Soviet Union — 60
2. Great Britain — 32
3. Poland — 28
4. United States and Germany — 27
6. Australia — 26

#### 1968
1. United States — 40
2. Soviet Union — 30
3. Australia — 27
4. East Germany and Rumania — 24
6. Hungary — 21
7. Great Britain — 17

#### 1972
1. East Germany — 93½
2. West Germany — 49½
3. Soviet Union — 36
4. Bulgaria — 25
5. United States — 21
6. Australia — 16
7. Great Britain — 14

## Record Achievements (Men)

Most gold medals won is nine by Paavo Nurmi (Finland), who between 1920 and 1928 was victorious in six individual and three team races.

Most individual wins is eight by Ray Ewry (USA) in the standing jump events between 1900 and 1908.

Most gold medals at one Olympics is five by Nurmi in 1924 (1500 m.,

146

3000 m. team, 5000 m., cross-country team and individual winner).

Most individual gold medals at one Olympics is four by Alvin Kraenzlein (USA)—60 m., 110 and 200 m. hurdles and long jump champion in 1900.

Most gold medals in one event is four by Al Oerter (USA) in the discus, 1956-1968 inclusive.

Most medals of any denomination is 12 by Nurmi.

Most medals by a British athlete is four by Guy Butler: 400 m. and 4 x 400 m. relay in 1920 and 1924.

## Record Achievements (Women)

Most gold medals won is four by Fanny Blankers-Koen (Netherlands): the 100 m., 200 m., 80 m. hurdles and 4 x 100 m. relay in 1948; and Betty Cuthbert (Australia): the 100m., 200 m. and 4 x 100 m. relay in 1956 and the 400 m. in 1964.

Most gold medals at one Olympics is four by Blankers-Koen as above.

Most individual gold medals at one Olympics is three by Blankers-Koen as above.

Most gold medals in one event is two by Annette Rogers, USA (relay in 1932 and 1936); Barbara Jones, USA (relay in 1952 and 1960); Shirley De La Hunty, Australia (80 m. hurdles in 1952 and 1956); Nina Ponomaryeva, USSR (discus in 1952 and 1960); Iolanda Balas, Rumania (high jump in 1960 and 1964); Tamara Press, USSR (shot in 1960 and 1964); and Wyomia Tyus, USA (100 m. in 1964 and 1968).

Most medals of any denomination is seven by De La Hunty between 1948 and 1956.

Most individual medals by a British athlete is three by Dorothy Hyman (100 m. and 200 m. in 1960, 4 x 100 m. relay in 1964) and Mary Rand (long jump, pentathlon and 4 x 100 m. relay in 1964).

Most appearances in an Olympics is six by Rumanian discus thrower Lia Manoliu: 6th in 1952, 9th in 1956, 3rd in 1960, 3rd in 1964, 1st in 1968 and 9th in 1972.

## Unofficial Olympics

An unofficial Olympic celebration was staged in Athens in 1906. For the record, the winners were as follows:

100 m., A. Hahn (USA) 11.2 sec.; 400 m., P. H. Pilgrim (USA) 53.2 sec.; 800 m., P. H. Pilgrim (USA) 2 min. 11.2 sec.; 1500 m., J. D. Lightbody (USA) 4 min. 12.0 sec.; 5 mi., H. Hawtrey (GB) 26 min. 26.2 sec.; Marathon, W. J. Sherring (Canada) 2 hr. 51 min. 23.6 sec.; 110 m. hurdles, R. G. Leavitt (USA) 16.2 sec.; High jump, C. Leahy (Ireland) 5 ft. 9 in.; Standing high jump, R. C. Ewry (USA) 5 ft. 1$\frac{1}{4}$ in.; Pole vault, F. Gonder (France) 11 ft. 6 in.; long jump, M. Prinstein (USA) 23 ft. 7$\frac{1}{4}$ in.; Standing long jump, R. C. Ewry (USA) 10 ft. 10 in.; Triple jump, P. J. O'Connor (Ireland) 46 ft. 2 in.; Shot, M. J. Sheridan (USA) 40 ft. 5 in.; Discus, M. J. Sheridan (USA) 136 ft. 0$\frac{1}{4}$ in.; Discus (Greek Style), W. Jarvinen (Finland) 115 ft. 4 in.; Javelin, E. Lemming (Sweden) 175 ft. 6 in.; throwing the stone (14 lb.), Georgeantas (Greece) 65 ft. 4$\frac{1}{4}$ in.; pentathlon, Mellander (Sweden).

## OWENS, J. C. (USA)

That Jesse Owens was the supreme physical genius of his age is less an opinion than a statement of fact. His sparkling career culminated in his quadruple success at the 1936 Olympic Games yet it is open to debate whether even that superlative achievement (winning the 100 m., 200 m., long jump and 4 x 100 m. relay) eclipses his feat at Ann Arbor, Michigan, on May 25th, 1935.

The sequence of events on that afternoon was as follows: 3.15—Owens equals 100 yd. world record of 9.4 sec.; 3.25—Owens takes one long jump . . . a very long jump of 26 ft. 8$\frac{1}{4}$ in., a world record destined to survive for quarter of a century; 3.45—Owens sets new world record of 20.3 sec. for the straight 220 yd., automatically collecting the 200 metres mark en route; 4.00—Owens covers the straight 220 yd. hurdles in 22.6 sec. for new world figures at that event and 200 m. hurdles . . . and two of the three watches showed 22.4 sec. Six records in 45 minutes! The world will never again witness the like.

Perhaps his finest single competitive performance was winning the Olympic long jump in Berlin. He began disastrously, managing to qualify

147

on his third and last try. In the final, after a thrilling struggle, he pulled out a magnificent leap of 26 ft. 5¼ in. to which the inspired German, Luz Long (25 ft. 9¾ in.), had no reply. Ever the sportsman, Owens even massaged his rival's leg during the competition at a vital stage.

He displayed his athletic gifts at an early age, recording 9.9 sec. for 100 yd., high jumping 6 ft. 2¾ in. and long jumping 23 ft. 0 in. when he was 15. In 1932, aged 18, he ran a wind-aided 100 m. in 10.3 sec. and next year, still at school, clocked 9.4 sec. for 100 yd., 20.7 sec. for the straight furlong and jumped 24 ft. 11¼ in.

Had he not turned professional shortly after the Olympics, he might have developed into the world's fastest quarter-miler, for he ran an effortless 29.5 sec. for 300 yd. in a time trial in 1936. His natural ability (he once high jumped 6 ft. 6 in. in training without any special preparation) stayed with him for many years. He claims to have run 100 yd. in 9.7 sec. and long jumped 25 ft. 11 in. in 1948, and 9.8 sec. in 1955 (aged 41).

His best marks were 9.4 sec. for 100 yd., 10.2 sec. for 100 m., 20.7 sec. for 200 m. (turn), 20.3 sec. for 220 yd. (straight), 22.6 sec. for 220 yd. hurdles (straight) and 26ft. 8¼in. long jump. He was born at Danville, Alabama, on Sept. 12th, 1913.

100 yd., 12.0 sec. (and wind-assisted 11.7 sec.) for 100 m., 23.7 sec. for 200 m., 52.2 sec. for 400 m., 54.3 sec. for 440 yd., 2 min. 01.1 sec. for 800 m., 2 min. 12.0 sec. for 880 yd., 11.4 sec. for 80 m. hurdles, 5ft. 3in. high jump, 19ft. 5in. long jump, 33ft. 5in. shot and 4,294 point pentathlon. Ann, who is now Mrs. Robbie Brightwell, was born at Moulsford (Berkshire) on March 8th, 1942.

## PACKER, A. E. (GB)

Whereas Fanny Blankers-Koen began her sparkling career as an 800 m. runner and found lasting fame as a sprinter, hurdler and jumper, Ann Packer started as a sprinter, hurdler and jumper and found lasting fame as an 800 m. runner. And whereas Fanny was 30 when she achieved Olympic immortality and continued in serious competition for a further eight years, Ann decided to retire immediately after her Olympic success aged only 22.

She can look back upon an extraordinarily varied career. She won the 100 yd. at the 1959 English Schools Championships, took the Women's AAA long jump title (in Mary Rand's absence) in 1960 and gained her first international in that event. Against all odds she reached the 200 m. final at the 1962 European Championships and later that year placed sixth in the Commonwealth Games 80 m. hurdles final and won a silver medal in the relay. In 1963 she moved up to the quarter-mile and, in only her fourth race, burst into the highest world class with 53.4 sec. for 400 m. Finally, in 1964, she added yet another string to her bow by taking up the 800 m.— with astonishing results.

She travelled to Tokyo with only five two-lap races behind her, the main objective being to win the Olympic 400 m. Despite returning a superb 52.2 sec. (a European record) she had to settle for second place in that event behind Betty Cuthbert but three days later she ran in simply inspired fashion to win the 800 m. in the world record time of 2 min. 01.1 sec.

Her best marks were 10.9 sec. for

## PADDOCK, C. W. (USA)

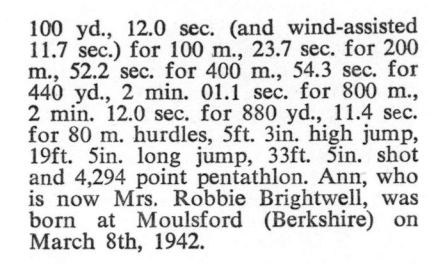

One of the most colourful personalities in sprinting history was Charley Paddock, famed for his "long jump" finish in which he literally leapt the final four or five yards to the tape. This spectacular gimmick paid off well, for it is said that no man ever passed Paddock once he took off.

During his career he set world's bests at every sprint distance from 50 yd. to 300m. After equalling the 100 yd. record of 9.6 sec. on five occasions between 1921 and 1924 he became the first to clock 9.5 sec. in 1926. His greatest performance, though, dated back to 1921 when he covered 110 yd. in 10.2 sec.—a fifth of a second better than his own record for the shorter 100 m. (109.36 yd.) event! It was 29 years before anyone ran faster.

He won two Olympic gold medals (100 m. and relay in 1920) and two silver (200 m. in 1920 and 1924), but placed only fifth in the 1924 100 m. won by Harold Abrahams. Best marks: 9.5 sec. for 100 yd., 10.2 sec. for 110 yd., 20.8 sec. for 220 yd. (straight), 21.2 sec. for 200 m. (turn), 30.2 sec. for 300 yd. and 33.2 sec. for 300 m. He was born at Gainesville, Texas, on Aug. 11th, 1900 and died in an air crash over Alaska in 1943.

## PAN-AMERICAN GAMES

The Pan-American Games were instituted in 1951, the first being held in Buenos Aires. Subsequent venues have been Mexico City (1955), Chicago 1959), Sao Paulo (1963), Winnipeg (1967) and Cali (1971). Past winners:—

| 100 Metres | sec. |
|---|---|
| 1951 R. Fortun (Cuba) | 10.6 |

| 1955 | R. Richard (USA) | 10.3 |
|------|------------------|------|
| 1959 | R. Norton (USA) | 10.3 |
| 1963 | E. Figuerola (Cuba) | 10.3 |
| 1967 | H. Jerome (Canada) | 10.2 |
| 1971 | D. Quarrie (Jamaica) | 10.2 |

## 200 Metres

| | | sec. |
|------|------------------|------|
| 1951 | R. Fortun (Cuba) | 21.3 |
| 1955 | R. Richard (USA) | 20.7 |
| 1959 | R. Norton (USA) | 20.6 |
| 1963 | R. Romero (Venezuela) | 21.2 |
| 1967 | J. Carlos (USA) | 20.5 |
| 1971 | D. Quarrie (Jamaica) | 19.8 |

## 400 Metres

| | | sec. |
|------|------------------|------|
| 1951 | M. Whitfield (USA) | 47.8 |
| 1955 | L. Jones (USA) | 45.4 |
| 1959 | G. Kerr (West Indies) | 46.1 |
| 1963 | J. Johnson (USA) | 46.7 |
| 1967 | L. Evans (USA) | 44.9 |
| 1971 | J. Smith (USA) | 44.6 |

## 800 Metres

| | | min. sec. |
|------|------------------|------|
| 1951 | M. Whitfield (USA) | 1 53.2 |
| 1955 | A. Sowell (USA) | 1 49.7 |
| 1959 | T. Murphy (USA) | 1 49.1 |
| 1963 | D. Bertoia (Canada) | 1 48.3 |
| 1967 | W. Bell (USA) | 1 49.2 |
| 1971 | K. Swenson (USA) | 1 48.0 |

## 1500 Metres

| | | min. sec. |
|------|------------------|------|
| 1951 | B. Ross (USA) | 4 00.4 |
| 1955 | J. Miranda (Argentina) | 3 53.2 |
| 1959 | D. Burleson (USA) | 3 49.1 |
| 1963 | J. Grelle (USA) | 3 43.5 |
| 1967 | T. Von Ruden (USA) | 3 43.4 |
| 1971 | M. Liquori (USA) | 3 42.1 |

## 5000 Metres

| | | min. sec. |
|------|------------------|------|
| 1951 | R. Bralo (Arg) | 14 51.2 |
| 1955 | O. Suarez (Arg) | 15 30.6 |
| 1959 | W. Dellinger (USA) | 14 28.4 |
| 1963 | O. Suarez (Arg) | 14 25.8 |
| 1967 | V. Nelson (USA) | 13 47.4 |
| 1971 | S. Prefontaine (USA) | 13 52.6 |

## 10,000 Metres

| | | min. sec. |
|------|------------------|------|
| 1951 | C. Stone (USA) | 31 08.6 |
| 1955 | O. Suarez (Arg) | 32 42.6 |
| 1959 | O. Suarez (Arg) | 30 17.2 |
| 1963 | P. McArdle (USA) | 29 52.2 |
| 1967 | V. Nelson (USA) | 29 17.4 |
| 1971 | F. Shorter (USA) | 28 50.8 |

## Marathon

| | | hr. min sec. |
|------|------------------|------|
| 1951 | D. Cabrera (Arg) | 2 25 00.2 |
| 1955 | D. Flores (Guatemala) | 2 59 09.2 |
| 1959 | J. Kelley (USA) | 2 27 54.2 |
| 1963 | F. Negrete (Mexico) | 2 27 55.6 |

| 1967 | A. Boychuk (Canada) | 2 22 00.4 |
|------|------------------|------|
| 1971 | F. Shorter (USA) | 2 22 40.4 |

## 3000 m. Steeplechase

| | | min. sec. |
|------|------------------|------|
| 1951 | C. Stone (USA) | 9 32.0 |
| 1955 | G. Sola (Chile) | 9 46.8 |
| 1959 | P. Coleman (USA) | 8 56.4 |
| 1963 | J. Fishback (USA) | 9 08.0 |
| 1967 | C. McCubbins (USA) | 8 38.2 |
| 1971 | M. Manley (USA) | 8 42.2 |

## 110 Metres Hurdles

| | | sec. |
|------|------------------|------|
| 1951 | R. Attlesey (USA) | 14.0 |
| 1955 | J. Davis (USA) | 14.3 |
| 1959 | H. Jones (USA) | 13.6 |
| 1963 | B. Lindgren (USA) | 13.8 |
| 1967 | E. McCullouch (USA) | 13.4 |
| 1971 | R. Milburn (USA) | 13.4 |

## 400 Metres Hurdles

| | | sec. |
|------|------------------|------|
| 1951 | J. Aparicio (Colombia) | 53.4 |
| 1955 | J. Culbreath (USA) | 51.5 |
| 1959 | J. Culbreath (USA) | 51.2 |
| 1963 | J. Dyrzka (Arg) | 50.2 |
| 1967 | R. Whitney (USA) | 50.7 |
| 1971 | R. Mann (USA) | 49.1 |

## 4 x 100 Metres

| | | sec. |
|------|------------------|------|
| 1951 | United States | 41.0 |
| 1955 | United States | 40.7 |
| 1959 | United States | 40.4 |
| 1963 | United States | 40.4 |
| 1967 | United States | 39.0 |
| 1971 | Jamaica | 39.2 |

## 4 x 400 Metres

| | | min. sec. |
|------|------------------|------|
| 1951 | United States | 3 09.9 |
| 1955 | United States | 3 07.2 |
| 1959 | The West Indies | 3 05.3 |
| 1963 | United States | 3 09.6 |
| 1967 | United States | 3 02.0 |
| 1971 | United States | 3 00.6 |

## High Jump

| | | ft. in. |
|------|------------------|------|
| 1951 | V. Severns (USA) | 6 4¾ |
| 1955 | E. Shelton (USA) | 6 7¼ |
| 1959 | C. Dumas (USA) | 6 11 |
| 1963 | G. Johnson (USA) | 6 11 |
| 1967 | E. Caruthers (USA) | 7 2¼ |
| 1971 | P. Matzdorf (USA) | 6 10¾ |

## Pole Vault

| | | ft. in. |
|------|------------------|------|
| 1951 | R. Richards (USA) | 14 9¼ |
| 1955 | R. Richards (USA) | 14 9¼ |
| 1959 | D. Bragg (USA) | 15 2 |
| 1963 | D. Tork (USA) | 16 0¾ |
| 1967 | R. Seagren (USA) | 16 0¾ |
| 1971 | J. Johnson (USA) | 17 5¾ |

| *Long Jump* | ft. in. |
|---|---|
| 1951 G. Bryan (USA) | 23 5¼ |
| 1955 R. Range (USA) | 26 4¼ |
| 1959 I. Roberson (USA) | 26 1¾ |
| 1963 R. Boston (USA) | 26 7¼ |
| 1967 R. Boston (USA) | 27 2½ |
| 1971 A. Robinson (USA) | 26 3¾ |

| *Triple Jump* | ft. in. |
|---|---|
| 1951 A. F. da Silva (Brazil) | 49 10 |
| 1955 A. F. da Silva (Braz) | 54 4 |
| 1959 A. F. da Silva (Braz) | 52 2 |
| 1963 W. Sharpe (USA) | 49 8½ |
| 1967 C. Craig (USA) | 54 3¼ |
| 1971 P. Perez (Cuba) | 57 1 |

| *Shot* | ft. in. |
|---|---|
| 1951 J. Fuchs (USA) | 56 7¼ |
| 1955 P. O'Brien (USA) | 57 8½ |
| 1959 P. O'Brien (USA) | 62 5½ |
| 1963 D. Davis (USA) | 60 9¼ |
| 1967 R. Matson (USA) | 65 0¾ |
| 1971 A. Feuerbach (USA) | 64 10 |

| *Discus* | ft. in. |
|---|---|
| 1951 J. Fuchs (USA) | 160 5 |
| 1955 F. Gordien (USA) | 174 2 |
| 1959 A. Oerter (USA) | 190 8 |
| 1963 R. Humphreys (USA) | 189 8 |
| 1967 G. Carlsen (USA) | 188 8 |
| 1971 R. Drescher (USA) | 204 3 |

| *Hammer* | ft. in. |
|---|---|
| 1951 G. Ortiz (Arg) | 157 6 |
| 1955 R. Backus (USA) | 180 2 |
| 1959 A. Hall (USA) | 195 10 |
| 1963 A. Hall (USA) | 205 10 |
| 1967 T. Gage (USA) | 214 4 |
| 1971 A. Hall (USA) | 216 0 |

| *Javelin* | ft. in. |
|---|---|
| 1951 R. Heber (Arg) | 223 4 |
| 1955 F. Held (USA) | 228 11 |
| 1959 B. Quist (USA) | 229 6 |
| 1963 D. Studney (USA) | 248 0 |
| 1967 F. Covelli (USA) | 243 8 |
| 1971 C. Feldmann (USA | 267 5 |

| *Decathlon* (1950 Tables) | Pts. |
|---|---|
| 1951 H. Figueroa (Chile) | 6,610 |
| 1955 R. Johnson (USA) | 7,985 |
| 1959 D. Edstrom (USA) | 7,245 |
| 1963 J. D. Martin (USA) | 7,335 |
| 1967 W. Toomey (USA) | 8,044 |
| 1971 R. Wanamaker (USA) | 7,648 |

| *20 Kilometres Walk* | h. min. sec. |
|---|---|
| 1963 A. Oakley (Canada) | 1 42 43.2 |
| 1967 R. Laird (USA) | 1 33 05.2 |
| 1971 G. Klopfer (USA) | 1 37 30.0 |

| *50 Kilometres Walk* | h. min. sec |
|---|---|
| 1951 S. Idanez (Arg) | 5 06 06.8 |
| 1967 L. Young (USA) | 4 26 20.8 |
| 1971 L. Young (USA) | 4 38 31.0 |

## Women's Events

| *60 Metres* | sec. |
|---|---|
| 1955 B. Diaz (Cuba) | 7.5 |
| 1959 I. Daniels (USA) | 7.4 |

| *100 Metres* | sec. |
|---|---|
| 1951 J. Sanchez (Peru) | 12.2 |
| 1955 B. Jones (USA) | 11.5 |
| 1959 L. Williams (USA) | 12.1 |
| 1963 E. McGuire (USA) | 11.5 |
| 1967 B. Ferrell (USA) | 11.5 |
| 1971 I. Davis (USA) | 11.2 |

| *200 Metres* | sec. |
|---|---|
| 1951 J. Patton (USA) | 25,3 |
| 1959 L. Williams (USA) | 24.2 |
| 1963 V. Brown (USA) | 23.9 |
| 1967 W. Tyus (USA) | 23.7 |
| 1971 S. Berto (Canada) | 23.5 |

| *400 Metres* | sec. |
|---|---|
| 1971 M. Neufville (Jamaica) | 52.3 |

| *800 Metres* | min. sec. |
|---|---|
| 1963 A. Hoffman (Can) | 2 10.2 |
| 1967 M. Manning (USA) | 2 02.3 |
| 1971 A. Hoffman (Canada) | 2 05.5 |

| *80 Metres Hurdles* | sec. |
|---|---|
| 1951 E. Gaete (Chile) | 11.9 |
| 1955 E. Gaete (Chile) | 11.7 |
| 1959 B. Diaz (Cuba) | 11.2 |
| 1963 J. A. Terry (USA) | 11.3 |
| 1967 C. Sherrard (USA) | 10.8 |

| *100 Metres Hurdles* | sec. |
|---|---|
| 1971 P. Johnson (USA) | 13.1 |

| *4 x 100 Metres* | sec. |
|---|---|
| 1951 United States | 48.7 |
| 1955 United States | 47.0 |
| 1959 United States | 46.4 |
| 1963 United States | 45.6 |
| 1967 Cuba | 44.6 |
| 1971 United States | 44.5 |

| *4 x 400 Metres* | min. sec. |
|---|---|
| 1971 United States | 3 32.4 |

| *High Jump* | ft. in. |
|---|---|
| 1951 J. Sandiford (Ecuador) | 4 9½ |
| 1955 M. McDaniel (USA) | 5 6½ |
| 1959 A. Flynn (USA) | 5 3½ |
| 1963 E. Montgomery (USA) | 5 6 |

| 1967 | E. Montgomery (USA) | 5 | 10 |
| 1971 | D. Brill (Canada) | 6 | 0¾ |

*Long Jump* ft. in.
| 1951 | B. Kretschmer (Chile) | 17 | 9½ |
| 1959 | A. Smith (USA) | 18 | 9¾ |
| 1963 | W. White (USA) | 20 | 2¼ |
| 1967 | I. Martinez (Cuba) | 20 | 9 |
| 1971 | B. Eisler (Canada) | 21 | 1¼ |

*Shot* ft. in.
| 1951 | I. de Preiss (Arg) | 40 | 10¼ |
| 1959 | E. Brown (USA) | 48 | 2 |
| 1963 | N. McCredie (Can) | 50 | 3¼ |
| 1967 | N. McCredie (Can) | 49 | 9¾ |
| 1971 | L. Graham (USA) | 51 | 8¼ |

*Discus* ft. in.
| 1951 | I. de Preiss (Arg) | 126 | 5 |
| 1955 | I. Pfuller (Arg) | 141 | 8 |
| 1959 | E. Brown (USA) | 161 | 9 |
| 1963 | N. McCredie (Can) | 164 | 8 |
| 1967 | C. Moseke (USA) | 161 | 7 |
| 1971 | C. Romero (Cuba) | 187 | 8 |

*Javelin* ft. in.
| 1951 | H. Garcia (Mex) | 129 | 5 |
| 1955 | K. Anderson (USA) | 161 | 3 |
| 1959 | M. Ahrens (Chile) | 148 | 10 |
| 1963 | M. Ahrens (Chile) | 163 | 9 |
| 1967 | B. Friedrich (USA) | 174 | 9 |
| 1971 | A. Nunez (Cuba) | 177 | 2 |

*Pentathlon* Pts.
| 1967 | P. Bank (USA) | 4860 |
| 1971* | D. Van Kiekebelt (Can) | 4290 |

\* New tables

## PENTATHLON

The pentathlon is a five-event test of all-round ability. The men's version comprises the long jump, javelin, 200 m., discus and 1500 m. in that order on one day. The event is staged occasionally in West Germany, the Soviet Union and United States but is rarely held elsewhere. Scoring is on the same basis as the decathlon.

The pentathlon has long been a most popular women's event, and was introduced into the Olympic schedule in 1964. The events are 100 m. hurdles, shot and high jump on the first day; long jump and 200 m. on the second. Sometimes the whole event is staged on one day.

Alexandra Chudina broke the world record four times between 1949 and 1955; Galina Bystrova, European

champion in 1958 and 1962, pushed the record up twice in 1957 and 1958; and from 1959 to 1966 the event was controlled by Irina Press, the inaugural Olympic champion in 1964. All three athletes were from the USSR.

The event was modified in 1969 when the 100 m. hurdles (2ft. 9in.) replaced the 80 m. hurdles (2ft. 6in.), and there was a further change in scoring when revised points tables came into force in 1972. Mary Peters (GB and NI) broke all previous records with her score of 4801 pts. in winning the 1972 Olympic title.

See also: BLANKERS-KOEN, F. E.; PETERS, M. E.; RAND, M. D.; and ROSENDAHL, H.

## PETERS, J. H. (GB)

Jim Peters was largely responsible for the radical advance in marathon times during the 1950s. Until he appeared on the scene the marathon was regarded as an ultra-long distance race in which one's resources had to be very carefully husbanded. Peters, by virtue of his spartan training regime and forceful racing tactics, did for marathon running what Emil Zatopek did for long distance track racing a few years earlier. In effect, the marathon became an extension of the 6 and 10-mile track runs.

Between 1952 and 1954 he lowered the world's best time of 2 hr. 26 min. 07 sec. by almost 8½ minutes, and his fastest time of 2 hr. 17 min. 39.4 sec. represented an average of about 5¼ minutes per mile—which only a few years earlier was considered good speed for a 10 miles race.

Peters had two careers. In 1946 he won the AAA 6 mi., next year added the 10 mi. title and in 1948 (aged 29) clocked 30 min. 07.0 sec. for 6 mi. and placed ninth in the Olympic 10,000 m.

Little was heard of him in the next two seasons but in 1951, coached by " Johnny " Johnston, he burst back as a marathon runner, winning the Windsor to Chiswick event in the British record time of 2 hr. 29 min. 24 sec. In 1952 he travelled to Helsinki as favourite after setting his first " world record " of 2 hr. 20 min. 42.2 sec., but in the Olympics—after leading for about 10 miles—he was forced out of the race by cramp at 20 miles while in fourth place.

He carried all before him in 1953: twice he lowered the world's best (2:18:40.2 and 2:18:34.8), he captained England's cross-country team, broke Walter George's 69-year-old English hour record and represented Britain on the track.

His final season, 1954, was notable for his final record-shattering run of 2 hr. 17 min. 39.4 sec. and his tragic experience in the Commonwealth Games at Vancouver. Refusing to compromise with the hot, humid conditions he entered the stadium with a 17 minutes lead—but was unable to complete those last few hundred yards, so weak was he. Later he received a special gold medal from the Duke of Edinburgh inscribed " To J. Peters as a token of admiration for a most gallant marathon runner."

His best track marks included 14 min. 09.8 sec. for 3 mi., 28 min. 57.8 sec. for 6 mi. and 11 mi. 986 yd. in the hour. He was born at Homerton (London), on Oct. 24th, 1918.

## PETERS, M. E. (GB & NI)

After 17 years of pentathlon competition, Mary Peters " overnight " became one of the world's great sports stars and a household name throughout the British Isles when in Munich in 1972 she joined the immortals by winning an Olympic title with a world record performance—in the tradition established by Britain's only previous female Olympic champions. Mary Rand and Ann Packer.

Her story is one of perseverance. Overshadowed as a pentathlete by Mary Rand (now Mrs. Bill Toomey) and never quite making world class as a shot-putter, her career might well have ended after a disappointing showing at the 1968 Olympics where, hampered by an injured ankle, she placed 9th. She was already 29 and had she quit then she would have been remembered as a very good and big hearted athlete (4th in the 1964 Olympics) but not truly a great one.

Instead she took off 1969 in order to regain her zest and at her fourth Commonwealth Games, in 1970, she won gold medals in both the shot and pentathlon — representing Northern Ireland. Her score of 5,148 pts. (4,524 on the new tables) re-established her among the world's elite after a gap of six years.

Mary again passed up competition in 1971, but the following indoor season saw her transformed as a high jumper. Previously just a competent straddle jumper with a best of 5 ft. 6 in., she was now a Fosbury-flopper of close to world class. This dramatic improvement was worth over 100 pts. in that one event and was the key to her Olympic pentathlon aspirations.

During the Olympic build-up period she raised her UK record to 4,630 pts., which ranked her fifth among the pentathlon contenders. From the very first event in Munich it was apparent she was in superb form and afraid of nobody. She clocked 13.3 sec. for the hurdles, her fastest without wind assistance; put the shot 53 ft. 1¼ in. which was only a few inches below her UK record; and ended the first day with an inspired high jump of 5 ft. 11½ in., another personal best. Her overnight score of 2,969 pts., a " world record ", gave her a lead of 97 pts.

On the second day she reached a near personal best long jump of 19 ft. 7½ in. and just held off the tremendous challenge of Heide Rosendahl (W. Germany) by clocking her fastest ever 200 m. time of 24.1 sec. Her final score of 4,801 pts. (5,430 on the old tables), a world record, was ten points more than Rosendahl's.

Her best marks are 11.1 sec. for 100 yd., 24.1 sec. for 200 m., 11.0 sec. for 80 m. hurdles, 13.3 sec. for 100 m. hurdles (and 13.1 sec. wind assisted), 5 ft. 11½ in. high jump, 19 ft. 9¾ in. long jump, 53 ft. 6¼ in. shot (53 ft. 9¾ in. indoors), 127 ft. discus (standing throw) and 4,801 pentathlon. Her annual progress in the pentathlon (she has competed in 46 of them!); 1955—3,253, 1956—3,679, 1957—3,913, 1958—3,720, 1959—3,905, 1961—3,940, 1962—4,586, 1963—4,527, 1964—4,823, 1965—4,512, 1966—4,625, 1968—4,803, 1970—5,148 (4,524 new tables), 1972—5,430 (4,801 new tables). She was born at Halewood (Lancs) on July 6th, 1939.

## PIRIE, D. A. G. (GB)

While Jim Peters was transforming the face of marathon running, his young countryman Gordon Pirie was leading British track distance running from the depths into which it had plunged following Sydney Wooderson's retirement to unprecedented heights. For a full decade, 1951 to 1961, this controversial figure held captive the imagination of British athletics fans.

Pirie's career began in 1943 and as early as 1948, when only 17, he ran 6 mi. in 33 min. 40 sec. That year, after watching Emil Zatopek in the Olympic 10,000 m., he vowed to emulate the Czech star.

He reached top class in 1951, winning his first AAA 6 mi. title in the English record time of 29 min. 32.0 sec. He broke more national records in 1952 but was not quite ready for success in Olympic competition and placed seventh in the 10,000 and fourth in the 5000 m. It was in Helsinki that he met Waldemar Gerschler, the German coach who was to guide Pirie for the rest of his career.

In 1953, during a fabulously successful season, he captured the first of his three successive English cross-country titles, set a 6 mi. world record of 28 min. 19.4 sec., helped a British team to a world 4 x 1500 m. relay record and even defeated America's star miler Wes Santee in 4 min. 06.8 sec. He predicted that one day he would run 5000 m. in 13 min. 40 sec., although the world record then existing stood at 13 min. 58.2 sec. Statements like this infuriated his detractors—but three years later he seized the record with a time of 13 min. 36.8 sec. in defeating Vladimir Kuts.

Within five days of this remarkable achievement he tied the 3000 m. world record of 7 min. 55.6 sec. and won over 1500 m. in 3 min. 43.7 sec. against Klaus Richtzenhain, the German who was destined to win the Olympic silver medal later in the year. Pirie reduced the 3000 m. mark to 7 min. 52.8 sec. against the combined forces of the Hungarian trio of Istvan Rozsavolgyi, Sandor Iharos and Laszlo Tabori.

At the Olympics, though, Kuts avenged his earlier defeat. He took both the 5000 and 10,000 m., with Pirie finishing eighth in the longer event (after cracking in the last mile following a murderous duel) and second in the 5000 m. Pirie's record was somewhat spotty in the seasons that followed but in 1960 he recaptured his dashing form of old, only to feature in one of the most sensational upsets in track history by failing even to qualify for the Olympic 5000 m. final. He came back for one last season in 1961 and succeeded in breaking the British 3 mi. record once more and turning in his fastest 1500 m. Later he became a professional.

His best marks included 1 min. 53.0 sec. for 880 yd., 3 min. 42.5 sec. for 1500 m., 3 min. 59.9 sec. for the mile, 5 min. 09.8 sec. for 2000 m., 7 min. 52.8 sec. for 3000 m., 8 min. 39.0 sec. for 2 mi., 13 min. 16.4 sec. for 3 mi., 13 min. 36.8 sec. for 5000 m., 28 min. 09.6 sec. for 6 mi., 29 min. 15.2 sec. for 10,000 m., 22 mi. 278 yd. in two hours, and 3000 m. steeplechase in 9 min. 06.6 sec. Pirie, who married the international sprinter Shirley Hampton in 1956, was born in Leeds on Feb. 10th, 1931.

## POLE VAULT

Pole vaulting dates back about 100 years. For some 25 years there were two schools of vaulting in existence: the English (Ulverston) style entailed the athlete climbing up the heavy ash, cedar or hickory pole and levering himself over the bar in a sitting position, while the method used elsewhere was similar to that practised today in that the athlete was forbidden to move his upper hand once he had left the ground.

The heavy poles in use in the 19th century were equipped with three iron spikes in the base. Light bamboo poles were introduced from Japan in the early years of this century. In place of spikes, the base of the pole was equipped with a plug that fitted into a box sunk level with the ground. The next development was the advent of aluminium poles and, in recent years, the controversial fibre-glass models that have revolutionised the event.

Apart from knocking off the bar, a failure is registered when the athlete

154

places his lower hand above the upper one or moves the upper hand higher on the pole after leaving the ground, when he leaves the ground for the purpose of making a vault and fails to clear the bar, or when before taking off he touches the ground beyond the vertical plane of the upper part of the stopboard. It is not counted a failure if the athlete's pole breaks while making an attempt.

The IAAF rule decrees that "the pole may be of any material and of any length or diameter."

In the years when both styles were flourishing, the slightly greater heights were achieved by the British vaulters, most of whom hailed from the Lake District. Edwin Woodburn (GB) was the first to exceed 11 ft. in 1876, seven years before Hugh Baxter (USA) did the trick with the fixed hand style. When the English technique fell into disuse the record stood to the credit of Richard Dickinson at 11 ft. 9 in. in 1891. Norman Dole (USA) ushered in the era of 12 foot vaulting in 1904; eight years later Robert Gardner (USA) became the first man to lever himself over 13 feet.

American supremacy was broken in the early 1920s by Charles Hoff (Norway), who held the world record from 1922 to 1927 with a best of 13 ft. 11¼ in. A foot injury prevented his challenging for the 1924 Olympic title—though he managed to reach the 800 m. final! Sabin Carr (USA) achieved the long awaited 14-foot leap in 1927.

The 1937 season was particularly notable, the Americans Earle Meadows and William Sefton between them lifting the record six times. Finally the "Heavenly Twins," as they were dubbed, tied at 14 ft. 11 in. and were prevented from trying 15 feet because the bar could not be raised any higher.

The first 15-footer was posted by Cornelius Warmerdam (USA) in 1940. Although no other man cleared 15 ft. until 1951 Warmerdam totalled 43 such clearances during the war years and his final world marks of 15 ft. 7¾ in. (outdoors) and 15 ft. 8½ in. (indoors) lasted many years. The next great figure was Bob Richards (USA), who never beat Warmerdam's records but became the first vaulter successfully to defend his Olympic title.

Bob Gutowski (USA), who died while in his prime, and the 1960 Olympic champion Don Bragg (USA) paved the way towards 16 feet—an honour that befell John Uelses, a German-born American, in 1962. Uelses used a glass pole, as do all the world's leading vaulters now, and the record has been climbing steeply since athletes have been learning to take full advantage of the glass pole's catapult-like properties. During 1963 the record rose ten times in the hands of Americans John Pennel (first to clear 17 ft.) and Brian Sternberg, whose career was cut short when he suffered grave injury while training. Chris Papanicolaou (Greece) opened the 18 foot era in 1970, and the record was broken several times in 1972, ending with Bob Seagren (USA) vaulting 18 ft. 5¾ in.

Britain's record in this event has been abysmal during this century. Only three vaulters have achieved anything of international significance: Richard Webster, who tied with ten others for sixth place in the 1936 Olympics; Geoff Elliott, the Commonwealth champion in 1954 and 1958; and Mike Bull, of Northern Ireland, who won the 1970 Commonwealth title and raised the UK record to 17 ft. 1 in. in 1972.

See also: NORDWIG, W.; SEAGREN, R.; and WARMERDAM, C. A.

## PROFESSIONAL ATHLETICS

Until an American-organised circuit began operations in 1973, professional athletics—particularly popular during much of the 19th century—had dwindled into insignificance. However, the International Track Association, by signing up such big names as Jim Ryun, Randy Matson, Lee Evans and Bob Seagren, was hoping to rekindle the public's interest in this side of the sport.

The most notable outdoor performances of recent years have been recorded by British athletes. George McNeill ran 110 m. in 11.0 sec. (passing 100 m. in 10.1 sec.) and Robbie Hutchinson clocked 10.1 sec. for 100 m. in 1971, and former European champion Arthur Rowe put the shot 64 ft. 0 in. in 1962.

Professional indoor records which are superior to the amateur counterparts—all set in 1973—are: 100 m.. 10.2 sec. Warren Edmonson (USA); 500 yd., 53.9 sec. Larry James (USA); 500 m., 62.0 sec. Lee Evans (USA); 600 m., 76.7 sec. Evans; 100 m., 2 min. 19.7 sec. Chris Fisher (Aus); High jump, 7 ft. 4¾ in. John Radetich (USA); Shot, 70 ft. 10½ in. Brian Oldfield (USA).

# PUTTEMANS, E. (Belgium)

Even though he had to settle for a silver medal in Munich, Emiel Puttemans' 1972 season was remarkable: he broke world records held by Ron Clarke, Kip Keino and Lasse Viren.

His international track career began in 1968, when he finished 12th in the Olympic 5000 m., and his progress was gradual if somewhat inconspicuous: 7th in the 1969 European Championships, 6th in the 1971 edition. Then, just a few days after the latter race, he caused a sensation by breaking Ron Clarke's world 2 mi. record with 8 min. 17.8 sec., followed by a European 3000 m. mark of 7 min. 39.8 sec.

In Munich he covered the last 800 m. of the 10,000 m. final in a pulsating 1 min. 57.6 sec., yet in spite of recording a brilliant 27 min. 39.6 sec. it was Viren of Finland who won the gold. The 5000 m. final was his hard race of the Games and he was run out of it on the last lap, finishing 5th. Again he exploded in late season: in the space of six days he broke Keino's 3000 m. record with 7 min. 37.6 sec., easily beat Viren in another 3000 m. race, and broke Viren's newly set 5000 m. record with 13 min. 13.0 sec. after passing 3 mi. in 12 min. 47.8 sec. to succeed Clarke in the record books. His best event, though, may yet prove to be the steeplechase which, with minimum preparation, he has run in 8 min. 27.8 sec.

In an astonishing indoor run early in 1973 he covered 2 mi. in 8 min. 13.2 sec. (Faster than the outdoor world record) after passing 1500 m. in 3 min. 43.0 sec. (his personal best is 3 min. 41.9 sec.) 2000 m. in 5 min. dead and 3000 m. in 7 min. 39.2 sec. Annual progress at 5000 and 10,000 m.: 1966—14:54.2; 1967—14:25.8; 1968—13:51.6, 29:23.8; 1969—13:53.2; 1970—13:47.0; 1971—13:24.6, 28.01.4; 1972—13.13.0, 27:39.6. He was born at Vossem on Oct. 8th, 1947.

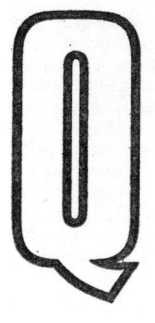

## QUARRIE, D. (Jamaica)

A precocious sprint talent, Don Quarrie had won six important gold medals by the time he was 20. He won the 100 m. and 200 m. and was a member of the victorious Jamaican 4 x 100 m. relay team at both the 1970 Commonwealth and 1971 Pan-American Games. His performance in the Pan-Am Games at Cali (Colombia) was all the more notable for his time in the 200 m. Taking half a second off his previous fastest, he equalled Tommie Smith's world record of 19.8 sec.

The Olympics have brought Quarrie nothing but disappointment. In 1968, as a 17-year-old who had already run 10.3 sec. for 100 m., he injured himself in training in Mexico City and was unable to take his place in the relay team; while in 1972 he pulled a muscle during his 200 m. semi-final.

His best marks are 9.3 sec. (and wind assisted 9.1 sec.) for 100 yd., 10.1 sec. (and windy 9.9 sec.) for 100 m. and 19.8 sec. for 200 m. Annual progression: 1965—10.9 (100 yd.); 1966—10.2; 1967—10.1; 1968—10.3 (100 m.), 21.2 (220 yd.); 1969—10.4; 1970—10.3, 20.5 (200 m.); 1971—10.2, 19.8; 1972—10.1, 20.4 (220 yd.). He was born in Kingston on Feb. 25th, 1951.

## RAND, M. D. (GB)

" The greatest thing of all would be to do a world record at the Olympics —like Herb Elliott, for instance. That would be wonderful. Needless to say, that's what I would like to do in Tokyo!" Those were the words of Mary Rand when interviewed by the author on Sept. 22nd, 1964. Twenty-two days later her hopes were translated into deeds in Tokyo's Olympic stadium . . . victory, a world record of 22ft. 2¼in., the greatest series of jumps on record (the *worst* of her six leaps was 21ft. 6⅛in.), the first Olympic gold medal to be won by a British woman athlete. And that was by no means all, for later in the Games she performed brilliantly in the pentathlon for a silver medal and second place on the world all-time list with 5,035 points, and later still contributed to the British team's third place in the 4 x 100m. relay.

Long before her marriage she had achieved fame as Mary Bignal. She set her first national record in the pentathlon (4,046 pts.) as early as 1957, when she was 17. Next year she gained a silver medal in the Commonwealth Games long jump and finished a creditable seventh in the European pentathlon championship.

An attack of nerves ruined her chances in the 1960 Olympic long jump. She led the qualifiers with a magnificent UK record of 20ft. 9½in. but in the final placed no higher than ninth—one of the very rare occasions on which she has failed to do herself justice in major competition. She made partial amends by unexpectedly taking fourth place in the hurdles.

Only a few months after the birth of her daughter in 1962 she made a remarkable comeback to earn the bronze medal in the European long jump. She enjoyed a glorious season in 1963 (including a share in a world relay record) and reached the summit of athletic endeavour in 1964.

She won the 1966 Commonwealth long jump title but was frustrated by injury in her attempt to make the British Olympic team in 1968 and retired. Her second marriage, to Olympic decathlon champion Bill Toomey (USA), took place in 1969.

Best marks: 10.6 sec. for 100yd., 11.7 sec. for 100m., 23.9 (and wind-assisted 23.6) for 200m., 56.5 sec. for 440 yd., 10.8 sec. for 80m. hurdles, 13.4 sec. (and 13.3 sec. wind-assisted) for 100m. hurdles, 5ft. 7¾in. high jump, 22ft. 2¼in. long jump, 40ft. 2¼in. shot and 5,035 pt. pentathlon. She was born at Wells, Somerset, on Feb. 10th, 1940.

## RECORDS

See Commonwealth Records, European Records, United Kingdom Records, World Records.

## RELAYS

No fewer than 17 relay events, ten men's and seven women's, are included in the IAAF's world record schedule —ranging from 4 x 100 m. to 4 x 1 mile or 4 x 800 m. for women. Olympic and European championships are staged at 4 x 100 m. and 4 x 400 m.

Chalk lines are drawn across the track to mark the distances of the stages and to denote the scratch line. Other lines are drawn 10 m. (11 yd.) before and after the scratch line, denoting the take-over zone within which the baton must be passed. Under a rule brought into force in 1963, in races up to 4 x 220 yd. the second, third and fourth runners may start running up to 10 m. outside the take-over zone but the baton must be passed only when both athletes are in the take-over zone. This new ruling has had the effect of speeding up the times of well drilled sprint relay teams.

The baton, which is passed from athlete to athlete, must be carried in the hand throughout the race. Should it be dropped, it must be recovered by the athlete who dropped it. Disqualification is incurred when the baton is passed outside the 20 m. (22 yd.) take-over zone.

It has been estimated that in the average 4 x 110 yd. relay, the first (lead-off) runner covers about 118 yards with the baton, the second and third runners about 110 yards each, and the final (anchor) runner about 102 yards.

The first relay race recorded was a two miles event at Berkeley, California, on Nov. 17th, 1883, nearly 12 years before the first relay held in Britain. Relay events entered the Olympic programme from 1908.

# ROELANTS, G. (Belgium)

Until 1972 it was unusual for Ron Clarke to lose a world record; yet in Oct. 1966 Gaston Roelants slashed over a minute off the Australian's figures for 20,000m. and carried on to add over a quarter of a mile to his one hour record!

It is as a steeplechaser, though, that he is best known. Famed for his front running, Roelants was a runaway winner of the 1962 European title after having placed fourth at the 1960 Olympics. He scored another great victory at the 1964 Olympics but was defeated at the 1966 European Championships, thus terminating an unbeaten steeplechase record stretching back all of five years. He was the first to run the distance inside 8¼ minutes.

On the flat, Roelants is a former European 10,000m. record holder, and in 1972—the year in which he won his fourth International Cross-Country Championship—he broke his own world records for 20,000m. and the hour. He has also promised much in the marathon, European silver medallist in 1969.

Best marks: 3 min. 44.4 sec. for 1500m., 7 min. 48.6 sec. for 3000m., 13 min. 34.6 sec. for 5000m., 28 min. 03.8 sec. for 10,000m., 57 min. 44.4 sec. for 20,000m., 12mi. 1,609yd. in the hour, 8 min. 26.4 sec. for the steeplechase, and 2 hr. 17 min. 22.2 sec. for the marathon.

Annual progress at steeplechase and 10,000m.: 1957—9:37.8; 1958—9:

16.4; 1959—8:56.6, 30:16.0; 1960—8:45.8, 29:19.4; 1961—8:38.2; 1962—8:32.6, 29:18.6; 1963—8:29.6, 29:07.2; 1964—8:30.8, 28:41.8; 1965—8:26.4, 28:10.6; 1966—8:27.2, 28:20.2; 1967—8:28.6, 28:26.6; 1968—8:29.2, 28:46.2; 1969—28:19.0; 1970—28:25.4; 1971—28:22.0; 1972—28:03.8. He was born at Opvelp on Feb. 5th, 1937.

# ROSENDAHL, H.
## (West Germany)

Few could have begrudged Heide Rosendahl her success at the Munich Olympics. The greatest long jumper in the world and one of the finest all-rounders, she had been plagued by misfortune on several major occasions. All she had to show in terms of gold medals for several years of brilliant endeavour was the 1971 European pentathlon crown.

She gave an early glimpse of her potential when, aged 19, she placed 2nd in the 1966 European pentathlon only 22 pts. behind the winner, but she was right out of luck at the 1968 Olympics—illness reduced her to 8th in the long jump and after pulling a muscle warming up she wasn't even able to start in the pentathlon. Another setback came at the 1969 European Championships; the West German team withdrew from all individual events as a protest against Jurgen May being ruled ineligible to run for West Germany.

A momentous season in 1970 was capped by a world record long jump of 22 ft. 5¼ in. and the following year she gained that elusive gold medal. Her luck was turning and at the 1972 Olympics she endeared herself still further with an adoring public. After winning the long jump she ran Mary Peters to ten points in the pentathlon, breaking the former world record herself, and on the anchor leg of the 4 x 100 m. relay she outpaced East Germay's Renate Stecher to bring West Germany in first in world record equalling time. Two golds and a silver!

The daughter of a German discus champion, Heide can point to a staggering range of personal bests: 11.3 sec. (11.2 sec. wind assisted) 100 m., 23.0 sec. 200 m., 13.1 sec. 100 m.

159

hurdles, 5 ft. 7 in. high jump, 22 ft. 5¼ in. long jump (and over 23 ft. from take-off to landing), 46 ft. 10 in. shot, 142 ft. 7 in. discus, 158 ft. 1 in. javelin and 4,791 pts. pentathlon (new tables). She is even said to have run 800 m. in 2 min. 11 sec. in training.

Annual progress at long jump and pentathlon: 1961—17ft. 3½in.; 1962—18ft. 7¾in.; 1963—19ft. 8½in.; 1964—19ft. 11¾in.; 1965—20ft. 2½in., 4,538 pts.; 1966—20ft. 7¾in., 4,765; 1967—20ft. 10in., 4,573; 1968—21ft. 8¾in., 5,129; 1969—21ft. 9½in., 5,155; 1970—22ft. 5¼in., 5,399; 1971—22ft. 0¾in., 5,299; 1972—22ft. 3in. (wind assisted 22ft. 5in.), 4,791 (new tables). She was born at Huckeswagen on Feb. 14th, 1947.

## RUDOLPH, W. G. (USA)

At four years of age her left leg was paralysed after a severe illness; not until she was seven was she able to walk normally. Yet at 16 Wilma Rudolph won a bronze medal as a member of the United States sprint relay team at the Melbourne Olympics and four years later she developed into the fastest female runner up till that time.

Her speed, grace and three gold medals combined to make her the outstanding personality of the 1960 Olympic Games. She had come to Rome as world record holder for 200 m. (22.9 sec.) but something of an unknown quantity though by no means a novice. She won both individual sprints with some three yards to spare, her time for the 100 m. (with the following wind just over the permissible limit) being a phenomenal 11.0 sec.

The following year she gained sole possession of the 100 m. world record with a time of 11.2 sec. The tall, slim (5 ft. 11 in., 130 lb.) American did not run the furlong after 1960 and she announced her retirement in 1964. Her best marks were 10.6 sec. for 100yd., 11.2 sec. for 100m. and 22.9 sec. for 200m. She was born at Clarksville, Tennessee, on June 23rd, 1940.

## RYAN, P. (Australia)

Although the ultimate prize of an Olympic gold medal eluded her on three occasions, Pam Ryan (née Kilborn) won just about every other honour in the sport, and few athletes can rival her consistency over such a long period. The 5 ft. 2 in. Australian was a world-class hurdler from 1960 to 1972, and in the latter season she equalled the world record of 12.5 sec. for the 100 m. barrier event. Earlier world records came her way in 1964, 1965, 1969 and 1971 in the 80 m. hurdles, 200 m. hurdles (she holds the current mark of 25.7 sec.) and 4 x 220 yd. relay.

Ever a tenacious competitor, she won the 80 m. hurdles and long jump at the 1962 Commonwealth Games, gained the bronze medal at the 1964 Olympics (sharing Karin Balzer's winning time), won another two golds apiece at the Commonwealth Games of 1966 and 1970 (hurdles and sprint relay) and, running with a shoulder injury, took the silver in the 1968 Olympic 80 m. hurdles. She placed 4th in the 1972 Olympic 100 m. hurdles.

Her best marks include 10.6 sec. for 100 yd. (10.4 sec. wind assisted), 11.4 sec. for 100 m. (windy 11.2 sec.), 23.6 sec. for 200 m., 10.4 sec. for 80 m. hurdles (windy 10.3 sec.), 12.5 sec. for 100 m. hurdles, 25.7 sec. for 200 m. hurdles, 20 ft. 5¾ in. long jump and 4,672 pts. pentathlon (old tables). Annual hurdling progress: 1960—10.9, 1961—10.6, 1962—10.6, 1963—10.6, 1964—10.5, 1965—10.4, 1966—10.4, 1967—10.4, 1968—10.4/13.4; 1969—13.3, 25.8; 1970—13.1, 26.2; 1971—13.4, 25.7; 1972—12.5, 26.4. She was born on Aug. 12th, 1939.

## RYUN, J. R. (USA)

Who could have guessed when Peter Snell broke Herb Elliott's world mile record in Jan. 1962 that a then 14-year-old American who had never run a mile in his life would, 4½ years later, be timed at 3 min. 51.3 sec. The rise to fame of Jim Ryun was indeed bewilderingly swift.

His very first mile race, on Sept. 7th, 1962, occupied as long as 5 min. 38 sec., but shortly before his 16th birthday he returned a highly promising 4 min. 26.4 sec. Here is how he has cut down his mile time since then (with age in years and months in brackets):—

| | | |
|---|---|---|
| 4:16.2 | May 3rd, 1963 | (16.0) |
| 4:08.2 | May 25th, 1963 | (16.0) |
| 4:07.8 | June 8th, 1963 | (16.1) |
| 4:06.4 | May 16th, 1964 | (17.0) |
| 4:01.7 | May 23rd, 1964 | (17.0) |
| 3:59.0 | June 5th, 1964 | (17.1) |
| 3:58.3 | May 15th, 1965 | (18.0) |
| 3:58.1 | May 29th, 1965 | (18.1) |
| 3:56.8 | June 4th, 1965 | (18.1) |
| 3:55.3 | June 27th, 1965 | (18.1) |
| 3:53.7 | June 4th, 1966 | (19.1) |
| 3:51.3 | July 17th, 1966 | (19.2) |
| 3:51.1 | June 23rd, 1967 | (20.1) |

In addition to these astonishing figures, Ryun can claim the world records of 1 min. 44.9 sec. for 880 yd. and 3 min. 33.1 sec. for 1500 m. He was unlucky, though, in his three Olympic appearances. In 1964, at 17 the youngest member of the USA team, he was hampered by a heavy cold and failed to reach the Final; in 1968 he ran brilliantly to clock 3 min. 37.8 sec. at high altitude but found Kip Keino 20 m. ahead, and in 1972 he tripped over in his heat. He turned professional shortly afterwards.

His best marks are 21.6 sec. for 220 yd. relay leg, 47.0 sec for 440 yd. relay leg, 1 min. 44.9 sec. for 880 yd., 3 min. 33.1 sec. for 1500 m., 3 min. 51.1 sec. for the mile, 8 min. 25.2 sec. for 2 mi. and 13 min. 38.2 secs. for 5000 m.

Annual progress at 880 yd. and mile: 1962—2:00.5, 5:38.0; 1963—1:53.6, 4:07.8; 1964—1:50.3, 3:59.0; 1965—1:47.7 (relay leg), 3:55.3; 1966—1:44.9, 3:51.3; 1967—1:47.2, 3:51.1 (and 3:33.1 1500 m.); 1968—1:47.9, 3:55.9; 1969—1:48.7, 3:55.9; 1971—3:54.8; 1972—1:45.2 (800 m.), 3:52.8, He was born at Wichita, Kansas, on Apr. 29th, 1947.

## SANEYEV, V. (USSR)

A knee injury caused Viktor Saneyev to switch from his first love, the high jump, but success in other fields came quickly. He placed second in both long and triple jumps at the 1964 European Junior Games.

After reaching 25 ft. 11 in. and 54 ft. 8¼ in. in 1967 he decided to concentrate on the triple jump for the following year's Olympics. It was a wise choice. No one would have beaten Bob Beamon at those Games, but in the greatest and most thrilling triple jump competition of all time Saneyev emerged the champion with his final effort of 57 ft. 0¾ in.—a massive improvement on the pre-Games world record of 55 ft. 10½ in. by Poland's Jozef Szmidt.

He scored another brilliant victory at the 1969 European Championships (56 ft. 10¾ in.) and though he lost this title in 1971 to his keenest rival, Jorg Drehmel (E. Germany), he was again in exceptional form for the Olympics —his opening leap of 56 ft. 11¼ in. proved 1¾ in. too much for Drehmel. Later in 1972 Saneyev regained the world record he had lost the previous year to Pedro Perez (Cuba) by registering 57 ft. 2¾ in. in his Georgian birthplace.

His other best marks include 10.5 sec. for 100 m., 6 ft. 2¾ in. high jump (at 17) and 25 ft. 11 in. long jump. Annual progress: 1963—48ft. 10in., 1964—51ft. 9¼in., 1965—51ft. 10in., 1967—54ft. 8¼in., 1968—57ft. 0¾in., 1969—56ft. 3¼in., 1970—56ft. 10¾in., 1971—56ft. 8¾in., 1972—57ft. 2¾in. He was born at Sukhumi on Oct. 3rd, 1945.

## SCHMIDT, W. (West Germany)

Such are the vicissitudes of top-level athletics that Walter Schmidt, who in 1971 became the first man to throw the hammer over 250 feet, could not even qualify for the West German Olympic team the following season. In any case, Schmidt's world record of 250 ft. 8 in. (he warmed up with a measured throw of 254 ft. 10 in.) came out of the blue. His previous best was 240 ft. 11 in. and in the European Championships three weeks before the record he had thrown only 231 ft. 5 in. for 5th place.

His annual progression: 1966— 185ft. 11in. (13 lb), 1967—213ft. 3in., 1968—222ft. 0in., 1969—226ft. 8in., 1970—239ft. 3in., 1971—250ft. 8in., 1972—240ft. 9in. He was born at Lahr on Aug. 7th, 1948, and at 6 ft. 3½ in. and 280 lb. is the largest of the top-class hammer throwers.

## SEAGREN, R. L. (USA)

Bob Seagren's pole vaulting career began when he was 11 and he and elder brother Art (later a 15 ft. 4 in. performer) would leap on to garage roofs using makeshift bamboo poles. Five years later, in 1963, he levered himself over 14 ft. for the first time and in successive seasons he topped 15, 16 and 17 ft. It was in the latter year, 1966, that he set his first world record of 17 ft. 5½ in.; it lasted two months.

In 1967 he regained the record from John Pennel with 17 ft. 7 in., only to lose it within a fortnight to Paul Wilson. He became world record-holder for the third time in 1968, vaulting 17 ft. 9 in. a month before he won the Olympic gold medal at half an inch lower.

He looked the man most likely to top 18 ft., but the honour went first to Greece's Chris Papanicolaou in 1970. Seagren joined the "club" in 1972, making up for the delay by re-capturing the world record and ending up with a breath-taking 18 ft. 5¾ in. clearance. Deprived by a last-minute IAAF ruling of using a pole with which he was familiar, he was naturally unable to show his best form in Munich and took second place with

17 ft. 8¼ in. He later signed up for a new professional group.

With little preparation, Seagren ran 52.3 sec. for 440 yd. hurdles. His annual vaulting progress: 1959—8ft. 0in., 1960—8ft. 6in., 1961—9ft. 6in., 1962—12ft. 4in., 1963—14ft. 4in., 1964 —15ft. 0¼in., 1965—16ft. 4in., 1966—17ft. 5¼in., 1967—17ft. 7in., 1968—17ft. 9in., 1969—17ft. 8¾in., 1970—17ft. 2in., 1971—17ft. 5¼in. (indoors), 1972—18ft. 5¾in. He was born at Pomona, California, on Oct. 17th, 1946.

## SHORTER, F. (USA)

It was one of the minor irritations of a tragic Olympics that Frank Shorter did not receive the public acclaim he so richly deserved when winning the marathon at Munich. A practical joker who entered the stadium posing as the winner so thoroughly confused the crowd that Shorter, himself a native of Munich (of American parents), was accorded at best a mixed reception.

He utterly dominated the race. moving away after about 7 miles and extending his lead to over two minutes by the finish, which he reached in a personal best time of 2 hr. 12 min. 19.8 sec. Earlier in the Games he had set an American record of 27 min. 58.2 sec. in his 10,000 m. heat, improving to 27 min. 51.4 sec. for fifth place in the final.

Shorter's marathon career has been brief but brilliant. He was 2nd in the 1971 AAU championship behind Kenny Moore; won the Pan-American title (as well as the 10,000 m.) and ended 1971 with victory in the Japanese open marathon in 2 hr. 12 min. 50.4 sec. In 1972 he tied for first place with Moore at the US Olympic Trials, won the Olympic title and, in December, won again at Fukuoka (Japan), this time in 2 hr. 10 min. 30 sec. for third place on the world all-time list.

His best track marks include 7 min. 51.4 sec. for 3000 m., 8 min. 26.2 sec. for 2 mi. (indoors), 13 min. 02.4 sec. for 3 mi., 13 min. 35.0 sec. for 5000 m. and 27 min. 51.4 sec. for 10,000 m. Annual 10,000 m. progress: 1969— 29:16.4, 1970—28:22.8, 1971—27:24.4 (6 mi.), 1972—27:51.4. He was born in Munich on Oct. 31st, 1947.

## SHOT

A shot (or weight) is a ball made of solid iron, brass or any metal not softer than brass, or a shell of such metal filled with lead or other material. The men's shot weighs 16 lb. It is delivered from a circle of 7 feet diameter (the same as for the hammer.) A stop board, firmly fastened to the ground, is placed at the middle of the circumference in the front half of the circle. The shot must land within a sector of 45 degrees.

The shot must not be thrown; it is put from the shoulder with one hand only. The IAAF rule states: "At the time the competitor takes a stance in the ring to commence a put, the shot shall touch or be in close proximity to the chin and the hand shall not be dropped below this position during the action of putting. The shot must not be brought behind the line of the shoulders." A competitor is allowed to touch the inside of the stop board but it is a foul if he touches the top of the stop board or the ground outside.

Three names are especially prominent in the early history of the event. George Gray (Canada) took the record to 47 ft. 0 in. in 1893 and he was succeeded by the remarkable Irish athlete Dennis Horgan, who in 1904 improved to 48 ft. 10 in. from a seven foot square—the custom in Britain until 1908. Horgan is noted particularly for his string of 13 AAA titles between 1893 and 1912, a record number for one event. The third man was the 6 ft. 6 in. tall Ralph Rose (USA), who pushed the record beyond 50 feet (51 ft. 0 in. in 1909) and was Olympic champion in 1904 and 1908 and runner-up in 1912. He had the bad luck of tying for first in the 1904 discus, only to lose the gold medal in a throw-off with countryman Martin Sheridan.

Rose's record stood until 1928 and progress was slow until 1934, a season that drastically altered all previous concepts of shot-putting standards. The man responsible was the giant American, Jack Torrance. He began with 53 ft. 6in. in Apr. and finished with 57 ft. 1 in. in Aug. There the world record stayed until Charles Fonville (USA) reached 58 ft. 0¼ in.

163

in 1948.

Jim Fuchs (USA) ruled the roost for the next few seasons—he recorded 58 ft. 10 ¾ in. in 1950—but even his performances were made to look puny by comparison with those of his successor, Parry O'Brien (USA), the inventor of a technique that permitted distances far in excess of 60 feet. O'Brien, winner of two Olympic titles, improved the world record 16 times between 1953 (59 ft. 0¾ in.) and 1959 (63 ft. 4 in.), but he in turn has been superseded by his American colleagues Bill Nieder, the first to better 65 feet and 20 metres; Dallas Long (67ft. 10in.); and Randy Matson, the pioneer 70-footer.

Another factor that has led to a tremendous upsurge in standards in this and other throwing events has been the widespread use in recent years of anabolic steroids despite being forbidden by the IAAF.

Arthur Rowe, European champion in 1958, has been Britain's greatest ever shot artist. His 64 ft. 2 in. put in 1961 lasted as a UK record until 1972 when Geoff Capes reached 66 ft. 2¼ in.

See also KOMAR, W.; MATSON, J. R.; and O'BRIEN, W. P.

## Women

Women use a shot weighing 8 lb. 13 oz. Two nations, Germany and the Soviet Union, have dominated the event since its inception in 1927.

The four leading individuals have been Gisela Mauermeyer (Germany), the 1936 Olympic discus champion (there was no Olympic shot until 1948) whose 47 ft. 2¼ in. in 1934 stood unmolested for 11 years; Galina Zybina (USSR), the O'Brien of women's putting who set a dozen world records between 1952 (49 ft. 10 in.) and 1956 (54 ft. 11¼ in.) and was Olympic champion in 1952; Tamara Press (USSR), the first to reach such landmarks as 55 feet, 17 metres, 18 metres and 60 feet; and Nadyezhda Chizhova (USSR) whose eight world records range from 61 ft. 3 in. in 1968 to 69 ft. 0 in. when winning her 1972 Olympic title.

See also under CHIZHOVA, N. and PETERS, M. E.

## SHRUBB, A. (GB)

During his heyday in the early years of the century, Alf Shrubb held just about every British running record from 1¼ miles to one hour—many of them surviving over 30 years, the last for all of 49 years. Not only was he outstanding from a British point of view; he was certainly the greatest in the world in the years prior to the rise of Jean Bouin (France) and the line of " Flying Finns."

World records can be judged by their longevity. Shrubb's 10 mi. time of 50 min. 40.6 sec. lasted 24 years, his 9 min. 09.6 sec. 2 mi. stood 22 years, 14 min. 17.2 sec. 3 mi. for 18 years, 11 mi. 1,137 yd. hour run for nine years, 29 min. 59.4 sec. 6 mi. and 31 min. 02.4 sec. 10,000 m. for seven years. All these performances were established in 1904, but unfortunately he was deprived of certain Olympic victory because Britain did not send a team to St. Louis.

He began running in 1898 and won his first national titles at crosscountry, 4 mi. and 10 mi. in 1901. He won each of these championships four years running and also won the AAA mile and the International crosscountry titles in 1903 and 1904.

He was declared a professional in Oct. 1905 and enjoyed a varied career in the paid ranks, his contests including a 10 miles race against a horse! Later he became Oxford University's first professional coach (1920-1926) and he lived in Canada from 1928. At the age of 75 he was reinstated by the AAA. He was born at Slinfold, Sussex, on Dec. 12th, 1878, and died in Canada on Apr. 23rd, 1964.

## SILVESTER, L. J. (USA)

It has been Jay Silvester's misfortune to be a contemporary of Al Oerter's. No other discus thrower can point to so many very long throws over such a lengthy period, but whereas the great occasions, and especially the Olympics, always brought out the best in Oerter, the reverse has held true for Silvester. Three times he has been a strong contender for the Olympic title, and three times he has fallen short of expectations.

He finished 4th in 1964, throwing over 10 ft. below his then best; in 1968, having set a phenomenal world record of 224 ft. 5 in. only a few weeks before, he threw a mere 202 ft. 8 in. for 5th place; and in 1972—free at last from Oerter's presence—he was overtaken by Ludvik Danek (Czechoslovakia) in the final round, his own throw of 208 ft. 4 in. again being well below his best.

It is as a record breaker that Silvester will be remembered. In 1961 he became the first to exceed 60 metres (196 ft. 10 in.) and in 1968 he carried the record out to 224 ft. 5 in. He did even better in 1971, with 230 ft. 11 in., but the performance did not conform to all the requirements for a record. He has thrown the staggering distance of 242 ft. 5 in. in training!

His annual discus progress 1956—157ft. 10in., 1957—172ft. 4in., 1958—181ft. 8in., 1959—184ft. 0in., 1960—190ft. 11in., 1961—199ft. 2in., 1962—199ft. 7in., 1963—204ft. 7in., 1964—200ft. 9in., 1965—210ft. 6in., 1966—200ft. 9in., 1967—205ft. 4in., 1968—224ft. 5in., 1969—211ft. 2in., 1970—217ft. 5in., 1971—230ft. 11in., 1972—218ft. 4in. He has put the shot 65ft. 7¾in. He was born at Plymouth, Utah, on Aug. 27th, 1937.

## SMITH, T. C. (USA)

It was thought, when Henry Carr retired in 1964, that the world would have to wait many years for another furlong cum quarter-mile runner of his calibre. In fact, Tommie Smith almost immediately stepped into Carr's shoes and quickly bettered his records. During his great 1966 season he set four world records (200 m. and 220 yd. straight and turn), was timed to run a lap (43.8 sec. 400 m. relay leg) faster than any man ever, missed the 100 m. world record by only a tenth of a second and casually long jumped 25ft. 11in. (actually measured at 26ft. 10in. from point of take-off)!

He collected further world records in 1967 (44.5 400 m. and 44.8 440 yd.) and 1968 (19.8 200 m. when winning the Olympic title). He later turned professional.

His best performances are 9.3 sec. (and 9.2 sec. wind-assisted) for 100 yd., 10.1 sec. for 100 m., 19.5 sec. for 220 yd. straight, 19.8 sec. for 200 m. turn, 44.5 sec. for 400 m., 44.8 sec. for 440 yd. and 25ft. 11in. long jump. He was born at Acworth, Texas, on Jan. 12th, 1944.

## SNELL, P. G. (New Zealand)

Early in 1962 Peter Snell clipped a tenth of a second from Herb Elliott's mile world record of 3 min. 54.5 sec. and followed up one week later with an even more dazzling exploit—records at 800 m. (1 min. 44.3 sec.) and 880 yd. (1 min. 45.1 sec.). If he achieved nothing else these records would suffice to earn Snell immortality.

In fact, Snell can boast of an enviable competitive record. He lost several unimportant races but was undefeated in his five major championship outings: the 1960 Olympic 800 m., 1962 Commonwealth 880 yd. and mile, and 1964 Olympic 800 m. and 1500 m. His double in Tokyo was the first at those events since Albert Hill in 1920.

Snell travelled to Rome in 1960 as New Zealand half-mile record holder at 1 min. 49.2 sec. and an unknown quantity. At the Olympics he scored a sensational upset victory over Belgium's Roger Moens in 1 min. 46.3 sec. and shortly afterwards was timed in a scorching 1 min. 44.9 sec. (50.0 sec. first lap!) for an 880 yd. relay leg in London, the official world record standing then at 1 min. 46.8 sec. He retired in 1965.

His best marks were 47.9 sec. for 440 yd. (relay leg), 1 min. 44.3 sec. for 800 m., 1 min. 45.1 sec. for 880 yd., 2 min. 06.0 sec. for 1000 yd. (an indoor world's best), 2 min. 16.6 sec. for 1000 m., 3 min. 37.6 sec. for 1500 m., 3 min. 54.1 sec. for the mile, 5 min. 12.6 sec. for 2000 m., 2 hr. 41 min. 11 sec. for the marathon and 9 min. 38.8 sec. for 3000 m. steeplechase. He was born at Opunake on Dec. 17th, 1938.

## SPRINTS

The sprinting events are those races up to and including 440 yd., the three Olympic distances in this category being 100 m. (nearly 9½ yards over 100 yd.), 200 m. (almost four feet less than 220 yd.) and 400 m. (about 2½ yd. under 440 yd). World records are recognised for all six events, and in the case of 200 m. and 220 yd. separate records are listed for races on a straight track and around a complete turn. Only performances made on a track no longer than 440 yards can qualify as records for the furlong and quarter.

The start is a vital part of a sprint race, and there have been two major advances in this department in the last century.

Until 1888 amateur sprinters invariably used a standing start. They would lean forward with the front foot on the starting line, the other seven or eight inches behind. The crouch start was invented by Charles Sherrill (later General Sherrill, US Ambassador to Turkey), the American 100 yd. champion in 1887, and his coach Mike Murphy, and was used in competition for the first time by Sherrill in May 1888. It was introduced into England in 1890 by T. L. Nicholas, that year's AAA 440 yd. champion.

The second significant advance occurred in 1927 when starting blocks were invented by the American coach, George Bresnahan. In 1929 George Simpson (USA) ran 100 yd. in 9.4 sec. from blocks but the performance, though genuine in every respect, was rejected as a world record since blocks were then still against the rules. Tests have indicated that the advantage of blocks over holes amounts to about one thirtieth of a second—roughly a foot in terms of distance. They were not used in the Olympic Games until 1948.

## 100 Yards and 100 Metres

The first recorded instance of an "even time" (10.0 sec.) 100 yd. under regular conditions was by C. A. Absalom (GB) in 1868. Since then the record has been reduced, as distinct from equalled, on seven occasions: John Owen, 9.8 sec. in 1890; Arthur Duffey, 9.6 sec. in 1902; Charley Paddock, 9.5 sec. in 1926; George Simpson, 9.4 sec. in 1929; Mel Patton, 9.3 sec. in 1948; Frank Budd, 9.2 sec. in 1961; and Bob Hayes, 9.1 sec. in 1963. All these athletes are American.

Harald Andersson, later Arbin (Sweden) clocked 11.0 sec. for 100 m. in 1890. There have been seven subsequent record breakers: Luther Cary (USA), 10.8 sec. in 1891; Knut Lindberg (Sweden), 10.6 sec. in 1906; Richard Rau (Germany), 10.5 sec. in 1911; Charley Paddock (USA), 10.4 sec. and 10.2 sec. in 1921; Lloyd La Beach (Panama), 10.1 sec. in 1950; Armin Hary (W. Germany), 10.0 sec. in 1960; and Jim Hines (USA), 9.9 sec. in 1968.

Of the men named above only four won Olympic titles at 100 m.—Paddock in 1920, Hary in 1960, Hayes in 1964 and Hines in 1968, though Duffey was unfortunate to pull a tendon while leading in the 1900 final. Most Olympic finals have been won by a foot or less, the "easiest" victor being Hayes, who won in 1964 by at least two yards.

The highest speed ever attained by a sprinter may be 26.9 m.p.h. by Hayes during a 100 yd. race in 1964.

Britain's most auspicious short sprint success was Harold Abrahams' victory in the 1924 Olympic 100 m. Four years later Jack London won the silver medal.

## 200 Metres and 220 Yards

The straight furlong used to be a popular event, particularly in that cauldron of hot sprint times, the United States. Recently, this form of furlong racing has fallen into relative disuse in favour of races around a turn. The differential between the two events is calculated to be 0.4 sec.

James Carlton (Australia) was the first to break 21 sec. around a turn, although his timing of 20.6 sec. in 1932 is treated with reserve by some. Nineteen years elapsed before Andy Stanfield (USA) tied the record. Peter Radford (GB) broke new ground with 20.5 sec. in 1960 and there the record stood until Carr clocked 20.3 sec. in 1963, and 20.2 sec. in 1964. Tommie Smith (USA) set new records of 20.0 sec. (turn) and 19.5 sec. (straight) in 1966; and in 1968 both John Carlos (USA) and Smith bettered 20 sec. around a turn.

No Briton has won the 200 m. at

the Olympics but medals were obtained in each final between 1912 and 1928. On the world record plane, Radford had two predecessors in Charles Wood, who in 1887 became the first man to crack 22.0 sec., and Willie Applegarth, whose 21.2 sec. in 1914 survived until Carlton's feat in 1932.

## 400 Metres and 440 Yards

Apart from the intrusion of two Germans (Rudolf Harbig and Carl Kaufmann, both of whom posted world records for 400 m.) the history of one-lap running is bound up with the United States, Britain and tiny Jamaica.

Lon Myers (USA) was the first to duck under 50 sec. with 49.2 sec. for 440 yd. in 1879. The record was whittled down little by little until suddenly in 1932 Ben Eastman (USA) sliced a complete second off the previous best with 46.4 sec. Jamaican Herb McKenley (who in two Olympics finished second to a team-mate) ran 46.0 sec. flat in 1948 and Adolph Plummer (USA) broke threequarters of a minute for the first time with 44.9 sec. in 1963—thus duplicating the metric world record which had been set by Otis Davis (USA) and Kaufmann in their epic duel at the 1960 Olympics. Lee Evans (USA) became the first to break 44 sec. when winning the 1968 Olympic crown.

Britain has a grand record in this event. Wyndham Halswelle won the 1908 Olympic title in a walk-over after his two American rivals scratched in protest against one of their colleagues being disqualified in a heat. Fellow Scotsman Eric Liddell ran away with the 1924 gold medal, and silver medals were secured by Guy Butler in 1920 and Godfrey Brown in 1936. The European title has been won by a Briton five times in nine races from 1938 onwards.

See also ABRAHAMS, H. M.; BORZOV, V.; CARLOS, J.; DAVIS, G. A.; EVANS, L.; HAYES, R. L.; HINES, J. R.; JENKINS, D. A.; LIDDELL, E. H.; MATTHEWS, V.; MORROW, B. J.; MYERS, L. E.; OWENS, J. C.; PADDOCK, C. W.; QUARRIE, D.; and SMITH, T.

## Women

From 1948, when the 200 m. was added to the schedule, until 1960 the winner of the Olympic 100 m. always went on to score in the longer event also. Fanny Blankers-Koen (Netherlands) was the first to gain this sprint double and she was followed by Marjorie Jackson (Australia) in 1952, Betty Cuthbert (Australia) in 1956 and Wilma Rudolph (USA) in 1960. The sequence was broken in 1964 but in 1972 Renate Stecher (E. Germany) also achieved the double. In the 100 m. she succeeded Wyomia Tyus (USA), the only sprinter ever to retain an Olympic title. Miss Tyus was timed at 23.78 m.p.h. in 1965.

Britain has produced a string of accomplished sprinters over the years, the most successful being Dorothy Hyman with two Olympic medals, two Commonwealth Games gold medals, and a European title.

The first to break 53 sec and 52 sec. for 400 m. was the mysterious Sin Kim Dan of North Korea, whose unratified time of 51.2 sec. in 1964 was not bettered until Marilyn Neufville (Jamaica) ran 51.0 sec in 1970, a mark tied by Monika Zehrt (E. Germany) in 1972.

Among the greatest names in British quarter-miling history are Nellie Halstead, who held the 440 yd. world best for nearly quarter of a century; Ann Packer, the 1964 Olympic silver medallist and European record breaker at 400 m.; and Lillian Board, who was narrowly beaten for the 1968 Olympic title. Verona Bernard won the 1973 European indoor championship, equalling the world best of 53.0 sec.

See also under BLANKERS-KOEN, F. E.; BOARD, L. B.; CHI CHENG; CUTHBERT, B.; DE LA HUNTY, S. B.; HYMAN, D.; NEUFVILLE, M. F.; PACKER, A. E.; RUDOLPH, W. G.; STECHER, R.; SZEWINSKA, I.; TYUS, W.; WALASIEWICZ, S.; and ZEHRT, M.

## STECHER, R. (East Germany)

One of the strongest as well as fleetest of all the great women sprinters, the 5 ft. 7 in., 152 lb. Renate Stecher (née Meissner) has carried all before her since 1970.

Her international career actually began in 1966 when, only 16, she won a gold medal in the 4 x 100 m. relay at the European Junior Games. At the next Games, two years later, she gained silver medals in the 100, 200 and relay. A late addition to the team, she increased her medal tally with a gold in the relay and a silver in the 200 in the senior European Championships of 1969.

The first of several world records (11.0 sec. for 100 m.) came in 1970 and the following season she won both European titles with ease. Superbly consistent, she was predictably at her very best for the 1972 Olympics and there she won the 100 m. in 11.1 sec and the 200 m. in a world record equalling 22.4 sec. Only an inspired run by West Germany's Heide Rosendahl prevented her collecting a third gold medal in the 4 x 100 m. relay.

Her best marks include 11.0 sec for 100 m., 22.4 sec. for 200 m., 18 ft. 6½ in. long jump, 36 ft. 4¼ in. shot and 4,297 pts. pentathlon (old tables). (Her annual sprint progress: 1963— 12.9; 1964—12.7; 1965—12.2; 1966— 12.0, 24.6; 1967—11.8, 24.4; 1968— 11.6, 23.9; 1969—11.5, 23.2; 1970— 11.0, 22.7; 1971—11.0, 22.6; 1972— 11.0, 22.4. She was born at Suptitz on May 12th, 1950.

## STEEPLECHASE

The standard steeplechasing distance is 3000 m., which is approximately 239 yards less than 2 miles. The race comprises 28 hurdles and seven water jumps. All the obstacles are three feet in height. Unlike those used in conventional hurdle races, the steeplechase barriers are solid and weigh between 176½ and 220½ lb. The width of the top of the hurdle is five inches, which enables an athlete to step on and off if he chooses. The water jump is 12 feet in length and width, the water being 2 ft. 3½ in. deep immediately in front of the hurdle. The trough slopes to ground level at the further end.

The first steeplechase to be traced was held over open country near Oxford in 1850, the 2 miles course including 24 obstacles. The event was introduced into the Oxford University sports in 1860 for a few years and two races (2500 and 4000 m.) were held at the 1900 Olympics.

The distance was internationally standardised at 3000 m. in 1920— Percy Hodge (GB) winning the first Olympic title over that length course. An official's error at the 1932 Olympics resulted in the runners covering one lap (460 m.) too many! The winner, Volmari Iso-Hollo (Finland) successfully defended his title in 1936 and is regarded as the father of modern steeplechasing.

Nine minutes was beaten for the first time in 1944 by Erik Elmsater (Sweden). Nineteen years later Gaston Roelants (Belgium) broke 8½ minutes and the record is now close to 8 min. 20 sec. Because of variations in the placing and number of hurdles, official world records were not recognised until 1954. The event is now fully standardised, although the design of hurdles and water jumps varies from stadium to stadium and at some tracks the water jump is located inside the main track, outside at others.

Welshman John Disley, the 1952 Olympic bronze medallist, was the first Briton to break nine minutes. In 1956 Chris Brasher won Britain's first individual Olympic gold medal on the track since 1932 with a time of 8 min. 41.2 sec.—six seconds faster than he had ever run before. Maurice Herriott was 2nd in the 1964 Olympics.

See also under BEDFORD, D. C.; BRASHER, C. W.; JIPCHO, B.; KEINO, K. and ROELANTS, G.

## STRICKLAND, S. B. (Australia)

See DE LA HUNTY, S. B.

## SZEWINSKA, I. (Poland)

Even before her 21st birthday Irena Szewinska (née Kirszenstein) had established herself as one of the most distinguished of all women athletes. As an inexperienced 18-year-old at the Tokyo Olympics she captured silver medals in the long jump (with a national record of 21 ft. 7¼ in.) and 200 m. (in a European record of 23.1 sec.) and ran in Poland's winning and world record-breaking 4 x 100 m. relay team.

The following season, 1965, she really showed her paces with world record sprints of 11.1 sec for 100 m. and 22.7 sec for 200 m. Again, at the 1966 European Championships, she produced her best form at the opportune time by winning the 200 m. and long jump, finishing a close second in the 100 m. and helping Poland win the sprint relay.

Even better was to come: she won the Olympic 200 m. crown in 1968 with a world record 22.5 sec. and filled third place in the 100 m. Since the birth of her baby she has picked up two more bronze medals in the 200 m. at the 1971 European Championships and 1972 Olympics.

Her best marks include 10.5 sec. for 100 yd., 11.1 sec for 100 m. (and wind assisted 11.0 sec.), 22.5 sec. for 200 m., 14.0 sec. for 100 m. hurdles, 5 ft. 6 in. high jump, 21ft. 10¾ in. long jump and 4,705 pts. pentathlon (old tables). Her annual sprint progress: 1961—12.6, 27.9; 1962—11.9, 25.4; 1963—11.6, 24.2; 1964—11.5, 23.1; 1965—11.1, 22.7; 1966—11.2, 23.1; 1967—11.2, 22.7; 1968—11.2, 22.5; 1969—11.3, 23.0; 1971—11.2, 22.8; 1972—11.2, 22.7. She was born in Leningrad (USSR) on May 24th, 1946.

## SZMIDT, J. (Poland)

Jozef Szmidt is one of those enviable sportsmen who always seemed to be at their very best on the occasions that mattered most. In his prime he won four major triple jump titles: the European championship in 1958 and 1962 and the Olympic gold medal in 1960 and 1964.

He became the first man to exceed the classic distances of 55 ft. and 17 metres when he established a new world record of 55 ft. 10½ in. (17.03 m.) in 1960, despite an awkward landing—an outstanding performance for the era before all-weather runways which stood unbroken for eight years. In spite of a series of leg injuries he maintained a high standard for many years and in placing 7th at the 1968 Games he bettered his previous Olympic winning marks with 55 ft. 5 in. Aged 37 he was still in international class in 1972.

His other best marks are 10.4 sec. for 100 m. (equalling the personal best of his elder brother Edward) and long jumps of 25 ft. 8¾ in. and wind-assisted 26 ft. 1½ in. Annual triple jump progress: 1955—47 ft. 3 in.; 1956—49 ft. 6½ in.; 1957—51 ft. 2¾ in.; 1958—53 ft. 11 in.; 1959—53 ft. 5½ in.; 1960—55 ft. 10½ in.; 1961—53 ft. 9¾ in.; 1962—54 ft. 4½ in.; 1963—55 ft. 9 in.; 1964—55 ft. 3½ in.; 1965—54 ft. 11¼ in.; 1966—54 ft. 7¼ in.; 1967—55 ft. 3 in.; 1968—55 ft. 5 in.; 1969—52 ft. 11½ in.; 1970—54 ft. 7½ in.; 1971—53 ft. 2¾ in.; 1972—53 ft. 3¾ in. He was born at Michalkowice on March 28th, 1935.

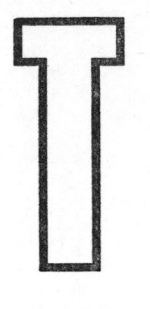

## TARMAK, J. (USSR)

Only a late change of heart by the Soviet team selectors enabled the 6 ft. 4 in. tall Juri Tarmak to seize his chance and win the 1972 Olympic high jump title. He had cleared 7 ft. 4¼ in. (and attempted a world record 7 ft. 6½ in.) in the qualifying round of the Soviet Championships only to finish fifth in the final at 7 ft. 1¾ in. In Munich his powerful straddle carried him over 7 ft. 3¾ in. His only previous international championship medals were a silver from the 1971 European Indoor and a bronze from the 1972 meeting. A prolific competitor he has jumped 2 metres (6 ft. 6¾ in.) or higher in some 230 separate competitions during a seven-year period.

Annual progress: 1960—4 ft. 11 in.; 1961—5 ft. 5 in.; 1962—5 ft. 8¼ in.; 1963—5 ft. 8¾ in.; 1964—6 ft. 1¼ in.; 1965—6 ft. 6¾ in.; 1966—6 ft. 10¾ in.; 1967—6 ft. 11½ in.; 1968—6 ft. 10¼ in.; 1969—7 ft. 0¼ in.; 1970—7 ft. 1½ in.; 1971—7 ft. 3 in. (indoors); 1972—7 ft. 4¼ in. He has put the shot 44 ft. 3½ in. He was born at Tallinn (Estonia) on July 21st, 1946.

## THOMPSON, D. J. (GB)

Britain's hero at the Rome Olympic Games of 1960 was diminutive (5 ft. 6¼ in., 126 lb.) Don Thompson, winner of the 50,000 m. road walk in the Olympic record time of 4 hr. 25 min. 30 sec. This popular victory wiped out the memory of Thompson's greatest disappointment: dropping out three miles from the finish of the 1956 Olympic event.

He took up walking in 1951 by accident . . . literally. A strained Achilles tendon prevented his running,
so he trained as a walker instead, won his first race and continued. His first major success came in 1955 when he won the London to Brighton (52 mi.) race for the first of eight successive years. The next season he chalked up his first national 50,000 m. title (an event he was to win for the following six years). On the track he set UK records at 20 mi., 30 mi. and 50,000 m.

He has competed in three European Championships, finishing fifth in 1958, third in 1962 and ninth in 1966. Illness caused him to miss much of the 1963 season but he made a gallant comeback in 1964 to finish 10th in the Olympics

His best marks include 14 min. 48 sec. for 2 mi. (track), 53 min. 19 sec. for 7 mi. (track), 94 min. 45 sec. for 20,000 m. (road), 2 hr. 41 min. 43.8 sec. for 20 mi. (track), 4 hr. 08 min. 11.6 sec. for 30 miles (track), 4 hr. 12 min. 19 sec. for 50,000 m. (road), 4 hr. 17 min. 29.8 sec. for 50,000 m. (track) and 7 hr. 35 min. 12 sec. for London to Brighton. He was born at Hillingdon, Middlesex, on Jan. 20th, 1933.

## THORPE, J. (USA)

Although more than sixty years have passed and the great man himself is dead, the disqualification of Jim Thorpe for professionalism and the resulting forfeiture of his two hard earned Olympic titles is still a talking point in track and field circles. It is true that Thorpe did receive money playing baseball in 1909 and 1910 but he was not aware that this would debar him from amateur athletics.

It was not until Jan. 1913, several months after his Olympic victories in the pentathlon and decathlon, that the story of his baseball activities came to light. Thorpe was stripped of his medals and records along with his amateur status but the fact remains he was the outstanding all-round athlete of his generation, and for many years to follow.

His best marks included 10.0 sec. for 100 yd., 51.0 sec. for 440 yd., 4 min. 40.1 sec. for 1500 m., 15.0 sec. for 110 m. hurdles, 23.8 sec. for 220 yd. hurdles (straight), 6ft. 5in. high jump, 10ft. 8in. pole vault, 23ft. 6in. long jump, 47ft. 9in. shot, 125ft. 8in. discus, 163ft. 0in. javelin and 6,756 points decathlon (under 1964 scoring tables.)

Following his disqualification, Thorpe played professional baseball and football until he was 41 and was voted the greatest football player of the half-century. Of part American Indian ancestry, he was born in Oklahoma in 1888 and died in 1953.

## TIMEKEEPING

The IAAF lays down that there should be three official timekeepers and one or two alternate timekeepers for every event. Where two of the official watches agree, that time is the official time. If all three watches disagree, the middle time becomes the official time.

The time is taken from the flash of the starting pistol to the moment at which any part of the athlete's torso (which excludes the neck) reaches the edge of the finish line which is nearer to the start. Times are recorded to one-tenth of a second in races up to and including the mile; to one-fifth of of a second in longer events.

### Electrical Timekeeping

Electrical timekeeping is the official form of timing at the Olympics and other major championships.

As most electric apparatus times to 1/100 sec., the following conversion table is used for returning times to the nearest 1/10 sec.:

.95 sec. to .04 sec. to be returned as .0
.05 sec. to .14 sec. to be returned as .1
.15 sec. to .24 sec. to be returned as .2
etc.

Where timing is required to 1/5 sec. the following conversions are used:
.85 sec. to .04 sec. to be returned as .0
.05 sec. to .24 sec. to be returned as .2
.25 sec. to .44 sec. to be returned as .4
etc.

On average, electrically recorded times in the sprints tend to be about 0.15 sec. slower than hand timing.

## TOOMEY, M. D. (GB)
See RAND, M. D.

## TOOMEY, W. (USA)

Bill Toomey's ambition was to become the world's greatest quarter miler but, by 1963 sensing he was doomed to failure, he turned instead to the decathlon. It was a wise move for in 1966 he ran up a world's best score of 8,234 points (which was not ratified, however), in 1968 he won the Olympic title—including a sensational 45.6 sec. 400 m.—and the following year he set an official world record of 8,417 points. Between 1966 and 1969 he lost only 3 of his 22 completed decathlons. Illness and injury caused two of the defeats; it took a world record by Russ Hodge (USA) to beat him in the other—by just 11 points. He married Mary Rand in 1969 and, although long " retired ", scored 7,421 in 1972.

His best marks are 10.3 sec. for 100 m., 45.6 sec. for 400 m., 4 min. 12.7 sec. for 1500 m., 14.3 sec. for 110 m. hurdles, 51.7 sec. for 400 m. hurdles, 6 ft. 6¾ in. high jump, 14 ft. 0¼ in. pole vault, 25 ft. 10 in. long jump, 47 ft. 2¼ in. shot, 154 ft. 2 in. discus, 225 ft. 8 in. javelin and 8,417 decathlon. He was born in Philadelphia on Jan. 10th, 1939.

## TOWNS, F. G. (USA)

A few weeks after winning the 1936 Olympic 110 m. hurdles in Berlin, Forrest Towns brought off one of the most dramatic statistical *coups* in athletics history by slashing no less than four-tenths of a second from the world record with a time of 13.7 sec. This performance was viewed sceptically by many at the time but nowadays, in view of similarly inspired performances in later years, it is generally accepted as genuine.

Towns, who never clocked faster than 14.1 sec. before or since, held the world record for nearly a dozen years. His best time for 220 yd. hurdles (straight) was 23.2 sec. and for 100 yd. 9.9 sec. He was born at Fitzgerald, Georgia, on Feb. 6th, 1914.

# TRIPLE JUMP

Basically, the rules for the triple jump (formerly known as the hop, step and jump) are identical with those governing the long jump. Specific regulations are that in the hopping phase of the event the competitor must land upon the same foot from which he took off; in the step he lands on the other foot, from which the jump is performed. If the competitor while jumping touches the ground with the " sleeping" leg it is counted as a failure.

The early history of the event is somewhat confused, since more often than not the pioneers took two hops and a jump. James Connolly (USA) performed in this manner to win the first Olympic title in 1896.

Americans and Irishmen (who competed for Britain) had things much their own way until just before the First World War. Myer Prinstein (USA) gained Olympic honours in 1900 and 1904 and he was succeeded in 1908 by Ireland's Tim Ahearne, whose winning jump of 48 ft. 11¼ in. was a world record. His brother Dan Ahearn relieved him of the record two years later in becoming the first man to exceed 50 ft.

Keen competition seems to bring out the best in triple jumpers, for on no fewer than five other occasions the Olympic title has been won at a world record distance. Tony Winter (Australia) scored in 1924 with 50 ft. 11¼ in., Chuhei Nambu (Japan) in 1932 with 51 ft. 7 in., Naoto Tajima (Japan) in 1936 with 52 ft. 6 in., Adhemar da Silva (Brazil) in 1952 with 53 ft. 2½ in. and Viktor Saneyev (USSR) in 1968 with 57 ft. 0¾ in.

The first to surpass the twin landmarks of 55 ft. and 17 m. (55 ft. 9¼ in.) was Poland's Jozef Szmidt, who shortly before winning the 1960 Olympic crown leapt 55 ft. 10½ in. British triple jumpers have been rather quiet internationally. However, Ken Wilmshurst won at the 1954 Commonwealth Games and in 1964 Fred Alsop jumped 54 ft. for the 4th place at the 1964 Olympics.

See also under DA SILVA, A. F.; SANEYEV, V.; and SZMIDT, J.

# TYLER, D. J. B. (GB)

Dorothy Odam high jumped over 5 ft. for the first time in 1935; as Mrs. Tyler she was still clearing close to that height in 1966, aged 46! Her seemingly endless career is strewn with medals and records, but the supreme competitive honours narrowly eluded her.

At both the 1936 and 1948 Olympics she cleared the height of the winner only to take second place in accordance with the rules then in operation for deciding ties. Under later rules, both times Dorothy would have been declared champion. She competed in four Olympics in all, covering a span of 20 years, finishing equal seventh in 1952 and equal 12th in 1956. She placed second also in the 1950 European and 1954 Commonwealth Games competitions.

Her three major successes (not that the foregoing can be considered as failures!) were winning the Commonwealth title in 1938 and 1950 and setting a world record of 5 ft. 5¼ in. in 1939. Between 1936 and 1956 she won eight outdoor and four indoor WAAA high jump titles, and also took the long jump and pentathlon in 1951.

It was in that year, aged 31, that she changed her style from the outmoded scissors to the western roll. In 1957 she cleared her own physical height of 5 ft. 6 in., only one-eighth of an inch below her all-time best of nine years earlier.

Other best marks include 11.8 sec. for 80 m. hurdles, 18ft. 9½in. long jump, 111ft. 6in. javelin and 3,953 point pentathlon. She was born at Stockwell (London) on Mar. 14th, 1920.

# TYUS, W. (USA)

Wyomia Tyus showed promise for a 17-year-old on a European tour in 1963 and created a minor sensation when in Feb. 1964 she set an indoor 70 yd. best performance of 7.5 sec. Outdoors, however, she was overshadowed by Edith McGuire ... until she arrived in Tokyo for the Olympics. There she hacked three-tenths of a second off her best 100 m. time to equal Wilma Rudolph's world

172

record of 11.2 sec. in a heat and went on to win the final by a good two yards. The following season she tied the world records for 100 yd. (10.3 sec.) and 100 m. (11.1 sec.) and in 1968 she clocked a world record 11.0 sec. at the Olympics where she became the first sprinter to defend successfully. Her best 200 m. time was 23.0 sec. She is now Mrs. Simburg, and was born at Griffin, Georgia, on Aug. 29th, 1945.

# UNITED KINGDOM RECORDS

Listed below are the best performances on record as at June 3rd, 1973.

| | | | | |
|---|---|---|---|---|
| 100 yd. | | 9.4 | Peter Radford | May 28 1960 |
| 100 m. | | 10.1 | Brian Green | June 3 1972 |
| (unofficial) | | 10.1 | David Jenkins | May 20 1972 |
| 200 m. | | 20.3 | David Jenkins | Aug. 19 1972 |
| 220 yd. | | 20.5 | Peter Radford | May 28 1960 |
| 400 m. | | 45.3 | David Jenkins | June 27 1972 |
| 440 yd. | | 45.9 | Robbie Brightwell | July 14 1962 |
| 800 m. | | 1:46.1 | Colin Campbell | July 26 1972 |
| 880 yd. | | 1:47.2 | Chris Carter | June 3 1968 |
| 1000 m. | | 2:18.2 | John Boulter | Sept. 6 1969 |
| 1500 m. | | 3:38.2 | Peter Stewart | July 15 1972 |
| | | 3:38.2 | Brendan Foster | Sept. 9 1972 |
| Mile | | 3:55.3 | Peter Stewart | June 10 1972 |
| 2000 m. | | 5:03.2 | Dave Bedford | July 8 1972 |
| 3000 m. | | 7:46.2 | Dave Bedford | June 21 1972 |
| 2 mi. | | 8:22.0 | Ian Stewart | Aug. 22 1972 |
| 3 mi. | | 12:52.0 | Dave Bedford | July 14 1972 |
| 5000 m. | | 13:17.2 | Dave Bedford | July 14 1972 |
| 6 mi. | | 26:51.6 | Dave Bedford | July 10 1971 |
| 10,000 m. | | 27:47.0 | Dave Bedford | July 10 1971 |
| 10 mi. | | 46:44.0 | Ron Hill | Nov. 9 1968 |
| 20,000 m. | | 58:39.0 | Ron Hill | Nov. 9 1968 |
| 1 hour | 12 mi | 1268 yd. | Ron Hill | Nov. 9 1968 |
| 15 mi. | | 1:12:48.2 | Ron Hill | July 21 1965 |
| 25,000 m. | | 1:15:22.6 | Ron Hill | July 21 1965 |
| 30,000 m. | | 1:31:30.4 | Jim Alder | Sept. 5 1970 |
| Marathon | | | | |
| (unofficial) | | 2:09:28.0 | Ron Hill | July 23 1970 |
| 3000 m. steeplechase | | 8:26.4 | Andy Holden | Sept. 15 1972 |
| 110 m. hurdles | | 13.6 | David Hemery | July 5 1969 |
| | | 13.6 | David Hemery | Sept. 13 1970 |
| 200 m. hurdles | | 23.0 | Alan Pascoe | June 5 1969 |
| 400 m. hurdles | | 48.1 | David Hemery | Oct. 15 1968 |
| 440 yd. hurdles | | 50.2 | David Hemery | July 13 1968 |
| | | 50.2 | David Hemery | June 11 1972 |
| High jump | (2.08m.) | 6ft. 10in. | Gordon Miller | May 18 1964 |
| | (2.08m.) | 6ft. 9¾in. | Mike Campbell | Aug. 6 1971 |
| Pole Vault | | 17ft. 1in. | Mike Bull | July 15 1972 |
| Long jump | | 27ft. 0in. | Lynn Davies | June 30 1968 |
| Triple jump | | 54ft. 0in. | Fred Alsop | Oct. 16 1964 |
| Shot | | 66ft. 2½in. | Geoff Capes | July 26 1972 |
| Discus | | 203ft. 3in. | Bill Tancred | May 27 1973 |
| Hammer | | 228ft. 2in. | Barry Williams | June 2 1973 |
| Javelin | | 273ft. 9in. | Dave Travis | Aug 2 1970 |
| Decathlon | | 7,903 | Peter Gabbett | June 5/6 1971 |

| (unofficial) | 8,040 | Peter Gabbett | May 21/22 1972 |
| 4 x 100 m. | 39.3 | Olympic Team | Oct. 19 1968 |
| 4 x 400 m. | 3:00.5 | Olympic Team | Sept. 10 1972 |

## Walking Events

| | | | |
|---|---|---|---|
| 3000 m. | 11:51.2 | Paul Nihill | June 5 1971 |
| 2 mi. | 13:02.4 | Stan Vickers | July 16 1960 |
| 5 mi. | 34:21.2 | Ken Matthews | Sept. 28 1959 |
| 10,000 m. | 41:55.6 | Phil Embleton | April 14 1971 |
| 7 mi. | 48:22.2 | Ken Matthews | June 6 1964 |
| 1 hr. | 8 mi. 1151 yd. | Ken Matthews | June 6 1964 |
| 10 mi. | 1:09:40.6 | Ken Matthews | June 6 1964 |
| 20 km. | 1:28:45.8 | Ken Matthews | June 6 1964 |
| (road) | 1:24:50.0 | Paul Nihill | July 30 1972 |
| 2 hr. | 16 mi. 315 yd. | Ron Wallwork | July 31 1971 |
| 30 km. | 2:28:44.0 | Paul Nihill | April 9 1972 |
| 20 mi. | 2:40:42.6 | Paul Nihill | April 9 1972 |
| 30 mi. | 4:08:11.6 | Don Thompson | Oct. 14 1960 |
| 50 km. | 4:17:29.8 | Don Thompson | Oct. 14 1960 |
| (road) | 4:11:31.2 | Paul Nihill | Oct. 18 1964 |

## Women

| | | | |
|---|---|---|---|
| 100 yd. | 10.6 | Heather Young | July 22 1958 |
| | 10.6 | Dorothy Hyman | July 7 1962 |
| | 10.6 | Dorothy Hyman | July 4 1964 |
| | 10.6 | Mary Rand | July 4 1964 |
| | 10.6 | Daphne Arden | July 4 1964 |
| 100 m. | 11.3 | Dorothy Hyman | Oct. 2 1963 |
| | 11.3 | Dorothy Hyman | Oct. 3 1963 |
| | 11.3 | Val Peat | Oct. 14 1968 |
| | 11.3 | Anita Neil | May 3 1971 |
| 200 m. | 23.2 | Dorothy Hyman | Oct. 3 1963 |
| | 23.2 | Margaret Critchley | Aug. 2 1970 |
| 220 yd. | 23.6 | Daphne Arden | July 4 1964 |
| 400 m. | 52.1 | Lillian Board | Oct. 16 1968 |
| | 52.1 | Verona Bernard | May 31 1973 |
| 440 yd. | 54.1 | Deirdre Watkinson | Aug 8 1966 |
| 800 m. | 2:00.2 | Rosemary Stirling | Sept. 3 1972 |
| 880 yd. | 2:04.2 | Anne Smith | July 2 1966 |
| 1500 m. | 4:04.8 | Sheila Carey | Sept. 9 1972 |
| Mile | 4:37.0 | Anne Smith | June 3 1967 |
| 3000 m. | 9:05.8 | Joyce Smith | Sept. 18 1972 |
| 100 m. hurdles | 13.2 | Judy Vernon | July 26 1972 |
| 200 m. hurdles | 26.7 | Sharon Colyear | July 16 1971 |
| High jump | 6ft. 1½in. | Barbara Inkpen | Sept. 15 1972 |
| Long jump | 22ft. 2¼in | Mary Rand | Oct. 14 1964 |
| Shot | 53ft. 6¼in. | Mary Peters | June 1 1966 |
| Discus | 190ft. 4 in. | Rosemary Payne | June 3 1972 |
| Javelin | 182ft. 5in. | Susan Platt | June 15 1968 |
| Pentathlon | 4,801 | Mary Peters | Sept. 2/3 1972 |
| 4 x 100 m. | 43.7 | Olympic Team | Oct. 20 1968 |
| | 43.7 | Olympic Team | Sept. 10 1972 |
| 4 x 400 m. | 3:28.7 | Olympic Team | Sept. 10 1972 |

## USA CHAMPIONSHIPS

See AAU CHAMPIONSHIPS.

# VASALA, P. (Finland)

It was one of the great disappointments of the 1972 Olympics that the eagerly awaited clash between Jim Ryun and Kip Keino in the 1500 m. final did not materialise. It is debatable, though, if even Ryun would have been able to hold Pekka Vasala in the closing stages of that race as it was run. Keino, at full stretch, posed few problems for the Flying Finn who covered the final 400 m. in 53.6 sec., the last 800 m. in an extraordinary 1 min. 49.2 sec. His final time was a personal best of 3 min. 36.3 sec.

It was in an earlier race against Keino, in 1971, that Vasala made his name—winning in a Finnish record of 3 min. 38.6 sec.—but he disappointed in that year's European Championships by placing only ninth. He made a vast improvement in his speed in 1972, lowering his best 800 m. time from 1 min. 48.5 sec. to a European record of 1 min. 44.5 sec., only a fifth of a second outside the world record. That turn of speed, plus good stamina (7 min. 50.8 sec. 3000 m. and 13 min. 45.8 sec 5000 m.), a long, elegant stride and shrewd racing brain, all add up to a man capable of breaking Ryun's 1500 m. and mile records.

Annual progress at 800 and 1500 m.: 1967—1:51.4, 3:51.9; 1968—1:49.5, 3:41.8; 1969—3:41.9; 1970—1:49.1, 3:41.0; 1971—1:48.5, 3:38.6; 1972—1:44.5, 3:36.3. He was born at Riihimaeli on Apr. 17th, 1948.

# VETERANS

One of the fastest growing aspects of athletics in recent years has been competition for veterans, i.e. athletes aged 40 or over on the day of the competition. Britain, the USA and West Germany have been in the forefront of this trend, and well supported international meetings have been held with particular success in San Diego, London and Cologne. Special competitions for "lady veterans" (35 and over) have just begun in Britain.

Several past Olympic champions and world record-holders have returned to competition as "vets", as this list of world best performances by the 40-and-over brigade will show:—

100 m.: 10.7 sec. by Thane Baker (USA) (gold medallist Olympic 4 x 100 m. 1956) in 1972.

200 m.: 22.3 sec. by Dean Smith (USA) (gold medallist 4 x 100 m. 1952) in 1972; and George Rhoden (Jamaica) (Olympic 400 m. champion in 1952) in 1972.

400 m.: 50.8 sec. by Jim Dixon (GB) in 1973.

880 yd.: 1 min. 55.8 sec. by Frank McBride (USA) in 1971.

1500 m.: 3 min. 59.3 sec. by Terry Kilmartin (GB) in 1972.

5000 m.: 14 min. 10.0 sec. by Michel Bernard (France) in 1972.

10,000 m.: 29 min. 57.4 sec. by Alain Mimoun (France) (1956 Olympic marathon champion) in 1964.

Marathon: 2 hr. 14 min. 53.4 sec. by Jack Foster (New Zealand) in 1973.

3000 m. Steeplechase: 9 min. 36.2 sec. by Hal Higdon (USA) in 1972.

110 m. Hurdles: 14.4 sec. by Don Finlay (GB) (1936 Olympic silver medallist) in 1949.

400 m. Hurdles: 54.8 sec. by Jim Dixon (GB) in 1973.

High Jump: 6 ft. 8¾ in. by Egon Nilsson (Sweden) in 1966.

Pole Vault: 15 ft. 1 in. by Roger Ruth (Canada) in 1972.

Long Jump. 22 ft. 9½ in. by Dave Jackson (USA) in 1971

Triple Jump: 45 ft. 11½ in. by Axel Johnsson (Sweden) in 1966 and 1967.

Shot: 64 ft. 11¼ in. by Pierre Colnard (France) in 1971.

Discus: 183 ft. 5 in. by Adolfo Consolini (Italy) (1948 Olympic champion and ex-world record holder) in 1958.

Hammer: 224 ft. 1 in by Harold Connolly (USA) (1956 Olympic champion and ex-world record holder) in

1972.
Javelin: 238 ft. 0 in. by Jan Smiding (Sweden) in 1972.
Decathlon: 5,638 pts. by Phil Mulkey (USA) (unofficial ex-world record holder) in 1972.

## Women

100 m., 220 yd., 400 m., 100 m. Hurdles, 200 m. Hurdles, and Pentathlon; Maeve Kyle (Rep. of Ireland) with 12.0 sec. (1970), 25.1 sec. (1969), 55,3 sec. (1970), 15.1 sec. (1969), 29.0 sec. (1969), and 4,041 pts. old tables (1969).

800 m. and 1500 m.: 2 min. 06.5 sec. and 4 min. 36.0 sec. by Anne Mc-Kenzie (S. Africa) in 1967.

High Jump: 5 ft. 4 in. by Dorothy Tyler (GB) (silver medallist 1936 and 1948 Olympics) in 1961.

Long Jump: 18 ft. 5½ in. by Stella Walsh (Poland/USA) (Olympic 100 m. champion 1932) in 1957.

Shot: 60 ft. 1¼ in. (indoors) by Antonina Ivanova (USSR) in 1973.

Discus: 203 ft. 7 in. by Lia Manoliu (Rumania) (Olympic champion in 1968) in 1972.

Javelin: 167 ft. 2 in. by Dana Zatopkova (Czechoslovakia) (Olympic champion in 1952 and ex-world record holder) in 1963.

## VIREN, L. (Finland)

Between 1912 and 1936 there was a total of twelve Olympic 5000 m. or 10,000 m. races; ten of them were won by Finnish runners! Names like Hannes Kolehmainen, Paavo Nurmi and Ville Ritola are still revered in Finland and the country has long awaited an heir to this great tradition. Juha Vaatainen's double at the 1971 European Championships in Helsinki was hailed with emotion, but it was Lasse Viren in Munich in 1972 who brought Finnish distance running Olympic honours again after such a long interval. And what honours! Not only did he win both the 5000 m. and 10,000 m., but his time in the latter event of 27 min. 38.4 sec. broke Ron Clarke's world record . . . in spite of his having fallen over just before halfway! He covered the final 800 m. in an amazing 1 min. 56.6 sec., and produced another remarkable display in the 5000 m. (13 min. 26.4 sec.) in zipping through the last four laps in 3 min. 59.8 sec.

Viren, who was barely noticed in the 1971 European meet where he placed 7th in the 5000 m., claimed the world 2 mile record with 8 min. 14.0 sec. shortly before the 1972 Olympics and set a short-lived 5000 m. record of 13 min. 16.4 sec. in the late season. Faster than Ron Clarke at the two classic distances, and with a pair of Olympic titles to his credit already at the age of 23, Viren is adding further lustre to his proud nation's athletics heritage.

His annual progress at 5000 m. and 10,000 m.: 1967—14:59.4; 1968—15:07.8, 32:18.8; 1969—13:55.0; 1970—13:43.0, 29:15.8; 1971—13:29.8, 28:17.4; 1972—13:16.4, 27:38.4. He has also run 1500 m. in 3 min. 44.2 sec., and 3000 m. in 7 min. 43.2 sec. He was born at Myrskyla on July 22nd, 1949.

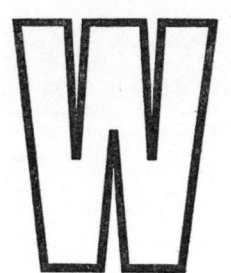

## WALASIEWICZ, S.
### (Poland/USA)

Known to the English speaking world as Stella Walsh (now Mrs. Olson), Stanislawa Walasiewicz was born in Poland on Apr. 11th, 1911 and taken to the United States at the age of two. She has spent all but 12 years of her life there and became an American citizen in 1947.

It was as a representative of Poland that she collected her numerous championship honours: Olympic 100 m. champion in 1932 and runner-up in 1936; European 100 and 200 m. champion and long jump silver medallist in 1938; 60, 100 and 200 m. winner at the 1930 Women's World Games: 60 m. victor and second in the 100 and 200 m. at the 1934 Games. She represented Poland for the last time at the 1946 European Championships.

At one time or another she held world records at 60 m., 100 yd. (unofficially), 100 m., 200 m. (her time of 23.6 sec. stood almost 17 years), 220 yd. and long jump (unofficially). She began serious competition in 1926 and was still an active participant at the age of 53! She has won over 40 American titles and in recent years long jumped 18 ft. 5½ in. in 1957, ran 440 yd. in 59.9 sec. in 1958 and 400 m. in 61.3 sec. in 1960.

Her best marks include 7.3 sec. for 60 m., 10.8 sec. for 100 yd., 11.6 sec. for 100 m., 23.6 sec. for 200 m., 24.3 sec. for 220 yd., 57.6 sec. for 400 m., 2 min. 18.4 sec. for 800 m., 3 min. 02.5 sec. for 1000 m., 12.2 sec. for 80 m. hurdles, 19ft. 9¾in. long jump, 127 ft. 7 in. discus and 127 ft. 9 in. javelin.

## WALKING

The IAAF defines walking as " progression by steps so taken that unbroken contact with the ground is maintained. At each step, the advancing foot of the walker must make contact with the ground before the rear foot leaves the ground. During the period of each step in which a foot is on the ground, the leg must be straightened (i.e. not bent at the knee) at least for one moment, and in particular, the supporting leg must be straight in the vertically upright position." The judges have the power to disqualify any competitor whose mode of progression they consider fails to comply with the definition of walking.

When an athlete is moving around the track at about 9 m.p.h. it can be difficult for the judges to decide whether he is " lifting " (having both feet off the ground for a split second). Several controversial decisions over the years led to the removal of track walking from the Olympic programme in 1928, 1932, 1936 and since 1952. The two international championship distances on the road are 20 kilometres (12 mi. 753 yd.) and 50 kilometres (31 mi. 122 yd.).

Britain has an enviable record at both these events, having supplied the winner of the 20 km. at the 1958, 1962 and 1969 European Championships and 1964 Olympic Games, and of the 50 km. in the 1932, 1936 and 1960 Olympic Games. Norman Read (New Zealand), the 1956 Olympic 50 km. champion, is English by birth.

The Race Walking Association (known as the Road Walking Association until 1954), which came into existence in 1907, is the governing body for road walking in England and Wales and their annual road races at 10 mi., 20 mi. 20 km. and 50 km. are recognised as English Championships. Winner:—

| 10 Miles | | min. sec. |
|---|---|---|
| 1947 | H. G. Churcher | 81 23.0 |
| 1948 | H. G. Churcher | 75 10.4 |
| 1949 | L. Allen | 75 09.0 |
| 1950 | L. Allen | 74 38.0 |
| 1951 | L. Allen | 75 41.0 |
| 1952 | R. Hardy | 73 16.0 |
| 1953 | R. Hardy | 74 53.4 |

| 1954 | R. Hardy | 74 16.0 |
|---|---|---|
| 1955 | R. Hardy | 74 47.0 |
| 1956 | R. Hardy | 74 31.0 |
| 1957 | S. F. Vickers | 76 51.0 |
| 1958 | S. F. Vickers | 73 44.0 |
| 1959* | K. J. Matthews | 71 00.4 |
| 1960 | K. J. Matthews | 70 57.0 |
| 1961 | K. J. Matthews | 74 21.0 |
| 1962 | K. J. Matthews | 76 10.0 |
| 1963 | K. J. Matthews | 73 00.0 |
| 1964 | K. J. Matthews | 70 22.0 |
| 1965 | V. P. Nihill | 74 55.0 |
| 1966 | P. McCullagh (Australia) | 74 05.0 |
| 1967 | R. Wallwork | 75 06.0 |
| 1968 | V. P. Nihill | 72 28.0 |
| 1969 | V. P. Nihill | 71 14.0 |
| 1970 | W. Wesch (W. Germany) | 72 07.0 |
| 1971 | P. B. Embleton | 69 29.0 |
| 1972 | V. P. Nihill | 73 33.0 |
| 1973 | J. A. Webb | 72 43.0 |

* course about 350 yd. short.

| *20 Miles* | | hr. min. sec. |
|---|---|---|
| 1908 | H. V. L. Ross | 2 56 32.0 |
| 1909 | S. C. A. Schofield | 2 56 48.4 |
| 1910 | H. V. L. Ross | 2 53 45.4 |
| 1911 | T. Payne | 2 50 30.0 |
| 1912 | H. V. L. Ross | 2 51 21.4 |
| 1913 | H. V. L. Ross | 2 49 53.4 |
| 1914 | H. V. L. Ross | 2 50 37.4 |
| 1920 | H. V. L. Ross | 2 57 59.6 |
| 1921 | W. Hehir | 2 58 56.4 |
| 1922 | W. Hehir | 2 50 12.0 |
| 1923 | F. Poynton | 2 51 35.0 |
| 1924 | F. Poynton | 2 57 17.5 |
| 1925 | F. Poynton | 2 48 17.4 |
| 1926 | No race | |
| 1927 | T. Lloyd Johnson | 2 55 53.0 |
| 1928 | L. Stewart | 2 50 20.6 |
| 1929 | A. E. Plumb | 2 50 18.0 |
| 1930 | A. E. Plumb | 2 46 30.4 |
| 1931 | T. Lloyd Johnson | 2 52 41.0 |
| 1932 | A. E. Plumb | 2 43 38.0 |
| 1933 | A. H. G. Pope | 2 48 38.0 |
| 1934 | T. Lloyd Johnson | 2 49 58.0 |
| 1935 | J. Medlicott | 2 47 46.0 |
| 1936 | H. A. Hake | 2 47 23.0 |
| 1937 | S. A. Fletcher | 2 47 54.0 |
| 1938 | J. Hopkins | 2 49 10.0 |
| 1939 | H. H. Whitlock | 2 51 03.0 |
| 1946 | H. J. Forbes | 2 50 43.0 |
| 1947 | H. J. Forbes | 2 47 40.0 |
| 1948 | G. B. R. Whitlock | 2 52 07.0 |
| 1949 | L. Allen | 2 51 18.0 |
| 1950 | L. Allen | 2 52 16.0 |
| 1951 | L. Allen | 2 51 52.0 |
| 1952 | J. W. Proctor | 2 52 07.0 |
| 1953 | R. F. Goodall | 2 50 40.0 |

| 1954 | L. Allen | 2 47 48.0 |
|---|---|---|
| 1955 | G. W. Coleman | 2 40 08.0 |
| 1956 | R. Hardy | 2 38 27.0 |
| 1957 | E. W. Hall | 2 45 12.0 |
| 1958 | L. Allen | 2 43 21.0 |
| 1959 | T. W. Misson | 2 45 19.0 |
| 1960 | S. F. Vickers | 2 41 41.0 |
| 1961 | D. J. Thompson | 2 44 49.0 |
| 1962 | K. J. Matthews | 2 38 39.0 |
| 1963 | V. P. Nihill | 2 39 43.0 |
| 1964 | V. P. Nihill | 2 40 13.0 |
| 1965 | V. P. Nihill | 2 44 03.0 |
| 1966 | N. R. Read (New Zealand) | 2 39 33.0 |
| 1967 | R. J. Lodge | 2 42 43.0 |
| 1968 | V. P. Nihill | 2 35 07.0 |
| 1969 | V. P. Nihill | 2 44 51.0 |
| 1970 | W. Wesch (W. Germany) | 2 38 15.0 |
| 1971 | V. P. Nihill | 2 30 35.0 |
| 1972 | J. Warhurst | 2 35 19.0 |

| *20 Kilometres* | | hr. min.sec. |
|---|---|---|
| 1965 | V. P. Nihill | 1 33 33.0 |
| 1966 | V. P. Nihill | 1 33 45.0 |
| 1967 | R. E. Wallwork | 1 37 21.0 |
| 1968 | V. P. Nihill | 1 31 19.0 |
| 1969 | V. P. Nihill | 1 30 07.0 |
| 1970 | W. Wesch (W. Germany) | 1 31 47.0 |
| 1971 | V. P. Nihill | 1 32 06.0 |
| 1972 | V. P. Nihill | 1 28 45.0 |
| 1973 | R. G. Mills | 1 31 13.0 |

| *50 Kilometres* | | hr. min.sec. |
|---|---|---|
| 1930 | T. W. Green | 4 35 36 |
| 1931 | T. Lloyd Johnson | 4 55 48 |
| 1932 | F. Pretti (Italy) | 4 41 54 |
| 1933 | H. H. Whitlock | 4 39 00 |
| 1934 | T. Lloyd Johnson | 4 36 30 |
| 1935 | H. H. Whitlock | 4 39 08 |
| 1936 | H. H. Whitlock | 4 30 38 |
| 1937 | H. H. Whitlock | 4 38 43 |
| 1938 | H. H. Whitlock | 4 43 01 |
| 1939 | H. H. Whitlock | 4 40 43 |
| 1946 | C. Megnin | 4 53 25 |
| 1947 | H. J. Forbes | 4 40 06 |
| 1948 | G. B. R. Whitlock | 4 35 35 |
| 1949 | T. Lloyd Johnson | 4 51 50 |
| 1950 | J. W. Proctor | 4 43 04 |
| 1951 | D. Tunbridge | 4 45 34 |
| 1952 | D. Tunbridge | 4 38 02 |
| 1953 | F. G. Bailey | 4 46 10 |
| 1954 | J. Ljunggren (Sweden) | 4 32 47 |
| 1955 | A. Johnson | 4 31 32 |
| 1956 | D. J. Thompson | 4 24 39 |
| 1957 | D. J. Thompson | 4 41 48 |
| 1958 | D. J. Thompson | 4 21 50 |
| 1959 | D. J. Thompson | 4 12 19 |

| | | | | |
|---|---|---|---|---|
| 1960 | D. J. Thompson | 4 | 32 | 55 |
| 1961 | D. J. Thompson | 4 | 22 | 51 |
| 1962 | D. J. Thompson | 4 | 27 | 26 |
| 1963 | R. C. Middleton | 4 16 | 43.2 | |
| 1964 | V. P. Nihill | 4 | 17 | 10 |
| 1965 | R. C. Middleton | 4 | 17 | 23 |
| 1966 | D. J. Thompson | 4 | 28 | 26 |
| 1967 | S. Lightman | 4 | 26 | 56 |
| 1968 | V. P. Nihill | 4 | 18 | 59 |
| 1969 | B. Eley | 4 | 19 | 13 |
| 1970 | R. W. Dobson | 4 | 20 | 22 |
| 1971 | V. P. Nihill | 4 | 15 | 05 |
| 1972 | J. Warhurst | 4 | 18 | 31 |

## Women

Winners of English women's road walking titles:—

| | |
|---|---|
| 1933 | J. Probbekk |
| 1934 | J. Howes |
| 1935 | J. Howes |
| 1936 | E. Littlefair |
| 1937 | D. Harris |
| 1938 | D. Harris |
| 1939 | F. Pengelly |
| 1946 | D. Hart |
| 1947 | J. M. Heath |
| 1948 | J. M. Heath |
| 1949 | J. M. Heath |
| 1950 | J. M. Heath |
| 1951 | L. Deas |
| 1952 | No race |
| 1953 | D. Williams |
| 1954 | D. Williams |
| 1955 | No race |
| 1956 | D. Williams |
| 1957 | J. Williams |
| 1958 | P. Myatt |
| 1959 | B. E. M. Randle |
| 1960 | S. Jennings |
| 1961 | S. Jennings |
| 1962 | J. Farr |
| 1963 | J. Farr |
| 1964 | J. Farr |
| 1965 | J. Farr |
| 1966 | S. Jennings |
| 1967 | B. A. Jenkins |
| 1968 | J. Farr |
| 1969 | B. A. Jenkins |
| 1970 | J. Farr |
| 1971 | B. A. Jenkins |
| 1972 | B. A. Jenkins |

See also FRENKEL, P.; GOLUBNICHIY, V.; KANNENBERG, B.; MATTHEWS, K. J.; NIHILL, V. P.; THOMPSON, D. J.

## WALSH, S. (Poland/USA)

See under WALASIEWICZ, S.

## WARMERDAM, C. A. (USA)

A fifteen-foot pole vault may be routine in this fibre-glass era but it was not until 1940 that Cornelius Warmerdam registered the first such leap. Utilising a bamboo pole, the American-born son of Dutch parents raised the world record several more times, finishing with 15 ft. 7¾ in. outdoors (1942) and 15ft. 8½ in. indoors (1943).

He cleared 15 ft. or over on 43 occasions before withdrawing from amateur competition in 1944. No other man up to that time had vaulted higher than 14 ft. 11 in. and it was only in 1951 that another athlete managed to scale 15 ft.

Warmerdam would almost certainly have won the Olympic gold medals of 1940 and 1944 had the world not been preoccupied with war. As it was, he had to settle for the American title every year from 1937 to 1944 except for 1939. In 1952 he made an exhibition vault of 14 ft. 4 in. and in Apr. 1957 (aged 41) cleared 13 ft. 0 in. using one of the then experimental fibre-glass poles.

Other best marks included 10.2 sec. for 100 yd., 25.5 sec. for 220 yd. hurdles, 5ft. 11in. high jump, 21ft. 6in. long jump, 40ft. shot, and 125ft. discus. He was born at Long Beach, California, on June 22nd, 1915.

## WEIGHT

See SHOT.

## WHITFIELD, M. G. (USA)

Mal Whitfield, one of the supreme racers of all-time, won the Olympic 800 m. twice—in 1948 and 1952—clocking 1 min. 49.2 sec. both times. He collected three other Olympic medals: gold in the 1948 4 x 400 m. relay, silver in the 1952 relay and bronze in the 1948 400 m.

A beautiful stylist, he was always more interested in simply winning than setting fast times, though he held world records at 880 yd. and 1000 m. His km. record of 2 min. 20.8 sec. in 1953 was followed just an hour later by an American 440 yd. standard of 46.2 sec.!

Between June 1948 and the end of 1954 he lost only three of his 69 races at 800 m. and 880 yd. He made an unsuccessful attempt at miling in 1955 and retired in 1956 after failing to qualify for the Olympic team.

His best marks: 10.7 sec. for 100 m., 45.9 sec. for 400 m., 46.2 sec. for 440 yd., 1 min. 17.3 sec. for 660 yd., 1 min. 47.9 sec. for 800 m., 1 min. 48.6 sec. for 880 yd., 2 min. 20.8 sec. for 1000 m., 3 min. 59.4 sec. for 1500 m. and 4 min. 12.6 sec. for the mile. He was born at Bay City, Texas, on Oct. 11th, 1924.

## WILLIAMS, R. (USA)

Randy Williams brought a touch of innocence to the Munich Olympics as he clutched his teddy bear mascot after winning the long jump title. Just turned 19, he was the youngest competitor in his event and at 5 ft. 9in. and 160 lb. one of the smallest.

A wind-assisted jump of 27 ft. 4½ in. prior to the Games underlined his undoubted ability but with so little experience of international competition there were reservations over his Olympic chances. These vanished when he jumped 27 ft. 4½ in., this time legally, in the qualifying round, and his opening shot in the final of 27 ft. 0½ in. was never equalled. None of his later leaps was better than 25 ft. 7½ in. but, having heard something go "pop" in his leg while warming up, he had to put everything into that first jump. He leapt a windy 27 ft. 9 in. in May 1973.

His annual progress: 1970—25 ft. 0 in., 1971—25 ft. 4½ in. (wind-assisted 26 ft. 3¾ in.), 1972—27 ft. 4½ in. He triple jumped 52 ft. 3½ in. at the age of 17. He was born at Fresno, California, on Aug. 23rd, 1953.

## WOLFERMANN, K. (West Germany)

The most thrilling javelin throwing duel of all time took place at the Munich Olympics, and the winner by a single inch was Klaus Wolfermann, who chose the occasion to unleash the longest throw of his career: 296 ft. 10 in. Defending champion and world record holder Janis Lusis (USSR) led until Wolfermann clicked with his great throw in the fifth round. Lusis, one of the supreme competitors, had one chance to retain his title; his throw was a beauty but it touched down at 296 ft. 9 in. and Wolfermann had become the first German to win this event since Gerhard Stock in 1936.

His previous championship record was unimpressive: a non-finalist at the 1968 Olympics and sixth at the 1971 European Championships. His annual progress: 1961—147 ft. 8 in.; 1962—157 ft. 6 in.; 1963—165 ft. 6 in.; 1964—221 ft. 11 in.; 1965—239 ft. 10 in.; 1966—257 ft. 6 in.; 1967—238 ft. 2 in.; 1968—269 ft. 7 in.; 1969—274 ft. 3 in.; 1970—283 ft. 8 in.; 1971—283 ft. 1 in.; 1972—296 ft. 10 in. He was born at Altdorf on Mar. 31st, 1946. He set a world record of 308 ft. 8 in. in May 1973.

## WOMEN'S AMATEUR ATHLETIC ASSOCIATION

The WAAA, which was founded in 1922, is the governing body for women's athletics in England and Wales. The Association promotes annual Championships.

The most titles gained in one event is ten by walker Judy Farr, including nine in succession, 1962–1970. Dorothy Tyler won the high jump eight times over a 20-year period, 1936–1956.

### Champions

| 60 Metres | | sec. |
|---|---|---|
| 1935 | A. Wade | 8.0 |
| 1936 | B. Lock | 7.6 |
| 1937 | B. Lock | 7.8 |
| 1938 | B. Lock | 7.6 |
| 1939 | B. Lock | 7.6 |
| 1946 | I. Stretton | 8.1 |
| 1947 | I. Royce* | 7.9 |
| 1948 | D. Batter | 9.1 |
| 1949 | D. Batter | 7.7 |
| 1950 | Q. Shivas | 7.8 |

\* née Stretton

| 100 Yards | | sec. |
|---|---|---|
| 1923 | M. Lines | 12.0 |
| 1924 | E. W. Edwards | 11.4 |
| 1925 | R. E. Thompson | 11.8 |
| 1926 | F. C. Haynes | 12.0 |
| 1927 | E. W. Edwards | 11.4 |
| 1928 | M. A. Gunn | 11.6 |
| 1929 | I. K. Walker | 11.4 |

| 1930 | E. M. Hiscock | 11.4 |
|------|---------------|------|
| 1931 | N. Halstead | 11.4 |
| 1932 | E. Johnson | 11.0 |
| 1952 | H. J. Armitage | 10.9 |
| 1953 | A. Pashley | 11.0 |
| 1954 | A. Pashley | 11.1 |
| 1955 | S. M. Francis | 10.8 |
| 1956 | J. F. Paul (1) | 10.6 |
| 1957 | H. J. Young (2) | 10.9 |
| 1958 | V. M. Weston | 10.6 |
| 1959 | D. Hyman | 10.8 |
| 1961 | J. Smart | 10.7 |
| 1962 | D. Hyman | 10.6 |
| 1963 | D. Hyman | 10.9 |
| 1964 | D. Arden | 10.6 |
| 1965 | I. Kirszenstein (Poland) | 10.6 |
| 1966 | D. Slater (3) | 10.5 |
| 1967 | J. Cornelissen (S. Africa) | 10.5 |

(1) *née* Foulds
(2) *née* Armitage.
(3) *née* Arden

*100 Metres*

| | | sec. |
|------|---------------|------|
| 1933 | E. M. Hiscock | 12.2 |
| 1934 | E. M. Hiscock | 12.2 |
| 1935 | E. M. Hiscock | 12.2 |
| 1936 | B. Burke (S. Africa) | 12.8 |
| 1937 | W. S. Jeffrey | 12.2 |
| 1938 | B. Lock | 12.2 |
| 1939 | B. Lock | 12.4 |
| 1945 | W. S. Jordan* | 12.8 |
| 1946 | M. A. J. Gardner | 12.6 |
| 1947 | W. S. Jordan* | 12.1 |
| 1948 | W. S. Jordan* | 12.6 |
| 1949 | S. Cheeseman | 12.1 |
| 1950 | J. F. Foulds | 12.6 |
| 1951 | J. F. Foulds | 12.3 |
| 1960 | D. Hyman | 11.7 |
| 1968 | V. Peat | 11.5 |
| 1969 | Chi Cheng (Taiwan) | 11.9 |
| 1970 | D. A. Neil | 11.6 |
| 1971 | S. Berto (Canada) | 11.4 |
| 1972 | D. P. Pascoe | 11.9 |

* *née* Jeffrey

*200 Metres*

| | | sec. |
|------|---------------|------|
| 1933 | E. M. Hiscock | 25.8 |
| 1934 | N. Halstead | 25.6 |
| 1935 | E. M. Hiscock | 25.3 |
| 1936 | B. Burke (S. Africa) | 25.2 |
| 1937 | L. Chalmers | 24.9 |
| 1938 | D. S. Saunders | 25.0 |
| 1939 | L. Chalmers | 25.6 |
| 1945 | W. S. Jordan | 26.7 |
| 1946 | S. Cheeseman | 25.7 |
| 1947 | S. Cheeseman | 25.0 |
| 1948 | S. Cheeseman | 25.7 |
| 1949 | S. Cheeseman | 25.4 |
| 1950 | D. G. Manley | 25.2 |
| 1951 | S. Cheeseman | 25.0 |

| 1968 | V. Peat | 23.6 |
|------|---------------|------|
| 1969 | D. Hyman | 23.7 |
| 1970 | M. A. Critchley | 23.8 |
| 1971 | S. Berto (Canada) | 23.5 |
| 1972 | D-M. L. Murray | 24.0 |

*220 Yards*

| | | sec. |
|------|---------------|------|
| 1922 | M. Lines | 26.8 |
| 1923 | E. W. Edwards | 27.0 |
| 1924 | E. W. Edwards | 26.2 |
| 1925 | V. Palmer | 26.8 |
| 1926 | V. Palmer | 26.8 |
| 1927 | E. W. Edwards | 25.8 |
| 1928 | K. Hitomi (Japan) | 26.2 |
| 1929 | W. Weldon | 26.4 |
| 1930 | N. Halstead | 25.2 |
| 1931 | N. Halstead | 25.5 |
| 1932 | N. Halstead | 25.6 |
| 1952 | S. Cheeseman | 25.0 |
| 1953 | A. E. Johnson | 25.0 |
| 1954 | A. E. Johnson | 25.1 |
| 1955 | J. E. Scrivens | 24.9 |
| 1956 | J. F. Paul | 23.8 |
| 1957 | H. J. Young | 24.2 |
| 1958 | H. J. Young | 24.5 |
| 1959 | D. Hyman | 24.5 |
| 1960 | D. Hyman | 24.0 |
| 1961 | J. Smart | 24.0 |
| 1962 | D. Hyman | 23.8 |
| 1963 | D. Hyman | 24.3 |
| 1964 | D. Arden | 23.6 |
| 1965 | J. M. Simpson | 23.9 |
| 1966 | J. M. Simpson | 24.1 |
| 1967 | J. Cornelissen (S. Africa) | 24.0 |

*400 Metres*

| | | sec. |
|------|---------------|------|
| 1933 | N. Halstead | 58.8 |
| 1934 | V. Branch | 60.0 |
| 1935 | O. M. Hall | 61.9 |
| 1936 | O. M. Hall | 58.6 |
| 1937 | N. Halstead | 60.1 |
| 1938 | O. M. Hall | 60.0 |
| 1939 | L. Chalmers | 59.5 |
| 1946 | M. Walker | 59.3 |
| 1947 | J. Upton | 61.6 |
| 1948 | V. M. Ball | 60.8 |
| 1949 | V. M. Ball | 59.4 |
| 1950 | V. M. Ball | 57.5 |
| 1951 | V. M. Ball | 58.2 |
| 1968 | H. van der Hoeven (Netherlands) | 53.6 |
| 1969 | J. B. Pawsey | 54.3 |
| 1970 | M. F. Neufville | 52.6 |
| 1971 | J. V. Roscoe | 53.9 |
| 1972 | V. M. Bernard | 53.2 |

*440 Yards*

| | | sec. |
|------|---------------|------|
| 1923 | M. Lines | 62.4 |
| 1924 | V. Palmer | 65.0 |
| 1925 | V. Palmer | 61.4 |

| | | |
|---|---|---|
| 1926 | V. Palmer | 61.8 |
| 1927 | D. Proctor | 62.4 |
| 1928 | F. C. Haynes | 60.8 |
| 1929 | M. King | 59.2 |
| 1930 | E. E. Wright | 59.8 |
| 1931 | N. Halstead | 58.8 |
| 1932 | N. Halstead | 56.8 |
| 1945 | W. S. Jordan | 61.8 |
| 1952 | V. M. Ball | 59.3 |
| 1953 | V. M. Winn* | 57.6 |
| 1954 | G. Goldsborough | 57.1 |
| 1955 | J. E. Ruff | 56.9 |
| 1956 | J. E. Ruff | 56.5 |
| 1957 | J. E. Ruff | 56.4 |
| 1958 | S. Pirie | 56.4 |
| 1959 | M. J. Pickerell | 55.9 |
| 1960 | P. Piercy | 57.2 |
| 1961 | M. E. E. Kyle (Ireland) | 56.3 |
| 1962 | J. Sorrell | 55.1 |
| 1963 | E. J. Grieveson | 55.9 |
| 1964 | A. E. Packer | 54.3 |
| 1965 | E. J. Grieveson | 55.1 |
| 1966 | H. Slaman (Netherlands) | 54.7 |
| 1967 | L. B. Board | 55.3 |

\* *née* Ball

| | | |
|---|---|---|
| 1932 | G. A. Lunn | 2 20.4 |
| 1945 | P. Richards | 2 26.7 |
| 1952 | M. Taylor | 2 17.5 |
| 1953 | I. E. A. Oliver | 2 15.0 |
| 1954 | D. S. Leather | 2 09.0 |
| 1955 | D. S. Leather | 2 09.7 |
| 1956 | P. E. M. Perkins | 2 13.2 |
| 1957 | D. S. Leather | 2 09.4 |
| 1958 | J. W. Jordan | 2 13.3 |
| 1959 | J. W. Jordan | 2 09.5 |
| 1960 | J. W. Jordan | 2 09.1 |
| 1961 | J. W. Jordan | 2 11.0 |
| 1962 | J. W. Jordan | 2 08.0 |
| 1963 | P. E. M. Perkins | 2 12.2 |
| 1964 | A. R. Smith | 2 08.0 |
| 1965 | A. R. Smith | 2 07.2 |
| 1966 | A. R. Smith | 2 04.2 |
| 1967 | A. R. Smith | 2 04.8 |

*1500 Metres* — min. sec.

| | | |
|---|---|---|
| 1968 | R. Lincoln | 4 25.3 |
| 1969 | M. Gommers (Netherlands) | 4 16.0 |
| 1970 | R. Ridley* | 4 15.4 |
| 1971 | R. Ridley* | 4 14.3 |
| 1972 | E. Tittel (W. Germany) | 4 17.2 |

(UK champion: J. Smith 4 17.6)

\* *née* Lincoln

*800 Metres* — min. sec.

| | | |
|---|---|---|
| 1933 | R. Christmas | 2 23.0 |
| 1934 | G. A. Lunn | 2 18.3 |
| 1935 | N. Halstead | 2 15.6 |
| 1936 | O. M. Hall | 2 20.2 |
| 1937 | G. A. Lunn | 2 18.5 |
| 1938 | N. Halstead | 2 20.4 |
| 1939 | O. M. Hall | 2 21.0 |
| 1946 | P. Richards | 2 21.0 |
| 1947 | N. Batson | 2 23.1 |
| 1948 | N. Batson | 2 20.3 |
| 1949 | H. Spears | 2 19.4 |
| 1950 | M. K. Hume | 2 20.5 |
| 1951 | N. Batson | 2 18.4 |
| 1968 | V. Nikolic (Yugoslavia) | 2 00.5 |
| 1969 | P. B. Lowe | 2 03.3 |
| 1970 | S. J. Carey | 2 03.6 |
| 1971 | A. Hoffman (Canada) | 2 04.8 |
| 1972 | M. Tracey (Ireland) | 2 03.0 |

(UK champion: P. B. Cropper* 2 03.7)

\* *née* Lowe

*Mile* — min. sec.

| | | |
|---|---|---|
| 1936 | G. A. Lunn | 5 23.0 |
| 1937 | G. A. Lunn | 5 17.0 |
| 1938 | D. Harris | 5 29.4 |
| 1939 | E. Forster | 5 15.3 |
| 1945 | P. M. Sandall | 5 40.2 |
| 1946 | B. E. Harris | 5 33.6 |
| 1947 | N. Batson | 5 37.6 |
| 1948 | N. Batson | 5 31.8 |
| 1949 | E. D. Garritt | 5 20.0 |
| 1950 | M. J. Heath | 5 25.8 |
| 1951 | H. Needham | 5 23.4 |
| 1952 | I. E. A. Oliver | 5 11.0 |
| 1953 | E. Harding | 5 09.8 |
| 1954 | P. E. M. Green | 5 09.6 |
| 1955 | P. E. M. Perkins* | 5 05.2 |
| 1956 | D. S. Leather | 5 01.0 |
| 1957 | D. S. Leather | 4 55.3 |
| 1958 | M. A. Bonnano | 5 02.6 |
| 1959 | J. S. Briggs | 5 02.2 |
| 1960 | R. Ashby | 4 54.2 |
| 1961 | R. Ashby | 5 01.8 |
| 1962 | J. Beretta (Australia) | 4 57.0 |
| 1963 | P. Davies | 5 10.8 |
| 1964 | A. Leggett | 4 56.0 |
| 1965 | J. Smith | 4 53.5 |
| 1966 | R. Lincoln | 4 47.9 |
| 1967 | R. Lincoln | 4 51.4 |

\* *née* Green

*880 Yards* — min. sec.

| | | |
|---|---|---|
| 1923 | E. F. Trickey | 2 40.2 |
| 1924 | E. F. Trickey | 2 24.0 |
| 1925 | E. F. Trickey | 2 26.6 |
| 1926 | E. F. Trickey | 2 28.0 |
| 1927 | E. F. Trickey | 2 32.4 |
| 1928 | J. Barber | 2 27.6 |
| 1929 | V. Streater | 2 25.8 |
| 1930 | G. A. Lunn | 2 18.2 |
| 1931 | G. A. Lunn | 2 22.4 |

*3000 Metres* — min. sec.

| | | |
|---|---|---|
| 1968 | C. Firth | 10 06.4 |

| 1969 | A. O'Brien (Ireland) | 9 47.6 |
|---|---|---|
| 1970 | A. O'Brien (Ireland) | 9 34.4 |
| 1971 | J. Smith | 9 23.4 |
| 1972 | A. Yeoman | 9 30.8 |

| 1970 | M. E. Peters | 14.0 |
|---|---|---|
| 1971 | V. Bufanu (Rumania) | 13.5 |
| 1972 | P. Ryan (Australia) | 13.4 |
| | (UK champion: J. A. Vernon 13.8) | |

### 80 Metres Hurdles

| | | sec. |
|---|---|---|
| 1929 | H. M. Hatt | 12.4 |
| 1930 | M. A. Cornell (1) | 12.4 |
| 1931 | E. E. Green | 12.0 |
| 1932 | E. E. Green | 12.2 |
| 1933 | E. E. Green | 12.0 |
| 1934 | E. E. Green | — |
| 1935 | E. E. Green | 12.3 |
| 1936 | B. Burke (S. Africa) | 11.9 |
| 1937 | B. Burke (S. Africa) | 12.1 |
| 1938 | K. Robertson | 12.2 |
| 1939 | K. Robertson | 12.4 |
| 1945 | L. Hancock | 13.6 |
| 1946 | B. Crowther | 12.8 |
| 1947 | M. A. J. Gardner | 11.5 |
| 1948 | M. A. J. Gardner | 12.0 |
| 1949 | J. C. Desforges | 11.9 |
| 1950 | M. A. J. Dyson (2) | 11.6 |
| 1951 | M. A. J. Dyson | 11.7 |
| 1952 | J. C. Desforges | 11.4 |
| 1953 | J. C. Desforges | 11.5 |
| 1954 | J. C. Desforges | 11.4 |
| 1955 | S. M. Francis | 11.3 |
| 1956 | P. G. Elliott | 11.1 |
| 1957 | T. E. Hopkins | 11.4 |
| 1958 | C. L. Quinton | 10.9 |
| 1959 | M. D. Bignal | 11.3 |
| 1960 | C. L. Quinton | 10.8 |
| 1961 | B. R. H. Moore (Australia) | 10.8 |
| 1962 | B. R. H. Moore (Australia) | 10.7 |
| 1963 | P. A. Nutting | 11.2 |
| 1964 | P. A. Pryce (3) | 10.7 |
| 1965 | P. A. Jones | 11.2 |
| 1966 | D. Straszynska (Poland) | 10.9 |
| 1967 | P. A. Jones | 11.0 |
| 1968 | P. A. Pryce | 10.9 |

(1) née Gunn.
(2) neé Gardner.
(3) neé Nutting.

### 100 Yards Hurdles

| | | sec. |
|---|---|---|
| 1927 | M. A. Gunn | 14.6 |
| 1928 | M. Clark (S. Africa) | 13.8 |

### 100 Metres Hurdles (2ft. 6in)

| | | sec. |
|---|---|---|
| 1963 | P. A. Nutting | 14.1 |
| 1964 | P. A. Pryce | 13.4 |
| 1965 | P. A. Jones | 13.8 |
| 1966 | M. D. Rand | 13.7 |

### 100 Metres Hurdles (2ft. 9in.)

| 1967 | P. A. Jones | 13.8 |
|---|---|---|
| 1968 | C. Perera | 13.5 |
| 1969 | Chi Cheng (Taiwan) | 13.5 |

### 120 Yards Hurdles

| | | sec. |
|---|---|---|
| 1922 | D. Wright | 20.4 |
| 1923 | M. Lines | 18.8 |
| 1924 | H. M. Hatt | 19.0 |
| 1925 | H. M. Hatt | 19.0 |
| 1926 | H. M. Hatt | 18.2 |

### 200 Metres Hurdles

| | | sec. |
|---|---|---|
| 1961 | P. A. Nutting | 28.3 |
| 1962 | P. A. Nutting | 28.9 |
| 1963 | P. A. Nutting | 28.9 |
| 1964 | P. A. Jones | 27.9 |
| 1965 | S. M. Mills | 28.0 |
| 1966 | P. A. Jones | 27.7 |
| 1967 | P. A. Jones | 27.3 |
| 1968 | C. Perera | 27.8 |
| 1969 | S. M. Hayward (1) | 28.5 |
| 1970 | C. Bell (2) | 27.4 |
| 1971 | S. Colyear | 26.7 |
| 1972 | P. Ryan (Australia ) | 26.8 |
| | (UK champion: J. S. Wood 29.9) | |

(1) née Mills
(2) née Perera

### High Jump

| | | ft. | in. |
|---|---|---|---|
| 1922 | S. Stone | 4 | 6¼ |
| 1923 | H. M. Hatt | 4 | 9 |
| 1924 | H. M. Hatt | 4 | 9¼ |
| 1925 | P. Green | 5 | 0 |
| 1926 | P. Green | 4 | 10 |
| 1927 | P. Green | 5 | 2¼ |
| 1928 | M. Clark (S. Africa) | 5 | 0 |
| 1929 | M. F. O'Kell | 4 | 10 |
| 1930 | C. Gisolf (Netherlands) | 5 | 2 |
| 1931 | M. F. O'Kell | 4 | 11 |
| 1932 | M. Milne | 5 | 1 |
| 1933 | M. Milne | 4 | 11 |
| 1934 | E. Bergman | 5 | 1 |
| 1935 | M. Milne | 5 | 1 |
| 1936 | D. J. B. Odam | 5 | 0½ |
| 1937 | D. J. B. Odam | 5 | 4¼ |
| 1938 | D. J. B. Odam | 5 | 2 |
| 1939 | D. J. B. Odam | 5 | 5 |
| 1945 | D. K. Gardner | 5 | 0 |
| 1946 | D. K. Gardner | 5 | 1 |
| 1947 | G. E. Young | 5 | 1 |
| 1948 | D. J. B. Tyler (1) | 5 | 4 |
| 1949 | D. J. B. Tyler | 5 | 3 |
| 1950 | S. Alexander | 5 | 4 |
| 1951 | S. Lerwill (2) | 5 | 7½ |
| 1952 | D. J. B. Tyler | 5 | 5 |
| 1953 | S. Lerwill | 5 | 5 |
| 1954 | S. Lerwill | 5 | 4 |
| 1955 | T. E. Hopkins | 5 | 5 |
| 1956 | D. J. B. Tyler | 5 | 3 |
| 1957 | T. E. Hopkins | 5 | 5 |

| | | | |
|---|---|---|---|
| 1958 | M. D. Bignal | 5 | 5 |
| 1959 | N. Zwier (Netherlands) | 5 | 5 |
| 1960 | D. A. Shirley | 5 | 6 |
| 1961 | D. A. Shirley | 5 | 7 |
| 1962 | I. Balas (Rumania) | 6 | 0 |
| 1963 | I. Balas (Rumania) | 5 | 7 |
| 1964 | F. M. Slaap | 5 | 8 |
| 1965 | F. M. Slaap | 5 | 7 |
| 1966 | D. A. Shirley | 5 | 7 |
| 1967 | L. Y. Knowles | 5 | 7 |
| 1968 | D. A. Shirley | 5 | 6 |
| 1969 | B. J. Inkpen | 5 | 7¾ |
| 1970 | D. A. Shirley | 5 | 6 |
| 1971 | D. Brill (Canada) | 6 | 0 |
| 1972 | R. Few | 5 | 8½ |

(1) *née* Odam
(2) *née* Alexander

| *Long Jump* | | ft. | in. |
|---|---|---|---|
| 1923 | M. Lines | 16 | 3½ |
| 1924 | M. Lines | 16 | 11 |
| 1925 | H. M. Hatt | 16 | 1 |
| 1926 | P. Green | 16 | 6 |
| 1927 | M. A. Gunn | 17 | 9 |
| 1928 | M. A. Gunn | 18 | 7¾ |
| 1929 | M. A. Cornell (1) | 18 | 11½ |
| 1930 | M. A. Cornell | 18 | 5¾ |
| 1931 | M. A. Cornell | 18 | 1 |
| 1932 | P. Bartholomew | 18 | 8¼ |
| 1933 | P. Bartholomew | 17 | 8½ |
| 1934 | P. Bartholomew | 18 | 2¾ |
| 1935 | E. M. Raby | 18 | 0½ |
| 1936 | E. M. Raby | 17 | 10½ |
| 1937 | E. M. Raby | 19 | 0½ |
| 1938 | E. M. Raby | 17 | 0 |
| 1939 | E. M. Raby | 18 | 6 |
| 1945 | K. Duffy | 15 | 7½ |
| 1946 | E. M. Raby | 16 | 7 |
| 1947 | K. Duffy | 17 | 3½ |
| 1948 | J. C. Shepherd | 18 | 8½ |
| 1949 | M. Erskine | 17 | 7½ |
| 1950 | M. Erskine | 17 | 10¾ |
| 1951 | D. J. B. Tyler | 18 | 3¾ |
| 1952 | S. Cawley | 18 | 5 |
| 1953 | J. C. Desforges | 18 | 10¼ |
| 1954 | J. C. Desforges | 19 | 1½ |
| 1955 | T. E. Hopkins | 18 | 11 |
| 1956 | S. H. Hoskin | 18 | 6½ |
| 1957 | C. M. Cops | 19 | 3¼ |
| 1958 | S. H. Hoskin | 19 | 6¾ |
| 1959 | M. D. Bignal | 19 | 9¾ |
| 1960 | A. E. Packer | 18 | 7½ |
| 1961 | M. D. Rand (2) | 19 | 6¼ |
| 1962 | J. Bijleveld (Netherlands) | 20 | 4½ |
| 1963 | M. D. Rand | 19 | 4¾ |
| 1964 | M. D. Rand | 21 | 7¼ |
| 1965 | M. D. Rand | 21 | 0 |
| 1966 | B. Berthelsen (Norway) | 20 | 8¼ |
| 1967 | B. Berthelsen (Norway) | 21 | 2¾ |

| | | | |
|---|---|---|---|
| 1968 | S. H. Sherwood | 21 | 0¾ |
| 1969 | S. H. Sherwood | 20 | 5¼ |
| 1970 | I. Mickler (W. Germany) | 21 | 4 |
| 1971 | S. H. Sherwood | 21 | 4¾ |
| 1972 | S. H. Sherwood | 20 | 10¾ |

(1) *née* Gunn
(2) *née* Bignal

| *Shot* (Two hands aggregate) | | | |
|---|---|---|---|
| 1923 | F. Birchenough | 53 | 0½ |
| 1924 | F. Birchenough | 53 | 8 |
| 1925 | M. Weston | 58 | 0¾ |
| 1926 | F. Birchenough | 54 | 5 |
| 1927 | F. Birchenough | 56 | 5½ |
| 1928 | M. Weston | 62 | 0 |
| 1929 | M. Weston | 62 | 5¾ |

| *Shot* | | ft. | in. |
|---|---|---|---|
| 1930 | E. Otway | 29 | 1¼ |
| 1931 | I. Phillips | 31 | 9¾ |
| 1932 | I. Phillips | 29 | 6½ |
| 1933 | G. de Kock (Netherlands) | 33 | 8 |
| 1934 | K. Tilley | 32 | 11¼ |
| 1935 | K. Tilley | 33 | 0¾ |
| 1936 | B. Steyl (S. Africa) | 35 | 3 |
| 1937 | K. Tilley | 34 | 9 |
| 1938 | B. A. Reid | 38 | 0¾ |
| 1939 | B. A. Reid | 37 | 5½ |
| 1945 | K. Dyer (1) | 30 | 9¾ |
| 1946 | K. Dyer | 33 | 5¼ |
| 1947 | B. A. Reid | 36 | 2¼ |
| 1948 | B. A. Reid | 40 | 5¾ |
| 1949 | B. A. Reid | 40 | 6 |
| 1950 | J. Linsell | 36 | 3¾ |
| 1951 | B. A. Shergold (2) | 38 | 8 |
| 1952 | J. Linsell | 39 | 8½ |
| 1953 | J. Linsell | 39 | 9 |
| 1954 | S. Allday | 41 | 1 |
| 1955 | J. Page | 39 | 0½ |
| 1956 | S. Allday | 43 | 11¼ |
| 1957 | J. Cook (3) | 41 | 4¼ |
| 1958 | S. Allday | 46 | 5 |
| 1959 | S. Allday | 43 | 3½ |
| 1960 | S. Allday | 46 | 11 |
| 1961 | S. Allday | 45 | 0¾ |
| 1962 | S. Allday | 45 | 6½ |
| 1963 | M. Klein (W. Germany) | 50 | 9½ |
| 1964 | M. E. Peters | 46 | 7¾ |
| 1965 | G. Schafer (W. Germany) | 48 | 7¼ |
| 1966 | B. R. Bedford | 47 | 7¾ |
| 1967 | B. R. Bedford | 49 | 9¾ |
| 1968 | M. Gummel (E. Germany) | 55 | 9 |
| 1969 | B. R. Bedford | 49 | 11¼ |
| 1970 | M. E. Peters | 48 | 8¾ |
| 1971 | J. E. Roberts (Australia) | 51 | 10½ |

| | | ft. | in. |
|---|---|---|---|
| 1972 | J. E. Roberts (Australia) | 50 | 4 |

(UK champion: B. R. Bedford: 48 3½)

(1) *née* Tilley
(2) *née* Reid
(3) *née* Page

*Discus*

| | | ft. | in. |
|---|---|---|---|
| 1923 | F. Birchenough | 78 | 10 |
| 1924 | F. Birchenough | 84 | 9 |
| 1925 | F. Birchenough | 89 | 2 |
| 1926 | F. Birchenough | 91 | 7 |
| 1927 | F. Birchenough | 93 | 8¾ |
| 1928 | F. Birchenough | 91 | 7½ |
| 1929 | M. Weston | 100 | 1 |
| 1930 | L. Fawcett | 96 | 1½ |
| 1931 | I. Phillips | 97 | 8½ |
| 1932 | A. Holland | 101 | 3 |
| 1933 | A. Holland | 108 | 11¾ |
| 1934 | I. Phillips | 101 | 8¼ |
| 1935 | A. Holland | 101 | 6 |
| 1936 | I. Phillips | 101 | 1 |
| 1937 | I. Phillips | 106 | 11¾ |
| 1938 | B. A. Reid | 116 | 2½ |
| 1939 | B. A. Reid | 111 | 0½ |
| 1945 | K. Dyer | 99 | 8 |
| 1946 | M. O. Lasbrey | 93 | 0½ |
| 1947 | M. Lucas | 119 | 5 |
| 1948 | B. A. Reid | 120 | 6 |
| 1949 | B. A. Reid | 121 | 3½ |
| 1950 | J. M. Smith | 108 | 4¾ |
| 1951 | B. A. Shergold (1) | 130 | 10¼ |
| 1952 | S. Farmer | 129 | 0½ |
| 1953 | S. Farmer | 131 | 3 |
| 1954 | M. Giri | 129 | 4 |
| 1955 | M. Giri | 136 | 9 |
| 1956 | S. Allday (2) | 154 | 3 |
| 1957 | S. J. Needham | 131 | 11½ |
| 1958 | S. Allday | 156 | 6 |
| 1959 | S. Allday | 148 | 4 |
| 1960 | S. Allday | 148 | 5½ |
| 1961 | S. Allday | 148 | 7 |
| 1962 | L. Boling (Netherlands) | 155 | 1 |
| 1963 | L. Manoliu (Rumania) | 162 | 1 |
| 1964 | K. Limberg (W. Germany) | 167 | 1 |
| 1965 | E. Ricci (Italy) | 165 | 10½ |
| 1966 | C. R. Payne | 163 | 8 |
| 1967 | C. R. Payne | 153 | 1 |
| 1968 | K. Illgen (E. Germany) | 187 | 9 |
| 1969 | L. Manoliu (Rumania) | 182 | 4 |
| 1970 | C. R. Payne | 172 | 6 |
| 1971 | L. Westermann (W. Germany) | 191 | 9 |
| 1972 | C. R. Payne | 176 | 5 |

(1) *née* Reid
(2) *née* Farmer

*Javelin* (Two hands aggregate)

| | | ft. | in. |
|---|---|---|---|
| 1923 | S. C. Elliott-Lynn | 117 | 4 |
| 1924 | S. C. Elliott-Lynn | 155 | 1½ |
| 1925 | I. Wilson | 156 | 7 |
| 1926 | L. Fawcett | 161 | 4 |
| 1927 | E. Willis | 135 | 7¾ |

*Javelin*

| | | ft. | in. |
|---|---|---|---|
| 1928 | K. Hitomi (Japan) | 118 | 0 |
| 1929 | M. Weston | 85 | 0 |
| 1930 | L. Rombout (Netherlands) | 106 | 5 |
| 1931 | L. Fawcett | 96 | 0 |
| 1932 | E. Halstead | 107 | 9¾ |
| 1933 | G. de Kock (Netherlands) | 118 | 5½ |
| 1934 | E. Halstead | 101 | 10½ |
| 1935 | R. Caro | 113 | 3 |
| 1936 | K. Connal | 118 | 1 |
| 1937 | G. A. Lunn | 108 | 2 |
| 1938 | K. Connal | 113 | 9½ |
| 1939 | K. Connal | 114 | 9 |
| 1945 | G. M. Clark | 104 | 1 |
| 1946 | M. O. Lasbrey | 113 | 0 |
| 1947 | M. Taiblova | 103 | 4 |
| 1948 | B. A. Reid | 102 | 0½ |
| 1949 | E. J. Allen | 103 | 9 |
| 1950 | D. Coates | 128 | 1¾ |
| 1951 | D. Coates | 124 | 9½ |
| 1952 | D. Coates | 148 | 7½ |
| 1953 | A. M. Collins | 119 | 11½ |
| 1954 | A. J. Dukes | 129 | 9 |
| 1955 | D. Coates | 137 | 1 |
| 1956 | D. Orphall | 133 | 11 |
| 1957 | A. M. Williams | 132 | 0 |
| 1958 | A. M. Williams | 142 | 8 |
| 1959 | S. Platt | 160 | 10½ |
| 1960 | S. Platt | 166 | 9½ |
| 1961 | S. Platt | 157 | 1 |
| 1962 | S. Platt | 166 | 5 |
| 1963 | A. Gerhards (W. Germany) | 165 | 0½ |
| 1964 | A. Gerhards (W. Germany) | 170 | 0 |
| 1965 | A. Koloska (W. Germany) | 174 | 5 |
| 1966 | S. Platt | 148 | 3 |
| 1967 | S. Platt | 161 | 3 |
| 1968 | S. Platt | 174 | 9 |
| 1969 | S. Platt | 161 | 10 |
| 1970 | A. Koloska (W. Germany) | 177 | 7 |
| 1971 | I. Fallo (Norway) | 156 | 5 |
| 1972 | P. E. French | 167 | 4 |

*Pentathlon*

| | | |
|---|---|---|
| 1949 | B. Crowther | 3901 |
| 1950 | B. Crowther | 3829 |
| 1951 | D. J. B. Tyler | 3953 |
| 1952 | S. Sewell | 3514 |

| 1953 | J. C. Desforges | 3997 |
| 1954 | J. C. Desforges | 3973 |
| 1955 | M. Rowley | 3943 |
| 1956 | M. Rowley | 3812 |
| 1957 | M. Rowley | 4183 |
| 1958 | J. P. Gaunt | 3887 |
| 1959 | M. D. Bignal | 4679 |
| 1960 | M. D. Bignal | 4568 |
| 1961 | C. A. Hamby | 3986 |
| 1962 | M. E. Peters | 4190 |
| 1963 | M. E. Peters | 4385 |
| 1964 | M. E. Peters | 4801 |
| 1965 | M. E. Peters | 4413 |
| 1966 | M. E. Peters | 4625 |
| 1967 | J. L. Oldall | 3965 |
| 1968 | M. E. Peters | 4723 |
| 1969 | M. L. Walls | 4591 |
| 1970 | M. E. Peters | 4841 |
| 1971 | J. L. Honour* | 4571 |
| 1972 | A. S. Wilson | †4292 |
| 1973 | M. E. Peters | †4429 |

\* *née* Oldall
†new tables

*880 Yards Walk* min. sec.

| 1923 | E. F. Trickey | 4 35.0 |
| 1924 | F. B. Faulkener | 4 20.0 |
| 1925 | F. B. Faulkener | 4 15.0 |
| 1926 | D. E. Crossley | 4 06.0 |
| 1927 | M. F. Heggarty | 3 54.2 |

*1600 Metres Walk* min. sec.

| 1933 | J. Probbekk | 7 51.2 |
| 1934 | J. Probbekk | 7 38.2 |
| 1935 | J. Howes | 7 57.8 |
| 1936 | J. Howes | 8 14.2 |
| 1937 | F. Pengelly | 8 36.5 |
| 1938 | E. Webb | 8 39.0 |
| 1939 | F. Pengelly | 8 19.9 |
| 1946 | D. Mann | 8 38.6 |
| 1947 | J. D. Riddington | 8 36.4 |
| 1948 | M. J. Heath | 8 17.8 |
| 1949 | M. J. Heath | 8 25.0 |
| 1950 | M. J. Heath | 8 17.0 |
| 1951 | M. J. Heath | 7 50.0 |

*Mile Walk* min. sec.

| 1928 | L. L. Howes | 8 27.4 |
| 1929 | L. L. Howes | 8 18.0 |
| 1930 | C. Mason | 8 14.4 |
| 1931 | C. Mason | 7 45.6 |
| 1932 | C. Mason | 7 47.8 |
| 1945 | J. D. Riddington | 8 42.8 |
| 1952 | B. E. M. Day | 7 58.2 |
| 1953 | B. E. M. Randle* | 7 48.2 |
| 1954 | B. E. M. Randle* | 7 38.4 |
| 1955 | B. E. M. Randle* | 7 59.4 |
| 1956 | D. Williams | 7 47.6 |
| 1957 | D. Williams | 8 08.4 |
| 1958 | B. A. Franklin | 8 09.4 |

\* *née* Day

*1½ Miles Walk* min. sec.

| 1959 | B. A. Franklin | 12 56.4 |
| 1960 | J. Farr | 12 31.2 |
| 1961 | S. Jennings | 12 18.4 |
| 1962 | J. Farr | 12 20.0 |
| 1963 | J. Farr | 12 26.4 |
| 1964 | J. Farr | 12 06.8 |
| 1965 | J. Farr | 12 14.2 |
| 1966 | J. Farr | 12 09.2 |
| 1967 | J. Farr | 12 09.2 |
| 1968 | J. Farr | 12 39.0 |

*2500 Metres Walk* min.sec.

| 1969 | J. Farr | 12 45.8 |
| 1970 | J. Farr | 12 34.0 |
| 1971 | B. J. Cook | 12 39.8 |
| 1972 | B. A. Jenkins* | 12 31.2 |

\* *née* Franklin

*Cross-Country*

| 1927 | A. M. A. Williams |
| 1928 | L. D. Styles |
| 1929 | L. D. Styles |
| 1930 | L. D. Styles |
| 1931 | G. A. Lunn |
| 1932 | G. A. Lunn |
| 1933 | L. D. Styles |
| 1934 | L. D. Styles |
| 1935 | N. Halstead |
| 1936 | N. Halstead |
| 1937 | L. D. Styles |
| 1938 | E. Forster |
| 1939 | E. Forster |
| 1946 | P. Sandall |
| 1947 | R. M. Wright |
| 1948 | I. Kibbler |
| 1949 | E. Johnson |
| 1950 | A. Gibson |
| 1951 | P. E. M. Green |
| 1952 | P. E. M. Green |
| 1953 | D. S. Leather |
| 1954 | D. S. Leather |
| 1955 | D. S. Leather |
| 1956 | D. S. Leather |
| 1957 | J. Bridgland |
| 1958 | R. Ashby |
| 1959 | J. Byatt |
| 1960 | J. Byatt |
| 1961 | R. Ashby |
| 1962 | R. Ashby |
| 1963 | M. C. Ibbotson |
| 1964 | M. C. Ibbotson |
| 1965 | P. Davies |
| 1966 | P. Davies |
| 1967 | P. Davies |
| 1968 | P. Davies |
| 1969 | R. Ridley |
| 1970 | R. Ridley |
| 1971 | R. Ridley |
| 1972 | R. Ridley |
| 1973 | J. Smith (née Byatt) |

# WOMEN'S ATHLETICS

Barred on pain of death from even watching the Olympic Games, the women of Ancient Greece held their own Heraea Games every four years —named after their reputed founder Hera, wife of Zeus. The events included foot races of about 165 yd.

Women took part in the sports meetings held at English fairs and wakes in the 18th and early 19th centuries but the "modern" history of women's athletics stretches back only about 70 years. The first governing body to come into existence was the French Women's Sports Federation in 1917. Two years later women's athletics began to be held on an organised basis in England.

The year of 1921 marked the beginning of international competition. Five nations were represented at the Monte Carlo Games, at which British athletes scored six wins in 11 events, and later in the year an unofficial British team met France in Paris and won six of the eight events.

An international governing body called the Fédération Sportive Féminine Internationale was formed in Paris on Oct. 31st, 1921. Britain, Czechoslovakia, France, Italy, Spain and the USA were the co-founders. The FSFI requested the International Olympic Committee to add women's athletics to the 1924 Olympic programme. The request was refused, and consequently the FSFI organised their own "Women's Olympic Games" in Paris in August 1922. Five nations sent teams, with Britain emerging the most successful.

Winners: — 60 m. M. Mejzlikova (Czechoslovakia) 7.6 sec.; 100 yd., N. E. Callebout (GB) 12.0 sec.; 300 m., M. Lines (GB) 44.8 sec.; 1000 m., L. Breard (France) 3 min. 12.0 sec.; 100 yd. hurdles, C. Sabie (USA) 14.4 sec.; High jump, H. Hatt (GB) and N. Voorhees (USA), 4ft. 9¼in.; Long jump, M. Lines (GB) 16ft. 7¼in.; Standing long jump. C. Sabie (USA) 8ft. 1¾in.; 8 lb. Shot (aggregate of both hands), L. Godbold (USA) 66ft. 4in.; 800 gr. Javelin (aggregate), F. Pianzola (Switzerland) 141ft. 10in.; 4 x 110 yd. relay, GB (Lines, Callebout, Leach, Porter) 51.8 sec.

The second "Women's Olympics" —now entitled the "Women's World Games" following protests by the IAAF and IOC—were held in Gothenburg in 1926. Britain again fared best of the ten participating nations.

Winners:—60 m., M. Radideau (France) 7.8 sec.; 100 yd., Radideau 11.8 sec.; 250 m., E. Edwards (GB) 33.4 sec.; 1000 m., E. Trickey (GB) 3 min. 08.8 sec.; 100 yd. hurdles, L. Sychrova (Czechoslovakia) 14.4 sec.; High jump, Bons (France) 4ft. 11 in.; Long jump, K. Hitomi (Japan) 18 ft. 0½ in.; Standing long jump, Hitomi 8 ft. 2 in.; Shot (aggregate), Vidiakova (Czechoslovakia) 64 ft. 1¼ in.; Discus H. Konopacka (Poland) 123ft. 8in.; Javelin (aggregate), A. L. Adelskold (Sweden) 161 ft. 3 in.; 1000 m. Walk, D. E. Crossley (GB) 5 min. 10 sec.; 4 x 100 m. relay, GB (D. E. Scouler, F. C. Haynes, E. Edwards, R. Thompson) 49.8 sec.

Five women's events were included in the 1928 Olympics but Britain was not one of the 21 competing nations.

For a list of all Olympic champions, see under OLYMPIC GAMES.

Meanwhile the FSFI, with British support, continued to promote their "Women's World Games." Winners in Prague in 1930:—60 m., S. Walasiewicz (Poland) 7.7 sec.; 100 m., Walasiewicz 12.5 sec.; 200 m. Walasiewicz 25.7 sec.; 800 m., G. Lunn (GB) 2 min. 21.9 sec.; 80 m. hurdles, M. Jacobson (Sweden) 12.4 sec.; High Jump, I. Braumuller (Germany) 5 ft. 1¼ in.; Long jump, K. Hitomi (Japan) 19 ft. 4¼ in.; Shot, G. Heublein (Germany) 40 ft. 11¾ in.; Discus, H. Konopacka (Poland), 120 ft. 9 in.; Javelin, L. Schumann (Germany), 138 ft. 10 in.; Triathlon (Javelin, high jump, 100 m.), Braumuller; 4 x 100 m. relay, Germany (Kellner, Karrer, Holger, L. Gelius), 49.9 sec.

Britain made her debut in Olympic competition in Los Angeles in 1932. Women's events were introduced into the Commonwealth Games in 1934 (see COMMONWEALTH GAMES for list of winners).

The fourth and final "Women's World Games" were held in London in 1934. Winners:—60 m., S. Walasiewicz (Poland) 7.6 sec.; 100 m., K. Krauss (Germany) 11.9 sec.; 200 m., Krauss 24.9 sec.; 800 m., Z. Koubkova (Czechoslovakia) 2 min. 12.8

188

sec.; 80 m. hurdles, R. Englehardt (Germany) 11.6 sec.; High jump, S. Grieme (Germany) 5 ft. 1 in.; Long jump, G. Koppner (Germany) 19 ft. 0¼ in.; Shot, G. Mauermeyer (Germany) 44 ft. 10¼ in.; Discus, J. Wajsowna (Poland) 143 ft. 8 in.; Javelin, G. Gelius (Germany) 139 ft. 2 in.; Pentathlon, Mauermeyer; 4 x 100 m. relay, Germany (M. Grieme, Krauss, M. Dollinger, I. Dorffeldt) 48.6 sec.

In 1936 the FSFI handed over full control of international women's athletics to the IAAF. Two years later the first European Championships were staged by the IAAF in Vienna (see EUROPEAN CHAMPIONSHIPS for list of all European champions.)

## WOODERSON, S. C. (GB)

No man looked less like the popular image of a world champion athlete than small (5 ft. 6 in., 125 lb.), bespectacled Sydney Wooderson. He was not even possessed of good health. Yet this was the man who won his way into the hearts of a whole nation with his world records and courageous racing at distances ranging from 440 yd. to 10 mi. cross-country. Not forgetting, of course, that the British love to see a good little one beat a good big one.

Wooderson never won an Olympic title or medal, for a cracked bone in his ankle put paid to his chances in Berlin, but he did win two European championships: the 1500 m. in 1938 and the 5000 m. in 1946.

This latter performance was probably the finest of a superlative career. At the age of 32 (less one week) he drew clean away from a notable field to win by 30 yd. in 14 min. 08.6 sec., the second fastest time on

record at that date. Placing fifth and sixth in the race were two rising stars of whom much more was to be heard, Emil Zatopek and Gaston Reiff.

When he was 18 Sydney ran a mile in 4 min. 29.8 sec. Today this would be regarded as rather slow but in 1933 this time was the fastest ever recorded by a schoolboy and it made his name. He never looked back. In 1934 he improved drastically to 4 min. 13.4 sec. and even managed to finish in front of Jack Lovelock in one race.

He set his first British record in 1936, a 4 min. 10.8 sec. mile—a time he cut to 4 min. 06.4 sec. in 1937 for a new world record. In 1938 he prepared for the European Championships by concentrating on the half-mile . . . to such good effect that he posted world records of 1 min. 48.4 sec. for 800 m. and 1 min. 49.2 sec. for 880 yd. and in an earlier race defeated the great Mario Lanzi, of Italy.

Wooderson raced Arne Andersson (Sweden) twice in 1945, losing both times but clocking his fastest mile of 4 min. 04.2 sec. on the second occasion after leading at 1500 m. in 3 min. 48.4 sec. The European 5000 m. victory marked the end of his track career but in 1948 he set the final seal on a remarkable athletic lifetime by winning the English cross-country title.

His best marks were 49.3 sec. for 440 yd., 1 min. 48.4 sec. for 800 m., 1 min. 49.2 sec. for 880 yd., 2 min. 59.5 sec. for ¾ mi., 3 min. 48.4 sec. for 1500 m., 4 min. 04.2 sec. for the mile, 9 min. 05.0 sec. for 2 mi., 13 min. 53.2 sec. for 3 mi. and 14 min. 08.6 sec. for 5000 m. He was born in London on Aug. 30th, 1914.

## WORLD RECORDS

Listed below are the world records as at June 1st 1973:

|        | min. sec. |                        |               |
|--------|-----------|------------------------|---------------|
| *100 yd.* | 9.1    | Bob Hayes (USA)        | June 21 1963  |
|        | 9.1       | Harry Jerome (Canada)  | July 15 1966  |
|        | 9.1       | Jim Hines (USA)        | May 13 1967   |
|        | 9.1       | Charlie Greene (USA)   | June 15 1967  |
|        | 9.1       | John Carlos (USA)      | May 10 1969   |
|        | *9.1      | Steve Williams (USA)   | May 12 1973   |
| *100 m.* | 9.9     | Jim Hines (USA)        | June 20 1968  |
|        | 9.9       | Ronnie Ray Smith (USA) | June 20 1968  |
|        | 9.9       | Charlie Greene (USA)   | June 20 1968  |
|        | 9.9       | Jim Hines (USA)        | Oct. 14 1968  |

189

| | | | | |
|---|---|---|---|---|
| | 9.9 | Eddie Hart (USA) | July 1 | 1972 |
| | 9.9 | Rey Robinson (USA) | July 1 | 1972 |
| *200 m.* | 19.8 | Tommie Smith (USA) | Oct. 16 | 1968 |
| | 19.8 | Don Quarrie (Jamaica) | Aug. 3 | 1971 |
| *220 yd.* | 20.0 | Tommie Smith (USA) | June 11 | 1966 |
| *220 yd. (straight)* | 19.5 | Tommie Smith (USA) | May 7 | 1966 |
| *400 m.* | 43.8 | Lee Evans (USA) | Oct. 18 | 1968 |
| *440 yd.* | 44.5 | John Smith (USA) | June 26 | 1971 |
| *800 m.* | 1:44.3 | Peter Snell (New Zealand) | Feb. 3 | 1962 |
| | 1:44.3 | Ralph Doubell (Australia) | Oct. 15 | 1968 |
| | 1:44.3 | Dave Wottle (USA) | July 1 | 1972 |
| *880 yd.* | *1:44.6 | Rick Wohlhuter (USA) | May 27 | 1973 |
| *1000 m.* | 2:16.2 | Jurgen May (E. Germany) | July 20 | 1965 |
| | 2:16.2 | Franz-Josef Kemper (W. Germany) Sept. 21 | | 1966 |
| *1500 m.* | 3:33.1 | Jim Ryun (USA) | July 8 | 1967 |
| *Mile* | 3:51.1 | Jim Ryun (USA) | June 23 | 1967 |
| *2000 m.* | 4:56.2 | Michel Jazy (France) | Oct. 12 | 1966 |
| *3000 m.* | 7:37.6 | Emiel Puttemans (Belgium) | Sept.14 | 1972 |
| *2 mi.* | 8:14.0 | Lasse Viren (Finland) | Aug. 14 | 1972 |
| *3 mi.* | 12:47.8 | Emiel Puttemans (Belgium) | Sept. 20 | 1972 |
| *5000 m.* | 13:13.0 | Emiel Puttemans (Belgium) | Sept. 20 | 1972 |
| *6 mi.* | 26:47.0 | Ron Clarke (Australia) | July 14 | 1965 |
| *10,000 m.* | 27:38.4 | Lasse Viren (Finland) | Sept. 3 | 1972 |
| *10 mi.* | 46:04.2 | Willy Polleunis (Belgium) | Sept. 20 | 1972 |
| *20,000 m.* | 57:44.4 | Gaston Roelants (Belgium) | Sept. 20 | 1972 |
| *1 Hour* | 12mi. 1,609yd. | Gaston Roelants (Belgium) | Sept. 20 | 1972 |
| *15 mi.* | 1:12:48.2 | Ron Hill (GB) | July 21 | 1965 |
| *25,000 m.* | 1:15:22.6 | Ron Hill (GB) | July 21 | 1965 |
| *30,000 m.* | 1:31:30.4 | Jim Alder (GB) | Sept. 5 | 1970 |
| *3000 m. Steeplechase* | 8:20.8 | Anders Garderud (Sweden) | Sept. 14 | 1972 |
| | *8:20.8 | Ben Jipcho (Kenya) | Jan 15 | 1973 |
| *120 yd. Hurdles* | 13.0 | Rod Milburn (USA) | June 25 | 1971 |
| *110 m. Hurdles* | 13.2 | Martin Lauer (W. Germany) | July 7 | 1959 |
| | 13.2 | Lee Calhoun (USA) | Aug. 21 | 1960 |
| | 13.2 | Earl McCullouch (USA) | July 16 | 1967 |
| | 13.2 | Willie Davenport (USA) | July 4 | 1969 |
| | 13.2 | Rod Milburn (USA) | Sept. 7 | 1972 |
| *200 m. Hurdles* | 22.5 | Martin Lauer (W. Germany) | July 7 | 1959 |
| | 22.5 | Glenn Davis (USA) | Aug. 20 | 1960 |
| *220 yd. Hurdles (straight)* | 21.9 | Don Styron (USA) | April 2 | 1960 |
| *400 m. Hurdles* | 47.8 | John Akii-Bua (Uganda) | Sept. 2 | 1972 |
| *440 yd. Hurdles* | 48.8 | Ralph Mann (USA) | June 20 | 1970 |
| *High Jump* | 7ft. 6¼in. | Pat Matzdorf (USA) | July 3 | 1971 |
| *Pole Vault* | 18ft. 5¾in. | Bob Seagren (USA) | July 2 | 1972 |
| *Long Jump* | 29ft. 2½in | Bob Beamon (USA) | Oct. 18 | 1968 |
| *Triple Jump* | 57ft. 2¾i.n | Viktor Saneyev (USSR) | Oct 17 | 1972 |
| *Shot* | *71ft. 7in. | Al Feuerbach (USA) | May 5 | 1973 |
| *Discus* | 224ft. 5in. | Jay Silvester (USA) | Sept 18 | 1968 |
| | 224ft. 5in. | Ricky Bruch (Sweden) | July 5 | 1972 |
| *Hammer* | 250ft. 8in. | Walter Schmidt (W. Germany) Sept. 4 | | 1971 |
| *Javelin* | *308ft. 8in. | Klaus Wolfermann (W. Ger) May 5 | | 1973 |
| *Decathlon* | 8,454 | Nikolay Avilov (USSR) | Sept.7/8 | 1972 |
| *20,000 m. Walk* | 1:25:19.4 | Peter Frenkel (E. Germany) | June 24 | 1972 |
| | 1:25:19.4 | Hans-Georg Reimann (E. Ger) June 24 | | 1972 |
| *2 Hours Walk* | 16mi. 1,269yd. | Karl-Heinz Stadtmuller (E. Germany) April 16 | | 1972 |
| *30,000 m. Walk* | 2:14:45.6 | Karl-Heinz Stadtmuller (E. Germany) April 16 | | 1972 |
| *20 mi. Walk* | 2:31:33.0 | Anatoliy Vedyakov (USSR) | Aug. 23 | 1958 |

| | | | | |
|---|---|---|---|---|
| *30 mi. Walk* | *3:51:48.6 | Gerhard Weidner (W. Ger) | Apr. 8 | 1973 |
| *50,000 m. Walk* | *4:00:27.0 | Gerhard Weidner (W. Ger) | Apr. 8 | 1973 |
| *4 x 100 m.* | 38.2 | USA (Charlie Greene, Mel Pender, Ronnie Ray Smith, Jim Hines) | Oct. 20 | 1968 |
| | 38.2 | USA (Larry Black, Robert Taylor, Gerald Tinker, Eddie Hart) | Sept. 10 | 1972 |
| *4 x 110 yd.* | 38.6 | University of Southern California (Earl McCullouch, Fred Kuller, O. J. Simpson, Lennox Miller) | June 17 | 1967 |
| *4 x 200 m.* | 1:21.5 | Italy (F. Ossola, P. Abeti, L. Benedetti, Pietro Mennea) | July 21 | 1972 |
| *4 x 220 yd.* | 1:21.7 | Texas A & M College (Donnie Rogers, Rocky Woods, Marvin Mills, Curtis Mills) | Apr. 24 | 1970 |
| *4 x 400 m.* | 2:56.1 | USA (Vince Matthews, Ron Freeman, Larry James, Lee Evans) | Oct. 20 | 1968 |
| *4 x 440 yd.* | 3:02.8 | Trinidad & Tobago (Lennox Yearwood, Kent Bernard, Ed. Roberts, Wendell Mottley) | Aug 13 | 1966 |
| *4 x 800 m.* | 7:08.6 | West Germany (Manfred Kinder, Walter Adams, Dieter Bogatzki, Franz-Josef Kemper) | Aug 13 | 1966 |
| *4 x 880 yd.* | *7:10.4 | Univ. of Chicago Track Club (Tom Bach, Ken Sparks, Lowell Paul, Rick Wohlhuter) | May 12 | 1973 |
| *4 x 1500 m.* | 14:49.0 | France (Gerard Vervoort, Claude Nicolas, Michel Jazy, Jean Wadoux) | June 25 | 1965 |
| *4 x 1 mile* | 16:02.8 | New Zealand (Kevin Ross, Tony Polhill, Richard Tayler, Dick Quax) | Feb. 3 | 1972 |

\* awaiting ratification

---

# Evolution of World Records

These lists show how the world's best performances in the standard events have been improved during the post-war years. Many marks listed have never been officially accepted as world records by the International Amateur Athletic Federation (which began recognising records in 1913) but have satisfied statisticians as to their authenticity. Performances marked by an asterisk have been accorded official status by the IAAF. It should be noted that many of the most recent record-breaking performances are currently awaiting ratification.

For earlier records, see the 1967 edition of " Encyclopaedia of Athletics ".

*100 Yards*
sec.
9.4  George Simpson (USA)
       June 8 1929
9.4\* Frank Wykoff (USA)
       May 10 1930
9.4  Hubert Meier (USA)
       May 24 1930
9.4  Wykoff  June 7 1930

9.4* Daniel Joubert
   (S. Africa)     May 16 1931
9.4  James Carlton (Australia)
               Nov. 15 1931
9.4  Jesse Owens (USA)
               June 17 1933
9.4  Ralph Metcalfe (USA)
               June 17 1933
9.4  George Anderson (USA)
               May 12 1934
9.4  Owens        May 18 1935
9.4* Owens        May 25 1935
9.4  Owens        June 13 1936
9.4* Owens        June 20 1936
9.4* Clyde Jeffrey (USA)
               Mar. 16 1940
9.4  Hal Davis (USA) May 16 1942
9.4* Mel Patton (USA)
               May 24 1947
9.4  Patton       June 20 1947
9.4  Lloyd La Beach
     (Panama)     Mar. 13 1948
9.4  Wendell Belfield (USA)
               May 15 1948
9.3* Patton       May 15 1948
9.3* Hec Hogan (Aus) Mar. 13 1954
9.3* Jim Golliday (USA)
               May 14 1955
9.3* Leamon King (USA)
               May 12 1956
9.3* Dave Sime (USA) May 19 1956
9.3* Sime         June 9 1956
9.3  King         Oct. 20 1956
9.3* Sime         May 18 1957
9.3* Bobby Morrow (USA)
               June 14 1957
9.3  Ira Murchison (USA)
               June 14 1957
9.3* Ray Norton (USA)
               Apr. 12 1958
9.3* Bill Woodhouse (USA)
               May 5 1959
9.3  Norton      May 9 1959
9.3* Roscoe Cook (USA)
               May 30 1959
9.3* Norton      Apr. 2 1960
9.3* Dennis Johnson
     (Jamaica)    Mar. 11 1961
9.3  Johnson     Apr. 1 1961
9.3* Johnson     Apr. 15 1961
9.3* Johnson     May 5 1961
9.3* Frank Budd (USA)
               May 6 1961
9.3* Harry Jerome (Canada)
               May 20 1961
9.3  Bob Hayes (USA) June 2 1961
9.3  Budd        June 11 1961
9.2* Budd        June 24 1961
9.2  Hayes       Feb. 17 1962
9.2* Jerome     Aug. 25 1962

9.2* Jerome     Sept. 3 1962
9.1* Hayes      June 21 1963
9.1  Hayes      Jan. 1 1964
9.1  Hayes      Apr. 18 1964
9.1  Hayes      May 2 1964
9.1* Jerome     July 15 1966
9.1* Jim Hines (USA) May 13 1967
9.1* Charlie Greene (USA)
               June 15 1967
9.1* John Carlos (USA)
               May 10 1969
9.1  Willie McGee (USA)
               May 8 1970
9.1  Steve Williams (US) May 12 1973

*100 Metres*
10.2  Charles Paddock (USA)
               June 18 1921
10.2  Eddie Tolan (USA)
               July 1 1930
10.2  Ralph Metcalfe (USA)
               June 11 1932
10.2* Jesse Owens (USA)
               June 20 1936
10.2* Hal Davis (USA) June 6 1941
10.2* Lloyd La Beach
     (Panama)    May 15 1948
10.2  La Beach    June 4 1948
10.2* Barny Ewell (USA)
               July 9 1948
10.1  La Beach    Oct. 7 1950
10.1* Willie Williams (USA)
               Aug. 3 1956
10.1* Ira Murchison (USA)
               Aug. 4 1956
10.1  Williams    Aug. 5 1956
10.1* Leamon King (USA)
               Oct. 20 1956
10.1* King        Oct. 27 1956
10.1* Ray Norton (US) Apr. 18 1959
10.1  Charles Tidwell (USA)
               June 10 1960
10.0* Armin Hary (W.
     Germany)    June 21 1960
10.0* Harry Jerome (Canada)
               July 15 1960
10.0* Horacio Esteves (Venez-
     uela)        Aug. 15 1964
10.0* Bob Hayes (USA) Oct. 15 1964
10.0  Chen Chia-chuan (China)
               Oct. 24 1965
10.0* Jim Hines (USA) May 27 1967
10.0  Willie Turner (USA)
               May 27 1967
10.0* Enrique Figuerola (Cuba)
               June 17 1967
10.0* Paul Nash (S. Africa)
               Apr. 2 1968
10.0  Nash        Apr. 6 1968

| | | | |
|---|---|---|---|
| 10.0 | Paul Nash (S. Africa) | Apr. 6 | 1968 |
| 10.0 | Charlie Greene (USA) | Apr. 20 | 1968 |
| 10.0* | Oliver Ford (USA) | May 31 | 1968 |
| 10.0* | Greene | June 20 | 1968 |
| 10.0* | Roger Bambuck (France) | June 20 | 1968 |
| 9.9* | Hines | June 20 | 1968 |
| 9.9* | Ronnie Ray Smith (USA) | June 20 | 1968 |
| 9.9* | Greene | June 20 | 1968 |
| 9.9* | Hines | Oct. 14 | 1968 |
| 9.9* | Eddie Hart (USA) | July 1 | 1972 |
| 9.9* | Rey Robinson (USA) | July 1 | 1972 |

*Note*: Paddock's 10.2 in 1921 was for 110 yd., a slightly longer distance.

IAAF records not shown above:

| | | | |
|---|---|---|---|
| 10.2 | McDonald Bailey (GB) | Aug. 25 | 1951 |
| 10.2 | Heinz Futterer (W. Germany) | Oct. 31 | 1954 |
| 10.2 | Bobby Morrow (USA) | May 19 | 1956 |
| 10.2 | Ira Murchison (USA) | June 1 | 1956 |
| 10.2 | Morrow | June 22 | 1956 |
| 10.2 | Murchison | June 29 | 1956 |
| 10.2 | Morrow | June 29 | 1956 |

*220 Yards* (Straight)
sec.

| | | | |
|---|---|---|---|
| 20.3* | Jesse Owens (USA) | May 25 | 1935 |
| 20.3 | Lloyd La Beach (Panama) | June 4 | 1948 |
| 20.3 | La Beach | Apr. 23 | 1949 |
| 20.2* | Mel Patton (USA) | May 7 | 1949 |
| 20.1 | Mike Agostini (Trinidad) | Mar. 17 | 1956 |
| 20.1* | Dave Sime (USA) | May 11 | 1956 |
| 20.0* | Sime | June 9 | 1956 |
| 20.0* | Frank Budd (USA) | May 12 | 1962 |
| 19.5* | Tommie Smith (USA) | May 7 | 1966 |

Performances for 200 m. are identical to above, with this addition to IAAF list:

| | | | |
|---|---|---|---|
| 20.0 | Tommie Smith (USA) | Mar. 13 | 1965 |

*200 Metres* (Turn)
sec.

| | | | |
|---|---|---|---|
| 20.6 | James Carlton (Australia) | Jan. 16 | 1932 |
| 20.6* | Andy Stanfield (USA) | May 26 | 1951 |
| 20.6 | Stanfield | June 28 | 1952 |
| 20.6 | Bobby Morrow (USA) | June 16 | 1956 |
| 20.6* | Thane Baker (USA) | June 23 | 1956 |
| 20.6 | Stanfield | June 23 | 1956 |
| 20.6 | Morrow | June 30 | 1956 |
| 20.6 | Baker | Oct. 27 | 1956 |
| 20.6* | Morrow | Nov. 27 | 1956 |
| 20.6* | Manfred Germar (W. Germany) | Oct. 1 | 1958 |
| 20.6 | Ray Norton (USA) | May 2 | 1959 |
| 20.6 | Norton | Aug. 4 | 1959 |
| 20.6* | Norton | Mar. 19 | 1960 |
| 20.6* | Norton | Apr. 30 | 1960 |
| 20.5* | Peter Radford (GB) | May 28 | 1960 |
| 20.5* | Stone Johnson (USA) | July 2 | 1960 |
| 20.5* | Norton | July 2 | 1960 |
| 20.5* | Livio Berruti (Italy) | Sept. 3 | 1960 |
| 20.5* | Berruti | Sept. 3 | 1960 |
| 20.5* | Paul Drayton (USA) | June 23 | 1962 |
| 20.5 | Bob Hayes (USA) | Feb. 10 | 1963 |
| 20.5 | Hayes | Mar. 2 | 1963 |
| 20.3* | Henry Carr (USA) | Mar. 23 | 1963 |
| 20.2* | Carr | Apr. 4 | 1964 |
| 20.0* | Tommie Smith (USA) | June 11 | 1966 |
| 19.7 | John Carlos (USA) | Sept. 12 | 1968 |

IAAF records not shown above:

| | | | |
|---|---|---|---|
| 19.8 | Tommie Smith (USA) | Oct. 16 | 1968 |
| 19.8 | Don Quarrie (Jamaica) | Aug. 3 | 1971 |

*220 Yards* (Turn)
sec.

| | | | |
|---|---|---|---|
| 20.6 | James Carlton (Australia) | Jan. 16 | 1932 |
| 20.6* | Andy Stanfield (USA) | May 26 | 1951 |
| 20.6* | Ray Norton (USA) | Mar. 19 | 1960 |
| 20.5* | Peter Radford (GB) | May 28 | 1960 |
| 20.5* | Paul Drayton (USA) | June 23 | 1962 |
| 20.5 | Bob Hayes (USA) | Mar. 2 | 1963 |

20.3* Henry Carr (USA)
                Mar. 23 1963
20.2* Carr          Apr.  4 1964
20.0* Tommie Smith (USA)
                June 11 1966

### 400 Metres
sec.
46.0* Rudolf Harbig
   (Germany)      Aug. 12 1939
46.0* Grover Klemmer (USA)
               June 29 1941
46.0* Herb McKenley
   (Jamaica)     June  5 1948
45.9* McKenley     July  2 1948
45.8* George Rhoden
   (Jamaica)     Aug. 22 1950
45.4* Lou Jones (USA) Mar. 18 1955
45.2* Jones        June 30 1956
44.9* Otis Davis (USA) Sept.  6 1960
44.9* Carl Kaufmann (W.
   Germany)     Sept.  6 1960
44.9* Adolph Plummer
   (USA)        May 25 1963
44.9* Mike Larrabee (USA)
               Sept. 12 1964

44.5* Tommie Smith (USA)
               May 20 1967
44.4  Vince Matthews (USA)
               Aug. 31 1968
44.0  Lee Evans (USA) Sept. 14 1968
43.8* Evans       Oct. 18 1968

IAAF record not shown above:
44.1  Larry James (USA)
               Sept. 14 1968

### 440 Yards
sec.
46.4* Ben Eastman (USA)
               Mar. 26 1932
46.4* Grover Klemmer (USA)
               May 31 1941
46.2  Herb McKenley
   (Jamaica)     June  1 1946
46.2  McKenley     June 21 1947
46.0* McKenley     June  5 1948
45.8* Jim Lea (USA)  May 26 1956
45.8* Glenn Davis (USA)
               May 24 1958
45.7* Davis       June 14 1958
44.9* Adolph Plummer (USA)
               May 25 1963
44.8* Tommie Smith (USA)
               May 20 1967
44.7* Curtis Mills (USA)
               June 21 1969
44.5* John Smith (USA)
               June 26 1971

IAAF record not shown above:
46.3  Herb McKenley
   (Jamaica)     June 28 1947

### 800 Metres
min. sec.
1:46.6* Rudolf Harbig
   (Germany)     July 15 1939
1:45.7* Roger Moens
   (Belgium)     Aug.  3 1955
1:44.3* Peter Snell (New
   Zealand)      Feb.  3 1962
1:44.3* Ralph Doubell
   (Australia)     Oct. 15 1968
1:44.3* Dave Wottle (USA)
               July  1 1972

### 880 Yards
min. sec.
1:49.2* Sydney Wooderson
   (GB)         Aug. 20 1938
1:49.2* Mal Whitfield (USA)
               Aug. 19 1950
1:48.6* Whitfield   July 17 1953
1:48.6* Gunnar Nielsen
   (Denmark)     Sept. 30 1954
1:47.5* Lon Spurrier (USA)
               Mar. 26 1955
1:46.8* Tom Courtney (USA)
               May 24 1957
1:45.1* Peter Snell (New
   Zealand)      Feb.  3 1962
1:44.9* Jim Ryun (US) June 10 1966
1:44.6  Rick Wohlhuter (US)
               May 27 1973

### 1000 Metres
2:21.5* Rudolf Harbig
   (Germany)     May 24 1941
2:21.4* Rune Gustafsson
   (Sweden)     Sept.  4 1946
2:21.4* Marcel Hansenne
   (France)      Aug. 27 1948
2:21.3* Olle Aberg (Sweden)
               Aug. 10 1952
2:21.2* Stanislav Jungwirth
   (Czechoslovakia) Oct. 27 1952
2:20.8* Mal Whitfield (USA)
               Aug. 16 1953
2:20.4* Audun Boysen (Norway)         Sept. 17 1953
2:19.5* Boysen     Aug. 18 1954
2:19.0* Boysen     Aug. 30 1955
2:19.0* Istvan Rozsavolgyi
   (Hungary)     Sept. 21 1955
2:18.1* Dan Waern (Sweden)
               Sept. 19 1958
2:18.0  Waern      Aug. 10 1959
2:17.8* Waern      Aug. 21 1959
2:16.7* Siegfried Valentin
   (E. Germany)   July 19 1960

2:16.6* Peter Snell (New
Zealand)      Nov. 12 1964
2:16.2* Jurgen May
(E. Germany)    July 20 1965
2:16.2* Franz-Josef Kemper
(W. Germany)   Sept. 21 1966

*1500 Metres*
min. sec.
3.43.0* Gunder Hagg
(Sweden)       July  7 1944
3:43.0* Lennart Strand
(Sweden)       July 15 1947
3:43.0* Werner Lueg (W.
Germany)      June 29 1952
3:43.0  Roger Bannister (GB)
May  6 1954
3:42.8* Wes Santee (USA)
June  4 1954
3:41.8* John Landy
(Australia)    June 21 1954
3:40.8* Sandor Iharos
(Hungary)      July 28 1955
3:40.8* Laszlo Tabori
(Hungary)      Sept.  6 1955
3:40.8* Gunnar Nielsen
(Denmark)      Sept.  6 1955
3:40.5* Istvan Rozsavolgyi
(Hungary)      Aug.  3 1956
3:40.2* Olavi Salsola (Finland)          July 11 1957
3:40.2* Olavi Salonen (Finland)          July 11 1957
3:38.1* Stanislav Jungwirth
(Czechoslovakia) July 12 1957
3:36.0* Herb Elliott
(Australia)    Aug. 28 1958
3:35.6* Elliott      Sept.  6 1960
3:33.1* Jim Ryun (USA)
July  8 1967

*Note:* The 3:40.5 mark above was
ratified as 3:40.6.

*Mile*
min. sec.
4:01.6* Arne Andersson
(Sweden)       July 18 1944
4.01.3* Gunder Hagg
(Sweden)       July 17 1945
3:59.4* Roger Bannister (GB)
May  6 1954
3:57.9* John Landy (Australia)
June 21 1954
3:57.2* Derek Ibbotson (GB)
July 19 1957
3:54.5* Herb Elliott
(Australia)    Aug.  6 1958
3:54.4* Peter Snell (New
Zealand)       Jan. 27 1962

3:54.1* Snell         Nov. 17 1964
3:53.6* Michel Jazy (France)
June  9 1965
3:51.3* Jim Ryun (USA)
July 17 1966
3:51.1* Ryun          June 23 1967

*Note:* The 4:01.3 mark above was
ratified as 4:01.4; 3:57.9 as
3:58.0.

*2000 Metres*
min. sec.
5:11.8* Gunder Hagg
(Sweden)       Aug 23 1942
5:06.9* Gaston Reiff
(Belgium)      Sept. 29 1948
5:02.2* Istvan Rozsavolgyi
(Hungary)      Oct.  2 1955
5:01.5* Michel Jazy (France)
June 14 1962
5:01.1* Josef Odlozil (Czechoslovakia)      Sept.  8 1965
4:57.8* Harald Norpoth (W
Germany)       Sept. 10 1966
4:56.2* Jazy          Oct. 12 1966

*Note:* The 5:06.9 mark above was
ratified as 5:07.0; 5:01.5 as
5:01.6; 5:01.1 as 5:01.2.

*3000 Metres*
min. sec.
8:01.2* Gunder Hagg
(Sweden)       Aug. 28 1942
7:58.7* Gaston Reiff (Belgium)
Aug. 12 1949
7:55.6* Sandor Iharos
(Hungary)      May 14 1955
7:55.5* Gordon Pirie (GB)
June 22 1956
7:52.8* Pirie        Sept.  4 1956
7:49.2* Michel Jazy (France)
June 27 1962
7:49.0* Jazy         June 23 1965
7:46.0* Siegfried Herrmann
(E. Germany)   Aug.  5 1965
7:39.5* Kipchoge Keino (Kenya)
Aug. 27 1965
7:37.6* Emiel Puttemans
(Belgium)      Sept. 14 1972

*Note:* The 7:58.7 mark above was
ratified as 7:58.8; 7:55.5 as
7:55.6; 7:39.5 as 7:39.6.

*2 Miles*
8:42.8* Gunder Hagg
(Sweden)       Aug.  4 1944

195

8:40.4* Gaston Reiff
(Belgium)          Aug. 26 1952
8:33.4* Sandor Iharos
(Hungary)          May 30 1955
8:32.0* Albert Thomas
(Australia)        Aug.  7 1958
8:30.0* Murray Halberg
(New Zealand)      July  7 1961
8:29.8* Jim Beatty (USA)
                   June  8 1962
8:29.6* Michel Jazy (France)
                   June  6 1963
8:26.4* Bob Schul (USA)
                   Aug. 29 1964
8:22.6* Jazy       June 23 1965
8:19.8* Ron Clarke
(Australia)        June 27 1967
8:19.6* Clarke     Aug. 24 1968
8:17.8* Emiel Puttemans
(Belgium)          Aug. 21 1971
8:14.0* Lasse Viren (Finland)
                   Aug. 14 1972

*3 Miles*
min. sec.
13:32.4* Gunder Hagg
(Sweden)           Sept. 20 1942
13:31.4  Vladimir Kuts
(USSR)             Sept. 20 1953
13:27.4* Kuts      Aug. 29 1954
13:27.0* Kuts      Oct. 13 1954
13:26.4* Kuts      Oct. 23 1954
13:23.2* Chris Chataway (GB)
                   July 30 1955
13:14.2* Sandor Iharos
(Hungary)          Oct. 23 1955
13:10.8* Albert Thomas
(Australia)        July  9 1958
13:10.0* Murray Halberg (New
Zealand)           July 25 1961
13:07.6* Ron Clarke (Australia)
                   Dec.  3 1964
13:00.4* Clarke    June  4 1965
12:52.4* Clarke    July 10 1965
12:50.4* Clarke    July  5 1966
12:47.8* Emiel Puttemans
(Belgium)          Sept. 20 1972

IAAF records not shown above:
13:32.2  Freddie Green (GB)
                   July 10 1954
13:32.2  Chris Chataway (GB)
                   July 10 1954

*5000 Metres*
min. sec.
13:58.2* Gunder Hagg
(Sweden)           Sept. 20 1942
13:57.2* Emil Zatopek
(Czechoslovakia)   May 30 1954
13:56.6* Vladimir Kuts (USSR)
                   Aug. 29 1954

13:51.6* Chris Chataway (GB)
                   Oct. 13 1954
13:51.2* Kuts      Oct. 23 1954
13:50.8* Sandor Iharos
(Hungary)          Sept. 10 1955
13:46.8* Kuts      Sept. 18 1955
13:40.6* Iharos    Oct. 23 1955
13:36.8* Gordon Pirie (GB)
                   June 19 1956
13:35.0* Kuts      Oct. 13 1957
13:34.8* Ron Clarke (Australia)
                   Jan. 16 1965
13.33.6* Clarke    Feb.  1 1965
13:25.8* Clarke    June  4 1965
13:24.2* Kipchoge Keino (Kenya)
                   Nov. 30 1965
13:16.6* Clarke    July  5 1966
13:16.4* Lasse Viren
(Finland)          Sept. 14 1972
13:13.0* Emiel Puttemans
(Belgium)          Sept. 20 1972

*6 Miles*
min. sec.
28:38.6* Viljo Heino (Finland)
                   Aug. 25 1944
28:30.8* Heino     Sept.  1 1949
28:19.4* Gordon Pirie (GB)
                   July 10 1953
28:08.4* Emil Zatopek (Czechoslovakia)          Nov.  1 1953
27:59.2* Zatopek   June  1 1954
27:54.0* Dave Stephens
(Australia)        Jan. 25 1956
27:43.8* Sandor Iharos
(Hungary)          July 15 1956
27:17.8* Ron Clarke (Australia)
                   Dec. 18 1963
27:11.6* Billy Mills (USA)
                   June 27 1965
27:11.6* Gerry Lindgren (USA)
                   June 27 1965
26:47.0* Clarke    July 14 1965

*10,000 Metres*
min. sec.
29:35.4* Viljo Heino (Finland)
                   Aug. 25 1944
29:28.2* Emil Zatopek (Czechoslovakia)          June 11 1949
29:27.2* Heino     Sept.  1 1949
29:21.2* Zatopek   Oct. 22 1949
29:02.6* Zatopek   Aug.  4 1950
29:01.6* Zatopek   Nov.  1 1953
28:54.2* Zatopek   June  1 1954
28:42.8* Sandor Iharos
(Hungary)          July 15 1956
28:30.4* Vladimir Kuts (USSR)
                   Sept. 11 1956

196

28:18.8* Pyotr Bolotnikov  
(USSR) Oct. 15 1960  
28:18.2* Bolotnikov Aug. 11 1962  
28:15.6* Ron Clarke (Australia)  
Dec. 18 1963  
27:39.4* Clarke July 14 1965  
27:38.4* Lasse Viren  
(Finland) Sept. 3 1972  

*10 Miles*  
min. sec.  
50:15.0* Paavo Nurmi (Fin-  
land) Oct. 7 1928  
49:41.6* Viljo Heino (Fin-  
land) Sept. 30 1945  
49:22.2* Heino Sept. 14 1946  
48:12.0* Emil Zatopek (Czecho-  
slovakia) Sept. 29 1951  
47:47.0* Basil Heatley (GB)  
Apr. 15 1961  
47:26.8* Mel Batty (GB)  
Apr. 11 1964  
47:12.8* Ron Clarke (Australia)  
Mar. 3 1965  
47:02.2* Ron Hill (GB) Apr. 6 1968  
46:44.0* Hill Nov. 9 1968  
46:37.4* Jerome Drayton  
(Canada) Sept. 6 1970  
46:04.2* Willy Polleunis  
(Belgium) Sept. 20 1972  

*20,000 Metres*  
hr. min. sec.  
1:03:01.2* Andras Csaplar  
(Hungary) Oct. 26 1941  
1:02:40.0* Viljo Heino (Fin-  
land) Sept. 22 1949  
1:01:16.0* Emil Zatopek  
(Czechoslovakia) Sept. 15 1951  
59:51.8* Zatopek Sept. 29 1951  
59:28.6* Bill Baillie (New  
Zealand) Aug. 24 1963  
59:22.8* Ron Clarke (Australia)  
Oct. 27 1965  
58:06.2* Gaston Roelants (Belgium)  
Oct. 28 1966  
57:44.4* Roelants Sept. 20 1972  

*1 Hour*  
11 mi. 1649 yd.* Paavo Nurmi  
(Finland) Oct. 7 1928  
12 mi. 29 yd.* Viljo Heino  
(Finland) Sept. 30 1945  
12 mi. 268 yd.* Emil Zatopek  
(Czechoslovakia) Sept. 15 1951  
12 mi. 809 yd.* Zatopek  
Sept. 29 1951  
12 mi. 960 yd.* Bill Baillie  
(New Zealand) Aug. 24 1963  
12 mi. 1006 yd.* Ron Clarke  
(Australia) Oct. 27 1965  

12 mi. 1478 yd.* Gaston Roelants  
(Belgium) Oct. 28 1966  
12 mi. 1609 yd.* Roelants  
Sept. 20 1972  

*15 Miles*  
hr. min. sec.  
1:19:48.6* Erkki Tamila (Fin-  
land) Aug. 29 1937  
1:18:48.0* Mikko Hietanen  
(Finland) Aug. 20 1947  
1:17:28.6* Hietanen May 23 1948  
1:16:26.4* Emil Zatopek  
(Czechoslovakia) Oct. 26 1952  
1:14:01.0* Zatopek Oct. 29 1955  
1:12:48.2* Ron Hill (GB)  
July 21 1965  

*25,000 Metres*  
hr. min. sec.  
1:21:27.0* Erkki Tamila (Fin-  
land) Sept. 3 1939  
1:20:14.0* Mikko Hietanen  
(Finland) May 23 1948  
1:19:11.8* Emil Zatopek  
(Czechoslovakia) Oct. 26 1952  
1:17:34.0* Albert Ivanov  
(USSR) Sept. 27 1955  
1:16:36.4* Zatopek Oct. 29 1955  
1:15:22.6* Ron Hill (GB)  
July 21 1965  

*30,000 Metres*  
hr. min. sec.  
1:40:57.6* Jose Ribas (Argen-  
tine) May 27 1932  
1:40:49.8* Mikko Hietanen (Fin-  
land) Sept. 28 1947  
1:40:46.4* Hietanen June 20 1948  
1:39:14.6* Fyeodosiy Vanin  
(USSR) Nov. 1 1949  
1:38:54.0* Yakov Moskachenkov  
(USSR) Oct. 3 1951  
1:35:23.8* Emil Zatopek  
(Czechoslovakia) Oct. 26 1952  
1:35:03.6* Antti Viskari (Fin-  
land) Oct. 21 1956  
1:35:01.0* Albert Ivanov  
(USSR) June 6 1957  
1:34:41.2* Aurel Vandendries-  
sche (Belgium) Oct. 3 1962  
1:34:32.2* Viktor Baikov  
(USSR) June 22 1963  
1:34:01.8* Jim Alder (GB)  
Oct. 17 1964  
1:32:34.6* Tim Johnston (GB)  
Oct. 16 1965  
1:32:25.4* Jim Hogan (GB)  
Nov. 12 1966  
1:31:30.4* Alder Sept. 5 1970

3000 Metres Steeplechase
min. sec.
8:59.6  Erik Elmsater
        (Sweden)         Aug.  4 1944
8:49.8  Vladimir Kazantsev
        (USSR)           July 10 1951
8:48.6  Kazantsev        June 12 1952
8:45.4  Horace Ashenfelter
        (USA)            July 25 1952
8:44.4  Olavi Rinteenpaa (Fin-
        land)            July  2 1953
8:41.2* Jerzy Chromik (Poland)
                         Aug. 31 1955
8:40.2* Chromik          Sept. 11 1955
8:39.8* Semyon Rzhishchin
        (USSR)           Aug. 14 1956
8:35.6* Sandor Rozsnyoi
        (Hungary)        Sept. 16 1956
8:35.6* Rzhishchin       July 21 1958
8:32.0* Chromik          Aug.  2 1958
8:31.3* Zdzislaw Krzyszkowiak
        (Poland)         June 26 1960
8:31.2* Grigoriy Taran (USSR)
                         May 28 1961
8:30.4* Krzyszkowiak     Aug. 10 1961
8:29.6* Gaston Roelants
        (Belgium)        Sept.  7 1963
8:26.4* Roelants         Aug.  7 1965
8:24.2* Jouko Kuha
        (Finland)        July 17 1968
8:22.2* Vladimir Dudin
        (USSR)           Aug. 19 1969
8:22.0* Kerry O'Brien
        (Australia)      July  4 1970
8:20.8* Anders Garderud
        (Sweden)         Sept. 14 1972
8:20.8  Ben Jipcho (Kenya)
                         Jan. 15 1973

Note: The 8:31.3 mark above was
ratified as 8:31.4.

IAAF records not shown above:
8:49.6  Sandor Rozsnyoi
        (Hungary)        Aug. 28 1954
8:47.8  Pentti Karvonen (Fin-
        land)            July  1 1955
8:45.4  Karvonen         July 15 1955
8:45.4  Vasiliy Vlasenko
        (USSR)           Aug. 18 1955

120 Yards and 110 Metres Hurdles
sec.
13.7m* Forrest Towns (USA)
                         Aug. 27 1936
13.7   Fred Wolcott (USA)
                         May  3 1940
13.7m* Wolcott           June 29 1941
13.6*  Harrison Dillard (USA)
                         Apr. 17 1948

13.5*  Dick Attlesey (USA)
                         May 13 1950
13.5m* Attlesey          July 10 1950
13.5*  Jack Davis (USA) June  9 1956
13.4m* Davis             June 22 1956
13.4*  Milton Campbell (USA)
                         May 31 1957
13.4   Elias Gilbert (USA)
                         May 31 1957
13.2m* Martin Lauer (W.
        Germany)         July  7 1959
13.2m* Lee Calhoun (USA)
                         Aug. 21 1960
13.2m* Earl McCullouch
        (USA)            July 16 1967
13.2   Willie Davenport (USA)
                         Aug. 31 1968
13.2*  Erv Hall (USA)   June 19 1969
13.2m* Davenport         July  4 1969
13.2   Thomas Hill (USA)
                         June 13 1970
13.0*  Rod Milburn (USA)
                         June 25 1971

Note: m signifies mark at 110 metres
(10 inches over 120 yards).

IAAF records not shown above:
13.6m Dick Attlesey (USA)
                         June 24 1950
13.2m Rod Milburn (USA)
                         Sept.  7 1972

220 Yards Hurdles (Straight)
sec.
22.5*  Fred Wolcott (USA)
                         June  8 1940
22.5*  Harrison Dillard (USA)
                         June  8 1946
22.5   Dillard           May 20 1947
22.2*  Dave Sime (USA) May  5 1956
22.2*  Ancel Robinson (USA)
                         June 15 1957
22.1*  Elias Gilbert (USA)
                         May 17 1958
21.9*  Don Styron (USA)
                         Apr.  2 1960

200 Metres Hurdles (Turn)
sec.
22.9   Fred Wolcott (USA)
                         July  4 1939
22.8   Elias Gilbert (USA)
                         June  8 1957
22.7   Charles Tidwell (USA)
                         June 14 1958
22.7   Tidwell           May 16 1959
22.6   Tidwell           June 20 1959
22.5*  Martin Lauer (W.
        Germany)         July  7 1959

198

22.5* Glenn Davis (USA) Aug. 20 1960

*220 Yards Hurdles* (Turn)
sec.
23.1 Fred Wolcott (USA) June 22 1940
23.0 Harrison Dillard (USA) June 22 1946
22.8 Elias Gilbert (USA) June 8 1957
22.7 Charles Tidwell (USA) June 14 1958
22.7 Tidwell May 16 1959

*400 Metres Hurdles*
sec.
50.6* Glenn Hardin (USA) July 26 1934
50.4* Yuriy Lituyev (USSR) Sept. 20 1953
49.5* Glenn Davis (USA) June 29 1956
49.2* Davis Aug. 6 1958
49.2* Salvatore Morale (Italy) Sept. 14 1962
49.1* Rex Cawley (USA) Sept. 13 1964
48.8* Geoff Vanderstock (USA) Sept. 11 1968
48.1* David Hemery (GB) Oct. 15 1968
47.8* John Akii-Bua (Uganda) Sept. 2 1972

*440 Yards Hurdles*
sec.
52.2* Roy Cochran (USA) Apr. 25 1942
52.2* Richard Ault (USA) Aug. 31 1949
51.9* Armando Filiput (Italy) Oct. 8 1950
51.9* Charles Moore (USA) Aug. 4 1952
51.6* Moore Aug. 9 1952
51.3* Yuriy Lituyev (USSR) Oct. 13 1954
50.7* Gerhardus Potgieter (S. Africa) Apr. 20 1957
50.5* Josh Culbreath (USA) Aug. 9 1957
49.9* Glenn Davis (USA) June 20 1958
49.7* Potgieter July 22 1958
49.3* Potgieter Apr. 16 1960
48.8* Ralph Mann (USA) June 20 1970

*High Jump*
ft. in.
6 11* Les Steers (USA) June 17 1941
6 11½* Walt Davis (USA) June 27 1953
7 0½* Charles Dumas (USA) June 29 1956
7 1½* John Thomas (USA) Apr. 30 1960
7 1¾* Thomas May 21 1960
7 2* Thomas June 24 1960
7 3¾* Thomas July 1 1960
7 3¾* Valeriy Brumel (USSR) June 18 1961
7 4¼* Brumel July 16 1961
7 4½* Brumel Aug. 31 1961
7 5* Brumel July 22 1962
7 5¼* Brumel Sept. 29 1962
7 5¾* Brumel July 21 1963
7 6¼* Pat Matzdorf (USA) July 3 1971

IAAF record not shown above:
7 1 Yuriy Styepanov (USSR) July 13 1957

*Pole Vault*
ft. in.
15 7¾* Cornelius Warmerdam (USA) May 23 1942
15 8¼* Bob Gutowski (USA) Apr. 27 1957
15 9¾ Gutowski June 15 1957
15 10¼* George Davies (USA) May 20 1961
16 0¾* John Uelses (USA) Mar. 31 1962
16 2* Dave Tork (USA) Apr. 28 1962
16 2½* Pentti Nikula (Finland) June 22 1962
16 3 John Pennel (USA) Mar. 22 1963
16 4 Pennel Apr. 10 1963
16 5* Brian Sternberg (USA) Apr. 27 1963
16 6¾ Pennel Apr. 30 1963
16 7 Sternberg May 25 1963
16 8* Sternberg June 7 1963
16 8¾ Pennel July 13 1963
16 8¾ Pennel July 26 1963
16 10¼* Pennel Aug. 5 1963
17 0¾* Pennel Aug. 24 1963
17 1 Fred Hansen (USA) June 5 1964
17 2* Hansen June 13 1964
17 4* Hansen July 25 1964
17 5½* Bob Seagren (USA) May 14 1966

17 5½ Seagren July 2 1966
17 6¼* Pennel July 23 1966
17 7* Seagren June 10 1967
17 7¾* Paul Wilson (USA) June 23 1967
17 9* Seagren Sept. 12 1968
17 10¼* Pennel June 21 1969
17 10½* Wolfgang Nordwig (E. Germany) June 17 1970
17 11* Nordwig Sept. 3 1970
18 0¼* Chris Papanicolaou (Greece) Oct. 24 1970
18 1* Kjell Isaksson (Sweden) Apr. 8 1972
18 2* Isaksson Apr. 15 1972
18 4¼ Seagren May 23 1972
18 4¼ Isaksson May 23 1972
18 5¾* Seagren July 2 1972

IAAF records not shown above:

15 9¼ Don Bragg (USA) July 2 1960
18 2½ Kjell Isaksson (Sweden) June 12 1972

*Long Jump*

ft. in.
26 8¼* Jesse Owens (USA) May 25 1935
26 11¼* Ralph Boston (USA) Aug. 12 1960
27 0½* Boston May 27 1961
27 2* Boston July 16 1961
27 3¼* Igor Ter-Ovanesyan (USSR) June 10 1962
27 3¼* Boston Aug. 15 1964
27 4¼* Boston Sept. 12 1964
27 5* (8.35m.) Boston May 29 1965
27 4¾* (8.35m.) Ter-Ovanesyan Oct. 19 1967
29 2½* Bob Beamon (USA) Oct. 18 1968

*Triple Jump*

ft. in.
52 6* Naoto Tajima (Japan) Aug. 6 1936
52 6* Adhemar da Silva (Brazil) Dec. 3 1950
52 6½* da Silva Sept. 30 1951
52 10¾* da Silva July 23 1952
53 2¾* da Silva July 23 1952
53 3* Leonid Shcherbakov (USSR) July 19 1953
54 4* da Silva Mar. 16 1955
54 5¼* Olyeg Ryakhovskiy (USSR) July 28 1958
54 9½* Olyeg Fyedoseyev (USSR) May 3 1959
55 10½* Jozef Szmidt (Poland) Aug. 5 1960

56 1¼* Giuseppe Gentile (Italy) Oct. 16 1968
56 6* Gentile Oct. 17 1968
56 6½* Viktor Saneyev (USSR) Oct. 17 1968
56 8* Nelson Prudencio Brazil) Oct. 17 1968
57 0¾* Saneyev Oct. 17 1968
57 1* Pedro Perez (Cuba) Aug. 5 1971
57 2¾* Saneyev Oct. 17 1972

*Shot*

ft. in.
57 1* Jack Torrance (USA) Aug. 5 1934
58 0¼* Charles Fonville (USA) Apr. 17 1948
58 4½* Jim Fuchs (USA) July 28 1949
58 5½* Fuchs Apr. 29 1950
58 8¾* Fuchs Aug. 20 1950
58 10¾* Fuchs Aug. 22 1950
59 0¾* Parry O'Brien (USA) May 9 1953
59 2¼* O'Brien June 5 1953
59 9¾ O'Brien Apr. 24 1954
60 5¼* O'Brien May 8 1954
60 5¾* O'Brien May 21 1954
60 6 O'Brien June 11 1954
60 10* O'Brien June 11 1954
61 1* O'Brien May 5 1956
61 4* O'Brien June 15 1956
61 4½ O'Brien Aug. 18 1956
62 3 O'Brien Sept. 3 1956
62 6¼* O'Brien Sept. 3 1956
62 8 O'Brien Nov. 1 1956
63 2* O'Brien Nov. 1 1956
63 2* Dallas Long (USA) Mar. 28 1959
63 2¼ Long May 2 1959
63 2½ O'Brien July 18 1959
63 4* O'Brien Aug. 1 1959
63 7* Long Mar. 5 1960
63 10* Bill Nieder (USA) Mar. 19 1960
64 6½* Long Mar. 26 1960
65 7* Nieder Apr. 2 1960
65 10* Nieder Aug. 12 1960
65 10½* Long May 18 1962
65 11¼* Long Apr. 4 1964
66 7¼ Long May 9 1964
67 10* Long July 25 1964
67 11¼ Randy Matson (USA) Apr. 9 1965
69 0¾ Matson Apr. 30 1965
70 7¼* Matson May 8 1965
71 5½* Matson Apr. 22 1967
71 7 Al Feuerbach (USA) May 5 1973

IAAF record not shown above:
66  3¼  Dallas Long (USA)
                May 29 1964

*Discus*
175  0*  Adolfo Consolini
         (Italy)        Oct. 26 1941
177 11*  Consolini      Apr. 14 1946
180  3*  Robert Fitch (USA)
                        June  8 1946
181  6*  Consolini      Oct. 10 1948
185  3*  Fortune Gordien (USA)
                        July  9 1949
186 11*  Gordien        Aug. 14 1949
190  0*  Sim Iness (USA)
                        June 20 1953
190  7*  Gordien        July 11 1953
194  6*  Gordien        Aug. 22 1953
196  6*  Edmund Piatkowski
         (Poland)       June 14 1959
198  8*  Jay Silvester (USA)
                        Aug. 11 1961
199  2*  Silvester      Aug. 20 1961
200  5*  Al Oerter (USA)
                        May 18 1962
202  3*  Vladimir Trusenyov
         (USSR)         June  4 1962
204 10*  Oerter         July  1 1962
205  5*  Oerter         Apr. 27 1963
206  6*  Oerter         Apr. 25 1964
211  9*  Ludvik Danek
         (Czechoslovakia) Aug.  2 1964
214  0*  Danek          Oct. 12 1965
216  9   Danek          June  7 1966
218  4*  Silvester      May 25 1968
224  5*  Silvester      Sept. 18 1968
224  5*  Ricky Bruch
         (Sweden)       July  5 1972

IAAF record not shown above:
196  6   Rink Bakba (USA)
                        Aug. 12 1960

*Hammer*
ft. in.
195  4   Pat O'Callaghan
         (Ireland)      Aug. 22 1937
195  5*  Imre Nemeth
         (Hungary)      Sept.  4 1949
196  5*  Nemeth         May 19 1950
197 11*  Jozsef Csermak
         (Hungary)      July 24 1952
200 11*  Sverre Strandli
         (Norway)       Sept. 14 1952
204  7*  Strandli       Sept.  5 1953
207 10*  Mikhail Krivonosov
         (USSR)         Aug. 29 1954
210  1*  Stanislav Nyenashev
         (USSR)         Dec. 12 1954
211  0*  Krivonosov     Aug.  4 1955

211  8*  Krivonosov     Sept. 19 1955
216  0*  Krivonosov     Apr. 25 1956
216  4*  Cliff Blair (USA)
                        July  4 1956
217  9*  Krivonosov     July  8 1956
218 10   Hal Connolly (USA)
                        Oct.  3 1956
220 10*  Krivonosov     Oct. 22 1956
224 10*  Connolly       Nov.  2 1956
225  4*  Connolly       June 20 1958
230  9*  Connolly       Aug. 12 1960
231 10*  Connolly       July 21 1962
233  2*  Connolly       May 29 1965
233  9*  Connolly       June 20 1965
241 11*  Gyula Zsivotzky
         (Hungary)      Sept  4 1965
242  0*  Zsivotzky      Sept. 14 1968
244  6*  Romuald Klim
         (USSR)         June 15 1969
245  0*  Anatoliy Bondarchuk
         (USSR)         Sept. 20 1969
247  8*  Bondarchuk     Oct. 12 1969
250  8*  Walter Schmidt (W.
         Germany)       Sept.  4 1971

IAAF record not shown above:
193  8   Imre Nemeth
         (Hungary)      July 14 1948

*Javelin*
ft. in.
258  2*  Yrjo Nikkanen
         (Finland)      Oct. 16 1938
263 10*  Bud Held (USA)
                        Aug.  8 1953
266  8   Bill Miller (USA)
                        Aug. 21 1954
266  8   Held           May 21 1955
268  2*  Held           May 21 1955
274  2*  Soini Nikkinen (Fin-
         land)          June 24 1956
274  6*  Janusz Sidlo (Poland)
                        June 30 1956
281  2*  Egil Danielsen (Nor-
         way)           Nov. 26 1956
282  3*  Al Cantello (USA)
                        June  5 1959
284  7*  Carlo Lievore (Italy)
                        June  1 1961
285 10*  Terje Pedersen (Nor-
         way)           July  1 1964
300 11*  Pedersen       Sept.  1 1964
301  9*  Janis Lusis (USSR)
                        June 23 1968
304  1*  Jorma Kinnunen
         (Finland)      June 18 1969
307  9*  Lusis          July  6 1972
308  8   Klaus Wolfermann
         (W. Germany)   May  5 1973

201

*Decathlon* (1962 Tables)
7421* Glenn Morris (USA
Aug 7/8 1936
7453* Bob Mathias (USA
June 29/30 1950
7690 Mathias July 1/2 1952
7731* Mathias July 25/26 1952
7758* Rafer Johnson (USA)
June 10/11 1955
7760* Vasiliy Kuznyetsov (USSR)
May 17/18 1958
7896* Johnson July 27/28 1958
7957* Kuznyetsov May 16/17 1959
8063* Johnson July 8/9 1960
8089* Yang Chuan-kwang
(Taiwan) Apr. 27/28 1963
8230 Russ Hodge (USA)
July 23/24 1966
8319* Kurt Bendlin (W.
Germany) May 13/14 1967
8417* Bill Toomey (USA)
Dec 10/11 1969
8454* Nikolay Avilov (USSR)
Sept. 7/8 1972

*Walking records as ratified by IAAF*

*20,000 Metres Walk*
1 : 32 : 28.4 John Mikaelsson
(Sweden) July 12 1942
1 : 30 : 26.4 Josef Dolezal
(Czechoslovakia) Nov. 1 1953
1 : 30 : 02.8 Vladimir Golubnichiy (USSR) Oct. 2 1955
1 : 28 : 45.2 Leonid Spirin
(USSR) June 13 1956
1 : 27 : 58.2 Mikhail Lavrov
(USSR) Aug.13 1956
1 : 27 : 38.6 Grigoriy Panichkin
(USSR) May 9 1958
1 : 27 : 05.0 Golubnichiy
Sept. 23 1958
1 : 26 : 45.8 Gennadiy Agapov
(USSR) Apr. 6 1969
1 : 25 : 50.0 Peter Frenkel (E.
Germany) July 4 1970
1 : 25 : 19.4 Frenkel June 24 1972
1 : 25 : 19.4 Han-Georg Reimann
(E. Germany) June 24 1972

*2 Hours Walk*
15 mi. 1228 yd. Edgar Bruun
(Norway) Oct. 8 1939
15 mi. 1521 yd. Olle Andersson
(Sweden) Sept. 15 1945
15 mi. 1591 yd. Josef Dolezal
(Czechoslovakia) Oct. 12 1952
15 mi. 1707 yd. Dolezal
May 14 1955

16 mi. 126 yd. Anatoliy Vedyakov
(USSR) Oct. 7 1955
16 mi. 403 yd. Ted Allsop
(Australia) Sept. 22 1956
16 mi. 743 yd. Anatoliy Yegorov
(USSR) July 15 1959
16 mi. 993 yd. Peter Frenkel
(E. Germany) Apr. 11 1971
16 mi. 1269 yd. Karl-Heinz Stadtmuller (E. Germany)
Apr. 16 1972

*30,000 Metres Walk*
hr. min. sec.
2 : 28 : 57.4 Harry Olsson (Sweden)
Aug. 15 1943
2 : 27 : 44.6 Sandor Laszlo (Hungary)
May 18 1952
2 : 27 : 42.0 John Ljunggren (Sweden)
Aug. 3 1952
2 : 21 : 38.6 Josef Dolezal (Czechoslovakia) Oct. 12 1952
2 : 20 : 40.2 Anatoliy Vedyakov
(USSR) Oct. 7 1955
2 : 19 : 43.0 Vedyakov Aug. 23 1958
2 : 17 : 16.8 Anatoliy Yegorov (USSR)
July 15 1959
2 : 15 : 16.0 Christoph Hohne (E.
Germany) Apr. 11 1971
2 : 14 : 45.6 Karl-Heinz Stadtmuller
(E. Germany) Apr. 16 1972

*20 Miles Walk*
hr. min. sec.
2 : 41 : 07.0 Harry Olsson (Sweden)
Aug. 15 1943
2 : 39 : 22.8 John Ljunggren (Sweden)
Aug. 3 1952
2 : 33 : 09.4 Josef Dolezal (Czechoslovakia) May 14 1954
2 : 31 : 33.0 Anatoliy Vedyakov
(USSR) Aug 23 1958

*30 Miles Walk*
hr. min. sec.
4 : 24 : 54.2 Florimond Cornet
(France) Oct. 11 1942
4 : 21 : 38.2 John Ljunggren (Sweden)
July 29 1951
4 : 21 : 12.6 Antal Roka (Hungary)
June 1 1952
4 : 21 : 11.0 Ljunggren Aug. 8 1953
4 : 20 : 10.6 Roka Oct. 30 1955
4 : 16 : 14.8 Milan Skront (Czechoslovakia) Apr. 30 1956
4.12 : 03.4 Ladislav Moc (Czechoslovakia) June 21 1956
4 : 07 : 11.0 Sergey Lobastov (USSR)
Aug. 23 1958

4:04:56.8 Abdon Pamich (Italy)
    Nov. 19 1961
4:02:33.0 Christoph Hohne
  (E. Germany)    May 16 1965
4:00:06.4 Hohne    Oct. 18 1969
3:56:12.6 Peter Selzer (E.
  Germany)    Oct. 3 1971

*50,000 Metres Walk*
hr. min. sec.
4:34:03.0* Paul Sievert (Germany)
    Oct. 5 1924
4:32:52.0 John Ljunggren (Sweden)
    July 29 1951
4:31:21.6 Antal Roka (Hungary)
    June 1 1952
4:29:58.0 Ljunggren  Aug. 8 1953

4:27:28.4 Ladislav Moc (Czechoslovakia)    Oct. 13 1955
4:26:05.2 Milan Skront (Czechoslovakia)    Apr. 30 1956
4:21:07.0 Moc    June 21 1956
4:16:08.6 Sergey Lobastov (USSR)
    Aug. 23 1958
4:14:02.4 Abdon Pamich (Italy)
    Nov. 19 1961
4:10:51.8 Christoph Hohne
  (E. Germany)    May 16 1965
4:08:05.0 Hohne    Oct. 18 1969
4:04:19.8 Peter Selzer
  (E. Germany)    Oct. 3 1971
4:03:42.6 Veniamin Soldatenko
  (USSR)    Oct. 5 1972

* performance made on road

# Women

Best performances on record:

| | | | |
|---|---|---|---|
| *100 yd.* | 10.0 | Chi Cheng (Taiwan) | June 13 1970 |
| *100 m.* | 11.0 | Wyomia Tyus (USA) | Oct. 15 1968 |
| | 11.0 | Chi Cheng (Taiwan) | July 18 1970 |
| | 11.0 | Renate Stecher (E. Germany) Aug. 2 1970 | |
| | 11.0 | Renate Stecher (E. Germany) July 31 1971 | |
| | 11.0 | Ellen Stropahl (E. Germany) June 18 1972 | |
| | 11.0 | Eva Gleskova (Czechoslovakia) July 1 1972 | |
| *200 m.* | 22.4 | Chi Cheng (Taiwan) | July 12 1970 |
| | 22.4 | Renate Stecher (E. Germany) Sept. 7 1972 | |
| *220 yd.* | 22.6 | Chi Cheng (Taiwan) | July 3 1970 |
| *400 m.* | 51.0 | Marilyn Neufville (Jamaica) July 23 1970 | |
| | 51.0 | Monika Zehrt (E. Germany) July 4 1972 | |
| *440 yd.* | 52.4 | Judy Pollock (Australia) | Feb. 27 1965 |
| *800 m.* | 1:58.5 | Hildegard Falck (W. Germany) July 11 1971 | |
| *880 yd.* | 2:02.0 | Dixie Willis (Australia) | Mar. 3 1962 |
| | 2:02.0 | Judy Pollock (Australia) | July 5 1967 |
| | *2:02.0 | Madeline Jackson (USA) | May 13 1972 |
| *1500 m.* | 4:01.4 | Lyudmila Bragina (USSR) | Sept. 9 1972 |
| *Mile* | 4:35.3 | Ellen Tittel (W. Germany) Aug. 20 1971 | |
| *100 m. Hurdles* | 12.5 | Annelie Ehrhardt (E. Germany) June 15 1972 | |
| | 12.5 | Pam Ryan (Australia) | June 28 1972 |
| | 12.5 | Annelie Ehrhardt (E. Germany) Aug. 13 1972 | |
| *200 m. Hurdles* | 25.7 | Pam Ryan (Australia) | Nov. 25 1971 |
| *High Jump* | 6ft. 4½in. | Yordanka Blagoyeva (Bulgaria) Sept. 24 1972 | |
| *Long Jump* | 22ft. 5¼in. | Heide Rosendahl (W. Germany) Sept. 3 1970 | |
| *Shot* | 69ft. 0in. | Nadyezhda Chizhova (USSR) Sept. 7 1972 | |
| *Discus* | 219ft. 0in. | Faina Melnik (USSR) | Aug. 4 1972 |
| | 221ft. 3in. | Faina Melnik (USSR) | May 25 1973 |
| *Javelin* | 213ft. 5in. | Ruth Fuchs (E. Germany) | June 11 1972 |
| *Pentathlon* | 4,801 | Mary Peters (GB & NI) | Sept. 2/3 1972 |

| 4 x 100 m. | 42.8 | USA (Barbara Ferrell, Margaret Bailes, Mildrette Netter, Wyomia Tyus | Oct. 20 1968 |
| | 42.8 | West Germany (Christine Krause, Ingrid Mickler, Annegret Richter, Heide Rosendahl) | Sept. 10 1972 |
| 4 x 200 m. | 1:33.8 | Gt. Britain (Maureen Tranter, Della Pascoe, Janet Simpson, Val Peat) | Aug. 24 1968 |
| 4 x 220 yd. | 1:35.8 | Australia (Marion Hoffman, Raelene Boyle, Pam Ryan, Jenny Lamy) | Nov. 9 1969 |
| 4 x 400 m. | 3:23.0 | East Germany (Dagmar Kasling, Rita Kuhne, Helga Seidler, Monika Zehrt) | Sept. 10 1972 |
| 4 x 800 m. | 8:16.8 | West Germany (Ellen Tittel, Sylvia Schenk, Christa Merten, Hildegard Falck) | July 31 1971 |

# Evolution of Women's World Records

100 Yards
sec.

| | | | |
|---|---|---|---|
| 10.8 | Stanislawa Walasiewicz (Poland) | May 30 | 1930 |
| 10.8 | Walasiewicz | Aug. 4 | 1930 |
| 10.8 | Myrtle Cook (Canada) | Aug. 4 | 1930 |
| 10.8 | Helen Stephens (USA) | Aug. 31 | 1935 |
| 10.8* | Fanny Blankers-Koen (Netherlands) | May 18 | 1944 |
| 10.8 | Cynthia Thompson (Jamaica) | Aug. 4 | 1947 |
| 10.8* | Marjorie Jackson (Australia) | Jan. 4 | 1950 |
| 10.8* | Jackson | Feb. 4 | 1950 |
| 10.8 | Jackson | Feb. 6 | 1950 |
| 10.7* | Jackson | Mar. 31 | 1950 |
| 10.4* | Jackson | Mar. 8 | 1952 |
| 10.4 | Betty Cuthbert (Australia) | Mar. 1 | 1958 |
| 10.4* | Cuthbert | Mar. 1 | 1958 |
| 10.4 | Marlene Willard (Australia) | Mar. 1 | 1958 |
| 10.4 | Willard | Mar. 20 | 1958 |
| 10.3* | Willard | Mar. 20 | 1958 |
| 10.3* | Wyomia Tyus (USA) | July 17 | 1965 |
| 10.3* | Tyus | June 8 | 1968 |
| 10.3 | Chi Cheng (Taiwan) | May 23 | 1969 |
| 10.3 | Chi Cheng | July 29 | 1969 |
| 10.3 | Chi Cheng | Mar. 28 | 1970 |
| 10.0* | Chi Cheng | June 13 | 1970 |

100 Metres
sec.

| | | | |
|---|---|---|---|
| 11.5 | Helen Stephens (USA) | Aug. 10 | 1936 |
| 11.5 | Fanny Blankers-Koen (Netherlands) | Sept. 5 | 1943 |
| 11.5* | Blankers-Koen | June 13 | 1948 |
| 11.5 | Marjorie Jackson (Australia) | July 22 | 1952 |
| 11.5* | Jackson | July 22 | 1952 |
| 11.5 | Blankers-Koen | Sept. 28 | 1952 |
| 11.4* | Jackson | Oct. 4 | 1952 |
| 11.3* | Shirley De La Hunty (Australia) | Aug. 4 | 1955 |
| 11.3* | Vyera Krepkina (USSR) | Sept. 13 | 1958 |
| 11.3* | Wilma Rudolph (USA) | Sept. 2 | 1960 |
| 11.3 | Rudolph | July 15 | 1961 |
| 11.2* | Rudolph | July 19 | 1961 |
| 11.2* | Wyomia Tyus (USA) | Oct. 15 | 1964 |
| 11.1* | Irena Szewinska (Poland) | July 9 | 1965 |
| 11.1* | Tyus | July 31 | 1965 |
| 11.1* | Barbara Ferrell (USA) | July 2 | 1967 |
| 11.1 | Tyus | Apr. 21 | 1968 |
| 11.1* | Ludmila Samotyosova (USSR) | Aug. 15 | 1968 |
| 11.1 | Margaret Bailes (USA) | Aug. 18 | 1968 |
| 11.1* | Szewinska | Oct. 14 | 1968 |
| 11.1 | Ferrell | Oct. 14 | 1968 |
| 11.0* | Tyus | Oct. 15 | 1968 |
| 11.0* | Chi Cheng (Taiwan) | July 18 | 1970 |
| 11.0* | Renate Stecher (E. Germany) | Aug. 2 | 1970 |

| | | | | |
|---|---|---|---|---|
| 11.0* | Stecher | July 31 1971 | | |
| 11.0 | Stecher | June 3 1972 | | |
| 11.0* | Ellen Stropahl (E. | | | |
| | Germany) | June 18 1972 | | |
| 11.0* | Eva Gleskova (Czecho- | | | |
| | slovakia) | July 1 1972 | | |
| 11.0 | Stecher | Aug. 20 1972 | | |

*200 Metres* (Turn)
sec.

| | | | |
|---|---|---|---|
| 23.6* | Stanislawa Walasiewicz | | |
| | (Poland) | Aug. 15 1935 | |
| 23.6* | Marjorie Jackson (Australia) | | |
| | | July 25 1952 | |
| 23.4* | Jackson | July 25 1952 | |
| 23.2* | Betty Cuthbert (Australia) | | |
| | | Sept. 16 1956 | |
| 23.2* | Cuthbert | Mar. 7 1960 | |
| 22.9* | Wilma Rudolph (USA) | | |
| | | July 9 1960 | |
| 22.9* | Margaret Burvill (Australia) | | |
| | | Feb. 22 1964 | |
| 22.7* | Irena Szewinska (Poland) | | |
| | | Aug. 8 1965 | |
| 22.7 | Szewinska | July 2 1967 | |
| 22.5* | Szewinska | Oct. 18 1968 | |
| 22.4* | Chi Cheng (Taiwan) | | |
| | | July 12 1970 | |
| 22.4* | Renate Stecher (E. | | |
| | Germany) | Sept. 7 1972 | |

*220 Yards* (Turn)
sec.

| | | | |
|---|---|---|---|
| 24.3* | Stanislawa Walasiewicz | | |
| | (Poland) | June 9 1935 | |
| 24.3* | Marjorie Jackson (Australia) | | |
| | | Feb. 9 1950 | |
| 24.2* | Fanny Blankers-Koen | | |
| | (Netherlands) | June 29 1950 | |
| 24.0 | Jackson | Feb. 20 1954 | |
| 24.0* | Jackson | Aug. 5 1954 | |
| 23.8 | Christa Stubnick (E. | | |
| | Germany) | May 29 1955 | |
| 23.6* | Maria Itkina (USSR) | | |
| | | July 22 1956 | |
| 23.6* | Betty Cuthbert (Australia) | | |
| | | Jan. 18 1958 | |
| 23.5* | Cuthbert | Mar. 8 1958 | |
| 23.4* | Marlene Willard (Australia) | | |
| | | Mar. 22 1958 | |
| 23.2* | Cuthbert | Mar. 7 1960 | |
| 23.2* | Margaret Burvill (Australia) | | |
| | | Jan. 12 1963 | |
| 22.9* | Burvill | Feb. 22 1964 | |
| 22.7* | Chi Cheng (Taiwan) | | |
| | | June 13 1970 | |
| 22.6* | Chi Cheng | July 3 1970 | |

*400 Metres*
sec.

| | | | |
|---|---|---|---|
| 56.8 | Nellie Halstead (GB) | | |
| | | July 9 1932 | |

| | | | |
|---|---|---|---|
| 56.7 | Zoya Petrova (USSR) | | |
| | | Sept. 19 1950 | |
| 56.0 | Petrova | July 15 1951 | |
| 56.0 | Valentina Pomogayeva | | |
| | (USSR) | Aug. 15 1951 | |
| 55.7 | Ursula Donath (E. Germany) | | |
| | | June 25 1953 | |
| 55.7 | Polina Solopova (USSR) | | |
| | | June 12 1954 | |
| 55.5 | Nina Otkalenko (USSR) | | |
| | | July 25 1954 | |
| 55.0 | Donath | Aug. 7 1954 | |
| 54.8 | Zinaida Safronova (USSR) | | |
| | | July 21 1955 | |
| 54.4 | Donath | Aug. 6 1955 | |
| 53.9 | Maria Itkina (USSR) | | |
| | | Oct. 1 1955 | |
| 53.6* | Itkina | July 6 1957 | |
| 53.6 | Itkina | June 14 1958 | |
| 53.4* | Itkina | Sept. 12 1959 | |
| 53.0 | Sin Kim Dan (N. Korea) | | |
| | | Oct. 22 1960 | |
| 53.0 | Sin Kim Dan | June 30 1962 | |
| 51.9* | Sin Kim Dan | Oct. 23 1962 | |
| 51.4 | Sin Kim Dan | Nov. 12 1963 | |
| 51.2 | Sin Kim Dan | Oct. 21 1964 | |
| 51.0* | Marilyn Neufville | | |
| | (Jamaica) | July 23 1970 | |
| 51.0* | Monika Zehrt | | |
| | (E. Germany) | July 4 1972 | |

IAAF records not shown above:

sec.

| | | | |
|---|---|---|---|
| 57.0 | Marlene Willard (Australia) | | |
| | | Jan. 6 1957 | |
| 57.0 | Marise Chamberlain (New | | |
| | Zealand) | Feb. 16 1957 | |
| 56.3 | Nancy Boyle (Australia) | | |
| | | Feb. 24 1957 | |
| 55.2 | Polina Lazareva (USSR) | | |
| | | May 10 1957 | |
| 54.0 | Maria Itkina (USSR) | | |
| | | June 8 1957 | |
| 53.4 | Itkina | Sept. 14 1962 | |
| 51.7 | Nicole Duclos (France) | | |
| | | Sept. 18 1969 | |
| 51.7 | Colette Besson (France) | | |
| | | Sept. 18 1969 | |

*440 Yards*
sec.

| | | | |
|---|---|---|---|
| 56.8 | Nellie Halstead (GB) | | |
| | | July 9 1932 | |
| 56.6 | Pamela Bryant (Australia) | | |
| | | Feb. 27 1954 | |
| 56.6 | Diane Leather (GB) | | |
| | | Aug. 21 1954 | |

56.5   Janet Ruff (GB)   Aug. 11 1956
56.3*  Nancy Boyle (Australia)
                         Feb. 24 1957
56.1*  Marise Chamberlain (New
       Zealand)          Mar.  8 1958
55.6*  Molly Hiscox (GB)
                         Aug.  2 1958
55.6*  Betty Cuthbert (Australia)
                         Jan. 17 1959
55.6*  Chamberlain      Mar. 14 1959
54.3*  Cuthbert         Mar. 21 1959
53.7*  Maria Itkina (USSR)
                         Sept. 12 1959
53.5*  Cuthbert         Mar. 11 1963
53.3*  Cuthbert         Mar. 23 1963
52.4*  Judy Pollock (Australia)
                         Feb. 27 1965

IAAF records not shown above:

57.0   Marlene Willard (Australia)
                         Jan.  6 1957
57.0   Marise Chamberlain (New
       Zealand)          Feb. 16 1957

*800 Metres*
min. sec.
2:12.0   Yevdokiya Vasilyeva
         (USSR)         Aug.  5 1943
2:12.0*  Nina Otkalenko (USSR)
                        Aug. 26 1951
2:11.7   Polina Solopova (USSR)
                        May 27 1952
2:08.5*  Otkalenko      June 15 1952
2:08.2   Otkalenko      June  7 1953
2:07.3*  Otkalenko      Aug. 27 1953
2:06.6*  Otkalenko      Sept. 16 1954
2:06.4   Otkalenko      Sept. 19 1955
2:05.0*  Otkalenko      Sept. 24 1955
2:04.3*  Lyudmila Shevtsova
         (USSR)         July  3 1960
2:04.3*  Shevtsova      Sept.  7 1960
2:01.2   Sin Kim Dan (N. Korea)
                        May  1 1961
2:01.2*  Dixie Willis (Australia)
                        Mar.  3 1962
1:59.1   Sin Kim Dan   Nov. 12 1963
1:58.0   Sin Kim Dan   Sept.  5 1964

IAAF records not shown above:

2:15.9   Anna Larsson (Sweden)
                        Aug. 28 1944
2:14.8   Larsson        Aug. 19 1945
2:13.8   Larsson        Aug. 30 1945
2:13.0   Yevdokiya Vasilyeva
         (USSR)         July 17 1950
2:12.2   Valentina Pomogayeva
         (USSR)         July 26 1951
2:01.1   Ann Packer (GB)
                        Oct. 20 1964

2:01.0   Judy Pollock (Australia)
                        June 28 1967
2:00.5   Vera Nikolic (Yugo-
         slavia)        July 20 1968
1:58.5   Hildegard Falck (W.
         Germany)       July 11 1971

*880 Yards*
min. sec.
2:17.4*  Olive Hall (GB)
                        July 25 1936
2:15.6*  Anna Larsson (Sweden)
                        Sept.  5 1945
2:14.4   Enid Harding (GB)
                        Aug. 30 1952
2:12.6*  Ursula Jurewitz (E.
         Germany)       Aug. 19 1953
2:11.6*  Aranka Kazi (Hungary)
                        May 29 1954
2:09.0*  Diane Leather (GB)
                        June 19 1954
2:08.4*  Nina Otkalenko (USSR)
                        July 18 1954
2:06.6*  Otkalenko      June 10 1956
2:06.1*  Joy Jordan (GB)
                        Sept. 24 1960
2:02.0*  Dixie Willis (Australia)
                        Mar.  3 1962
2:02.0*  Judy Pollock (Australia)
                        July  5 1967
2:02.0   Madeline Jackson (USA)
                        May 13 1972

IAAF record not shown above:
2:14.5   Valerie Winn (GB)
                        Sept. 17 1952

*1500 Metres*
min. sec.
4:38.0   Yevdokiya Vasilyeva
         (USSR)         Aug. 17 1944
4:37.8   Olga Ovsyannikova
         (USSR)         Sept. 15 1946
4.37.0   Nina Otkalenko (USSR)
                        Aug. 30 1952
4:35.4   Phyllis Perkins (GB)
                        May 17 1956
4:30.0   Diane Leather (GB)
                        May 16 1957
4:29.7   Leather        July 19 1957
4:19.0   Marise Chamberlain
         (NZ)           Dec.  8 1962
4:17.3*  Anne Smith (GB)
                        June  3 1967
4:15.6*  Maria Gommers
         (Netherlands)  Oct. 24 1967
4:12.4*  Paola Pigni (Italy)
                        July  2 1969
4:10.7*  Jaroslava Jehlickova
         (Czechoslovakia) Sept. 20 1969

4:09.6* Karin Burneleit (E.
Germany)          Aug 15 1971
4:06.9* Lyudmila Bragina
(USSR)            July 18 1972
4:06.5* Bragina         Sept.  4 1972
4:05.1* Bragina         Sept.  7 1972
4:01.4* Bragina         Sept.  9 1972

*Mile*
min. sec.
5:15.3  Evelyne Forster (GB)
July 22 1939
5:11.0  Anne Oliver (GB)
June 14 1952
5:09.8  Enid Harding (GB)
July  4 1953
5:08.0  Oliver          Sept. 12 1953
5:02.6  Diane Leather (GB)
Sept. 30 1953
5:00.3  Edith Treybal
(Rumania)         Nov.  1 1953
5:00.2  Leather         May 26 1954
4:59.6  Leather         May 29 1954
4:50.8  Leather         May 24 1955
4:45.0  Leather         Sept. 21 1955
4:41.4  Marise Chamberlain
(NZ)              Dec.  8 1962
4:39.2  Anne Smith (GB)
May 13 1967
4:37.0* Smith           June  3 1967
4:36.8* Maria Gommers
(Netherlands)     June 14 1969
4:35.3* Ellen Tittel (W.
Germany)          Aug. 20 1971

*100 Metres Hurdles*
(event officially inaugurated on May
1 1969)
sec.
13.3* Karin Balzer (E.
Germany)          June 20 1969
13.3* Teresa Sukniewicz
(Poland)          June 20 1969
13.0* Balzer          July 27 1969
12.9* Balzer          Sept.  5 1969
12.8* Sukniewicz      June 20 1970
12.8* Chi Cheng (Taiwan)
July 12 1970
12.7* Balzer          July 26 1970
12.7* Sukniewicz      Sept. 20 1970
12.7* Sukniewicz      Sept. 27 1970
12.7* Balzer          July 25 1971
12.6* Balzer          July 31 1971
12.5* Annelie Ehrhardt (E.
Germany)          June 15 1972
12.5* Pam Ryan (Australia)
June 28 1972
12.5* Ehrhardt        Aug. 13 1972

*200 Metres Hurdles*
sec.
26.2* Chi Cheng (Taiwan)
May 25 1969
26.1* Pam Ryan (Australia)
Oct. 11 1969
26.0* Ryan            Nov.  9 1969
25.8* Ryan            Dec. 17 1969
25.8* Annelie Ehrhardt (E.
Germany)          July  5 1970
25.8* Teresa Sukniewicz
(Poland)          Aug.  9 1970
25.7* Ryan            Nov. 25 1971

*High Jump*
ft. in.
5  7¼* Fanny Blankers-Koen
(Netherlands)     May 30 1943
5  7½* Sheila Lerwill (GB)
July  7 1951
5  8*  Alexandra Chudina
(USSR)            May 22 1954
5  8½* Thelma Hopkins (GB)
May  5 1956
5  8¾* Iolanda Balas (Rumania)
July 14 1956
5  9¼* Mildred McDaniel (USA)
Dec.  1 1956
5  9¼* Balas           Oct. 13 1957
5  9¾* Cheng Feng-yung (China)
Nov. 17 1957
5 10*  Balas           June  7 1958
5 10¾* Balas           June 22 1958
5 11¼* Balas           July 31 1958
5 11½* Balas           Oct.  4 1958
6  0*  Balas           Oct. 18 1958
6  0½* Balas           Sept. 21 1959
6  0¾* Balas           June  6 1960
6  1¼* Balas           July  9 1960
6  1½* Balas           Apr. 15 1961
6  2*  Balas           June 18 1961
6  2¾* Balas           July  8 1961
6  3¼* Balas           July 16 1961
6  3½* Ilona Gusenbauer
(Austria)         Sept.  4 1971
6  3½* Ulrike Meyfarth (W.
Germany)          Sept.  4 1972
6  4¼* Yordanka Blagoyeva
(Bulgaria)        Sept. 24 1972

*Long Jump*
ft. in.
20  6* Fanny Blankers-Koen
(Netherlands)     Sept. 19 1943
20  7¼* Yvette Williams (New
Zealand)          Feb. 20 1954
20  7¼* Galina Vinogradova
(USSR)            Sept. 11 1955
20  8½* Vinogradova     Nov. 18 1955

| 190 | 0* | Elvira Ozolina (USSR) | | | |
| | | | May | 3 | 1960 |
| 195 | 4* | Ozolina | June | 4 | 1960 |
| 196 | 1* | Ozolina | July | 3 | 1963 |
| 201 | 4* | Ozolina | Aug. | 27 | 1964 |
| 204 | 9* | Yelena Gorchakova | | | |
| | | (USSR) | Oct. | 16 | 1964 |
| 205 | 8* | Ewa Gryziecka | | | |
| | | (Poland) | June | 11 | 1972 |
| 213 | 5* | Ruth Fuchs (E. | | | |
| | | Germany) | June | 11 | 1972 |

IAAF records not shown above:

| 158 | 2 | Hermina Bauma | | | |
| | | (Austria) | June | 29 | 1947 |
| 159 | 6 | Bauma | Sept. | 12 | 1948 |
| 162 | 8 | Natalya Smirnitskaya | | | |
| | | (USSR) | July | 25 | 1949 |

*Pentathlon* (1954 tables)
Pts.

| 4608 | Alexandra Chudina (USSR) | | |
| | | Oct. | 9 1949 |
| 4651 | Chudina | Sept. 21/22 | 1950 |
| 4692* | Fanny Blankers-Koen | | |
| | (Netherlands) | Sept. 15/16 | 1951 |
| 4704* | Chudina | Aug. 8/9 | 1953 |
| 4747* | Nina Vinogradova (USSR) | | |
| | | July 6/7 | 1955 |
| 4750* | Chudina | Sept. 6/7 | 1955 |
| 4767* | Vinogradova | Aug. 11/12 | 1956 |
| 4846* | Galina Bystrova (USSR) | | |
| | | Oct. 15/16 | 1957 |
| 4872* | Bystrova | Nov. 1/2 | 1958 |
| 4880* | Irina Press (USSR) | | |
| | | Sept. 13/14 | 1959 |
| 4902* | Press | May 21/22 | 1960 |
| 4959* | Press | June 25/26 | 1960 |
| 4972* | Press | Oct. 17/18 | 1960 |
| 5020 | Press | Aug. 16/17 | 1961 |
| 5137* | Press | Oct. 8/9 | 1961 |
| 5194 | Press | Aug. 29/30 | 1964 |
| 5246* | Press | Oct. 16/17 | 1964 |

*With 100 m. hurdles*

| 5352* | Liese Prokop (Austria) | | |
| | | Oct.4/5 | 1969 |
| 5406* | Burglinde Pollak (E. | | |
| | Germany) | Sept. 5/6 | 1970 |

*New Tables*

| 4791 | Heide Rosendahl (W. | | |
| | Germany) | Sept. 2/3 | 1972 |
| 4801* | Mary Peters (GB & NI) | | |
| | | Sept. 2/3 | 1972 |

## WOTTLE, D. (USA)

Prior to 1972 Dave Wottle was just a promising middle distance runner with times of 1 min. 47.8 sec. for 880 yd. and 3 min. 59.0 sec. for the mile to his credit. Both those marks were made in 1970 since he was out of action throughout 1971 due to stress fractures in both feet and bursitis in the knee.

It was at the US Olympic Trials that Wottle, wearing the battered golf cap that was to become so famous, caused an unsuspecting world to sit up and take notice. Running the 800 m., " just for some speed work before the 1500 ", he stormed home in 1 min. 44.3 sec. to equal the world record—three seconds faster than he had ever run before!

An Achilles tendon injury caused him to lose form in European races prior to the Olympics, but in the Munich final, after lagging far behind in last place for much of the race, he came through with a late burst to pip European champion Yevgeniy Arzhanov (USSR) on the tape in 1 min. 45.9 sec. His even-pace tactics (200 m. splits of 26.4, 26.9, 26.4, 26.2) had paid off. His habit of laying off the pace caused his downfall in the 1500 m.; however, and he failed to reach the final.

His best marks include 1 min. 44.3 sec. for 800 m., 3 min. 39.7 sec. for 1500 m., 3 min. 58.2 sec. for the mile and 8 min. 39 sec. for 2 mi. (indoors). Annual progress at 880 yd. and mile: 1968—4:20.2; 1969—1:54.9, 4:06.8; 1970—1:47.8, 3:59.0; 1972—1:44.3 (800 m.), 3:58.2. He was born at Canton, Ohio, on Aug. 7th, 1950.

O

# YOUNGEST

## Men

Youngest Olympic champion was Bob Mathias (USA), 1948 decathlon winner at the age of 17 yr. 8 mth.

Youngest British champion: Charles Lockton, winner of Amateur Athletic Club (English Championships) long jump in 1873, aged 16 yr. 9 mth.

Youngest British international: William Land, high jump in 1931 aged 16.

Youngest world record holder: John Thomas (USA) was 10 days short of his 18th birthday when in 1959 he jumped 7 ft. 1¼ in. for an indoor world best—superior to the existing outdoor record.

Youngest British record holder: Alan Paterson, high jump in 1946, aged 17 yr. 11 mth.

## Women

Youngest Olympic champion: Barbara Jones (USA), member of winning 4 x 100 m. relay team in 1952, aged 15 yr. 3 mth. Youngest individual gold medallist: Ulrike Meyfarth (W. Germany), high jump in 1972, aged 16 yr. 4 mth. These two girls are also the youngest world record breakers.

Youngest British champion: Betty Lock, WAAA 60 m. in 1936, aged 15.

Youngest British international: Sonia Lannaman, indoor 50 m. in 1971 aged 14 yr. 10 mth.

# Z

## ZATOPEK, E. (Czechoslovakia)

In the eyes of many athletics experts, Emil Zatopek's triple triumph at the 1952 Olympics represents the sport's supreme achievement. Even to attempt the 5000 m., 10,000 m. and marathon against the cream of the world's athletes is startling; to win all three—each in Olympic record time—is well nigh incredible.

This was the measure of Zatopek's feat in Helsinki: July 20th, first in 10,000 m. in 29 min. 17.0 sec. (won by 100 yd.); July 22nd, third in 5000 m. heat in 14 min. 26.0 sec.; July 24th, first in 5000 m. final in 14 min. 06.6 sec. (won by five yd.); July 27th, first in marathon in 2 hr. 23 min. 03.2 sec. (won by 750 yd.). What is more, he had never before run a marathon in competition!

Zatopek made his Olympic bow in London in 1948, winning the 10,000 m. (only two months after his debut in the event) and placing a close second in the 5000 m. His final Olympic appearance in 1956 resulted in his finishing sixth in the second marathon race of his career.

On the European Championship plane, he won both titles in 1950, the 10,000 m. in 1954 and was third in the 5000 m. He set world records at several distances between 5000 and 30,000 m. from 1949 to 1955 and was the first man to leap such barriers as 28 min. for 6 mi., 29 min. for 10,000 m. and 60 min. for 20,000 m.

Zatopek made himself the greatest runner of his generation, if not all-time, by virtue of his capacity for training longer and harder than anyone had previously attempted. He possessed little natural ability. For the record, his first race was a 1400 m. event in 1941 (at the age of 18) for which he was timed in an unimpressive 4 min. 24.6 sec.

His best marks included 56.2 sec. for 400 m.; 1 min. 58.7 sec for 800 m.; 3 min. 52.8 sec. for 1500 m.; 8 min. 07.8 sec. for 3000 m.; 13 min. 31.2 sec. for 3 mi.; 13 min. 57.0 sec for 5000 m.; 27 min. 59.2 sec. for 6 mi.; 28 min. 54.2 sec for 10,000 m.; 44 min. 54.6 sec for 15 km.; 48 min. 12.0 sec. for 10 mi.; 59 min. 51.8 sec. for 20 km.; 12 mi. 809 yd. in one hour; 1 hr. 14 min. 01 sec for 15 mi.; 1 hr. 16 min. 36.4 sec. for 25 km.; 1 hr. 35 min. 23.8 sec. for 30 km. and 2 hr. 23 min. 03.2 sec for the marathon.

Emil's wife, Dana Zatopkova (*née* Ingrova), was herself an Olympic champion—winner of the javelin in 1952. She won the silver medal in 1960 and was European champion in 1954 and 1958. She held the world record briefly in 1958, her best throw measuring 185 ft. 11 in.

Curiously, she and Emil were born on the same day: Sept. 19th, 1922— he at Koprivnice, she at Tryskat. He is the elder by six hours!

## ZEHRT, M. (East Germany)

Relentless progress has been the keynote of Monika Zehrt's career. In 1967, aged 14, she clocked 59.5 sec. in her first year of 400 m. running; she was down to 56.7 sec. in 1968, 55.3 in 1969, 52.9 sec. in 1970—the season she won the European junior title. Her best time of 52.5 sec. in 1971 was not quite good enough to win her selection for the individual 400 m. at the European Championships but she did earn herself a gold medal and world record in the 4 x 400 m. relay. By 1972 she was ready to take on the world although still only 19, and a splendid season was crowned by the Olympic title (in 51.5 sec.) and a share in Marilyn Neufville's world record of 51.0 sec. In addition she collected another gold medal as a member of East Germany's world record shattering relay team.

Born at Riesa on Sept. 29th, 1952, Monika has sprint times of 11.5 sec. (100 m.) and 22.8 sec. (200 m.) to her name.

211

# INDEX

Arese, F., 78, 114
Arizmendi, F., 69
Armitage, H. J., *see* Young, H. J.
Arzhanov, Y., 78, 105, 209
Asaad, N., 12
Asati, C., 12, 57, 59, 66, 141
Ashbaugh, W., 36
Ashby, R., 183, 187
Ashenfelter, H., 32, 33, 139, 198
Ashenfelter, W., 33
Ashworth, G. H., 140
Askew, H. E., 24
Astley, A., 16
Atkinson, S. J. M., 20, 140
Atterberry, W., 21, 34
Atterwall, A. L. F., 27, 80
Attlesey, K., 43
Attlesey, R. H., 33, 87, 150, 198
Audet, E., 36
Auerbach, R., 43, 44
Aukett, J. W., 102
Ault, R. F., 199
Avant, R., 34
Avery, G. G., 24
Avilov, N., 47, 72, 85, 143, 190, 202

B

Baba, T., 45
Babcock, H. S., 141
Babka, R., 37, 201
Bach, T., 191
Bacheler, J., 32
Backman, E., 18
Backus, R., 37, 151
Bacon, C. J., 140
Bacon, F. E., 16, 18
Badana, V., 46
Baddeley, E., 26
Badenski, A., 79, 84, 85, 105
Baghbanbashi, 45
Baik Ok-ja, 46
Baikov, V., 197
Bailes, M., 40, 144, 203, 204
Bailey, E. McD., 13, 14, 15, 136, 193
Bailey, F. G., 179
Bailey, G. W., 19, 20, 58, 62
Baillie, W. D., 197
Bair, R., 44
Baird, G., 141
Baker, B. H., 22
Baker, H., 16, 31
Baker, P. J. Noel-, 96, 136
Baker, S. H., 16
Baker, W. T., 30, 140, 176, 193
Bakhtawar Singh, 46
Balachowski, J., 85, 105

Balas, I., 48, 49, 81, 96, 106, 144, 147, 185, 207
Baldwin, A. G., 76
Balkar Singh, 45
Ball, E., 104
Ball, H. R., 15
Ball, V. M., *see* Winn, V. M.
Bally, E., 77
Balogh, L., 24
Balzer, K., 48, 75, 81, 84, 106, 108, 144, 160, 207
Bambuck, R., 77, 79, 85, 193
Bane, T., 37
Bangert, W., 36
Bank, P., 41, 42, 44, 152
Banks, J. H., 22
Bannister, R. G., 16, 17, 48, 49, 52, 55, 56, 57, 62, 76, 78, 101, 129, 195
Banthorpe, R., 102
Bantum, K., 36
Baraton, G., 17
Barber, J., 183
Barbuti, R. J., 30, 138, 141
Barkley, M., 41
Barksdale, D., 36
Barnes, J. G., 76
Barnes, L. S., 35, 141
Barrett, B-A., 104
Barrett, J., 25
Barron, H. E., 33
Barry, J. J., 17
Barry, W. J. M., 24, 26
Barten, H., 31
Barthel, J., 93, 138
Barthel, W., 115
Bartholomew, P., 61, 64, 185
Bartlett, L., 38
Barua, B. S., 44
Bates, A. H., 35
Batiste, J., 33
Batson, N., 183
Batter, D., 64, 181
Batty, M. R., 19, 68, 197
Bauer, R., 142
Bauma, H., 144, 209
Baumgartner, H., 106
Bausch, J. A. B., 38, 143
Baxter, H., 155
Baxter, I. K., 22, 141
Baxter, M. I., 17
Bayi, F., 12
Beacham, M. A., 104, 105, 106, 107
Beacham, P. J., 102
Beamon, R., 35, 36, 49, 51, 70, 108, 121, 141, 162, 190, 200
Beard, P., 33
Beasley, G., 60
Beatty, J. T., 31, 196
Beaudry, C., 38
Beaven, P., 115

Booysen, D., 25
Borah, C. E., 29, 30, 140
Borchmeyer, E., 78
Borck, H., 31
Boreham, C., 22
Borican, J., 31, 38
Borjesson, K. A., 28
Borowski, E., 79
Borzov, V., 51, 77, 85, 105, 108, 138
Bosmans, J., 21
Boston, R. H., 35, 49, 51, 54, 70, 121, 141, 151, 200
Botha, J., 25
Botley, M. Y., 104
Bouin, J., 68, 118, 164
Boulter, J. P., 16, 128, 174
Bourbeillon, P., 79
Dourland, C. F., 30, 141
Bowen, C. G., 27
Bowen, R. F., 30
Bowman, C., 29
Bowman, S., 36
Box, K. J., 14, 76
Boxberger, J., 105
Boyce, E., 24
Boyce, P., 66
Boychuk, A., 150
Boyd, I. H., 62
Boyes, M. G., 21
Boyle, N., 205, 206
Boyle, R. A., 41, 60, 61, 66, 115, 204
Boysen, A., 128, 194
Brabec, J., 106
Bradley, C. A., 14
Braekman, P., 21
Bragg, A., 29, 30
Bragg, D. G., 35, 141, 150, 155, 200
Bragina, L., 52, 86, 130, 143, 203, 207
Braithwaite, N. D., 104
Bralo, R., 150
Branch, V., 182
Brand, E. C., 144
Brangwin, K. C., 15, 58, 62
Brasher, C. W., 48, 52, 136, 139, 168
Brasser, R. J., 20, 25
Bratchikov, A., 105
Braumuller, I., 188
Braun, H., 16
Breach, W. E. N., 24
Breacker, A., 58, 62, 76
Breard, L., 188
Brechenmacher, G., 25
Bredin, E. C., 15, 16
Bresnahan, G., 166
Brewill, G. F., 14
Bridge, R., 27, 28
Bridges, C., 125
Bridgland, J., 187
Briesenick, H., 80. 84, 85, 106
Briggs, J. S., 183

Bright, N., 32
Brightwell, A. E., see Packer, A. E.
Brightwell, R. I., 15, 62, 76, 77, 136, 149, 174
Brill, D., 61, 66, 152, 185
Britton, H., 19
Britton, W., 26
Brix, H., 36
Broman, S., 43
Bronder, G. A., 38
Brooks, M. J., 95
Brough, E., 40
Brown, A., 137
Brown, A. G., 27
Brown, A. G. K., 15, 16, 76, 77, 136, 141, 167
Brown, B. (HJ), 42
Brown, B. (JT), 38
Brown, D., 41, 69
Brown, E., 43, 152
Brown, G., 35
Brown, H., 59
Brown, H. H., 138
Brown, J. R., 58
Brown, K., 23, 35
Brown, L., 34
Brown, M. M., 61
Brown, R., 34
Brown, R. K., 21, 62
Brown, V., 41, 151
Brown, W., 35, 36
Browne, P. M., 16
Brownlee, D. A., 64
Bruce, T., 24
Bruch, R., 84, 85, 190, 201
Bruggeman, R., 34
Brumel, V., 53, 79, 84, 85, 95, 108, 115, 126, 141, 199
Bruun, E., 202
Bryan, G., 35, 36, 151
Bryan, T. J. B., 102
Bryan-Jones, D. G., 20
Bryant, P., 205
Bryde, K., 66
Bryngeirsson, T., 23, 79
Buck, C., 35
Budd, F. J., 29, 93, 140, 166, 192, 193
Bues, M., 79
Bufanu, V., 108, 184
Buker, R., 31
Bulanchik, Y., 78
Bulger, D. D., 20, 23
Bull, M. A., 23, 59, 65, 103, 107, 155, 174
Bullivant, M. J., 18
Burg, A. B., 34
Burgard, W., 24
Burge, D., 60, 66
Burger, M. D., 27

215

Burgess, J., 30
Burgess, S., 64
Burghley, Lord, 20, 21, 53, 58, 62, 98, 99, 136, 140
Burke, B., 60, 103, 104, 137, 182, 184
Burke, E., 26, 38
Burke, T. E., 138
Burke, V., 34
Burleson, D., 31, 150
Burneleit, K., 81, 106, 207
Burns, J. A., 18, 62, 67
Burrell, O., 34
Burtin, A., 17
Burton, T. P., 103
Burvill, M. J., 205
Butcher, G., 41
Butler, G. M., 14, 15, 136, 140, 147, 167
Butler, J., 28
Butler, S., 35
Butt, M. S., 44
Butterfield, D., 64
Butterfield, G., 16, 17
Bystrova, G., 81, 82, 152, 209

C

Cabrejas, C., 36
Cabrera, D., 139, 150
Cacchi, P., see Pigni, P.
Caird, M., 115, 144
Calhoun, L. Q., 33, 54, 98, 129, 140, 190, 198
Callebout, N. E., 188
Calvert, S., 44
Camien, J., 17
Campbell, C. W. A., 102, 107, 174
Campbell, L., 31
Campbell, M. C., 22, 103, 174
Campbell, M. G., 33, 38, 143, 198
Campbell, M. T., 104
Campbell, T. S., 31
Campbell, W. M., 15
Cannon, H. S., 37
Cantello, A., 38, 201
Cantrell, J., 42
Capes, G. L., 25, 66, 103, 107, 164, 174
Capozzoli, C., 32
Carette, J., 79
Carew, M. L., 144
Carey, D., 26
Carey, S. J., 66, 104, 175, 183
Carlos, J., 30, 54, 150, 166, 189, 192, 193
Carlsen, G., 37, 151
Carlsson, S., 39
Carlton, J., 166, 167, 192, 193
Caro, R., 186

Carpenter, K. K., 37, 142
Carr, E. W., 57, 59
Carr, G. A., 62
Carr, H., 30, 138, 141, 165, 166, 193, 194
Carr, S. W., 141, 155
Carr, W. A., 30, 138, 141
Carroll, N., 16, 105
Carter, A., 103
Carter, A. W., 16, 76, 128
Carter, C. S., 128, 174
Carter, E. C., 17, 18
Carter, F. T., 28
Carter, L. R., 103
Carter, L. W., 58, 62
Cartmell, N. J., 14, 140
Cartwright, E., 40, 42
Caruthers, E., 34, 150
Cary, L. H., 14, 166
Casanas, A., 115
Casey, L., 36
Cassell, O. C., 30, 141
Cassidy, O., 33
Catherwood, E., 144
Cator, S., 121
Cawley, S., 137, 185
Cawley, W. J., 21, 34, 99, 140, 199
Cerutty, P. W., 75
Cerveny, J., 31
Chalmers, L., 64, 182
Chamberlain, M., see Stephen, M.
Chapelle, J., 19, 20
Charles, D. S., see Leather, D. S.
Charles, W., 38
Chataway, C. J., 17, 48, 52, 54, 55, 57, 62, 76, 118, 121, 196
Cheeseman, S., 64, 137, 182
Chefd'hotel, R., 79
Chemabwai, T., 12
Chen Chia-chuan, 192
Chenchik, T., 81, 106
Cheng Feng-yung, 207
Chhota Singh, 45
Chiang, L., 45
Chi Cheng, 40, 41, 42, 44, 46, 55, 100, 182, 184, 203, 204, 205, 207
Chil, C. Y., 44, 124
Chionis, 97, 121
Chisholm, D., 42
Chitty, M. A., 104
Chivas, S., 115
Chivers, A. H., 18, 62
Chizhova, N., 55, 82, 84, 86, 107, 108, 144, 164, 203, 208
Chmelkova, A., 81
Christiernsson, C. A., 21
Christmas, R., 183
Christophel, B., 43
Christopher, W., 35
Chromik, J., 78, 198

217

220

222

Hanks, E., 34
Hanlon, J. A. T., 14, 15, 62
Hanner, F., 38
Hansen, F. M., 23, 35, 141, 199
Hansenne, M., 194
Harbig, R., 78, 79, 93, 128, 167, 194
Hardin, G. F., 34, 93, 99, 140, 199
Hardin, W., 34, 93
Harding, E., 183, 206, 207
Hardy, C., 40, 41, 144
Hardy, R., 28, 178, 179
Harlow, C., 38
Harnden, A. H., 141
Harper, E., 19, 62, 67, 68, 125, 136
Harragin, A. E. A., 22
Harrington, P., 35
Harris, A., 37
Harris, B. E., 183
Harris, D., 180, 183
Harris, E., 30
Harris, R., 43
Harrison, H., 18
Harrison, M. A., 19
Harrison, R., 27
Hart, D., 180
Hart, E., 51, 140, 189, 191, 193
Hart, H. B., 25, 27, 59, 65
Hart, R. (Ghana), 12
Hart, R. (USA), 32
Harte, O., 24, 26
Harwood, P. G., 23
Hary, A., 77, 79, 85, 138, 140, 166, 192
Hasenfus, O., 40
Haskett, C., 116
Hatt, H. M., 184, 185, 188
Hauck, M. A., 62
Hause, D., 33
Havasi, I., 123
Haward, C. W., 20, 21
Hawkins, P., 42
Hawtrey, H., 147
Hay, E., 77, 81
Hayes, J. J., 124, 139
Hayes, R. L., 29, 93, 94, 138, 140, 166, 189, 192, 193
Hayes, W. D., 29
Haynes, F. C., 181, 183, 188
Hayward, B., 102
Hayward, S. M., 184
Healey, A. H., 20
Healion, B., 26
Healy, J., 34
Heap, J. C., 62
Heath, H. A., 67
Heath, M. J., 180, 183, 187
Heatley, B. B., 19, 68, 69, 125, 136, 197
Hebauf, A., 94
Heber, R., 151

Hedmark, L. Y., 77, 96, 104, 105, 185
Hegarty, A., 136
Heggarty, M. F., 187
Hehir, W., 28, 179
Hein, K., 26, 80, 142
Heine, J., 81
Heino, V. J., 78, 196, 197
Heinrich, I., 80
Heintzmann, J., 34
Held, F. D., 38, 113, 151, 201
Held, R., 113
Helffrich, A. B., 31, 140
Heljasz, Z., 25
Helten, I., 81
Hemery, D. P., 12, 21, 58, 62, 76, 85, 94, 99, 136, 140, 174, 199
Henderson, A., 32
Henke, A. H., 29
Henley, E. J., 136
Hennige, G., 85
Henning, H., 106
Herman, P., 38
Hernandez, V., 36
Herriott, M., 13, 20, 62, 136, 168
Herrmann, S., 195
Hesketh, W., 68
Heublein, G., 188
Hewson, B. S., 16, 17, 62, 76, 78, 128
Hewson, J., 40
Hibbins, F. N., 67, 136
Hickman, J. E., 67
Hicks, H. J., 19
Hicks, T. J., 139
Hietanen, M., 78, 197
Higdon, H., 176
Higdon, M. R., 103
Higgins, F. P., 15, 59, 62, 79, 136
Higgins, N., 39
Higgins, R., 61
Higgins, T. L., 62
Higginson, J., 24
Higham, C. E. E., 62
Hignell, A. F., 27
Hildreth, P. B., 21, 76, 99
Hill, A. G., 16, 17, 18, 52, 96, 128, 136, 138, 165
Hill, E., 43
Hill, J., 41
Hill, J. M., 16
Hill, R., 18, 19, 58, 63, 68, 76, 78, 85, 96, 125, 174, 190, 197
Hill, R. (USA), 32
Hill, T., 33, 198
Hill, W. A., 14
Hiller, J., 41
Hillman, H. L., 138, 140
Hills, R. G., 36
Hincks, P., 103
Hindmar, L., 28
Hines, C. B., 38

223

Hines, H., 24
Hines, J. R., 29, 30, 97, 138, 140, 166, 189, 191, 192, 193
Hires, H., 20
Hirota, T., 45
Hirscht, J., 105
Hiscock, E. M., 60, 64, 103, 137, 182
Hiscox, M. E., 77, 206
Hitomi, K., 122, 182, 186, 188
Hobbs, B., 40
Hobson, P. F., 59
Hockert, G., 139
Hodge, P., 20, 136, 139, 168
Hodge, R., 171, 202
Hodgson, W. H., 22
Hofer, R., 81
Hoff, C., 23, 155
Hoffman, A., 60, 66, 151, 183
Hoffman, H., 38
Hoffman, M., 61, 204
Hoffmann, D., 80
Hoffmeister, H., 73, 106
Hofmeister, F-P., 115
Hogan, H. D., 192
Hogan, J. J., 76, 78, 197
Hogan, J. M. W., 102
Hogarth, R. G., 23
Hogstrom, G., 23
Hohne, C., 80, 123, 143, 202, 203
Holden, J. A., 20, 174
Holden, J. T., 18, 19, 58, 63, 67, 68, 69, 76, 78, 125, 135
Holdorf, W., 143
Holger, 188
Holland, A. M., 186
Holland, J., 35
Hollie, W., 36
Hollings, S. C., 20
Hollingsworth, R. A., 26
Holman, S. K., 16
Holmer, G., 90
Holmes, C. B., 14, 15, 57, 63, 101
Holmes, W. J., 16
Holmvang, G., 80
Holst, Sorensen, N., 77
Holt, F. T., 20
Homonnay, T., 23
Honner, R. St. J., 23
Honour, J. L., 187
Honz, K., 85
Hooper, B. R. L., 103
Hopkins, J., 179
Hopkins, T. E., 61, 65, 77, 81, 96, 137, 184, 185, 207
Horgan, D., 13, 24, 25, 136, 163
Horine, G., 34, 95
Hornberger, G., 78, 79
Horwood, E., 23
Hoskin, S. H., 61, 64, 185
Houben, H., 14

Houghton, R. F., 21
Housden, F., 94
Houser, C. L., 36, 37, 73, 142
Houtzager, J. H., 26
Howard, R., 34
Howard, W. B., 67
Howe, B., 42
Howe, I. T., 29
Howe, J., 32
Howe, L., 34
Howes, J., 180, 187
Howes, L. L., 187
Howland, R. L., 13, 63, 103
Hoyt, W. W., 141
Hubbard, W. de H., 35, 36, 112, 141
Hudson, C., 41
Hudson, M., 144
Hulford, F. H., 18
Hulse, W., 31
Hume, M. K., 183
Hummel, W. A., 33
Humphreys, J. W., 59
Humphreys, R., 151
Humphreys, T., 136
Hunter, F. A. R., 21, 58, 64
Huseby, G., 25, 80
Hussey, F., 29, 140
Hutchinson, R., 155
Hutson, G. W., 17, 18, 36
Hutton, L., 59
Hyde, C. W., 28
Hyman, D., 60, 64, 77, 80, 83, 100, 137, 147, 167, 175, 182
Hyman, H. A., 14
Hymes, L., 40, 42
Hys, M., 115
Hyytiainen, T., 80

I

Ibarra, A., 43
Ibbotson, G. D., 17, 101, 102, 129, 136, 195
Ibbotson, M. C., 187
Idanez, S., 151
Iddings, L., 42
Ifeajuna, E. A., 59
Ignatyev, A., 77
Igun, S., 11, 12, 59
Iharos, S., 154, 195, 196
Illgen, K., 84, 186
Imuro, Y., 45
Inaoka, M., 46
Iness, S. G., 73, 142, 201
Inkpen, B. J., 66, 77, 96, 104, 107, 175, 185
Innocenti, D., 23
Inoue, K., 45
Inoue, O., 45

224

P 225

226

P*
227

228

231

P

235

237

239

240

241

243

# Late Additions

*1973 AAA Champions:* 100m: D. Halliday 10.6; 200m: C. Monk 21.1; 400m: D. Jenkins 46.5; 800m: A. Carter 1:45.1; 1500m: R. Dixon (NZ) 3:38.9 (UK champion: F. Clement 3:39.4); 5000m: B. Foster 13:23.8; 10,000m: D. Bedford 27:30.8; 3000mSC: S. Hollings 8:31.0; 110mH: B. Price 14.1; 400mH: A. Pascoe 49.8; HJ: C. Dunn (USA) 6ft. 9in. (UK champion: M. Campbell 6ft. 8in.); PV: B. Hooper 16ft. 11in.; LJ: G. Hignett 24ft. 2¼in.; TJ: A. Wadhams 51ft. 8½in.; SP: G. Capes 66ft 6in.; DT: W. Tancred 200ft. 10in.; HT: H. Payne 223ft. 0in.; JT: D. Travis 241ft. 5in.; 3000m Walk: R. Mills 12:16.8

*1973 WAAA Champions:* 100m: A. Lynch 11.7; 200m: H. Golden 24.2; 400m: J. Roscoe 53.8; 800m: M. Tracey (Ireland) 2:03.4 (UK champion: R. Wright 2:05.5); 1500m: J. Allison 4:15.7; 3000m: I. Knutsson (Sweden) 9:08.0 (UK champion: J. Smith 9:11.6); 100mH: J. Vernon 14.0; 400mH: S. Howell 61.4; HJ: I Gusenbauer (Austria) 6ft. 0¾in. (UK champion: B. Lawton 5ft. 11½in.); LJ: M. Nimmo 20ft. 9¼in.; SP: B. Bedford 48ft. 7½in.; DT: R. Payne 185ft. 0in.; JT: S. Corbett 176ft. 9in.; 3000m Walk: B. Jenkins 14:59.4.

*1973 AAU Champions:* 100y/220y: S. Williams 9.4/20.4; 440y: M. Peoples 45.2; 880y: R. Wohlhuter 1:45.6; Mile: L. Hilton 3:55.9; 3M: S. Prefontaine 12:53.4; 6M: G. Minty (GB) 27:20.8; 3000mSC: D. Brown

8:26.8; 120yH: T. Hill 13.2; 440yH: J. Bolding 49.2; HJ: D. Stones 7ft. 5in.; PV: M. Cotton 17ft. 4in.; LJ: R. Williams 26ft. 1in.; TJ: J. Craft 55ft. 8¾in.; SP: A. Feuerbach 68ft. 1in.; DT: M. Wilkins 211ft. 1in.; HT: T. Bregar 215ft. 4in.; JT: C. Feldmann 265ft. 3in.; Dec: J. Bennett 8121; Mar: D. Schmenk 2:15:48; *(Women)* 100y: I. Davis 10.3; 220y/440y: M. Fergerson 23.4/54.1; 880y: W. Koenig 2:04.7; Mile: F. Larrieu 4:40.3; 2M: E. Claugus 10:19.4; 100mH: P. Johnson 12.9; 400mH: G. Fitzgerald 61.1; HJ: D. Wilson 5ft. 9in.; LJ: M. Watson 21ft. 4¾in.; SP: M. Seidler 51ft. 8½in.; DT: J. Roberts (Australia) 173ft. 3in.; JT: K. Schmidt 194ft. 6in.

*World Records* (established between June 1st and August 14th 1973) 800m: 1:43.7 Marcello Fiasconaro (Italy); 1000m: 2:16.0 Danie Malan (S. Africa); 10,000m: 27:30.8 Dave Bedford (GB); 3000mSC: 8:14.0 Ben Jipcho (Kenya); 120yH: 13.0 Rod Milburn (USA) (equal); 110mH: 13.1 Milburn; HJ: 7ft. 6½in Dwight Stones (USA). *(Women)* 100m/200m: 10.8/22.1 Renate Stecher (E. Germany); Mile: 4:29.5 Paola Cacchi (Italy); 100mH: 12.3 Annelie Ehrhardt (E. Germany); DT: 221ft. 9in. Faina Melnik (USSR); Pen: 4831 Burglinde Pollak (E. Germany); 4x800m: 8:08.6 Bulgaria; 400mH (unofficial): 56.7 Danuta Piecyk (Poland). Note: Kathy Hammond (USA) set 440y record of 52.2 in 1972.